Hazardous Materials
for First Responders
3rd Edition

W9-CKC-484

Validated by the International Fire Service
Training Association

Published by Fire Protection Publications
Oklahoma State University

RECYCLABLE

Barbara Adams
Project Manager/Senior Editor

Leslie A. Miller
Writer/Senior Editor

Cover photo courtesy of Tom Clawson, Technical Resources, Inc.
Divider page background photo courtesy of Joan Hepler
Chapter divider page photos courtesy of Rich Mahaney

The International Fire Service Training Association

The International Fire Service Training Association (IFSTA) was established in 1934 as a "nonprofit educational association of fire fighting personnel who are dedicated to upgrading fire fighting techniques and safety through training." To carry out the mission of IFSTA, Fire Protection Publications was established as an entity of Oklahoma State University. Fire Protection Publications' primary function is to publish and disseminate training texts as proposed and validated by IFSTA. As a secondary function, Fire Protection Publications researches, acquires, produces, and markets high-quality learning and teaching aids as consistent with IFSTA's mission.

The IFSTA Validation Conference is held the second full week in July. Committees of technical experts meet and work at the conference addressing the current standards of the National Fire Protection Association and other standard-making groups as applicable. The Validation Conference brings together individuals from several related and allied fields, such as:

- Key fire department executives and training officers
- Educators from colleges and universities
- Representatives from governmental agencies
- Delegates of firefighter associations and industrial organizations

Committee members are not paid nor are they reimbursed for their expenses by IFSTA or Fire Protection Publications. They participate because of commitment to the fire service and its future through training. Being on a committee is prestigious in the fire service community, and committee members are acknowledged leaders in their fields. This unique feature provides a close relationship between the International Fire Service Training Association and fire protection agencies which helps to correlate the efforts of all concerned.

IFSTA manuals are now the official teaching texts of most of the states and provinces of North America. Additionally, numerous U.S. and Canadian government agencies as well as other English-speaking countries have officially accepted the IFSTA manuals.

ISBN 0-87939-244-4   Library of Congress Control Number: 2004111897

Third Edition, First Printing, November 2004   *Printed in the United States of America*

10   9   8   7   6

If you need additional information concerning the International Fire Service Training Association (IFSTA) or Fire Protection Publications, contact:

Customer Service, Fire Protection Publications, Oklahoma State University
930 North Willis, Stillwater, OK 74078-8045
800-654-4055   Fax: 405-744-8204

For assistance with training materials, to recommend material for inclusion in an IFSTA manual, or to ask questions or comment on manual content, contact:

Editorial Department, Fire Protection Publications, Oklahoma State University
930 North Willis, Stillwater, OK 74078-8045
405-744-4111   Fax: 405-744-4112   E-mail: editors@osufpp.org

Table of Contents

Preface

This is the third edition of the IFSTA manual dealing with hazardous materials for first responders. It is intended as a primary text for all personnel seeking to qualify as Awareness- and/or Operational-Level responders to hazardous materials incidents and as a reference text for those who have already qualified. This manual primarily addresses NFPA 472, *Professional Competence of Responders to Hazardous Materials Incidents,* (2002 Edition), for Awareness and Operational Levels. It also covers the Office of Domestic Preparedness *Emergency Responder Guidelines* (for terrorist incidents involving weapons of mass destruction) for Awareness Level and Performance Level A (Operational Level) for firefighters and law enforcement officers. Because the world of hazardous materials has changed so dramatically since the last edition of this manual, this edition has been completely revised and updated, and it contains many new sections, tables, photos, and illustrations.

Acknowledgement and special thanks are extended to the members of the material review committee who contributed their time, wisdom, and knowledge to the development of this manual.

IFSTA Hazardous Materials for First Responders, 3rd Edition Validation Committee

Chair
Richard C. Mahaney
Dona Ana County Office of Emergency Management
Santa Teresa, NM

Vice Chair
Edward Hartin
Gresham Fire & Emergency Services
Gresham, OR

Secretary
Glenn P. Jirka
Miami Township Fire Division
Miamisburg, OH

Committee Members

Gary E. Allen
Tampa Fire Rescue
Tampa, FL

Steve Hendrix
Arlington Fire Training
Arlington, TX

Sherry Arasim
Tualatin Valley Fire & Rescue
Aloha, OR

Joan Hepler
PMB 225
Canby, OR

Jimmie Badgett
Texas Department of Public Safety
Dallas, TX

Philip Linder
Quantum Emergency Response Inc.
Delta, B.C. CANADA

Steve George
Oklahoma Fire Service Training
Stillwater, OK

Jeff Tucker
Central Emergency Services
Soldotna, AK

Much appreciation is given to the following individuals and organizations for contributing information, photographs, and technical assistance instrumental in the development of this manual:

Midwest City (OK) Fire Department
    Steve Huff
    Rhett Murphy
    Steve Masoner
    Kelly McGlasson
    Rodney Foster
    Chris Denton

Oklahoma State University Environmental
   Health Services
    Brenda Sorenson
    James Isaacs

Stillwater (OK) Fire Department

Oklahoma State Fire Service Training

National Fire Protection Association

Canadian Centre for Occupational Health and Safety

Mohave Museum of History and Arts

Moore Memorial Library, Texas City, TX

International Tanker Owners Pollution Federation Ltd., Houndsditch London

Edward Feather Photography

Lab Safety Supply

Kidde Fire Fighting

Illinois Fire Service Institute

Kenneth Baum

Ray Elder

Judy Halmich

Chris E. Mickal

Howard Chatterton

Bob Parker

Rich Mahaney

Steve George

Joan Hepler

Phil Linder

Steve Hendrix

Sherry Arasim

Amy Hunt

Luke Ennis

Rahman Mahmudur

Daniel Tyler

Dr. Brandy White

Dr. Asfaha Iob

Dr. Loralee Ohrtman

Garry Hannes

Matt Hannes

Hank Welliver

Kristen Wooley

Mike Cordell

Vernon D. Phillips

Doug Sanders

Chad Love

Robert Wright

George Cushmac

Tom Allan

Delmer Billings

Shane Kelley

Mary Hillstrom

Richard Boyle

Robert Richard

John F. Lewis

J. Patrick Johnson

Lawrence W. Hepburn

Jennifer K. Smith and K. Christensen, MS, MC, LPC (for the information provided in the Psychological Hazards section)

Gene Carlson (for providing decontamination definitions and chapter review)

Tom Clawson, Technical Resources Group, Inc. (for pictures and much assistance on the radiological sections)

Kenneth E. Keaton (for reviewing the radiological sections)

Jimmie Badgett (for his hard work producing most of Appendix C)

Sherry Arasim (for providing Appendices B and F)

Edward Hartin (for providing Appendix G, the original scenario, and much of the GEBMO information)

Thanks also go to the many, many authors of the various government and noncopyrighted documents that were used throughout this manual from the following sources:

Health Canada

Los Alamos National Laboratory

Sandia National Laboratories

Transport Canada

Union Pacific Railroad

Oklahoma Highway Patrol Bomb Squad

Department of Fire Services, Commonwealth of MA

U.S. Agency for Toxic Substances and Disease Registry

U.S. Bureau of Alcohol, Firearms, Tobacco and Explosives

U.S. Centers for Disease Control and Prevention

U.S. Coast Guard

U.S. Department of Defense (particularly the U.S. Army Soldier and Biological Chemical Command)

U.S. Department of Energy (particularly the Transportation Emergency Preparedness Program)

U.S. Department of Homeland Security

U.S. Department of Justice

U.S. Department of Transportation

U.S. Environmental Protection Agency

U.S. Federal Bureau of Investigation

U.S. Federal Emergency Management Agency

U.S. Fire Administration

U.S. National Institute for Occupational Safety and Health

U.S. Nuclear Regulatory Commission

U.S. Occupational Safety and Health Administration

U.S. State Department

Colorado Regional Community Policing Institute, North Metro Task Force, and Rocky Mountain High Intensity Drug Trafficing Area

On a sad note, we extend special thanks to Joan Hepler, who passed away before final completion of this project. Joan was an active participant as a committee member, and she was always there to remind us to include law enforcement throughout the book. This book is much better because of her contributions.

Last, but certainly not least, gratitude is extended to the following members of the Fire Protection Publications staff whose contributions made the final publication of this manual possible.

Hazardous Materials for First Responders Project Team

Project Manager/Editor
Barbara Adams, Senior Editor

Technical Reviewers/Photography
Jeff Fortney, Senior Technical Editor
Fred Stowell, Senior Technical Editor

Proofreaders
Susan S. Walker, Instructional Developer
Bill Robinson, Curriculum Coordinator
Melissa Noakes, Curriculum Editor
Beth Ann Fulgenzi, Instructional Developer

Editorial Assistants
Tara Gladden
Robin Balderson

Research Technicians
Nathan York
Foster Cryer

Production Manager
Don Davis

Illustrators and Layout Designers
Ann Moffat, Production Coordinator
Ben Brock, Senior Graphic Designer
Lee Shortridge, Senior Graphic Designer
Clint Parker, Senior Graphic Designer
Missy Reese, Senior Graphic Designer
Jeff Mitchell, Graphics Technician

Library Researchers
Susan F. Walker, Librarian
Shelly Magee, Assistant Librarian

Introduction

To meet consumers' needs, billions of tons of chemical substances, materials, and products are manufactured, stored, used, and transported around the world every year. In addition to their necessary and beneficial uses, many of these materials pose considerable risks to the public and to the environment. Those substances that possess harmful characteristics are called *hazardous materials* (or *haz mat*) in the United States and *dangerous goods* in Canada and other countries. Accidents and emergencies involving these potentially harmful products are often referred to as *hazardous materials* or *haz mat incidents*. In this book, *emergency* and *incident* are often used interchangeably, with the understanding that the types of incidents addressed by this book are emergencies.

Hazardous materials are found in every jurisdiction, community, workplace, and modern household. Incidents involving these materials can be caused by such factors as human error, package failure, and transportation accidents. First responders (emergency personnel who are likely to arrive first at an incident scene) must also be aware of the potential for hazardous materials to be involved in fires, explosions, and criminal or terrorist activities. Because of the harmful characteristics of these substances, first responders must possess the skills necessary to address incidents involving hazardous materials in a safe and effective manner.

Purpose and Scope

This book is written for emergency first responders who are mandated by law and/or called upon by necessity to prepare for and respond to hazardous materials incidents and potential incidents. These first responders include the following individuals:

- Firefighters
- Law enforcement officers/personnel
- Emergency medical services personnel
- Military responders
- Industrial and transportation emergency response members
- Public works employees
- Utility workers
- Members of private industry
- Other emergency response professionals

The purpose of this book is to provide these first responders with the information they need to take appropriate initial actions when hazardous materials spills or releases are encountered. Its scope is limited to giving detailed information about the initial defensive operations. More advanced procedures require hazardous materials technicians who have specialized training.

Related regulations/standards are referenced in this book as applicable, but this book primarily addresses the training requirements of the following National Fire Protection Association (NFPA), Occupational Safety and Health Administration (OSHA), and Office for Domestic Preparedness (ODP) documents:

- NFPA 472, *Standard for Professional Competence of Responders to Hazardous Materials Incidents* (2002 edition), for the Awareness and Operational Levels

- OSHA regulations in Title 29 *Code of Federal Regulations (CFR)* 1910.120, *Hazardous Waste Operations and Emergency Response (HAZWOPER)*, paragraph (q), for first responders at the Awareness and Operational Levels
- Office for Domestic Preparedness, *Emergency Responder Guidelines*, 2002, Law Enforcement and Fire Service Awareness and Operational Levels for response to terrorist incidents involving weapons of mass destruction (WMD)

This book is designed to meet the requirements for NFPA, OSHA, and ODP first responder Awareness and Operations Levels. It addresses the first responders' responsibilities to recognize the presence of hazardous materials, secure the area, provide personnel protection, and request the assistance of trained technicians. Additionally, it addresses the control of hazardous materials releases from a safe distance using defensive operations.

Book Organization

The chapters of this book are divided into three parts in order to present the information in a logical, sequential order, starting with the basics (What are hazardous materials) and building from there. Additional information is contained in appendices, and many of the government and noncopyrighted reference materials cited in the book are provided on a supplemental compact disk (CD). The supplemental CD also contains a photo section with pictures of many different hazardous materials containers.

Part 1 (Introduction to Hazardous Materials) of the book includes Chapters 1 and 2 that introduce the subject of hazardous materials. Chapter 1 provides an overview of pertinent hazardous materials legislation, regulations, and standards. It introduces many of the important terms associated with hazardous materials and gives relevant statistical information. Chapter 2 provides an explanation of various hazardous materials properties, including an overview of potential physical and health hazards.

Part 2 (Incident Problem-Solving Process) includes Chapters 3 through 7 that explain the problem-solving processes used by responders at actual hazardous materials incidents. A sample hazardous materials incident or scenario is given in Chapter 3, Hazardous Materials Identification, and this incident is referred to throughout the other chapters in this part. This sample gives first responders a point of reference for the different aspects of managing an incident from the initial identification of the material to decontamination and cleanup. It is important to understand that emergencies involving hazardous materials may be extremely complex, and while information in this book is presented in a linear fashion, responding appropriately at such an incident is not necessarily a linear process. For example, whereas personal protective equipment (PPE) is not discussed in great detail until Chapter 6, Personal Protective Equipment, first responders need to be wearing PPE from the moment they arrive on scene until they finish their assigned duties.

Part 3 (Special Topics) include Chapters 8 and 9; they present stand-alone topics that are not addressed in the problem-solving context. The chapter on terrorist and other criminal activities is a new subject in this 3rd edition.

Chapter Organization

Part 1. Introduction to Hazardous Materials

Chapter 1: Hazardous Materials Regulations, Definitions, and Statistics

Chapter 2: Hazardous Materials Properties and Hazards

Part 2. Incident Problem-Solving Process

Chapter 3: Hazardous Materials Identification

Chapter 4: Incident Management Elements

Chapter 5: Strategic Goals and Tactical Objectives

Chapter 6: Personal Protective Equipment

Chapter 7: Contamination and Decontamination

Part 3. Special Topics

Chapter 8: Incident-Specific Strategies and Tactics

Chapter 9: Terrorist and Other Criminal Activities

Key Information

Various types of information in this book are given in shaded boxes marked by symbols or icons (sidebars, information, key information, and case histories). Smart operations tips and *what does this mean to you* notices are given in boxes indicated by a safety-alert icon. See the following examples:

Haz Mat Sidebar

Atmospheric pressure is greatest at low altitudes; consequently, its pressure at sea level is used as a standard. At sea level, the atmosphere exerts a pressure of 14.7 psi (101 kPa) {1.01 bar}. A common method of measuring atmospheric pressure is to compare the weight of the atmosphere with the weight of a column of mercury: the greater the atmospheric pressure, the taller the column of mercury.

Haz Mat Information

Some experts make this differentiation: Acids are *corrosive*, while bases are *caustic*. In the world of emergency response; however, both acids and bases are called *corrosives*. The U.S. Department of Transportation (DOT) and Transport Canada (TC), for example, do not differentiate between the two. Any materials that destroy metal or skin tissue are considered corrosives by these agencies.

Key Information

Volatility refers to a substance's ability to become a vapor at a relatively low temperature. Essentially, volatile chemical agents have low boiling points at ordinary pressures and/or high vapor pressures at ordinary temperatures. The volatility of a chemical agent often determines how it is used.

Case History

The Love Canal saga (1978) began nearly 100 years before the environmental nightmare came to the world's attention. In the 1890s, industrialist William T. Love devised a plan to dig a canal around Niagara Falls. The canal would allow marine traffic around the falls, provide a water source for inexpensive hydroelectric power, and create a distinct boundary for a model *planned industrial community.* The U.S. economy entered a sharp decline shortly after the project began, and the development ceased. The open canal was publicly auctioned and by 1920 was in use as a local dump and swimming hole.

What Does This Mean to You? Be Aware!

Some chemicals may have multiple routes of entry. For example, toluene (a solvent) can cause moderate irritation to the skin through skin contact, but it can also cause dizziness, lack of coordination, coma, and even respiratory failure when inhaled in sufficient concentrations. Other chemicals with multiple routes of entry include azide, methyl ethyl ketone (MEK), benzene, and other solvents.

Information pertinent to Awareness Level and Operational Level tasks are designated by a spyglass icon and a wrench icon, respectively:

Information relating to the different countries in North America and the United Nations (UN) is symbolized by its flag:

Information relating to the problem-solving process scenario is symbolized by the scenario icon and is indicated by short red lines above and below the paragraph or paragraphs.

Three key signal words are found in the book: **WARNING, CAUTION,** and **NOTE.** Definitions and examples of each are as follows:

- **WARNING** indicates information that could result in death or serious injury to fire and emergency services personnel. See the following example:

WARNING

Any clothing saturated with a cryogenic material must be removed immediately, particularly if the vapors are flammable or oxidizing. The first responder could not escape flames from clothing-trapped vapors if the vapors were to ignite.

- **CAUTION** indicates important information or data that fire and emergency service responders need to be aware of in order to perform their duties safely. See the following example:

CAUTION

All personnel working at hazardous materials incidents must use appropriate personal protective equipment, including appropriate respiratory protection equipment.

- **NOTE** indicates important operational information that helps explain why a particular recommendation is given or describes optional methods for certain procedures. See the following example:

NOTE: *Vapor* is a gaseous form of a substance that is normally in a solid or liquid state at room temperature and pressure. It is formed by evaporation from a liquid or sublimation from a solid.

Part One

Introduction to Hazardous Materials

Chapter 1

Hazardous Materials Regulations, Definitions, and Statistics

This chapter provides information that will assist the reader in meeting the following first responder competencies from NFPA 472, *Professional Competence of Responders to Hazardous Materials Incidents*, 2002 Edition. The numbers are noted directly in the text under the section titles where they are addressed.

NFPA 472

Chapter 3   Definitions

3.3.25   First Responder at the Awareness Level. Those persons who, in the course of their normal duties, could be the first on the scene of an emergency involving hazardous materials and who are expected to recognize the presence of hazardous materials, protect themselves, call for trained personnel, and secure the area.

3.3.26   First Responder at the Operational Level. Those persons who respond to releases or potential releases of hazardous materials as part of the initial response to the incident for the purpose of protecting nearby persons, the environment, or property from the effects of the release and who are expected to respond in a defensive fashion to control the release from a safe distance and keep it from spreading.

3.3.29   Hazardous Material. A substance (solid, liquid, or gas) that when released is capable of creating harm to people, the environment, and property.

Chapter 4   Competencies for the First Responder at the Awareness Level

4.1.1.1   First responders at the awareness level shall be trained to meet all competencies of this chapter.

4.1.1.2   They also shall receive any additional training to meet applicable United States Department of Transportation (DOT), United States Environmental Protection Agency (EPA), Occupational Safety and Health Administration (OSHA), and other state, local, or provincial occupational health and safety regulatory requirements.

4.1.2.1   The goal of the competencies at the awareness level shall be to provide first responders with the knowledge and skills to perform the tasks in 4.1.2.2 safely.

4.1.2.2   When first on the scene of an emergency involving hazardous materials, the first responder at the awareness level shall be able to perform the following tasks:

(1)   Analyze the incident to determine both the hazardous materials present and the basic hazard and response information for each hazardous material by completing the following tasks:

    (a)   Detect the presence of hazardous materials

    (b)   Survey a hazardous materials incident from a safe location to identify the name, UN/NA identification number, or type placard applied for any hazardous materials involved

    (c)   Collect hazard information from the current edition of the Emergency Response Guidebook

(2)   Implement actions consistent with the local emergency response plan, the organization's standard operating procedures, and the current edition of the Emergency Response Guidebook by initiating and completing the following tasks:

    (a)   Protective actions

    (b)   Notification process

4.2.1   Detecting the Presence of Hazardous Materials. Given various facility or transportation situations, or both, with and without hazardous materials present, the first responder at the awareness level shall identify those situations where hazardous materials are present and also shall meet the following requirements:

(1)   Identify the definition of hazardous materials (or dangerous goods, in Canada).

(4)   Identify the difference between hazardous materials incidents and other emergencies.

4.4.1   Initiating Protective Actions. Given examples of facility and transportation hazardous materials incidents, the local emergency response plan, the organization's standard operating procedures, and the current edition of the Emergency Response Guidebook, first responders at the awareness level shall be able to identify the actions to be taken to protect themselves and others and to control access to the scene and shall also meet the following requirements:

(2)   Identify the role of the first responder at the awareness level during a hazardous materials incident.

Chapter 5   Competencies for the First Responder at the Operational Level

5.1.1.2   First responders at the operational level also shall receive any additional training to meet applicable DOT, EPA, OSHA, and other state, local, or provincial occupational health and safety regulatory requirements.

5.1.2.1   The first responder at the operational level shall be able to perform the following tasks:

(1)   Analyze a hazardous materials incident to determine the magnitude of the problem in terms of outcomes by completing the following tasks:

    (b)   Collect hazard and response information from MSDS; CHEMTREC/CANUTEC/SETIQ; local, state, and federal authorities; and shipper/manufacturer contacts

5.2.2   Collecting Hazard and Response Information. Given known hazardous materials, the first responder at the operational level shall collect hazard and response information using MSDS; CHEMTREC/CANUTEC/SETIQ; local, state, and federal authorities; and contacts with the shipper/manufacturer and also shall meet the following requirements:

(4) Identify the following:

(a) Type of assistance provided by CHEMTREC/CANUTEC/SETIQ and local, state, and federal authorities

(b) Procedure for contacting CHEMTREC/CANUTEC/SETIQ and local, state, and federal authorities

(c) Information to be furnished to CHEMTREC/CANUTEC/SETIQ and local, state, and federal authorities

Emergency Responder Guidelines

This chapter provides information that will assist the reader in meeting the following first responder guidelines for fire service and law enforcement from the Office for Domestic Preparedness (ODP) *Emergency Responder Guidelines,* 2002 Edition. The numbers are noted directly in the text under the section titles where they are addressed.

ODP Emergency Responder Guidelines*

Fire Service and Law Enforcement

Awareness Level for Events Involving Weapons of Mass Destruction

I. **Recognize hazardous materials incidents.** The responder should:

    a. Understand what hazardous materials are, as well as the risks associated with these materials in an emergency incident or event.

III. **Know and follow self-protection measures for WMD events and hazardous materials events.** The responder should:

    d. Understand the role of the first responder as well as other levels of response in the department's emergency response plan.

Performance Level for Events Involving Weapons of Mass Destruction

I. **Have successfully completed adequate and proper training at the awareness level for events involving hazardous materials, and for weapons of mass destruction (WMD) and other specialized training.** The responder should:

    a. Complete training in (or have equivalent training and experience) and understand the guidelines at the awareness level for fire service.

III. **Know and follow self-protection measures and rescue and evacuation procedures for WMD events.** The responder should:

    g. Understand the role of the Performance Level A responder, as well as the role of other levels of response, in the department's emergency response plan.

* While law enforcement and fire service guidelines for these two levels are virtually identical, some modifications to the original text of the guidelines have been made throughout the book in order to incorporate them together. The complete and unedited ODP *Emergency Responder Guidelines* are included on the supplemental CD accompanying this book.

Hazardous Materials Regulations, Definitions, and Statistics

[NFPA 472: 4.2.1(4)] [ODP Awareness I.a.]

A *hazardous materials* (*haz mat* or *HM) incident* involves a substance that poses an unreasonable risk to people, the environment, and/or property. It may involve a substance (product or chemical) that has been (or may be) released from a container or a substance that is on fire. The incident may be the result of an accident (such as a container of chemical falling off a forklift) or a deliberate attack (such as a terrorist attack using a deadly gas). It is almost certain that hazardous materials incidents will be more complex than the *routine* emergency incidents faced by any first responder.

First responders must understand the role they play at hazardous materials incidents. They must know their limitations and realize when they cannot proceed any farther. In part, this role is spelled out in government laws and national consensus standards that set forth the training requirements and response limitations imposed on personnel responding to these emergencies. Additionally, responders need a basic understanding of how hazardous materials are regulated because these regulations affect how these materials are transported, used, stored, and disposed of.

Hazardous Materials: A Citizen's Orientation

An online training program from the United States (U.S.) Government provides an excellent introduction to the complex issue of hazardous materials. The paragraphs that follow include material adapted from that program.

In the years since World War II, new technologies have developed at a stunning pace. Nearly every household in our consumer society has grown accustomed to daily use of manufactured products that offer people increased convenience and efficiency: detergents, toilet-bowl cleaners, air fresheners, specialized glues, caulks, and insecticides **(Figure 1.1).**

Many of these products make use of materials that do not exist in nature. It is estimated that over 1,000 new synthetic chemicals will enter our communities every year. Many will require careful handling during manufacture, transport, storage, use, and disposal in order to avoid causing harm to people, other living things, and the environment. many of these

Figure 1.1 Many common household products contain hazardous materials.

chemicals are not *biodegradable* (able to be broken down into their components by microorganisms). For such chemicals in particular, the potential for adverse health effects can continue for decades or even centuries.

Hazardous Materials: A Citizen's Orientation *(continued)*

We are becoming increasingly aware of the limited space that our planet has to offer for the disposal of toxic products. According to 1987 data based on industry reports of toxic discharges compiled by the U.S. Environmental Protection Agency (EPA), over 7 billion pounds (3.2 billion kg) of toxic substances were released directly into our environment (air, land, and water) by industry manufacturers alone. Numerous small businesses, such as printing industries and vehicle maintenance shops, also released toxic chemicals not included in these estimates. Few communities are eager to have hazardous waste deposited in their *backyards. While products that contain hazardous materials attract us by promising to make our lives easier, they often confront us with complex problems — many of which have no easy or immediate solutions.*

Naturally occurring toxic substances can also pose problems. For example, ponds near a wildlife refuge in California became contaminated by selenium, an element commonly found in alkaline desert soil. The high level of selenium was the result of irrigation methods used at nearby farms. Water removed the selenium from the soil, dissolved it, and carried enough of the element to nonfarm portions of the refuge to threaten wildlife. As waterfowl ingested (ate) the selenium, deformities were found more frequently in developing embryos. Naturally occurring substances have sometimes led to expensive cleanup operations comparable to those required for human-created hazardous waste.

Sometimes, the challenge posed by hazardous materials glares at us in headlines and stories. While the following examples happened in the past, similar incidents are still occurring today:

- In Bhopal, India, 44 tons of methyl isocyanate (a highly volatile liquid) spewed into the atmosphere, killing at least 1,700 persons and injuring tens of thousands.

- In a small southern U.S. community, tank railcars containing toxic substances derailed and burned. The fire caused a column of toxic smoke 3,000 feet (914 m) high that forced 7,500 area residents to evacuate.

- In Florida, vandals broke the valves of chemical tanks at a local swimming pool supply company.

The chemicals mixed to form a toxic acid, and a poisonous cloud of vapors sent 45 persons to the hospital.

- In Louisiana, up to 41,000 pounds (18 144 kg) of hydrobromic acid fouled part of the Mississippi River after two ships collided.

- In Pennsylvania, a garbage truck operator found his load on fire after loading mixed chemicals discarded by a high school science department. The operator dumped the load in a residential driveway, and the released cyanide vapors sent 100 persons to the hospital.

- Two New Jersey workers were killed and five were injured by vapors inhaled as they cleaned a chemical mixing vat at a local company.

Often, however, problems posed by hazardous materials are less clear-cut. Many of the effects attributed to toxic substances, such as certain types of cancer, have multiple causes. In any single case of illness or death, it is difficult to point at a specific instance of exposure to a particular hazardous material. In fact, one study found traces of over 200 industrial chemicals and pesticides in members of an American sample group. Determining at what exposure level each of these common substances becomes harmful to human health is not only a scientific question but also social, political, and economic issues.

The legal system seeks to control these materials at every level of government — federal, state/provincial and local — but it is hampered by funding limitations, debates over emerging technologies, lack of definitive research in certain areas, and competing rights and interests. Laws and regulations at all three levels of government address various aspects of the hazardous materials problem by specifying the following:

- How chemicals must be stored

- What employees are told about chemicals they handle at work

- How chemicals are labeled

- What containers are needed to transport specific chemicals

- What emissions levels are acceptable from industries

In each instance, the *local* government's role in regulating its own hazardous materials problems is critical.

This chapter explains the role of different North American government agencies in regulating hazardous materials as well as their different definitions for such materials. Many other countries have similar regulations. The chapter also defines the roles of first responders who become involved with hazardous materials, provides hazardous materials incident statistics, and describes North American emergency response centers.

First Responder Roles

[NFPA 472: 4.1.1.1, 4.1.1.2, 5.1.1.2] [ODP Awareness III.d.] [ODP Operations I.a., III.g.]

The United States (U.S.) Occupational Safety and Health Administration (OSHA) and the U.S. Environmental Protection Agency (EPA) require that responders to hazardous materials incidents meet specific training standards. The OSHA versions of these legislative mandates are outlined in paragraph (q) of Title 29 (Labor) *Code of Federal Regulations (CFR)* 1910.120, *Hazardous Waste Operations and Emergency Response (HAZWOPER)* **(Figure 1.2).** The training requirements found in 29 *CFR* 1910.120 are included by reference in the EPA regulations in Title 40 (Protection of Environment) *CFR* 311, *Worker Protection.* This EPA regulation provides protection to those responders not covered by an OSHA-approved State Occupational Health and Safety Plan. See **Appendix A,** OSHA Plan States, for a list of state-plan and non-state-plan states. The U.S. Department of Justice through the Office for Domestic Preparedness (ODP) has also published federal guidelines for first responders at terrorist incidents involving weapons of mass destruction (WMD).

In addition to U.S. Government regulations, the National Fire Protection Association (NFPA) has several standards that apply to personnel who respond to hazardous materials emergencies. The requirements in these standards are recommendations, not laws or regulations, unless they are adopted as such by the authority having jurisdiction (AHJ). However, because they are a national standard, they can be used as a basis for *accepted practice.* The NFPA's hazardous materials requirements are detailed in the following standards:

- NFPA 471, *Recommended Practice for Responding to Hazardous Materials Incidents* (2002)

- NFPA 472, *Standard for Professional Competence of Responders to Hazardous Materials Incidents* (2002)

- NFPA 473, *Standard for Competencies for EMS Personnel Responding to Hazardous Materials Incidents* (2002)

In Canada, the Ministry of Labour (in most provinces) or the Workers Compensation Board (WCB) in British Columbia are the regulatory bodies governing response to haz mat incidents and the training requirements for first responders. In addition to governing minimum training standards, these provincial bodies require employers to provide standard operating guidelines (SOGs) or standard operating procedures (SOPs) to protect their employees. Canadian firefighters and most

Figure 1.2 In the United States, training requirements for first responders at haz mat incidents are mandated in Title 29 *Code of Federal Regulations (CFR)* 1910.120, *Hazardous Waste Operations and Emergency Response.*

emergency responders are trained to the same NFPA standards as their U.S. counterparts. While Canada does not have the definitive equivalent of OSHA 29 *CFR* 1910.120, the minimum acceptable level of training for firefighters is NFPA 472.

Mexico is in the process of developing and implementing a variety of national laws dealing with the handling and regulation of hazardous materials. However, it does not currently have any national laws applying to the training of emergency haz mat first responders. Local jurisdictions may have their own training standards.

What Does This Mean to You?

 If you are a first responder to haz mat incidents in the U.S., by law your employer must meet the requirements set forth in the *HAZWOPER* regulation (29 *CFR* 1910.120). If your authority having jurisdiction (AHJ) has formally adopted the applicable NFPA standards as law, your employer is required to meet them as well. If you belong to a volunteer fire and emergency services organization, you will also have to meet these regulations. Under 40 *CFR* 311, volunteers are considered employees. Many employers are also training first responders to meet the ODP guidelines for response to terrorist incidents involving WMDs.

 If you are a first responder to haz mat incidents in Canada, your employer must provide you with standard operating guidelines (or standard operating procedures) and the training required by your province. If you are a firefighter, you must be trained in accordance with the requirements in NFPA 472.

 Mexico does not have any national laws applying to the training of haz mat first responders. Local jurisdictions may have their own standards.

NFPA 472 and the OSHA regulations in 29 *CFR* 1910.120 identify two levels of first responders: *Awareness* and *Operational*. They also identify higher levels of response personnel who perform more complex operations. It is important to know and understand the responder's role at each of these levels; however, this book addresses the requirements of the *Awareness* and *Operational*

Levels only. OSHA identifies three levels above the Operational Level: (1) *Hazardous Materials Technician*, (2) *Hazardous Materials Specialist*, and (3) *On Scene Incident Commander (OIC)*. NFPA 472 identifies five levels above the Operational Level: (1) *Hazardous Materials Technician* (plus three specialties), (2) *Hazardous Materials Branch Officer*, (3) *Hazardous Materials Branch Safety Officer*, (4) *Hazardous Materials Incident Commander*, and (5) *Private Sector Specialist Employee*.

The ODP *Emergency Responder Guidelines* (for terrorist incidents involving WMDs) specify training for three levels of responders: (1) *Awareness Level*, (2) *Performance Level*, and (3) *Planning and Management Level*. Each of these levels has separate guidelines for different groups such as law enforcement, fire services, emergency medical services, emergency management, and public works. The Performance Level is subdivided into *Performance Level A (Operations Level)* and *Performance Level B (Technician Level)*. This book covers guidelines for fire services and law enforcement Awareness Level and Performance Level A (Operations Level) only. The ODP requirements for these levels are very similar to OSHA and NFPA requirements, with specific emphasis placed on response to terrorist attacks and understanding of WMDs.

Personnel trained to the Awareness and Operational Levels perform only defensive tasks at haz mat incidents, with a few exceptions (see Operational Level section/information box). Hazardous materials technicians perform offensive and defensive actions. Offensive and defensive tasks are explained in greater detail in Chapter 5, Strategic Goals and Tactical Objectives, under Modes of Operation section.

Awareness Level
[NFPA 472: 4.1.2.1, 4.4.1(2)]

First responders who are trained and certified to the Awareness Level are individuals who, in the course of their normal duties, may be the first to arrive at a hazardous materials incident. These responders must know basic hazards and response information and be able to analyze the incident to determine the hazardous material present and implement protective actions and the notification process **(Figure 1.3)**. **Table 1.1, p. 14,** compares

Figure 1.3 First responders at the Awareness Level are expected to recognize the presence of hazardous materials, protect themselves, call for trained personnel, and secure the area.

Figure 1.4 First responders at the Operational Level are able to perform defensive actions such as confining a spill by digging a retention area in order to prevent a released liquid from spreading.

OSHA and NFPA Awareness-Level first responder roles in a simple bulleted-list format. To summarize both OSHA and NFPA requirements, individuals trained to the Awareness Level are expected to assume the following responsibilities when faced with an incident involving hazardous materials:

- Recognize the presence or potential presence of a hazardous material.

- Recognize the type of container at a site and identify the material in it if possible.

- Transmit information to an appropriate authority and call for appropriate assistance.

- Identify actions to protect themselves and others from hazards.

- Establish scene control by isolating the hazardous area and denying entry.

Operational Level
[NFPA 472: 5.1.1.1]

First responders who are trained and certified to the Operational Level are individuals who respond to releases (or potential releases) of hazardous materials as part of their normal duties. This responder is expected to protect individuals, the environment, and property from the effects of the release in a defensive manner **(Figure 1.4***)*.

Responsibilities of the first responder at the Operational Level include the Awareness-Level responsibilities *plus* confining a release in a defensive fashion from a safe distance. **Table 1.2, p. 15,** compares OSHA and NFPA Operational-Level first responder roles in a simple bulleted-list format. To summarize both OSHA and NFPA requirements, first responders at the Operational Level must be able to perform the following actions:

Table 1.1
Awareness-Level First Responder Roles:
OSHA and NFPA Comparisons

OSHA 29 *CFR* 1910.120 and EPA 40 *CFR* 311	NFPA 472*

[29 1910.120 (q)(6)(i)]
 	
First responders at the awareness level are individuals who are likely to witness or discover a hazardous substance release and who have been trained to initiate an emergency response sequence by notifying the proper authorities of the release. They would take no further action beyond notifying the authorities of the release. First responders at the awareness level shall have sufficient training or have had sufficient experience to objectively demonstrate competency in the following areas:
 	
• An understanding of what hazardous substances are, and the risks associated with them in an incident.
 	
• An understanding of the potential outcomes associated with an emergency created when hazardous substances are present.
 	
• The ability to recognize the presence of hazardous substances in an emergency.
 	
• The ability to identify the hazardous substances, if possible.
 	
• An understanding of the role of the first responder awareness individual in the employer's emergency response plan including site security and control and the *Emergency Response Guidebook*.
 	
• The ability to realize the need for additional resources, and to make appropriate notifications to the communication center.
 	
[40 311.1]
 	
The substantive provisions found at 29 *CFR* 1910.120 on and after March 6, 1990, and before March 6, 1990, found at 54 *CFR* 9317 (March 6, 1989), apply to State and local government employees engaged in hazardous waste operations, as defined in 29 *CFR* 1910.120(a), in States that do not have a State plan approved under section 18 of the Occupational Safety and Health Act of 1970.
 	
[40 311.2]
 	
Employee in Sec. 311.1 is defined as a compensated or non-compensated worker who is controlled directly by a State or local government, as contrasted to an independent contractor.
	[3.3.25]
	
	First Responder at the Awareness Level. Those persons who, in the course of their normal duties, could be the first on the scene of an emergency involving hazardous materials. First responders at the awareness level are expected to:
	
	• Recognize the presence of hazardous materials,
	
	• Protect themselves,
	
	• Call for trained personnel, and
	
	• Secure the area.
	
	[4.1.2.2]
	
	Therefore, when first on the scene of an emergency involving hazardous materials, the first responder at the awareness level shall be able to perform the following tasks:
	
	• Analyze the incident to determine both the hazardous materials present and the basic hazard and response information for each hazardous material by completing the following tasks:
	
	  1. Detect the presence of hazardous materials.
	
	  2. Survey a hazardous materials incident from a safe location to identify the name, UN/NA identification number, or type of placard applied for any materials involved.
	
	  3. Collect hazard information from the current edition of the *Emergency Response Guidebook*.
	
	• Implement actions consistent with the local emergency response plan, the organization's standard operating procedures,** and the current edition of the *Emergency Response Guidebook* by completing the following tasks:
	
	  1. Initiate protective actions.
	
	  2. Initiate the notification process.

---

* Reprinted with permission from NFPA 472, *Standard on Professional Competence of Responders to Hazardous Materials Incidents*, Copyright © 2002, National Fire Protection Association, Quincy, MA 00269. This reprinted material is not the complete and official position of the National Fire Protection Association on the referenced subject, which is represented only by the standard in its entirety.

** The Incident Management System (IMS) requires standard operating procedures (SOPs); however, in many places, SOPs have been dropped in favor of standard operating guidelines (SOGs).

OSHA 29 *CFR* 1910.120 and EPA 40 *CFR* 311	NFPA 472*

[29 1910.120 (q) (6) (ii)]
 	
First responders at the operational level are individuals who respond to releases or potential releases of hazardous substances as part of the initial response to the site for the purpose of protecting nearby persons, property, or the environment from the effects of the release. They are trained to respond in a defensive fashion without actually trying to stop the release. Their function is to contain the release from a safe distance, keep it from spreading, and prevent exposures. First responders at the operational level shall have received at least eight hours of training or have had sufficient experience to objectively demonstrate competency in the following areas in addition to those listed for the awareness level and the employer shall so certify:
 	
• Knowledge of the basic hazard and risk assessment techniques.
 	
• Know how to select and use proper personal protective equipment provided to the first responder operational level.
 	
• An understanding of basic hazardous materials terms.
 	
• Know how to perform basic control, containment and/or confinement operations within the capabilities of the resources and personal protective equipment available with their unit.
 	
• Know how to implement basic decontamination procedures.
 	
• An understanding of the relevant standard operating procedures and termination procedures.
 	
[40 311.1]
 	
The substantive provisions found at 29 *CFR* 1910.120 on and after March 6, 1990, and before March 6, 1990, found at 54 *CFR* 9317 (March 6, 1989), apply to State and local government employees engaged in hazardous waste operations, as defined in 29 *CFR* 1910.120(a), in States that do not have a State plan approved under section 18 of the Occupational Safety and Health Act of 1970.
 	
[40 311.2]
 	
Employee in Sec. 311.1 is defined as a compensated or non-compensated worker who is controlled directly by a State or local government, as contrasted to an independent contractor
	[3.3.26]
	
	First Responder at the Operational Level. Those persons who respond to releases or potential releases of hazardous materials as part of the initial response to the incident for the purpose of protecting nearby persons, the environment, or property from the effects of the release. First responders at the operational level are expected to:
	
	• Respond in a defensive fashion to control the release from a safe distance and
	
	• Keep it from spreading.
	
	[5.1.2.1]
	
	Therefore, in addition to being competent at the awareness level, the first responder at the operational level shall be able to perform the following tasks:
	
	• Analyze a hazardous materials incident to determine the magnitude of the problem in terms of outcomes by completing the following tasks:
	
	  1. Survey the hazardous materials incident to identify the containers and materials involved, determine whether hazardous materials have been released, and evaluate the surrounding conditions.
	
	  2. Collect hazard and response information from MSDSs; CHEMTREC/CANUTEC/SETIQ; local, state, and federal authorities; and shipper/manufacturer contacts.
	
	  3. Predict the likely behavior of a hazardous material as well as its container.
	
	  4. Estimate the potential harm at a hazardous materials incident.
	
	• Plan an initial response within the capabilities and competencies of available personnel, personal protective equipment, and control equipment by completing the following tasks:
	
	  1. Describe the response objectives for hazardous materials incidents.
	
	  2. Describe the defensive options available for a given response objective.
	
	  3. Determine whether the personal protective equipment provided is appropriate for implementing each defensive option.
	
	  4. Identify the emergency decontamination procedures.

Continued

OSHA 29 *CFR* 1910.120 and EPA 40 *CFR* 311	NFPA 472*
	• Implement the planned response to favorably change the outcomes consistent with the local emergency response plan and the organization's standard operating procedures by completing the following tasks:
	1. Establish and enforce scene control procedures including control zones, emergency decontamination, and communications.
	2. Initiate an incident management system (IMS) for hazardous materials incidents.
	3. Don, work in, and doff personal protective equipment provided by the authority having jurisdiction.
	4. Perform defensive control functions identified in the plan of action.
	• Evaluate the progress of the actions taken to ensure that the response objectives are being met safely, effectively, and efficiently by completing the following tasks:
	1. Evaluate the status of the defensive actions being taken in accomplishing the response objectives.
	2. Communicate the status of the planned response.

• Identify the hazardous material(s) involved in an incident if possible.

• Analyze an incident to determine the nature and extent of the problem.

• Protect themselves, nearby persons, the environment, and property from the effects of a release.

• Develop a defensive plan of action to address the problems presented by the incident (plan a response).

• Implement the planned response to control a release from a safe distance (initiate defensive actions to lessen the harmful incident [known as *mitigation*]) and keep it from spreading.

• Evaluate the progress of the actions taken to ensure that response objectives are safely met.

Fire and emergency services organizations commonly respond initially to a variety of hazardous materials incidents. NFPA 1001, *Standard for Fire Fighter Professional Qualifications* (2002), and NFPA 472 identify tactical operations for firefighters and first responders at the Operational Level that are, or may be, offensive in nature (such as flammable liquid and gas fire control). **Table**

1.3, p. 18, provides the appropriate NFPA 1001 job performance requirements for these tasks in a simplified bulleted list format.

Exceptions to the Rule: Offensive Tasks Allowed for Operational-Level Responders in the U.S. and Canada

U.S. OSHA and the Canadian government recognize that first responders at the Operational Level who have appropriate training (including demonstration of competencies and certification by employers — see Table 1.3), appropriate protective clothing, and adequate/appropriate resources can perform offensive operations (sometimes referred to as an Operations Plus level of training) involving flammable liquid and gas fire control of the following materials:

- Gasoline
- Diesel fuel
- Natural gas
- Liquefied petroleum gas (LPG)

Each fire and emergency services organization should have written procedures describing appropriate actions consistent with the level of training. A sample of such a guideline is found in **Appendix B,** Sample Standard Operating Guideline.

Hazardous Materials Regulations and Definitions

[NFPA 472: 4.2.1(1), 3.3.29]
[29 CFR 1910.119, 1910.120, 1910.120(q)(6)(i)(A)]
[U.S. DOT 49 CFR, Parts 170–179, Sections 171.8, 172.101]
[U.S. DOT 49 CFR, Sections 171.8, 172.101 (Appendix A)]
[U.S. EPA 40 CFR, Parts 261.33, 262, 302, 302.4, 355]

This section explains the roles of different North American government agencies in regulating hazardous materials, as well as their definitions for such materials. Today, laws and regulations are often viewed as restrictive or limiting and, therefore, negative. For this reason, it is important for today's first responder to realize that the regulations affecting hazardous materials emergency response have been developed in response to a long string of hazardous materials emergencies, disasters, and environmental damage incidents. For example, the Love Canal environmental emergency and disaster directly led to the enactment of the Comprehensive Environmental Response, Compensation, and Liability Act (CERCLA) of 1980 (often referred to as the *Superfund*) (see case history box, p. 19).

In 1986, fire service professional organizations representing both labor and management testified before the U.S. Congress and requested inclusion of emergency responders in the provisions of the Superfund Amendment and Reauthorization Act (SARA). Emergency responders requested this inclusion based on a history of harmful and deadly incidents that have affected the emergency response community. In response to the emergency response community's request, Congress directed both OSHA and EPA to include emergency responders in the 29 *CFR* 1910.120 and 40 *CFR* 311 regulations (see First Responder Roles section). In fact, the team that authored 29 *CFR* 1910.120 included individuals with strong fire-fighting and emergency-response backgrounds.

U.S. Regulations/Definitions

In the U.S., the four main agencies involved in the regulation of hazardous materials and/or wastes at the federal level are as follows:

- Department of Transportation (DOT)
- Environmental Protection Agency (EPA)
- Department of Labor (DOL)
- Nuclear Regulatory Commission (NRC)

Department of Transportation

The DOT issues transportation regulations in Title 49 (Transportation) *CFR*. There are seven volumes of transportation regulations. These legally binding regulations are enforced at the federal, state, and local levels. The regulations specifically governing the transportation of hazardous materials found in Title 49 *CFR* are sometimes referred to as the *Hazardous Materials Regulations* or *HMR*. They address the transportation of hazardous materials in all modes: air, highway, pipeline, rail, and water.

6.3 **Fireground Operations.** This duty involves performing activities necessary to insure

- Life safety,

- Fire control, and

- Property conservation, according to the following job performance requirements.

NOTE: Many organizations now teach this order as *L*ife safety, *I*ncident stabilization and control, and *P*rotection of property and the environment (sometimes referred to as *LIP service*). The priority of property versus environment may change depending on the situation and location. For example, in Canada, protection of the environment may be stressed over protection of property.

6.3.1 Extinguish an ignitable liquid fire, operating as a member of a team, given an assignment, an attack line, personal protective equipment, a foam proportioning device, a nozzle, foam concentrates, and a water supply, so that

- The correct type of foam concentrate is selected for the given fuel and conditions.

- A properly proportioned foam stream is applied to the surface of the fuel to create and maintain a foam blanket.

- Fire is extinguished.

- Reignition is prevented.

- Team protection is maintained with a foam stream.

- The hazard is faced until retreat to safe haven is reached.

(A) Requisite Knowledge:

— Methods by which foam prevents or controls a hazard

— Principles by which foam is generated

— Causes for poor foam generation and corrective measures

— Difference between hydrocarbon and polar solvent fuels and the concentrates that work on each

— The characteristics, uses, and limitations of fire-fighting foams

— The advantages and disadvantages of using fog nozzles versus foam nozzles for foam application

— Foam stream application techniques

— Hazards associated with foam usage

— Methods to reduce or avoid hazards

6.3.3 Control a flammable gas cylinder fire operating as a member of a team, given an assignment, a cylinder outside of a structure, an attack line, personal protective equipment, and tools, so that

- Crew integrity is maintained.

- Contents are identified.

- Safe havens are identified prior to advancing.

- Open valves are closed.

- Flames are not extinguished unless the leaking gas is eliminated.

- The cylinder is cooled.

- Cylinder integrity is evaluated.

- Hazardous conditions are recognized and acted upon.

- The cylinder is faced during approach and retreat.

(A) Requisite Knowledge:

— Characteristics of pressurized flammable gases

— Elements of a gas cylinder

— Effects of heat and pressure on closed cylinders

— Boiling liquid expanding vapor explosion (BLEVE) signs and effects

— Methods for identifying contents

— How to identify safe havens before approaching flammable gas cylinder fires

— Water stream usage and demands for pressurized cylinder fires

— What to do if the fire is prematurely extinguished

Continued

(B) Requisite Skills:

— The ability to prepare a foam concentrate supply for use.

— Assemble foam stream components.

— Master various foam application techniques.

— Approach and retreat from spills as part of a coordinated team.

A.6.3.1 The Fire Fighter II should be able to accomplish this task with each type of foam concentrate used by the jurisdiction. This could include the use of both Class A and B foam concentrates on appropriate fires. . . . The intent of this JPR can be met in training through the use of training foam concentrates or gas-fired training props.

— Valve types and their operation

— Alternative actions related to various hazards and when to retreat

(B) Requisite Skills:

— The ability to execute effective advances and retreats.

— Apply various techniques for water application.

— Assess cylinder integrity and changing cylinder conditions.

— Operate control valves.

— Choose effective procedures when conditions change.

A.6.3.3 Controlling flammable gas cylinder fires can be a very dangerous operation. The Fire Fighter II should act as a team member, under the direct supervision of an officer, during these operations.

---

* Reprinted with permission from NFPA 1001, *Standard for Fire Fighter Professional Qualifications*, Copyright © 2002, National Fire Protection Association, Quincy, MA 00269. This reprinted material is not the complete and official position of the National Fire Protection Association on the referenced subject, which is represented only by the standard in its entirety.

Why Do We Have All These Regulations?

• *Love Canal, Niagara Falls (1978)* — The Love Canal saga began nearly 100 years before the environmental nightmare came to the world's attention. In the 1890s, industrialist William T. Love devised a plan to dig a canal around Niagara Falls. The canal would allow marine traffic around the falls, provide a water source for inexpensive hydroelectric power, and create a distinct boundary for a model *planned industrial community*. The U.S. economy entered a sharp decline shortly after the project began, and the development ceased. The open canal was publicly auctioned and by 1920 was in use as a local dump and swimming hole.

In 1942, Hooker Chemical Company (later purchased by Occidental Chemical) purchased the site and used it as a waste disposal site for its Niagara Falls Plant. Between 1942 and 1954, Hooker dumped an estimated 22,000+ tons (22 352+ tonnes) of chemical waste into the 3,000-foot long, 60-foot wide, 40-foot deep (194 m long, 18 m wide, 12 m deep) canal and several 25-foot (8 m) deep trenches built near the canal. In 1952, the local school board asked Hooker to sell a small portion of the filled canal to the board for the site of a new school. Hooker initially declined, and the school board subsequently threatened to forcibly acquire the section of the canal.

In 1953, Hooker agreed to provide the district with the property for $1 provided the school district took the entire canal site, Hooker was relieved of any liability for the site, and Hooker was allowed to continue dumping on the site until construction began. The deed-transfer paperwork carried specific warnings to the school board about not

Why Do We Have All These Regulations? *(continued)*

disturbing parts of the site. The school board built a school on the site, and the surrounding area was developed.

In 1978, a series of news reports identified local health issues and the presence of high levels of toxic materials including dioxins and polychlorinated biphenyls (PCBs) **(Figure 1.5)**. The reports led to the evacuation of the entire area, the declaration of a federal emergency, and the development of the Comprehensive Environmental Response, Compensation, and Liability Act (CERCLA).

- ***Torrey Canyon tank ship, England and France (March 18, 1967)*** — On March 18, 1967, one of the world's first oil supertankers (*Torrey Canyon*) to sail the sea ran aground off the southern coast of England. The mishap, caused by a series of navigational miscalculations, resulted in the release of approximately 31,000,000 gallons (125 000 000 L) of Kuwaiti oil from the *Torrey Canyon*. The spill caused extensive damage to marine life and shorelines of France and England. Additionally, since no one had ever planned for an event like this one, mitigation techniques only worsened the damage.

Attempts to mitigate the spill used over 10,000 tons (10 160 tonnes) of dispersing agents that became more toxic than the oil itself. Additionally, the wreckage and oil remaining in the ship were bombed and napalmed in attempts to burn the oil. Aviation gas was even dumped into the spill in an attempt to get it to burn more completely.

As a result of the incident, many countries instituted national plans for dealing with spills of large quantities of oil off their shores. The U.S. passed legislation providing for such planning, and designated the U.S Coast Guard (USCG) as the agency responsible for protecting U.S. coastlines from oil spills and other hazardous materials emergencies. The Coast Guard also placed in service what are called *USCG Strike Teams.*

- ***Kansas City, MO (November 29, 1988)***— Kansas City (MO) Fire Department Engine Companies 41 and 30 responded to a report of a pickup truck fire at a highway construction site in the early morning hours of November 29, 1988. Security guards who phoned in the call reported explosives were stored on site, and that information was communicated to the responding units. Arriving units found multiple fires on the site including two smoldering truck trailers that were loaded with explosives. The trailers' contents (which were not required to be marked or labeled) contained a total of nearly 50,000 pounds (22 680 kg) of ammonium nitrate, fuel-oil-mixture-based explosives. Other explosives stored on site were labeled. Shortly after arrival, the smoldering trailers detonated **(Figure 1.6)**. The first blast killed the six firefighters on scene instantly and destroyed the two pumping apparatus. The explosion left an 80-foot (24 m) diameter and 8-foot (2.4 m) deep crater. Sadly, the fire had been intentionally set.

Nearly 10 years later, U.S. Department of Transportation regulations regarding when placards can be removed from vehicles were changed as a direct result of the incident.

Figure 1.5 Love Canal was used as a chemical waste disposal site before being sold to a local school board for development in 1953. The resulting health problems eventually led to evacuation of the area and passage of the Comprehensive Environmental Response, Compensation, and Liability Act (CERCLA). *Courtesy of the U.S. Environmental Protection Agency.*

Figure 1.6 U.S. Department of Transportation regulations regarding placards were changed after an unmarked trailer containing 50,000 pounds (22 680 kg) of ammonium nitrate exploded in Kansas City in 1988 killing six firefighters. *Courtesy of Ray Elder.*

Why Do We Have All These Regulations? *(continued)*

Figure 1.7 After this tank car exploded in Kingman, Arizona, in 1973, the U.S. Department of Transportation changed its thermal protection standards for railcars. *Courtesy of Mohave Museum of History and Arts.*

- *Kingman, AZ (July 5, 1973)* — Two workers had been preparing a railcar for unloading at the Kingman Doxol Gas plant. During the process, a leak was detected and as workers attempted to stop it, a fire ignited, seriously burning one of the workers and killing the other **(Figure 1.7)**. The Kingman Fire Department was dispatched at 13:57, and first arriving units were on scene at 14:00. Fire department personnel initially deployed handlines and worked to secure water supply for deck-gun operations from the closest hydrant (approximately 1,200 feet [366 m] away).

Less than 20 minutes from the time the fire started, the railcar tank shell failed, releasing the propane contents in what has come to be known as a *BLEVE (boiling liquid expanding vapor explosion).* The BLEVE killed four firefighters instantly and burned seven others so badly that they succumbed to their injuries in the following days. One member of the fire department who had climbed into a truck to talk on the radio suffered severe burns but survived.

As a result of the incident, the Department of Transportation required all railcars in flammable gas service at the time to be retrofitted with thermal protection that would provide significant protection of the tank during similar fire conditions. Today's flammable gas railcars are thermally protected to protect the tank from 100 minutes of exposure to a 1,600°F fire (871°C) and at least 30 minutes of 2,200°F (1 204°C) impingement as a direct result of this incident.

- *Texas City, TX (April 16, 1947)* — The greatest industrial disaster in U.S. history occurred in April of 1947 when a French ship, the *Grandcamp,* caught fire during loading in Texas City, Texas. The ship was already loaded with tobacco, twine, cotton, other commodities, and ammonium nitrate fertilizer when workers were completing the loading process in Hold 4 of the ship. The hold contained more than 800 tons (813 tonnes) of ammonium nitrate fertilizer and was being loaded with more when a fire ignited (thought to be caused by workers smoking and other lax safety practices). The crew attempted to fight the fire but was driven from the cargo hold rapidly by thick smoke. The crew sounded a dock alarm at about 08:30.

By 08:45, the Texas City Fire Department was on scene and had deployed hoselines. By 09:00, extensive flames were coming from the ship, and at 09:12 the ship disintegrated, killing all 27 firefighters of the Texas City Fire Department and 34 vessel crew members and causing additional explosions and fires at nearby refineries and on adjacent ships. The initial blast sent the *Grandcamp's* 3,200-pound (1 452 kg) anchor flying over 1.6 miles (2.6 km) inland. The initial explosion and subsequent events killed over 550 people and injured well over 3,000 **(Figure 1.8)**.

Figure 1.8 Over 550 people were killed and well over 3,000 injured in Texas City, Texas, in 1947 when a ship carrying ammonium nitrate fertilizer exploded at dock. *Courtesy of Moore Memorial Library, 1701 9th Avenue North, Texas City, TX 77590.*

Why Do We Have All These Regulations? *(continued)*

As a result of this incident, the USCG Board of Investigation recommended establishment of a federal office to do the following:

— Collect, evaluate, and disseminate information on fire prevention and extinguishment on board merchant vessels.

— Prepare and publish a fire prevention and fire extinguishment manual for use on board merchant vessels.

— Establish and operate a fire-fighting school for training of key operating personnel of merchant ship operators and stevedores.

— Conduct other related marine safety activities.

It also served to increase awareness that fire departments in general are at great risk when responding to hazardous materials incidents and fires.

- ***Shreveport, LA (September 17, 1984)*** — On September 17, 1984, the Shreveport (LA) Fire Department responded to an anhydrous ammonia leak at Dixie Cold Storage. While working to control the leak in the warehouse, a spark ignited the ammonia. The explosion and flash fire severely burned two firefighters who were working in the area in chemical protective clothing. One firefighter died from his injuries a few days later. As a direct result of the incident, the NFPA standards on chemical protective clothing now address the hazards of flash fires and require garments to be constructed of materials that will not contribute to injuries in similar situations.

The purpose of the HMR is to provide adequate protection against the risks to life, property, and the environment inherent in transporting hazardous materials in commerce by improving the regulatory and enforcement authority of the Secretary of Transportation. The DOT Research and Special Programs Administration (RSPA) agency carries out these duties through a program of regulation, enforcement, emergency response education and training, and data collection and analysis.

Environmental Protection Agency

The EPA is responsible for researching and setting national standards for a variety of environmental programs. It delegates the responsibility for issuing permits, monitoring, and enforcing compliance to states and tribes. It also works closely with other federal agencies, state and local governments, and Indian tribes to develop and enforce regulations under existing environmental laws. The EPA also works with industries and all levels of government in a wide variety of voluntary pollution prevention programs and energy conservation efforts.

Several pieces of environmental legislation are of particular interest to first responders. The first is the Comprehensive Environmental Response, Compensation, and Liability Act (CERCLA), commonly known as the *Superfund Act,* which was

enacted by Congress on December 11, 1980. This law created a tax on the chemical and petroleum industries and provided broad federal authority to respond directly to releases or threatened releases of hazardous substances that may endanger public health or the environment. Over 5 years, $1.6 billion was collected, and the tax went to a trust fund for cleaning up abandoned or uncontrolled hazardous waste sites. CERCLA was responsible for the following actions:

- Established prohibitions and requirements concerning closed and abandoned hazardous waste sites

- Provided for liability of persons responsible for releases of hazardous waste at these sites

- Established a trust fund to provide for cleanup when no responsible party could be identified.

The law authorizes the following two kinds of response actions:

- Short-term removals where actions may be taken to address releases or threatened releases requiring prompt response

- Long-term remedial response actions that permanently and significantly reduce the dangers associated with releases or threats of releases of hazardous substances that are serious, but not immediately life-threatening (see EPA's National Priorities List for more information)

CERCLA also enabled the revision of the National Contingency Plan (NCP). The NCP provided the guidelines and procedures needed to respond to releases and threatened releases of hazardous substances, pollutants, or contaminants. CERCLA was amended by the Superfund Amendments and Reauthorization Act (SARA) on October 17, 1986.

SARA reflected the EPA's experience in administering the complex Superfund program during its first 6 years and made several important changes and additions to the program. SARA was responsible for the following actions:

- Stressed the importance of permanent remedies and innovative treatment technologies in cleaning up hazardous waste sites

- Required Superfund actions to consider the standards and requirements found in other state and federal environmental laws and regulations

- Provided new enforcement authorities and settlement tools

- Increased state involvement in every phase of the Superfund program

- Increased the focus on human health problems posed by hazardous waste sites

- Encouraged greater citizen participation in making decisions on how sites should be cleaned up

- Increased the size of the trust fund to $8.5 billion

The Environmental Protection and Community Right-to-Know Act (EPCRA) (also known as Title III of SARA) was enacted by Congress as the national legislation on community safety. This law was designated to help local communities protect public health, safety, and the environment from chemical hazards. To implement EPCRA, Congress required each state to appoint a State Emergency Response Commission (SERC). The SERCs were required to divide their states into Emergency Planning Districts and to name a Local Emergency Planning Committee (LEPC) for each district. Broad representation by emergency responders, health officials, government and media representatives, community groups, industrial facilities, and emergency managers ensures that all necessary elements of the planning process are represented.

The Resource Conservation and Recovery Act (RCRA) gave the EPA the authority to control hazardous waste from the *cradle-to-grave*. This control includes the generation, transportation, treatment, storage, and disposal of hazardous waste. RCRA also set forth a framework for the management of nonhazardous wastes.

The 1986 amendments to RCRA enabled the EPA to address environmental problems that could result from underground tanks storing petroleum and other hazardous substances. RCRA focuses only on active and future facilities and does not address abandoned or historical sites.

The Toxic Substances Control Act (TSCA) of 1976 was enacted by Congress to give the EPA the ability to track the 75,000 industrial chemicals currently produced or imported into the U.S. The EPA repeatedly screens these chemicals and can require reporting or testing of those that may pose an environmental or human-health hazard. The EPA can ban the manufacture and import of those chemicals that pose an unreasonable risk.

Also, the EPA has mechanisms in place to track the thousands of new chemicals that industry develops each year with either unknown or dangerous characteristics. The EPA then can control these chemicals as necessary to protect human health and the environment. TSCA supplements other federal statutes, including the Clean Air Act and the Toxic Release Inventory under EPCRA. The EPA issues legislation to protect the environment in Title 40 *CFR*.

Department of Labor

The DOL is responsible for overseeing U.S. labor laws. The U.S. Congress passed the Occupational Safety and Health (OSH) Act in 1970. One year later a new department, the Occupational Safety and Health Administration, was created to oversee compliance with the Act under the jurisdiction of the DOL.

OSHA issues legislation relating to worker safety under Title 29 *CFR*. OSHA legislation of interest to first responders includes the *HAZWOPER* regulation (29 *CFR* 1910.120) discussed earlier as well as the *Hazard Communication* regulation (29 *CFR* 1910.1200) and the *Process Safety Management of Highly Hazardous Chemicals* regulation (29 *CFR* 1910.119).

The Hazard Communication Standard (HCS) is designed to ensure that information about chemical hazards and associated protective measures is disseminated to workers and employers. This dissemination is accomplished by requiring chemical manufacturers and importers to evaluate the hazards of the chemicals they produce or import and provide information about them through labels on shipped containers and material safety data sheets (MSDSs).

The Process Safety Management (PSM) of Highly Hazardous Chemicals (HHCs) standard is intended to prevent or minimize the consequences of a catastrophic release of toxic, reactive, flammable, or explosive HHCs from a process. A *process* is any activity or combination of activities including any use, storage, manufacturing, handling, or on-site movement of HHCs. A process includes any group of vessels that are interconnected and separate vessels that are located such that a HHC could be involved in a potential release.

Nuclear Regulatory Commission

The NRC regulates U.S. commercial nuclear power plants and the civilian use of nuclear materials as well as the possession, use, storage, and transfer of radioactive materials through Title 10 (Energy) *CFR 20, Standards for Protection Against Radiation.* The NRC's primary mission is to protect the public's health and safety and the environment from the effects of radiation from nuclear reactors, materials, and waste facilities. Title 10 *CFR* 20 includes information on the following items:

- Radiation dose limits for workers and members of the public

- Requirements for monitoring and labeling of radioactive materials

- Requirements for posting of radiation areas

- Requirements for reporting the theft or loss of radioactive materials

- Tables of individual radionuclide exposure limits

Other Agencies

Several other U.S. agencies are involved with hazardous materials:

- *Department of Homeland Security (DHS)* — Has three primary missions: (1) Prevent terrorist attacks within the U.S., (2) Reduce America's vulnerability to terrorism, and (3) Minimize the damage from potential attacks and natural disasters. DHS was created in the aftermath of the September 11, 2001, terrorist attacks and assumes primary responsibility for ensuring that emergency response professionals are prepared for any situation in the event of a terrorist attack, natural disaster, or other large-scale emergency. *Details:*

  — Responsibilities include providing a coordinated, comprehensive federal response to any large-scale crisis and mounting a swift and effective recovery effort.

  — The Federal Emergency Management Agency (FEMA) and U.S. Coast Guard (USCG) are located within DHS.

- *Consumer Product Safety Commission (CPSC)* — Oversees and enforces compliance with the Federal Hazardous Substances Act (FHSA), which requires that certain hazardous household products (hazardous substances) carry cautionary labeling to alert consumers to the potential hazards that those products present and inform them of the measures they need to protect themselves from those hazards. Under this Act, the Commission also has the authority to ban a product if the hazardous substance it contains is so hazardous that the cautionary labeling required by the Act is inadequate to protect the public.

- *Department of Energy (DOE)* — Manages the national nuclear research and defense programs, including the storage of high-level nuclear waste.

- *Department of Defense Explosives Safety Board (DDESB), Department of Defense (DOD)* — Provides oversight of the development, manufacture, testing, maintenance, demilitarization, handling, transportation, and storage of explosives, including chemical agents on DOD facilities worldwide.

- *Bureau of Alcohol, Tobacco, Firearms and Explosives (ATF), Department of Treasury* — Enforces the federal laws and regulations relating to alcohol, tobacco products, firearms, explosives, and arson.
- *Department of Justice (DOJ)* — Assigns primary responsibility for operational response to threats or acts of terrorism within U.S. territory to the Federal Bureau of Investigation (FBI). The FBI then operates as the on-scene manager for the federal government. It is ultimately the lead agency on terrorist incident scenes. *FBI duties:*
  - Investigates the theft of hazardous materials
  - Collects evidence for crimes
  - Prosecutes criminal violations of federal hazardous materials laws and regulations

The Office for Domestic Preparedness (ODP) also falls under the jurisdiction of the DOJ. The ODP issues federal emergency responder guidelines for WMD events.

U.S. Summary

Table 1.4, p. 26, lists the main U.S. agencies involved in the regulation of hazardous materials, their spheres of responsibility, and associated pieces of legislation. The table also includes the hazardous material terms and definitions coming from the respective regulations that are of primary concern to first responders. First responders need to be aware of the context in which these different terms are used.

Canadian Regulations/Definitions

In Canada the four main agencies that are involved in the regulation of hazardous materials and/or wastes at the national level are as follows:

- Transport Canada (TC)
- Environment Canada
- Health Canada
- Canadian Nuclear Safety Commission (CNSC)

Transport Canada

TC is the focal point for the national program to promote public safety during the transportation of *dangerous goods* (the Canadian term for hazardous materials in transport). The department's Transport Dangerous Goods (TDG) Directorate serves as the major source of regulatory development, information, and guidance on dangerous goods transport for the public, industry employees, and government employees, particularly in regards to the Transportation of Dangerous Goods Act, the Canadian equivalent of the U.S. HMR. The Directorate also operates the Canadian Transport Emergency Centre (CANUTEC) (see Emergency Response Centers section).

Environment Canada

Environment Canada shares with Health Canada the task of assessing and managing the risks associated with toxic substances. Under the Canadian Environmental Protection Act (CEPA), 1999, the potential risks of environmental pollutants and toxic substances are evaluated. The Act also addresses pollution prevention and the protection of the environment and human health. In order to distinguish new substances from existing ones and prescribe reporting requirements for new substances, Environment Canada has established the following substance inventories or lists:

- Domestic Substances List
- Export Control List
- National Pollutant Release Inventory
- Non-Domestic Substances List
- Priority Substances List
- Toxic Substances List
- Waste or other matter that may be disposed of at sea

Health Canada

Health Canada provides national leadership to develop health policy, enforce health regulations, promote disease prevention, and enhance healthy living for all Canadians. The Minister of Health has total or partial responsibility for administration of the following Acts:

- *Hazardous Products Act* — Controls the sale, advertising, and importation of hazardous products used by consumers in the workplace that are not covered by other acts and listed as prohibited or restricted products. The Act covers

Agency	Sphere of Responsibility	Important Legislation	Hazardous Material Terms/Definitions
Department of Transportation (DOT) Research and Special Programs Administration (RSPA)	Transportation Safety	Title 49 (Transportation) *CFR* 100-185 Hazardous Materials Regulations (HMR)	***Hazardous Material:*** a substance or material (including hazardous wastes, marine pollutants, and elevated temperature materials) that has been determined by the U.S. Secretary of Transportation to be capable of posing an unreasonable risk to health, safety, and property when transported in commerce and which has been so designated*
Environmental Protection Agency (EPA)	Public Health and the Environment	Title 40 (Protection of Environment) *CFR* 302.4 Designation of Hazardous Substances	***Hazardous Substance:*** a chemical that if released into the environment above a certain amount must be reported and, depending on the threat to the environment, federal involvement in handling the incident can be authorized
		40 *CFR* 355 Superfund Amendments and Reauthorization Act (SARA)	***Extremely Hazardous Substance:*** any chemical that must be reported to the appropriate authorities if released above the threshold reporting quantity** ***Toxic Chemical:*** one whose total emission or release must be reported annually by owners and operators of certain facilities that manufacture, process, or otherwise use a listed toxic chemical***
		40 *CFR* 261 Resource Conservation and Recovery Act (RCRA)	***Hazardous Wastes:*** chemicals that are regulated under the Resource Conservation and Recovery Act (40 *CFR* 261.33 provides a list of hazardous wastes)

Continued

Agency	Sphere of Responsibility	Important Legislation	Hazardous Material Terms/Definitions
Department of Labor (DOL) Occupational Safety and Health Administration (OSHA)	Worker Safety	29 (Labor) *CFR* 1910.1200 Hazard Communications	***Hazardous Chemical:*** any chemical that would be a risk to employees if exposed in the workplace (Hazardous chemicals cover a broader group of chemicals than the other chemical lists.)
		29 *CFR* 1910.120 Hazardous Waste Operations and Emergency Response (HAZWOPER)	***Hazardous Substance:*** every chemical regulated by the U.S. DOT and EPA.
		29 *CFR* 1910.119 Process Safety Management of Highly Hazardous Chemicals	***Highly Hazardous Chemicals:*** those chemicals that possess toxic, reactive, flammable, or explosive properties (A list of these chemicals is published in Appendix A of 29 *CFR* 1910.119.)
Consumer Product Safety Commission (CPSC)	Hazardous Household Products (chemical products intended for consumers)	Title 16 (Commercial Practices) *CFR* 1500 Hazardous Substances and Articles Federal Hazardous Substances Act (FHSA)	***Hazardous Substance:*** any substance or mixture of substances that is toxic; corrosive; an irritant; a strong sensitizer; flammable or combustible; or generates pressure through decomposition, heat, or other means and if such substance or mixture of substances may cause substantial personal injury or substantial illness during or as a proximate result of any customary or reasonably foreseeable handling or use, including reasonably foreseeable ingestion by children. ***Also:*** any radioactive substance if, with respect to such substance as used in a particular class of article or as packaged, the Commission determines by regulation that the substance is sufficiently hazardous to require labeling in accordance with the Act in order to protect the public health****

Continued

Agency	Sphere of Responsibility	Important Legislation	Hazardous Material Terms/Definitions
Nuclear Regulatory Commission (NRC)	Radioactive Materials (use, storage, and transfer)	Title 10 (Energy) *CFR* 20 Standards for Protection Against Radiation	

* DOT uses the term *hazardous materials* to cover 9 hazard classes, some of which have subcategories called *divisions*. DOT includes in its regulations *hazardous substances* and *hazardous wastes*, both of which are regulated by the U.S. EPA if their inherent properties would not otherwise be covered. The different DOT hazard classes are discussed in Chapter 3, Hazardous Materials Identification.

** Each substance has a threshold reporting quantity. The list of *extremely hazardous substances* is identified in Title III of SARA of 1986 (see 40 *CFR* 355).

*** The list of *toxic chemicals* is provided in Title III of SARA (see 40 *CFR* 355). The EPA regulates these materials because of public health and safety concerns. While regulatory authority is granted under the Resource Conservation and Recovery Act, the DOT regulates the transport of these materials.

**** The complete definition of *hazardous substance* as found in the FHSA contains five parts (A–E) and includes such items as toys and other articles intended for use by children. Only parts A and C are cited here in their entirety.

consumer products that are poisonous, toxic, flammable, explosive, corrosive, infectious, oxidizing, and reactive. It also covers workplace hazardous materials; products intended for domestic or personal use, gardening, sports, or other recreational activities; and products for lifesaving or children (such as toys, games, and equipment), which pose or are likely to pose a hazard to public health and safety because of their design, construction, or contents.

• *Pest Control Products Act (and regulations)* — Intended to protect people and the environment from risks posed by pesticides, which include a variety of products such as insecticides, herbicides, and fungicides. Any pesticide imported, sold, or used in Canada must first be registered under this Act, which is administered by the Pest Management Regulatory Agency of Health Canada.

Canadian Nuclear Safety Commission

The Canadian Nuclear Safety Commission can be best described as the watchdog over the use of nuclear energy and materials in Canada. In addition to nuclear power plants and nuclear research facilities, the CNSC regulates numerous other uses of nuclear material. Some examples include radioisotopes used in the treatment of cancer, the operation of uranium mines and refineries, and the use of radioactive sources for oil exploration and in instruments such as precipitation measurement devices.

Canadian Summary

Table 1.5 lists the main Canadian agencies, their spheres of responsibility, important legislation, and the hazardous materials terms and definitions associated with the legislation. **Table 1.6, p. 31** provides a brief summary of the regulatory programs administered by other agencies of the Canadian government relating to chemical substances.

Table 1.5
Main Canadian Agencies Involved in the
Regulation of Hazardous Materials

Agency	Sphere of Responsibility	Important Legislation	Hazardous Material Terms/Definitions
Transport Canada (TC) Transport Dangerous Goods (TDG) Directorate	Transportation Safety	Transportation of Dangerous Goods Act	***Dangerous Goods:*** any product, substance, or organism included by its nature, or by the regulation, in any of the classes listed in the schedule of the nine United Nations (UN) Classes of Hazardous Materials*
Environment Canada	Public Health and the Environment	Canadian Environmental Protection Act 1999	***Toxic Substance:*** a substance that if it is entering or may enter the environment in a quantity or concentration or under conditions that it (a) Has or may have an immediate or long-term harmful effect on the environment or its biological diversity (b) Constitutes or may constitute a danger to the environment on which life depends (c) Constitutes or may constitute a danger in Canada to human life or health
Transboundary Movement Division	Transportation of Hazardous Waste	Canadian Environmental Protection Act, 1999 Export and Import of Hazardous Wastes Regulations (EIHWR)	***Hazardous Waste:*** any substance specified in Parts I, II, III, or IV of the List of Hazardous Wastes Requiring Export or Import Notification in Schedule III, (*déchets dangereux*); or any product, substance, or organism that is dangerous goods, as defined in Section 2 of the Transportation of Dangerous Goods Act, 1992, that is no longer used for its original purpose and that is recyclable material or intended for treatment or disposal, including storage prior to treatment or disposal, but does not include a product, substance or organism that is (i) Household in origin

Continued

Agency	Sphere of Responsibility	Important Legislation	Hazardous Material Terms/Definitions
			(ii) Returned directly to a manufacturer or supplier of the product, substance, or organism for reprocessing, repackaging, or resale, including a product, substance or organism that is (A) Defective or otherwise not usable for its original purpose (B) In surplus quantities but still usable for its original purpose (iii) Included in Class 1 or 7 of the *Transportation of Dangerous Goods Regulations*
Health Canada	Worker Safety	Hazardous Product Act	***Hazardous Product:*** any product, material, or substance that is, or contains, a poisonous, toxic, flammable, explosive, corrosive, infectious, oxidizing, or reactive product, material, or substance (or other product, material or substance of a similar nature) that the Governor in Council is satisfied is (or is likely to be) a danger to the health or safety of the public
Workplace Hazardous Materials Information System Division (WHMIS Division)	Worker Safety/ Chemicals Intended for the Workplace	Hazardous Product Act Workplace Hazardous Materials Information System (WHMIS)	***Controlled Product:*** any product, material, or substance specified by the regulations to be included in any of the classes listed in Schedule II of the Hazardous Product Act

* Internationally, hazardous materials in transport are generally referred to as *dangerous goods.*

**Table 1.6
Other Canadian Agencies Involved
with Hazardous Materials**

Canadian Authority	Program
Health Canada, Consumer Products Division	Chemicals on the retail market
Natural Resources Canada, Explosives Regulatory Division	Explosives
Environment Canada, Waste Management and Remediation	Management of hazardous wastes, assessment and remediation of contaminated sites, and the control of waste disposal at sea
Canadian Nuclear Safety Commission	Nuclear substances
Health Canada, Pest Management Regulatory Agency	Pesticides
Health Canada, Radiation Protection Bureau	Radioactive substances
National Energy Board	Transportation of chemical products (oil and natural gas) via pipeline

Mexican Regulations/Definitions

The three main agencies that are involved in the regulation of hazardous materials and/or wastes at the national level in Mexico are as follows:

- *Secretaría de Comunicaciones y Transportes (SCT)* — Ministry of Communications and Transport

- *Secretaría de Medio Ambiente y Recursos Naturales (SEMARNAT)* — Ministry of Environment and Natural Resources

- *Secretaría del Trabajo y Previsión Social (STPS)* — Ministry of Labor and Social Welfare

Secretaría de Comunicaciones y Transportes

The Ministry of Communications and Transport is responsible for publishing and maintaining the official Mexican standards (NOMs) covering the *Mexican Hazardous Materials Land Transportation Regulation.* The Mexican NOMs are fairly consistent with the *United Nations Recommendations on the Transport of Dangerous Goods (UN Recommendations).* Since the U.S. Hazardous Materials Regulations are also based on the *UN Recommendations,* the HMR and the Mexican regulations are fairly consistent. The significant differences between the two are discussed in Chapter 3, Hazardous Materials Identification.

Something You Should Know!

Don't get caught up in the specific definitions of different material terms. To an emergency responder, they are all *hazardous.* However, since you may hear other terms being used, be aware that the location where you find a hazardous material and how it is being used may determine what it is called for government purposes.

For example, when xylene is being transported in the U.S., the DOT regulates it, and it would be called a *hazardous material.* (If it were being transported in Canada, it would be called a *dangerous good.*) In the industry (or place of employment) where it is being used or manufactured, it becomes subject to the OSHA requirements protecting employees who work with it, and it would be considered a *hazardous chemical.* If it were marketed to consumers for pur-

chase and use, it would fall subject to the Consumer Product Safety Commission, and it would be called a *hazardous substance.*

If at any point xylene was accidentally discharged from its packaging into the environment, it would become a hazardous substance as regulated by the EPA. When xylene completes its useful life in a plant or workplace and must be disposed of (in any manner), it becomes a *hazardous waste* and would be subject to both the EPA and DOT regulations (during transport). Additionally, if xylene was used to kill or injure a large number of people in a terrorist attack, it might be called a *weapon of mass destruction* by federal law enforcement authorities such as the FBI (see Chapter 9, Terrorist and Other Criminal Activities).

Secretaría de Medio Ambiente y Recursos Naturales

The Ministry of Environment and Natural Resources is roughly equivalent to the U.S. EPA. Its main purpose is to create a state environmental protection policy and oversee the Federal General Law of Ecological Equilibrium and the Protection of the Environment (LGEEPA). Included in LGEEPA are regulations for manufacturing, handling, storage, and disposal of hazardous wastes.

Secretaría del Trabajo y Previsión Social

Labor is the responsibility of the Ministry of Labor and Social Welfare, and there is one labor law in Mexico: Ley Federal del Trabajo or LFT (Federal Labor Law). In the Federal Labor Law, there are two regulations: (1) Regulation for Safety, Health, and Environment in the Workplace (RFSHMAT) and (2) Regulation for the Inspection and Application of Sanctions for Violations of Labor Legislation. Of particular interest to the emergency responder are the following NOMs outlining the requirements and responsibilities set forth in RFSHMAT:

- *System for the Identification and Communication of Hazards and Risks for Dangerous Chemical Substances in the Workplace (NOM-018-STPS-2000)* — Equivalent to the U.S. Hazard Communication Standard in that it sets forth requirements dealing with chemical labels, employee training and communication, and material safety data sheets; also provides a list of substances divided by classification and grade of risk

- *Signs and Colors for Safety and Health, and Identification of Risk of Accidents by Fluids Conducted in Pipes (NOM-026-STPS-1998)* — Spells out the color and signage requirements for pipelines carrying various hazardous materials

- *Health and Safety Conditions in the Workplace for the Handling, Transport, and Storage of Hazardous Chemical Substances (NOM-005-STPS-1998)* — Details the requirements for handling, transport, and warehousing of hazardous materials, including programs relating to confined spaces, personal protective equipment, training, and medical monitoring as well as maintenance of machinery, containers, installations, and other equipment

Mexican Summary

Table 1.7 lists the Mexican agencies, their spheres of responsibility, important legislation, and the hazardous material terms and definitions with which first responders need to be familiar.

Emergency Response Centers

[NFPA 472: 5.1.2.1(1)(b); 5.2.2(4)(a–c)]

In addition to the government agencies responsible for regulating hazardous materials, Canada and Mexico have government-operated emergency response centers. The U.S. has several emergency response centers that are not government operated. These centers are staffed with experts who can provide 24-hour assistance to emergency responders dealing with haz mat emergencies.

The Canadian Transport Emergency Centre (CANUTEC) is operated by Transport Canada. This national bilingual (English and French) advisory center is part of the Transportation of Dangerous Goods Directorate. CANUTEC has a scientific data bank on chemicals manufactured, stored, and transported in Canada and is staffed by professional scientists who specialize in emergency response and are experienced in interpreting technical information and providing advice. Mexico has two emergency response centers: (1) National Center for Communications of the Civil Protection Agency (CECOM) and (2) Emergency Transportation System for the Chemical Industry (SETIQ), which is operated by the National Association of Chemical Industries.

In the U.S., several emergency response centers, such as the Chemical Transportation Emergency Center (CHEMTREC®), are not government operated. CHEMTREC®, for example, was established by the chemical industry as a public service hotline for firefighters, law enforcement responders, and other emergency service responders to obtain information and assistance for emergency incidents involving chemicals and hazardous materials.

A full list of emergency response centers and their telephone numbers is provided in the current *Emergency Response Guidebook (ERG)* (also see sidebar) **(Figure 1.9, p. 35)**. The *ERG* is discussed in more detail in later chapters of this book.

Table 1.7
Mexican Agencies Involved in the Regulation of
Hazardous Materials

Agency	Sphere of Responsibility	Important Legislation	Hazardous Material Terms/Definitions
Secretaría de Communicaciones y Transportes Ministry of Communications and Transportation	Transportation Safety	• Mexican Hazardous Materials Land Transportation Regulation • NOM-004-SCT-2000: System of Identification of Units Designated for the Transport of Hazardous Substances, Materials, and Wastes • NOM-005-SCT-2000: Emergency Information for the Transport of Hazardous Substances, Materials, and Wastes	
Secretaría de Medio Ambiente y Recursos Naturales Ministry of the Environment and Natural Resources	Public Health and the Environment	• La Ley General de Equilibrio Ecológico y Protección al Ambiente: Federal General Law of Ecological Equilibrium and the Protection of the Environment (LGEEPA) • Regulation of LGEEPA in the area of hazardous wastes	

Continued

Table 1.7 (continued)
Mexican Agencies Involved in the Regulation of
Hazardous Materials

Agency	Sphere of Responsibility	Important Legislation	Hazardous Material Terms/Definitions
Secretaría del Trabajo y Previsión Social Ministry of Labor and Social Welfare	Worker Safety/ Labor	• NOM-018-STPS-2000: System for the Identification and Communication of Hazards and Risks for Dangerous Chemical Substances in the Workplace	***Sustancias químicas peligrosas (dangerous chemical substances):*** those chemicals that through their physical and chemical properties upon being handled, transported, stored, or processed present the possibility of fire, explosion, toxicity, reactivity, radioactivity, corrosive action, or harmful biological action and can affect the health of the persons exposed or cause damage to installations and equipment
		• NOM-005-STPS-1998: Health and Safety Conditions in the Workplace for the Handling, Transport, and Storage of Hazardous Chemical Substances	***Sustancias tóxicas (toxic substances):*** those chemicals in solid, liquid, or gaseous state that can cause death or damage to health if they are absorbed by the worker even in relatively small amounts
		• NOM-026-STPS-1998: Signs and Colors for Safety and Health, and Identification of Risk of Accidents by Fluids Conducted in Pipes	***Fluidos de bajo riesgo (dangerous fluids):*** those liquids and gases that can cause injury or illness on the job because of their intrinsic hazards such as flammables, unstable combustibles that can cause explosion, irritants, corrosives, toxics, reactives, radioactives, biological agents, or those that are subjected to extreme pressure or temperature as part of a process

How to Contact Emergency Response Centers

Collect and provide to the center as much of the following information as safely possible:

- Caller's name, callback telephone number, and FAX number
- Location and nature of problem (spill, fire, etc.)
- Name and identification number of material(s) involved
- Shipper/consignee/point of origin
- Carrier name, railcar, or truck number
- Container type and size
- Quantity of material transported/released
- Local conditions (weather, terrain, proximity to schools, hospitals, waterways, etc.)
- Injuries and exposures
- Local emergency services that have been notified

Figure 1.9 In addition to providing emergency response guidelines for hundreds of different chemicals, the *Emergency Response Guidebook (ERG)* lists contact information for emergency response centers in North America.

How to Contact Emergency Response Centers *(continued)*

The emergency response center will do the following:

- Confirm that a chemical emergency exists.
- Record details in writing and on tape.
- Provide immediate technical assistance to the caller.
- Contact the shipper of the material or other experts.
- Provide the shipper/manufacturer with the caller's name and callback number so that the shipper/manufacturer can deal directly with the party involved.

United States Centers

- CHEMTREC®: 800-424-9300 (Business CHEMTREC: 202-887-1255, 9–4 p.m. EST)
- CHEM-TEL, INC.: 800-255-3924
- INFOTRAC: 800-535-5053
- 3ECOMPANY: 800-451-8346
- National Response Center: 800-424-8802
- U.S. Army Operations Center (DOD shipments involving explosives and ammunition): 703-697-0218 (call collect)
- Defense Logistics Agency (DOD shipments involving other dangerous goods): 800-851-8061

Canada Centers

- CANUTEC: 613-996-6666 collect (Emergency only)
- Alberta: 800-272-9600
- British Columbia: 800-663-3456
- Manitoba: 204-945-4888
- New Brunswick: 800-565-1633
- Newfoundland: 709-772-2083
- Northwest Territories: 867-920-8130
- Nova Scotia: 800-565-1633
- Nunavut: 800-693-1666 or 867-979-6262
- Ontario, Quebec: Local police
- Prince Edward Island: 800-565-1633
- Saskatchewan: 800-667-7525
- Yukon Territory: 867-667-7244

Mexico Centers

- SETIQ: 01-800-00-214-00
- CENACOM: 01-800-00-413-00

Brazil Center

- PRÓ-QUÍMICA: 0-800-118270

Hazardous Materials Incident Statistics

Hazardous materials incidents are not infrequent occurrences. It is likely that all emergency first responders will have to deal with hazardous materials at some point in their careers. In fact, hazardous material spills, releases, and incidents are so common that there are seven different U.S. government databases dedicated to tracking them **(Table 1.8).**

Because certain hazardous materials are more commonly used and/or used in greater quantities than others, they are statistically more likely to be involved in incidents and accidents. Additionally, clandestine, illegal methamphetamine labs with their variety of hazardous products are increasing problems in many jurisdictions. Records have shown that the majority of haz mat incidents involve the following products (not necessarily in this order):

- Flammable/combustible liquids (petroleum products, paint products, resins, adhesives, etc.)
- Corrosives (sulfuric acid, hydrochloric acid, sodium hydroxide, etc.)
- Anhydrous ammonia
- Chlorine

Many incidents occur while hazardous materials are being transported, and statistics indicate that the majority of haz mat transportation incidents occur while the materials are being transported via highway rather than by air, rail, or water. **Table 1.9** shows the numbers of incidents divided by mode (or means of transport) reported to the U.S. DOT between the years 1992 and 2001.

Some statistics are also kept for releases at fixed facilities and pipelines. **Table 1.10** shows a pipeline accident summary by commodity provided by the U.S. Office of Pipeline Safety for the year 2002. While there were no fatalities related to these incidents, there was 1 injury. Almost all pipeline incidents involved flammable or combustible liquids with crude oil topping the list. If emergency responders are called to the scene of a pipeline incident, they need to be concerned about flammability hazards.

The U.S. Agency for Toxic Substances and Disease Registry (ATSDR) maintains the Hazardous Substances Emergency Events Surveillance (HSEES) database. In 1998, 16 state health departments had cooperative agreements with ATSDR to participate in HSEES: Alabama, Colorado, Iowa, Louisiana, Minnesota, Mississippi, Missouri, New Jersey, New York, North Carolina, Oregon, Rhode Island, Texas, Utah, Washington, and Wisconsin.

Table 1.8
U.S. Government Databases Tracking Hazardous Material Spills, Incidents, and Releases

Acronym	Database	Lead Agency
IRIS	Incident Reporting Information System	NRC
ERNS	Emergency Response Notification System	EPA
ARIP	Accidental Release Information Program	EPA
HMIRS	Hazardous Materials Incident Reporting System	DOT
HLPAD	Hazardous Liquid Pipeline Accident Database	DOT
IMIS	Integrated Management Information System	OSHA
HSEES	Hazardous Substances Emergency Events Surveillance	ATSDR

Table 1.9
Hazardous Materials Incident Numbers by Mode and Incident Year: U.S. Department of Transportation

Mode	1992	1993	1994	1995	1996	1997	1998	1999	2000	2001	Total
Air	414	622	929	813	918	1,029	1,386	1,583	1,420	1,077	10,191
Highway	7,842	11,095	13,995	12,764	11,916	11,864	13,111	14,992	15,093	15,582	128,255
Railway	1,128	1,113	1,157	1,153	1,112	1,103	989	1,074	1,053	894	10,776
Water	8	8	6	12	6	5	14	8	17	4	88
Total	9,393	12,838	16,087	14,742	13,952	14,001	15,500	17,657	17,583	17,557	149,310

Table 1.10
Hazardous Liquid Pipeline Accident Summary by Commodity: 2002

Commodity	Number of Accidents	Percent of Total Accidents	Barrels Lost	Property Damages	Injuries/Fatalities
Crude Oil	39	27.27	12,010	$10,793,431	0
Gasoline	13	9.09	6,445	$2,548,656	0
Diesel Fuel	8	6.2	3,445	$2,548,656	0
Propane	9	6.29	12,001	$324,388	0
Anhydrous Ammonia	1	0.69	28	$6,839	0
Ethylene	2	1.39	660	$100,296	0
Butane	4	2.79	28	$26,543	1
Fuel Oil	6	4.19	890	$1,066,876	0
Jet Fuel (JP8)	2	1.39	286	$115,900	0
Natural Gasoline	2	1.39	228	$50,000	0
Unleaded Gasoline	8	5.59	4,444	$2,303,643	0
Jet A Turbine Fuel	1	0.69	19	$330,000	0
Carbon Dioxide	2	1.39	3,912	$10,430	0
Gasoline and Diesel	1	0.69	950	$76,000	0
No Data	5	3.49	231	599,946	0
TOTAL	100		41,712	$19,129,883	1

Table 1.11
Profiles of Events With Fatalities in Fixed Facilities:
HSEES Database, 1998

Event	Industry/ Location	Type of Release	Chemicals (quantity)	Factors	Victim Category	Injury	Number of Deaths
1	Lumber/wood treatment	Spill	Creosote (2 gallons [7.6L])	Operator	Employee	Trauma	1
2	Explosive incinerator	Explosion	Explosives	Unknown	Employee	Trauma	1
3	Fish and marine animal oil products	Air emission	Hydrogen sulfide	Decaying organic matter	Employee	Hydrogen sulfide (H_2S) poison	1
4	Dairy agriculture	Air emission	Nitrogen dioxide	Operator error	Employee	Respiratory, chemical burns, chemical asphyxia	1
5	Industrial yard	Explosion	Acetylene	Operator error	Employee	Trauma	1
6	Food/chem./ pharm. processing	Spill + air emission	Ammonia	Operator error	Employee	Respiratory, chemical burns	1
7	Vineyard, winery	Air emission	Carbon dioxide	Equipment failure	Employee	Suffocation	1
8	Construction	Fire + explosion	Indeterminate (1 gallon [3.8 L])	Operator error	Employee	Respiratory, chemical, and thermal burns	1
9	Construction	Air emission	Carbon monoxide/hydrogen sulfide (CO/H_2S) (10 pounds [4.5 kg])	Unknown	Employee	Respiratory, suffocation	1
10	Tavern	Spill + air emission	Ammonia (1,000 cubic feet [28 m³])	Operator error	Employee	Chemical burns	1
11	Silicon computer chip	Fire + explosion	Hydrochloric acid, silicon tetrachloride (33,000 pounds [14 969 kg])	Equipment failure	Employee	Chemical burns	2
12	Multiple family residence	Air emission	Arsenic trioxide, hydrochloric acid	Drugs	General public	Chemical death	1
13	Petroleum refinery	Fire + explosion	Coke oven emission	Equipment failure	Employee	Thermal burns, smoke inhalation	6

Note: HSEES = Hazardous Substances Emergency Events Surveillance

Table 1.11 provides insight into the types of incidents that resulted in fatalities at fixed facilities in 1998. During the same year, the HSEES recorded a total of 2,783 injuries (both at fixed facilities and during transport), the largest percentage of which (32.4 percent) involved injuries to the respiratory system.

Summary

First responders must understand their roles and limitations at haz mat emergencies. These are, in part, spelled out by government laws such as U.S. OSHA 29 *CFR* 1910.120, *Hazardous Waste Operations and Emergency Response (HAZWOPER)* and consensus standards such as NFPA 472, *Standard for Professional Competence of Responders to Hazardous Materials Incidents* (2002), and NFPA 473, *Standard for Competencies for EMS Personnel Responding to Hazardous Materials Incidents* (2002). Additionally, numerous government agencies and government regulations play important roles in how hazardous materials are manufactured, used, transported, and disposed of. It is important for first responders to be familiar with this legal framework in order to understand how and why hazardous materials are handled, packaged, used, and transported the way they are.

First responders also need to be aware of the various emergency response centers in Canada, U.S., and Mexico. These emergency response centers are listed in the current *ERG,* and they can greatly assist first responders in the event of a hazardous materials incident by providing important information about the products involved. First responders must not hesitate to contact these organizations when the need arises.

Most commonly, haz mat incidents involve flammable and combustible liquids, corrosives, anhydrous ammonia, and chlorine. However, first responders must be prepared to deal with emergencies involving any of the thousands of chemical products in use today.

Part One

Introduction to Hazardous Materials

Chapter 2

Hazardous Materials Properties and Hazards

First Responder Competencies

This chapter provides information that will assist the reader in meeting the following first responder competencies from NFPA 472, *Professional Competence of Responders to Hazardous Materials Incidents,* 2002 Edition. The numbers are noted directly in the text under the section titles where they are addressed.

NFPA 472

Chapter 4   Competencies for the First Responder at the Awareness Level

4.2.1   Detecting the Presence of Hazardous Materials. Given various facility or transportation situations, or both, with and without hazardous materials present, the first responder at the awareness level shall identify those situations where hazardous materials are present and also shall meet the following requirements:

(3) Identify the primary hazards associated with each of the UN/DOT hazard classes and divisions of hazardous materials by hazard class or division.

(4) Identify the difference between hazardous materials incidents and other emergencies.

4.4.1   Initiating Protective Actions. Given examples of facility and transportation hazardous materials incidents, the local emergency response plan, the organization's standard operating procedures, and the current edition of the Emergency Response Guidebook, first responders at the awareness level shall be able to identify the actions to be taken to protect themselves and others and to control access to the scene and shall also meet the following requirements:

(3) Identify the following basic precautions to be taken to protect themselves and others in a hazardous materials incident:

(b) Identify typical ignition sources found at the scenes of hazardous materials incidents.

(c) Identify the ways hazardous materials are harmful to people, the environment, and property at hazardous materials incidents.

(d) Identify the general routes of entry for human exposure to hazardous materials for each hazard class.

A.4.4.1(3)(c) This would include thermal, mechanical, poisonous, corrosive, asphyxiation, radiation, and etiologic. This can also include psychological harm.

Chapter 5   Competencies for the First Responder at the Operational Level

5.2.2   Collecting Hazard and Response Information. Given known hazardous materials, the first responder at the operational level shall collect hazard and response information using MSDS; CHEMTREC/CANUTEC/SETIQ;

local, state, and federal authorities; and contacts with the shipper/manufacturer and also shall meet the following requirements:

(3) Using an MSDS for a specified material, identify the following hazard and response information:

(a) Physical and chemical characteristics

(b) Physical hazards of the material

(c) Health hazards of the material

(d) Signs and symptoms of exposure

(e) Routes of entry

(f) Permissible exposure limits

(8) Describe the properties and characteristics of the following:

(a) Alpha particles

(b) Beta particles

(c) Gamma rays

(d) Neutrons

5.2.3   Predicting the Behavior of a Material and its Container. Given an incident involving a single hazardous material, the first responder at the operational level shall predict the likely behavior of the material and its container and also shall meet the following requirements:

(1) Given two examples of scenarios involving known hazardous materials, interpret the hazard and response information obtained from the current edition of the Emergency Response Guidebook; MSDS; CHEMTREC/CANUTEC/SETIQ; local, state, and federal authorities; and shipper/manufacturer contacts as follows:

(a) Match the following chemical and physical properties with their significance and impact on the behavior of the container and/or its contents:

i. Boiling point

ii. Chemical reactivity

iii. Corrosivity (pH)

iv. Flammable (explosive) range (LEL and UEL)

v. Flash point

vi. Ignition (autoignition) temperature

vii. Physical state (solid, liquid, gas)

viii. Specific gravity

ix. Toxic products of combustion

x. Vapor density

xi. Vapor pressure

xii. Water solubility

xiii. Radiation (ionizing and non-ionizing)

(b) Identify the differences between the following pairs of terms:

    iv. Radioactive material exposure (internal and external) and radioactive

(7) Identify the health and physical hazards that could cause harm.

(8) Identify the health hazards associated with the following terms:

    (a) Asphyxiant

    (b) Chronic health hazard

    (c) Convulsant

    (d) Irritant/corrosive

    (e) Sensitizer/allergen

    (f) Alpha, beta, gamma, and neutron radiation

5.2.4 Estimating the Potential Harm. The first responder at the operational level shall estimate the potential harm within the endangered area at a hazardous materials incident and also shall meet the following requirements:

(5) Describe the impact that time, distance, and shielding have on exposure to radioactive materials specific to the expected dose rate.

A.5.2.3(7) The health and physical hazards that could cause harm in a hazardous materials incident are thermal, mechanical, poisonous, corrosive, asphyxiation, radiation, and etiologic.

A.5.2.3(8)(b) Chronic health hazards include carcinogen, mutagen, and teratogen.

Reprinted with permission from NFPA 472, *Standard on Professional Competence of Responders to Hazardous Materials Incidents,* Copyright © 2002, National Fire Protection Association, Quincy, MA 00269. This reprinted material is not the complete and official position of the National Fire Protection Association on the referenced subject, which is represented only by the standard in its entirety.

Office for Domestic Preparedness

Emergency Responder Guidelines

This chapter provides information that will assist the reader in meeting the following first responder guidelines for fire service and law enforcement from the Office for Domestic Preparedness (ODP) *Emergency Responder Guidelines,* 2002 Edition. The numbers are noted directly in the text under the section titles where they are addressed.

ODP Emergency Responder Guidelines

Fire Service and Law Enforcement

Awareness Level for Events Involving Weapons of Mass Destruction

I. **Recognize hazardous materials incidents.** The responder should:

    e. Understand the potential outcomes or consequences of an emergency due to the presence of hazardous materials with and without fire.

Performance Level for Events Involving Weapons of Mass Destruction

I. **Have successfully completed adequate and proper training at the awareness level for events involving hazardous materials, and for weapons of mass destruction (WMD) and other specialized training.** The responder should:

    b. Understand the terminology (including any glossary of WMD terms), classes of materials and agents, and toxicology of hazardous materials and WMD agents and materials.

Chapter 2
Hazardous Materials Properties and Hazards

[NFPA 472: 4.2.1(4), 4.4.1(3)(c)] [ODP Awareness I.e.] [ODP Operations Level I.b.]

In order to deal with hazardous material incidents (as well as fully appreciate the dangers they present), first responders must understand the variety of hazardous materials that may be encountered, how these materials may potentially affect health, and the physical hazards that may be associated with them. By knowing some of these basic concepts, the hazardous materials first responder may be able to prevent or reduce injury, loss of life, and environmental/property losses caused by these incidents.

Hazardous materials may be elements, compounds, or mixtures found in gaseous, liquid, or solid states or combinations of these states. They may present a direct threat to health (such as with a poison) or be considered dangerous because of their physical hazards (such as with a flammable liquid). Hazardous materials that affect health include carcinogens, toxic or highly toxic agents, reproductive toxins, irritants, corrosives, sensitizers, and agents that damage the lungs, skin, eyes, or mucous membranes. Hazardous materials that present physical hazards include compressed gases, explosives, flammables, organic peroxides, oxidizers, pyrophoric chemicals, cryogenic materials, reactive chemicals, radioactive materials, and water-reactive materials.

The severity of hazards these materials present may range from insignificant to catastrophic, depending on the material and quantity involved. The flammability hazard may range from negligible (for materials that do not burn) to extremely flammable. Materials may range in reactivity from those that are usually stable to those that detonate unexpectedly. The radioactive and biochemical effects of hazardous materials may be short-lived or last for generations.

Exposures to hazardous materials may be *acute* (single occurrence) or *chronic* (long-term, reoccurring). Health effects can also be acute or chronic. *Acute health effects* are short-term effects that appear within hours or days such as vomiting or diarrhea. *Chronic health effects* are long-term effects that may take years to appear such as cancer. Many hazardous materials have major effects on human health. Working with these materials may require that emergency responders use special personal protective equipment (PPE). This equipment offers protection that is different from that provided by the clothing worn for standard structural fire fighting.

This chapter discusses many of the various properties and hazards that make these materials hazardous to living organisms. It includes information on how people may be exposed to various substances and how they may be affected by that exposure.

Hazardous Materials Properties

[NFPA 472: 4.4.1(3)(c), 5.2.2 (3)(a), 5.2.3(1)(a)]

An uncontrolled release of a hazardous material from a container can create a variety of problems. Awareness-Level responders need to understand the basic hazards associated with different classes of hazardous materials such as flammables, corrosives, and reactives. Operational-Level responders need to know how hazardous materials behave in addition to the symptoms and effects of an exposure (see Hazardous Materials Hazards section). The behavior of hazardous materials is often determined by the material's physical properties. The material's physical state, flammability, boiling point, chemical reactivity, and other properties affect how it behaves, determine the harm it can cause, and influence the effect it may have on its container (as well as the people, living organisms, and other chemicals it contacts and the environment).

Everything in the world is made of substances called *matter*. Matter is found in three states: *gas, liquid,* and *solid.* The first responder must understand that different hazardous materials may come in any one of these states and the material's state of matter influences its behavior **(Figure 2.1).** This behavior in turn can influence the nature of the hazards presented by the material. See the following definitions:

- *Gas* — Fluid that has neither independent shape nor volume; gases tend to expand indefinitely.

- *Liquid* — Fluid that has no independent shape but does have a specific volume; liquids flow in accordance with the laws of gravity.

- *Solid* — Substance that has both a specific shape (without a container) and volume.

The following sections discuss some of the physical properties of hazardous materials that emergency responders need to know. Such qualities as flammability, vapor pressure, boiling point, melting point/freezing point/sublimation, vapor density, solubility, miscibility, specific gravity, and reactivity of a hazardous material may play an important part in how responders manage an incident. Hazardous material radiological effects are discussed in the Hazardous Materials Hazards section. The explanations of the terms found in this book may vary slightly from those used in scientific circles, but they will aid first responders in applying technical data to real-world incidents.

Flammability

The majority of hazardous materials incidents involve materials that are flammable. The obvious hazard of flammable materials is the damage caused to life and property when they burn or explode. A flammable hazard depends on properties such as flash point, autoignition temperature or point, and flammable (explosive or combustible) range. Other important properties include boiling point, vapor pressure, vapor density, specific gravity, and solubility (see following sections). All of

Is It a Solid, Liquid, or Gas? Industry Terms Used to Describe Air Contaminants

Air contaminants are commonly classified as either particulate or gas and vapor contaminants. The most common particulate contaminants include dusts, fumes, mists, aerosols, and fibers. Definitions are as follows:

- *Dust* — Solid particle that is formed or generated from solid organic or inorganic materials by reducing its size through mechanical processes such as crushing, grinding, drilling, abrading, or blasting.

- *Fume* — Suspension of particles that form when material from a volatilized (vapor state) solid condenses in cool air. In most cases, the solid,

smokelike particles resulting from the condensation react with air to form an oxide.

- *Mist* — Finely divided liquid suspended in the atmosphere. Mists are generated by liquids condensing from a vapor back to a liquid or by breaking up a liquid into a dispersed state by splashing, foaming, or atomizing.

- *Aerosol* — Form of mist characterized by highly respirable, minute liquid particles.

- *Fiber* — Solid particle whose length is several times greater than its diameter.

- *Vapor* — Gaseous form of a substance that is normally in a solid or liquid state at room temperature and pressure. It is formed by evaporation from a liquid or sublimation from a solid. Examples can be found where cleaning and painting take place and solvents are used. Vapors are the volatile forms of these substances.

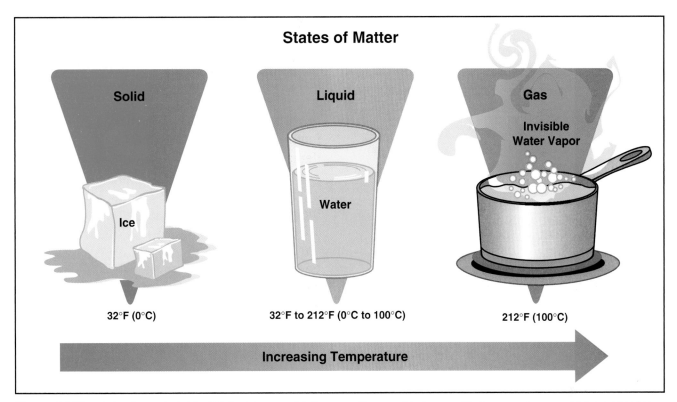

Figure 2.1 The state of a material (solid, liquid, or gas) influences the way it behaves. First responders must be prepared to deal with hazardous materials in all three states.

this information is vital for determining incident strategies and tactics.

Flash Point

Flash point is the minimum temperature at which a liquid or volatile solid gives off sufficient vapors to form an ignitable mixture with air near its surface. At this temperature, the vapors will flash in the presence of an ignition source but will *not* continue to burn. Do *not* confuse flash point with fire point. *Fire point* is the temperature at which enough vapors are given off to support continuous burning. The fire point temperature is usually only slightly higher than the flash point.

The liquids themselves do *not* burn but rather the vapors they produce burn. As the temperature of the liquid increases, more vapors are emitted. Vapors are emitted below the flash point but not in sufficient quantities to ignite. Therefore, if a substance is not at its flash-point temperature, it will not burn. Flammable gases have no flash points because they are already in the gaseous state **(Figure 2.2, p. 48)**.

Autoignition Temperature/Autoignition Point

The *autoignition temperature* or *autoignition point* of a substance is the minimum temperature to which the fuel in air must be heated to initiate self-sustained combustion *without* initiation from an independent ignition source. This temperature is the point at which a fuel spontaneously ignites. All flammable materials have autoignition temperatures/points, and these are considerably higher than the flash and fire points. For example, the autoignition temperature/point of gasoline is about 536°F (280°C), but the flash point of gasoline is -45°F (-43°C). This difference means that at -45°F (-43°C), gasoline will ignite if a match is waved through its vapors, whereas at 536°F (280°C) it ignites all by itself.

The term *ignition temperature* is often used synonymously with *autoignition temperature* or *autoignition point*. They are always the same temperature. However, NFPA defines *ignition temperature* as "the minimum temperature required to initiate or cause self-sustained combustion, independent of the heating or heated element." It defines *autoignition temperature* as "the temperature at which a mixture will spontaneously ignite."

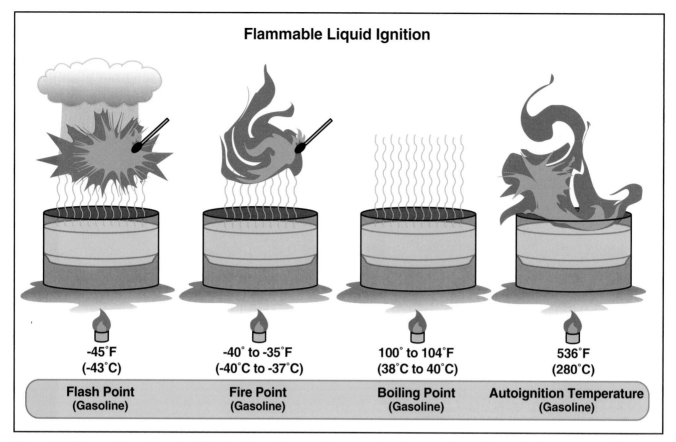

Flammable Liquid Ignition

-45°F (-43°C)	-40° to -35°F (-40°C to -37°C)	100° to 104°F (38°C to 40°C)	536°F (280°C)
Flash Point (Gasoline)	**Fire Point** (Gasoline)	**Boiling Point** (Gasoline)	**Autoignition Temperature** (Gasoline)

Figure 2.2 Flammable and combustible liquids produce varying amounts of vapors depending on their temperature. The *flash point* of a liquid is the temperature at which it gives off sufficient vapors to flash but not sustain combustion. It will sustain combustion at the fire point, boil at the boiling point, and automatically ignite at the autoignition point. Generally, the lower the flash point of a liquid, the greater the fire hazard is.

Is it Flammable or Combustible?

In everyday language, the terms *flammable* and *combustible* can be used interchangeably to denote a substance that will burn. In the world of hazardous materials, these terms take on very specific meanings, particularly in regards to liquids. It should be noted that the term *inflammable* means the same thing as *flammable* in many parts of the world. In other words, inflammable materials will burn; inflammable does not mean *nonflammable*. A nonflammable material does not ignite easily. In Mexico, for example, a tank truck carrying flammable liquids may read either *flammable* or *inflammable*. Transport Canada allows only the term *flammable*. However, Canadian responders should be aware that *inflammable* is the French word for *flammable*.

Flash Points Used to Determine Whether a Liquid Is Flammable or Combustible

Agency	Flammable Liquid	Combustible Liquid
Department of Transportation (DOT)	141°F (60.5°C) or less	Greater than 141°F (60.5°C) and below 200°F (93°C)
Occupational Safety and Health Administration (OSHA)	Less than 100°F (38°C)	100°F (38°C) or greater
National Fire Protection Association (NFPA)	Less than 100°F (38°C)	100°F (38°C) or greater
Environmental Protection Agency (EPA)	Less than 140°F (60°C) (Ignitable Waste)	

NOTE: Canada does not differentiate between flammable and combustible liquids for purposes of transportation. It uses only the term *flammable*.

Is it Flammable or Combustible? *(continued)*

The flash point is commonly used to determine how flammable a liquid is. Liquids that have low flash points and burn very easily are designated as *flammable liquids*, whereas liquids with higher flash points that do not burn as easily are called *combustible liquids*. However, different U.S. agencies reference different flash points in their designations of *flammable* and *combustible* substances.

Flammable liquids such as gasoline and acetone have flash points well below 100°F (38°C). Combustible liquids such as fuel oils and lubricating oils have flash points above 100°F (38°C). In general, the lower the flash point, the greater the fire hazard.

Ignition Sources at an Incident Scene

[NFPA 472: 4.4.1(3)(b)]

Many potential ignition sources may exist at the scene of a hazardous materials incident. Emergency responders need to be aware of the following items:

- Open flames
- Static electricity
- Existing pilot lights
- Electrical sources including non-explosion-proof electrical equipment
- Internal combustion engines in vehicles and generators
- Heated surfaces
- Cutting and welding operations
- Radiant heat
- Heat caused by friction or chemical reactions
- Cigarettes and other smoking materials
- Cameras
- Road flares

Explosive atmospheres can be ignited by several simple actions:

- Opening or closing a switch or electrical circuit (for example, a light switch)
- Turning on a flashlight
- Operating a radio
- Activating a cell phone

Flammable, Explosive, or Combustible Range

The *flammable, explosive, or combustible range* is the percentage of the gas or vapor concentration in air that will burn or explode if ignited. The *lower explosive limit (LEL)* or *lower flammable limit (LFL)* of a vapor or gas is the lowest concentration (or lowest percentage of the substance in air) that will produce a flash of fire when an ignition source is present. At concentrations lower than the LEL, the mixture is too *lean* to burn.

The *upper explosive limit (UEL)* or *upper flammable limit (UFL)* of a vapor or gas is the highest concentration (or highest percentage of the substance in air) that will produce a flash of fire when an ignition source is present. At higher concentrations, the mixture is too *rich* to burn **(Figure 2.3)**. Within the upper and lower limits, the gas or vapor concentration will burn rapidly if ignited. Atmospheres within the flammable range

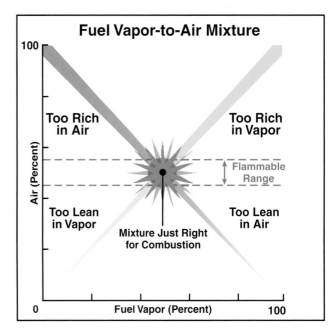

Figure 2.3 Illustration of the fuel vapor-to-air mixture: The flammable range is the point at which the mixture will ignite and sustain burning.

are particularly dangerous. **Table 2.1** provides the flammable ranges for selected materials.

What Does This Mean to You?

Products with a very low LEL and products with a wide range between the LEL and UEL are the most dangerous. Also, just because the concentration is above the UEL does not mean that you are safe. If the concentration drops for any reason (for example, more fresh air is introduced, which dilutes the concentration, or the concentration is less than the UEL in places where you didn't monitor), you could be in an explosive atmosphere anyway.

Vapor Pressure

Vapor pressure is the pressure exerted by a saturated vapor above its own liquid in a closed container, or more simply, it is the pressure produced or exerted by the vapors released by a liquid. Vapor pressure can be viewed as the measure of the tendency of a substance to evaporate.

Vapor pressure can be expressed in terms of *pounds per square inch (psi), kilopascals (kPa), bars,* or in *millimeters of mercury (mmHg)* or *atmospheres (atm)*. Vapor pressures reported in reference materials may use any of these units, but vapor pressures are usually reported in *mmHg* on material safety data sheets (MSDSs). See information box and sidebar for more information on these measurements and terms.

Measurements and Terms

- *Pounds per square inch (psi)* — Unit for measuring pressure in the English or Customary System. The International System of Units (SI) equivalent is kilopascal (kPa). Another equivalent unit of pressure is bar (*1 bar = 14.5038 psi*) {*1 bar = 100 kPa*}. This book uses the units of *psi* as the primary measurement of pressure. Metric equivalent pressures expressed in *bar* and *kPa* are also given.

- *Atmospheric pressure* — Force exerted by the weight of the atmosphere at the surface of the earth. See sidebar for more information.

Table 2.1
Flammable Ranges for Selected Materials

Material	Lower Flammable Limit (LFL) (percent by volume)	Upper Flammable Limit (UFL) (percent by volume)
Acetylene	2.5	100.0
Carbon Monoxide	12.5	74.0
Ethyl Alcohol	3.3	19.0
Fuel Oil No. 1	0.7	5.0
Gasoline	1.4	7.6
Hydrogen	4.0	75.0
Methane	5.0	15.0
Propane	2.1	9.5

Source: *Fire Protection Guide to Hazardous Materials*, 13th edition, 2002, by National Fire Protection Association.

Atmospheric Pressure

Atmospheric pressure is greatest at low altitudes; consequently, its pressure at sea level is used as a standard. At sea level, the atmosphere exerts a pressure of 14.7 psi (101 kPa) {1.01 bar}. A common method of measuring atmospheric pressure is to compare the weight of the atmosphere with the weight of a column of mercury: the greater the atmospheric pressure, the taller the column of mercury. A pressure of 1 psi (7 kPa) {0.069 bar} makes the column of mercury about 2.04 inches (52 mm) tall. At sea level, then, the column of mercury is 2.04 × 14.7, or 29.9 inches tall (759 mm). See the diagram in **Figure 2.4**.

The following facts regarding vapor pressure are important:

- The higher the temperature of a substance, the higher the vapor pressure will be. In other words, the vapor pressure of a substance at 100°F (38°C) will always be higher than the vapor pressure of the same substance at 68°F (20°C). Higher temperatures provide more energy to a liquid, which in turn allows more liquid to escape into the gas form. The gas rises above the liquid and exerts a downward pressure.

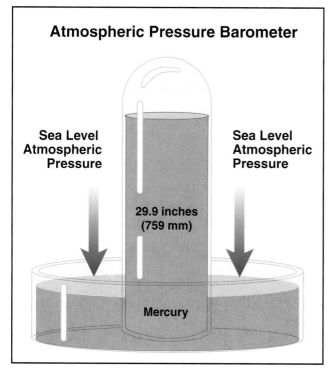

Atmospheric Pressure Barometer

Sea Level Atmospheric Pressure

Sea Level Atmospheric Pressure

29.9 inches (759 mm)

Mercury

Figure 2.4 Simple barometer showing atmospheric pressure.

- Vapor pressures reported on MSDSs in mmHg are usually very low; for comparison, 760 mmHg is equivalent to 14.7 psi or 1 atmosphere at standard temperature (*14.7 psi = 760 mmHg = 1 atm = 101 kPa = 1 bar*).

- The lower the boiling point of a substance, the higher its vapor pressure will be. The low boiling point means less heat is required to change some of the liquid into a gas. For example, we obviously think of boiling water, which requires a lot of heat, but some substances *boil* at room temperature, requiring much less heat.

Boiling Point

Boiling point is the temperature at which the vapor pressure of a liquid is equal to or greater than atmospheric pressure. In other words, it is the temperature at which a liquid changes to a gas at a given pressure. The boiling point is usually expressed in degrees Fahrenheit (Celsius) at sea level air pressure. For mixtures, the initial boiling point or boiling-point range may be given. Flammable materials with low boiling points generally present special fire hazards.

What Does This Mean to You?

Following are the vapor pressures of six substances at 68°F (20°C):

- **Motor oil:** less than 0.01 mmHg
- **Sarin:** 2.1 mmHg (at 70°F/21°C)
- **Water:** 25 mmHg
- **Acetone:** 180 mmHg
- **Isopropylamine:** 478 mmHg
- **Chlorine:** 5,168 mmHg

Vapor pressure can be used as a general gauge to tell how fast a product will evaporate under normal circumstances. A product like acetone evaporates much more quickly at room temperature and normal atmospheric pressure than something like water with a much lower vapor pressure — or even motor oil, which does not evaporate easily at all.

Knowledge of this fact is important to the safety of responders at an incident for many reasons. For example, under most normal conditions, a spill of a liquid with a high vapor pressure (such as isopropylamine) will produce more vapors in greater concentration than a substance with a low vapor pressure (such as sarin). These fumes or vapors could then be carried by the wind or travel distances on air currents and cause problems far from the spill itself (such as toxic or flammable vapors being blown into a residential neighborhood).

The vapor pressure may also be an indication of what state of matter a product is likely to be. For example, chlorine, with its extremely high vapor pressure, is likely to be released as a gas rather than a liquid because at normal atmospheric pressure and temperatures it will instantly evaporate. Also, the lower the vapor pressure, the less likely that the chemical will produce fumes or vapors that can be inhaled (and vice versa).

A *boiling liquid expanding vapor explosion (BLEVE)* (also called *violent rupture*) can occur when a liquid within a container is heated, causing the material inside to boil or vaporize (such as in the case of a liquefied petroleum gas tank exposed to a fire). If the resulting increase in internal vapor pressure exceeds the vessel's ability to relieve the excess pressure, it can cause the container to fail catastrophically. As the vapor is released, it expands rapidly and ignites, sending flames and pieces of tank flying in a tremendous explosion. BLEVEs most commonly occur when flames contact a tank shell above the liquid level or when insufficient water is applied to keep a tank shell cool.

BLEVE!!
A more practical way of explaining the results of a BLEVE is a "**B**last **L**eveling **E**verything **V**ery **E**venly." Don't let one happen on your shift.

Melting Point/Freezing Point/Sublimation

Melting point is the temperature at which a solid substance changes to a liquid state at normal atmospheric pressure. For example, an ice cube melts at just above 32°F (0°C) — its melting point.

Freezing point is the temperature at which a liquid becomes a solid at normal atmospheric pressure. For example, water freezes at 32°F (0°C) — its freezing point. Some substances will actually *sublime* or change directly from a solid into a gas without going into a liquid state in between. Dry ice (carbon dioxide) and mothballs both sublime rather than melt.

Vapor Density

Vapor density is the weight of a given volume of pure vapor or gas compared to the weight of an equal volume of dry air at the same temperature and pressure. A vapor density less than 1 indicates a vapor lighter than air, while a vapor density greater than 1 indicates a vapor heavier than air. Examples of materials with a vapor density less than 1 include acetylene, methane (primary component of natural gas), and hydrogen. Examples of materials with a vapor density greater than 1 include propane, hydrogen sulfide, ethane, butane, chlorine, and sulfur dioxide. The majority of gases have a vapor density greater than 1.

All vapors and gases will mix with air, but the lighter materials tend to rise and dissipate (unless confined). Heavier vapors and gases are likely to concentrate in low places along or under floors; in sumps, sewers, and manholes; and in trenches and ditches where they may create fire or health

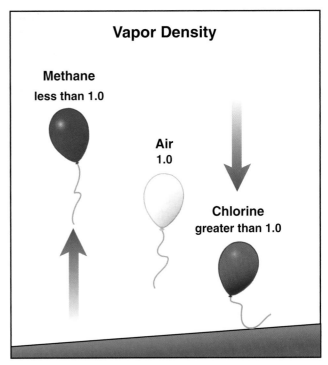

Figure 2.5 Vapor densities compare the weight of a specific volume of air to an equal volume of another gas. Methane weighs less than air, so its specific vapor density is less than 1. Chlorine weighs more than air, so its vapor density is greater than 1.

hazards. Unfortunately, the spread of vapors cannot be predicted exactly from the vapor density because topography, weather conditions, and the vapor mixture with air easily affect vapors. However, knowing the vapor density gives a general idea of what to expect from a specific gas. See **Figure 2.5.**

Solubility/Miscibility

Solubility in water is a term expressing the percentage of a material (by weight) that will dissolve in water at ambient temperature. Solubility information can be useful in determining spill cleanup methods and extinguishing agents. When a non-water-soluble liquid such as a *hydrocarbon* (gasoline, diesel fuel, pentane) combines with water, the two liquids remain separate. When a water-soluble liquid such as a *polar solvent* (alcohol, methanol, methyl ethyl ketone [MEK]) combines with water, the two liquids mix easily. A substance's solubility affects whether it mixes in water.

Water solubility is also an important contributor for symptom development. Irritant agents that are water-soluble usually cause early upper respiratory tract irritation, resulting in coughing and throat irritation. Partially water-soluble chemicals penetrate into the lower respiratory system, causing delayed (12 to 24 hours) symptoms that include breathing difficulties, pulmonary edema, and coughing up blood.

What Is Slightly Soluble?

The following are generally accepted terms for degrees of solubility:

- *Negligible (insoluble)* — Less than 0.1 percent dissolved in water

- *Slight (slightly soluble)* — Percents from 0.1 to 1 dissolved in water

- *Moderate (moderately soluble)* — Percents from 1 to 10 dissolved in water

- *Appreciable (partly soluble)* — More than 10 to 25 percent dissolved in water

- *Completely (soluble)* — Percents from 25 to 100 percent dissolved in all proportions in water

Miscibility/Immiscibility is the degree or readiness to which two or more gases or liquids are able to mix with or dissolve into each other. Two liquids that dissolve into each other in any proportion are considered *miscible*. Typically, two materials that do **not** readily dissolve into each other are considered *immiscible*. For example, water and fuel oil are immiscible, which can create a hazard because the oil (which weighs less than water) will rise to the top and could ignite and burn on top of the water **(Figure 2.6)**.

Specific Gravity

Specific gravity is the ratio of the density (heaviness) of a material to the density of some standard material at standard conditions of pressure and temperature. The weight of a substance compared to the weight of an equal volume of water is an expression of the density of a material. For example, if a volume of a material weighs 8 pounds (3.6 kg), and an equal volume of water weighs 10 pounds (4.5 kg), the material is said to have a specific gravity of 0.8. Materials with specific gravities less than 1 will float in (or on) water. Materials with specific gravities greater than 1 will sink in water.

Solubility plays an important role in specific gravity in that highly soluble materials will mix or dissolve more completely in water (distributing themselves more evenly throughout), rather than sinking or floating (without dissolving) according to their specific gravities. Most (but not all)

Figure 2.6 Water and fuel oil are immiscible, meaning they don't mix with each other. This fact can create a hazard because oil (which weighs less than water) rises to the top and could ignite and burn on top of water. In this example, the tank vessel *Haven* wrecked and burned in 1991. *Courtesy of International Tanker Owners Pollution Federation Ltd., Houndsditch London.*

flammable liquids have specific gravities less than 1 and, if not soluble, will float on water. This fact is an important consideration for fire-suppression activities. See **Figure 2.7.**

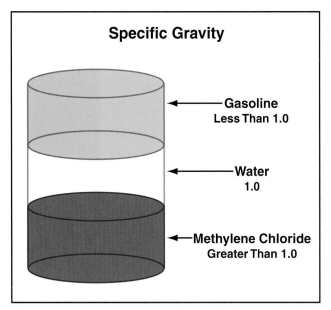

Specific Gravity

Gasoline
Less Than 1.0

Water
1.0

Methylene Chloride
Greater Than 1.0

Figure 2.7 Specific gravity example: Equal volumes of water, gasoline, and methylene chloride do not weigh the same. Gasoline weighs less than water, so it has a specific gravity less than 1. Methylene chloride weighs more than water, so it has a specific gravity more than 1. In general, hydrocarbons float on water, and chlorinated solvents sink.

Reactivity

The *reactivity* of a substance is its relative ability to undergo a chemical reaction with another material. Undesirable effects such as pressure buildup, temperature increase, and/or formation of noxious, toxic, or corrosive byproducts may occur as a result of a reaction. Substances referred to in the industrial world as *reactive* commonly react vigorously or violently with air, water, heat, light, each other, or other materials.

Many first responders are familiar with the fire tetrahedron or the four elements necessary to produce combustion: oxygen, fuel, heat, and a chemical chain reaction. Fire is just one type of chemical reaction, and a *reactivity triangle* can be used to explain the basic components of many (though not all) chemical reactions: an oxidizing agent (oxygen), a reducing agent (fuel), and an activation energy source (often heat, but not always so) **(Figure 2.8).**

All reactions require some energy to get them started, which is commonly referred to as *activation energy.* How much energy is needed depends on the particular reaction. In some cases, the energy can be in the form of added heat from an

What Does This Mean to You?

Let's look at heptane, a major component of gasoline. Heptane has the following physical and chemical properties:

- *Vapor Pressure:* 45 mmHg
- *Flash Point:* 25°F (-4°C)
- *Boiling Point:* 210°F (98°C)
- *Vapor Density:* 3.5
- *Solubility in Water:* Negligible
- *Specific Gravity:* 0.7

By understanding how to interpret this information, an emergency responder can predict how the material is likely to behave. If, for example, a significant amount of heptane is spilled into a pond or waterway, a responder might follow this chain of thought:

- First, because the heptane is spilled into the water, it is important to determine what the material is going to do relative to the water. Is it going to mix with the water? Is it going to sink or float? Since heptane's solubility in water is negligible, you can

gather that it's going to stick together in the water rather than dissolve or mix in it. Because its specific gravity is less than 1, you know it is going to float to the surface of water. So, you can deduce that heptane is going to float on top of the water.

- Next, since you know that heptane will burn, you will want to know what it might be doing on top of the water in terms of emitting vapors or fumes that could be ignited accidentally. Its vapor pressure (higher than that of water) tells you that it will likely evaporate (emit some vapors) under most normal conditions. A flash point of 25°F (-4°C) tells you that those vapors will burn if exposed to most ignition sources, so keeping ignition sources away from the vapors (or visa versa) is an important priority.

- So what are the vapors likely to be doing and where are they going? Are they rising in the air or staying close to the surface of the water? A vapor density of 3.5 tells you (assuming no wind or other disturbances) that they will tend to stay low or close to the surface of the water.

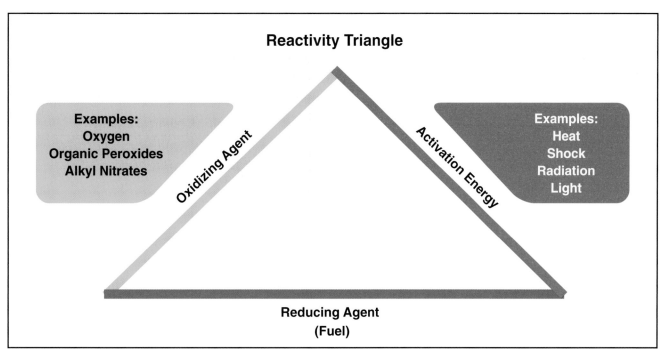

Reactivity Triangle

Examples:
Oxygen
Organic Peroxides
Alkyl Nitrates

Oxidizing Agent

Activation Energy

Examples:
Heat
Shock
Radiation
Light

Reducing Agent
(Fuel)

Figure 2.8 The reactivity triangle consists of an oxidizing agent, an activation energy source, and a reducing agent.

external source (such as when starting a fire with a match). In some instances, radio waves, radiation, or another waveform of energy may provide the needed energy to the molecules (such as when food is heated in a microwave oven). In other reactions the energy could come from a shock or pressure change (such as might occur when nitroglycerin is jostled).

Reactions that have very low activation energies happen very easily or need very little help to begin the process. For example, materials that are generally classified as water-reactive typically react with water easily at room temperature simply because the heat being provided from the surroundings is sufficient to start the reaction. In addition to other major categories of chemical reactives, first responders may see terms like *light-sensitive, heat-sensitive,* or *shock-sensitive* on MSDSs and/or manufacturers' labels, indicating that those products have an increased susceptibility to those particular sources of activation energy. See **Table 2.2, p. 56,** for a summary of the different ways in which chemicals can be reactive. This table supplies the definition and chemical examples of nine reactive hazard classes.

The oxidizing agent in the reactivity triangle provides the oxygen necessary for the chemical reaction. *Strong oxidizers* are materials that encourage a strong reaction (by readily accepting electrons) from reducing agents (fuels). Many people are familiar with the concept that the greater the concentrations of oxygen present in the atmosphere, the hotter, faster, and brighter a fire will burn. The same principle applies to oxidation reactions — generally speaking, the stronger the oxidizer, the stronger the reaction. For example, many hydrocarbons (such as petroleum products) ignite spontaneously when they come into contact with a strong oxidizer. If liquid oxygen (a cryogenic liquid) is spilled on an asphalt roadway and sufficient activation energy is supplied (from shock or friction such as someone stepping on it), the roadway could explode.

The reducing agent in the fire tetrahedron acts as the fuel source for the reaction, which basically means that it is combining with the oxygen (or losing electrons to the oxidizer) in such a way that energy is being released. Oxidation-reduction reactions can be extremely violent and dangerous because they are releasing a tremendous amount of energy. Obviously, some reducing agents (fuels) are more volatile than others. Wood, for example, is not as prone to undergo rapid oxidation (that is, it won't burn as easily) as a highly flammable liquid like MEK.

Table 2.2
Nine Reactive Hazard Classes: Chemical Emergency
Preparedness and Prevention Office

Reactive Hazard Class	Definition	Chemical Examples
Highly Flammable	Substances having flash points less than 100°F (38°C) and mixtures that include substances with flash points less than 100°F (38°C)	Gasoline, Acetone, Pentane, Ethyl Ether, Toluene, Methyl Ethyl Ketone (MEK), Turpentine
Explosive	A material synthesized or mixed deliberately to allow the very rapid release of chemical energy; also, a chemical substance that is intrinsically unstable and liable to detonate under conditions that might reasonably be encountered	Dynamite, Nitroglycerin, Perchloric Acid, Picric Acid, Fulminates, Azide
Polymerizable	Capable of undergoing self-reactions that release energy; some polymerization reactions generate a great deal of heat. (The products of polymerization reactions are generally less reactive than the starting materials.)	Acrylic Acid, Butadiene, Ethylene, Styrene, Vinyl Chloride, Epoxies
Strong Oxidizing Agent	Oxidizing agents gain electrons from other substances and are themselves thereby chemically reduced, but strong oxidizing agents accept electrons particularly well from a large range of other substances. The ensuing oxidation-reduction reactions may be vigorous or violent and may release new substances that may take part in further additional reactions. Keep strong oxidizing agents well separated from strong reducing agents. In some cases, the presence of a strong oxidizing agent can greatly enhance the progress of a fire.	Hydrogen Peroxide, Fluorine, Bromine, Calcium Chlorate, Chromic Acid, Ammonium Perchlorate

Continued

Reactive Hazard Class	Definition	Chemical Examples
Strong Reducing Agent	Reducing agents give up electrons to other substances and are thereby oxidized, but strong reducing agents donate electrons particularly well to a large range of other substances. The ensuing oxidation-reduction reactions may be vigorous or violent and may generate new substances that take part in further additional reactions.	Alkali metals (Sodium, Magnesium, Lithium, Potassium), Beryllium, Calcium, Barium, Phosphorus, Radium, Lithium Aluminum Hydride
Water-Reactive	Substances that may react rapidly or violently with liquid water and steam, producing heat (or fire) and often toxic reaction products	Alkali metals (Sodium, Magnesium, Lithium, Potassium), Sodium Peroxide, Anhydrides, Carbides
Air-Reactive	Likely to react rapidly or violently with dry air or moist air; may generate toxic and corrosive fumes upon exposure to air or catch fire	Finely divided metal dusts (Nickel, Zinc, Titanium), Alkali metals (Sodium, Magnesium, Lithium, Potassium), Hydrides (Diborane, Barium Hydrides, Diisobutyl Aluminum Hydride)
Peroxidizable Compound	Apt to undergo spontaneous reaction with oxygen at room temperature, to form peroxides and other products. Most such auto-oxidations are accelerated by light or trace impurities. Many peroxides are explosive, which makes peroxidizable compounds a particular hazard. Ethers and aldehydes are particularly subject to peroxide formation (the peroxides generally form slowly after evaporation of the solvent in which a peroxidizable material had been stored).	Isopropyl Ether, Furan, Acrylic Acid, Styrene, Vinyl Chloride, Methyl Isobutyl Ketone, Ethers, Aldehydes
Radioactive Material	Spontaneously and continuously emitting ions or ionizing radiation. Radioactivity is not a chemical property, but an additional hazard that exists in addition to the chemical properties of a material.	Radon, Uranium

Source: U.S. Environmental Protection Agency's CEPPO (Chemical Emergency Preparedness and Prevention Office) Computer-Aided Management of Emergency Operations (CAMEO) software was used to identify this information.

Another term with which first responders should be familiar is *polymerization,* which is a chemical reaction in which a catalyst causes simple molecules to combine to form long chain molecules. Examples of catalysts include light, heat, water, acids, or other chemicals. If this reaction is uncontrolled, it often results in a tremendous release of energy. Materials that may undergo violent polymerization if subjected to heat or contamination are designated with a *P* in the blue and yellow sections of the *Emergency Response Guidebook* (*ERG*) (see Clue 5, Written Resources section in Chapter 3, Hazardous Materials Identification).

Inhibitors are materials that are added to products that easily polymerize in order to control or prevent an undesired reaction. Inhibitors may be *time-sensitive* in that they may be *exhausted* over a period of time or when exposed to circumstances/unexpected contamination that cause them to be consumed more rapidly, such as being overwhelmed by exposure to heat or other reaction triggers. Shipments of polymerizing materials may become extremely unstable if delayed during transport or involved in accidents. For example, time-sensitive inhibitors are added to liquid styrene when it is shipped in order to prevent the styrene from polymerizing during transport. If containers holding the styrene rupture or emergency responders add water, the inhibitor becomes exhausted, and the polymerization reaction begins. A BLEVE may result because of the resulting release of heat and expanding gas.

Remember that some reactive materials are special concerns to emergency responders because they are oxidizers. Others are concerns because they are volatile reducing agents or because the reduction reaction is started in an unusual way (such as by exposure to water). Additionally, emergency responders must be concerned with the various ways in which activation energy may be supplied to certain chemicals in order to prevent a reaction from occurring. Under emergency conditions, reactive materials can be extremely destructive to life and property. Knowledge and extreme caution are vital factors in handling emergencies involving reactive materials. Keep people and equipment upwind, uphill, and back a safe distance or in protected locations until pertinent facts are

established and definite plans can be formulated. With advances in modern technology, more and more reactive and unstable materials are being used for various processes, and responders must be prepared to deal with them.

Hazardous Materials Properties Summary

Hazardous materials have a variety of properties that affect how they behave and how dangerous they may be. First responders, particularly at the Operational Level, need to be aware of how these properties may affect the behavior of containers (such as the potential for BLEVE) and/or their contents (such as the material's flammability). **Table 2.3** (in both English and SI units) provides a list of common hazardous materials and summaries of their properties.

Hazardous Materials Hazards

[NFPA 472: 4.2.1(3), 4.4.1(3)(c), 5.2.2(3)(b), 5.2.2 (3)(c), 5.2.3 (7), 5.2.3 (8)]

Hazardous materials can be dangerous in many ways, but generally the threats they pose can be divided into two categories: health hazards and physical hazards. *Health hazards* include materials that may directly affect an individual's health once they enter or come in contact with the body (such as with poisons or corrosives). *Physical hazards* present a threat because of the materials' physical properties (such as temperature or radioactivity).

The U.S. National Fire Academy (NFA) uses a simple classification system for identifying the hazards faced (or types of harm that can be caused) at emergency incidents. This classification is commonly known by the acronym *TRACEM* (or *TRACEMP,* with a *P* for *Psychological harm* added). This book discusses the potential hazards of hazardous materials following the *TRACEMP* model and is described as follows:

- *Thermal* — Thermal harm is the result of exposure to the extremes of heat and cold.

- *Radiological* — Radiological refers to nuclear radiation (alpha, beta, gamma), not radiation as a type of heat transfer.

- *Asphyxiation* — Asphyxiants interfere with oxygen flow during normal breathing. There

Table 2.3
Hazardous Materials Properties Summary
(English Units)

Chemical Name	Lbs Per Gallon	Solid/Liquid/ Gas	Vapor Pressure (at 68°F)	Vapor Density (air=1)	Soluble (degree of solubility)	Specific Gravity (water=1)	Boiling Point (°F)	Melting Point (°F)	Freezing Point (°F)	Flash Point (°F)	LEL/ UEL	Ignition Temperature (°F)
Acetone	6.6	L	3.5 psi	2.0	Yes	0.791	133	-138	-138	0	2.5/13.0	869
Acrolein	7.0	L	4.1 psi	1.94	Yes (40%)	0.843	127	-125	-125	-15	2.8/31	428
Acrylonitrile	6.7	L	1.6 psi	1.83	Yes (7%)	0.800	171	-117	-117	32	3/17	898
Ammonia Anhydrous	6.0	G/L	14.7 psi	0.6	Yes (34%)	0.68	-28	-108	-108	N/A	15.5/27	1204
Chlorine	13	G/L	92.6 psi	2.5	Yes (0.7%)	1.424	-29	-150	-150	N/A	N/A	N/A
Ethylene Oxide	7.2	L/G	21 psi	1.5	Yes	0.974	51	-79	-79	-20	3.0/100	1058
Benzene	7.3	L	1.5 psi	2.7	No	0.879	176	42	42	12	1.3/7.9	928
Bromine	26.0	L	3.3 psi	5.5	Yes (4%)	3.12	138	19	19	N/A	N/A	N/A
Acetylene		G	587.8 psi	0.91	No	0.613 at 112°F	-118	-115.2	-115.2	0	2.5/100	581
Sulfuric Acid	15	L	0.019 psi at 295°F	3.3	Yes	1.84	554	37	37	N/A	N/A	N/A
Hydrochloric Acid	10.1	L	58.8 psi	1.3	Yes	1.19	123	-173.7	-173.7	N/A	N/A	N/A
Sodium Hydroxide	12.5	L/S	0 psi	1.4	Yes	2.13	2534	604	604	N/A	N/A	N/A
Ethyl Ether		L	8.5 psi	2.6	Yes (8%)	0.714	95	-177	-177	-49	1.9/36.0	356
Ethylene Diamine	7.5	L	0.2 psi	2.1	Yes	0.909	242	52	52	99	4.2/14.4	715
Hydrofluoric Acid	9.6 or 10.5	L	7.7 psi at 36.5°F	0.7	Yes	1.25	152	-117.6	-117.6	N/A	N/A	N/A
Isopropyl Alcohol		L	0.6 psi	2.1	Yes	0.8	181	-128	-128	53	2/12.7	750
Methyl Ethyl Ketone	6.7	L	1.4 psi	2.5	Yes	0.8	175.3	-123	-123	16	1.4/11.5	759
Carbon Dioxide		G/L	14.7 psi	1.53	Yes	1.56	Sublimes	-109	-109	N/A	N/A	N/A
Phenol	9.9	L/S	0.008 psi	3.2	Yes (9%)	1.058	358	106	106	175	1.7/8.6	1319

Table 2.3
Hazardous Materials Properties Summary
(International System Units)

Chemical Name	Kgs Per Gallon	Solid/Liquid/ Gas	Vapor Pressure (at 20°C)	Vapor Density (air=1)	Soluble (degree of solubility)	Specific Gravity (water=1)	Boiling Point (°C)	Melting Point (°C)	Freezing Point (°C)	Flash Point (°C)	LEL/ UEL	Ignition Temperature (°C)
Acetone	2.99	L	180 mmHg	2.0	Yes	0.791	56	-94	-94	-18	2.5/13.0	465
Acrolein	3.18	L	210 mmHg	1.94	Yes (40%)	0.843	53	-87	-87	-26	2.8/31	220
Acrylonitrile	3.04	L	83 mmHg	1.83	Yes (7%)	0.800	77	-82.8	-82.8	0	3/17	481
Ammonia Anhydrous	2.7	G/L	760 mmHg	0.6	Yes (34%)	0.68	-33	-78	-78	N/A	15.5/27	651
Chlorine	6.0	G/L	6.3 atm or 4 788 mmHg	2.5	Yes (0.7%)	1.424	-34	-101	-101	N/A	N/A	N/A
Ethylene Oxide	3.27	L/G	1.43 atm or 1 086.8 mmHg	1.5	Yes	0.974	11	-62	-62	-29	3.0/100	570
Benzene	3.31	L	75 mmHg	2.7	No	0.879	80	6	6	-11	1.3/7.9	498
Bromine	12	L	172 mmHg	5.5	Yes (4%)	3.12	59	-7	-7	N/A	N/A	N/A
Acetylene		G	40 atm	0.91	No	0.613 at 44°C	-83	-82	-82	-18	2.5/100	305
Sulfuric Acid	6.8	L	1 mmHg at 146°C	3.3	Yes	1.84	290	3	3	N/A	N/A	N/A
Hydrochloric Acid	4.6	L	4 atm or 3 040 mmHg	1.3	Yes	1.19	51	-114	-114	N/A	N/A	N/A
Sodium Hydroxide	5.7	L/S	0 mmHg	1.4	Yes	2.13	1 390	318	318	N/A	N/A	N/A
Ethyl Ether		L	440 mmHg	2.6	Yes (8%)	0.714	35	-116	-116	-45	1.9/36.0	180
Ethylene Diamine	3.4	L	11 mmHg	2.1	Yes	0.909	117	11	11	37	4.2/14.4	379
Hydrofluoric Acid	4.4 or 4.8	L	400 mmHg at 2.5°C	0.7	Yes	1.25	67	-83.1	-83.1	N/A	N/A	N/A
Isopropyl Alcohol		L	33 mmHg	2.1	Yes	0.8	83	-89	-89	12	2/12.7	399
Methyl Ethyl Ketone	3.04	L	71.2 mmHg	2.5	Yes	0.8	80	-86	-86	-9	1.4/11.5	404
Carbon Dioxide		G/L	760 mmHg	1.53	Yes	1.56	Sublimes	-78	-78	N/A	N/A	N/A
Phenol	4.5	L/S	0.4 mmHg	3.2	Yes (9%)	1.058	181	41	41	79	1.7/8.6	715

are two types: simple and chemical. *Simple asphyxiants* are usually inert gases that displace or dilute oxygen below the level needed by the human body. *Chemical asphyxiants* (referred to as *blood poisons*) interrupt the flow of oxygen in the blood or to body tissues.

- *Chemical* — Two broad types of chemicals can cause harm: toxic materials and corrosives. Toxic materials produce harmful effects depending on the concentration of the materials and the length of exposure to them. Corrosive materials cause visible destruction or irreversible alterations in human skin tissue at the site of contact.

- *Etiological* — Etiological harm involves exposure to a living microorganism (or toxin) that causes, or may cause, human disease.

- *Mechanical* — Contact with mechanical or physical hazards is the most common type of harm causing trauma. One form of mechanical injury might be sustained when shrapnel is created and spread during an explosion.

- *Psychological* — Any incident that causes an unusually strong emotional reaction in an emergency responder can cause psychological harm in the form of stress (such as critical incident stress [CIS] or posttraumatic stress disorder [PTSD]).

NFPA Categories

[NFPA 472: 4.4.1(3)(c), A.4.4.1(3)(c)]

NFPA 472, *Standard on Professional Competence of Responders to Hazardous Materials Incidents* (2002), specifically recognizes the following health and physical hazards that could cause harm in a hazardous materials incident:

- Thermal
- Mechanical
- Poisonous
- Corrosive
- Asphyxiation
- Radiation
- Etiologic
- Psychological

NFPA's terms *poisonous* and *corrosive* would both be grouped under *TRACEMP's chemical* category.

Thermal

[NFPA 472: 4.4.1(3)(c)]

Thermal hazards are related to temperature extremes. Hazardous materials themselves can cause temperature extremes such as with elevated-temperature materials, exothermic reactions (sudden release of heat energy that might occur during oxidation or polymerization), fires, explosions, or cryogenic liquids. Thermal hazards can also be caused by conditions on the scene such as extreme external air temperature or the use of PPE. The latter is discussed in Chapter 6, Personal Protective Equipment. Cold hazards presented by cryogenic liquids and liquefied gases and the heat hazards presented by elevated-temperature materials, fires, or explosions are discussed in the sections that follow.

Cold Temperatures

Cold exposure is a concern when dealing with cryogenic and liquefied gases. A *liquefied gas* (such as propane or carbon dioxide) is one that at the charging pressure is partially liquid at 70°F (21°C). A *cryogen* (sometimes called *refrigerated liquefied gas*) is a gas that turns into a liquid at or below -130°F (-90°C) at 14.7 psi (101 kPa) {1.01 bar}. Examples of cryogenic materials include liquid oxygen (LOX), nitrogen, helium, hydrogen, argon, and liquefied natural gas (LNG). These substances are commonly stored and transported in their liquid states. At these extremely cold temperatures, cryogens have the ability to instantly freeze materials (including human tissue) on contact. Some cryogens have other hazardous properties in addition to the cold hazard. An example of this type would be fluorine, which is also a corrosive, an oxidizer, and a poison.

Cryogenic and liquefied gases vaporize rapidly when released from their containers. A liquid spill or leak will boil into a much larger vapor cloud. These vapor clouds can be extremely dangerous if the vapors are flammable. Both types of liquids cause freeze burns, which are treated as cold injuries according to their severity. Working in extremely cold weather and cold injuries are also discussed in the Climate Concerns and Health Issues section of Chapter 6, Personal Protective

**Table 2.4
Conditions and Symptoms of
Cold Exposure**

Condition	Symptoms
Frost Nip/Incipient Frostbite	Whitening or blanching of skin
Superficial Frostbite	• Waxy or white skin • Firm touch to outer layer of skin; underlying tissue is resilient (flexible)
Deep Frostbite	• Cold skin • Pale skin • Solid, hard skin • Black skin tissue
Systemic Hypothermia	• Shivering • Sleepiness, apathy, listlessness • Core temperature of 95°F (35°C) or less • Slow pulse • Slow breathing • Glassy eyes • Unconsciousness • Freezing of extremities • Death

Equipment. The conditions and symptoms of cold exposure detailed in **Table 2.4** apply to any situation where cold exposure is a factor.

> ### WARNING
> Any clothing saturated with a cryogenic material must be removed immediately. This action is particularly important if the vapors are flammable or oxidizers. A first responder could not escape flames from clothing-trapped vapors if they were to ignite.

Another source of cold exposure is from anhydrous ammonia, which is sometimes used as a refrigerant in cold-storage facilities. This material, too, can cause cold injuries, and its vapors are toxic and may catch fire.

Elevated Temperatures

Elevated-temperature materials such as molten sulphur and molten aluminum can present a thermal hazard in the form of heat. Molten aluminum, for example, is generally shipped at temperatures above 1,300°F (704°C). First responders must be extremely cautious around these materials to avoid being burned. Molten aluminum and other high-temperature materials can ignite flammable and combustible materials (including wood). Working around or near elevated-temperature materials can increase the heating effect of wearing PPE due to high ambient air temperatures (see Chapter 6, Personal Protective Equipment). The U.S. Department of Transportation (DOT) defines an *elevated-temperature material* as one that when offered for transportation or transported in a bulk packaging has one of the following properties:

● Liquid phase and at a temperature at or above 212°F (100°C)

● Liquid phase with a flash point at or above 100°F (38°C) that is intentionally heated and offered for transportation or transported at or above its flash point

● Solid phase and at a temperature at or above 464°F (240°C)

Emergency responders (particularly firefighters) also encounter temperature extremes caused by the heat of combustion in fires, steam, radiation, and the incendiary thermal effects of explosions (see Mechanical Trauma section). **Table 2.5** provides the three types (or degrees) of thermal burns with their symptoms. Chapter 6, Personal Protective Equipment, discusses symptoms of heat illness, a common concern when working in warm temperatures while wearing PPE.

Table 2.5
Thermal Burn Types and Symptoms

Thermal Burn Type	Symptoms
First-Degree Burn — involves the first (top) layer of skin	• Redness • Tenderness (painful to touch) • Mild swelling
Second-Degree Burn — involves the first two layers of skin	• Deep reddening of the skin • Pain • Blisters • Glossy appearance from leaking fluid • Possible loss of some skin
Third-Degree Burn — penetrates the entire thickness of the skin and permanently destroys tissue	• Loss of skin layers • Often painless (Pain may be caused by patches of first- and second-degree burns, which often surround third-degree burns.) • Dry and leathery skin • Skin may appear charred or have patches which appear white, brown or black

Radiological

[NFPA 472: 4.4.1(3)(c)]

The potential for radiation exposure exists when first responders respond to incidents at facilities such as medical centers, industrial operations, nuclear power plants, and research facilities and possibly at terrorist attack incidents. Different types of radiation exist, and some are more energetic than others. For example, nonionizing radiation has enough energy to move atoms around but not enough to change them chemically. Examples of nonionizing radiation include radio waves, electromagnetic field (EMF) radiation, infrared radiation, and microwaves. The most energetic form of radiation is ionizing radiation, and when *radiation* is discussed throughout the rest of this manual, it is (for the most part) referring to *ionizing radiation* **(Figure 2.9)**.

Ionizing radiation is radiation that has sufficient energy to remove electrons from atoms. The removal of electrons can disrupt chemical bonds, resulting in a chemical change in the atom. The process of removing electrons from atoms is called *ionization* and also is the method by which radia-

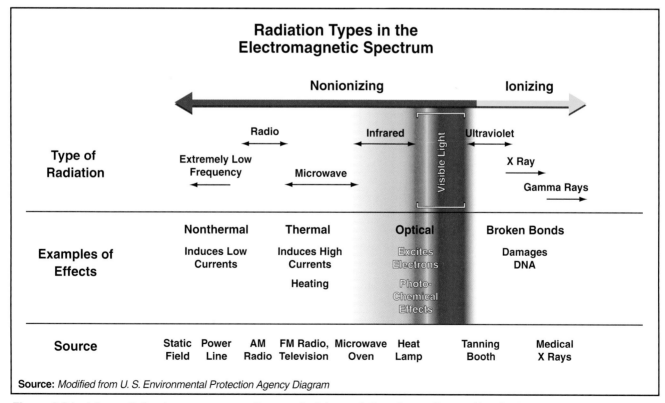

Source: *Modified from U. S. Environmental Protection Agency Diagram*

Figure 2.9 Ionizing radiation has more energy than nonionizing radiation. Generally speaking, ionizing radiation is of more concern to first responders because of the potential health effects associated with exposure.

tion causes damage to the human body. One source of such radiation is the nuclei of unstable atoms. For these radioactive atoms (also referred to as *radionuclides* or *radioisotopes*) to become stable, the nuclei eject or emit subatomic particles and high-energy photons (gamma rays) — a process called *radioactive decay* (see information box *{right}*).

Unstable isotopes of radium, radon, uranium, and thorium exist naturally. Others are continually being made naturally or by human activities such as the splitting of atoms in a nuclear reactor. Either way, they release ionizing radiation. The major

Measuring Radioactivity

Units called *curies (Ci)* and *becquerels (Bq)* are used to measure radioactivity, indicating the number of nuclear decays/disintegrations a radioactive material undergoes in a certain period of time. A Ci represents a large amount of activity, whereas a Bq represents a small amount of activity. These units come from two different measurement systems: English System and SI. Curies, part of the English System, are still commonly used in the U.S., whereas becquerels are more commonly used in other parts of the world.

Types of Radiation

[NFPA 472: 5.2.2(8)]

- **Alpha particles** — Energetic, positively charged particles (helium nuclei) emitted from the nucleus during radioactive decay that rapidly lose energy when passing through matter. They are commonly emitted in the radioactive decay of the heaviest radioactive elements such as uranium and radium as well as by some manmade elements. *Details:*

  — Alpha particles lose energy rapidly in matter and do not penetrate very far; however, they can cause damage over their short path through human tissue. They are usually completely blocked by the outer dead layer of the human skin, so alpha-emitting radioisotopes are not a hazard outside the body. However, they can be very harmful if the material emitting the alpha particles is ingested or inhaled.

  — Alpha particles can be stopped completely by a sheet of paper. See **Figure 2.10.**

- **Beta particles** — Fast moving, positively or negatively charged electrons emitted from the nucleus during radioactive decay. Humans are exposed to beta particles from manufactured and natural sources such as tritium, carbon-14, and strontium-90. *Details:*

  — Beta particles are more penetrating than alpha particles but less damaging over equally traveled distances. Some beta particles are capable of penetrating the skin and causing radiation damage; however, as with alpha emitters, beta emitters are generally more hazardous when they are inhaled or ingested.

  — Beta particles travel appreciable distances in air (up to 20 feet [6.1 m]) but can be reduced or stopped by a layer of clothing or by a few millimeters (less than 0.08 inch) of a substance such as aluminum. See Figure 2.10.

- **Gamma rays** — High-energy photons (weightless packets of energy like visible light and X rays). Gamma rays often accompany the emission of alpha or beta particles from a nucleus. They have neither a charge nor a mass but are very penetrating. One source of gamma rays in the environment is naturally occurring potassium-40. Manufactured sources include plutonium-239 and cesium-137. *Details:*

  — Gamma rays can easily pass completely through the human body or be absorbed by tissue, thus constituting a radiation hazard for the entire body.

  — Several feet (about 0.6 m) of concrete or a few inches (about 50 mm) of lead may be required to stop the more energetic gamma rays. Standard fire-fighting clothing provides **no** protection against the penetrating power of gamma rays. See Figure 2.10.

- **X rays** — High-energy photons produced by the interaction of charged particles with matter. X rays and gamma rays have essentially the same properties, but differ in origin; that is, X rays are emitted from processes outside the nucleus, while gamma rays originate inside the nucleus. *Details:*

  — X rays are generally lower in energy and therefore less penetrating than gamma rays. Literally thousands of X-ray machines are used daily in medicine and industry for examinations, inspections, and process

Types of Radiation *(continued)*

controls. Because of their many uses, X rays are the single largest source of manufactured radiation exposure.

— A few millimeters (less than 0.08 inch) of lead can stop medical X rays.

• *Neutrons* — Ultrahigh energy particles that have a physical mass like alpha or beta radiation but have no electrical charge. Neutrons are highly penetrating. Fission reactions produce neutrons

along with gamma radiation. Neutron radiation is difficult to measure in the field and is usually estimated based on gamma measurements. *Details:*

— Neutron radiation is not commonly used in commercial or industrial operations. It is most likely to be encountered in research laboratories or operating nuclear power plants.

— The health hazard that neutrons present arises from the fact that they cause the release of secondary radiation.

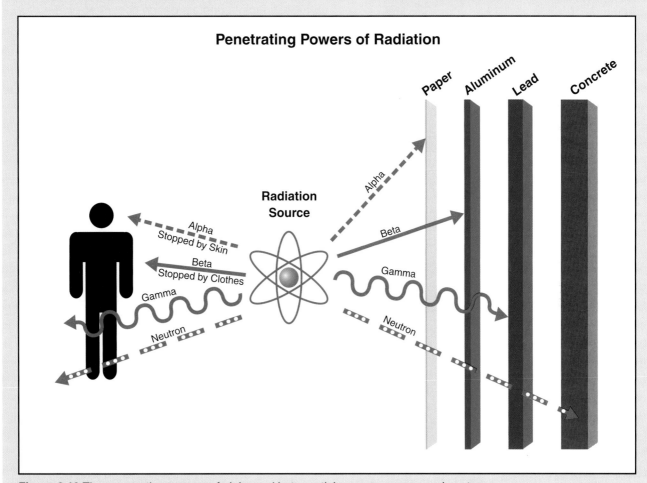

Figure 2.10 The penetrating powers of alpha and beta particles, gamma rays, and neutrons.

types of radiation emitted as a result of spontaneous decay are alpha and beta particles, and gamma rays. X rays, another major type of radiation, are very similar to gamma rays except that they arise from processes outside the nucleus. Neutrons are ultrahigh energy particles that are ejected from the nucleus (see information box *{left}*).

The sources of radiation exposure (both natural and manufactured), exposure pathways, and the health hazards of exposure are given in the sections that follow. The risks of radiation and radionuclides chemical health hazards and radiation protection strategies are also given.

Sources of Radiation Exposure

The ionizing radiations of primary concern are alpha and beta particles, gamma rays, and X rays. Alpha and beta particles and gamma rays can come from natural sources or be technologically produced. Most of the X-ray exposure that people receive is technologically produced. Radiation is used on an ever-increasing scale in medicine, dentistry, and industry. Radioactive materials are also used in common consumer products such as digital and luminous-dial wristwatches, ceramic glazes, artificial teeth, and smoke detectors.

Natural radiation comes from the following sources:

- The sun
- Cosmic rays from space (energetic protons, electrons, gamma rays, and X rays)
- Naturally occurring radioactive elements found in the earth's crust (uranium, thorium, and potassium and their radioactive derivatives that emit alpha and beta particles or gamma rays)
- Radioactive decay products such as radon (which emanates from the ground); the group that represents the majority of the radiation exposure of the general public

In addition to these natural sources, radiation can come from other technological sources. Many of the following facilities generate some radioactive waste, and some release a controlled amount of radiation into the environment.

- Medical facilities (hospitals, medistations/urgent-care clinics, physician offices, and dentist offices) and pharmaceutical facilities
- Research and teaching institutions
- Pipe X-ray equipment
- Nuclear reactors and their support facilities such as uranium mills and fuel preparation plants
- Certain manufacturing processes
- Federal facilities involved in nuclear weapons production as part of their normal operation

Any release of radioactive material is a potential source of radiation exposure to the population. In addition to exposure from external sources, radiation exposure can occur internally by ingesting, inhaling, injecting, or absorbing radioactive materials. Both external and internal sources may irradiate the whole body or a portion of it.

What's the Difference Between Radioactive Material Exposure and Radioactive Contamination?

[NFPA 472: 5.2.3(1)(b)(iv)]

Radioactive *contamination* occurs when a material that contains radioactive atoms is deposited on surfaces, skin, clothing, or any place where it is not desired. It is important to remember that radiation does *not* spread; rather, it is radioactive material/contamination that is spread. *Exposure* to radiation occurs when a person is near a radiation source and is exposed to the energy from that source. Exposure to radiation alone does *not* contaminate a person. Contamination can occur when a person comes in contact with radioactive material. A person can become contaminated externally, internally, or both. Radioactive material can enter the body via one or more exposure pathways (see Exposure Pathways section). An unprotected person contaminated with radioactive material receives radiation exposure until the source of radiation (radioactive material) is removed. Note the following situations:

- A person is *externally* contaminated (and receives external exposure) when radioactive material is on the skin or clothing.
- A person is *internally* contaminated (and receives internal exposure) when radioactive material is breathed, swallowed, or absorbed through wounds.
- The *environment* is contaminated when radioactive material is spread about or is unconfined. Environmental contamination is another potential source of external exposure.

The amount of radiation exposure is usually expressed in a unit called *rem* (for a large amount of radiation) or *millirem (mrem)*. However, several terms are used to express radiation dose and exposure that first responders should be familiar with (see information box). These units may be used on radiation dose instruments (dosimeters) and radiation survey meters.

Measuring Radiation Exposure

As with curies and becquerels, two systems of units are used to measure and express radiation exposure and radiation dose (energy absorbed from the exposure). The U.S. still commonly uses the English System, and these units are as follows:

- *Roentgen (R)* — Used for exposure, applied only to gamma and X-ray radiation; the unit used on most U.S. dosimeters; R per hour (R/hr) is used on radiation survey meters.

- *Radiation absorbed dose (rad)* — Used to measure the amount of radiation energy absorbed by a material. This unit applies to any material and all types of radiation, but it does *not* take into account the potential effect that different types of radiation have on the human body. For example, 1 rad of alpha radiation is 20 times more damaging to the human body than 1 rad of gamma radiation.

- *Roentgen equivalent in man (rem)* — Used for the absorbed dose equivalence as pertaining to a human body; applied to all types of radiation. This unit takes into account the energy absorbed (as measured in rad) and the biological effect on the body due to different types of radiation. Rem is used to set dose limits for emergency responders.

For gamma and X-ray radiation, a common *conversion factor* between exposure, absorbed dose, and dose equivalent is as follows:

1 R = 1 rad = 1 rem

The SI unit used to measure absorbed dose is called *gray (Gy)* whereas the unit for dose equivalence is *seivert (Sv)*. Seivert is used on some newer radioactive survey meters and meters outside the U.S. The U.S. Department of Defense also uses survey meters that read in units of gray per hour (Gy/hr).

In the U.S. the average person is exposed to an effective dose equivalent of approximately 360 mrems (whole-body exposures) per year from all sources. **Figure 2.11** shows potential sources of natural and manufactured radiation and the approximate percentages for each.

Exposure Pathways

Each of the different pathways (or routes) by which people can be exposed to radioactive material results in exposure to different parts of the

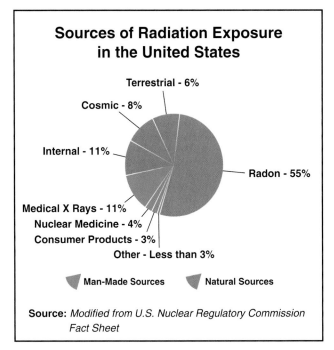

Sources of Radiation Exposure in the United States

Terrestrial - 6%
Cosmic - 8%
Internal - 11%
Radon - 55%
Medical X Rays - 11%
Nuclear Medicine - 4%
Consumer Products - 3%
Other - Less than 3%

Man-Made Sources   Natural Sources

Source: *Modified from U.S. Nuclear Regulatory Commission Fact Sheet*

Figure 2.11 Naturally occurring radon is the most significant source of radiation exposure in the U.S., followed by medical X rays.

body. According to the Environmental Protection Agency (EPA), the three basic radiation exposure pathways are as follows (also see Routes of Entry section under Chemical section):

- *Inhalation* — Exposure occurs when people breathe radioactive materials into the lungs. The chief concerns are radioactively contaminated dust, smoke, or gaseous radionuclides such as radon. Inhalation is of most concern for radionuclides that are alpha or beta particle emitters. *Details:*

  — Radioactive particles can lodge in the lungs and remain for a long time. As long as they remain and continue to decay, the exposure continues.

  — For radionuclides that decay slowly, the exposure continues over a very long time.

  — Alpha and beta particles can transfer large amounts of energy to surrounding tissue, damaging deoxyribonucleic acid (DNA) or other cellular material. This damage can eventually lead to cancer or other diseases and mutations.

- *Ingestion* — Exposure occurs when someone swallows radioactive materials. Alpha- and beta-emitting radionuclides are of most concern for ingested radioactive materials. They release large amounts of energy directly to tissue, causing DNA and other cell damage. *Details:*

— Ingested radionuclides can expose the entire digestive system.

— Some radionuclides can also be absorbed and expose the kidneys and other organs as well as the bones.

• **Direct exposure (skin contact/penetration)** — External exposure from radioactive material is a concern that varies depending on the type. *Examples:*

— The threat of harm from alpha particles is reasonably limited since they cannot penetrate the outer layer of skin. However, they may still pose a risk if the skin is broken such as with an open wound.

— Beta particles can burn the skin in very high doses and/or damage the eyes.

— The greatest threat is from gamma rays. While different radionuclides emit gamma rays of different strength, they can travel long distances and penetrate the entire body.

Radiation Health Hazards
[NFPA 472: 5.2.3(8)(f)]

Scientists have determined that the effects of ionizing radiation occur at the cellular level. The human body is composed of many organs, and each organ of the body is composed of specialized cells. Ionizing radiation can affect the normal operation of these cells.

Radiation causes damage to any material by ionizing the atoms in that material — changing the material's atomic structure. When atoms are ionized, the chemical properties of those atoms are altered. Radiation can damage a cell by ionizing the atoms and changing the resulting chemical behavior of the atoms and/or molecules in the cell. If a person receives a sufficiently high dose of radiation and many cells are damaged, there may be noticeable (observable) health effects. Some human cells are more sensitive to environmental factors than others. These environmental factors include viruses, toxins, and ionizing radiation. Radiation damage to cells depends on how sensitive the cells are to ionizing radiation.

Generally, the most sensitive cells are those that divide rapidly or are in the process of dividing. These cells are most vulnerable because it is difficult or impossible for them to repair any damage that may occur during cell division. Examples of highly vulnerable cells include blood-forming cells, cells that line our intestinal tract, hair follicle cells, and cells in an embryo or fetus. Cells that divide more slowly and are more specialized (brain and muscle cells) are not as easily damaged by ionizing radiation.

The biological effects of ionizing radiation depend on how much and how fast a radiation dose is received. There are two categories of radiation doses: acute and chronic radiation doses.

Acute doses. Exposure to a large dose of radiation received in a short period of time is an acute dose. The body can't repair or replace cells fast enough after a large acute dose of radiation, so physical effects may be seen. Some possible health effects from acute doses of radiation include reduced blood count, hair loss, nausea, and fatigue. The physical reaction to an acute dose of radiation is the result of extensive cell damage over a short period of time.

Radiation therapy patients (those undergoing cancer treatment) receive high doses of radiation over a short period of time, generally applied to a small portion of the body. Ionizing radiation is used to treat cancer because cancer cells divide rapidly and are sensitive to ionizing radiation. It takes a large acute dose of radiation before people experience any observable physical effects. Physical effects may take days to manifest themselves and may include nausea, vomiting, and diarrhea. Other than radiation therapy patients, acute doses have only been received by atomic bomb survivors exposed at the Japanese cities of Hiroshima and Nagasaki and by people at a few radiation incidents at nuclear facilities.

Most radioactive material shipments contain very small amounts of radioactivity. Federal packaging regulations require that the level of radiation (measured on the external surface of shipping packages) be low enough that those who handle packages or are potentially exposed to the packages will not experience any adverse health effects. When highly radioactive material is shipped, special packages are used that have been designed to withstand severe accident conditions without breaching or releasing their radioactive contents. The probability that first responders will receive an acute dose of radiation while responding to a transportation incident is extremely low.

Chronic doses. Small amount of radiation received over a long period of time is a chronic dose. The body is better equipped to handle a chronic dose of radiation than it is an acute radiation dose. The body can repair the damage from chronic doses because a smaller percentage of cells will need repair at any given time. The body has enough time to replace dead or nonfunctioning cells with healthy ones.

Chronic doses do not result in the detectable health effects seen with acute doses. Because of cell repair, even a sophisticated blood analysis will not reveal any biological effects. Examples of chronic radiation doses include the everyday doses we receive from natural background radiation and those received by workers in nuclear and medical facilities.

Radionuclides Chemical Health Hazards

Radioactive elements and compounds behave chemically exactly like their nonradioactive forms. For example, radioactive lead has the same chemical properties as nonradioactive lead. The chemical properties of a radionuclide can determine where health effects occur. To function properly, many organs require certain elements. They cannot distinguish between radioactive and nonradioactive forms of an element and accumulate one as quickly as the other. Examples are as follows:

- ***Radioactive iodine*** — The thyroid needs iodine to function normally and cannot tell the difference between stable and radioactive isotopes. As a result, radioactive iodine tends to concentrate in the thyroid and may contribute to thyroid cancer.

- ***Strontium-90 and radium-226*** — Each element has chemical properties similar to calcium, thus strontium and radium tend to collect in calcium-rich areas of the body such as bones and teeth.

Radiation Protection Strategies

[NFPA 472: 5.2.4(5)]

Time, distance, and shielding are three ways to provide protection from external radiation during an emergency. The three protection principles are explained as follows:

- ***Time*** — The amount of radiation exposure increases or decreases according to the time spent near the source of radiation. The shorter the exposure time, the smaller the total radiation dose is.

- ***Distance*** — The farther the distance from the source, the less the exposure is. Generally, doubling the distance reduces the exposure by a factor of four. Halving the distance increases the exposure by a factor of four (see sidebar, p. 70). Since alpha and beta particles don't travel very far, distance is a prime concern when dealing with gamma rays.

- ***Shielding*** — Certain materials such as lead, earth, concrete, and water prevent penetration of some types of radiation. The thickness of the shielding depends on the type of material, the type of radiation, and the distance from the source **(Figure 2.12)**.

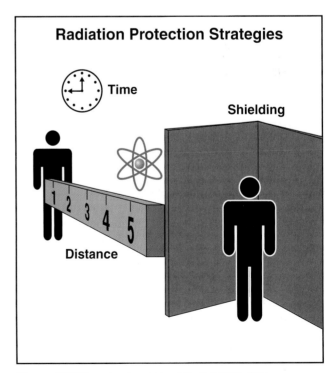

Figure 2.12 To reduce exposure to radiation, first responders should use the protection strategies of time, distance, and shielding.

Why Does Exposure Change More Rapidly Than the Distance?

The area of a circle depends on the distance from the center of the circle to the edge (radius). The area is proportional to the square of the radius. As a result, if the radius doubles, the area increases four times. Think of the radiation source as a bare lightbulb. The bulb emits light equally in every direction in a circle. The energy from the light is distributed evenly over the whole area of the circle. When the radius doubles, the radiation spreads over four times as much area, so the dose is only one-fourth as much **(Figure 2.13)**. In addition, as the distance from the source increases, so does the likelihood that some gamma rays will lose their energy. Therefore, the exposure of an individual sitting 4 feet (1.2 m) from a radiation source will be one-fourth the exposure of an individual sitting 2 feet (0.6 m) from the same source.

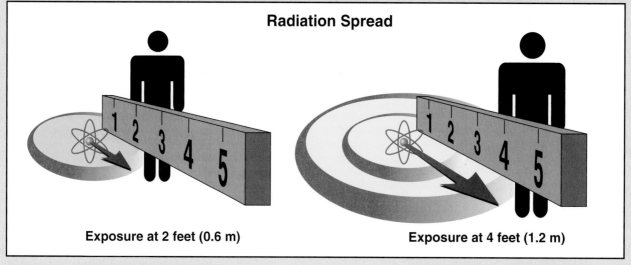

Radiation Spread

Exposure at 2 feet (0.6 m)   Exposure at 4 feet (1.2 m)

Figure 2.13 Doubling the distance from a radiation source reduces the exposure by a factor of four because the radiation is spread over four times as much area.

CAUTION

Wearing personal protective equipment (including self-contained breathing apparatus) generally protects emergency response personnel from external and internal contaminates. It *does not* protect against exposure to gamma rays.

Asphyxiation

[NFPA 472: 4.4.1(3)(c), 5.2.3(8)(a)]

Asphyxiants are substances that affect the oxygenation of the body and generally lead to suffocation. Asphyxiants can be divided into two classes: simple and chemical. *Simple asphyxiants* are gases that displace the oxygen necessary for breathing. These gases dilute the oxygen concentration below the level required by the human body. These gases may also displace the oxygen normally present — just as a gas that is heavier than air will fill a basement or other low-lying area that doesn't have natural or mechanical ventilation. Examples are acetylene, carbon dioxide, helium, hydrogen, nitrogen, methane, and ethane. *Chemical asphyxiants* are substances that prohibit the body from using oxygen. Even though oxygen is available, these substances starve the cells of the body for oxygen. Examples are hydrogen cyanide, aniline, acetonitrile, carbon monoxide, and hydrogen sulfide.

Chemical

[NFPA 472: 4.4.1(3)(c), 5.2.3(7), A.5.2.3(7), 5.2.3(8)(a–e), A.5.2.3(8)]

Exposure to hazardous chemicals may produce a wide range of adverse health effects. The likelihood of an adverse health effect occurring and the severity of the effect depend on the following factors:

- Toxicity of the chemical

- Pathway or route of exposure

- Nature and extent of exposure

- Factors that affect the susceptibility of the exposed person such as age and the presence of certain chronic diseases

Toxic chemicals often produce injuries at the site where they come into contact with the body. A chemical injury at the site of contact (typically the skin and mucous membranes of the eyes, nose, mouth, or respiratory tract) is termed a *local toxic effect*. Irritant gases such as chlorine and ammonia can, for example, produce a localized toxic effect in the respiratory tract, while corrosive acids and bases can result in local damage to the skin.

In addition, a toxic chemical may be absorbed into the bloodstream and distributed to other parts of the body, producing *systemic effects*. Many pesticides, for example, absorb through the skin, distribute to other sites in the body, and produce adverse effects such as seizures or cardiac, pulmonary, or other problems.

It is important to recognize that exposure to chemical compounds can result not only in the development of a single systemic effect but also in the development of multiple systemic effects or a combination of systemic and local effects. Some of these effects may be delayed, sometimes for as long as 48 hours or more.

The following sections discuss the routes of entry that chemicals use to get into the body, toxicity and exposure limits, types of hazardous chemicals or substances (such as irritants, convulsants, corrosives, carcinogens, mutagens, teratogens, and sensitizers/allergens), and signs and symptoms of chemical exposure.

Routes of Entry
[NFPA 472: 4.4.1(3)(d), 5.2.2 (3)(e)]

The Centers for Disease Control and Prevention (CDC) and the National Institute for Occupational Safety and Health (NIOSH) list the following three main routes of entry through which hazardous materials can enter the body and cause harm (see information box, p. 72, for others):

- ***Inhalation*** — Process of taking in materials by breathing through the nose or mouth. Hazardous vapors, smoke, gases, liquid aerosols, fumes, and suspended dusts may be inhaled into the body. When a hazardous material presents an inhalation threat, respiratory protection is required. Respiratory protection is discussed in more detail in Chapter 6, Personal Protective Equipment.

- ***Ingestion*** — Process of taking in materials through the mouth by means other than simple inhalation. Taking a pill is a simple example of how a chemical might be deliberately ingested. However, poor hygiene after handling a hazardous material can lead to its ingestion accidentally. *Other examples:*

  — Chemical residue on the hands can be transferred to food and then ingested while eating. Hand washing is very important to prevent accidental ingestion of hazardous materials.

  — Ingestion can also occur when particles of insoluble materials become trapped in the mucous membranes and are swallowed after being cleared from the respiratory tract **(Figure 2.14)**.

- ***Skin contact (also includes contact with mucous membranes)*** — Occurrence when a chemical or hazardous material (in any state — solid, liquid, or gas) contacts the skin or exposed surface of

Figure 2.14 Using disposable cups and practicing good hygiene (such as washing hands before eating and drinking) at hazardous materials incidents reduces the likelihood of accidental ingestion of chemicals.

the body (such as the mucous membranes of the eyes, nose, or mouth). If the skin is damaged or abraded, it is easier for substances to absorb into the body through the breaks in the skin's protective barrier. Toxic substances are also more readily absorbed into the body when the skin is wet (particularly from sweat). When this contact occurs, one of the following four things is likely to occur:

— The skin and its associated film of lipid (fat) act as an effective barrier against penetration, injury, or other forms of disturbance (that is, the skin prevents any harm from being done).

— The substance reacts with the skin surface and causes primary irritation or dermatitis (such as might happen when the skin is burned by an acid).

— The substance penetrates the skin and conjugates with tissue protein, resulting in skin sensitization (meaning the substance can cause an allergic reaction such as what many people experience when contacting poison ivy).

— The substance penetrates the skin, enters the blood stream, and acts as a potential systemic poison. This penetration is most

likely to occur through two main absorption pathways:

○ Epidural (skin) cells *(transepidermal)*

○ Hair follicles and sebaceous (sweat) glands *(pilosebaceous)*

CAUTION

All personnel working at hazardous materials incidents must use appropriate personal protective equipment, including appropriate respiratory protection equipment.

Eating and Drinking Can be Dangerous . . .

. . . on the scene of a hazardous material incident. If hazardous materials at an incident site contaminate food or water, the chemicals can be ingested into the body where they can cause harm. Therefore, you **never** want to eat or drink in areas where hazardous materials may be present. Make sure that water comes from a clean source and is dispensed in disposable cups. Always place rehabilitation areas well away from any sources of contamination. Finally, wash your hands and be certain that you are completely decontaminated before eating or drinking.

Other Routes of Entry
[NFPA 472: 4.4.1(3)(d)]
While this manual discusses the routes of entry as described by CDC and NIOSH, many sources designate four main routes of entry: *inhalation* and *ingestion* (the same as the CDC definitions given earlier) plus *injection* and *absorption (*terms used in place of *skin contact)*. These entry routes are defined as follows:

• **Injection** — Process of taking in materials through a puncture or break in the skin. Protection from injection must be a consideration when dealing with any sort of contaminated (or potentially contaminated) objects easily capable of cutting or puncturing the skin (such as broken glass, nails, sharp metal edges, tools like utility knives, or other sharps).

• **Absorption** — Process of taking in materials through the skin or eyes. Some materials pass

easily through the mucous membranes or areas of the body where the skin is the thinnest, allowing the least resistance to penetration. The eyes, nose, mouth, wrists, neck, ears, hands, groin, and underarms are areas of concern. Many poisons are easily absorbed into the body system in this manner. Others can enter the system easily through the unknowing act of touching a contaminated finger to one's eye.

NFPA 472 identifies the routes of entry as contact (essentially the same as skin contact), absorption, inhalation, and ingestion. Additionally, some experts define a fifth route of entry in regards to radiation as follows:

• **Penetration** — Radioactive particles and energy waves can *penetrate* (go through) the human body, rather than being absorbed by it or injected into it. This penetrating radiation can cause a variety of health effects.

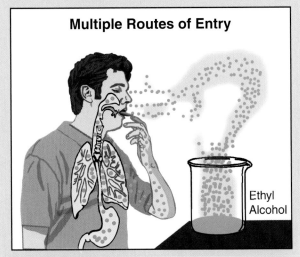

Multiple Routes of Entry

Ethyl Alcohol

Figure 2.15 Chemicals often have multiple routes of entry. First responders must ensure that all routes are protected against exposure.

Toxic Materials
[NFPA 472: 5.2.2(3)(f), 5.2.3(8)(b)]

Many poisons (toxins) have fast-acting, acute toxic effects while others may have chronic effects that aren't manifested for many years. Exposures to poisons can cause damage to organs or other parts of the body and may even cause death. Numerous types of poisons exist such as the following examples:

- *Nephrotoxic agents* — Agents such as halogenated hydrocarbons affect the kidneys.

- *Hematotoxic agents* — Agents such as benzene, nitrites, naphthalene, and arsine affect the blood.

- *Neurotoxic agents* — Organophosphates such as the pesticide parathion and the nerve agent sarin affect the nervous system.

- *Hepatotoxic agents* — Agents such as alcohol, trichloroethylene, carbon tetrachloride, and phenols affect the liver.

Some chemicals affect the lungs, while others may attack the reproductive system. Types of toxins, their target organs, and chemical examples are given in **Table 2.6, p. 74.**

The methods by which poisons attack the body vary depending on the type of poison. Irritants and chemical asphyxiants interfere with oxygen flow to the lungs and the blood. Nerve poisons act on the body's nervous system by disrupting nerve impulses.

According to the CDC, the effect produced by a toxic compound is primarily a function of the dose (amount of a substance ingested or administered through skin contact) and the concentration (amount of the substance inhaled in this context) of the compound **(Figure 2.16. p. 75)**. This principle, termed the *dose-response relationship,* is a key concept in toxicology. Many factors affect the normal dose-response relationship, but typically, as the dose increases, the severity of the toxic response increases **(Figure 2.17, p. 76)**. For example, people exposed to 100 parts per million (ppm) (see information box, p. 77) of tetrachloroethylene (solvent commonly used for dry cleaning fabrics) may experience relatively mild symptoms such as headache and drowsiness. However, exposure to 200 ppm of tetrachloroethylene can result in a loss of motor coordination in some individuals, and exposure to 1,500 ppm for 30 minutes may result in a loss of consciousness. The severity of the toxic effect also depends on the duration of exposure, a factor that influences the dose of the compound in the body. **Table 2.7, p. 77,** gives factors influencing toxicity.

Poisons and the measurements of their toxicity are often expressed in terms of *lethal dose (LD)* for amounts ingested and *lethal concentration (LC)* for amounts inhaled. These terms are often found on MSDSs. While first responders at the Awareness and Operational Levels may have little practical use for the information the terms provide, it should be understood that as a general rule, the smaller the value presented, the more toxic the substance is. Obviously, the lower the dose or concentration needed to kill, the more dangerous it is. These

Table 2.6
Types of Toxins and Their Target Organs

Toxin	Target Organ	Chemical Examples
Nephrotoxins	Kidney	Halogenated Hydrocarbons, Mercury, Carbon Tetrachloride
Hemotoxins	Blood	Carbon Monoxide, Cyanides, Benzene, Nitrates, Arsine, Naphthalene, Cocaine
Neurotoxins	Nervous System	Organophosphates, Mercury, Carbon Disulphide, Carbon Monoxide, Sarin
Hepatoxins	Liver	Alcohol, Carbon Tetrachloride, Trichloroethylene, Vinyl Chloride, Chlorinated HC
Immunotoxins	Immune System	Benzene, Polybrominated Biphenyls (PBBs), Polychlorinated Biphenyls (PCBs), Dioxins, Dieldrin
Endocrine Toxins	Endocrine System (including the pituitary, hypothalamus, thyroid adrenals, pancreas, thymus, ovaries, and testes)	Benzene, Cadmium, Chlordane, Chloroform, Ethanol, Kerosene, Iodine, Parathion
Musculoskeletal Toxins	Muscles/Bones	Fluorides, Sulfuric Acid, Phosphine
Respiratory Toxins	Lungs	Hydrogen Sulfide, Xylene, Ammonia, Boric Acid, Chlorine
Cutaneous Hazards	Skin	Gasoline, Xylene, Ketones, Chlorinated Compounds
Eye Hazards	Eyes	Organic Solvents, Corrosives, Acids
Mutagens	DNA	Aluminum Chloride, Beryllium, Dioxins
Teratogens	Embryo/Fetus	Lead, Lead Compounds, Benzene
Carcinogens	All	Tobacco Smoke, Benzene, Arsenic, Radon, Vinyl Chloride

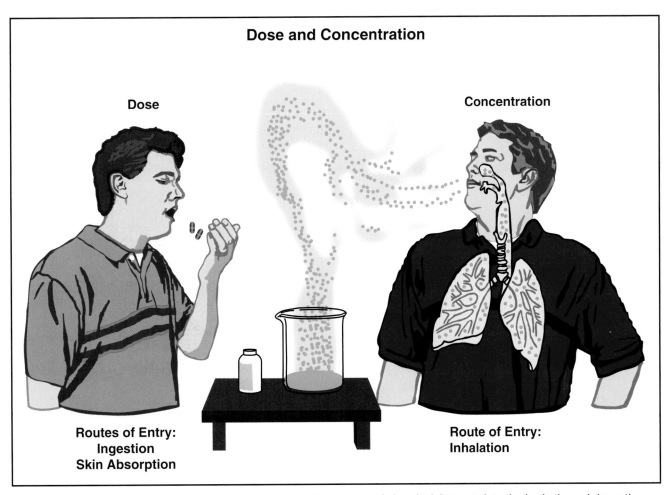

Dose and Concentration

Dose

Concentration

Routes of Entry:
Ingestion
Skin Absorption

Route of Entry:
Inhalation

Figure 2.16 For purposes of measuring toxicity, a *dose* is the amount of chemical that gets into the body through ingestion or skin contact (such as being absorbed through the skin). *Concentration* refers to the amount of a chemical inhaled.

values are normally established by testing the effects of exposure on animals (rats or rabbits) under laboratory conditions over a set period of time. Dose terms are defined as follows:

- *Lethal dose (LD)* — Minimum amount of solid or liquid that when ingested, absorbed, or injected through the skin will cause death. Sometimes the lethal dose is expressed in conjunction with a percentage such as LD_{50} (most common) or LD_{100}. The number refers to the percentage of an animal test group that was killed by the listed dose (usually administered orally).

- *Median lethal dose (LD_{50})* — Statistically derived single dose of a substance that can be expected to cause death in 50 percent of animals when administered by the oral route. The LD_{50} value is expressed in terms of weight of test substance per unit weight of test animal (mg/kg) (see information box, p. 77). It should also be

understood that the term LD_{50} does not mean that the other half of the subjects are necessarily completely well. They may be very sick or almost dead, but only half will actually die.

- *Lethal dose low (LD_{LO} or LDL)* — Lowest administered dose of a material capable of killing a specified test species.

Concentration terms are defined as follows:

- *Lethal concentration (LC)* — Minimum concentration of an inhaled substance in the gaseous state that will be fatal to the test group (usually within 1 to 4 hours). Like lethal dose, the lethal concentration is often expressed as LC_{50}, indicating that half of the test group was killed by concentrations at the listed value. Keep in mind that the 50 percent of the population not killed may suffer effects ranging from no response to severe injury. LC may be expressed in the following ways:

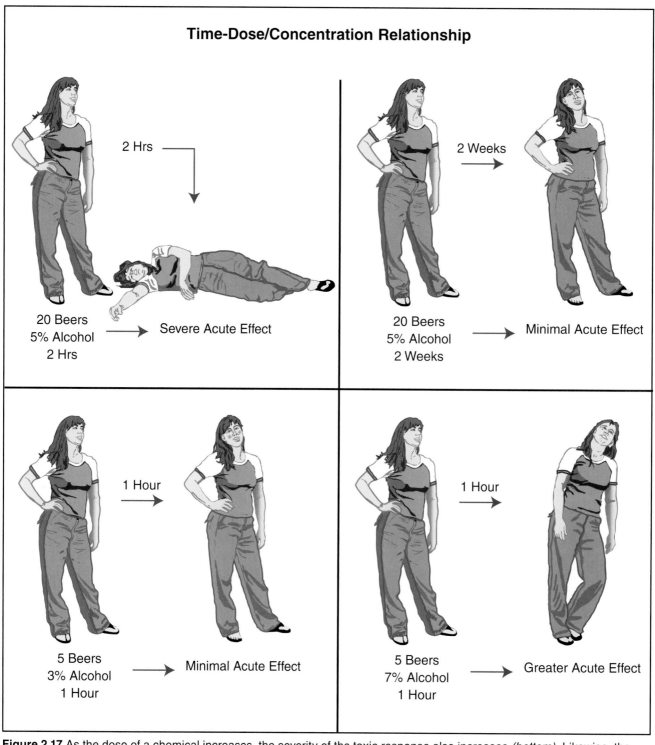

Time-Dose/Concentration Relationship

20 Beers
5% Alcohol
2 Hrs → Severe Acute Effect

20 Beers
5% Alcohol
2 Weeks → Minimal Acute Effect

5 Beers
3% Alcohol
1 Hour → Minimal Acute Effect

5 Beers
7% Alcohol
1 Hour → Greater Acute Effect

Figure 2.17 As the dose of a chemical increases, the severity of the toxic response also increases *(bottom)*. Likewise, the duration of exposure has an affect on the toxic response. A dose spread over a long period of time may have less effect than the same dose administered over a shorter period *(top)*.

— Parts per million (ppm)

— Milligrams per cubic meter (mg/m³)

— Micrograms of material per liter of air (μg/L)

— Milligrams per liter (mg/L) (see information box)

● *Lethal concentration low* $(LC_{LO}$ *or LCL)*—Lowest concentration of a gas or vapor capable of killing a specified species over a specified time.

Table 2.7
Factors Influencing Toxicity

Type of Factor	Examples
Factors related to the chemical	Composition (salt, freebase, etc.), physical characteristics (size, liquid, solid, etc.), physical properties (volatility, solubility, etc.), presence of impurities, breakdown products, carriers
Factors related to exposure	Dose, concentration, route of exposure (inhalation, ingestion, etc.), duration
Factors related to person exposed	Heredity, immunology, nutrition, hormones, age, sex, health status, preceding diseases
Factors related to environment	Media (air, water, soil, etc.), additional chemicals present, temperature, air pressure

Source: U.S. Centers for Disease Control and Prevention (CDC).

While lethal dose and lethal concentration values are obtained under laboratory conditions using test animals, emergency responders should be aware that exertion, stress, and individual metabolism or chemical sensitivities (allergies) may make persons more vulnerable to the harmful effects of hazardous materials.

The *incapacitating dose (ID)* for an organism (such as a human being) is expressed similarly to lethal dose and lethal concentration. Incapacitation can vary from moderate (unable to see, breathless) to severe (convulsions). The term is often used in the context of chemical warfare agents. Incapacitating doses are expressed as follows:

- ID_{50} — Dose that incapacitates 50 percent of the population of interest
- ID_{10} — Dose that incapacitates 10 percent of the population of interest

Expressing Concentration

For purposes of exposure limits (values expressing the maximum dose or concentration to which workers should be exposed given a specific time frame) and other measurements, the concentration of a substance is often expressed in the following terms:

- *Parts per million (ppm)* — Concentration of a gas or vapor in air; parts (by volume) of the gas or vapor in a million parts of air; also the concentration of a particular substance in a liquid or solid

- *Parts per billion (ppb)* — Concentration of a gas or vapor in air; parts (by volume) of the gas or vapor in a billion parts of air; usually used to express extremely low concentrations of unusually toxic gases or vapors; also the concentration of a particular substance in a liquid or solid

- *Milligrams per cubic meter (mg/m3)* — Unit for expressing concentrations of dusts, gases, or mists in air

- *Grams per kilogram (g/kg)* — Expression of dose used in oral and dermal toxicology testing to denote grams of a substance dosed per kilogram of animal body weight

- *Milligrams per kilogram (mg/kg)* — Expression of toxicological dose to denote milligrams of a substance dosed per kilogram of animal body weight

- *Micrograms of material per liter of air (µg/L)* — Unit for expressing concentrations of chemicals in air

- *Milligrams per liter (mg/L)* — Unit for expressing concentrations of chemicals in water

Exposure limits may be expressed in terms such as *threshold limit value (TLV®), short-term exposure limit (STEL), threshold limit value-ceiling (TLV®-C),* and *permissible exposure limit (PEL).* Concentrations that are high enough to kill or cause serious injury or illness are expressed in terms of *immediately dangerous to life or health (IDLH).* **Table 2.8, p. 78,** provides definitions and exposure periods for the various limits as well as the organizations responsible for establishing them.

Table 2.8
Exposure Limits

Term	Definition	Exposure Period	Organization
IDLH Immediately Dangerous to Life or Health	An atmospheric concentration of any toxic, corrosive, or asphyxiating substance that poses an immediate threat to life. It can cause irreversible or delayed adverse health effects and interfere with the individual's ability to escape from a dangerous atmosphere.*	Immediate (This limit represents the maximum concentration from which an unprotected person can expect to escape in a 30-minute period of time without suffering irreversible health effects.)	**NIOSH** National Institute for Occupational Safety and Health
IDLH Immediately Dangerous to Life or Health	An atmosphere that poses an immediate threat to life, would cause irreversible adverse health effects, or would impair an individual's ability to escape from a dangerous atmosphere.	Immediate	**OSHA** Occupational Safety and Health Administration
PEL Permissible Exposure Limit**	A regulatory limit on the amount or concentration of a substance in the air. PELs may also contain a skin designation. The PEL is the maximum concentration to which the majority of healthy adults can be exposed over a 40-hour workweek without suffering adverse effects.	8-hours Time-Weighted Average (TWA)*** (unless otherwise noted)	**OSHA** Occupational Safety and Health Administration
PEL (C) PEL Ceiling Limit	The maximum concentration to which an employee may be exposed at any time, even instantaneously.	Instantaneous	**OSHA** Occupational Safety and Health Administration
STEL Short-Term Exposure Limit	The maximum concentration allowed for a 15-minute exposure period.	15 minutes (TWA)	**OSHA** Occupational Safety and Health Administration
TLV® Threshold Limit Value†	An occupational exposure value recommended by ACGIH® to which it is believed nearly all workers can be exposed day after day for a working lifetime without ill effect.	Lifetime	**ACGIH®** American Conference of Governmental Industrial Hygienists

Continued

Table 2.8 (continued)
Exposure Limits

Term	Definition	Exposure Period	Organization
TLV®-TWA Threshold Limit Value-Time-Weighted Average	The allowable time-weighted average concentration.	8-hour day or 40-hour workweek (TWA)	**ACGIH®** American Conference of Governmental Industrial Hygienists
TLV®-STEL Threshold Limit Value-Short-Term Exposure Limit	The maximum concentration for a continuous 15-minute exposure period (maximum of four such periods per day, with at least 60 minutes between exposure periods, provided the daily TLV®-TWA is not exceeded).	15 minutes (TWA)	**ACGIH®** American Conference of Governmental Industrial Hygienists
TLV®-C Threshold Limit Value-Ceiling	The concentration that should not be exceeded even instantaneously.	Instantaneous	**ACGIH®** American Conference of Governmental Industrial Hygienists
BEIs® Biological Exposure Indices	A guidance value recommended for assessing biological monitoring results.		**ACGIH®** American Conference of Governmental Industrial Hygienists
REL Recommended Exposure Limit	A recommended exposure limit made by NIOSH.	10-hours (TWA) ††	**NIOSH** National Institute for Occupational Safety and Health
AEGL-1 Acute Exposure Guideline Level-1	The airborne concentration of a substance at or above which it is predicted that the general population, including "susceptible" but excluding "hypersusceptible" individuals, could experience notable discomfort. †††	Multiple exposure periods: 10 minutes 30 minutes 1 hour 4 hours 8 hours	**EPA** Environmental Protection Agency

Continued

Table 2.8 (continued)
Exposure Limits

Term	Definition	Exposure Period	Organization
AEGL-2 Acute Exposure Guideline Level-2	The airborne concentration of a substance at or above which it is predicted that the general population, including "susceptible" but excluding "hypersusceptible" individuals, could experience irreversible or other serious, long-lasting effects or impaired ability to escape. Airborne concentrations below AEGL-2 but at or above AEGL-1 represent exposure levels that may cause notable discomfort.	Multiple exposure periods: 10 minutes 30 minutes 1 hour 4 hours 8 hours	**EPA** Environmental Protection Agency
AEGL-3 Acute Exposure Guideline Level-3	The airborne concentration of a substance at or above which it is predicted that the general population, including "susceptible" but excluding "hypersusceptible" individuals, could experience life-threatening effects or death. Airborne concentrations below AEGL-3 but at or above AEGL-2 represent exposure levels that may cause irreversible or other serious, long-lasting effects or impaired ability to escape.	Multiple exposure periods: 10 minutes 30 minutes 1 hour 4 hours 8 hours	**EPA** Environmental Protection Agency

* It should be noted that the NIOSH definition only addresses airborne concentrations. It does not include direct contact with liquids or other materials.

** PELs are issued in Title 29 *CFR* 1910.1000, particularly Tables Z-1, Z-2, and Z-3, and are enforceable as law.

*** Time-weighted average means that changing concentration levels can be averaged over a given period of time to reach an average level of exposure.

† TLVs® and BEIs® are guidelines for use by industrial hygienists in making decisions regarding safe levels of exposure. They are not considered to be consensus standards by the ACGIH®, and they do not carry the force of law unless they are officially adopted as such by a particular jurisdiction.

†† NIOSH may also list STELs (15-minute TWA) and ceiling limits.

††† Airborne concentrations below AEGL-1 represent exposure levels that could produce mild odor, taste, or other sensory irritation.

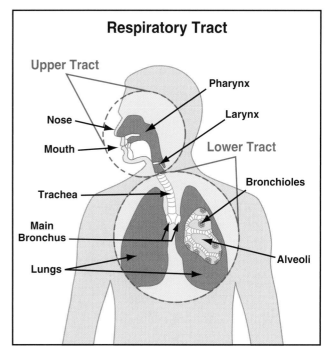

Figure 2.18 Respiratory irritants in the respiratory tract.

Irritants

[NFPA 472: 5.2.3(8)(d)]

Irritants are toxins that cause temporary but sometimes severe inflammation to the eyes, skin, or respiratory system. Irritants attack the mucous membranes of the body such as the surfaces of the eyes, nose, mouth, throat, and lungs. Respiratory irritants are classified as *upper,* meaning they affect the respiratory tract above the voice box, and *lower,* meaning they affect the respiratory tract below the voice box, including the lungs **(Figure 2.18).**

Convulsants

[NFPA 472: 5.2.3(8)(c)]

Convulsants are toxic materials that can cause convulsions (involuntary muscle contractions). Some chemicals considered to be convulsants

are strychnine, organophosphates, carbamates, and infrequently used drugs such as picrotoxin. A person exposed to a convulsant may feel a sense of suffocation and dyspnea (painful or difficult breathing and rapid shallow respirations) followed by muscular rigidity. Painful muscle spasms may occur at varying intervals from 3 to 30 minutes, and these spasms may be triggered by seemingly harmless stimuli such as touching the victim. Death can result from asphyxiation or exhaustion.

Corrosives

[NFPA 472: 5.2.3 (8)(d)]

Chemicals that destroy or burn living tissues and have destructive effects (cause corrosion, particularly to metals) are often called *corrosives.* With the exception of liquid and gas fuels, corrosives comprise the largest usage class (by volume) in industry. Corrosives are commonly divided into two broad categories: *acids* and *bases* (bases are sometimes called *alkalis* or *caustics*). However, it is important to note that some corrosives (such as hydrogen peroxide) are neither acids nor bases. Definitions are as follows:

- *Acid* — Any chemical that ionizes (breaks down) to yield hydrogen ions in water. Acids have pH values of 0 to 6. An acid may cause severe chemical burns to flesh and permanent eye damage. Contact with an acid typically causes immediate pain. Hydrochloric acid, nitric acid, and sulfuric acid are examples of common acids. See information boxes.

- **Base (alkalis)** — Water-soluble compound that breaks apart in water to form a negatively charged hydroxide ion. Bases react with an acid to form a salt by releasing an unshared pair of electrons to the acid or by receiving a proton (hydrogen ion) from the acid. Bases have pH values of 8 to 14. A base breaks down fatty skin tissues and can penetrate deeply into the body. They can also cause severe eye damage because they tend to adhere to the tissues in the eye, which makes bases difficult to remove. Bases often cause more eye damage than acids because of the longer duration of exposure. Contact with a base does not normally cause immediate pain. A sign of exposure to a base is a greasy or slick feeling of the skin, which is caused by the breakdown of fatty tissues. Caustic soda, potassium hydroxide, and other alkaline materials commonly used in drain cleaners are examples of bases. See information boxes.

In some cases, corrosives (particularly strong acids) can cause a fire or an explosion if they come in contact with combustibles because their corrosive actions can generate enough heat to start a fire. Some acids (for example, hydrochloric acid) can react with metal to form hydrogen gas (which is explosive). Additionally, acids and bases can react very violently when mixed together or water is added to them. This consideration is important during decontamination and spill cleanup.

Acids and bases can be toxic, flammable, reactive, and/or explosive and many can polymerize. Some of them are oxidizers as well. Because of the wide variety of hazards presented by corrosives, it is important that emergency responders do not focus solely on the corrosive properties when considering appropriate actions for managing incidents involving these materials.

Is it Corrosive, Caustic, an Acid, a Base, or an Alkali?

Some experts make this differentiation: acids are *corrosive*, while bases are *caustic*. In the world of emergency response, however, both acids and bases are called *corrosives*. The U.S. Department of Transportation (DOT) and Transport Canada (TC), for example, do not differentiate between the two. Any materials that destroy metal or skin tissue are considered corrosives by these agencies.

The terms *base* and *alkali* are often used interchangeably, but some chemical dictionaries define alkalis as *strong bases*. Base solutions are usually referred to as *alkaline* rather than *basic*, but, again, the two terms are often used synonymously. Just be aware that if you hear the terms *caustic*, *alkali*, or *alkaline*, they are referring to bases or basic solutions.

Be Aware!

The pH of a substance by itself may not be a reliable indicator of the potential harm presented by an acid or a base. However, a pH of approximately 3 or less, or 11 or higher will likely cause damage to flesh or metal (such as metal containers).

Carcinogens

[NFPA 472: A.5.2.3(8)(b)]

Carcinogens are cancer-causing agents. Examples of known or suspected carcinogenic hazardous materials are polyvinyl chloride, benzene, asbestos, some chlorinated hydrocarbons, arsenic, nickel, some pesticides, and many plastics. Some carcinogens may be contained within the smoke from structure fires. Exact data is not available on the level and duration or dose of exposure needed for individual chemicals to cause cancer. However, exposures to only small amounts of some substances have long-term consequences. Often, the long-term effects of exposure are unknown. Disease and complications can occur as long as 10 to 40 years after exposure (see sidebar, p. 84).

Properties of Acids and Bases: Concentration, Strength, and pH

- **Concentration** — Acids and bases are usually created by dissolving a chemical (usually a liquid or a gas) in water. The degree to which the chemical is diluted determines the solution's *concentration*. Thus, the concentration reflects the amount of acid or base that is mixed with water. A 95-percent solution of formic acid is composed of 95 percent formic acid and 5 percent water. Generally, the higher the concentration, the more damage the acid or base will do (or the more corrosive it will be) relative to itself. For example, a 98-percent solution of sulfuric acid will burn the skin much more quickly and badly than an equal amount of a 1-percent sulfuric acid solution.

- **Strength** — The strength of an acid or base is determined by the number of hydrogen ions or hydroxyl ions, respectively, produced when the solution is created. *Details:*

  — The higher the number of hydrogen ions in the solution, the stronger the acid and the more corrosive it will be relative to other acids of equal concentration. For example, a 98-percent solution of hydrochloric acid (a strong acid) is far more corrosive than a 98-percent solution of acetic acid (a much weaker acid).

  — The higher the number of hydroxyl ions produced in making a solution, the stronger the base will be. For example, sodium hydroxide is far more caustic than lime.

- **pH** — The pH of a solution is a measurement of the hydrogen ions in a solution, indicating its strength. The higher the pH of bases, or the lower the pH of acids, the stronger the base or acid is, respectively. The pH scale ranges from 0 to 14. A pH of 7 is neutral. Any substance that is neither acidic nor basic is neutral. A pH less than 7 is acidic, and a pH greater than 7 is basic.

Each whole pH value below 7 is 10 times more acidic than the next higher value. For example, a pH of 4 is 10 times more acidic than a pH of 5 and 100 times (10 × 10) more acidic than a pH of 6. The same holds true for pH values above 7, each of which is 10 times more alkaline than the value below it. For example, a pH of 10 is 10 times more alkaline than a pH of 9. At the extremes of the scale, a pH of 1 is 1,000,000 times more acidic than a substance with a pH of 7, and a pH of 14 is 1,000,000 times more alkaline. Pure water is neutral, with a pH of 7.0.

Not all substances that are acidic or basic end with the terms *acid* or *-oxide.* For example, vinegar, chlorine, and lemon juice are acidic substances, while laundry detergents, anhydrous ammonia/ammonia, and lye (sodium hydroxide) are basic.

pH Scale		
Concentration of Hydrogen Ions Compared to Distilled Water	pH	Examples of Solutions at this pH
10,000,000	0	Strong Hydrofluoric Acid
1,000,000	1	Hydrochloric Acid, Battery Acid
100,000	2	Lemon Juice, Vinegar
10,000	3	Apple Juice, Orange Juice
1,000	4	Acid Rain, Wine
100	5	Black Coffee
10	6	Milk, Saliva
1	7	*Pure* Water, Human Blood
1/10	8	Seawater
1/100	9	Baking Soda
1/1,000	10	Milk of Magnesia
1/10,000	11	Ammonia
1/100,000	12	Lime
1/1,000,000	13	Lye
1/10,000,000	14	Sodium Hydroxide

Delay in Knowing Health Effects

Unlike corrosives that burn the skin on contact, some harmful substances do not hurt the body right away. In some cases, it may take many years for a chemical, agent, or substance to cause a disease like cancer. Because of this *delay* (sometimes called *latency period*), it can be difficult to establish a direct chain of cause and effect between an exposure to a particular substance and the resulting disease.

The history of asbestos demonstrates how long it can take before enough evidence is gathered to produce action in the form of government intervention. Asbestos was first used in the U.S. in the early 1900s to insulate steam engines. It wasn't until the 1940s, however, that asbestos began to be used extensively. In particular, it was used in U.S. Navy shipyards to insulate the country's growing fleet of warships during World War II.

While some articles documenting the harmful effects of asbestos were published as early as the 1930s, it wasn't until the 1960s (15- to 40-year latency period) that studies began to show an unquestionably clear relationship between the inhalation of asbestos fibers and the development of lung cancer, asbes- tosis, and mesothelioma in groups such as the U.S. Navy shipyard workers. As a result of these studies and a growing public awareness of the hazard, the U.S. government began regulating asbestos in the 1970s.

Many substances (acetaldehyde, chloroform, progesterone, and polychlorinated biphenyls [PCBs]) are listed by the U.S. Department of Health and Human Services as *reasonably anticipated to be carcinogens* or *suspected carcinogens* because the body of evidence concerning their chronic effects is still being gathered and evaluated. Saccharin, for example, was listed as a suspected carcinogen for nearly 20 years before it was removed from the list in 2000 due to a lack of evidence that it caused cancer. In the same year, diesel exhaust particulate was added to the list.

Our understanding of the health effects associated with chemical products and substances is often changing, and new products are continually being developed. First responders should keep in mind that chronic health effects of substances may not be known for many years, and what is considered safe today, may not be tomorrow.

Mutagens

[NFPA 472: A.5.2.3(8)(b)]

Mutagens are substances or agents that are capable of altering the genetic material in a living cell; in other words, they affect DNA. Mutagens cause changes (mutations) in the genetic system of a cell in ways that can be transmitted during cell division. Exposed individuals may transmit undesirable mutations to a later generation. In simple terms, individuals who are exposed to a mutagen may not be hurt, but their offspring can be. Radiation is one mutagen where the exposure and the effect have been correlated. Other mutagens include ethidium bromide, aluminum chloride, benzidine, nitrous acid, and ethylene oxide.

Teratogens

[NFPA 472: A.5.2.3(8)(b)]

Teratogens are substances or agents that are capable of causing developmental abnormalities *in utero*; in other words, exposure to these substances by a pregnant female can result in malformations in her fetus. Some materials classified as teratogens are ionizing radiation, ethyl alcohol, methyl mercury, thalidomide, and dioxins. Some infections such as rubella are also classified as teratogens because they interfere with the normal growth of an embryo, causing malformations in the developing fetus. The major difference between a teratogen and a mutagen is that a mutagen affects the genetic system (DNA) and a teratogen affects an embryo. Therefore, a teratogen is not hereditary, whereas a mutagen's effects may be.

Sensitizers/Allergens

[NFPA 472: 5.2.3(8)(e)]

Allergens are substances that cause allergic reactions in people or animals. *Sensitizers* are chemicals that cause a substantial proportion of exposed people or animals to develop an allergic reaction after *repeated* exposure to the chemical. Common examples of sensitizers and allergens include latex, bleach, nickel compounds, chromates, formaldehyde, isocyanates, certain phenols, toluene diisocyanate, chlorinated hydrocarbons, chromium compounds, and urushiol (the chemical found in the sap of poison ivy, oak, and sumac).

Some individuals exposed to a material may not be abnormally affected at first but may experience significant and dangerous effects in the presence of the material when exposed again. An example is an individual's severe reaction to a subsequent bee sting. See sidebar.

Latex Allergies

One example of *sensitization* is the allergy that many people develop when repeatedly exposed to latex. Studies indicate that 8 to 12 percent of health-care workers regularly exposed to latex become sensitized to it. These latex allergies result from contact with the proteins in natural rubber latex. Reactions usually begin within minutes of exposure to latex, but they can occur hours later. They can produce a variety of symptoms including skin rash (and inflammation), respiratory irritation, asthma, and, in rare cases, anaphylactic shock.

Emergency responders, particularly emergency medical services (EMS) personnel, who wear latex gloves may be at risk for latex allergy. The amount of exposure needed to sensitize individuals to natural rubber latex is not known, but reductions in exposure to latex proteins have been reported to decrease sensitization and symptoms. Latex allergy is also associated with allergies to certain foods such as avocados, potatoes, bananas, tomatoes, chestnuts, kiwi fruit, and papaya. The following are some recommendations to reduce the risk of developing latex allergy:

1. Use nonlatex gloves as inner gloves and for activities that are not likely to involve contact with infectious materials (food preparation, routine housekeeping, maintenance, etc.).

2. Use powder-free gloves with reduced protein content when using latex gloves.

3. Do not use oil-based hand creams or lotions when wearing latex gloves unless they have been shown to reduce latex-related problems.

4. Learn to recognize the symptoms of latex allergy: skin rashes; hives; flushing; itching; nasal, eye, or sinus symptoms; asthma; and shock.

5. Avoid direct contact with latex gloves and products if you develop symptoms of latex allergy until you can see a physician experienced in treating latex allergy.

General Symptoms of Exposure
[NFPA 472: 5.2.2(3)(d)]

Hazardous materials produce a wide range of physical symptoms that may not be immediately apparent and can be masked by common illnesses like flu or by smoke inhalation. At the first signs or symptoms of exposure, withdraw to a predetermined safe area and immediately report these conditions. Some general symptoms of exposure to hazardous materials include the following:

- Confusion, light-headedness, anxiety, and dizziness
- Blurred or double vision
- Changes in skin color or blushing
- Coughing or painful respiration
- Tingling or numbness of extremities
- Loss of coordination
- Nausea, vomiting, abdominal cramping, and diarrhea
- Changes in behavior or mannerisms
- Unconsciousness
- Burning eyes, throat, or nose
- Headache
- Irregular heartbeat
- Tightness in chest
- Abnormal euphoria

CAUTIONS

Many harmful hazardous materials cannot be detected by the senses. Others may deaden or *fool* the senses. See the following examples:

- **Carbon monoxide is invisible, has no odor, and cannot be detected without special monitoring equipment.**
- **Hydrogen sulfide (H2S) may deaden the sense of smell and lead to a false sense of safety.**

Etiological

[NFPA 472: 4.4.1(3)(c)]

An *etiological* hazard is the exposure to a microorganism or its toxin that may result in a severe, disabling disease. Examples of diseases associated with etiological events are malaria, acquired immunodeficiency syndrome (AIDS), tuberculosis, and typhoid. These microorganisms are present in biological and medical laboratories or when dealing with people who are carriers of such diseases. Most of these diseases are carried in body fluids and are transmitted by contact with the fluids. In most cases, simple protective garments provide an effective barrier against these fluids.

Emergency responders may also be exposed to biological agents used as weapons in terrorist attacks and criminal activities. Biological agents include microorganisms such as anthrax, smallpox, and plague. Biological weapons and their etiological effects are discussed in Chapter 9, Terrorist and Other Criminal Activities.

Mechanical Trauma

[NFPA 472: 4.4.1(3)(c)]

Mechanical trauma refers to damage that occurs as a result of direct contact with an object. The two most common types are *striking* and *friction* exposures. Trauma can be mild, moderate, or severe and can occur in a single event.

In hazardous materials situations, a striking injury could be the result of an explosion caused by the failure of a pressurized container (BLEVE), a bomb (or explosive booby trap), or the reactivity of the hazardous material itself **(Figure 2.20)**. See Chapter 9, Terrorist and Other Criminal Activities, for information on bombs. An explosion can cause the following four hazards (three mechanical and one thermal):

- *Blast pressure wave (shock wave)* — Gases being released rapidly create a shock wave that travels outward from the center. As the wave increases in distance, the strength decreases. This blast pressure wave is the primary reason for injuries and damage. *Details:*

  — The positive-pressure phase is the result of the blast wave moving away from the seat of

Bloodborne Pathogens

Bloodborne pathogens are etiological agents that are familiar to most emergency responders. Bloodborne pathogens are transmitted through contact with infected blood or body fluids. Common examples of bloodborne pathogens include the following:

- Hepatitis B
- Hepatitis C
- HIV (human immunodeficiency virus which causes AIDS)

Because of the risk of contracting one of these diseases, you should always use the following universal precautions while providing medical assistance:

- Use PPE (including rubber gloves and safety glasses).
- Sterilize contaminated surfaces and equipment (using a 10-percent bleach solution).
- Wash your hands frequently.
- Always assume that blood and other body fluids are potentially harmful and take appropriate actions to protect yourself by minimizing contact with them **(Figure 2.19)**.

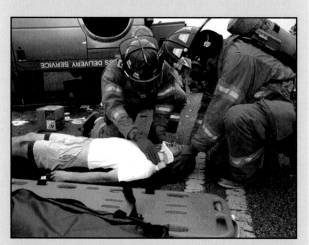

Figure 2.19 First responders must always use universal precautions (such as wearing latex gloves) to protect against bloodborne pathogens and other etiological agents. *Courtesy of Tom Clawson, Technical Resources Group, Inc.*

the blast as gases are expanding. The positive-pressure phase is responsible for the majority of damage because of its power.

— The negative-pressure phase occurs in the same way as the positive-pressure phase, except that it displaces and heats the sur-

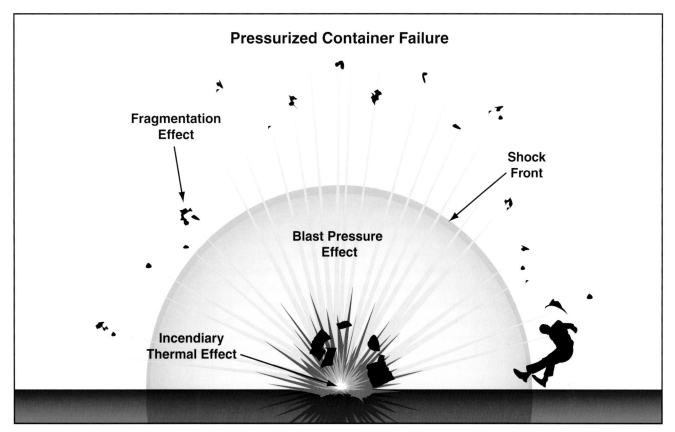

Figure 2.20 BLEVEs and other explosions can cause mechanical trauma.

rounding air creating low air pressure at the seat or origin. As the positive-pressure phase moves outward, a negative-pressure phase or low-pressure region is formed behind the pressure wave. The result is air rushing back towards the explosion center. This negative-pressure wave results in additional structural damage.

- ***Shrapnel fragmentation*** — Small pieces of debris are thrown from a container or structure that ruptures from containment or restricted blast pressure. Shrapnel may be thrown over a wide area and great distances (fragmentation), causing personal injury and other types of damage to surrounding structures or objects. Shrapnel can result in bruises, punctures, or even avulsions (part of the body being torn away) when the container or pieces of the container strike a person.

- ***Seismic effect*** — When a blast occurs at or near ground level, the air blast creates a ground shock or crater (earth vibration similar to an earthquake). As shock waves move across or underground, a seismic disturbance is formed.

The distance the shock wave travels depends on the type and size of the explosion and type of soil.

- ***Incendiary thermal effect*** — During an explosion, thermal heat energy in the form of a fireball is the result of burning combustible gases or flammable vapors and ambient air at very high temperatures. The thermal heat fireball is present for a limited time after the explosive event.

Friction injuries are less common in hazardous materials operations. These injuries occur as a result of portions of the body rubbing against an abrasive or otherwise irritating surface, causing raw skin, blisters, and brush burns. In hazardous material situations, contact between protective clothing and the skin most commonly causes friction injuries.

Psychological
[NFPA 472: 4.4.1(3)(c)]

Any incident that causes an unusually strong emotional reaction in an emergency responder can cause psychological harm in the form of stress. Incidents involving mass casualties, death or serious injury to fellow emergency responders, or other traumatic components are considered *critical incidents*. Critical incidents may cause emergency responders an unusual amount of stress, sometimes called *critical incident stress (CIS)*. The terms *critical incident stress disorder (CISD)*, *critical incident stress syndrome (CISS)*, *posttraumatic stress disorder (PTSD)*, and *posttraumatic stress syndrome (PTSS)* are sometimes used synonymously to describe the conditions caused by CIS. However CIS should be divided into two separate types of events: *acute* and *posttraumatic*.

Acute stress disorder and posttraumatic stress disorder are closely related in that they are caused by the same events and display similar symptoms. Generally, the disorders are caused when persons have been exposed to a traumatic event where they have experienced, witnessed, or been confronted with an event or events that involve actual death, threatened death, serous injury, or threat of physical integrity of self or others. The response of these people involved intense fear, helplessness, or horror. A list of common symptoms is as follows:

- Experiences stressful recollections or recurring dreams of the event or reliving the event by way of hallucinations and illusions; also becomes distressed when exposed to aspects that resemble the event

- Exhibits lack of ability to recall parts of the event and/or avoids thoughts, feelings, activities, places, and people associated with the event

- Exhibits lack of interest in activities once enjoyed or difficulty sleeping, controlling anger, or

concentrating; may also have hyperactive startle responses

- Shows distress in social, work, or home environments

Acute stress disorder and posttraumatic stress disorder differ in their timing. Acute stress disorder symptoms appear within the first 30 days and do not last more than 4 weeks. Posttraumatic stress disorder symptoms occur 30 days to years after the event. Acute stress disorder may become posttraumatic if symptoms persist past 30 days.

Summary

First responders need the ability to predict how a hazardous material will behave when it escapes its container. This behavior is often determined by the material's physical properties such as its flammability, boiling point, vapor pressure, chemical reactivity, and others. The physical properties of a material determine such things as whether or not it will burn, how fast it will evaporate, at what temperature it will freeze and/or boil, whether or not it is likely to react with other materials, and other important factors.

It is also important for first responders to understand how hazardous materials can cause harm. The broad categories of hazards (or causes of harm) generally associated with hazardous materials can be identified by the acronym TRACEMP: thermal, radiological, asphyxiation, chemical, etiological, mechanical, and psychological.

Part Two

Incident Problem-Solving Process

Chapter 3

Hazardous Materials Identification

First Responder Competencies

This chapter provides information that will assist the reader in meeting the following first responder competencies from NFPA 472, *Professional Competence of Responders to Hazardous Materials Incidents,* 2002 Edition. The numbers are noted directly in the text under the section titles where they are addressed.

NFPA 472

Chapter 4 Competencies for the First Responder at the Awareness Level

4.1.2.2 When first on the scene of an emergency involving hazardous materials, the first responder at the awareness level shall be able to perform the following tasks:

(1) Analyze the incident to determine both the hazardous materials present and the basic hazard and response information for each hazardous material by completing the following tasks:

   (a) Detect the presence of hazardous materials

   (b) Survey a hazardous materials incident from a safe location to identify the name, UN/NA identification number, or type placard applied for any hazardous materials involved

   (c) Collect hazard information from the current edition of the Emergency Response Guidebook

4.2.1 Detecting the Presence of Hazardous Materials. Given various facility or transportation situations, or both, with and without hazardous materials present, the first responder at the awareness level shall identify those situations where hazardous materials are present and also shall meet the following requirements:

(3) Identify the primary hazards associated with each of the UN/DOT hazard classes and divisions of hazardous materials by hazard class or division.

(5) Identify typical occupancies and locations in the community where hazardous materials are manufactured, transported, stored, used, or disposed of.

(6) Identify typical container shapes that can indicate the presence of hazardous materials.

(7) Identify facility and transportation markings and colors that indicate hazardous materials, including the following:

   (c) Military hazardous materials markings

   (d) Special hazard communication markings for each hazard class

   (e) Pipeline markings

   (f) Container markings

(8) Given an NFPA 704 marking, describe the significance of the colors, numbers, and special symbols.

(9) Identify U.S. and Canadian placards and labels that indicate hazardous materials.

(10) Identify the following basic information on material safety data sheets (MSDS) and shipping papers that indicates hazardous materials:

   (a) Identify where to find MSDS.

   (b) Identify entries on an MSDS that indicate the presence of hazardous materials.

   (c) Identify the entries on shipping papers that indicate the presence of hazardous materials.

   (d) Match the name of the shipping papers found in transportation (air, highway, rail, and water) with the mode of transportation.

   (e) Identify the person responsible for having the shipping papers in each mode of transportation.

   (f) Identify where the shipping papers are found in each mode of transportation.

   (g) Identify where the papers can be found in an emergency in each mode of transportation.

(11) Identify examples of clues (other than occupancy/location, container shape, markings/color, placards/labels, MSDS, and shipping papers) that use the senses of sight, sound, and odor to indicate hazardous materials.

(12) Describe the limitations of using the senses in determining the presence or absence of hazardous materials.

4.2.2 Surveying the Hazardous Materials Incident from a Safe Location. Given examples of facility and transportation situations involving hazardous materials, the first responder at the awareness level shall identify the hazardous material(s) in each situation by name, UN/NA identification number, or type placard applied, and also shall meet the following requirements:

(1) Identify difficulties encountered in determining the specific names of hazardous materials in both facilities and transportation.

(2) Identify sources for obtaining the names of, UN/NA identification numbers for, or types of placard associated with hazardous materials in transportation.

(3) Identify sources for obtaining the names of hazardous materials in a facility.

4.2.3 Collecting Hazard Information. Given the identity of various hazardous materials (name, UN/NA identification number, or type placard), the first responder at the awareness level shall identify the fire, explosion, and health hazard information for each material by using the current edition of the *Emergency Response Guidebook* and also shall meet the following requirements:

(1) Identify the three methods for determining the guide page for a hazardous material.

(2) Identify the two general types of hazards found on each guide page.

4.4.1   Initiating Protective Actions. Given examples of facility and transportation hazardous materials incidents, the local emergency response plan, the organization's standard operating procedures, and the current edition of the Emergency Response Guidebook, first responders at the awareness level shall be able to identify the actions to be taken to protect themselves and others and to control access to the scene and shall also meet the following requirements:

(1) Identify the location of both the local emergency response plan and the organization's standard operating procedures.

(4) Given the identity of various hazardous materials (name, UN/NA identification number, or type placard), identify the following response information:

    (a) Emergency action (fire, spill, or leak and first aid)

    (b) Personal protective equipment necessary

    (c) Initial isolation and protective action distances

(5) Given the name of a hazardous material, identify the recommended personal protective equipment from the following list:

    (a) Street clothing and work uniforms

    (b) Structural fire-fighting protective clothing

    (c) Positive pressure self-contained breathing apparatus

    (d) Chemical-protective clothing and equipment

(7) First responders at the awareness level shall identify the shapes of recommended initial isolation and protective action zones.

(8) First responders at the awareness level shall describe the difference between small and large spills as found in the table of initial isolation and protective action distances in the Emergency Response Guidebook.

(9) First responders at the awareness level shall identify the circumstances under which the following distances are used at a hazardous materials incident:

    (a) Table of initial isolation and protective action distances

    (b) Isolation distances in the numbered guides

(10) First responders at the awareness level shall describe the difference between the isolation distances in the orange-bordered guide pages and the protective action distances in the green-bordered pages in the document.

Chapter 5   Competencies for the First Responder at the Operational Level

5.2.1.1   Given three examples each of liquid, gas, and solid hazardous materials, including various hazard classes, the first responder at the operational level shall identify the general shapes of containers in which the hazardous materials are typically found.

(A) Given examples of the following tank cars, the first responder at the operational level shall identify each tank car by type as follows:

(1) Cryogenic liquid tank cars

(2) High-pressure tube cars

(3) Nonpressure tank cars

(4) Pneumatically unloaded hopper cars

(5) Pressure tank cars

(B) Given examples of the following intermodal tanks, the first responder at the operational level shall identify each intermodal tank by type and identify at least one material and its hazard class that is typically found in each tank as follows:

(1) Nonpressure intermodal tanks, such as the following:

    (a) IM-101 (IMO Type 1 internationally) portable tank

    (b) IM-102 (IMO Type 2 internationally) portable tank

(2) Pressure intermodal tanks

(3) Specialized intermodal tanks, such as the following:

    (a) Cryogenic intermodal tanks

    (b) Tube modules

(C) Given examples of the following cargo tanks, the first responder at the operational level shall identify each cargo tank by type as follows:

(1) Nonpressure liquid tanks

(2) Low pressure chemical tanks

(3) Corrosive liquid tanks

(4) High pressure tanks

(5) Cryogenic liquid tanks

(6) Dry bulk cargo tanks

(7) Compressed gas tube trailers

(D) Given examples of the following tanks, the first responder at the operational level shall identify at least one material, and its hazard, that is typically found in each tank as follows:

(1) Nonpressure tank

(2) Pressure tank

(3) Cryogenic liquid tank

(E) Given examples of the following nonbulk packages, the first responder at the operational level shall identify each package by type as follows:

(1) Bags

(2) Carboys

(3) Cylinders

(4) Drums

(F) Given examples of the following radioactive material containers, the first responder at the operational level shall identify each container/package by type as follows:

(1) Type A

(2) Type B

(3) Industrial

(4) Excepted

(5) Strong, tight containers

5.2.1.2 Given examples of facility and transportation containers, the first responder at the operational level shall identify the markings that differentiate one container from another.

(A) Given examples of the following marked transport vehicles and their corresponding shipping papers, the first responder at the operational level shall identify the vehicle or tank identification marking as follows:

(1) Rail transport vehicles, including tank cars

(2) Intermodal equipment including tank containers

(3) Highway transport vehicles, including cargo tanks

(B) Given examples of facility containers, the first responder at the operational level shall identify the markings indicating container size, product contained, and/or site identification numbers.

5.2.1.3 Given examples of facility and transportation situations involving hazardous materials, the first responder at the operational level shall identify the name(s) of the hazardous material(s) in each situation.

(A) The first responder at the operational level shall identify the following information on a pipeline marker:

(1) Product

(2) Owner

(3) Emergency telephone number

(B) Given a pesticide label, the first responder at the operational level shall identify each of the following pieces of information, then match the piece of information to its significance in surveying the hazardous materials incident:

(1) Name of pesticide

(2) Signal word

(3) Pest control product (PCP) number (in Canada)

(4) Precautionary statement

(5) Hazard statement

(6) Active ingredient

(C) Given a label for a radioactive material, the first responder at the operational level shall identify vertical bars, contents, activity, and transport index.

5.2.2 Collecting Hazard and Response Information. Given known hazardous materials, the first responder at the operational level shall collect hazard and response information using MSDS; CHEMTREC/CANUTEC/SETIQ; local, state, and federal authorities; and contacts with the shipper/manufacturer and also shall meet the following requirements:

(1) Match the definitions associated with the UN/DOT hazard classes and divisions of hazardous materials, including refrigerated liquefied gases and cryogenic liquids, with the class or division.

(2) Identify two ways to obtain an MSDS in an emergency.

(3) Using an MSDS for a specified material, identify the following hazard and response information:

(a) Physical and chemical characteristics

(b) Physical hazards of the material

(c) Health hazards of the material

(d) Signs and symptoms of exposure

(e) Routes of entry

(f) Permissible exposure limits

(g) Responsible party contact

(h) Precautions for safe handling (including hygiene practices, protective measures, procedures for cleanup of spills or leaks)

(i) Applicable control measures including personal protective equipment

(j) Emergency and first-aid procedures

(5) Identify two methods of contacting the manufacturer or shipper to obtain hazard and response information.

5.2.4 Estimating the Potential Harm. The first responder at the operational level shall estimate the potential harm within the endangered area at a hazardous materials incident and also shall meet the following requirements:

(3) Identify resources available for determining the concentrations of a released hazardous material within an endangered area.

5.4.3 Using Personal Protective Equipment. The first responder at the operational level shall demonstrate the ability to don, work in, and doff the personal protective equipment provided by the authority having jurisdiction, and shall meet the following related requirements:

(3) Identify the safety precautions to be observed when approaching and working at hazardous materials incidents.

Emergency Responder Guidelines

This chapter provides information that will assist the reader in meeting the following first responder guidelines for fire service and law enforcement from the Office for Domestic Preparedness (ODP) *Emergency Responder Guidelines,* 2002 Edition. The numbers are noted directly in the text under the section titles where they are addressed.

ODP Emergency Responder Guidelines

Fire Service and Law Enforcement

Awareness Level for Events Involving Weapons of Mass Destruction

I.   **Recognize hazardous materials incidents.** The responder should:

  b. Identify if hazardous materials are present in an emergency incident or event.

  c. Know how to use the *Emergency Response Guidebook (ERG)* published by the U.S. Department of Transportation.

  d. Use the *ERG* (or other available resources) to identify the hazardous material.

Performance Level for Events Involving Weapons of Mass Destruction

I.   **Have successfully completed adequate and proper training at the awareness level for events involving hazardous materials, and for weapons of mass destruction (WMD) and other specialized training.** The responder should:

  b. Understand the terminology (including any glossary of WMD terms), classes of materials and agents, and toxicology of hazardous materials and WMD agents and materials.

Chapter 3

Hazardous Materials Identification

[NFPA 472: 4.1.2.2(1), 4.2.1, 4.2.1(7), 4.2.1(9), 4.2.2] [ODP Awareness I.b.]

First responders must be able to detect and identify the presence of hazardous materials. Historically, the failure of responders to recognize the presence and potential harm of hazardous materials at accidents, fires, spills, and other emergencies has caused unnecessary casualties. Haz mat incidents can be controlled only when the personnel involved have sufficient information to make informed decisions. Part of this information is learned from size-ups of all materials that may be hazardous. The time and effort devoted to a positive identification of the contents of buildings, vehicles, and containers result in greater safety for first responders and the community.

Once the presence of a hazardous material is detected, first responders can use a number of resources to accurately identify the material and its hazards and specify recommended protective measures. First responders who know the properties of substances can perform tasks confidently and evaluate changing conditions accurately. First responders must be diligent and observant of the hazardous materials present at every emergency.

This chapter is divided into three parts and begins with an incident scenario **(Part 1)** that will be referenced throughout the rest of this book. The chapter explains the seven clues **(Part 2)** that are used to detect the presence of hazardous materials, including occupancy types and locations, pre-incident surveys, container shapes, placards and labels, markings and colors, written resources, the responder's own senses, and monitoring and detection devices. Be aware that these are general guidelines. It is possible that hazardous materials will be mislabeled or incorrectly marked (if at all) and found in incorrect containers and other unexpected conditions. **Part 3** is the chapter summary.

Part 1
Sample Hazardous Materials Incident Scenario

This incident scenario is not designed to be all-inclusive or used as a definitive model to approach all hazardous materials emergencies. It is an example provided to illustrate some of the principles discussed throughout the manual. There are many different ways to mitigate (control) hazardous materials emergencies — this scenario is only one of them. Additionally, this scenario will be using terms that may not be explained or defined until later in the text. See the information box for the scene layout.

Scene Layout
Ace Trucking, 19201 N.W. Industrial Drive 10 a.m., Tuesday

Equipment: On Scene: Engine 1 initially; when upgraded to Level II: Engines 2 and 4, Truck 1, Haz Mat 3, Medic 1, Battalion 1
At Staging: Engine 5, Medic 2

Players:
Engine 1 Lieutenant: Adams
Engine 1 Reconnaissance Group: Firefighters Linder and George
Engine 1 Driver/Operator/Paramedic: Miller
Facility Manager/Responsible Party, Ace Trucking: Tucker
Truck 1 Captain: Hendrix
Engine 2 Lieutenant: Allen
Engine 2 Firefighter: Jirka
Engine 2 Driver/Operator: Badgett
Engine 4 Lieutenant: Hartin
Engine 4 Firefighters: Hepler and Lewis
Battalion 1: Battalion Chief: Arasim
Haz Mat 3: Captain: Mahaney

Once Upon a Time ... There Was a Hazardous Materials Incident

Dispatch: Engine 1, respond on a haz mat investigation at Ace Trucking, 19201 N.W. Industrial Drive. The caller reports a sharp chemical odor in the warehouse.

Engine 1: Engine 1 responding to 19201 N.W. Industrial Drive.

As Engine 1 leaves the station at 10 a.m. on Tuesday, Lieutenant (Lt.) Adams examines the pre-incident survey for Ace Trucking. From information on the survey and her familiarity with the first-due district, she knows that this trucking company handles a wide range of products, including many hazardous materials in nonbulk containers.

Lt. Adams selects a response route that approaches uphill and upwind. See **Scenario Diagram 1.**

Dispatch: Engine 1, the caller reports that a 300-gallon (1 136 L) intermediate bulk container of butylene oxide has been damaged and is leaking inside the warehouse.

Lt. Adams confirms the spelling of the product name with the dispatcher/telecommunicator. While en route, she consults the current *Emergency Response Guidebook (ERG)* for initial response information. Referring to the alphabetical index in the blue pages (see **Scenario Sample 1**), she locates 1,2-butylene oxide, stabilized. The index lists Guide 127P for this product. Lt. Adams recognizes that the letter *P* indicates that this material has the potential to polymerize.

Scenario Diagram 1

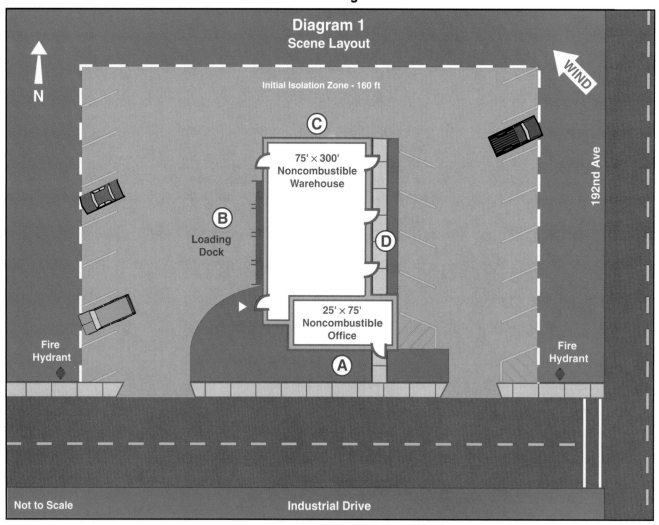

Scenario Sample 1

Name of Material	Guide No.	ID No.	Name of Material	Guide No.	ID No.
Bromobenzene	129	2514	Butyl alcohol	129	1120
Bromobenzyl cyanides	159	1694	n-Butylamine	132	1125
1-Bromobutane	129	1126	N-Butylaniline	153	2738
2-Bromobutane	130	2339	Butylbenzenes	128	2709
Bromochlorodifluoromethane	126	1974	n-Butyl bromide	129	1126
Bromochloromethane	160	1887	Butyl chloride	130	1127
1-Bromo-3-chloropropane	159	2688	n-Butyl chloroformate	155	2743
2-Bromoethyl ethyl ether	130	2340	sec-Butyl chloroformate	155	2742
Bromoform	159	2515	tert-Butyl cumene peroxide	145	2091
1-Bromo-3-methylbutane	130	2341	tert-Butyl cumyl peroxide	145	2091
Bromomethylpropanes	130	2342	tert-Butylcyclohexyl chloroformate	156	2747
2-Bromo-2-nitropropane-1,3-diol	133	3241	n-Butyl-4,4-di-(tert-butylperoxy)valerate	146	2140
2-Bromopentane	130	2343			
2-Bromopropane	130	2344	n-Butyl-4,4-di-(tert-butylperoxy)valerate	145	2141
Bromopropanes	130	2344			
3-Bromopropyne	129	2345	Butylene	115	1012
Bromotrifluoroethylene	116	2419	Butylene	115	1075
Bromotrifluoromethane	126	1009	1,2-Butylene oxide, stabilized	127P	3022
Brown asbestos	171	2212	Butyl ethers	127	1149
Brucine	152	1570	n-Butyl formate	129	1128
Burnt cotton, not picked	133	1325	tert-Butyl hydroperoxide	147	2093
Butadienes, inhibited	116P	1010	tert-Butyl hydroperoxide	147	2094
Butane	115	1011	tert-Butyl hydroperoxide, not more than 80% in Di-tert-butyl peroxide and/or solvent	147	2092
Butane	115	1075			
Butanedione	127	2346			
Butane mixture	115	1011	tert-Butyl hypochlorite	135	3255
Butane mixture	115	1075	N,n-Butylimidazole	152	2690
Butanols	129	1120	n-Butyl isocyanate	155	2485
Butoxyl	127	2708	tert-Butyl isocyanate	155	2484
Butyl acetates	129	1123	tert-Butyl isopropyl benzene hydroperoxide	145	2091
Butyl acid phosphate	153	1718			
Butyl acrylate	129P	2348	Butyl mercaptan	130	2347
Butyl acrylates, inhibited	129P	2348	n-Butyl methacrylate	129P	2227

Page 114

ERG List of Dangerous Goods in Alphabetical Order

Guide 127 in the orange section (see **Scenario Sample 2**) indicates that this material is a polar/water-miscible flammable liquid. A quick scan of the guide page indicates that the primary hazard presented by this material is flammability. However, 1,2-butylene oxide presents health hazards on contact with the skin or when inhaled. Lt. Adams advises her crew that the initial isolation distance recommended in the *ERG* is 80 to 160 feet (24 m to 49 m) and that structural fire-fighting clothing provides limited protection.

Scenario Sample 2

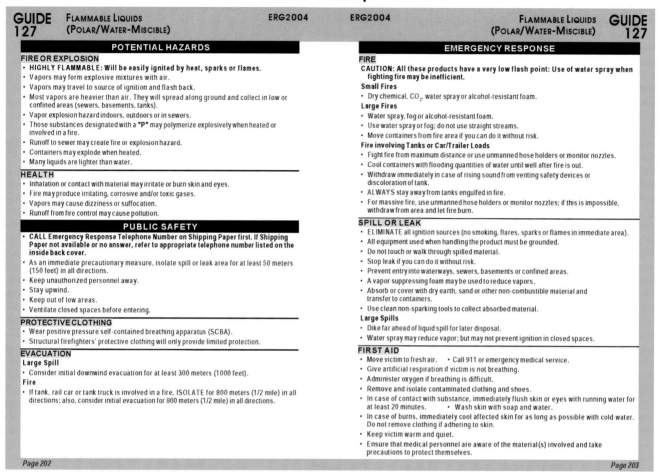

GUIDE 127 — FLAMMABLE LIQUIDS (POLAR/WATER-MISCIBLE)   ERG2004   ERG2004   FLAMMABLE LIQUIDS (POLAR/WATER-MISCIBLE) — GUIDE 127

POTENTIAL HAZARDS

FIRE OR EXPLOSION
- HIGHLY FLAMMABLE: Will be easily ignited by heat, sparks or flames.
- Vapors may form explosive mixtures with air.
- Vapors may travel to source of ignition and flash back.
- Most vapors are heavier than air. They will spread along ground and collect in low or confined areas (sewers, basements, tanks).
- Vapor explosion hazard indoors, outdoors or in sewers.
- Those substances designated with a "P" may polymerize explosively when heated or involved in a fire.
- Runoff to sewer may create fire or explosion hazard.
- Containers may explode when heated.
- Many liquids are lighter than water.

HEALTH
- Inhalation or contact with material may irritate or burn skin and eyes.
- Fire may produce irritating, corrosive and/or toxic gases.
- Vapors may cause dizziness or suffocation.
- Runoff from fire control may cause pollution.

PUBLIC SAFETY
- CALL Emergency Response Telephone Number on Shipping Paper first. If Shipping Paper not available or no answer, refer to appropriate telephone number listed on the inside back cover.
- As an immediate precautionary measure, isolate spill or leak area for at least 50 meters (150 feet) in all directions.
- Keep unauthorized personnel away.
- Stay upwind.
- Keep out of low areas.
- Ventilate closed spaces before entering.

PROTECTIVE CLOTHING
- Wear positive pressure self-contained breathing apparatus (SCBA).
- Structural firefighters' protective clothing will only provide limited protection.

EVACUATION
Large Spill
- Consider initial downwind evacuation for at least 300 meters (1000 feet).

Fire
- If tank, rail car or tank truck is involved in a fire, ISOLATE for 800 meters (1/2 mile) in all directions; also, consider initial evacuation for 800 meters (1/2 mile) in all directions.

EMERGENCY RESPONSE

FIRE
CAUTION: All these products have a very low flash point: Use of water spray when fighting fire may be inefficient.

Small Fires
- Dry chemical, CO_2, water spray or alcohol-resistant foam.

Large Fires
- Water spray, fog or alcohol-resistant foam.
- Use water spray or fog; do not use straight streams.
- Move containers from fire area if you can do it without risk.

Fire involving Tanks or Car/Trailer Loads
- Fight fire from maximum distance or use unmanned hose holders or monitor nozzles.
- Cool containers with flooding quantities of water until well after fire is out.
- Withdraw immediately in case of rising sound from venting safety devices or discoloration of tank.
- ALWAYS stay away from tanks engulfed in fire.
- For massive fire, use unmanned hose holders or monitor nozzles; if this is impossible, withdraw from area and let fire burn.

SPILL OR LEAK
- ELIMINATE all ignition sources (no smoking, flares, sparks or flames in immediate area).
- All equipment used when handling the product must be grounded.
- Do not touch or walk through spilled material.
- Stop leak if you can do it without risk.
- Prevent entry into waterways, sewers, basements or confined areas.
- A vapor suppressing foam may be used to reduce vapors.
- Absorb or cover with dry earth, sand or other non-combustible material and transfer to containers.
- Use clean non-sparking tools to collect absorbed material.

Large Spills
- Dike far ahead of liquid spill for later disposal.
- Water spray may reduce vapor; but may not prevent ignition in closed spaces.

FIRST AID
- Move victim to fresh air.   • Call 911 or emergency medical service.
- Give artificial respiration if victim is not breathing.
- Administer oxygen if breathing is difficult.
- Remove and isolate contaminated clothing and shoes.
- In case of contact with substance, immediately flush skin or eyes with running water for at least 20 minutes.   • Wash skin with soap and water.
- In case of burns, immediately cool affected skin for as long as possible with cold water. Do not remove clothing if adhering to skin.
- Keep victim warm and quiet.
- Ensure that medical personnel are aware of the material(s) involved and take precautions to protect themselves.

Page 202   Page 203

ERG Guide 127

Engine 1: *Dispatch, upgrade the assignment to a Level 2 haz mat incident. Also request law enforcement to provide perimeter control.*

Dispatch: *Engines 2 and 4, Truck 1, Haz Mat 3, Medic 1, and Battalion 1 respond on a Level 2 haz mat incident at Ace Trucking, 19201 N.W. Industrial Drive. This response is for a reported leaking 300-gallon (1 136 L) intermediate bulk container of butylene oxide.*

Engine 1 arrives at Ace Trucking, and Lt. Adams observes a number of people standing in the parking lot and others exiting the building. She also notices an NFPA 704 placard on an entrance door with a *3* in the blue diamond, a *3* in the red diamond, a *2* in the yellow diamond, and *OX* in the white special hazard diamond.

Engine 1: *Dispatch, Engine 1 on-scene, Ace Trucking, 19201 N.W. Industrial Drive, 1-story, noncombustible warehouse, people exiting the building. Engine 1 is assuming Command on Side Alpha and*

is investigating. Designate this unit as Ace Command. Staging will be at 192nd Avenue and Industrial Drive. Advise responding companies that the wind is blowing from the southeast, blowing from Alpha/Delta to Bravo/Charlie.

Engine 1 is positioned uphill and upwind from the building. Then Lt. Adams locates Mr. Tucker, the responsible party (RP). He indicates that a 300-gallon (1 136 L) intermediate bulk container of 1,2-butylene oxide was damaged while workers were unloading a truck. He provides the material safety data sheet (MSDS) for the product. The leaking container is inside the warehouse adjacent to the loading dock. Mr. Tucker advises Lt. Adams that two maintenance workers are investigating the extent of the release. Lt. Adams asks Mr. Tucker to account for all other personnel who were in the building. Knowing that the presence of oxidizers indicated by the NFPA 704 placard could seriously complicate an incident involving a flammable liquid, she also asks Mr. Tucker where the oxidizers are located in relation to the spill. Mr. Tucker informs her that fertilizers are stored in their own bay, separated from the leak by concrete walls.

Engine 1: *Dispatch, have confirmed with the responsible party that this release involves a 300-gallon (1 136 L) intermediate bulk container of 1,2-butylene oxide. We are using Guide 127 for Flammable Liquids. This material is a liquid that mixes with water.*

At this point, Lt. Adams has identified several problems presented by the incident, including the following:

- Reported (and potentially other) exposed occupants
- Breach of a flammable liquid container with dispersion of both liquid and vapor
- Limited access to the incident area
- Potential ignition of flammable vapors
- Exposure of the remainder of the building in the event that ignition occurs

Initial notification strategies have already been addressed by the upgrade to a Level 2 haz mat incident. See **Scenario Table 1, p. 100.** Items are not necessarily presented in chronological order in this table. These items are typical Operational-Level haz mat first-responder actions upon arrival at an incident.

Lt. Adams assigns two firefighters from Engine 1 to perform reconnaissance (recon) from outside the hazard areas. Wearing structural fire-fighting clothing, Firefighters Linder and George (recon group) don self-contained breathing apparatus (SCBA) and proceed to the loading dock on Side Bravo (outside the anticipated hazard area) with a four-gas combustible gas indicator (CGI) (which measures percent of lower explosive limit [LEL], oxygen, carbon monoxide, and hydrogen sulfide). They will perform off-site reconnaissance and determine if the maintenance workers have identified the extent of the release.

As they approach, they observe a storm drain approximately 200 feet (61 m) away from Side B of the building. From outside the initial isolation zone, they see the two maintenance workers exiting the building through an open overhead door. Both are exhibiting signs of respiratory distress.

The recon group directs the workers to a safe area. One worker indicates that he was splashed with the leaking product while attempting to identify the location of the leak. The workers also tell Linder and George that the spill covers a 20- × 10-foot (6 m by 3 m) area on the floor of the warehouse and is spreading slowly towards the loading dock. See **Scenario Diagram 2, p. 102.**

Recon Group: *Ace Command, we have two victims on Side Bravo. They are exhibiting difficulty in breathing; one is contaminated. The victims report that the spill is 20 × 10 feet (6 m by 3 m) and is slowly spreading towards the loading dock.*

Ace Command: *Engine 1, set up emergency decontamination (decon) at the Alpha/Bravo corner of the building, outside the initial isolation zone.*

Engine 1's driver/operator/paramedic, Firefighter Miller, gets the company's decon kit and sets up an emergency decon area at the Alpha/Bravo corner. Firefighter Miller first stretches a hoseline to the decon location to provide immediate capability to rinse the contaminated victims. She then puts detergent, water solution, and large sponges in the decon kit's bucket. She also prepares *bag suits,* consisting of large plastic bags with head and arm openings to protect the victims' privacy during decon, and paper coveralls for the victims to don after decon.

Ace Command: *Dispatch, update on conditions: We have two victims in respiratory distress who have left the building and a report of a 20- × 10-foot (6 m by 3 m) spill inside the warehouse. Give me an additional engine, medic, and electric and gas utilities.*

Dispatch: *Engine 5 and Medic 2 respond on a Level 2 haz mat incident at Ace Trucking, 19201 N.W. Industrial Drive. Engine 1 on scene with a butylene oxide spill and two patients. Staging is at 192ⁿᵈ Avenue and Industrial Drive. Ace Command reports that the wind is from the southeast, blowing from Alpha/Delta to Bravo/Charlie. Electric and gas utilities have been notified.*

Engine 1's recon group firefighters question the two workers about their actions inside the warehouse and determine that only one of them actually had contact with the liquid product. Driver/Operator/Paramedic Miller provides sup-

Scenario Table 1
Incident Problems Identified

Priorities	Problems	Strategic Goal	Tactical Objectives	Task
Life Safety	Safety of Emergency responders	Protection	Use Personal Protective Equipment (PPE)	Don appropriate PPE
	Release of hazardous material with potential exposure to both the public and emergency responders	Isolation	Establish initial isolation zone	Follow *ERG* guidelines for initial isolation distances — communicate this information to responders and the public
	Access control and isolation	Isolation	• Establish hot zone • Verify hot zone through atmospheric monitoring • Isolate and deny entry	• Delineate the hot zone boundary with cones • Perform atmospheric monitoring • Establish a safe refuge area • Request law enforcement assistance for access control
	Two missing employees, other potential victims	Rescue (if appropriate)	• Locate missing employees • Account for all occupants	• Gather information, conduct interviews • Determine location of the two maintenance employees and notify them to evacuate (without entering the initial isolation area) • Request headcount to ensure all others are safely evacuated • Establish decontamination station if necessary

Continued

Priorities	Problems	Strategic Goal	Tactical Objectives	Task
Life Safety (Continued)	People in adjacent properties	Possibly: Protection	Possibly: Evacuation or shelter in place	• Assess exposures • Determine appropriate protective actions
Incident Stabilization	Command and control	Establish incident command	Implement Incident Management System	• Identify command • Designate command post
	Insufficient resources to mitigate incident	Notification	Upgrade incident to Level 2	Call for additional units
	Container breach and release	Spill control	Protect storm drain and environment	Dike storm drain downhill from the point of release (outside of hot zone) without coming in contact with the material
	Potential ignition of flammable vapors	Fire hazard control	• Establish fire control capability • Control vapors • Eliminate ignition sources	• Deploy a foam handline for vapor suppression • Establish horizontal positive-pressure ventilation • Turn off utilities
Property/ Environmental Protection	Potential environmental contamination	Spill control	Prevent liquid from reaching the storm drain	Dike storm drain

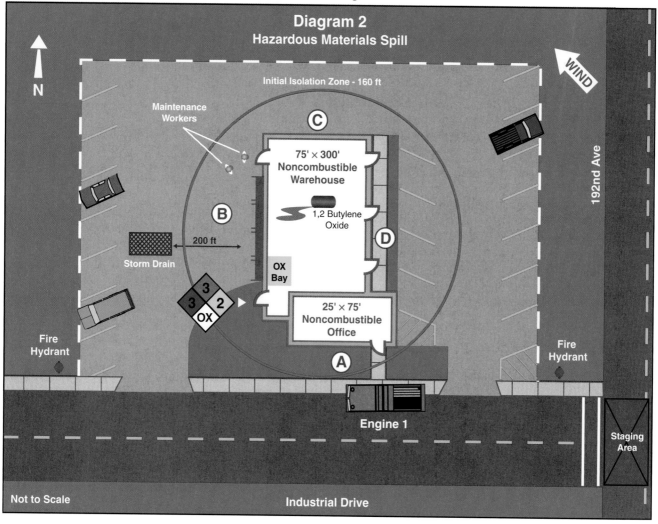

Diagram 2
Hazardous Materials Spill

portive care to the uncontaminated patient. The group then assists the contaminated worker in performing emergency decontamination. Firefighter Linder provides the contaminated employee with a bag suit and has him place it over his torso with his head exposed and then remove his clothing. He then directs the victim to wash the contaminated areas of his body with detergent and water. Firefighter George rinses the contaminated area with a hoseline at low pressure after the victim has completed washing. Firefighter Linder then assists the victim in donning a set of paper coveralls.

The local police shift supervisor arrives on scene and reports to the command post. Lt. Adams asks law enforcement to provide access control on Industrial Drive and 192nd Avenue. The shift supervisor instructs additional units to respond to 192nd Avenue and initially positions his vehicle on Industrial Drive west of Ace Trucking to divert traffic from the area. As additional law enforcement units arrive, Lt. Adams knows that the perimeter will be extended to the nearest intersections on either side, but for now (with limited resources), law enforcement units will be securing the immediate area.

As more fire department resources begin to arrive, Lt. Adams begins to make additional tactical assignments, and she assigns Driver/Operator/Paramedic Miller as the incident safety officer. Firefighter Miller begins to create the site safety and control plan.

Ace Command: *Medic 1, you have two patients who have been exposed to 1,2-butylene oxide. Only one needed decontamination; they are located at Engine 1 on Side Alpha.*

Ace Command: Truck 1, you are assigned to site-access control. Establish the hot-zone boundary as the exterior walls of the warehouse and 160 feet (49 m) from the exterior of the building on Side Bravo adjacent to the loading dock. The exterior walls of the building will define the hot zone on Sides Alpha, Charlie, and Delta. Identify a safe refuge area for occupants exiting from the location of the release.

Ace Command: Engine 2, deploy supply line to Side Delta, and set up positive-pressure ventilation (PPV) from Alpha and Delta to Bravo. An overhead door is already open on Bravo. Deploy a 2½-inch (65 mm) foam handline to the doorway on Side Delta.

Ace Command: Engine 4, dike the storm drain on Side Bravo, adjacent to the loading dock.

Truck 1 (site-access control) positions at the Charlie/Delta corner of the building to block access to the west parking lot. Captain Hendrix, assigns the truck's firefighters to deploy cones on Side Bravo to establish a 160-foot (49 m) radius hot zone. The firefighters proceed to Side Bravo to accomplish this task wearing structural fire-fighting clothing and SCBA. While deploying the cones, the firefighters monitor the atmosphere with a four-gas CGI.

Engine 2 arrives shortly after Truck 1 and lays a 5-inch (125 mm) supply line from the hydrant just to the east of Ace Trucking to Side Delta. Lt. Allen directs Driver/Operator Badgett to set up a fan to the entry door on Side Delta to initiate positive-pressure ventilation (Delta to Bravo). Concurrently, he and Firefighter Jirka extend a 2½-inch (65 mm) hoseline to the access door. Driver/Operator Badgett then supplies this hoseline with a 3-percent aqueous film forming foam (AFFF) solution using an alcohol-type concentrate (AFFF-ATC).

Engine 4 parks at staging located at 192nd Avenue and Industrial Drive. Lt. Hartin ensures that his crew is wearing structural fire-fighting clothing and SCBA and directs them to proceed to Side Bravo with absorbents, plastic sheeting, hand tools and a CGI. Conferring with Captain Hendrix from Truck 1, they determine that the storm drain is currently outside the hot zone. Lt. Hartin directs his crew to cover the storm drain and construct a circle dike around it while he monitors the atmosphere in the work area. Firefighters Hepler and Lewis quickly remove the storm drain grate, cover it with plastic sheeting, and replace it, which provides an effective barrier to liquid entry. They then construct a circle dike around the storm drain using the absorbents to limit any liquid infiltration. See **Scenario Diagram 3, p. 104.**

With the location of the two maintenance workers determined, Mr. Tucker confirms that all employees are accounted for. Lt. Adams reviews the MSDS (**Scenario Table 2, p. 105**) for 1,2-butylene oxide received earlier and verifies the information from the *ERG*.

Ace Command: Dispatch, all building occupants have been accounted for. Primary search will not be conducted.

Lt. Adams notes that the MSDS gives the following information: With a flash point of -7°F (-22°C) and a lower explosive limit of 3.9 percent, 1,2-butylene oxide presents a significant flammability hazard. In addition, the vapor pressure at 207 mmHg at 68°F (20°C) indicates that this particular brand is more volatile than acetone (which has a vapor pressure of 180 mmHg at the same temperature). With a vapor density of 2.49, the vapors are heavier than air. Given the vapor pressure and vapor density, the vapors vented from the structure have significant potential to move downwind and downhill.

The MSDS also indicates that no occupational exposure limits have been established for this material, but it is a respiratory and skin irritant and potential human carcinogen. The MSDS indicates that 1,2-butylene oxide has temperature sensitivity (avoid exposure to excessive heat) and is reactive to strong mineral acids, bases, and oxidizers. Excessive heat and contact with peroxides and polymerization catalysts may cause hazardous polymerization.

Battalion 1 arrives on scene, and Battalion Chief Arasim confers face to face with Lt. Adams. Lt. Adams provides a summary of the history of the incident, status of the incident, actions being taken, and the overall plan.

Ace Command: Dispatch, Battalion 1 is assuming Command of the incident at Ace Command.

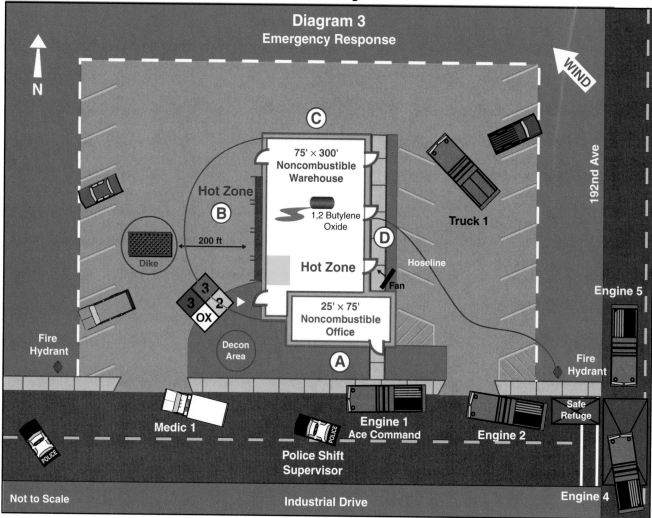

Diagram 3
Emergency Response

Battalion Chief Arasim evaluates the incident action plan established by Lt. Adams and identifies additional strategies and tactics that will be necessary to permit offensive operations to control the release from the container. See **Scenario Diagram 4, p. 109.**

Ace Command: Haz Mat 3, you are Haz Mat Branch, and you will have Engines 1 and 5 and Medic 2.

Haz Mat 3 positions in the parking lot just to the east of the warehouse, and Captain Mahaney reports to Ace Command for a briefing. Chief Ara-

sim and Lt. Adams provide Captain Mahaney with an overview of conditions and current operations. Captain Mahaney reviews the pre-incident survey and confirms the location of the leaking container with Mr. Tucker.

After this point, Operational-Level personal are primarily involved in conducing defensive activities while assisting technicians and conducting support duties. Support activities may include assisting entries, obtaining equipment needed by technicians, and assisting with decontamination functions.

Scenario Table 2
1,2-Butylene Oxide Material Safety Data Sheet

BADAMS-MILLER INC. Date Prepared: 01/26/04
BUTYLENE OXIDE-1,2 Date Printed: 06/18/04

1. CHEMICAL PRODUCT AND COMPANY IDENTIFICATION

Material Identity
Product Name: BUTYLENE OXIDE-1,2
General or Generic ID: EPOXIDE

Company
BAdams-Miller Inc.
P.O. Box 1234
Chemsink, OK 11111
555-777-8888

Emergency Telephone Number:
1-555-333-4444
24 hours everyday

2. COMPOSITION/INFORMATION ON INGREDIENTS

Ingredients (s)	CAS Number	% (by weight)
1,2-EPOXYBUTANE	106-88-7	100.0

3. HAZARDS IDENTIFICATION

Potential Health Effects

Eye
Contact may cause eye irritation

Skin
Contact may cause mild skin irritation. Prolonged or repeated contact may cause blistering of the skin.

Inhalation
Breathing 1,2-Butylene Oxide can irritate the nose, throat, and lungs, causing coughing, wheezing, and/or shortness of breath. High exposure may lead to lightheadedness or loss of consciousness.

Target Organ Effects

Developmental Information

Cancer Information
1,2-Butylene Oxide may be a carcinogen in humans

Other Health Effects

Primary Route (s) of Entry
Inhalation, through the skin, ingestion

4. FIRST AID MEASURES

Eye
If symptoms develop, move victim into fresh air. Flush eyes gently with water for at least 15 minutes while holding eyelids apart; seek immediate medical attention.

Skin
Remove contaminated clothing. Flush exposed area with large amounts of water. If skin is damaged, seek immediate medical attention. If skin is not damaged and symptoms persist, seek medical attention.

Continued

Swallowing

Seek medical attention immediatley. If individual is drowsy or unconscious, do not give fluids or any thing by mouth. Contact a physician, medical facility, or poison control center for advice.

Inhalation

If symptoms develop, immediately move individual into fresh air. Seek immediate medical attention; keep individual warm and quiet. If the individual is not breathing, begin artificial respiration. If heart has stopped, initiate cardiopulmonary resuscitation (CPR).

5.   FIRE-FIGHTING MEASURES

Flash Point
-7°F (-22°C)

Explosive Limit
Vol % in air: 3.9 - 20.6

Autoignition Temperature
822°F (439°C)

Hazardous Products of Combustion
May form carbon dioxide, carbon monoxide, and other toxic gases.

Fire and Explosion Hazards
This material gives off vapors that are heavier than air. They may travel along the ground or be moved by ventilation. Vapors may be ignited by pilot lights or other distant ignition sources.

Extinguishing Media
Carbon dioxide, dry chemical, and water fog. Water may be ineffective.

Fire-Fighting Instructions
Wear positive-pressure self-contained breathing apparatus (SCBA) with appropriate turnout gear and appropriate chemical-resistant personal protective equipment.

NFPA Rating
Health - 2, Flammability - 3, Reactivity - 2

6.   ACCIDENTAL RELEASE MEASURES

Spills

Evacuate danger area in case of large spills and contact emergency response agency. Collect leaking liquid in sealable containers. Absorb remaining liquid in sand or inert absorbent and remove to safe place. Do NOT wash away into sewer. Remove/extinguish all ignition sources.

7.   HANDLING AND STORAGE

Handling

Source of ignition such as smoking and open flames are prohibited in locations where this material is used, handled, or stored. Metal containers involving transfer of this material should be grounded and bonded. Use nonsparking tools and equipment when working with 1,2-Butylene Oxide, particularly when opening and closing containers. Even empty containers may contain flammable vapors and residue.

8.   EXPOSURE CONTROLS/PERSONAL PROTECTION

Eye Protection
Chemical splash goggles.

Skin Protection

Wear resistant gloves such as neoprene. To prevent repeated or prolonged skin contact, wear impervious clothing and boots.

Continued

Respiratory Protections
> Where potential for overexposure exists, use a NIOSH/MSHA approved air-supplied respirator. Engineering controls may also be implemented to reduce exposure.

Engineering Controls
> Provide sufficient ventilation to maintain exposure below level of overexposure.

Exposure Guidelines
> No exposure limits established

9. PHYSICAL AND CHEMICAL PROPERTIES

Boiling Point
> 146°F (63.3°C)

Vapor Pressure
> 207 mmHg at 68°F (20°C)

Specific Vapor Density
> 2.49 @ AIR = 1

Specific Gravity
> 0.826 @ 68°F (20°C)

Liquid Density
> 6.88 lbs/gal @ 68°F (20°C)
> 0.826 kg/l @ 20°C

Description
> Colorless liquid with disagreeable odor

10. STABILITY AND REACTIVITY

Hazardous Polmerization
> The substance may polymerize on contact with acids, alkalies, tin, aluminum, and iron chlorides, with fire or explosion hazard. Reacts with strong oxidants (such as peroxides), causing fire hazard. Avoid exposure to excessive heat and polymerization catalysts.

Hazardous Decomposition
> May form carbon dioxide, carbon monoxide, and various hydrocarbons.

Chemical Stability
> Stable.

Incompatibility
> Avoid contact with strong alkalies, strong mineral acids, and strong oxidizing agents.

11. TOXICOLOGICAL INFORMATION

No data

12. ECOLOGICAL INFORMATION

No data

13. DISPOSAL CONSIDERATION

Waste Management Information
> Contact local, state, or federal authorities for specific recommendations.

Continued

Scenario Table 2 (continued)
1,2-Butylene Oxide Material Safety Data Sheet

14. TRANSPORT INFORMATION

DOT Information - 49 *CFR* 172.101

DOT Description: 1,2 - BUTYLENE OXIDE, STABILIZED, 3, UN 3022, II

Container/Mode: 55 GAL DRUM/TRUCK PACKAGE

NOS Component: 1,2 BUTYLENE OXIDE

RQ (Reportable Quantity) - 49 *CFR* 172.101

Product Quantity (lbs)	Component
100	1,2 - BUTYLENE OXIDE

15. REGULATORY INFORMATION

U.S. Federal Regulations

TSCA (Toxic Substances Control Act) Status

TSCA (UNITED STATES) The intentional ingredients of this product are listed.

CERCLA RQ - 40 *CFR* 302.4 (a)

Component	RQ (lbs)
1,2 - BUTYLENE OXIDE	100

SARA 302 Components - 40 *CFR* 355 Appendix A

None

Section 311/312 Hazard Class - 40 *CFR* 370.2

Immediate (X) Delayed ( ) Fire (X) Reactive (X)

Sudden Release of Pressure ( )

SARA 313 Components - 40 *CFR* 372.65

Section 313 Component (s)	CAS Number	%
1,2 - BUTYLENE OXIDE	106-88-7	100.00

International Regulations

Inventory Status

Not determined

State and Local Regulations

California Proposition 65

None

New Jersey RTK Label Information

1,2 - BUTYLENE OXIDE 106-88-7

Pennsylvania RTK Label Information

OXIRANE, ETHYL- 106-88-7

16. OTHER INFORMATION

The information provided in this MSDS was derived from a variety of sources, none of which warrent complete accuracy of their information. Therefore, while the information provided in this MSDS is believed to be correct, BAdams-Miller Inc. cannot guarantee it.

Scenario Diagram 4

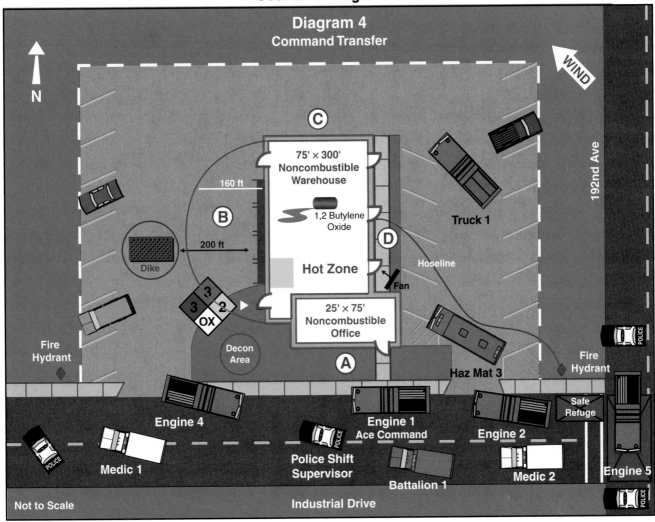

Diagram 4
Command Transfer

N

WIND

192nd Ave

C

75' × 300'
Noncombustible
Warehouse

160 ft

B

1,2 Butylene
Oxide

Truck 1

200 ft

D

Dike

Hoseline

Hot Zone

Fan

3
3 2
OX

25' × 75'
Noncombustible
Office

Fire
Hydrant

Decon
Area

A

Haz Mat 3

Fire
Hydrant

Safe
Refuge

Engine 4

Engine 1
Ace Command

Engine 2

POLICE

Medic 1

Police Shift
Supervisor

Medic 2

Engine 5

Battalion 1

Not to Scale

Industrial Drive

Part 2
Seven Clues to the Presence of Hazardous Materials

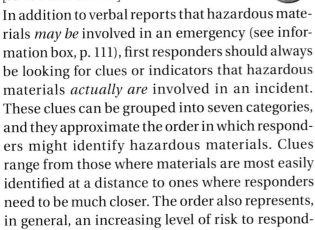

[NFPA 472: 5.2.1.1]

In addition to verbal reports that hazardous materials *may be* involved in an emergency (see information box, p. 111), first responders should always be looking for clues or indicators that hazardous materials *actually are* involved in an incident. These clues can be grouped into seven categories, and they approximate the order in which responders might identify hazardous materials. Clues range from those where materials are most easily identified at a distance to ones where responders need to be much closer. The order also represents, in general, an increasing level of risk to respond-

ers. The closer responders need to be in order to identify the material, the greater their chances of being in an area where they could be exposed to its harmful effects (**Figure 3.1. p. 110**).

The seven clues as presented here may differ from the clues described by other organizations and texts. These changes have been made to avoid confusion regarding terminology and to clarify the categories (for example, see information box, Is It a Placard, Label, or Marking? under Clue 3, p. 155). The seven clues to the presence of hazardous materials are as follows:

1. Occupancy types, locations, and pre-incident surveys

2. Container shapes

3. Transportation placards, labels, and markings

4. Other markings and colors (nontransportation)

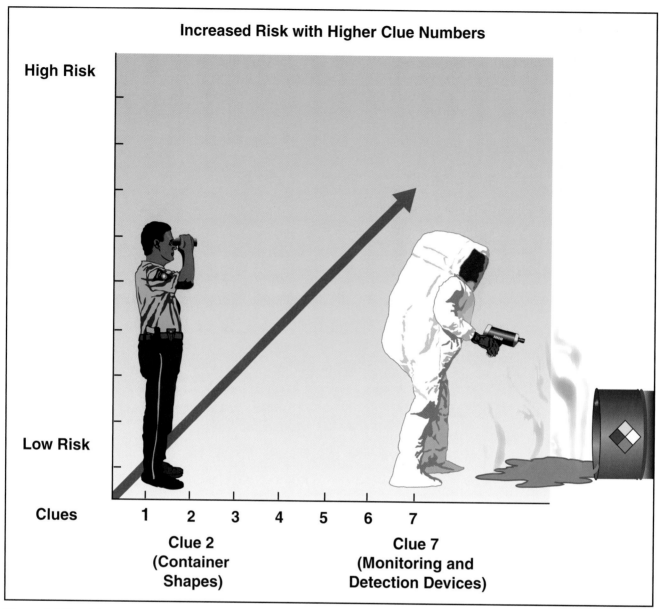

Increased Risk with Higher Clue Numbers

High Risk

Low Risk

Clues   1   2   3   4   5   6   7

Clue 2
(Container
Shapes)

Clue 7
(Monitoring and
Detection Devices)

Figure 3.1 The risk to responders increases as they move closer to the hazardous material. It is much safer to identify a material from a distance based on a container shape than it is to physically sample the substance with a monitoring device.

5. Written resources

6. Senses

7. Monitoring and detection devices

Clue 1
Occupancy Types, Locations, and Pre-incident Surveys

Simply stated, hazardous materials are found everywhere — from residential garages to the custodial closet in the local library. Not all locations or occupancies are as obvious as a local manufacturing plant, and responders may have little or no warning of materials being transported through their jurisdictions by road, rail, or waterway. However, pre-incident surveys (sometimes called *preplans*) and the occupancy type for a particular structure may provide the first clue to the emergency responder that hazardous materials may be involved in an incident.

Pre-incident Surveys

The complexity and potential harm from haz mat incidents require that all first responders make a firm commitment to preparation. It is important to use the talents of every member of the responsible fire and emergency services organization. To form

Verbal Reports

As given in the sample incident scenario, the first evidence that hazardous materials are present at an emergency often comes from a knowledgeable or responsible person at the site (such as the facility manager). This person may have vital information about the events that led to the emergency, materials involved, and humans or property exposed. Whether a telecommunicator/dispatcher questions this person over the telephone or first responders question the person at the scene, emergency personnel must be prepared to make maximum use of this resource. After receiving verbal reports of the involvement of hazardous materials, officials at the scene determine and record answers to the following questions:

- Who are the reporting persons, and how did they get the information?

- What materials are involved, and how did the reporting persons identify them?

- How much material is involved, exposed, spilled, or leaking?

- Are materials leaking from vessels/containers or escaping under pressure? If so, what are estimated flow rates? Is a spill static or flowing? Are sealed containers subject to the physical damage of fire exposure?

- Do any personnel need rescuing? If so, how many, where are they located, and what are their physical conditions?

- Is any other information pertinent or peculiar to the situation?

a cohesive response, everyone must participate in planning, preparing, and training for haz mat incidents.

The very nature of haz mat incidents places extreme pressure on first responders to make decisions quickly and accurately. First responders can reduce the number of on-site decisions by conducting pre-incident surveys and being familiar with local emergency response plans (see sidebar, right). With the groundwork laid, first responder companies can concentrate on the situation and operate more safely and efficiently. Planning reduces oversights, confusion, and duplication of efforts, and it results in a desirable outcome. Furthermore, pre-incident surveys identify the following items:

- Exposures (people, property, and environment)

- Types, quantities, and locations of hazardous materials in the area

- Dangers of the hazardous materials

- Building features (location of fixed fire-suppression systems, etc.)

- Site characteristics

- Possible access/egress difficulties

- Inherent limitations of the responding organizations to control certain types of haz mat emergencies

Planning is an ongoing process that includes reviewing surveys and updating them regularly. Pre-incident surveys are not always accurate, however, because inventories, businesses, and other factors may change without notice. Compliance with existing reporting rules and regulations cannot be guaranteed. First responders must always expect to find the unexpected.

Local Emergency Response Plans

[NFPA 4.4.1(1)]

In the U.S., federal law requires Local Emergency Planning Committees (LEPCs) to complete *local emergency response plans*. These plans must be reviewed once a year or more frequently when circumstances change in the community. Federal law also requires each LEPC to evaluate the need for resources necessary to develop, implement, and exercise the emergency plan. **Appendix C,** Emergency Response Plans, goes into greater detail about the requirements of local emergency response plans, emergency planning, and other planning sources and requirements.

In the scenario, Lt. Adams examined the pre-incident survey for Ace Trucking on the way to the scene. Before reaching the incident, she already had important information to assist in the decision-making process. For example, she knew that the company handled a wide variety of hazardous products in nonbulk containers. Furthermore, she was able to select a safe response route in order to approach the incident from uphill and upwind.

Occupancy Types

[NFPA 472: 4.2.1(5)]

Community emergency response planning helps first responders identify specific sites where hazardous materials are located, used, and stored. However, first responders should be aware that certain occupancies, such as the following, are always highly probable locations for finding significant quantities of hazardous materials:

- Fuel storage facilities
- Gas/service stations (and convenience stores)
- Paint supply stores
- Plant nurseries, garden centers, and agricultural facilities
- Pest control and lawn care companies
- Medical facilities
- Photo processing laboratories
- Dry cleaners
- Plastics and high-technology factories
- Metal-plating businesses
- Mercantile concerns (hardware stores, groceries stores, certain department stores) **(Figure 3.2)**
- Chemistry (and other) laboratories in educational facilities (including high schools)
- Lumberyards
- Feed/farm stores
- Veterinary clinics
- Print shops
- Warehouses
- Industrial and utility plants

Figure 3.2 Many different commercial stores have hazardous materials.

- Port shipping facilities (with changing cargo hazards)
- Treatment storage disposal (TSD) facilities

Private property is not exempt from danger because hazardous chemicals in the form of drain cleaners, pesticides, fertilizers, paint products, and flammable liquids (such as gasoline) are common household products. In rural areas, propane tanks provide fuel for heating, and farms may have large quantities of dangerous products such as pesticides.

It is possible for chemicals to be stored or used unsafely. Materials may be transferred from their original, labeled containers, or dangerous substances may be hidden to avoid detection by chance inspections.

 In the scenario, Lt. Adams knew from the preincident survey that Ace Trucking handled hazardous materials. Even without a pre-incident survey or report of a chemical odor, the fact that the incident was reported in a warehouse — an occupancy likely to contain hazardous materials — should have raised her suspicions that hazardous materials might be a factor.

Incident Locations
[NFPA 472: 4.2.1(5)]

The location of an emergency incident may also provide informal evidence of haz mat involvement. Locations such as mechanical rooms, supply stockrooms, and chemistry labs in schools are likely sites as are kitchens, storage sheds, and garages on private property. Ports, docks or piers, railroad sidings, airplane hangars, truck terminals, and other places of material transfer (such as trucking warehouses) are also likely locations for haz mat accidents. Any building with a fume hood exhaust stack (or stacks) on the roof (such as a high school or medical office building) probably has a functioning laboratory inside.

Local experience with transportation accidents also indicates where to expect haz mat incidents. Each of the following modes of transportation has particular locations where accidents may occur more frequently:

- *Roadways*
  — Designated truck routes
  — Blind intersections
  — Poorly marked or poorly engineered interchanges
  — Areas frequently congested by traffic
  — Heavily traveled roads
  — Sharp turns
  — Steep grades
  — Highway interchanges and ramps
  — Bridges, tunnels
- *Railways*
  — Depots, terminals, and switch or classification yards
  — Sections of poorly laid or poorly maintained tracks
  — Steep grades and severe curves
  — Shunts and sidings
  — Uncontrolled crossings
  — Bridges, trestles, and tunnels
- *Waterways*
  — Difficult passages at bends or other threats to navigation
  — Bridges and other crossings
  — Piers and docks
  — Shallow areas
  — Locks
  — Loading/unloading stations
- *Airways*
  — Fueling ramps
  — Repair and maintenance hangars
  — Freight terminals
  — Crop duster planes and supplies
- *Pipelines*
  — Exposed crossings over waterways or roads
  — Pumping stations
  — Construction and demolition sites
  — Intermediate or final storage facilities

Other locations may be identified by consulting with local law enforcement officials to determine problem spots based on traffic studies. First responders should also pay attention to the water level in rivers and tidal areas and be aware of the following facts:

- Many accidents occur because flow volume and tidal conditions were not considered. These flow and tidal variances affect clearance under bridges, many of which also have pipelines, water mains, gas lines, and the like attached to them.

- Occupancies in low-lying areas that may be affected by flood conditions must have a contingency plan to isolate and protect hazardous materials.

- Tidal and flow conditions are constantly changing. Areas that were once considered safe may become compromised by change of tide direction, flow rate, back eddies, etc.

- Once a material reaches an outside water source, it becomes a moving incident and is extremely difficult to contain, confine, and mitigate.

First responders should also be familiar with the types of haz mat shipments that come through their jurisdiction. For example, farming communities may be more likely to see tanks of anhydrous ammonia passing through, whereas a port serving an industrial complex with many refineries might see more petroleum products.

Approaching a Scene Safely

[NFPA 472: 5.4.3(3)]

Identify problem locations and hazardous occupancies; evaluate them during emergency response planning. Include some remote observation/assessment steps in the planned approach so that responding companies can stop briefly to assess the situation for unusual conditions before entering the scene. Always approach the scene of a hazardous materials incident from uphill, upwind, and upstream if at all possible.

Binoculars, spotting scopes, camera lenses, or sight scopes are invaluable pieces of equipment for observers during assessment. They allow responders to identify scene conditions from a safe, distant location. After assessment, report any unusual conditions to the telecommunications/dispatch center and reevaluate the situation. The assessment location can be used as a temporary staging area if reconnaissance teams must approach on foot.

Clue 2
Container Shapes

[NFPA 4.2.1(6), 5.2.1.1]

While first responders may recognize the location of an incident or type of occupancy as one that handles hazardous materials, the presence of certain storage vessels, tanks, containers, packages, or vehicles alerts them to their presence with certainty. These containers can provide useful information about the materials inside, so it is important for first responders to recognize the shapes of the different types of packaging and containers in which hazardous materials are stored and transported.

Types of containers can be categorized in different ways: bulk versus nonbulk (referring to capacity as defined by the U.S. Department of Transportation [DOT] and Transport Canada [TC]) (see information box), pressure versus nonpressure (referring to the design of the container based on the pressure within), or bulk-capacity fixed-facility containment systems versus transportation packaging (referring to the facility or mode). This Clue 2 section discusses (1) bulk-capacity containment systems at fixed facilities, (2) bulk transportation packaging, and (3) nonbulk containers in general. Pressure and nonpressure containers are discussed as appropriate under these three categories.

Bulk-Capacity Fixed-Facility Containers

[NFPA 472: 5.2.1.1(D)]

Containers at fixed facilities include buildings, aboveground storage tanks, machinery, underground storage tanks, pipelines, reactors, open piles or bins, vats, storage cabinets, and other fixed, on-site containers. This section focuses on storage tanks holding bulk quantities of hazardous materials. Nonbulk packages that may be found at fixed facilities are discussed in the Nonbulk Packaging section. Pipeline identification and other labeling and marking systems used to identify the materials in storage cabinets, bins, vats, and the like are discussed under Clue 4: Other Markings and Colors.

What Is Bulk/Nonbulk Packaging?

Bulk packaging refers to a packaging, other than that on a vessel or barge, in which materials are loaded with no intermediate form of containment. This packaging type includes a transport vehicle or freight container such as a cargo tank, railcar, or portable tank. Intermediate bulk containers (IBCs) and intermodal (IM) containers are also examples. To be considered bulk packaging, one of the following criteria must be met:

- Maximum capacity is greater than 119 gallons (450 L) as a receptacle for a liquid.

- Maximum net mass is greater than 882 pounds (400 kg) or maximum capacity is greater than 119 gallons (450 L) as a receptacle for a solid.

- Water capacity is 1,001 pounds (454 kg) or greater as a receptacle for a gas.

Nonbulk packaging is packaging that is smaller than the minimum criteria established for bulk packaging. Drums, boxes, carboys, and bags are examples. Composite packages (packages with an outer packaging and an inner receptacle) and combination packages (multiple packages grouped together in a single outer container such as bottles of acid packed inside a cardboard box) may also be classified as nonbulk packaging.

As soon as Lt. Adams was told that the 1,2-butylene oxide was in a nonbulk container, she knew that she was probably not dealing with more than 119 gallons (450 L) of product (another useful piece of information in terms of planning an appropriate response). Depending on circumstances, incidents involving bulk containers may take considerably more resources to handle appropriately and safely.

In general, aboveground storage tanks are divided into two major categories: (1) atmospheric and nonpressure tanks and (2) pressure tanks. Underground storage tanks may be atmospheric or pressurized, and they are discussed in the same sections as atmospheric tanks and pressure tanks, respectively. See information box, right. The following sections highlight the features of these tanks.

What Is the Difference Between Nonpressure, Atmospheric, Low-pressure, Cryogenic, and Pressure Storage Tanks?

NFPA categorizes fixed-facility storage tanks as *pressure* and *nonpressure.* See **Table 3.1** for pressure ranges. NFPA also singles out *cryogenic liquid tanks* for special recognition. Descriptions are as follows:

- *Nonpressure tanks (also called atmospheric tanks)* — If these tanks are storing any product, they will normally have a small amount of pressure (up to 0.5 psi [3.45 kPa] {0.03 bar}) inside, which makes the term *nonpressure* something of a misnomer under most circumstances. Responders should be aware that even *nonpressure* tanks probably have *some* internal pressure.

- *Pressure tanks* — These tanks are divided into the following two categories:

  — Low-pressure storage tanks that have pressures between 0.5 psi to 15 psi (3.45 kPa to 103 kPa) {0.03 bar to 1.03 bar}.

  — Pressure vessels that have pressures above 15 psi (103 kPa) {1.03 bar}.

- *Cryogenic liquid tanks* — These tanks have varying pressures, but some can be very high (over 300 psi [2 068 kPa] {20.7 bar}). They are usually heavily insulated with a vacuum in the space between the outer and inner shells.

Table 3.1
Fixed-Facility Container Pressures

Tank/Vessel	Pressure psi (kPa)
Atmospheric/ Nonpressure Tanks	0.5 psi (0 kPa to 4 kPa)
Low-Pressure Storage Tanks	0.5 to 15 psi (4 kPa to 103 kPa)
Pressure Vessels	15+ psi (103+ kPa)

Source: Reprinted with permission of the *Hazardous Materials Response Handbook,* 4th Edition, Copyright © 2002, National Fire Protection Association, Quincy, MA.

Atmospheric/Nonpressure Storage Tanks

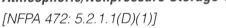

[NFPA 472: 5.2.1.1(D)(1)]

Atmospheric/nonpressure storage tanks are designed to hold contents under little pressure. The maximum pressure under which an atmospheric tank is capable of holding its contents is 0.5 psi (3.45 kPa) {1.03 bar}. Common types of atmospheric tanks are horizontal tanks, ordinary cone roof tanks, floating roof tanks, lifter roof tanks, and vapordome roof tanks. **Table 3.2, p. 116,** provides pictures and examples of various atmospheric storage tanks and also describes underground storage caverns.

According to the U.S. Environmental Protection Agency (EPA), catastrophic failures of aboveground atmospheric storage tanks can occur when flammable vapors in a tank explode and break either the shell-to-bottom or side seam. These failures have caused tanks to rip open and (in rare cases) hurtle through the air. A properly designed and maintained storage tank will break along the shell-to-top seam, which is more likely to limit the fire to the damaged tank and prevent the contents from spilling.

The following two examples of catastrophic shell-to-bottom seam failures illustrate the potential dangers:

- In 1995, the combustible vapor inside two large, 30-foot diameter by 30-foot high (9 m by 9 m) storage tanks exploded during a welding operation on the outside of one tank. The explosion propelled both tanks upward — one landing more than 50 feet (15 m) away. The flammable liquid inside was instantly released and ignited, resulting in a massive fire that caused five deaths and several serious injuries.

- In 1992, while workers were welding the outside of an empty liquid storage tank, residual vapor in the tank exploded and propelled it upward and into an adjacent river. Three workers were killed and one was injured.

Historically, shell-to-bottom seam failures are more common among old storage tanks. Steel storage tanks built before 1950 generally do not conform to current industry standards for explosion and fire venting situations. Atmospheric tanks used for storage of flammable and combustible liquids should be designed to fail along the shell-to-roof seam when an explosion occurs in the tank. This

Table 3.2
Atmospheric/Nonpressure Storage Tanks

Tank Type

Descriptions

Horizontal Tank

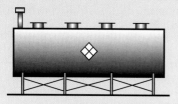

Horizontal tanks: Cylindrical tanks sitting on legs, blocks, cement pads, or something similar; typically constructed of steel with flat ends. Horizontal tanks are commonly used for bulk storage in conjunction with fuel-dispensing operations. Old tanks (pre-1950s) have bolted seams, whereas new tanks are generally welded. A horizontal tank supported by unprotected steel supports or stilts (prohibited by most current fire codes) may fail quickly during fire conditions.

Contents: Flammable and combustible liquids, corrosives, poisons, etc.

Cone Roof Tank

Cone roof tanks: Have cone-shaped, pointed roofs with weak roof-to-shell seams that break when or if the container becomes overpressurized. When it is partially full, the remaining portion of the tank contains a potentially dangerous vapor space.

Contents: Flammable, combustible, and corrosive liquids

Open Top Floating Roof Tank

Floating Deck

Open top floating roof tanks (sometimes just called *floating roof tanks*): Large-capacity, aboveground holding tanks. They are usually much wider than they are tall. As with all floating roof tanks, the roof actually floats on the surface of the liquid and moves up and down depending on the liquid's level. This roof eliminates the potentially dangerous vapor space found in cone roof tanks. A fabric or rubber seal around the circumference of the roof provides a weather-tight seal.

Contents: Flammable and combustible liquids

Covered Top Floating Roof Tank

Vents around rim provide differentation from Cone Roof Tanks

Internal floating roof tanks (sometimes called *covered [or covered top] floating roof tanks*): Have fixed cone roofs with either a pan or deck-type float inside that rides directly on the product surface. This tank is a combination of the open top floating roof tank and the ordinary cone roof tank.

Contents: Flammable and combustible liquids

Covered Top Floating Roof Tank with Geodesic Dome

NOTE: Floating roof tanks covered by geodesic domes are used to store flammable liquids.

Continued

Table 3.2 (continued)
Atmospheric/Nonpressure Storage Tanks

Tank Type

Descriptions

Lifter Roof Tank

Lifter roof tanks: Have roofs that float within a series of vertical guides that allow only a few feet (meters) of travel. The roof is designed so that when the vapor pressure exceeds a designated limit, the roof lifts slightly and relieves the excess pressure.

Contents: Flammable and combustible liquids

Vapordome Roof Tank

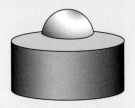

Vapordome roof tanks: Vertical storage tanks that have lightweight aluminum geodesic domes on their tops. Attached to the underside of the dome is a flexible diaphragm that moves in conjunction with changes in vapor pressure.

Contents: Combustible liquids of medium volatility and other nonhazardous materials

Atmospheric Underground Storage Tank

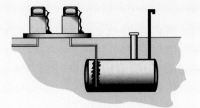

Atmospheric underground storage tanks: Constructed of steel, fiberglass, or steel with a fiberglass coating. Underground tanks will have more than 10 percent of their surface areas underground. They can be buried under a building or driveway or adjacent to the occupancy.

This tank has fill and vent connections located near the tank. Vents, fill points, and occupancy type (gas/service stations, private garages, and fleet maintenance stations) provide visual clues.

Many commercial and private tanks have been abandoned, some with product still in them. These tanks are presenting major problems to many communities.

Contents: Petroleum products

Fill Connections Cover

Underground storage caverns: Rare and technically are not "tanks." First responders should be aware that some natural and manmade caverns are used to store natural gas. The locations of such caverns should be noted in local emergency response plans.

feature prevents the tank from propelling upward or splitting along the side. Several organizations have developed standards and specifications for storage tank design. A published standard relevant to this design feature includes American Petroleum Institute (API) API-650, "Welded Steel Tanks for Oil Storage."

Some of the factors that might contribute to catastrophic failures include (but are not limited to) the following:

- Atmospheric storage tanks that do not meet API-650 or other applicable code(s) and contain flammable liquids or liquids that may produce combustible vapor

- Tanks with corrosion around the base and/or steel tanks whose base is in direct contact with the ground and exposed to moisture

- Tanks or associated structures (pipes) with weakened or defective welds

- Tanks used to store mixtures containing water and flammables where the water phase is at the tank bottom, which may contribute to internal bottom corrosion

- Tanks containing combustible vapor, which are not equipped with flame arrestors or vapor-control devices to limit emissions

- Possible ignition sources near tanks containing combustible vapor

Of course, many other safety issues arise once atmospheric tanks become involved in or are exposed to fire. Emergency response planning is essential to prevent injuries or deaths caused by the special problems presented by tank fires and emergencies.

Pressure Storage Tanks

[NFPA 472: 5.2.1.1(D)(2), 5.2.1.1(D)(3)]
Pressure tanks are designed to hold contents under pressure. NFPA uses the term *pressure tank* to cover both low-pressure storage tanks and pressure vessels (with higher pressures). Low-pressure storage tanks have operating pressures from 0.5 to 15 psi (3.45 kPa to 103 kPa) {0.03 bar to 1.03 bar}. Pressure vessels (including many large cryogenic liquid storage tanks) have pressures of 15 psi (103 kPa) {1.03 bar} or greater. **Table 3.3** provides pictures and examples of various pressure tanks.

Bulk Transportation Containers

It is important for first responders to recognize the most common types of bulk transportation containers. These containers can be divided into three main categories determined by the mode of transportation as follows:

- Rail tank cars (railroad)
- Cargo tank trucks (highway)
- Intermodal containers (highway, railroad, or marine vessel)

This section also covers *cargo vessels* (ships) that transport hazardous materials via waterways and *unit loading devices* used in air transportation, which technically are not considered bulk packaging by the U.S. DOT's definition. Intermediate bulk containers, ton containers/cylinders, and storage bladders are also discussed.

Rail Tank Cars

[NFPA 472: 5.2.1.1(A) (1–5)]
Some railroad tank cars have capacities in excess of 30,000 gallons (113 562 L). Because of the large quantities these cars hold, a sudden, pressurized/liquefied material release could overwhelm the capabilities of most responding organizations. By recognizing distinctive railroad cars, first responders can begin the identification process from the greatest possible distance. The type of car gives clues as to what material may be within as well as the material's weight and volume.

Tank cars carry the bulk of the hazardous materials transported by rail. These tank cars are divided into the following three main categories:

- Nonpressure tank cars
- Pressure tank cars
- Cryogenic liquid tank cars

Several other types of railroad cars may also carry hazardous materials:

- Hopper cars (including pneumatically unloaded hopper cars)
- Boxcars
- Special service (or specialized) cars

NOTE: The source for most of the following information on railroad tank cars is courtesy of "A General Guide to Tank Cars," prepared by the Union Pacific Railroad, April 2003.

Table 3.3
Low-Pressure Storage Tanks and Pressure Vessels

Tank/Vessel Type

Descriptions

Dome Roof Tank

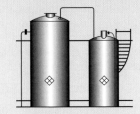

Dome roof tanks: Generally classified as low-pressure tanks with operating pressures as high as 15 psi (103 kPa). They have domes on their tops.

Contents: Flammable liquids, combustible liquids, fertilizers, solvents, etc.

Spheroid Tank

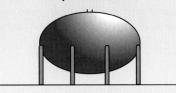

Spheroid tanks: Low-pressure storage tanks. They can store 3,000,000 gallons (11 356 200 L) or more of liquid.

Contents: Liquefied petroleum gas (LPG), methane, propane, and some flammable liquids such as gasoline and crude oil

Noded Spheroid Tank

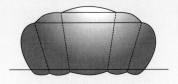

Noded spheroid tanks: Low-pressure storage tanks. They are similar in use to spheroid tanks, but they can be substantially larger and flatter in shape. These tanks are held together by a series of internal ties and supports that reduce stresses on the external shells.

Contents: LPG, methane, propane, and some flammable liquids such as gasoline and crude oil

Horizontal Pressure Vessel*

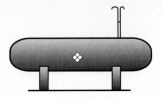

Horizontal pressure vessels:* Have high pressures and capacities from 500 to over 40,000 gallons (1 893 L to over 151 416 L). They have rounded ends and are not usually insulated. They usually are painted white or some other highly reflective color.

Contents: LPG, anhydrous ammonia, vinyl chloride, butane, ethane, liquefied natural gas (LNG), compressed natural gas (CNG), chlorine, hydrogen chloride, and other similar products

Spherical Pressure Vessel

Spherical pressure vessels: Have high pressures and capacities up to 600,000 gallons (2 271 240 L). They are often supported off the ground by a series of concrete or steel legs. They usually are painted white or some other highly reflective color.

Contents: Liquefied petroleum gases and vinyl chloride

Continued

Table 3.3 (continued)
Low-Pressure Storage Tanks and Pressure Vessels

Tank/Vessel Type	Descriptions
Cryogenic-Liquid Storage Tank 	**Cryogenic-liquid storage tanks:** Insulated, vacuum-jacketed tanks with safety-relief valves and rupture disks. Capacities can range from 300 to 400,000 gallons (1 136 L to 1 514 160 L). Pressures vary according to the materials stored and their uses. **Contents:** Liquid carbon dioxide, liquid oxygen, liquid nitrogen, etc.

* It is becoming more common for horizontal propane tanks to be buried underground. Underground residential tanks usually have capacities of 500 or 1,000 gallons (1 893 L or 3 785 L). Once buried, the tank may be noticeable only because of a small access dome protruding a few inches (millimeters) above the ground.

Nonpressure tank car. *[NFPA 472: 5.2.1.1(A)(3)]* Nonpressure tank cars (known as *general service* or *low-pressure* tank cars) transport hazardous and nonhazardous materials with vapor pressures below 25 psi (172 kPa) {1.7 bar} at 105 to 115°F (41°C to 46°C). First responders must be aware that even though these tank cars are called *nonpressure,* they have *some* internal pressure. Tank test pressures for nonpressure tank cars are 60 and 100 psi (414 and 689 kPa) {4.1 and 6.9 bar}. Capacities range from 4,000 to 45,000 gallons (15 142 to 170 343 L).

Nonpressure tank cars are cylindrical with rounded ends (heads). They have at least one manway for access to the tank's interior. Fittings for loading/unloading, pressure and/or vacuum relief, gauging, and other purposes are visible at the top and/or bottom of the car. Old nonpressure tank cars have at least one expansion dome with a manway.

Nonpressure tank cars may be compartmentalized with up to six compartments. Each compartment is constructed as a separate and distinct tank with its own set of fittings. Each compartment may have a different capacity and transport a different commodity. Nonpressure tank cars transport a variety of hazardous materials such as flammable liquids, flammable solids, reactive liquids, reactive solids, oxidizers, organic peroxides, poisons, irritants, and corrosive materials. They also transport nonhazardous materials such as fruit and vegetable juices, wine and other alcoholic beverages, tomato paste, and other agricultural products.

Another type of nonpressure tank car is a *tank-within-a-tank* car. This type of car consists of an inner tank (steel, alloy steel, or aluminum) covered with thick insulation and enclosed within an outer shell. These cars are used to transport temperature-sensitive materials such as food products and certain hazardous materials such as chloroprene, uninhibited methyl methacrylate, and super phosphoric acid. See **Table 3.4** for examples of nonpressure tank cars.

Pressure tank car. *[NFPA 472: 5.2.1.1(A)(5)]* Pressure tank cars typically transport hazardous materials including flammable, nonflammable, and poison gases at pressures greater than 25 psi (172 kPa) {1.7 bar} at 68°F (20°C). They also may transport flammable liquids. Tank test pressures from these tank cars are 100, 200, 300, 340, 400, 500, and 600 psi (689, 1 379, 2 068, 2 344, 2 758, 3 447, and 4 137 kPa) {6.9, 13.8, 20.7, 23.4, 27.6, 34.5, and 41.2 bar}. Pressure tank car capacities range from 4,000 to 45,000 gallons (15 142 to 170 343 L).

Pressure tank cars are cylindrical, noncompartmentalized metal (steel or aluminum) tanks with rounded ends (heads). They typically are top-loading cars with their fittings (loading/unloading, pressure-relief, and gauging) located inside the

Table 3.4
Nonpressure Tank Cars

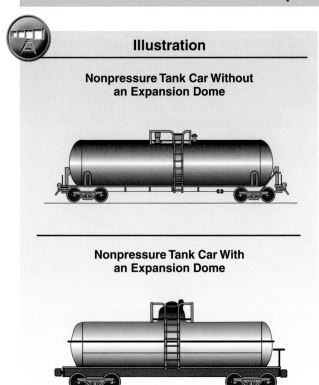 Illustration	Descriptions
Nonpressure Tank Car Without an Expansion Dome	**Nonpressure tank car without an expansion dome:** Fittings are visible.
	Carries: Flammable liquids, flammable solids, reactive liquids, reactive solids, oxidizers, organic peroxides, poisons, irritants, corrosive materials, and similar products
Nonpressure Tank Car With an Expansion Dome	**Nonpressure tank car with an expansion dome:** Old models have the expansion dome.
	Carries: Flammable liquids, flammable solids, reactive liquids, reactive solids, oxidizers, organic peroxides, poisons, irritants, corrosive materials, and similar products

Source: Information and drawings courtesy of Union Pacific Railroad.

protective housings mounted on the manway cover plates in the top center of the tanks. To distinguish visually between pressure and nonpressure tank cars, look at the fittings on top of the car. Most nonpressure tank cars have visible fittings or one or more expansion domes. Pressure tank cars typically have all fittings out of sight under the single protective housings on top of the tanks. However, some nonpressure tank cars also have protective housings.

Pressure tank cars may be insulated and/or thermally protected. Those without insulation and without jacketed thermal protection may have at least the top two-thirds of the tanks painted white. See **Table 3.5, p. 122,** for examples of pressure tank cars.

Cryogenic liquid tank car. Cryogenic liquid tank cars carry low-pressure (usually below 25 psi [172 kPa] {1.7 bar}) refrigerated liquids (-130°F and below [-90°C and below]). Materials found in these tanks include argon, hydrogen, nitrogen, and oxygen. Liquefied natural gas (LNG) and ethylene may be found at somewhat higher pressures. Fittings for loading/unloading, pressure relief, and venting are in ground-level cabinets at diagonal corners of the car or the center of one end of the car.

A cryogenic liquid tank car is in the *tank-within-a-tank* category with a stainless steel inner tank supported within a strong outer tank. The space between the inner tank and outer tank is filled with insulation. This space is also kept under a vacuum. The combination of insulation and vacuum protects the contents from ambient temperatures for only 30 days. The shipper tracks these *time-sensitive* shipments. An example of a cryogenic liquid tank car is given in **Table 3.6, p. 122.**

Other railroad cars. Other railroad cars include pneumatically unloaded hopper cars, other hopper cars, miscellaneous cars such as boxcars (see **Table 3.7, p. 123,** for examples), and high-pressure tube

Table 3.5
Pressure Tank Cars

Illustration

Descriptions

Typical Pressure Tank Car

Typical pressure tank car: Fittings are inside the protective housing.

Carries: Flammable, nonflammable, and poison gases as well as flammable liquids

Hydrogen Cyanide (Hydrocyanic Acid), HCN *Candy Stripe* Car

Hydrogen cyanide (hydrocyanic acid), HCN *candy stripe car*: In the past, some HCN cars were painted white with red bands (called *candy stripes*). This practice is becoming obsolete due to concerns about terrorism.

Table 3.6
Cryogenic Liquid Tank Car

Illustration

Descriptions

Typical Cryogenic Liquid Tank Car

Typical cryogenic liquid tank car: Fittings are in ground-level cabinets at diagonal corners of the car or in the center of one end of the car.

Carries: Argon, hydrogen, nitrogen, oxygen, LNG, and ethylene

NOTE: Cryogenic liquid tanks can also be enclosed inside a boxcar.

Table 3.7
Other Railroad Cars

Illustration

Descriptions

Pneumatically Unloaded Hopper Car

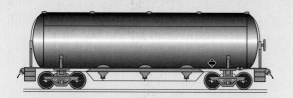

Covered Hopper Car

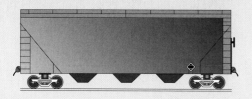

Open Top Hopper

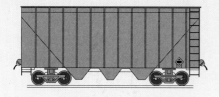

Miscellaneous: Boxcar

Miscellaneous: Gondola

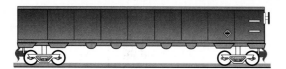

Pneumatically unloaded hopper car:

Carries: Dry caustic soda, ammonium nitrate fertilizer, other fine-powdered materials, plastic pellets, and flour

Covered hopper car:

Carries: Calcium carbide, cement, and grain

Open top hopper:

Carries: Coal, rock, gravel, and sand

Miscellaneous: boxcar:

Carries: All types of materials and finished goods

Miscellaneous: gondola:

Carries: Sand, rolled steel, and other materials that do not require protection from the weather

Continued

**Table 3.7 (continued)
Other Railroad Cars**

Illustration	Descriptions

Miscellaneous: Flat Bed Car with Intermodal Containers

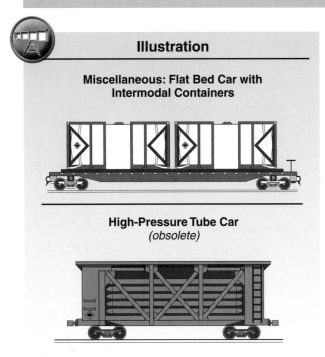

High-Pressure Tube Car
(obsolete)

Miscellaneous: flat bed car with intermodal containers:

Carries: 1 ton containers, intermodal containers (shown), large vehicles, and other commodities that do not require protection from the weather

High-pressure tube car *(obsolete)*:

Carried: Helium, hydrogen, methane, oxygen, and other compressed gases

cars (now obsolete). Descriptions of these tank cars are as follows:

- **Hopper cars** — *[NFPA 472: 5.2.1.1(A)(4)]* Tank pressures range from 20 to 80 psi (138 kPa to 552 kPa) {1.4 bar to 5.5 bar}. Types are as follows:

  — *Covered hopper cars* are often used to transport dry bulk materials such as grain, calcium carbide, and cement.

  — *Uncovered* (or *open top*) *hopper cars* may carry coal, sand, gravel, or rocks.

  — *Pneumatically unloaded hopper cars* are unloaded by air pressure and used to transport dry bulk loads such as ammonium nitrate fertilizer, dry caustic soda, plastic pellets, and cement.

- **Miscellaneous cars** — Boxcars are often used to carry other containers of hazardous materials. These cars can include mixed cargos of a variety of products in different types of packaging.

- **High-pressure tube car** —*[NFPA 472: 5.2.1.1(A)(2)]* This car is no longer in service, but was an open-frame car

containing seamless, uninsulated steel cylinders arranged horizontally and permanently attached to the car. The high-pressure cylinders were connected to a manifold at the end of the car. These cars were used to transport helium, hydrogen, oxygen, etc.

Cargo Tank Trucks
[NFPA 472: 5.2.1.1(C), 5.2.1.1(C)(1–7)]

Cargo tank trucks are also called *tank motor vehicles*, *tank trucks*, and *cargo tanks*. Cargo tank trucks are commonly used to transport hazardous materials via roadway. Most cargo tank trucks that haul hazardous materials are designed to meet government tank-safety specifications. These specifications set minimum tank construction material thicknesses, required safety features, and maximum allowable working pressures. The two specifications currently in use are the motor carrier (MC) standards and DOT/TC standards. Cargo tank trucks built to a given specification are designated using the *MC* or *DOT/TC* initials followed by a three-digit number identifying the specification (such as *MC 306* and *DOT/TC 406*).

Emergency responders can recognize these cargo tank trucks by their required construction features, fittings, attachments, and shapes.

Tanks not constructed to meet one of the common MC or DOT/TC specifications are commonly referred to as *nonspec* tanks. Nonspec tanks may haul hazardous materials if the tank was designed for a specific purpose and exempted from the DOT/TC requirements. Nonhazardous materials may be hauled in either nonspec cargo tank trucks or cargo tank trucks that meet a designated specification.

Cargo tank trucks are recognizable because they have construction features, fittings, attachments, or shapes characteristic of their uses. Even if first responders recognize one of the cargo tank trucks described in this section, the process of positive identification must proceed from placards to shipping papers or other formal sources of information. **Table 3.8** provides brief descriptions and illustrations of various cargo tank trucks.

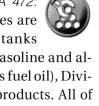

Nonpressure liquid tank. *[NFPA 472: 5.2.1.1(C)(1)]* Cargo tank truck types are MC 306 and DOT/TC 406. These tanks carry flammable liquids (such as gasoline and alcohol), combustible liquids (such as fuel oil), Division 6.1 poisons, and liquid food products. All of these materials are maintained at a vapor pressure less than 3 psi (21 kPa) {0.2 bar}. Distinguishing features of this tank include the following characteristics (**Figures 3.3 (below) and 3.4, p. 129**):

- Elliptical aluminum tank construction (old vehicles may be constructed of steel) (**Figure 3.5, p. 129**)

- Longitudinal rollover protection

- Valve assembly and unloading control box under tank

- Vapor-recovery system (piping and valves) on right side and rear (not all MC 306 trucks have a vapor-recovery system), manway assemblies, and vapor-recovery valves on top for each compartment

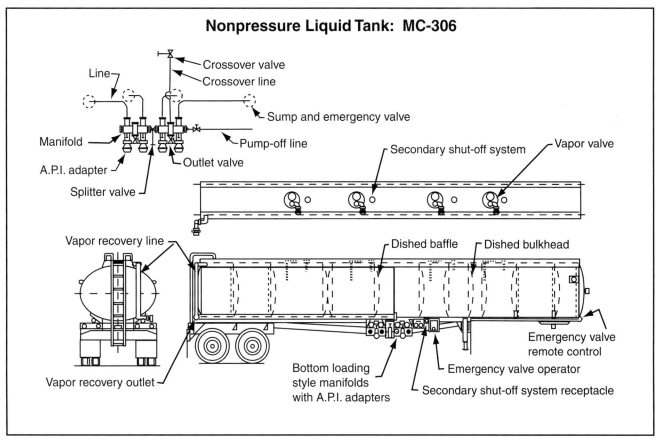

Figure 3.3 Nonpressure liquid tanks like the MC 306 and DOT/TC 406 are two of the more common cargo tank trucks, frequently carrying gasoline and other flammable and combustible liquids. *Reprinted with permission of the Hazardous Materials Response Handbook, 4th Edition, copyright © 2002, National Fire Protection Association, Quincy, MA.*

Table 3.8
Cargo Tank Trucks

  Illustration

 Descriptions

Nonpressure Liquid Tank (DOT/TC 406/MC 306)

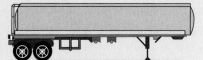

Nonpressure liquid tank (DOT/TC 406/MC 306):

- Pressure less than 3 psi (21 kPa)
- Typical maximum capacity: 9,000 gallons (34 069 L)
- New tanks made of aluminum
- Old tanks made of steel
- Oval shape
- Multiple compartments
- Recessed manways
- Rollover protection
- Bottom valves
- Vapor recovery likely

Carries: Gasoline, fuel oil, alcohol, other flammable/combustible liquids, other liquids, and liquid fuel products

Low-Pressure Chemical Tank (DOT/TC 407/MC 307)

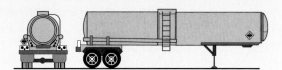

Low-pressure chemical tank (DOT/TC 407/MC 307):

- Pressure under 40 psi (172 kPa to 276 kPa)
- Typical maximum capacity: 7,000 gallons (26 498 L)
- Rubber lined or steel
- Single- or double-top manway
- Typically double shell
- Stiffening rings
- Rollover protection
- Single or multiple compartments
- Horseshoe or round shaped

Carries: Flammable liquids, combustible liquids, acids, caustics, and poisons

Corrosive Liquid Tank (MC 312)

Corrosive liquid tank (MC 312):

- Pressure less than 75 psi (517 kPa)
- Typical maximum capacity: 7,000 gallons (26 498 L)
- Rubber lined or steel
- Stiffening rings
- Rollover protection
- Rollover protection splash guard
- Top loading at rear or center
- Typically single compartment

Carries: Corrosive liquids (usually acids)

Continued

Table 3.8 (continued)
Cargo Tank Trucks

Illustration

Descriptions

High-Pressure Tank
(MC 331)

High-pressure tank (MC 331):

- Pressure above 100 psi (689 kPa)
- Typical maximum capacity: 11,500 gallons (43 532 L)
- Single steel compartment
- Noninsulated
- Bolted manway at front or rear
- Internal and rear outlet valves
- Typically painted white or other reflective color
- May be marked FLAMMABLE GAS and COMPRESSED GAS
- Round/dome-shaped ends

Carries: Pressurized gases and liquids, anhydrous ammonia, propane, butane, and other gases that have been liquefied under pressure

High-Pressure Bobtail Tank

High-pressure bobtail tank: Used for local delivery of liquefied petroleum gas and anhydrous ammonia

Cryogenic Liquid Tank
(MC 338)

Cryogenic liquid tank (MC 338):

- Pressure less than 22 psi (152 kPa)
- Well-insulated steel tank
- Possibly discharging vapor from relief valves
- Loading/unloading valves enclosed at rear
- Possibly marked REFRIGERATED LIQUID
- Round tank with flat ends and some type of cabinet at rear

Carries: Liquid oxygen, liquid nitrogen, liquid carbon dioxide, liquid hydrogen, and other gases that have been liquefied by lowering their temperatures

Continued

Table 3.8 (continued)
Cargo Tank Trucks

Illustration

Descriptions

Compressed-Gas/Tube Trailer

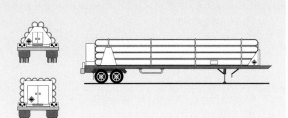

Compressed-gas/tube trailer:

- Pressure at 3,000 to 5,000 psi (20 684 kPa to 34 474 kPa) (gas only)
- Individual steel cylinders stacked and banded together
- Typically has over-pressure device for each cylinder
- Bolted manway at front or rear
- Valves at rear (protected)
- Manufacturer's name possibly marked on cylinders

Carries: Helium, hydrogen, methane, oxygen, and other gases

Dry Bulk Cargo Tank

 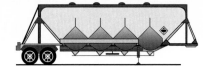

Dry bulk cargo tank:

- Pressure less than 22 psi (152 kPa)
- Typically not under pressure
- Top side manway
- Bottom valves
- Air-assisted loading and unloading
- Shapes vary, but has hoppers

Carries: Calcium carbide, oxidizers, corrosive solids, cement, plastic pellets, and fertilizers

---

- Possible permanent markings for compartment capacities, materials, or ownership that are locally identifiable

Low-pressure chemical tank. *[NFPA 472: 5.2.1.1(C)(2)]* Cargo tank truck types are MC 307 and DOT/TC 407. These tanks are designed to carry various chemicals with pressures not to exceed 40 psi (276 kPa) {2.76 bar} at 70°F (21°C). They may carry flammables, corrosives, or poisons. This tank can be recognized by the following characteristics **(Figures 3.6 and 3.7, p. 130):**

- Single- or double-top manway assembly protected by a flash box that also provides rollover protection

- Circumferential rollover protection at each end
- Single-outlet discharge piping at midship or rear
- Double shell with covered ring stiffeners (although some have external ring stiffeners)
- Fusible plugs, frangible disks, or vents (combination vacuum breakers and relief devices) outside the flash box on top of the tank
- Drain hose from the flash box down the side of the tank
- Rounded ends **(Figure 3.8, p. 131)**
- Permanent ownership markings that are locally identifiable

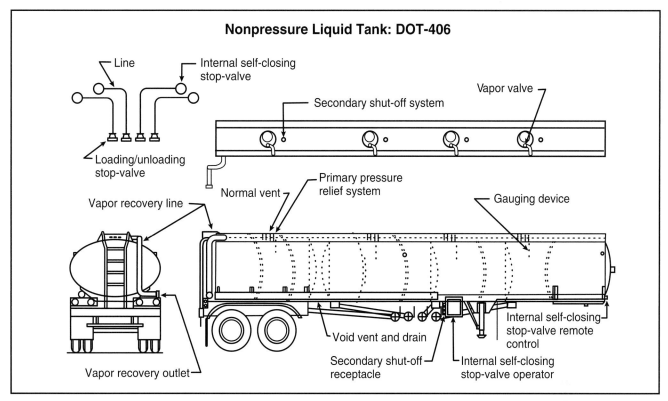

Nonpressure Liquid Tank: DOT-406

Line

Internal self-closing stop-valve

Secondary shut-off system

Vapor valve

Loading/unloading stop-valve

Vapor recovery line

Normal vent

Primary pressure relief system

Gauging device

Void vent and drain

Secondary shut-off receptacle

Internal self-closing stop-valve remote control

Internal self-closing stop-valve operator

Vapor recovery outlet

Figure 3.4 Nonpressure liquid tanks have vapor pressures less than 3 psi (21 kPa) {0.2 bar}. *Reprinted with permission of the Hazardous Materials Response Handbook, 4th Edition, copyright © 2002, National Fire Protection Association, Quincy, MA.*

Figure 3.5 Nonpressure liquid tanks can be recognized by their elliptical tank construction.

Corrosive liquid tank. *[NFPA 472: 5.2.1.1 (C)(3)]* Cargo tank truck types are MC 312 and DOT/TC 412. These tanks carry corrosive liquids, usually acids. Pressures may range up to 75 psi (517 kPa) {5.17 bar}. This tank can be identified by the following characteristics **(Figures 3.9 and 3.10, pp. 131–132):**

- Small-diameter round shape
- Exterior stiffening rings **(Figure 3.11, p. 132)**
- Rear or middle top-loading/unloading station with exterior piping extending to the bottom of the tank

- Splashguard serving as rollover protection around valve assembly
- Additional circumferential rollover protection at front of tank
- Flange-type rupture disk vent either inside or outside the splashguard
- Discoloration around loading/unloading area or area painted or coated with corrosive-resistant material
- Permanent ownership markings that are locally identifiable

High-pressure tank. *[NFPA 472: 5.2.1.1(C)(4)]* This cargo tank truck type is MC 331. This tank carries gases that have been liquefied by increasing the pressure and compressing them into the liquid state. Examples of materials that are carried include propane, butane, and anhydrous ammonia. A smaller (mini) version of this high-pressure tank is commonly called a *bobtail truck*. High-pressure tanks can be identified by the following characteristics **(Figure 3.12, p. 133):**

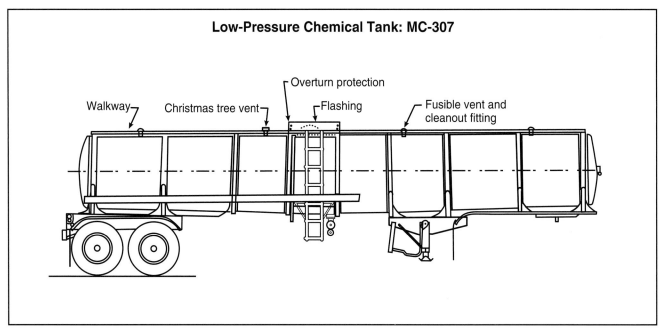

Low-Pressure Chemical Tank: MC-307

Walkway
Christmas tree vent
Overturn protection
Flashing
Fusible vent and cleanout fitting

Figure 3.6 Low-pressure chemical tanks like the MC 307 and DOT/TC 407 may carry flammables, corrosives, or poisons. *Reprinted with permission of the Hazardous Materials Response Handbook, 4th Edition, copyright © 2002, National Fire Protection Association, Quincy, MA.*

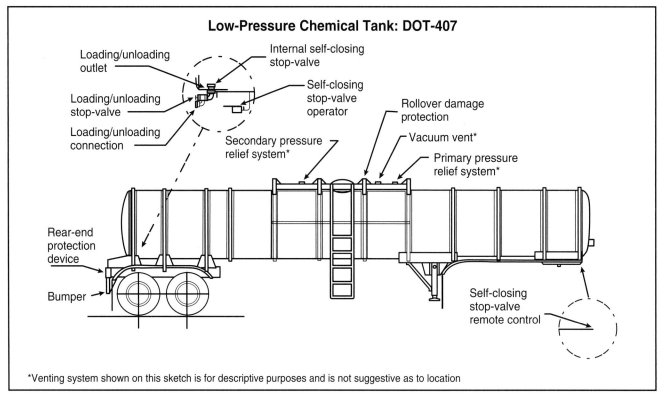

Low-Pressure Chemical Tank: DOT-407

Loading/unloading outlet
Internal self-closing stop-valve
Loading/unloading stop-valve
Self-closing stop-valve operator
Loading/unloading connection
Secondary pressure relief system*
Rollover damage protection
Vacuum vent*
Primary pressure relief system*
Rear-end protection device
Bumper
Self-closing stop-valve remote control

*Venting system shown on this sketch is for descriptive purposes and is not suggestive as to location

Figure 3.7 Low-pressure chemical tanks have pressures up to 40 psi (276 kPa) {2.76 bar} at 70°F (21°C). *Reprinted with permission of the Hazardous Materials Response Handbook, 4th Edition, copyright © 2002, National Fire Protection Association, Quincy, MA.*

Figure 3.8 Low-pressure chemical tanks can vary in their exterior look. Some, like the one pictured here, have a *horseshoe* shape. Others may be round. Some may have exterior ring stiffeners.

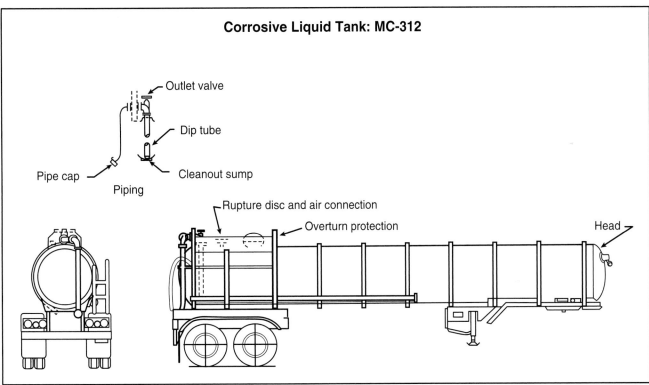

Corrosive Liquid Tank: MC-312

Outlet valve

Dip tube

Pipe cap

Cleanout sump

Piping

Rupture disc and air connection

Overturn protection

Head

Figure 3.9 As their name implies, corrosive liquid tanks like the MC 312 and DOT/TC 412 typically carry corrosive liquids, most commonly acids. *Reprinted with permission of the Hazardous Materials Response Handbook, 4ᵗʰ Edition, copyright © 2002, National Fire Protection Association, Quincy, MA.*

- Large hemispherical heads on both ends (**Figure 3.13, p. 133**)

- Bolted manway at the rear

- Guard cage around the bottom loading/ unloading piping

- Uninsulated tanks, single-shell vessels usually painted white

- Permanent markings such as FLAMMABLE GAS, COMPRESSED GAS, or identifiable manufacturer or distributor names

Cryogenic liquid tank. *[NFPA 472: 5.2.1.1(C)(5)]* This cargo tank truck type is MC 338. This tank carries gases that have been liquefied by temperature reduction. Typical materials that are carried include liquid oxygen (LOX), nitrogen, hydrogen, argon, and carbon dioxide. The tank can be identified by the following characteristics (**Figure 3.14, p. 133**):

- Large and bulky double shelling and heavy insulation

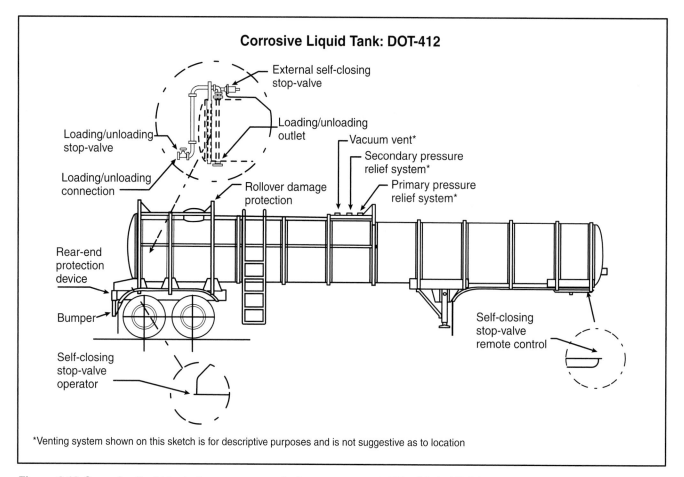

Corrosive Liquid Tank: DOT-412

External self-closing stop-valve

Loading/unloading outlet

Vacuum vent*

Secondary pressure relief system*

Primary pressure relief system*

Loading/unloading stop-valve

Loading/unloading connection

Rollover damage protection

Rear-end protection device

Bumper

Self-closing stop-valve remote control

Self-closing stop-valve operator

*Venting system shown on this sketch is for descriptive purposes and is not suggestive as to location

Figure 3.10 Corrosive liquid tanks have pressures that may range up to 75 psi (517 kPa) {5.17 bar}. *Reprinted with permission of the Hazardous Materials Response Handbook, 4th Edition, copyright © 2002, National Fire Protection Association, Quincy, MA.*

Figure 3.11 Corrosive liquid tanks can be recognized by their round, small-diameter tank construction and exterior stiffening rings.

- Ends that are basically flat
- Loading/unloading station attached either at the rear or in front of the rear dual wheels
- Permanent markings such as *REFRIGERATED LIQUID* or an identifiable manufacturer name

Dry bulk cargo tank. *[NFPA 472: 5.2.1.1(C)(6)]* This vehicle carries various types of hazardous materials in dry bulk and slurry forms that can burn and release toxic products of combustion. This tank can be identified by the following characteristics (**Figure 3.15, p. 133**):

- Large, sloping, *V*-shaped bottom-unloading compartments
- Rear-mounted, auxiliary-engine-powered compressor or tractor-mounted power-take-off air compressor
- Exterior loading and bottom unloading pipes
- Top manway assemblies

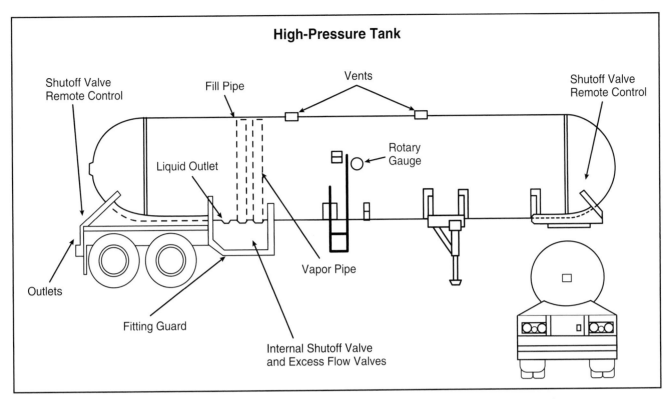

High-Pressure Tank

Shutoff Valve Remote Control

Fill Pipe

Vents

Shutoff Valve Remote Control

Liquid Outlet

Rotary Gauge

Outlets

Vapor Pipe

Fitting Guard

Internal Shutoff Valve and Excess Flow Valves

Figure 3.12 High-pressure tanks carry liquefied gases such as propane, butane, and anhydrous ammonia.

Figure 3.13 High-pressure tanks can be recognized by their large, round tanks with large hemispherical heads on both ends.

Figure 3.15 Dry bulk cargo tanks carry hazardous materials in dry bulk and slurry forms. They are most easily recognized by their side profiles because of large, sloping, *V*-shaped bottom-unloading compartments.

Figure 3.14 Cryogenic liquid tanks carry materials such as liquid oxygen (LOX), nitrogen, hydrogen, argon, and carbon dioxide. They can be recognized by their flat ends and rear loading/unloading station. These tanks are heavily insulated.

Figure 3.16 Compressed-gas tube trailers carry compressed gases rather than liquefied gases. Materials carried include air, argon, helium, hydrogen, nitrogen, oxygen, and refrigerant gases. *Courtesy of Rich Mahaney.*

Compressed-gas tube trailer. *[NFPA 472: 5.2.1.1(C)(7)]* This trailer carries compressed gases; it does *not* carry liquefied gases. The materials that are carried include air, argon, helium, hydrogen, nitrogen, oxygen, and refrigerant gases. This tank can be identified by the following characteristics:

- Several horizontal tubes on a trailer or intermodal unit (**Figure 3.16**)

- Manifold enclosed at the rear

- Permanent markings for the material or ownership that is locally identifiable

Intermodal Containers

[NFPA 472: 5.2.1.1(B), 5.2.1(B)(1)(a) and (b), 5.2.1(B)(2), 5.2.1.1(B)(3)(a) and (b)]
An *intermodal container* is a freight container that is used interchangeably in multiple modes of transport such as rail, highway, and ship (**Figure 3.17***).* The various types of intermodal containers can be divided into the following two main categories:

- ***Freight containers*** — Transport a wide range of products, from foodstuffs to dry goods. They come in a variety of types and sizes, most commonly in 20, 40, 48, and 53-foot (6 m, 12 m, 15 m, and 16 m) lengths. Several common types of freight containers are as follows (**Figure 3.18**):

  — Dry van intermodal containers (sometimes called *box containers*)

  — Refrigerated intermodal containers (also called *reefers*)

Figure 3.17 Intermodal containers can be transported by rail, highway, or ship. *Courtesy of Matt Hannes.*

  — Open top intermodal containers

  — Flat intermodal containers of various sorts

- ***Tank containers*** — Also called *intermodal tanks.* Three general classifications of intermodal tank containers are as follows:

  — Nonpressure intermodal tanks (also called *low-pressure intermodal tanks*)

  — Pressure intermodal tanks

  — Specialized intermodal tanks such as cryogenic intermodal tanks and tube modules

Some intermodal freight containers may contain hazardous materials. Others may contain mixed loads that include both hazardous and nonhazardous materials. With many freight containers, the shape of the container alone will not tell first responders whether it contains hazardous materials. Identification will have to be made from the intermodal container markings or shipping papers (see International Intermodal Container/Tank Markings section under Clue 3 and Shipping Papers section under Clue 5).

Intermodal tank containers generally have a cylinder enclosed at both ends. First responders may also see tube modules, cryogenic tanks, compartmentalized tanks, or other shapes. **Table 3.9, p. 136,** provides examples of the most common types of intermodal tanks. The tank container is placed in frames to protect it and provide for stacking, lifting, and securing. The two types of basic frames are the box type (with the tank enclosed in a cage) and beam type (with frame

Intermodal Freight Containers

Dry Van (box containers)

Refrigerated (reefers)

Open Top

Flat

Figure 3.18 Freight containers come in a variety of different types including dry van containers (sometimes called *box containers*), refrigerated containers (also called *reefers*), open top containers, and flat containers.

structures only at the ends of the tank) **(Figures 3.19 a and b)**. The capacities of these containers ordinarily do not exceed 6,340 gallons (24 000 L) **(Table 3.10, p. 137)**.

Nonpressure intermodal tank. *[NFPA 472: 5.2.1.1(B)(1), 5.2.1.1(B)(1)(a), 5.2.1.1(B)(1)(2)]* This tank is the most common intermodal tank used in transportation. Even though they are often called *nonpressure*, these tanks may have pressures as high as 100 psi (689 kPa) {6.9 bar}. For this reason, they are sometimes referred to as *low-pressure tanks*. They are also called *intermodal portable tanks* or *IM portable tanks*. The two common groups of nonpressure/low-pressure intermodal tank containers are as follows:

Figure 3.19a Box-type intermodal containers have the tank enclosed in a cage. *Courtesy of Gary Hannes.*

Figure 3.19b Beam-type intermodal containers have tanks supported by frame structures located only at the ends. *Courtesy of Matt Hannes.*

Table 3.9
Examples of Intermodal Tanks

Illustration	Descriptions
Nonpressure Intermodal Tank 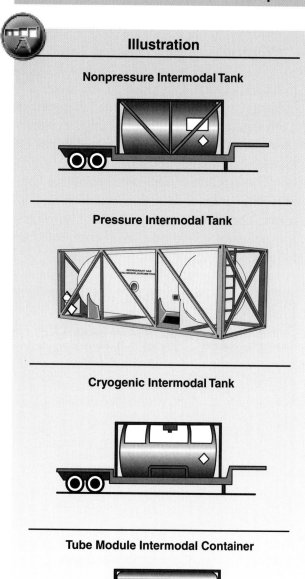	**Nonpressure intermodal tank:** • IM-101: 25.4 to 100 psi (175 kPa to 689 kPa) • IM-102: 14.5 to 25.4 psi (100 kPa to 175 kPa) **Contents:** Liquids or solids (both hazardous and nonhazardous)
Pressure Intermodal Tank	**Pressure intermodal tank:** 100 to 500 psi (689 kPa to 3 447 kPa) **Contents:** Liquefied gases, liquefied petroleum gas, anhydrous ammonia, and other liquids
Cryogenic Intermodal Tank	**Cryogenic intermodal tank:** **Contents:** Refrigerated liquid gases, argon, oxygen, helium
Tube Module Intermodal Container	**Tube module intermodal container:** **Contents:** Gases in high-pressure cylinders (3,000 or 5,000 psi [20 684 kPa or 34 474 kPa]) mounted in the frame

• *IM 101 portable tanks* — Built to withstand a working pressure of 25.4 to 100 psi (175 kPa to 689 kPa) {1.75 bar to 6.9 bar}. They transport both hazardous and nonhazardous materials. Internationally, they are called *International Maritime Organization (IMO) Type 1 tank containers* (**Figure 3.20, p. 137**).

• *IM 102 portable tanks* — Designed to handle maximum allowable working pressures of 14.5 to 25.4 psi (100 kPa to 175 kPa) {1 to 1.75 bar}. They transport materials such as alcohols, pesticides, resins, industrial solvents, and flammables with flash points between 32 and 140°F (0°C to 60°C). Most commonly, they transport

Table 3.10
Intermodal Tank Container Descriptions

Specification	Materials Transported	Capacity	Design Pressure
IM 101 Portable Tank	Hazardous and nonhazardous materials, including toxics, corrosives, and flammables with flash points below 32°F (0°C)	Normally range from 5,000 to 6,300 gallons (18 927 to 23 848 L)	25.4 to 100 psi (175 to 689 kPa) {1.75 to 6.89 bar}
IM 102 Portable Tank	Whiskey, alcohols, some corrosives, pesticides, insecticides, resins, industrial solvents, and flammables with flash points ranging from 32 to 140°F (0 to 60°C)	Normally range from 5,000 to 6,300 gallons (18 927 to 23 848 L)	14.5 to 25.4 psi (100 to 175 kPa) {1 to 1.75 bar}
Spec. 51 Portable Tank	Liquefied gases such as LPG, anhydrous ammonia, high vapor pressure flammable liquids, pyrophoric liquids (such as aluminum alkyls), and other highly regulated materials	Normally range from 4,500 to 5,500 gallons (17 034 to 0 820 L)	100 to 500 psi (689 to 3 447 kPa) {6.89 to 34.5 bar}

Figure 3.20 Though called nonpressure intermodal tanks, IM 101 portable tanks may have pressures from 25.4 to 100 psi (175 kPa to 689 kPa) {1.75 bar to 6.9 bar}.

Figure 3.21 IM 102 portable tanks have pressures from 14.5 to 25.4 psi (100 kPa to 175 kPa) {1 bar to 1.75 bar} (less than IM 101s). It is difficult to tell the difference between IM 101 and IM 102 tanks without looking at specification markings. *Courtesy of Rich Mahaney.*

nonregulated materials (those not specifically covered by regulations) such as food commodities. Internationally, they are called *IMO Type 2 tank containers* (**Figure 3.21**).

Pressure intermodal tank. *[NFPA 472: 5.2.1.1(B)(2)]* A pressure intermodal tank container is less common in transport. It is designed for working pressures of 100 to 500 psi (689 kPa to 3 447 kPa) {6.9 to 34.5 bar} and usually transports liquefied gases under pressure. DOT classifies this tank as *Spec. 51,* while internationally it is known as an *IMO Type 5 tank container* (**Figure 3.22**).

Figure 3.22 Spec. 51 tanks, internationally known as IMO Type 5 tank containers, usually transport liquefied gases under pressure. *Courtesy of Rich Mahaney.*

Specialized intermodal tank or container. *[NFPA 472: 5.2.1.1(B)(3), 5.2.1.1(B)(3)(a), 5.2.1.1(B)(3)(b)]* There are several types of specialized intermodal tank containers. Cryogenic liquid tank containers carry refrigerated liquid gases, argon, oxygen, and helium. Cryogenic-type containers are built to IMO Type 7 specifications **(Figure 3.23)**. The tube module transports gases in high-pressure cylinders (3,000 to 5,000 psi [20 684 kPa to 34 474 kPa] {207 bar to 345 bar}). Dry bulk intermodal containers carry materials such as fertilizer and cement **(Figure 3.24)**.

Figure 3.23 Cryogenic liquid tank containers carry refrigerated liquid gases and are built to IMO Type 7 specifications. *Courtesy of Rich Mahaney.*

Figure 3.24 Dry bulk intermodal containers may carry hazardous materials such as pesticides. *Courtesy of Rich Mahaney.*

Vessel Cargo Carriers

It is estimated that over 90 percent of the world's cargo is transported by marine vessels, and the amount of cargo transported by vessels is expected to increase as much as threefold by 2010. Hazardous materials incidents involving vessels can be minor (such as a small spill that occurs at a port during loading or unloading) or major such as a spill contaminating miles (kilometers) of river or coastline waters or a large spill inside a ship. Statistics on oil spills show that most spills result from routine operations such as loading and unloading, which normally occur in ports or at oil/chemical terminals. The majority of these operational spills are small, with some 91 percent involving quantities less than 7 tons (7.1 tonnes). First responders need to be aware of vessel types and cargos that are likely to contain hazardous materials.

Tanker. A vessel that exclusively carries liquid products in bulk is generally known as *tanker* or *tank vessel* **(Figure 3.25)**. Modern tankers are capable of transporting very large quantities of liquid products (see sidebar, p. 141). Tankers often carry a variety of products in segregated tanks. Tankers can be divided into the following three general categories:

- *Petroleum carriers* — Transport crude or finished petroleum products. They range in size from 200-foot (61 m), 15,000-barrel coastal tankers of 2,000 deadweight tons to 1,200-foot (366 m), 3,680,000-barrel ultra-large crude carriers of 480,000 deadweight tons. *Details:*

  — When entering the U.S. and Canada, the operator of any tank vessel carrying petroleum products is required by law to maintain vessel emergency response plans that identify and ensure the availability of both a salvage company with expertise and equipment and a company with pollution incident response capabilities in the area(s) in which the vessel operates.

  — The availability of preplanned resources should not be overlooked during a marine fire-fighting or emergency response.

- *Chemical carriers* — Transport multiple commodities; these carriers are sometimes nicknamed *floating drugstores* **(Figure 3.26)**. They may carry oils, solvents, gasoline, sulfur, and other commodities (many classified as hazardous materials) in 30 to 58 separate tanks. Each tank usually has its own pump (and piping), so the deck of a chemical carrier typically has a

Figure 3.25 Modern tankers transport very large quantities of liquid products such as crude oil or finished petroleum products. *Courtesy of Edward Feather Photography.*

Figure 3.26 Chemical carriers typically have mazes of piping and may carry oils, solvents, gasoline, sulfur, and other hazardous materials in 30 to 58 separate tanks. *Courtesy of Captain John F. Lewis.*

maze of piping. About 3,000 chemical carriers are in operation worldwide, and they have the lowest average annual loss rate of all cargo vessel types.

///////////////////////
CAUTION
Chemical carriers are not required to carry placards. The only way to positively identify a chemical cargo is to ask the master or mate (captain or first officer) or obtain the cargo plan that identifies where each commodity is stowed on the vessel.

• *Liquefied flammable gas carriers* — Transport LNG and liquefied petroleum gas (LPG) (propane and butane for example), and generally use large insulated spherical tanks for product storage **(Figures 3.27 a and b).** However, other configurations of gas carriers look very similar to ordinary tankers. The tanks are isolated within the vessel's hull by cofferdams (empty spaces between compartments) designed to contain low-volume leakage from the tanks. LPG carriers are usually identified by a large number of pressure vessels **(Figures 3.28 a and b).** Cargo piping is located above the main deck so that any piping leaks vent to the atmosphere rather than inside the vessel. *Details:*

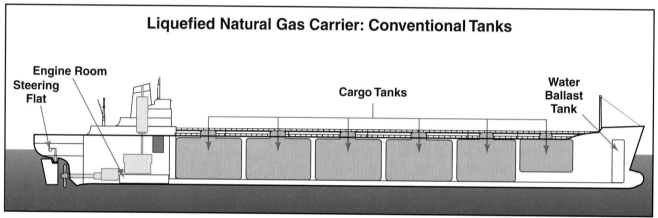

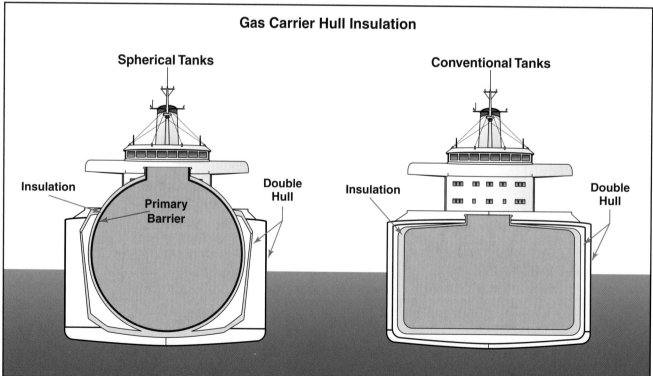

Figures 3.27 a and b Liquefied flammable gas carriers: (a) Conventional tanks *(top)*. (b) Gas carrier hull insulation for spherical and conventional tanks *(bottom)*.

Barge

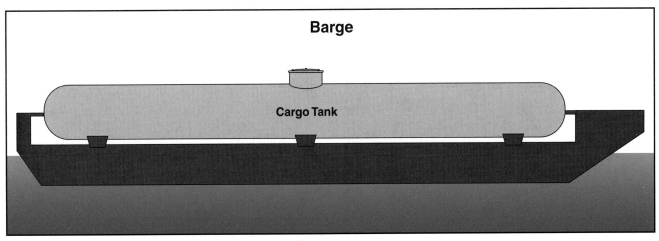

Cargo Tank

Liquefied Petroleum Gas Carrier

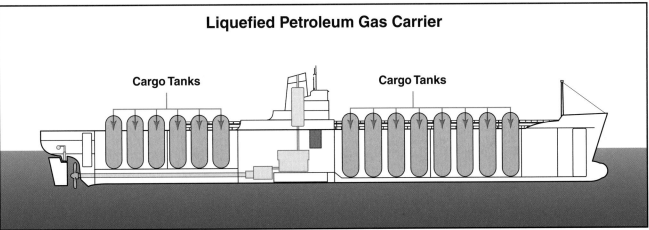

Cargo Tanks

Cargo Tanks

Figures 3.28 a and b LPG carriers are usually identified by a large number of pressure vessels. (a) Tanks on a barge *(top)*. (b) Tanks on a vessel *(bottom)*.

— In U.S. ports that handle LNG and LPG carriers, the Captain of the Port is required to maintain LNG/LPG vessel management and emergency contingency plans.

— In Canada, each port handling hazardous shipments is required to conduct an evaluation that defines all threats to the port and environment and prepare contingency plans to manage emergencies. These plans are consulted for area-specific guidance in handling emergencies involving these vessels.

Cargo vessel. The size of commercial cargo vessels can be overwhelming. Cargo vessels are typically 500 to 900 feet (152 m to 274 m) in length, 50 to 130 feet (15 m to 40 m) in beam, and have hold depths from 40 to 60 feet (12 m to 18 m). Cargo is shipped in the following four vessel types:

● *Bulk carrier* — Can be either liquid bulk (tanker) or dry bulk carrier **(Figure 3.29, p. 142).**

Tanker Capacity

A highway tank truck typically carries 45 to 200 barrels of product. A railway tank car typically carries 100 to 1,000 barrels of product. During the 1940s, standard tanker capacity was about 120,000 barrels of product. The first postwar (World War II) supertankers were limited in draft (distance between the water surface and lowest point of a vessel) by the depth of the Suez Canal and had a capacity of approximately 200,000 barrels of product.

In 1956, the Suez Canal was closed by military action. Tankers designed to sail around the Cape of Good Hope were built to hold capacities of approximately 1,800,000 barrels and were known as *very large crude carriers (VLCCs). Ultra-large crude carriers (ULCCs)* have capacities between 2,000,000 and 3,500,000 barrels of product. They operate between offshore terminals in deep water and cannot enter most ports when loaded because of their great drafts.

Figure 3.29 The bulk carrier *Paul R. Tregurtha* carries 75,000 tons (76 200 t) of iron ore. Bulk carriers can be either liquid bulk (tanker) or dry bulk. *Courtesy of Howard Chatterton.*

— Dry bulk vessels carry products such as coal, wood chips, grain, iron ore, sand, gravel, salt, grain, and fertilizers. The cargo is loaded directly into a hold without packaging, much like liquid in a tanker. Some of these cargoes generate dust (grain, for example), creating the possibility of an explosion.

— The two primary liquid bulk cargoes are chemicals (that may or may not be flammable) and liquid hydrocarbons. Liquid hydrocarbons carried in bulk include crude oils and refined oil products such as diesel fuel, gasoline, lubricating oils, and kerosene. These products vary widely in their characteristics, and some can be very volatile. The hazards are similar to those found at any petrochemical refinery or bulk storage facility.

• *Break bulk carrier* — Has large holds to accommodate a wide range of products such as vehicles, pallets of metal bars, liquids in drums, or items in bags, boxes, and crates **(Figure 3.30)**.

• *Container vessel* — Carries cargo in standard containers that measure 8 feet (2.4 m) wide with varying heights and lengths. Container vessels may transport intermodal tanks (each enclosed in an open framework with standard container-size dimensions). Several vessel capacities and hazardous considerations to take into account are as follows:

— The capacity of a container vessel is specified in 20-foot (6 m) equivalent units or TEUs. A 1,000-TEU container vessel can carry 1,000

Figure 3.30 Break bulk carriers have large holds to accommodate a wide range of products such as liquids in drums, crates, or pallets of bags and boxes. Pictured here are billets of aluminum. *Courtesy of Howard Chatterton.*

20-foot (6 m) containers, 500 40-foot (12 m) containers, or any mix of containers adding up to 1,000 TEUs. A large container vessel has the capacity of about 6,600 TEUs, stacked as many as 13 containers high **(Figure 3.31)**. In 1999 the newest container vessels had capacities of 8,500 TEUs; in 2001 the capacities had increased to 9,800 TEUs.

— Containers may show little, if any, indication of the product inside. Some containers have self-contained refrigeration units; some may carry liquids in flexible bladders or even vehicles. Any container or the hold in which a container is placed may have an oxygen-deficient atmosphere or a hazardous atmosphere due to the cargo within the container or leakage of a product from the container.

Roll-on/roll-off vessel — Has large stern and side ramp structures that are lowered to allow vehicles to be driven on and off the vessel **(Figure 3.32).** This vessel type can be visualized as a floating, moving, multilevel parking garage.

Barge. *Barges* are typically box-shaped, flat-decked vessels used for transporting cargo. Usually they are not self-propelled but are moved by towing or pushing vessels. Virtually anything can be on a barge, and they have more kinds of uses than any other vessel. Some barges are configured as floating barracks for military or construction crews; some are designed as bulk oil and chemical tankers. Other barges carry LNG in cylinders that may not be visible until a person is aboard. Barges may serve as floating warehouses with hazardous goods, vehicles, or rail cars inside.

Unit Loading Devices

Unit loading devices (ULDs) are containers and aircraft pallets used to consolidate air cargo into a single, transportable unit **(Figure 3.33, p. 144).** ULDs are designed and shaped to fit into the various decks and compartments of airplanes (com-

Figure 3.31 The *Evergreen* is a container vessel. Container vessels may transport intermodal tanks. *Courtesy of Howard Chatterton.*

Figure 3.32 Roll-on/roll-off vessels are characterized by large stern and side ramp structures that are lowered to allow vehicles to be driven on and off the vessel. *Courtesy of Howard Chatterton.*

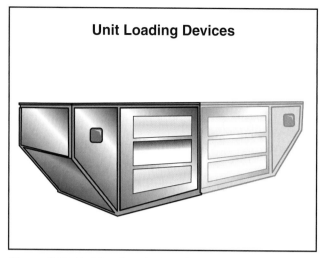

Figure 3.33 Unit loading devices (ULDs) are used to consolidate air cargo into a single, transportable unit. ULDs containing hazardous materials must be appropriately placarded and labeled.

Figure 3.34 Flexible intermediate bulk containers come in a variety of styles and carry both solid materials and fluids. *Courtesy of Howard Chatterton.*

mercial cargo planes), and in some cases they may be stacked. Hazardous materials may be shipped in ULDs provided they are in accordance with U.S. Federal Aviation Administration (FAA) and DOT regulations. ULDs containing hazardous materials are required to be labeled or placarded in accordance with Title 49 (Transportation) *CFR* 172.512 (a) and (b) (see Clue 3: Transportation Placards, Labels, and Markings).

Intermediate Bulk Containers

According to the U.S. DOT, an *intermediate bulk container (IBC)* is either a rigid or flexible portable packaging (other than a cylinder or portable tank) designed for mechanical handling. Design standards for IBCs in the U.S., Canada, and Mexico are based on *United Nations Recommendations on the Transportation of Dangerous Goods (UN Recommendations)*. The maximum capacity of an IBC is not more than three 3 cubic meters (3,000 L, 793 gal, or 106 ft³). The minimum capacity is not less than 0.45 cubic meters (450 L, 119 gal, or 15.9 ft³) or a maximum net mass of not less than 400 kilograms (882 lbs).

IBCs are divided into two types: flexible intermediate bulk containers (FIBCs) and rigid intermediate bulk containers (RIBCs). Both types are often called *totes,* although correctly, only FIBCs are truly totes. IBCs are authorized to transport a wide variety of materials and hazard classes:

- Aviation fuel (turbine engine)
- Gasoline
- Hydrochloric acid
- Methanol
- Toluene
- Corrosive liquids
- Solid materials in powder, flake, or granular forms

Flexible intermediate bulk container. FIBCs are sometimes called *bulk bags, bulk sacks, supersacks, big bags, tote bags,* or *totes.* They are flexible, collapsible bags or sacks that are used to carry both solid materials and fluids **(Figure 3.34)**. The designs of FIBCs are as varied as the products they carry. Often the bags used to transport wet or hazardous materials are lined with polypropylene or some other high-strength fabric. Others may be constructed of multiwall paper or other textiles. A common-sized supersack can carry the equivalent of four to five 55-gallon (208 L) drums and (depending on design and the material inside) be stacked one on top of another. Sometimes FIBCs are transported inside a rigid exterior container made of corrugated board or wood.

Rigid intermediate bulk container. RIBCs are typically made of steel, aluminum, wood, fiberboard, or plastic, and they are often designed to be stacked **(Figures 3.35 a and b)**. RIBCs can contain both solid materials and liquids. Some

Rigid Intermediate Bulk Containers

Figure 3.36 Metal bins such as those shown are also RIBCs. *Courtesy of Rich Mahaney.*

Figures 3.35 a and b Rigid intermediate bulk containers (RIBCs) come in a variety of shapes, sizes, and styles, and they are often designed to be stacked. RIBCs can contain (a) solid materials *(top)* and (b) liquids *(bottom)*. *Photo Courtesy of Rich Mahaney.*

Figure 3.37 Ton containers may have convex or concave ends and have two valves in the center of one end, one above the other. Ton containers often contain chlorine, but they may also contain other products such as anhydrous ammonia and other refrigerant gases. *Courtesy of Rich Mahaney.*

liquid containers may look like smaller versions of intermodal nonpressure tanks with metal or plastic tanks inside rectangular box frames. Other RIBCs may be large, square or rectangular boxes or bins **(Figure 3.36).** Rigid portable tanks may be used to carry liquids, fertilizers, solvents, and other chemicals, and they may have capacities up to 400 gallons (1 514 L) and pressures up to 100 psi (689 kPa) {6.9 bar}.

Ton Containers

Ton containers are tanks that have capacities of 1 short ton or approximately 2,000 pounds (907

kg or 0.9 tonne). Typically stored on their sides, the ends (heads) of the containers are convex or concave and have two valves in the center of one end, one above the other **(Figure 3.37).** One valve connects to a tube going into the liquid space; the other valve connects to a tube going into the vapor space above. They also have pressure-relief devices (fusible plugs) in case of fire or exposure to elevated temperatures. Ton containers commonly contain chlorine and are often found at water treatment plants, commercial swimming pools, etc. Ton containers may also contain other products such as sulphur dioxide, anhydrous ammonia, or Freon® refrigerant.

Leaks from ton containers require special equipment (and Technician-Level training) to patch, which is true for most of the containers in this chapter. Always ensure responders and civilians are evacuated to a safe distance to avoid the vapor cloud that escapes from these containers. Structural fire-fighting gear does not provide adequate protection against the hazardous materials commonly stored in ton containers.

Storage Bladders

On rare occasions, first responders may encounter flexible storage bladders (sometimes called *flexible tanks* or *pillow-type bladders*) **(Figure 3.38)**. Flexible storage bladders may contain oil, chemicals, fuels, or other liquids (such as water), and they vary in size from a capacity of a few gallons (liters) to 100,000 gallons (378 540 liters). Some are designed to float and can be towed through water while others are designed to be transported on flatbed tractor-trailers.

Nonbulk Packaging

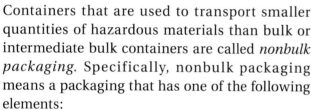

[NFPA 472: 5.2.1.1(E)]

Containers that are used to transport smaller quantities of hazardous materials than bulk or intermediate bulk containers are called *nonbulk packaging*. Specifically, nonbulk packaging means a packaging that has one of the following elements:

- Maximum capacity of 119 gallons (450 L) or less as a receptacle for a liquid

- Maximum net mass of 882 pounds (400 kg) or less and a maximum capacity of 119 gallons (450 L) or less as a receptacle for a solid

- Water capacity of less than 1,001 pounds (454 kg) as a receptacle for a gas

The number of transportation-related nonbulk packaging incidents has increased almost every year since 1992. The majority of these incidents occurred during highway transport. **Table 3.11** lists the various containers that are used to transport hazardous materials in the various hazard classes. Common types of nonbulk packaging include the following types of containers:

- Bags
- Carboys and jerricans
- Cylinders
- Drums
- Radioactive containers
- Others (including boxes, bottles, and composite packages)

Combination packaging (a combination of packaging for transport purposes, consisting of one or more inner packagings secured in a nonbulk outer packaging) is also categorized as nonbulk packaging. Infectious substances are packaged in combination packaging **(Figure 3.39, p. 148)**. Combination packages do not include *composite packages* (packaging consisting of an outer packaging and an inner receptacle, constructed so

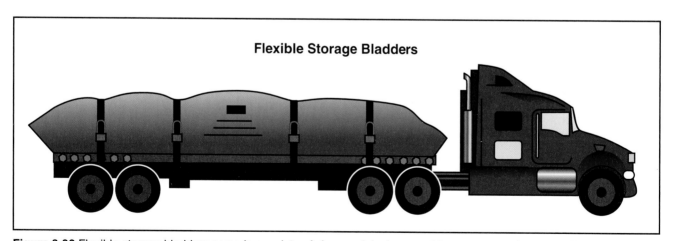

Figure 3.38 Flexible storage bladders come in a variety of sizes and designs, and they may contain water, oil, chemicals, fuels, or other liquids.

Table 3.11
Hazard Classes of Shipping Container Contents

Shipping Container	Hazard Class										
	Explosive	Compressed Gas	Flammable and Combustible Liquid	Flammable Solid	Oxidizer	Organic Peroxide	Poisonous Material	Etiologic Agent	Radioactive Material	Corrosive Material	Other Regulated Material
Pail			X	X	X	X	X				
Glass carboy in plywood drum or box										X	
Fiberboard box**	X		X	X	X	X		X	X	X	X
Wooden box**	X		X	X	X	X	X	X	X	X	X
Mailing tubes***	X			X	X	X	X	X			
Wooden barrel											X
Bag	X			X	X	X	X				X
Cylinder		X	X				X		X	X	
Fiberboard drum	X		X	X	X	X	X		X	X	
Metal drum	X		X	X	X	X	X		X	X	X
Metal keg	X									X	
Polystryrene case**										X	
Lead-shielded container**									X		
Portable tank		X	X		X	X	X			X	
Tank truck	X	X	X		X	X*	X			X	X
Tank car	X	X	X	X	X		X			X	X
Tanker (marine)		X	X		X		X			X	
Barge		X	X	X	X		X			X	

* Under exemption from U.S. Department of Transportation.
** Indicates outside package for inside containers.
*** Indicates shape of package only. They are *not* used to ship hazardous materials through the mail.

Packaging

Infectious Substances Packaging
(49 *CFR* 173.196)

- Watertight primary & secondary inner containers
- Primary *or* secondary inner containers capable of withstanding internal pressure of 95 kPa at -40°F to 131°F
- Outer packaging - smallest external dimension at least 100 mm (3.9 in)
- Capable of passing:
  - 9 m (30 ft) drop test
  - Penetration test
  - Vibration standard

A typical infectious substance packaging configuration (closures not shown):

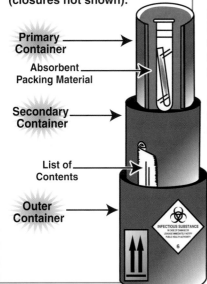

Primary Container
Absorbent Packing Material
Secondary Container
List of Contents
Outer Container

Exceptions
(49 *CFR* 173.134)

Regulated Medical Waste transported by a private or contract carrier is excepted from packaging and labeling requirements if:

- Packaged in rigid, non-bulk packagings conforming to general packaging requirements of §§ 173.24 and 173.24a, and

- Packaged and marked with the "BIOHAZARD" marking in accordance with the Department of Labor regulations in 29 *CFR* 1910.1030.

Diagnostic specimens and Biological products are not subject to the HMR, except when transported as regulated medical waste.

Certain wastes may not be subject to the HMR (see 49 *CFR* 173.134).

Regulated Medical Waste Packaging
(49 *CFR* 173.197)

- Nonbulk max capacity = 450 L (119) gal) or less
- Nonbulk max net mass = 400 kg (882 lbs) or less
- Meets UN packing Group II
- Rigid
- Leak resistant
- Impervious to moisture
- Of sufficient strength to prevent tearing or bursting under normal conditions of use and handling
- Sealed to prevent leakage during transport
- Puncture resistant for sharps
- Break-resistant
- Tightly lidded or stoppered for fluids in quantities greater than 20 cc

A typical regulated medical waste packaging configuration:

Figure 3.39 Infectious substances are packaged in combination packaging consisting of one or more inner packagings secured in a nonbulk outer packaging. *Courtesy of the U.S. Department of Transportation (DOT).*

that the inner receptacle and the outer packaging form an integral packaging). See Other Types section for more information.

Bags
[NFPA 472: 5.2.1.1(E)(1)]

A *bag* is a flexible packaging made of paper, plastic film, textiles, woven material, or other similar materials (**Figure 3.40**). Bags may transport explosives, flammable solids, oxidizers, organic peroxides, fertilizers, pesticides, and other regulated materials. They can be sealed in a variety of ways: ties, stitching, gluing, heat sealing, and crimping with metal. Typically, bags are stored and transported on pallets.

Figure 3.40 Bags may contain a variety of solid hazardous materials including explosives, oxidizers, organic peroxides, and toxic products such as pesticides.

Carboys and Jerricans
[NFPA 472: 5.2.1.1(E)(2)]

A *carboy* is a large glass or plastic bottle encased in a basket or box, primarily used to store and transport corrosive liquids, although its use has expanded to nonhazardous materials (such as water) as well. The outer packaging may be made of such materials as polystyrene or wood, and carboys may be round or rectangular. Their capacities may exceed 20 gallons (76 L), but 5-gallon (19 L) containers are more common.

Jerrican is another name for a rectangular plastic carboy and is the term used in UN regulations. Some people differentiate between carboys and jerricans, claiming that jerricans are rectangular metal containers typically transporting flammable and combustible liquids, whereas carboys transport corrosives **(Figure 3.41)**.

Cylinders
[NFPA 472: 5.2.1.1(E)(3)]

A *cylinder* is a pressure vessel designed for pressures higher than 40 psi (276 kPa) {2.76 bar} and has a circular cross section, but it does not include any of the containers, tanks, or vessels discussed in previous sections. Cylinders are used to store, transport, and dispense large volumes of gaseous materials. Compressed-gas cylinders range in size from small lecture bottles (small bottles used for classroom demonstrations) to large cylinders and have varying pressures **(Figure 3.42)**.

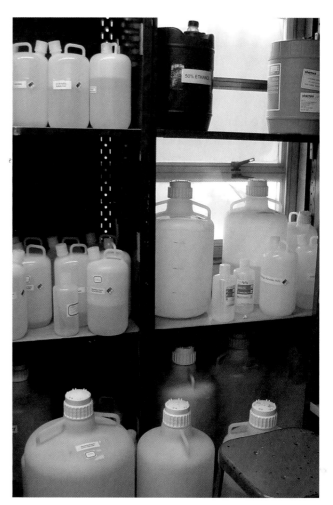

Figure 3.41 Carboys and jerricans are primarily used to store and transport corrosive liquids, but they may contain other hazardous and nonhazardous liquids as well.

Figure 3.42 Compressed-gas cylinders range in size from small to large.

All approved cylinders, with the exception of some that store poisons, are equipped with safety-relief devices. These devices may be spring-loaded valves that reclose after operation, heat-fusible plugs, or pressure-activated bursting disks that completely empty the container. All fittings and threads are standardized according to the material stored in the cylinder.

As yet, there is no nationally regulated color code that permits visual identification of cylinder materials by color. Some manufacturers use a single color for all their cylinders, while other manufacturers have their own color-coding system. If local manufacturers and distributors use an identification system, it should be identified in emergency response plans.

Drums

[NFPA 472: 5.2.1.1(E)(4)]

A *drum* is a flat-ended or convex-ended cylindrical packaging made of the following materials:

- Metal
- Fiberboard
- Plastic
- Plywood
- Other suitable materials

This definition also includes packagings of other shapes made of metal or plastic (for example, round taper-necked or pail-shaped), but it does *not* include the following items:

- Cylinders
- Jerricans
- Wood barrels
- Bulk packaging

The terms *drum* and *barrel* are often used interchangeably. Historically, however, a barrel has a cylindrical shape that is wider in the middle than it is on its ends (has a bulge in the center). See sidebar. Drum capacities range up to 100 gallons (379 L), but 55-gallon (208 L) drums are the most common. Drums that hold less than 12 gallons (45 L) are called *pails*. Drums may contain a wide variety of hazardous and nonhazardous materials in both liquid and solid form. The tops of drums come in the following two types (**Figure 3.43**):

- ***Open heads*** — Removable tops
- ***Tight (or closed) heads*** — Nonremovable tops with small openings plugged by bungs (stoppers)

Figure 3.43 Open-head drums have removable tops. The open-head drum in the foreground of this picture can be recognized by the screw used to tighten the binding ring that holds the lid in place. The drums in the rear of this picture have closed heads.

Is It a Drum or a Barrel?

Confusion may arise between the terms *drum* and *barrel* because *barrel (bbl)* is a unit of measurement as well. According to U.S. Customs, a barrel ranges from 31.5 to 42 gallons for liquids or 7,056 cubic inches (105 dry quarts or 115.63 L) for most fruits, vegetables, and other dry commodities. A barrel of petroleum, for example, is 42 gallons (159 L); in Canada, it is 45 gallons (170 L). A 15,000-barrel petroleum carrier, then, refers not to the number of drums it can carry, but rather to the number of gallons it can hold (15,000 × 42 = 630,000 gallons [2 384 802 L]).

Radioactive Containers

[NFPA 472: 5.2.1.1(F)(1–5)]

According to the U.S. government, all shipments of radioactive materials (sometimes called *RAM*), whether from industry or government, must be packaged and transported according to strict regulations. These regulations protect the public, transportation workers, and the environment from potential exposure to radiation. The types of radioactive materials that are shipped and the percent of shipments by type (according to the U.S. Department of Energy) are as follows:

- Uranium ores/compounds (10.7 percent)
- Nuclear fuel (1.8 percent)
- Spent fuel (0.2 percent)
- Radioactive waste (14.8 percent)
- Medical/research (including radioisotopes) (54.5 percent)
- Empty containers (6 percent)
- Miscellaneous radiological items (12 percent)

The type of packaging used to transport radioactive materials is determined by the activity, type, and form of the material to be shipped. Depending on these factors, radioactive material is shipped in one of four basic types of containers/packaging: Type A, Type B, industrial, or excepted **(Table 3.12, p. 152)**. A fifth type of packaging, *strong, tight,* is still used for some domestic shipments. Additional information about these packages (in order of increasing levels of hazard of the radioactive material contained within) is as follows:

- ***Strong, tight*** — Container used to ship materials of low radioactivity. These packages are authorized for domestic shipment only in vehicles solely dedicated to that purpose. Packaging may be made of wood, steel, or fiberboard. Like industrial packages, they are not identified as strong, tight on shipping papers or the packaging. *Material examples:*
  - Natural uranium
  - Rubble from decommissioned nuclear reactors
- ***Excepted*** — Packaging used for transportation of materials that have very limited radioactivity such as articles manufactured from natural or depleted uranium or natural thorium. Excepted packagings are only used to transport materials with extremely low levels of radioactivity that present no risk to the public or environment. Excepted packaging is not marked or labeled as such **(Figure 3.44a)**. *Other information:*

Figure 3.44a Excepted packaging is used for materials with extremely low levels of radioactivity that present no risk to the public or environment. Excepted packaging is exempt from many labeling and documentation requirements. *Courtesy of Department of Energy (DOE)/Sandia National Laboratories.*

Figure 3.44b Industrial packaging is used for materials that present limited hazard to the public and the environment such as smoke detectors. *Courtesy of Department of Energy (DOE)/Sandia National Laboratories.*

  - Empty packaging is also excepted.
  - Because of its low risk, excepted packaging is exempt from several labeling and documentation requirements.
- ***Industrial*** — Container that retains and protects the contents during normal transportation activities. Materials that present limited hazard to the public and the environment are shipped in these packages. Industrial packages are not identified as such on the packages or shipping papers **(Figure 3.44b)**. *Material examples:*
  - Slightly contaminated clothing
  - Laboratory samples
  - Smoke detectors
- ***Type A*** — Packages that must demonstrate their ability to withstand a series of tests without releasing their contents. The package

Table 3.12
Radioactive Container Descriptions

Excepted Packaging	Industrial Packaging (IP)	Type A Packaging	Type B Packaging
Designed to survive normal conditions of transport	Designed to survive normal conditions of transport (IP-1) and at least the DROP test and stacking test for Type A packaging (IP-2 and IP-3)	• Designed to survive normal transportation, handling, and minor accidents • Certified as Type A on the basis of performance requirements, which means it must survive certain tests	Must be able to survive severe accidents
Used for transportation of materials that are either Low Specific Activity (LSA) or Surface Contaminated Objects (SCO) and that are limited quantity shipments, instruments or articles, articles manufactured from natural or depleted uranium, or natural thorium; empty packagings are also excepted (49 *CFR* 173.421–428)	Used for transportation of materials with very small amounts of radioactivity (Low Specific Activity [LSA] or Surface Contaminated Objects [SCO])	Used for the transportation of limited quantities of radioactive material (RAM) that would not result in significant health effects if they were released	Used for the transportation of large quantities of radioactive material
Can be almost any packaging that meets the basic requirements, with any of the above contents; they are excepted from several labeling and documentation requirements	Usually metal boxes or drums	• May be cardboard boxes, wooden crates, or drums • Shipper and carrier must have documentation of the certification of the packages being transported	• May be a metal drum or a huge, massive shielded transport container • Must meet severe accident performance standards that are considerably more rigorous than those required for Type A packages • Either has a Certificate of Compliance (COC) by the Nuclear Regulatory Commission (NRC) or Certificate of Competent Authority (COCA) by the Department of Transportation (DOT)

Source: Courtesy of U.S. Department of Energy (DOE)/Sandia National Laboratories.

and shipping papers will have the words *Type A* on them. Regulations require that the package protect its contents and maintain sufficient shielding under conditions normally encountered during transportation. Radioactive materials with relatively high specific activity levels are shipped in Type A packages (**Figure 3.45a**). *Material examples:*

— Radiopharmaceuticals (radioactive materials for medical use)

— Certain regulatory qualified industrial products

• *Type B* — Packages must not only demonstrate their ability to withstand tests simulating normal shipping conditions, but they must also withstand severe accident conditions without releasing their contents. Type B packages are identified as such on the package itself as well as on shipping papers. The size of these packages can range from small containers to those weighing over 100 tons (102 tonnes). These large, heavy packages provide shielding against radiation. Radioactive materials that exceed the limits of Type A package requirements must be shipped in Type B packages (**Figure 3.45b**). *Material examples:*

— Materials that would present a radiation hazard to the public or the environment if there were a major release

— Materials with high levels of radioactivity such as spent fuel from nuclear power plants

Other Types

Several other nonbulk types of packaging are as follows:

• *Boxes* — Often used as outer packaging for other nonbulk packages such as chemical bottles or etiological agents; may contain almost any type of hazardous material. Boxes have complete rectangular or polygonal faces and are made of metal, wood, plywood, reconstituted wood, fiberboard, plastic, or other suitable material. For ease of handling or opening, DOT permits holes appropriate to the size and use of the packaging as long as they do not compromise the integrity of the packaging during transportation.

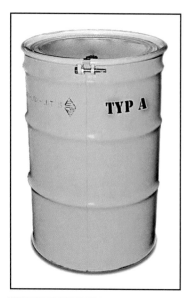

Figure 3.45a Materials with relatively high specific activity levels are shipped in Type A packages. *Courtesy of Department of Energy (DOE)/Sandia National Laboratories.*

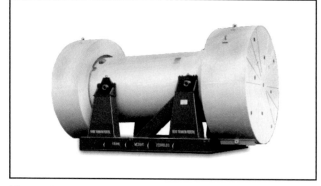

Figure 3.45b Type B packages are designed to withstand severe accident conditions. Type B packages contain materials with high levels of radioactivity. *Courtesy of Department of Energy (DOE)/Sandia National Laboratories.*

• *Bottles* — Used as inner packaging for the transport of solids and liquids; characterized by a neck of relatively smaller cross section than the body and an opening capable of holding a closure for retention of the contents. Bottles are usually made of metal or plastic. A bottle made of brown glass may indicate that its contents are light-sensitive or reactive.

• *Composite packages* — Single containers made of two different types of material; for example, a metal drum lined with a plastic inner receptacle for transporting an epoxy or glue or a metal pail lined with a plastic bag for transporting a solid of some sort. Generally, composite packages look like their outer packaging — a simple box, bag, or other container — but their construction of integral inner receptacle and outer packaging distinguish them from those categories.

Clue 2 Summary

Container shapes, sizes, and types provide valuable clues to first responders about the materials they may hold. The *What Does Clue 2 Mean to You* safety alert box provides a summary of things to remember.

What Does Clue 2 Mean to You?

As an Awareness-Level responder, you need to be able to identify the typical container shapes (fixed-facility tanks, transportation tanks, and bulk and nonbulk containers) that may contain hazardous materials. Here's a hint: If it looks like it might contain **something** — it probably does! The next step is to determine if that **something** is likely to be hazardous and take appropriate actions from there. For example, if you are the first to arrive on the scene of a highway accident involving a cargo tank truck that is now spilling a liquid, you should recognize the liquid as a potentially hazardous material and not rush forward to assist the driver in the cab.

As an Operational-Level responder, you need to be able to identify not only each of the specific types of containers discussed in this section but also what materials they are likely to contain. If you are the first to arrive on the scene of a highway accident involving a cargo tank truck, you should be able to recognize it as a corrosive liquid tank and immediately have a better understanding of the potential hazards associated with the liquid and how to act accordingly. This information also helps you make an exact identification of the material through other methods.

Clue 3
Transportation Placards, Labels, and Markings

[NFPA 472: 5.2.1.2]

The U.S., Canada, and Mexico have all adopted the *UN Recommendations*. Therefore, with a few country-specific variations, the majority of the placards, labels, and markings used to identify hazardous materials during transport are very similar in all three countries.

In relation to the seven clues and the increasing level of hazard associated with them, ideally, this section would discuss placards and certain markings that can be seen from a great distance, and the next section would discuss individual labels and markings to which a responder would probably need to be much closer. However, for purposes of this book, only placards, labels, and markings based on the UN system for classifying and identifying transported hazardous materials are discussed in this section, along with common intermodal markings and railcar specification markings. Placards, labels, markings, and colors associated with other systems (such as NFPA 704, *Standard System for the Identification of the Hazards of Materials for Emergency Response*, 2001, and military markings) are discussed in the next section, Clue 4: Other Markings and Colors.

UN Recommendations on the Transport of Dangerous Goods

The *UN Recommendations* provide a uniform basis for development of *harmonized regulations* for all modes of transport in order to facilitate trade and the safe, efficient transport of hazardous materials. The *UN Recommendations* were first published in 1957, establishing minimum requirements applicable to the transport of hazardous materials by all modes of transport. Since then, these recommendations have gained global acceptance as the basis for most international, regional, national, and modal transportation regulations. These recommendations enhance safety, improve enforcement capability, ease training requirements, and enhance global trade and economic development.

Safety is enhanced primarily because harmonized requirements simplify the complexity of the regulations, simplify training efforts, and decrease the likelihood of noncompliance. The UN's recommendations provide economic benefits by eliminating the costs of complying with a multitude of differing national, regional, and modal regulations. They also facilitate compatibility between modal requirements so that a consignment may be transported by more than one mode without intermediate reclassification, marking, labeling, or repackaging.

Is It a Placard, Label, or Marking?

The issue may be a confusing one, because the terms are used differently in different circumstances. Take a look at **Figures 3.46 a–e.** Depending on context, there are people who would make the following identifications:

- Picture (a) is a placard, (c) is a label, and everything else is a marking.

- Picture (a) is a placard, (b) is a marking, and everything else is a label.

- Pictures (a) and (b) are both placards, (c) and (d) are both labels, and (e) is a marking

- Pictures (a) and (b) are both placards, and everything else is a label.

- All of them are markings ("Hey dude, did you see the marking on that truck?").

- All of them are labels ("I'm pretty sure it had some kind of weird label on it!")

- None of the choices; they're all signs.

Part of this confusion is caused because the terms are used interchangeably in everyday language. For example, the *Merriam-Webster Collegiate Online Dictionary* defines placard as nothing more than "a notice posted in a public place." The U.S. Department of Transportation (DOT), however, has very specific definitions for *placard*, *label*, and *marking,* and those definitions are frequently used by emergency response personnel in the context of hazardous materials. These specific definitions are discussed in Clue 3: U.S. Transportation Placards, Labels, and Markings. Other organizations, on the other hand, tend to use the terms less specifically than the DOT. Therefore, first responders may hear these terms used in a variety of ways in different contexts.

The following is one explanation of the pictures:

- Pictures are (*a*) *a placard*, (*c*) *a label*, and (*e*) *a marking*; all based on the UN classification system and U.S. DOT definitions

- Picture (*b*) is a *placard* (everyday language), *sign*, or *marking* based on the NFPA 704 hazard identification system

- Picture (*d*) is a *label* (everyday language) based on the NFPA 704 system

a

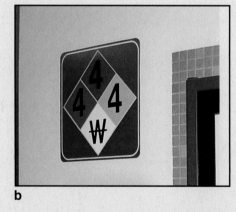

b

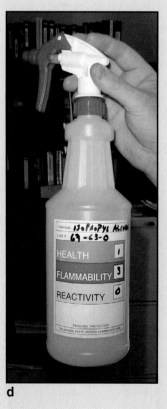

d

c

e

Figures 3.46 a–e

The *UN Recommendations* cover all aspects of transportation necessary to provide international uniformity. The publication includes a comprehensive criteria-based classification system for substances that pose a significant hazard in transportation. Hazards addressed include substances with the following characteristics:

- Explosive
- Flammable
- Toxic
- Corrosive to human tissue and metal
- Reactive (for example, oxidizing materials, self-reactive materials, pyrophoric substances, and substances that react with water)
- Radioactive
- Infectious
- Environmental contaminants

The recommendations prescribe standards for packaging and multimodal tanks used to transport hazardous materials. The publication also includes a system of communicating the hazards of substances in transport through hazard communication requirements. This system addresses labeling and marking of packages, placarding of tanks and freight units, and documentation and emergency response information required to accompany each shipment.

UN Hazard Classes

Under the UN system, nine hazard classes are used to categorize hazardous materials:

Class 1: Explosives

Class 2: Gases

Class 3: Flammable liquids

Class 4: Flammable solids, substances liable to spontaneous combustion, substances that emit flammable gases on contact with water

Class 5: Oxidizing substances and organic peroxides

Class 6: Toxic and infectious substances

Class 7: Radioactive materials

Class 8: Corrosive substances

Class 9: Miscellaneous dangerous substances and articles

To avoid redundancy, a detailed explanation of these nine major hazard classes is given in the U.S. Transportation Placards, Labels, and Markings section under DOT Placards (see Table 3.15). While there may be minor variances between the UN and the U.S. class definitions, because most North American first responders primarily deal with DOT or Transport Canada (TC) placards, labels, and markings, the unique UN placards are not detailed here. Examples of the UN class placards and labels are found in **Appendix D,** UN Class Placards and Labels.

UN Commodity Identification Numbers

[NFPA 472: 4.2.1(7)(a), 5.2.1.2(A)(3)]
The UN has also developed a system of four-digit numbers that is used in conjunction with illustrated placards in North America (NA). The UN system provides uniformity in recognizing regulated hazardous materials during international transport. By using the UN identification numbers, first responders can determine information on the general hazard class and the identity of certain predetermined commodities.

If Lt. Adams had been given the four-digit ID number for 1,2-butylene oxide rather than the name, she could have identified the material and found the correct guide in the orange section of the *ERG* just as quickly and easily.

The UN number must be displayed on bulk containers in one of the three ways illustrated by **Figure 3.49, p. 158**. In North America, UN numbers must be displayed on the following containers/packages:

- Rail tank cars
- Cargo tank trucks
- Portable tanks
- Bulk packages

UN Identification Numbers

[NFPA 472: 4.2.2(2), 5.2.1.2(A)(3)]

Each material listed in the Hazardous Materials Table appearing in the current *Emergency Response Guidebook (ERG)* has a four-digit UN identification (ID) number assigned to it. This number will often be displayed on placards, labels, orange panels, and/or white diamonds in association with materials being transported in cargo tanks, portable tanks, or tank cars. The number may be preceded by the letters *NA* for North America (which means it is not recognized for international transportation except in North America) or *UN* for United Nations (which means it is recognized for international transportation) **(Figure 3.47).**

The identification number also appears on shipping papers and should match the numbers displayed on the exteriors of tanks or shipping containers. UN numbers are found on vehicles or containers transporting large quantities of materials (at least 8,820 lbs or 4 000 kg), nonbulk packages containing a single hazardous material, and containers transporting

certain inhalation hazards (see Division 1.6, DOT Placards section).

The identification number can assist first responders in correctly identifying the material and referencing it in the *ERG*. For example, the UN number for 1,2-butylene oxide (stabilized) is 3022. The yellow pages of the *ERG* provide an index based on UN numbers. However, nonregulated materials (some of which may be hazardous) will not have a UN number.

Four-Digit UN ID Number

1090

Figure 3.47 The four-digit UN identification number can be used to identify hazardous materials in the *Emergency Response Guidebook.* Sometimes these four-digit numbers will be preceded by the letters *NA* or *UN,* standing for North America and United Nations.

Careful!

Don't be confused by an orange placard with two sets of numbers on intermodal tanks and containers **(Figure 3.48)**. The four-digit UN ID number is on the bottom. The top number is a hazard identification number (or code) required under European and some South American regulations. This number consists of two or three figures* indicating the following hazards:

2 — Emission of a gas due to pressure or chemical reaction

3 — Flammability of liquids (vapors) and gases or self-heating liquid

4 — Flammability of solids or self-heating solid

5 — Oxidizing (fire intensifying) effect

6 — Toxicity or risk of infection

7 — Radioactivity

8 — Corrosivity

9 — Risk of spontaneous violent reaction

---

* Doubling a number (such as *33, 44,* or *88*) indicates an intensification of that particular hazard. When the

hazard associated with a material is adequately indicated by a single number, it is followed by a zero (such as *30, 40,* or *60*). A hazard identification code prefixed by the letter *X* (such as *X88*) indicates that the material will react dangerously with water.

Figure 3.48 The UN ID number is on the bottom. The top number is a hazard identification number (code) required by some European and South American regulations.

Sample Displays of 4-Digit UN Identification Numbers

FLAMMABLE — 3

1090 — 3

1993 — 3

1090

Figure 3.49 The UN number will be displayed in one of the three ways shown on bulk containers (such as cargo tank trucks and rail tank cars) and certain nonbulk packages.

- Vehicle containers containing large quantities (at least 8,820 lbs or 4 000 kg) of hazardous materials

- Certain nonbulk packages (for example, poisonous gases in specified amounts)

U.S. Transportation Placards, Labels, and Markings

[NFPA 472: 4.2.1(9)]

The UN system is the basis for the DOT regulations. DOT classifies hazardous materials according to their primary danger and assigns standardized symbols to identify the classes. DOT regulations cover some additional categories of substances, including other regulated materials (ORM-Ds), materials of trade (MOTs), and fumigated loads. The major classes and a brief description of each are given in Table 3.15 in the next section.

DOT Placards

[NFPA 472: 4.2.1(2), 4.2.1(3), 5.2.2(1)] [ODP Operations Level I.b.]

A *placard* is a diamond-shaped, color-coded sign provided by shippers to identify the materials in transportation containers. Each of the nine haz-

ard classes has a specific placard that identifies the class of the material and assists the responder in identifying the hazards associated with the product. A material's hazard class is indicated either by its class (or division) number or name. The hazard class or division number must be displayed in the lower corner of placards corresponding to the primary hazard class of a material. **Figure 3.50** provides the required dimensions of DOT placards and summarizes the information conveyed by them. Placards may be found on the following types of containers:

- Bulk packages

- Rail tank cars

- Cargo tank vehicles

- Portable tanks

- Unit loading devices containing hazardous materials over 640 cubic feet (18 m³) in capacity

- Certain nonbulk containers

Specifically, placards are required on any container transporting any quantity of the materials given in **Table 3.13, p. 160,** (Placarding Table 1 of DOT Chart 12) or 1,001 pounds (454 kg) or more of the materials listed in **Table 3.14, p. 160,** (Placarding Table 2 of DOT Chart 12). A placard

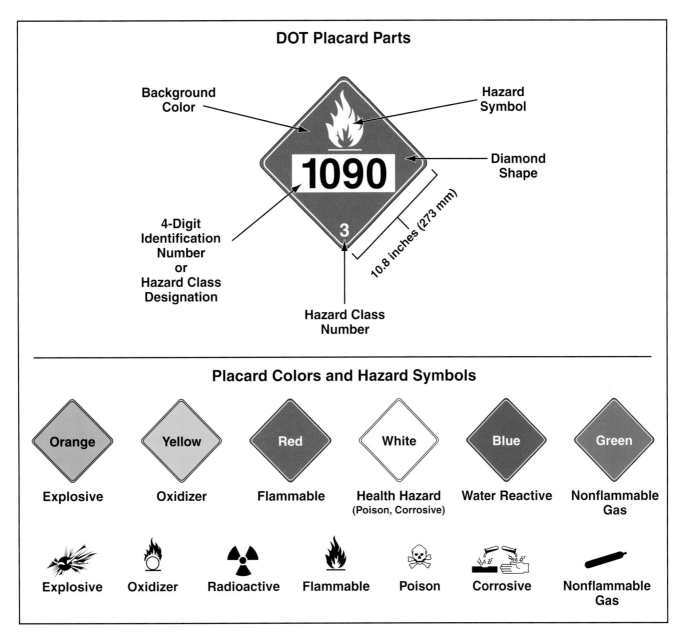

DOT Placard Parts

Background Color

Hazard Symbol

1090

Diamond Shape

10.8 inches (273 mm)

4-Digit Identification Number or Hazard Class Designation

Hazard Class Number

Placard Colors and Hazard Symbols

Orange	Yellow	Red	White	Blue	Green
Explosive	Oxidizer	Flammable	Health Hazard (Poison, Corrosive)	Water Reactive	Nonflammable Gas
Explosive	Oxidizer	Radioactive	Flammable	Poison	Corrosive	Nonflammable Gas

Figure 3.50 Placards provide many visual clues to the hazards presented by a material.

is not required when the gross weight of any of the materials covered in Table 3.14 is less than 1,001 pounds (454 kg) for any one shipment. Unfortunately, improperly marked, unmarked, and otherwise illegal shipments are common. These shipments may include incompatible products, products that contravene local, state/provincial, and federal laws, and waste products shipped and disposed of without permit.

Table 3.15, p. 161, provides an explanation of the DOT hazard classes and subdivisions, the Hazardous Material Regulation (HMR) references for each, and their associated placards.

The following is a list of important facts that relate to placards:

- A placard is not required for shipments of infectious substances, ORM-Ds, MOTs, limited quantities, small-quantity packages, radioactive materials (white label I or yellow label II; see DOT Labels section and Table 3.16), or combustible liquids in nonbulk packaging. See information box, p. 169.

- Some private agriculture and military vehicles may not have placards, even though they are carrying significant quantities of hazardous materials. For example, farmers may carry

Table 3.13
Materials Requiring Placarding Regardless of Quantity

Hazard Class or Division	Placard Name
1.1	Explosives 1.1
1.2	Explosives 1.2
1.3	Explosives 1.3
2.3	Poison Gas
4.3	Dangerous When Wet
5.2 (organic peroxide, Type B, liquid or solid, temperature controlled)	Organic Peroxide
6.1 (Inhalation Hazard Zone A or B)	Poison Inhalation Hazard
7 (Radioactive Yellow III Label only)	Radioactive

Source: U.S. Department of Transportation, Chart 12, Hazardous Materials Marking, Labeling & Placarding Guide, Table 1.

Table 3.14
Materials in Excess of 1,001 Pounds (454 kg) Requiring Placarding

Hazard Class or Division	Placard Name
1.4	Explosives 1.4
1.5	Explosives 1.5
1.6	Explosives 1.6
2.1	Flammable Gas
2.2	Nonflammable Gas
3	Flammable
Combustible Liquid	Combustible
4.1	Flamable Solid
4.2	Spontaneously Combustible
5.1	Oxidizer
5.2 (Other than organic peroxide, Type B, liquid or solid, temperature controlled)	Organic Peroxide
6.1 (Other than inhalation hazard, Zone A or B)	Poison
6.2	None
8	Corrosive
9	Class 9 [See 49 *CFR*, Part 172, subpart E, paragraph 172.504 (f)(9)]
ORM-D	None

Source: U.S. Department of Transportation, Chart 12, Hazardous Materials Marking, Labeling & Placarding Guide, Table 2.

fertilizer, pesticides, and fuel between fields of their farms or to and from their farms without any placarding.

- The hazard class or division number corresponding to the primary or subsidiary hazard class of a material must be displayed in the lower corner of a placard (**Figure 3.51, p. 168**).

- Other than Class 7 or the DANGEROUS placard, text indicating a hazard (for example, the word *FLAMMABLE*) is not required. Text may be omitted from the Oxygen placard only if the specific ID number is displayed.

- The shipper is required to provide placards. Drivers may not know what they are carrying or may have varying degrees of information about the hazardous materials in their vehicles.

DOT Labels
[NFPA 472: 4.2.1(9)]

Basically, DOT-required labels provide the same information as vehicle placards (**Figure 3.52, p. 168**). Labels on packages communicate the haz-

ards posed by the material in the event the package spills from the transport vehicle. Labels are 3.9-inch (100 mm), square-on-point diamonds, which may or may not have written text that identifies the hazardous material within the packaging. Class 7 Radioactive labels must always contain text.

First responders must be familiar with the pictogram and hazard class or division number for the material. Packaging will contain a primary label and a subsidiary label for materials that meet the definition of more than one hazard class. In **Figure 3.53, p. 169**, the label on the left is the primary la-

Table 3.15
U.S. DOT Placard Hazard Classes and Divisions

Class 1: Explosives (49 *CFR* 173.50)

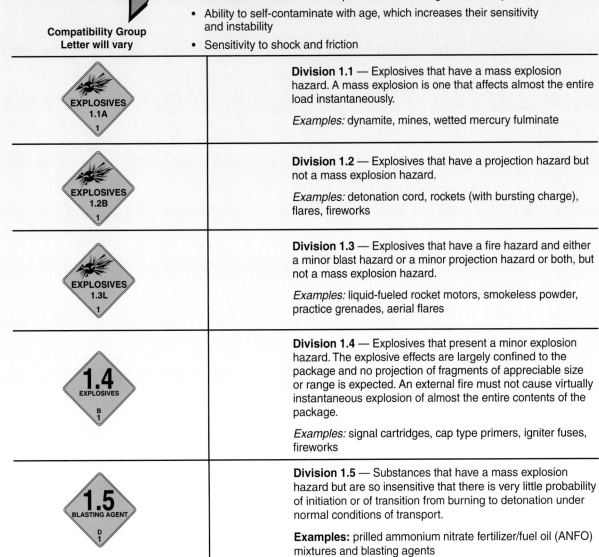

An **explosive** is any substance or article (including a device) that is designed to function by explosion (that is, an extremely rapid release of gas and heat) or (by chemical reaction within itself) is able to function in a similar manner even if not designed to function by explosion.

Explosive placards will have a *compatibility group* letter on them, which is a designated alphabetical letter used to categorize different types of explosive substances and articles for purposes of stowage and segregation. However, it is the division number that is of primary concern to first responders.

The primary hazards of explosives are thermal (heat) and mechanical, but may include the following:

- Blast pressure wave
- Shrapnel fragmentation
- Incendiary thermal effect
- Seismic effect
- Chemical hazards from the production of toxic gases and vapors
- Ability to self-contaminate with age, which increases their sensitivity and instability
- Sensitivity to shock and friction

Compatibility Group Letter will vary

Division 1.1 — Explosives that have a mass explosion hazard. A mass explosion is one that affects almost the entire load instantaneously.

Examples: dynamite, mines, wetted mercury fulminate

Division 1.2 — Explosives that have a projection hazard but not a mass explosion hazard.

Examples: detonation cord, rockets (with bursting charge), flares, fireworks

Division 1.3 — Explosives that have a fire hazard and either a minor blast hazard or a minor projection hazard or both, but not a mass explosion hazard.

Examples: liquid-fueled rocket motors, smokeless powder, practice grenades, aerial flares

Division 1.4 — Explosives that present a minor explosion hazard. The explosive effects are largely confined to the package and no projection of fragments of appreciable size or range is expected. An external fire must not cause virtually instantaneous explosion of almost the entire contents of the package.

Examples: signal cartridges, cap type primers, igniter fuses, fireworks

Division 1.5 — Substances that have a mass explosion hazard but are so insensitive that there is very little probability of initiation or of transition from burning to detonation under normal conditions of transport.

Examples: prilled ammonium nitrate fertilizer/fuel oil (ANFO) mixtures and blasting agents

Continued

Table 3.15 (continued)
U.S. DOT Placard Hazard Classes and Divisions

Class 1: Explosives (continued)

Division 1.6 — Extremely insensitive articles that do not have a mass explosive hazard. This division is comprised of articles that contain only extremely insensitive detonating substances and that demonstrate a negligible probability of accidental initiation or propagation.

Example: wetted cellulose nitrate

Class 2: Gases (49 *CFR* 173.115)

DOT defines *gas* as a material that has a vapor pressure greater than 43.5 psi (300 kPa) at 122°F (50°C) or is completely gaseous at 68°F (20°C) at a standard pressure of 14.7 psi (101.3 kPa).

NOTE: The DOT definition for gas is much more specific than the definition provided in Chapter 2, Hazardous Materials Properties and Hazards.

The potential hazards of gases may include thermal, asphyxiation, chemical, and mechanical hazards:

- Thermal hazards (heat) from fires, particularly associated with Division 2.1 and oxygen

- Thermal hazards (cold) associated with exposure to cryogens in Division 2.2

- Asphyxiation caused by leaking/released gases displacing oxygen in a confined space

- Chemical hazards from toxic and/or corrosive gases and vapors, particularly associated with Division 2.3

- Mechanical hazards from a boiling liquid expanding vapor explosion (BLEVE) for containers exposed to heat or flame

- Mechanical hazards from a ruptured cylinder rocketing after exposure to heat or flame

Division 2.1: Flammable Gas — Consists of any material that is a gas at 68°F (20°C) or less at normal atmospheric pressure or a material that has a boiling point of 68°F (20°C) or less at normal atmospheric pressure and that

(1) Is ignitable at normal atmospheric pressure when in a mixture of 13 percent or less by volume with air, or

(2) Has a flammable range at normal atmospheric pressure with air of at least 12 percent, regardless of the lower limit.

Examples: compressed hydrogen, isobutene, methane, and propane

Division 2.2: Nonflammable, Nonpoisonous Gas — Nonflammable, nonpoisonous compressed gas, including compressed gas, liquefied gas, pressurized cryogenic gas, and compressed gas in solution, asphyxiant gas and oxidizing gas; means any material (or mixture) which exerts in the packaging an absolute pressure of 40.6 psi (280 kPa) or greater at 68°F (20°C) and does not meet the definition of Divisions 2.1 or 2.3.

Examples: carbon dioxide, helium, compressed neon, refrigerated liquid nitrogen, cryogenic argon, anhydrous ammonia

Continued

Table 3.15 (continued)
U.S. DOT Placard Hazard Classes and Divisions

Class 2: Gases (continued)

Division 2.3: Gas Poisonous by Inhalation — Material that is a gas at 68°F (20°C) or less and a pressure of 14.7 psi (101.3 kPa) (a material that has a boiling point of 68°F [20°C] or less at 14.7 psi [101.3 kPa]), and that is known to be so toxic to humans as to pose a hazard to health during transportation; or (in the absence of adequate data on human toxicity) is presumed to be toxic to humans because of specific test criteria on laboratory animals.

Division 2.3 has *ERG*-designated hazard zones associated with it, determined by the concentration of gas in the air:

- Hazard Zone A — LC_{50} less than or equal to 200 ppm

- Hazard Zone B — LC_{50} greater than 200 ppm and less than or equal to 1,000 ppm

- Hazard Zone C — LC_{50} greater than 1,000 ppm and less than or equal to 3,000 ppm

- Hazard Zone D — LC_{50} greater than 3,000 ppm and less than or equal to 5,000 ppm

Examples: cyanide, diphosgene, germane, phosphine, selenium hexafluoride, and hydrocyanic acid

Oxygen Placard — Oxygen is not a separate division under Class 2, but first responders may see this oxygen placard on containers with 1,001 lbs (454 kg) or more gross weight of either compressed gas or refrigerated liquid.

Class 3: Flammable and Combustible Liquids (49 *CFR* 173.120)

A *flammable liquid* is generally a liquid having a flash point of not more than 141°F (60.5°C), or any material in a liquid state with a flash point at or above 100°F (37.8°C) that is intentionally heated and offered for transportation or transported at or above its flash point in a bulk packaging.

A *combustible liquid* is any liquid that does not meet the definition of any other hazard class and has a flash point above 141°F (60.5°C) and below 200°F (93°C). A flammable liquid with a flash point at or above 100°F (38°C) that does not meet the definition of any other hazard class may be reclassified as a combustible liquid. This provision does not apply to transportation by vessel or aircraft, except where other means of transportation is impracticable. An elevated temperature material that meets the definition of a Class 3 material because it is intentionally heated and offered for transportation or transported at or above its flash point may not be reclassified as a combustible liquid.

The primary hazards of flammable and combustible liquids are thermal, asphyxiation, chemical, and mechanical, and may include the following:

- Thermal hazards (heat) from fires and vapor explosions

- Asphyxiation from heavier than air vapors displacing oxygen in low-lying, and/or confined spaces

- Chemical hazards from toxic and/or corrosive gases and vapors

- Chemical hazards from the production of toxic and/or corrosive gases and vapors during fires

- Mechanical hazards from a BLEVE, for containers exposed to heat or flame

- Mechanical hazards caused by a vapor explosion

- Vapors that can mix with air and travel great distances to an ignition source

- Environmental hazards (pollution) caused by runoff from fire control

When responding to a transportation incident, first responders must keep in mind that a flammable liquid placard can indicate a product with a flash point as high as 140°F (60°C).

Continued

Table 3.15 (continued)
U.S. DOT Placard Hazard Classes and Divisions

Class 3: Flammable and Combustible liquids (continued)

FLAMMABLE 3	**Flammable Placard** *Examples:* gasoline, methyl ethyl ketone
GASOLINE 3	**Gasoline Placard** — May be used in the place of a flammable placard on a cargo tank or a portable tank being used to transport gasoline by highway
COMBUSTIBLE 3	**Combustible Placard** *Examples:* diesel, fuel oils, pine oil
FUEL OIL 3	**Fuel Oil Placard** — May be used in place of a combustible placard on a cargo tank or portable tank being used to transport fuel oil by highway.

Class 4: Flammable Solids, Spontaneously Combustible Materials, and Dangerous-When-Wet Materials (49 *CFR* 173.124)

This class is divided into three divisions: 4.1 Flammable Solids, 4.2 Spontaneously Combustible Materials, and 4.3 Dangerous When Wet (see definitions, p. 165).

First responders must be aware that fires involving Class 4 materials may be extremely difficult to extinguish. The primary hazards of Class 4 materials are thermal, chemical, and mechanical and may also include the following hazards:

- Thermal hazards (heat) from fires that may start spontaneously or upon contact with air or water
- Thermal hazards (heat) from fires and vapor explosions
- Thermal hazards (heat) from molten substances
- Chemical hazards from irritating, corrosive, and/or highly toxic gases and vapors produced by fire or decomposition
- Severe chemical burns
- Mechanical effects from unexpected, violent chemical reactions and explosions
- Mechanical hazards from a BLEVE, for containers exposed to heat or flame (or if contaminated with water, particularly for Division 4.3)
- Production of hydrogen gas from contact with metal
- Production of corrosive solutions on contact with water, for Division 4.3
- May spontaneously reignite after fire is extinguished
- Environmental hazards (pollution) caused by runoff from fire

Continued

Table 3.15 (continued)
U.S. DOT Placard Hazard Classes and Divisions

Class 4 (continued)

Division 4.1: Flammable Solid Material — Includes (1) wetted explosives, (2) self-reactive materials that can undergo a strongly exothermal decomposition, and (3) readily combustible solids that may cause a fire through friction, certain metal powders that can be ignited and react over the whole length of a sample in 10 minutes or less, or readily combustible solids that burn faster than 2.2 mm/second:

- **Wetted explosives:** Explosives with their explosive properties suppressed by wetting with sufficient alcohol, plasticizers, or water
- **Self-reactive materials:** Materials liable to undergo a strong exothermic decomposition at normal or elevated temperatures due to excessively high transport temperatures or to contamination
- **Readily combustible solids:** Solids that may ignite through friction or any metal powders that can be ignited

Examples: phosphorus heptasulfide, paraformaldehyde, magnesium

Division 4.2: Spontaneous Combustible Material — Includes (1) a pyrophoric material (liquid or solid) that, without an external ignition source, can ignite within 5 minutes after coming in contact with air and (2) a self-heating material that, when in contact with air and without an energy supply, is liable to self-heat

Examples: sodium sulfide, potassium sulfide, phosphorus (white or yellow, dry), aluminum and magnesium alkyls, charcoal briquettes

Division 4.3: Dangerous-When-Wet Material — Material that, by contact with water, is liable to become spontaneously flammable or to release flammable or toxic gas at a rate greater than 1 liter per kilogram of the material per hour

Examples: magnesium powder, lithium, ethyldichlorosilane, calcium carbide, potassium

Class 5: Oxidizers and Organic Peroxides (49 *CFR* 173.127 and 128)

This class is divided into two divisions: 5.1 Oxidizers and 5.2 Organic Peroxides (see definitions, p. 166). Oxygen supports combustion, so the primary hazards of Class 5 materials are fires and explosions with their associated thermal and mechanical hazards:

- Thermal hazards (heat) from fires that may explode or burn extremely hot and fast
- Explosive reactions to contact with hydrocarbons (fuels)
- Chemical hazards from toxic gases, vapors, and dust
- Chemicals hazards from toxic products of combustion
- Chemical burns
- Ignition of combustibles (including paper, cloth, wood, etc.)
- Mechanical hazards from violent reactions and explosions
- Accumulation of toxic fumes and dusts in confined spaces
- Sensitivity to heat, friction, shock, and/or contamination with other materials

Continued

Table 3.15 (continued)
U.S. DOT Placard Hazard Classes and Divisions

Class 5 (continued)

OXIDIZER 5.1	**Division 5.1: Oxidizer** — Material that may, generally by yielding oxygen, cause or enhance the combustion of other materials *Examples:* chromium nitrate, copper chlorate, calcium permanganate, ammonium nitrate fertilizer
ORGANIC PEROXIDE 5.2	**Division 5.2: Organic Peroxide** — Any organic compound containing oxygen (O) in the bivalent -O-O- structure and which may be considered a derivative of hydrogen peroxide, where one or more of the hydrogen atoms has been replaced by organic radicals *Examples:* liquid organic peroxide type B

Class 6: Poison (Toxic) and Poison Inhalation Hazard (49 *CFR* 173.132 and 134)

A poisonous material is a material, other than a gas, that is known to be toxic to humans. The primary hazards of Class 6 materials are chemical and thermal and may include the following:

- Toxic effects due to exposure via all routes of entry
- Chemicals hazards from toxic and/or corrosive products of combustion
- Thermal effects (heat) from substances transported in molten form
- Flammability and its associated thermal hazards (heat) from fires

POISON 6	**Division 6.1: Poisonous Material** — Material, other than a gas, that is known to be so toxic to humans as to afford a hazard to health during transportation or that is presumed to be toxic to humans based on toxicity tests on laboratory animals *Examples:* aniline, arsenic, liquid tetraethyl lead
No Placard for Division 6.2, see labels	**Division 6.2: Infectious Substance** — Material known to contain or suspected of containing a pathogen. A pathogen is a virus or microorganism (including its viruses, plasmids, or other genetic elements, if any) or a proteinaceous infectious particle (prion) that has the potential to cause disease in humans or animals.
PG III 6	**PG III** — For Division 6.1, packing group III* (PG III) materials, a POISON placard may be modified to display the text "PG III" below the mid line of the placard rather than the word "POISON" **A packing group is a DOT packaging category based on the degree of danger presented by the hazardous material. Packing Group I indicates great danger; Packing Group II, medium danger; and Packing Group III, minor danger. The PG III placard, then, might be used for materials that are not as dangerous as those that would be placarded with the "POISON" placard*

Continued

Table 3.15 (continued)
U.S. DOT Placard Hazard Classes and Divisions

Class 6: (continued)

Inhalation Hazard Placard — Used for any quantity of Division 6.1, Zones A or B inhalation hazard only (see Division 2.3 for hazard zones)

Harmful Placard — Used to indicate materials that should be kept away from food

Class 7: Radioactive Materials (49 *CFR* 173.403)

A radioactive material means any material having a specific activity greater than 70 c (becquerels) per gram (0.002 microcurie per gram). The primary hazard of Class 7 materials is radiological, including burns and biological effects

Radioactive Placard — Is required on certain shipments of radioactive materials; vehicles with this placard are carrying "highway route controlled quantities" of radioactive materials and must follow prescribed, predetermined transportation routes

Examples: solid thorium nitrate, uranium hexafluoride

Class 8: Corrosive Materials (49 *CFR* 173.136)

A corrosive material means a liquid or solid that causes full thickness destruction of human skin at the site of contact within a specific period of time or a liquid that has a severe corrosion rate on steel or aluminum. The primary hazards of Class 8 materials are chemical and thermal, and may include the following hazards:

- Chemical burns
- Toxic effects due to exposure via all routes of entry
- Thermal effects, including fire, caused by chemical reactions generating heat
- Reactivity to water
- Mechanical effects caused by BLEVEs and violent chemical reactions

Corrosive Placard

Examples: battery fluid, chromic acid solution, soda lime, sulfuric acid, hydrochloric acid (muriatic acid), sodium hydroxide, potassium hydroxide

Continued

Table 3.15 (continued)
U.S. DOT Placard Hazard Classes and Divisions

Class 9: Miscellaneous Dangerous Goods (49 *CFR* 173.140)

A miscellaneous dangerous good is a material that (1) has an anesthetic, noxious, or other similar property that could cause extreme annoyance or discomfort to flight crew members and would prevent their correct performance of assigned duties; (2) is a hazardous substance or a hazardous waste; or (3) is an elevated temperature material; or (4) is a marine pollutant.

Miscellaneous dangerous goods will primarily have thermal and chemical hazards. For example, polychlorinated biphenyls (PCBs) are carcinogenic, while elevated temperature materials may present some thermal hazards. However, hazardous wastes may present any of the hazards associated with the materials in normal use.

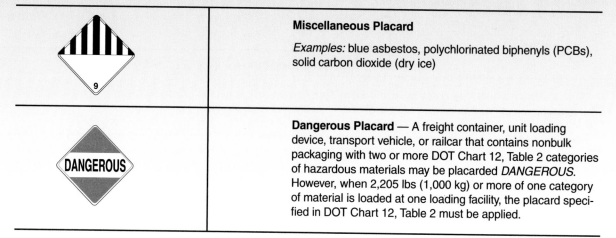

	Miscellaneous Placard *Examples:* blue asbestos, polychlorinated biphenyls (PCBs), solid carbon dioxide (dry ice)
	Dangerous Placard — A freight container, unit loading device, transport vehicle, or railcar that contains nonbulk packaging with two or more DOT Chart 12, Table 2 categories of hazardous materials may be placarded *DANGEROUS*. However, when 2,205 lbs (1,000 kg) or more of one category of material is loaded at one loading facility, the placard specified in DOT Chart 12, Table 2 must be applied.

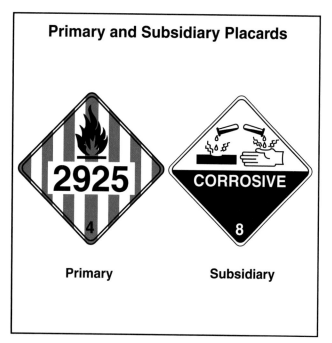

Figure 3.51 Both primary and subsidiary placards must have the hazard class or division number displayed.

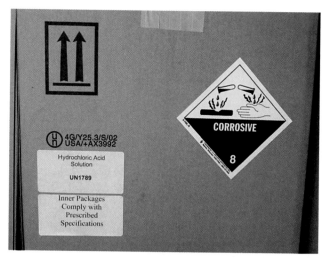

Figure 3.52 DOT-required labels provide the same basic information as vehicle placards, but they are used on nonbulk packaging such as drums, boxes, bags, and other small containers.

Figure 3.53 The oxidizer label is the primary label in this photo, while the corrosive label is the subsidiary.

Other Regulated Materials (ORM-Ds) and Materials of Trade (MOTs)*

ORM-Ds are consumer commodities that present a limited hazard during transportation due to their form, quantity, and packaging. No placards are required for ORM-Ds, but they are otherwise subject to the requirements of the Hazardous Materials Regulations (HMR). *Examples:* consumer commodities and small arms cartridges.

A *MOT* is a hazardous material, other than a hazardous waste, that is carried on a motor vehicle for the purposes listed. Placards, shipping papers, emergency response information, and formal record keeping and training are not required for them. MOT purposes:

- To protect the health and safety of motor vehicle operators or passengers. Examples: insect repellant, fire extinguishers, and self-contained breathing apparatus (SCBA)

- To support the operation or maintenance of motor vehicles, including its auxiliary equipment. Examples: spare batteries, gasoline, and engine starting fluid

- To directly support principal businesses (by private motor carriers) that are not transportation. Examples: lawn care, pest control, plumbing, welding, painting, and door-to-door sales

Many ORM-Ds (such as hairspray) may qualify as MOTs. However, self-reactive materials, poison inhalation hazard materials, and hazardous wastes are *never* eligible to qualify as MOTs.

---

* See 49 *CFR* 173.144 and 49 *CFR* 173.6.

Don't be Fooled!

Placarded materials may have many hazards not reflected by the placard classification. For example, many materials marked by a Flammable placard are toxic as well.

A specific example is anhydrous ammonia; it is placarded in the U.S. as a nonflammable gas. However, under certain conditions (particularly inside where fumes can become concentrated), it will burn. In 1984, in Shreveport, Louisiana, two hazardous material response team members entered a cold-storage facility to stop a leak of anhydrous ammonia. With a lower explosive limit (LEL) of 16 percent and an explosive range of 16 to 25 percent, the fumes inside the facility reached a flammable concentration. Unfortunately, a spark ignited the vapors, and one team member was killed. The other was seriously burned. Anhydrous ammonia can catch fire even though it is not classified as a flammable gas by DOT.

In other countries, anhydrous ammonia is classified as a corrosive (caustic) liquid and a poison gas because of its chemical effects. Anhydrous ammonia has a threshold limit value (TLV®) of 25 ppm in air. Inhaling concentrated fumes can kill a person even though it is not classified as an inhalation hazard by DOT!

bel, while the label on the right is the subsidiary. DOT regulations require that subsidiary labels have the class number displayed. There is a transition period through 2005 for that requirement, so subsidiary labels before that time may lack the class number. The regulations governing the use of labels are contained in Title 49 *CFR*.

Table 3.16, p. 170, provides examples of the unique DOT labels. Other labels for the nine hazard classes and subdivisions are essentially the same as the placards shown earlier in Table 3.15.

DOT Markings
[NFPA 472: 4.2.1(7)(a)]

By the DOT definition, a *marking* is a descriptive name, an identification number, a weight, or a specification and includes instructions, cautions, or UN marks (or combinations thereof) required on outer packagings of hazardous materials. This section, however, shows only those markings found on DOT Chart 12. Markings on intermodal

Table 3.16
Unique U.S. DOT Labels

Subsidiary Risk Labels

Subsidiary risk labels may be used for the following classes: Explosives, Flammable Gases, Flammable Liquids, Flammable Solids, Corrosives, Oxidizers, Poisons, Spontaneously Combustible Materials, and Dangerous-When-Wet Materials.

Explosive Subsidiary Risk Label

Class 3: Flammable Liquid

Flammable Liquid Label — Marks packages containing flammable liquids.

Examples: gasoline, methyl ethyl ketone

Class 6: Poison (Toxic), Poison Inhalation Hazard, Infectious Substance

Infectious Substances Label — Marks packages with infectious substances (viable microorganism, or its toxin, which causes or may cause disease in humans or animals).

This label may be used to mark packages of Class 6.2 materials as defined in 49 *CFR* 172.432 until October 1, 2005.

Examples: anthrax, hepatitis B virus, *escherichia* coli (E. coli)

Biohazard Label — Marks bulk packaging containing a regulated medical waste as defined in 49 *CFR* 173.134(a)(5).

Examples: used needles/syringes, human blood or blood products, human tissue or anatomical waste, carcasses of animals intentionally infected with human pathogens for medical research

Etiological Agents Label — Marks packages containing etiologic agents transported in interstate traffic per 42 *CFR* 72.3 and 72.6

Examples: rabies virus, rickettsia, Ebola virus, salmonella bacteria

Continued

Table 3.16 (continued)
Unique U.S. DOT Labels

Class 7: Radioactive Materials

Packages of radioactive materials must be labeled on two opposite sides, with a distinctive warning label. Each of the three label categories — RADIOACTIVE WHITE-I, RADIOACTIVE YELLOW-II, or RADIOACTIVE YELLOW-III — bears the unique trefoil symbol for radiation.

Class 7 Radioactive I, II, and III labels must always contain the following additional information:

- Isotope name
- Radioactive activity

Radioactive II and III labels will also provide the transport Index (TI) indicating the degree of control to be excercised by the carrier during transportation. The number in the transport index box indicates the maximum radiation level measured (in mrem/hr) at one meter from the surface of the package. Packages with the Radioactive I label have a Transport Index of 0.

	Radioactive I Label — Label with an all-white background color that indicates that the external radiation level is low and no special stowage controls or handling are required.
	Radioactive II Label — Upper half of the label is yellow, which indicates that the package has an external radiation level or fissile (nuclear safety criticality) characteristic that requires consideration during stowage in transportation.
	Radioactive III Label — Yellow label with three red stripes indicates the transport vehicle must be placarded RADIOACTIVE.
	Fissile Label — Used on containers of fissile materials (materials capable of undergoing fission such as uranium-233, uranium-235, and plutonium-239). The Criticality Safety Index (CSI) must be listed on this label. The CSI is used to provide control over the accumulation of packages, overpacks, or freight containers containing fissile material.
	Empty Label — Used on containers that have been emptied of their radioactive materials, but still contain residual radioactivity.

Continued

Table 3.16 (continued)
Unique U.S. DOT Labels

	Aircraft Labels
	Magnetized Material Label — Marks magnetized materials that could cause navigation deviations on aircraft.
	Danger - Cargo Aircraft Only — Used to indicate materials that cannot be transported on passenger aircraft.

containers, tank cars, and other packaging are discussed in later sections. **Table 3.17** shows the DOT Chart 12 markings.

Canadian Transportation Placards, Labels, and Markings

[NFPA 472: 4.2.1(9)]

TC and the Dangerous Goods Act govern transportation placards, labels, and markings in Canada. Like the U.S. HMR, the Dangerous Goods Act is based on the *UN Recommendations* and, therefore, is very similar. The nine hazard classes are identical. **Table 3.18, p. 174,** provides Canadian placards, labels, and markings divided by class. There are some differences, however, between Canadian and U.S. placards, labels, and markings such as the following:

- Most Canadian transport placards do not have any signal words written on them.

- Labels and markings may be in both English and French.

- Subsidiary labels and placards will not have the class number on them.

Mexican Transportation Placards, Labels, and Markings

Like Canada and the U.S., Mexican transportation placards, labels, and markings are based on the *UN Recommendations* and have the same hazard classes and subdivisions. In fact, Canadian and Mexican placards and labels are virtually the same. However, because international regulations authorize the insertion of text (other than the class or division number) in the space below the symbol as long as the text relates to the nature of the hazard or precautions to be taken in handling, placards and labels in Mexico may have text that is in Spanish **(Figure 3.54, p. 178).** Likewise, information provided on markings is likely to be written in Spanish. English-speaking first responders in Mexico or along the U.S./Mexican border should familiarize themselves with the more common Spanish hazard warning terms such as *peligro* (danger).

Some differences between the Mexican transportation regulations and the U.S. HMR are as follows:

- Mexican regulations do not authorize the *Stow-Away-from-Foodstuffs* label. The *Poison* or *Toxic* label is used instead.

Table 3.17
U.S. DOT Markings

Marking	Description
HOT	**Hot Marking** — Has the same dimensions as a placard and is used on elevated temperature materials. *Note:* Bulk containers of molten aluminum or molten sulfur must be marked MOLTEN ALUMINUM or MOLTEN SULFUR, respectively.
MARINE POLLUTANT	**Marine Pollutant Marking** — Must be displayed on packages of substances designated as marine pollutants. *Examples:* cadmium compounds, copper cyanide, mercury based pesticides
INHALATION HAZARD	**Inhalation Hazard Marking** — Used to mark materials that are poisonous by inhalation. *Examples:* anhydrous ammonia, methyl bromide, hydrogen cyanide, hydrogen sulfide
DANGER — THIS UNIT IS UNDER FUMIGATION — DO NOT ENTER	**Fumigant Marking** — Warning affixed on or near each door of a transport vehicle, freight container, or railcar in which the lading has been fumigated or is undergoing fumigation with any material. The vehicle, container, or railcar is considered a package containing a hazardous material unless it has been sufficiently aerated so that it does not pose a risk to health and safety.
↑↑ ↑↑	**Orientation Markings** — Markings used to designate the orientation of the package. Sometimes these markings will be accompanied by words such as "this side up."
CONSUMER COMMODITY — ORM-D	**ORM-D** — Used on packages of ORM-D materials. *Examples:* consumer commodities, small arms cartridges
CONSUMER COMMODITY — ORM-D-AIR	**ORM-D-AIR** — Used on packages of ORM-D materials shipped via air.
INNER PACKAGES COMPLY WITH PRESCRIBED SPECIFICATIONS	**Inner Packaging** — Used on authorized packages containing hazardous materials being transported in an overpack as defined in 49 *CFR* 171.8.

Table 3.18
Canadian Transportation Placards, Labels, and Markings

Class 1: Explosives	
Placard and Label	**Class 1.1** — Mass explosion hazard
Placard and Label	**Class 1.2** — Projection hazard but not a mass explosion hazard
Placard and Label	**Class 1.3** — Fire hazard and either a minor blast hazard or a minor projection hazard or both but not a mass explosion hazard
Placard and Label	**Class 1.4** — No significant hazard beyond the package in the event of ignition or initiation during transport * = Compatibility group letter
Placard and Label	**Class 1.5** — Very insensitive substances with a mass explosion hazard
Placard and Label	**Class 1.6** — Extremely insensitive articles with no mass explosion hazard

Class 2: Gases	
Placard and Label	**Class 2.1 — Flammable Gases**
Placard and Label	**Class 2.2 — Nonflammable and Nontoxic Gases**

Continued

Class 2: Gases (continued)

	Class 2.3 — Toxic Gases
Placard and Label	**Oxidizing Gases**

Class 3: Flammable Liquids

Placard and Label	**Class 3 — Flammable Liquids**

Class 4: Flammable Solids, Substances Liable to Spontaneous Combustion, and Substances that on Contact with Water Emit Flammable Gases (Water-Reative Substances)

Placard and Label	**Class 4.1 — Flammable Solids**
Placard and Label	**Class 4.2 — Substances Liable to Spontaneous Combustion**
Placard and Label	**Class 4.3 — Water-Reactive Substances**

Class 5: Oxidizing Substances and Organic Peroxides

Placard and Label	**Class 5.1 — Oxidizing Substances**
Placard and Label	**Class 5.2 — Organic Peroxides**

Continued

Class 6: Toxic and Infectious Substances	
Placard and Label	**Class 6.1 — Toxic Substances**
Label Only	**Class 6.2 — Infectious Substances** Text: INFECTIOUS In case of damage or leakage, Immediately notify local authorities AND INFECTIEUX En cas de Dommage ou de fuite communiquer Immédiatement avec les autorités locales ET CANUTEC 613-996-6666
Placard Only	**Class 6.2 — Infectious Substances**

Class 7: Radioactive Materials	
Label and Optional Placard	**Class 7 — Radioactive Materials** **Category I** — White RADIOACTIVE CONTENTS......................CONTENU ACTIVITY ....ACTIVITÉ
Label and Optional Placard	**Class 7 — Radioactive Materials** **Category II** — Yellow RADIOACTIVE CONTENTS......................CONTENU ACTIVITY ....ACTIVITÉ INDICE DE TRANSPORT INDEX
Label and Optional Placard	**Class 7 — Radioactive Materials** **Category III** — Yellow RADIOACTIVE CONTENTS......................CONTENU ACTIVITY ....ACTIVITÉ INDICE DE TRANSPORT INDEX

Continued

Class 7: Radioactive Materials (continued)

 Placard	**Class 7 — Radioactive Materials** The word RADIOACTIVE is optional.

Class 8: Corrosives

 Placard and Label	**Class 8 — Corrosives**

Class 9: Miscellaneous Products, Substances, or Organisms

 Placard and Label	**Class 9 — Miscellaneous Products, Substances, or Organisms**

Other Placards, Labels, and Markings

	Danger Placard
	Elevated Temperature Sign
	**Fumigation Sign** Text is in both English and French
	**Marine Pollutant Mark** The text is MARINE POLLUTANT or POLLUANT MARIN.

Mexican Placards and Labels

Figure 3.54 Placards and labels in Mexico may have text that is written in Spanish. English-speaking responders should still be able to recognize symbols, shapes, and colors that provide them with information about the hazards associated with the contents of the package or container.

- The official Mexican standards do not authorize the use of the *DANGEROUS* placard since NOM-004 does not include provisions for its use. However, *PELIGROSO (DANGEROUS)* placards may still be seen in Mexico.

- Package markings are consistent except that the proper shipping name is provided in Spanish in addition to English. NOM-002-SCT2/1994 provides the official Mexican proper shipping names.

- The *HOT* mark used for elevated temperature materials in the U.S. is not authorized in Mexico. In Mexico, the elevated temperature mark provided in the *UN Recommendations* must be used, which is the same as the Canadian elevated temperature mark (see p. 177).

- The Mexican regulations do not require the marine pollutants mark for surface transportation.

- The Mexican standards incorporate provisions for consumer commodities but do not authorize the use of the ORM-D description as a package marking.

- The Mexican standard regarding the classification of flammable liquids does not incorporate provisions for combustible liquids. Combustible liquid requirements only apply in the U.S.

- Like Canada, subsidiary placards and labels in Mexico may not have the class number in the bottom corner **(Figure 3.55).**

Mexican Subsidiary Placard: Water Reactive Solids

Figure 3.55 Subsidiary placards in Mexico and Canada may not have the hazard class or division number in the bottom corner.

Other North American Highway Vehicle Identification Markings

[NFPA 472: 5.2.1.2(A)(3)]

In addition to UN commodity identification numbers (often just called *ID numbers* or *four-digit ID numbers;* see UN Commodity Identification Numbers section), highway transportation vehicles may have other identification markings. These markings may include company names, logos, specific tank colors for certain tanks, stenciled commodity names (such as *Liquid Propane*), and manufacturers' specification plates. Specification plates provide information about the standards to which the container/tank was built (**Figure 3.56**).

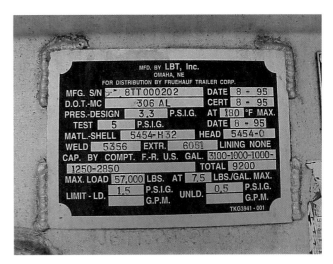

Figure 3.56 Manufacturers' specification plates provide a wealth of information about the standards to which the container/tank was built.

North American Railroad Tank Car Markings

[NFPA 472: 5.2.1.2(A)(1)]

There may be a variety of markings on railroad tank cars that responders can use to gain valuable information about the tank and its contents such as the following:

- Initials (reporting marks) and number
- Capacity stencil
- Specification marking

The *ERG* provides a key to these markings in the railcar identification chart, and more information is provided in sections that follow. Additionally, manufacturer's names on cars may provide some contact information. Dedicated railcars transporting a single material must have the name of that material painted on the car. Likewise, a number of hazardous materials transported by rail are required to have their names stenciled on the sides of the car in 4-inch (102 mm) letters. These hazardous chemicals are listed in **Table 3.19, p. 180**.

NOTE: The source for the following information on railroad tank car markings is courtesy of "A General Guide to Tank Cars," prepared by the Union Pacific Railroad, April, 2003.

Initials

Tank cars (like all other freight cars) are marked with their own unique sets of initials (called *reporting marks*) and numbers. The initials and numbers

are stenciled on both sides (to the left when facing the side of the car) and both ends (upper center) of the tank car tank (**Figure 3.57, p. 181**). Some shippers and car owners also stencil the top of the car with the car's initials and numbers to help identify the car in case an accident turns it on its side.

Initials and numbers may be used to get information about the car's contents from the railroad's computer or the shipper. These reporting marks and numbers should match the reporting marks and numbers provided on the shipping papers for the car.

Capacity Stencil

The *capacity stencil* shows the volume of the tank car tank. The volume in gallons (and sometimes liters) is stenciled on both ends of the car under the car's initials and number (**Figure 3.58, p. 181**). The volume in pounds (and sometimes kilograms) is stenciled on the sides of the car under the car's initials and number. The term *load limit* may be used to mean the same thing as *capacity*. For certain tank cars, the water capacity (water weight) of the tank, in pounds (and typically kilograms) is stenciled on the sides of the tank near the center of the car.

Specification Marking

The *specification marking* indicates the standards to which a tank car was built. The marking is stenciled on both sides of the tank. When facing

Table 3.19
Stenciled Commodity Names

ACROLEIN	LIQUEFIED HYDROCARBON GAS (may also be stenciled PROPANE, BUTANE, PROPYLENE, or ETHYLENE)
ANHYDROUS AMMONIA	
BROMINE	
BUTADIENE	LIQUEFIED PETROLEUM GAS (may also be stenciled PROPANE, BUTANE, PROPYLENE, or ETHYLENE)
CHLORINE	
CHLOROPRENE (when transported in DOT 115A specification tank car)	
	METHYL ACETYLENE PROPADIENE STABILIZED
DIFULOROETHANE*	
DIFLUOROMONOCHLORO-METHANE*	METHYL CHLORIDE
	METHYL MERCAPTAN
DIMETHYLAMINE, ANHYDROUS	METHYL CHLORIDE – METHYLENE CHLORIDE MIXTURE
DIMETHYL ETHER (transported only in ton cylinders)	
	MONOMETHYLAMINE, ANHYDROUS
ETHYLENE IMINE	MOTOR FUEL ANTIKNOCK COMPOUND or ANTIKNOCK COMOUND
ETHYLENE OXIDE	
FORMIC ACID	
FUSED POTASSIUM NITRATE AND SODIUM NITRATE	NITRIC ACID
	NITROGEN TETROXIDE
HYDROCYANIC ACID	NITROGEN TETROXIDE – NITRIC OXIDE MIXTURE
HYDROFLUORIC ACID	
HYDROGEN	PHOSPHORUS
HYDROGEN CHLORIDE (by exemption from DOT)	SULFUR TRIOXIDE
	TRIFLUOROCHLORO-ETHYLENE*
HYDROGEN FLUORIDE	TRIMETHYLAMINE, ANHYDROUS
HYDROGEN PEROXIDE	VINYL CHLORIDE
HYDROGEN SULFIDE	VINYL FLUORIDE INHIBITED
LIQUEFIED HYDROGEN	VINYL METHYL ETHER INHIBITED

* May be stenciled DISPERSANT GAS or REFRIGERANT GAS in lieu of name. Only *flammable* refrigerant or dispersant gases are stenciled.

the side of the car, the marking will be to the right (opposite from the initials and number) **(Figure 3.59a, p. 182)**. The specification marking is also stamped into the tank heads where it is not readily visible. Emergency responders can also get specification information from the railroad, shipper, car owner, or the Association of American Railroads (from the car's Certificate of Construction) by using the car's initials and number. **Figure 3.59b, p. 182,** provides a brief explanation of tank car specification markings.

International Intermodal Container/Tank Markings
[NFPA 472: 5.2.1.2(A)(2)]

In addition to DOT-required placards, intermodal tanks and containers are marked with initials (reporting marks) and tank numbers **(Figure 3.60, p. 183)**. These markings are generally found on the right-hand side of the tank or container as the emergency responder faces it from either the sides or the ends. The markings are either on the tank/

Tank Car Initials and Number

Acme Tank Car Co.
CELX 6430
LD LMT 000000 LB 00000 KG
LT WT 00000 LB   00000 KG
NEW   00 00

CELX 6430
Capy 00000 Gals US
00000 L

Figure 3.57 *CELX 6430* are the reporting marks and car number on this fictional tank car. The other stencils depicted here indicate such things as the tank capacity (*CAPY* on the end view), various weights (load limit [*LD LMT*] and light weight [*LT WT*, the weight of the car unloaded]), and the *NEW* date (month and year). On a real car, these numbers will not be all zeros.

Figure 3.58 An example of water capacity markings found on tank cars. On a real tank, the zeros will be replaced with actual weights.

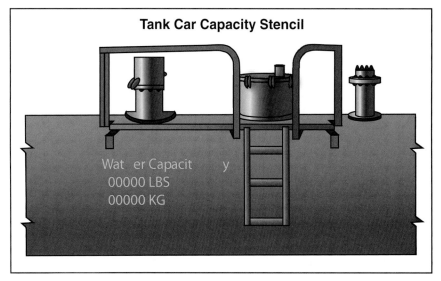

Tank Car Capacity Stencil

Wat er Capacit   y
00000 LBS
00000 KG

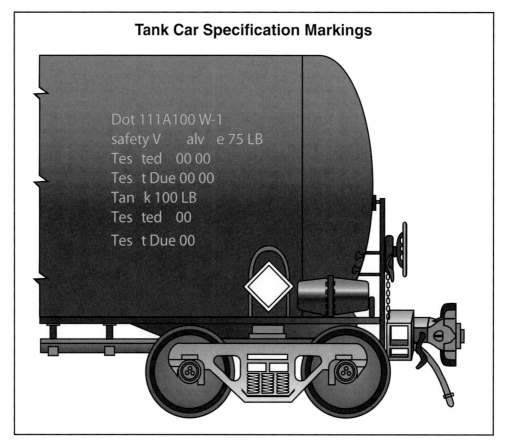

Tank Car Specification Markings

Dot 111A100 W-1
safety V   alv   e 75 LB
Tes ted   00 00
Tes t Due 00 00
Tan k 100 LB
Tes ted   00
Tes t Due 00

Figure 3.59a The top line of stencils (beginning with *DOT*) provides the specification markings indicating the standards to which the tank car was built.

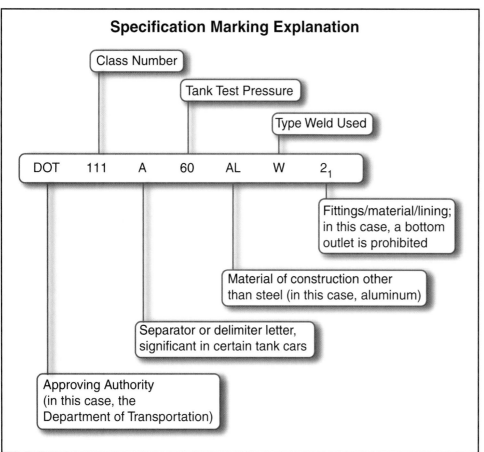

Specification Marking Explanation

Class Number

Tank Test Pressure

Type Weld Used

DOT   111   A   60   AL   W   2₁

Fittings/material/lining; in this case, a bottom outlet is prohibited

Material of construction other than steel (in this case, aluminum)

Separator or delimiter letter, significant in certain tank cars

Approving Authority (in this case, the Department of Transportation)

Figure 3.59b Key to tank car specification markings.

Figure 3.60 Intermodal tanks are also marked with initials (reporting marks) and tank numbers (top line of stencils: ICSU 029514 1). *Courtesy of Rich Mahaney.*

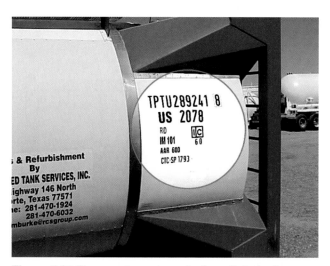

Figure 3.61 The country code and a four-digit size/type code are directly beneath the reporting marks and numbers on this tank. The *US* in the picture stands for United States, *20* indicates size, and *78* is a code for the type.

container or the frame. As with tank car reporting marks, emergency responders can use this information in conjunction with the shipping papers or computer data to identify and verify the contents of the tank or container.

The tank/container also displays a country code and size/type code (**Figure 3.61**). The four-digit size/type code follows the country code (**Table 3.20**). The first two numbers identify the container length and height; the second two numbers indicate the pressure range of the contents (see **Table 3.21, p. 184**).

Clue 4
Other Markings and Colors

[NFPA 472: 4.2.1(7)(f), 5.2.1.2, 5.2.1.2(B), 5.2.1.3]

In addition to DOT placards, labels, and markings, a number of other markings, marking systems, labels, labeling systems, colors, color-codes, and signs may indicate the presence of hazardous materials at fixed facilities, on pipelines, on piping systems, and on other containers. These other markings may be as simple as the word *chlorine* stenciled on the outside of a fixed-facility tank or as complicated as a site-specific hazard communication system using a unique combination of labels, placards, emergency contact information, and color codes. Some fixed-facility containers

Table 3.20
Common Intermodal Container Country Codes

BM (BER)..........Bermuda	**LIB**.........................Liberia
CH (CHS) ...... Switzerland	**NLX** .... Netherlands
DE............West Germany	**NZX** .... New Zealand
DKX...................Denmark	**PA (PNM)** .... Panama
FR (FXX) ....France	**PIX**................... Phillipines
GB .... Great Britain	**PRC** ..... People's Republic of China States
HKXX.............Hong Kong	
ILX ....Israel	**RCX** ....Republic of China (Taiwan)
IXX.............................Italy	**SGP** .... Singapore
JP (JXX).................Japan	**SXX** ....Sweden
KR ....Korea	**US (USA)** ... United States

may have identification numbers that correspond to site or emergency plans that provide details on the product, quantity, and other pertinent information.

First responders need to be familiar with some of the more widely used specialized marking systems for hazardous materials. The sections that follow highlight the most common specialized systems in North America, including NFPA 704, common hazardous communication labels, International Organization for Standardization (ISO) safety

Table 3.21
Common Intermodal Tank Size and Type Codes

| Common Size Codes | Common Type Codes (Maximum Allowable Working Pressures) | |
	Nonhazardous Commodities	Hazardous Commodities
20 = 20 feet (8 feet high) *[6 m (2.4 m high)]*	70 = less than 0.44 bar test pressure *(6.4 psi) {44 kPa}*	74 = less than 1.47 bar test pressure *(21.3 psi) {147 kPa}*
22 = 20 feet (8 feet 6 inches high) *[6 m (2.6 m high)]*	71 = 0.44 to 1.47 bar test pressure *(6.4 to 21.3 psi) {44 to 147 kPa}*	75 = 1.47 to 2.58 bar test pressure *(21.3 to 37.4 psi) {147 to 258 kPa}*
24 = 20 feet (greater than 8 feet 6 inches high) *[6 m (2.6 m high)]*	72 = 1.47 to 2.94 bar test pressure *(21.3 to 42.6 psi) {147 to 294 kPa}*	76 = 2.58 to 2.94 bar test pressure *(37.4 to 42.6 psi) {258 to 294 kPa}*
	73 = spare	77 = 2.94 to 3.93 bar test pressure *(42.6 to 3.93 psi) {294 to 393 kPa}*
		78 = greater than 3.93 bar test pressure *(57 psi) {393 kPa}*
		79 = spare

symbols, globally harmonized system symbols, military markings, pipeline identifications, piping systems, American Petroleum Institute (API) markings, pesticide labels, and color codes.

NFPA 704 System

[NFPA 472: 4.2.1.7(b), 4.2.1(8)]

The information in NFPA 704 gives a widely recognized method for indicating the presence of hazardous materials at commercial, manufacturing, institutional, and other fixed-storage facilities. Use of this system is commonly required by local ordinances for all occupancies that contain hazardous materials. It is designed to alert emergency responders to health, flammability, instability, and related hazards (specifically, oxidizers and water-reactive materials) that may present as short-term, acute

exposures resulting from a fire, spill, or similar emergency. The NFPA 704 system is *not* designed for the following situations or hazards:

• Transportation

• General public use

• Nonemergency occupational exposures

• Explosive and blasting agents, including commercial explosive materials

• Chronic health hazards

• Etiologic agents, and other similar hazards

The NFPA 704 system does, however, offer the following information:

• Provides the appropriate signal or alert to first responders that hazardous materials are present. The first-arriving responder who sees the NFPA 704 marker on a structure can determine the hazards of a single material in a marked container or the relative combined hazard severity of the collection of numerous materials in the occupancy (**Figure 3.62**).

- Identifies the general hazards and the degree of severity for health, flammability, and instability.

- Provides immediate information necessary to protect the lives of both the public and emergency response personnel.

Be Aware!

NFPA 704 markings provide very useful information, but the system does have its limitations. For example, an NFPA diamond doesn't tell you exactly what chemical or chemicals may be present in specific quantities. Nor does it tell you exactly where they may be located when the sign is used for a building, structure, or area (such as a storage yard) rather than an individual container. Positive identification of the materials needs to be made through other means such as container markings, employee information, company records, and pre-incident surveys.

Lt. Adams saw the NFPA 704 diamond on the outside of the trucking warehouse, and it alerted her to the presence of oxidizers, a fact that significantly increased the potential hazard of the situation. Keeping the extremely flammable 1,2-butylene oxide from coming in contact with the oxidizers would have been a top priority. However, the NFPA 704 diamond did not provide her with the pertinent information that the oxidizers were kept in a separate section of the warehouse from the 1,2-butylene oxide. That information came from the facility manager.

Specifically, the NFPA 704 system uses a rating system of numbers from *0* to *4*. The number *0* indicates a minimal hazard, whereas the number *4* indicates a severe hazard. The rating is assigned to three categories: health, flammability, and instability. The rating numbers are arranged on a diamond-shaped marker or sign. The health rating is located on the blue background, the flammability hazard rating is positioned on the

Figure 3.62 NFPA 704 markers provide useful information to first responders. The *3* in the blue diamond on this marker warns that there are significant health hazards associated with materials in this building.

red background, and the instability hazard rating appears on a yellow background. As an alternative, the backgrounds for each of these rating positions may be any contrasting color, and the numbers (*0* to *4*) may be represented by the appropriate color (blue, red, and yellow) (**Figure 3.63, p. 186**).

Special hazards are located in the six o'clock position and have no specified background color; however, white is most commonly used. Only two special hazard symbols are presently authorized for use in this position by the NFPA: *W* and *OX* (respectively, indicating unusual reactivity with water or that the material is an oxidizer). However, first responders may see other symbols on old placards, including the trefoil radiation symbol.

The general ratings for each hazard (health, flammability, and instability) are presented in **Figure 3.64, p. 186**. Detailed descriptions of the hazard ratings are provided in the NFPA 704

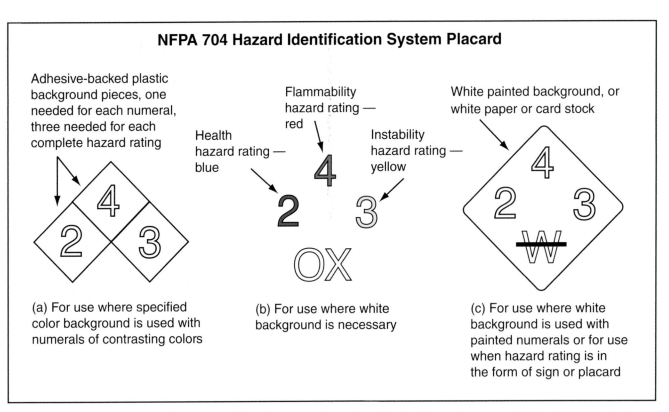

Figure 3.63 Layout of the NFPA 704 hazard identification system. *Reprinted with permission from NFPA 704-2001, System for the Identification of the Hazards of Materials for Emergency Response, Copyright © 2001, National Fire Protection Association, Quincy, MA. This reprinted material is not the complete and official position of the NFPA on the referenced subject, which is represented only by the standard in its entirety.*

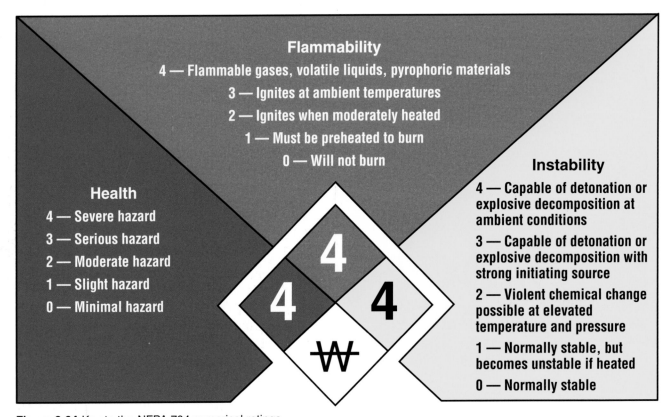

Figure 3.64 Key to the NFPA 704 numerical ratings.

standard itself. The NFPA 704 system is used in conjunction with NFPA 49, *Hazardous Chemicals Data,* and NFPA 325, *Guide to Fire Hazard Properties of Flammable Liquids, Gases, and Volatile Solids,* which are found in NFPA's *Fire Protection Guide to Hazardous Materials* (2001).

NFPA 49 and 325 describe the properties and hazards of various materials and provide information on personal protection and fire fighting when faced with these specific chemicals. Valuable information is given on assigning appropriate ratings to the NFPA 704 markers at facilities that contain listed chemicals.

Hazard Communications Labels and Markings
[NFPA 472: 4.2.1(7)(d)]

The OSHA Hazard Communication Standard (HCS) (Subpart Z, Toxic and Hazardous Substances, 29 *CFR* 1910.1200) requires employers to identify hazards in the workplace and train employees how to recognize those hazards. It also requires the employer to ensure that all hazardous material containers are labeled, tagged, or marked with the identity of the substances contained in them, along with appropriate hazard warnings. The standard does not specify what system (or systems) of identification must be used, leaving that to be determined by individual employers. First responders, then, may encounter a variety of different (and sometimes unique) labeling and marking systems in their jurisdictions **(Figure 3.65).** Conducting pre-incident surveys should assist responders in identifying and understanding these systems.

Hazard Communications Labels
[NFPA 472: 4.2.1(9)]

A variety of labeling systems are used to comply with the requirements of the HCS. Some of these systems are available commercially to the general public; individual companies or organizations develop others for their own private use. Many of these systems resemble NFPA 704 in that they are color-coded/numerical rating systems based on a rating scale of *0* to *4,* with *0* indicating the lowest level of hazard and *4* indicating the highest level. However, there may be some common differences

Figure 3.65 The OSHA Hazard Communications Standard requires employers to identify hazards in the workplace. First responders may encounter a variety of different identification systems used by employers in their area.

between NFPA 704 and these labeling systems such as the following:

- Most of these labels are intended to communicate the hazards of a material under normal, occupational conditions rather than emergency conditions.

- The *0* to *4* rating found on the label for a particular substance might not be the same as the NFPA rating for the same product. (While some people may consider the label rating and NFPA rating to be identical and/or synonymous, it is not necessarily the case.)

- Whereas NFPA 704 ratings are communicated on a diamond shape, the hazard communication label ratings are usually provided on vertically stacked bars **(Figure 3.66, p. 188).** *Details:*

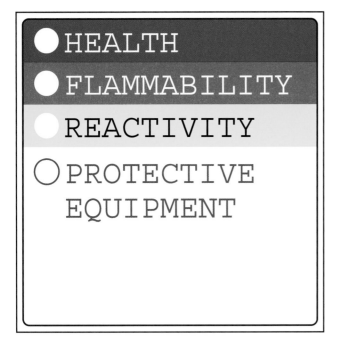

Figure 3.66 Hazardous Materials Information Guide (HMIG) labels are used to quickly identify the hazards associated with individual containers of product. *Courtesy of Lab Safety Supply, Inc.*

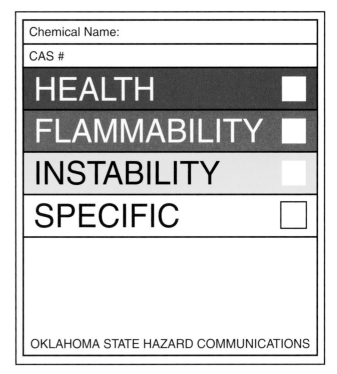

Figure 3.67 Hybrid labeling systems often look similar to HMIG labels but may have significant differences in how they should be interpreted.

— The white (specific hazard) portion of both labels usually provided information about what personal protective equipment should be used when working with the material.

— Information is often conveyed by a letter code, sometimes supplemented by pictograms. For example, the letter *A* in the white box/bar might indicate that safety glasses should be worn.

• Different systems may use colors to indicate different things. For example, whereas blue generally indicates *Health* and red indicates *Flammability*, NFPA uses yellow to indicate *Instability*, while the Hazardous Materials Information Guide (HMIG) system (a commercial labeling system marketed by Lab Safety Supply, Inc.) uses yellow to indicate *Reactivity*.

• An asterisk (*) or other symbol is sometimes used to indicate that the material has chronic health effects.

Again, be aware that many employers have devised their own hybrid labeling systems that are often very similar looking but may have significant differences in how they should be interpreted **(Figure 3.67)**. It is important that emergency responders use pre-incident surveys to become familiar with the systems used at facilities in their jurisdictions.

Manufacturers' Labels and Signal Words

Under the HCS, chemical manufacturers and importers are required to provide appropriate labels on their product containers. Manufacturers' labels provide a variety of information to first responders, including the name of the product, manufacturer's contact information, and precautionary hazard warnings. These labels may also provide directions for use and handling, names of active ingredients, first aid instructions, and other pertinent information.

Under the Federal Hazardous Substances Act (FHSA), labels on products destined for consumer households must incorporate one of the following four *signal words* to indicate the degree of hazard associated with the product **(Figure 3.68)**:

• *CAUTION* — Indicates the product may have minor health effects (such as eye or skin irritation)

• *WARNING* — Indicates the product has moderate hazards such as significant health effects or flammability

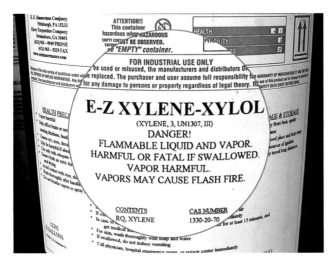

Figure 3.68 Signal words such as *CAUTION*, *WARNING*, and *DANGER* indicate the degree of hazard associated with the product. *DANGER* indicates the highest degree of hazard. An additional word, *POISON*, is required on highly toxic materials such as pesticides.

- *DANGER* — Indicates the highest degree of hazard (used on products that have potentially severe or deadly effects); also used on products that explode when exposed to heat

- *POISON* — Required in addition to DANGER on the labels of highly toxic materials such as pesticides

The FHSA requires labels to provide other information as well such as the following:

- Name and business address of the manufacturer, packer, distributor, or seller

- Common or usual or chemical name of each hazardous ingredient

- Affirmative statement of the principal hazard or hazards that the product presents, for example, *Flammable, Harmful if Swallowed, Causes Burns, Vapor Harmful,* and the like.

- Precautionary statements telling users what they must do or what actions they must avoid to protect themselves

- Instructions for first-aid treatment where it is appropriate in the event the product injures someone

- Instructions for consumers to follow to protect themselves when a product requires special care in handling or storage

- Statement, *Keep out of the reach of children*

The EPA mandates that appropriate signal words (CAUTION, WARNING, DANGER, or DANGER/POISON) be provided on the labels of pesticides. Most chemical manufacturers and importers incorporate these signal words into their labels based on the American National Standard Institute's (ANSI) "Hazardous Industrial Chemicals - Precautionary Labeling" document (ANSI Z129.1-2000) regardless of whether the product is intended for consumers or not.

Other Symbols and Signs

Other hazard communication symbols that first responders should be able to recognize are shown in **Table 3.22.** There may be other hazard communication symbols as well. Every facility may have its own system and its own symbols, signs, and markings.

The EPA requires a warning label on any containers, transformers, or capacitors that contain polychlorinated biphenyl (PCB), which is considered hazardous because it may cause cancer. **Figure 3.69, p. 190,** shows a typical U.S. PCB warning label, whereas **Figure 3.70, p. 190,** shows a Canadian PCB warning label.

Table 3.22 Hazard Communications Symbols*	
Symbol	**Description**
☣	**Biological Hazard**
⚗	**Chemical Hazard**
☢	**Nuclear/Radiological Hazard**
CANCER HAZARD	**Carcinogen/Cancer Hazard**

* These symbols may be presented in a variety of colors and/or formats. For example, they will not always be seen in the center of a circle or rectangle.

CAUTION
CONTAINS
PCBs
(Polychlorinated Biphenyls)

A toxic environmental contaminant requiring
special handling and disposal in accordance with
U.S. Environmental Protection Agency Regulations
40 CFR 761 - For Disposal Information contact
the nearest U.S. E.P.A. Office.

In case of accident or spill, call toll free the U.S.
Coast Guard National Response Center:
800:424-8802
Dow Chemical
504-353-8888

Figure 3.69 U.S. PCB warning labels are found on
containers, transformers, or capacitors that contain
polychlorinated biphenyls.

ATTENTION
PCB

CONTAINS POLYCHLORINATED BIPHENYLS	CONTIENT DES BIPHÉNYLES POLYCHLORÉS
A TOXIC SUBSTANCE LISTED IN SCHEDULE 1 OF THE CANADIAN ENVIRONMENTAL PROTECTION ACT. IN CASE OF ACCIDENT, SPILL OR FOR DISPOSAL INFORMATION, CONTACT THE NEAREST OFFICE OF THE ENVIROMENTAL PROTECTION BRANCH, ENVIRONMENT CANADA	UN PRODUIT TOXIQUE MENTIONNÉ DANS L'ANNEXE I DE LA LOI CANADIENNE SUR LA PROTECTION DE L'ENVIRONMENT. EN CASE D'ACCIDENT, OU DE DÉVERSMENT, OU POUR SAVOIR COMMENT L'ÉLIMINER, CONTACTER LE DUREAU DU SERVICE DE LA PROTECTION DE L'ENVIRONMENT, MINISTÈRE DE L'ENVIRONMENT, LE PLUS PRÈS.

PN

Figure 3.70 This example is one of several different styles
of Canadian PCB warning labels.

Canadian Workplace Hazardous Materials Information System

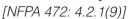

[NFPA 472: 4.2.1(9)]

Like the U.S. HCS, the Canadian Workplace Hazardous Materials Information System (WHMIS) requires that hazardous products be appropriately labeled and marked (see sidebar). A WHMIS label can be a mark, sign, stamp, sticker, seal, ticket, tag, or wrapper. It can be attached, imprinted, stenciled, or embossed on the controlled product or its container. However, there are two different types that are used most often: the supplier label and the workplace label.

Supplier Labels

A *supplier label* must appear on all controlled products received at workplaces in Canada and contain the following information **(Figure 3.71):**

- Product identifier (name of product)
- Supplier identifier (name of company that sold it)
- Statement that a MSDS is available
- Hazard symbols (pictures of the classifications)
- Risk phrases (words that describe the main hazards of the product)

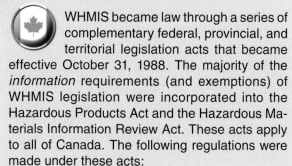

More on Canadian WHMIS

WHMIS became law through a series of complementary federal, provincial, and territorial legislation acts that became effective October 31, 1988. The majority of the *information* requirements (and exemptions) of WHMIS legislation were incorporated into the Hazardous Products Act and the Hazardous Materials Information Review Act. These acts apply to all of Canada. The following regulations were made under these acts:

- Controlled Products Regulations
- Ingredient Disclosure List
- Hazardous Materials Information Review Act Appeal Board Procedures Regulations
- Hazardous Materials Information Review Regulations

The occupational health and safety components of WHMIS that apply to federal employees and others covered by the Canada Labor Code (CLC) are specified in the CLC and the Canadian Occupational Safety and Health Regulations (Part X).

- Precautionary measures (how to work with the product safely)
- First aid measures (what to do in an emergency)

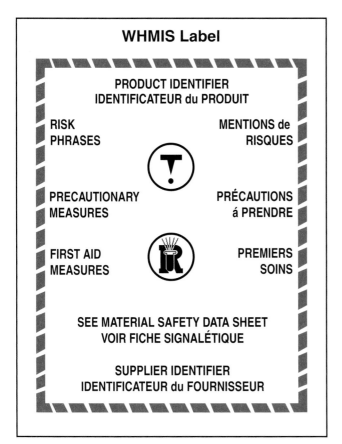

WHMIS Label

PRODUCT IDENTIFIER
IDENTIFICATEUR du PRODUIT

RISK PHRASES

MENTIONS de RISQUES

PRECAUTIONARY MEASURES

PRÉCAUTIONS á PRENDRE

FIRST AID MEASURES

PREMIERS SOINS

SEE MATERIAL SAFETY DATA SHEET
VOIR FICHE SIGNALÉTIQUE

SUPPLIER IDENTIFIER
IDENTIFICATEUR du FOURNISSEUR

Figure 3.71 An example of a blank Canadian supplier label. Completed supplier labels must be provided on all controlled products received at Canadian workplaces.

- All text in English and French
- WHMIS hatched border

If the product is always used in the container with the supplier label, no other label is required (unless the supplier label is lost or becomes unreadable). However, if the material is moved into another container for use in the workplace, this new container must have a workplace WHMIS label.

Workplace Labels

A *workplace label* must appear on all controlled products produced in a workplace or transferred to other containers by the employer and must provide the following information:

- Product identifier (product name)
- Information for the safe handling of the product
- Statement that the MSDS is available

The employer may wish to put more information on the labels such as the WHMIS hazard symbols or other pictograms, but it is not required under the law. Workplace labels may appear in placard form on controlled products received in bulk from a supplier. **Table 3.23, p. 192,** provides the WHMIS symbols and hazard classes.

NOTE: Material in this section was adapted from the Canadian Centre for Occupational Health and Safety (CCOHS), 250 Main Street East, Hamilton, Ontario L8N 1H6; Telephone: (905) 572-4400; Toll free: (800) 263-8466; Fax: (905) 572-4500.

Mexican Hazard Communication System

Mexico's equivalent to the HCS is NOM-018-STPS-2000. It, too, requires employers to ensure that hazardous chemical substances in the workplace are appropriately and adequately labeled. Essentially, it adopts NFPA 704 and a hybrid HMIG system as the official labeling and marking systems. However, employers can opt to use alternative systems as long as they comply with the objectives and purpose of the standard and are authorized by the Secretary of Labor and Social Welfare.

NOM-026-STPS-1998 ("Signs and Colors for Safety and Health") authorizes the use of some ISO safety symbols (ISO-3864, "Safety Colors and Safety Signs") on signs to communicate hazard information. General caution symbols in Mexico are triangular rather than round like those in Canada (WHMIS) or rectangular as typically found in the U.S.

ISO Safety Symbols

ISO defines the design criteria for international safety signs in its standard, ISO-3864. These symbols are being used more frequently in the U.S. in conjunction with OSHA-required hazard signs (designed per ANSI Standard Z535.4, "Product Safety Signs and Labels") as well as in Mexico, so first responders should be able to recognize the more common symbols that are used to indicate hazardous materials **(Table 3.24, p. 193).**

Globally Harmonized System

According to DOT, the U.S. and many other countries throughout the world have developed a Globally Harmonized System of Classification

Table 3.23
WHMIS Symbols and Hazard Classes

Symbol	Hazard Class	Description
	Class A: **Compressed Gas**	Contents under high pressure; cylinder may explode or burst when heated, dropped, or damaged
	Class B: **Flammable and Combustible Material**	May catch fire when exposed to heat, spark, or flame; may burst into flames
	Class C: **Oxidizing Material**	May cause fire or explosion when in contact with wood, fuels, or other combustible material
	Class D, Division 1: **Poisonous and Infectious Material:** **Immediate and serious toxic effects**	Poisonous substance; a single exposure may be fatal or cause serious or permanent damage to health
	Class D, Division 2: **Poisonous and Infectious Material:** **Other toxic effects**	Poisonous substance; may cause irritation; repeated exposure may cause cancer, birth defects, or other permanent damage
	Class D, Division 3: **Poisonous and Infectious Material:** **Biohazardous infectious materials**	May cause disease or serious illness; drastic exposures may result in death
	Class E: **Corrosive Material**	Can cause burns to eyes, skin, or respiratory system
	Class F: **Dangerously Reactive Material**	May react violently, causing explosion, fire, or release of toxic gases when exposed to light, heat, vibration, or extreme temperatures

Source: WHMIS = Canadian Workplace Hazardous Materials Information System. Table adapted from Canadian Centre for Occupational Health and Safety (CCOHS) with pictograms from Health Canada.

Table 3.24
Sample ISO-3864 Type Symbols*

| Corrosive | Explosive | Flammable | Toxic/ Poisonous |
| Biological Hazard | Radiation | Oxidizer | Irritant |

* ISO = International Organization for Standardization. This table is not comprehensive.

and Labeling of Chemicals (GHS). The purpose of GHS is to promote common, consistent criteria for classifying chemicals according to their health, physical, and environmental hazards and encourage the use of compatible hazard labels, MSDSs for employees, and other hazard communication information based on the resulting classifications.

While criteria for classifying and labeling transported dangerous goods have been internationally harmonized through the *UN Recommendations*, harmonized requirements have not been established for environmental, employee, or consumer safety regulations. A harmonized system for all regulatory purposes will lead to greater regulatory consistency among countries, thereby promoting safer transportation, handling, and use of chemicals. It is envisioned that international and domestic regulations will be harmonized on the basis of GHS in the future. Several key harmonized information elements of GHS are as follows:

- Uniform classification of hazardous substances and mixtures
- Hazard communications: labeling standards
  - Allocation of label elements
  - Symbols and pictograms **(Table 3.25, p. 194)**
  - Signal words: DANGER (most severe hazard categories) and WARNING (less severe hazard categories)

- Hazard statements
- Precautionary statements and pictograms
- Product and supplier identification
- Multiple hazards and precedence of information
- Arrangements for presenting GHS label elements
- Special labeling arrangements
- Hazard communications: Safety Data Sheet (SDS) content and format (similar to an MSDS)

Under GHS, chemical hazards are divided into the two following general categories and various subdivisions:

- *Physical hazards*
  - Explosives
  - Flammable gases
  - Flammable aerosols
  - Oxidizing gases
  - Gases under pressure
  - Flammable liquids
  - Flammable solids
  - Self-reactive substances
  - Pyrophoric liquids
  - Pyrophoric solids
  - Self-heating substances

Table 3.25
Globally Harmonized System of Classification and Labeling of Chemicals (GHS)

Flame	Flame Over Circle	Exploding Bomb	Corrosion	Gas Cylinder
Flammables/ Fire Hazard	Oxidizers	Explosives or Explosion Hazard	Corrosives	Compressed Gases
Exclamation Mark	Environment	Skull and Crossbones	Health Hazard	
Warnings	Environmental Hazards	Poison/Toxic	Variety of Health Hazards	

NOTE: The border and background colors may vary for different targeted groups. For multiple hazards, there will be an order of precedence allocating appropriate symbols, signal words, and hazard statements.

— Substances that emit flammable gases when in contact with water

— Oxidizing liquids

— Oxidizing solids

— Organic peroxides

— Corrosive to metals

- *Health and environmental hazards*

  — Acute toxicity

  — Skin corrosion/irritation

  — Serious eye damage/eye irritation

  — Respiratory and skin sensitization

  — Germ cell mutagenicity

  — Carcinogenicity

  — Reproductive toxicity

  — Specific target organ systemic toxicity — single exposure

  — Specific target organ systemic toxicity — repeated exposure

  — Aquatic environment damage

Military Markings

[NFPA 472: 4.2.1(7)(c)]

The U.S. and Canadian military services have their own marking systems for hazardous materials and chemicals in addition to DOT and TC transportation markings. These markings are used on fixed facilities, and they may be seen on military vehicles, although they are not required. Caution must be exercised, however, because the military placard system is not necessarily uniform. Some buildings and areas that store hazardous materials may not be marked due to security reasons.

First responders who approach a military vehicle that is involved in an accident or fire (either on or off a military base) should exercise extreme caution. Many military supplies (ordnance) are capable of inflicting great bodily harm and/or heavy property damage.

Identifying Military Cargos . . .

. . . may not be an easy thing. Although most military cargos are marked in accordance with federal regulations, some cargos may be unmarked. In some cases, military vehicle drivers may be under orders not to identify what they are carrying. In other cases, an armed escort may accompany the cargo to protect it. If this situation is the case, you should follow the instructions of the military personnel on the scene in the event of an accident or incident. However, there is one good piece of advice to always keep in mind when it comes to military cargos: Withdraw immediately if a military driver rapidly abandons a vehicle!

Figure 3.72 Pipeline markers in the U.S. and Canada include signal words, information describing the transported commodity, and the name and emergency telephone number of the carrier.

Table 3.26, p. 196, provides the U.S. and Canadian military markings for explosive ordnance and fire hazards, chemical hazards, and personal protective equipment requirements. **Table 3.27, p. 198,** provides emergency withdrawal distances for nonessential personnel. **Table 3.28, p. 199,** provides old symbols that may still be used on some military bases.

Posting fire-fighting symbols on nuclear, chemical, or conventional weapon storage sites is done at the discretion of the military. This situation recognizes that under some conditions, security considerations may make it undesirable to identify munitions with fire symbols at the actual storage locations. Also, supplemental symbols to indicate special hazards such as those of toxic chemicals may be used in addition to the fire-fighting symbols.

Pipeline Identification

[NFPA 472: 4.2.1(7)(e), 5.2.1.3(A)(1–3)]

Many types of materials, particularly petroleum varieties, are transported across both the U.S. and Canada in an extensive network of pipelines, most of which are buried in the ground. The DOT Office of Pipeline Safety regulates pipelines that carry hazardous materials across state borders, navigable waterways, and federal lands in the U.S. In Canada, the Canadian National Energy Board regulates oil and natural gas pipelines.

Where pipelines cross under (or over) roads, railroads, and waterways, pipeline companies must provide markers. They must be in sufficient numbers along the rest of the pipeline to identify the pipe's location. However, first responders should be aware that pipeline markers do not always mark the exact location of the pipeline, and they should not assume that the pipeline runs in a perfectly straight line between markers. Pipeline markers in the U.S. and Canada include the signal words *CAUTION, WARNING,* or *DANGER* (representing an increasing level of hazard) and contain information describing the transported commodity and the name and emergency telephone number of the carrier **(Figure 3.72).**

Piping Systems

Many industrial, commercial, and institutional facilities have miles (kilometers) of pipes carrying everything from hazardous chemicals to water and steam. Pipes carrying hazardous materials need to be appropriately marked and labeled. Many facilities in the U.S. and Canada follow ANSI's A13.1-1981 "Scheme for Identification of Piping Systems" to mark and label pipes. For aboveground piping systems, ANSI separates materials into the following three broad categories:

High-hazard materials — Corrosives, toxics, explosives and flammable materials, radioactive substances, and materials that (if released) would be hazardous due to extreme pressures or temperatures **(Figure 3.73, p. 199)**

Table 3.26
U.S. and Canadian Military Symbols

Symbol	Fire (Ordnance) Divisions
1	**Division 1: Mass Explosion** Fire Division 1 indicates the greatest hazard. This division is equivalent to DOT/UN Class 1.1 Explosives Division **Also, according to some U.S. military documents, this exact symbol may also be used for:** **Division 5: Mass Explosion — very insensitive explosives (blasting agents)** This division is equivalent to DOT/UN Class 1.5 Explosives Division
2	**Division 2: Explosion with Fragment Hazard** This division is equivalent to DOT/UN Class 1.2 Explosives Division **Also, according to some U.S. military documents, this exact symbol may also be used for:** **Division 6: Nonmass Explosion — extremely insensitive ammunition** This division is equivalent to DOT/UN Class 1.6 Explosives Division
3	**Division 3: Mass Fire** This division is equivalent to DOT/UN Class 1.3 Explosives Division
4	**Division 4: Moderate Fire — no blast** This division is equivalent to DOT/UN Class 1.4 Explosives Division

Symbol	Chemical Hazards
"Red You're Dead"	**Wear Full Protective Clothing (Set One)** Indicates the presence of highly toxic chemical agents that may cause death or serious damage to body functions.
"Yellow You're Mellow"	**Wear Full Protective Clothing (Set Two)** Indicates the presence of harassing agents (riot control agents and smokes).

Continued

Table 3.26 (continued)
U.S. and Canadian Military Symbols

Symbol	Chemical Hazards (continued)
"White is Bright"	**Wear Full Protective Clothing (Set Three)** Indicates the presence of white phosphorus and other spontaneously combustible material.
	Wear Breathing Apparatus Indicates the presence of incendiary and readily flammable chemical agents that present an intense heat hazard. This hazard and sign may be present with any of the other fire or chemical hazards/symbols.
	Apply No Water Indicates a dangerous reaction will occur if water is used in an attempt to extinguish the fire. This symbol may be posted together with any of the other hazard symbols.

Symbol	Supplemental Chemical Hazards
G	**G-Type Nerve Agents** — persistent and nonpersistent nerve agents *Examples: sarin (GB), tabun (GA), soman (GD)*
VX	**VX Nerve Agents** — persistent and nonpersistent V-nerve agents *Example: V-agents (VE, VG, VS)*
BZ	**Incapacitating Nerve Agent** *Examples: lacrymatory agent (BBC), vomiting agent (DM)*
H	**H-Type Mustard Agent/Blister Agent** *Example: persistent mustard/lewisite mixture (HL)*
L	**Lewisite Blister Agent** *Examples: nonpersistent choking agent (PFIB), nonpersistent blood agent (SA)*

Table 3.27
Emergency Withdrawal Distances for Nonessential Personnel

Fire (Ordnance) Division	Withdrawal Distance (Unknown Material Quantity)	Withdrawal Distance (Known Material Quantity)
Unknown, located in facility, truck, and/or tractor trailer	Approximately ¾ mile (4,000 feet/1 219 m)	4,000 feet (1 219 m)
Unknown, located in railcar	Approximately 1 m (5,000 feet/1 524 m)	5,000 feet (1 524 m)
1 and 5 *(See Note 1)*	Same as unknown facility, truck trailer or railcar as appropriate	• For transportation, use 2,500 feet (762 m) minimum distance for 500 pounds (227 kg) and below • Above 500 pounds (227 kg), for railcars, use 5,000 feet (1 524 m) minimum distance; otherwise use 4,000 feet (1 219 m) minimum distance • Use 4,000 feet (1 219 m) minimum distance for bombs and projectiles with caliber 5 inches (127 mm) or greater • For facilities, use 2,500 feet (762 m) minimum distance for 15,000 pounds (6 804 kg) and below • Use 4,000 feet (1 219 m) minimum distance for net explosive weights above 15,000 pounds (6 804 kg) and less than or equal to 50,000 pounds (22 680 kg) • Above 50,000 pounds (22 680 kg), use d (distance) = $105\,W^{1/3}$
2 and 6 *(See Note 1)*	2,500 feet (762 m)	2,500 feet (762 m)
3 *(See Note 2)*	600 feet (183 m)	Twice the inhabited building distance with a 600-foot (183 m) minimum range
4	300 feet (91 m)	300 feet (91 m)

Source: U.S. Department of Defense website

Note 1: For Divisions 1 and 2 items, if known, the maximum range fragments and debris will be thrown (including the interaction effects of stacks of items, but excluding lugs, strong backs, and/or nose and tail plates) may be used to replace the minimum range.

Note 2: For accidents involving propulsion units, it is not required to specify emergency withdrawal distances based upon the potential flight ranges of these items.

Table 3.28
Old U.S. Military Symbols

Symbol	Description
⊕	Flammable Liquids, Solvents, Oils, Paints
1	Fire Hazard
2	Limited Explosive Hazard
3	Intense Radiant Heat Hazard
4	High Explosive Hazard

Figure 3.73 According to ANSI A13.1-1981 "Scheme for Identification of Piping Systems," piping carrying hazardous materials (including steam) should be identified by markings.

- *Low-hazard materials* — Products that are not inherently hazardous and have a small chance of harming employees through mild temperatures and low pressures
- *Fire-suppression materials* — Fire-protection materials such as carbon dioxide (CO_2), foam,

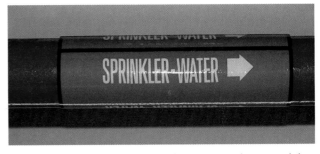

Figure 3.74 ANSI also requires fire-suppression materials to be marked.

halon, and water carried in automatic sprinkler systems **(Figure 3.74)**

Pipe markings identify the contents of the pipe and provide additional information if special hazards, such as high temperature or pressure, are concerns. An arrow shows the direction of flow within the pipe. **Table 3.29, p. 200,** shows the piping system colors associated with each of the material categories.

NOM-026-STPS-1998 spells out the piping systems signs and colors used for safety and health in Mexico. Those of special interest to first responders include piping systems marked in *red*, indicating a flammability

Table 3.29
Piping System Color Codes

Yellow (black letters on a yellow background)	High-Hazard Materials
Green (white letters on a green background)	Low-Hazard Liquids or Liquid Mixtures
Blue (white letters on a blue background)	Low-Hazard Gases or Gaseous Mixtures
Red (white letters on a red background)	Fire-Suppression Materials

hazard (as opposed to fire-suppression materials in the U.S. and Canada); piping systems marked in *yellow*, indicating dangerous fluids; and pipes marked in *green*, indicating low-risk fluids.

Pipes may be marked in appropriate warning colors by painting the entire pipe, applying colored bands, or applying colored labels. Colors may also be accompanied by the following captions:

- *Toxico* (toxic)
- *Inflamable* (flammable/inflammable)
- *Explosivo* (explosive)
- *Irritante* (irritant)
- *Corrosivo* (corrosive)
- *Reactivo* (reactive)
- *Riesgo Biologico* (biological risk)
- *Alta Temperatura* (high temperature)
- *Baja Temperatura* (low temperature)
- *Alta Presion* (high pressure)

American Petroleum Institute Markings

API has developed a uniform marking system designed to identify different grades of gasoline and fuel oils **(Table 3.30)**. These markings may be found at petroleum facilities and some service/filling stations, particularly at transfer valves and connections, loading racks, and fill point connections for service/filling station tanks.

Pesticide Labels

[*NFPA 472: 5.2.1.3(B)(1–6)*]

The EPA regulates the manufacture and labeling of pesticides. Each EPA label must contain the manufacturer's name for the pesticide and one of the following signal words: DANGER/POISON, WARNING, or CAUTION. The words DANGER/POISON are used for highly toxic materials, WARNING means moderate toxicity, and CAUTION is used for chemicals with relatively low toxicity **(Figure 3.75)**. The words EXTREMELY FLAMMABLE are also displayed on the label if the contents have a flash point below 80°F (27°C).

The label also lists an EPA registration number. This number normally is used to obtain information about the product from the manufacturer's 24-hour emergency contact. Another requirement is an establishment number that identifies the manufacturing facility. Other information that may be found on these labels includes routes of entry into the body, precautionary statements (such as *Keep out of the reach of children*), active ingredients, requirements for storage and disposal, first aid information, antidotes for poisoning (if known), and hazard statements indicating that the product poses an environmental hazard.

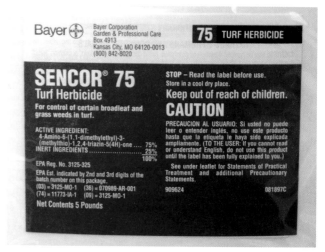

Figure 3.75 According to EPA requirements, pesticide labels must provide the name of the pesticide, the appropriate signal word, a precautionary statement, a hazard statement, and a list of active ingredients. Canadian pesticide labels will also have a PCP (Pest Control Products) Act number.

Table 3.30
American Petroleum Institute Color Code Marking System

Gasolines		Distillates
Leaded	**Unleaded**	**Distillates**
High Grade	High Grade	Diesel
Middle Grade	Middle Grade	No. 1 Fuel Oil
Low Grade	Low Grade	No. 2 Fuel Oil
Vapor Recovery		Kerosene

Symbols for Products with Extender (Optional)

Unleaded High Grade
Gasoline with Extender

Diesel with Extender

Source: Symbol Seeker®, Global Edition, Paul P. Burns, 2002.

Materials originating in Canada carry a Pest Control Products (PCP) Act number. The Canadian Transport Emergency Centre (CANUTEC) operated by TC provides information about these materials when given the PCP registration number. Canadian products also have the same signal words and required information as the U.S.

Color Codes

Colors can sometimes provide clues to the nature of hazardous materials in North America. For example, even if a DOT placard is too far away to clearly read the number, a first responder can deduce that the material inside is some kind of oxidizer if the placard background color is yellow. If the placard color is red, it can be determined that the material is flammable.

Another example of color providing a clue to contents was the *candy striping* on a hydrogen cyanide (also known as *hydrocyanic acid*) tank car. A white tank car with a horizontal red stripe around it and two vertical red stripes 3 feet (1 m) from each end used to transport hydrogen cyanide, which is extremely toxic.

Most flammable liquid storage cabinets are painted yellow. So are many portable containers of corrosive or unstable materials. Flammable liquid safety cans and portable containers are often red.

U.S. and Canadian Safety Color Codes

ANSI Z535.1 sets forth the following safety color code that is recommended for use in the U.S. and Canada:

- *Red* — Means *Danger* or *Stop;* is used on containers of flammable liquids, emergency stop bars, stop buttons, and fire-protection equipment **(Figure 3.76)**

- *Orange* — Means *Warning;* is used on hazardous machinery with parts that can crush or cut or energized equipment

- *Yellow* — Means *Caution;* solid yellow, yellow and black stripes, or yellow and black checkers may be used to indicate physical hazards such as tripping hazards; also used on containers of corrosive or unstable materials

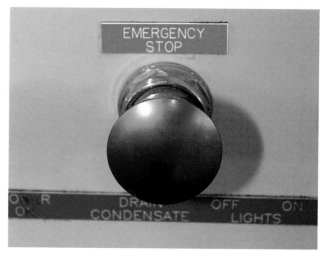

Figure 3.76 In ANSI's safety color code system, the color *red* means *Danger* or *Stop,* and it is used on containers of flammable liquids, emergency stop bars, stop buttons, and fire-protection equipment.

- *Green* — Marks safety equipment such as first-aid stations, safety showers, and exit routes

- *Blue* — Marks safety information signage such as labels or markings indicating the type of required personal protective equipment (PPE)

Mexican Safety Color Code

NOM-026-STPS-1998 describes the safety color code for Mexico provided in **Table 3.31**.

Clue 5
Written Resources

[NFPA 472: 4.2.2(3), 5.2.2(5)]

A variety of written resources are available to assist responders in identifying hazardous materials at both fixed facilities and transportation incidents. Fixed facilities should have MSDSs, inventory records, and other facility documents in addition to signs, markings, container shapes, and other labels. At transportation incidents, first responders should be able to use the current *ERG* as well as shipping papers. Operational-Level responders needing response information directly from the manufacturer or shipper can gather contact information from shipping papers and MSDSs or by contacting an emergency response agency such as Chemical Transportation Emergency Center (CHEMTREC®) of the American Chemistry

Table 3.31
Mexican Safety Color Code

Color	Meaning	Uses, Indications, and Clarifications
Rojo **(Red)**	• Stop • Prohibited • Material (equipment and systems for fighting fires)	• Emergency stops and disconnects • Signs prohibiting specific actions • Identification of pipes carrying fluids with flammability hazards • Identification and location of fire-fighting equipment
Amarillo **(Yellow)**	• Warning of Danger • Delineation of Areas • Warning of Ionizing Radiation	• Attention, precaution, verification, as well as the identification of dangerous fluids • Boundaries of restricted areas or areas of specific usage • Signs indicating the presence of radioactive materials
Verde **(Green)**	Safety/Safe Condition	• Identification of pipes carrying low-risk fluids • Signs for indicating emergency exits, evacuation routes, safety zones, and first-aid stations • Safety/emergency showers, eye washes, and others
Azul **(Blue)**	• Requirements • Obligations	Signs requiring specific actions (such as the use of PPE)

Council, Canadian Transport Emergency Centre (CANUTEC), or Emergency Transportation System for the Chemical Industry (SETIQ).

Shipping Papers
[NFPA 472: 4.2.1(10)(c–g)]

Shipments of hazardous materials must be accompanied by shipping papers that describe them. The information can be provided on a bill of lading, waybill, or similar document **(Figure 3.77, p. 204)**. The general location and type of paperwork change according to the mode of transport **(Table 3.32, p. 205)**. However, the exact location of the documents varies. The exceptions are hazardous waste shipments, which must be accompanied by a Uniform Hazardous Waste Manifest document. DOT/TC regulations require the following in descriptions of hazardous materials:

- Proper shipping name of the material
- Hazard class represented by the material
- Packing group assigned to the material
- Quantity of material

In addition, special description requirements apply to certain types of materials (for example, those that cause poison by inhalation, radioactive materials, and hazardous substances) and modes of transportation. Other information is also required on shipping papers. See **Table 3.33, p. 205,** for a list of the minimum requirements on shipping papers.

When first responders know that a close approach to an incident is safe, they can then examine the cargo shipping papers. Responders may need to check with the responsible party in order to locate these documents. If the responsible party is not carrying them, responders will need

THIS MEMORANDUM is an acknowledgement that a Bill of Lading has been issued and is not the Original Bill of Lading nor a copy or duplicate, covering the property named herein, and is intended solely for filing or record.
RECEIVED, subject to the classifications and lawfully filed tariffs in effect on the date of the receipt by the carrier of the property described in the Original Bill of Lading.

SHELL CHEMICAL COMPANY

SC-6084.4 (REV. 2-91)

BILLING OFFICE MEMORANDUM 1

AT	PAGE	OF	SHIPPER'S I.D. NO.	B/L SEQ. NO.	CARRIER NAME OR RAIL CAR INITIALS AND NO.	SCAC	SHIPPING DATE
DEER PARK		TX	141 A04602	978	MATLACK 6189	MTLK	11-05-94

SHIP VIA

FOR CHEMICAL EMERGENCY
Spill, Leak, Fire, Exposure or Accident
CALL CHEMTREC Day or night
800-424-9300

ROUTE CODE · ROUTE

SEAL NO.'S 188288-90

Subject to Section 7 of Conditions of applicable bill of lading; if this shipment is to be delivered to the consignee without recourse on the consignor, the consignor shall sign the following statement:
The carrier shall not make delivery of this shipment without payment of freight and all other lawful charges.
SHELL CHEMICAL COMPANY.
(Signature of Consignor)

CUSTOMER NO. 39300001 · CITY 100 · STATE 09 · DATE ORDERED · CUSTOMER ORDER NO. 90576 R-4

CONSIGNED TO:
JOHN OGORMAN
1123 DATELOG WAY
HOUSTON, TX 77090

BILL TO:
JPO INDUSTRIES
P. O. BOX 90674
HOUSTON, TX 77090

FREIGHT TERMS
CODE 2

SR DIST.	CR DIST.	ORDERED BY AND DATE DIST. · MO · DAY · YR.	SUGGESTED SHIPPING DATE	REQUESTED DELIVERY DATE	ORDERER'S INITIALS TELEPHONE & TWX
82	82	47 · 11 · 01 · 93	11 · 05 · 93	11 · 05 · AM	AMH 713-444-2430

SPLC CODES · ORIGIN · DEST.

DESCRIPTION OF ARTICLES, SPECIAL MARKS AND EXCEPTIONS

HM	NO. & KIND PACKAGES	TRUCK/TRAILER NUMBER	TRUCK/TRAILER OR T/C COMPT	CAPACITY	GALLONS OUTAGE AT LOADING TEMP.	LOADING TEMP. °F	LB./GAL AT LOAD TEMP.	GALLON CORR. FACTOR	NET WEIGHT OR GALLONS AT 60°F	GROSS WEIGHT (Subject to correction)
X	1 T/T EPICHLOROHYDRIN, 6.1, UN 2023, II, RQ, GUIDE 30									

LINE 01 4,500 GAL EPICHLOROHYDRIN
BULK
CA 32410

GROSS	TARE	NET
70,240	25,960	44,280

SPECIAL INSTRUCTIONS: ANY UNLOADING DETENTION CHARGES BILL TO CONSIGNEE EQUIP. T/T WITH 2" CAMLOCK FITTING FOR UNLOADING AND 2" MALE CAMLOCK FITTING FOR VENTING VAPORS. DELIVER 10 AM - 3 PM 11/5.

IF SHIPMENT IS PREPAID, MAIL FREIGHT BILL IN DUPLICATE WITH NO. 4 COPY OF B/L TO: Shell Chemical Company, P.O. Box 1876, Houston, Texas 77251 · Attention: Chemical Products Accounting, Freight Accounting · SHIPMENTS VIA MOTOR CARRIER · D.O.T. HAZARDOUS MATERIALS PLACARDS FURNISHED BY: ☐ SHIPPER ☐ CARRIER

1. The agreed or declared value of the property is hereby specifically stated by the shipper to be not exceeding 50 cents per pound where the rate is dependent on value. 2. Description and gross weight thereof as shown herein are correct, per Agreement filed with Weighing and Inspection Bureau, if applicable. 3. This is to certify that the above-named materials are properly classified, described, packaged, marked and labeled and are in proper condition for transportation according to the applicable regulations of the Department of Transportation.
SHELL CHEMICAL COMPANY, Shipper — is a division of, and means herein, SHELL OIL COMPANY, a Delaware Corporation

Per

Carrier certifies that the container supplied by Carrier for this shipment is a proper container for transportation of the Materials as above described.
Carrier
Per Agent

DELIVERY RECEIPT — Received in good order Customer/Customer's Carrier certifies that the container supplied by it for this shipment is a proper container for transportation
For
By

Figure 3.77 An example of a hazardous material shipping paper. Note the *X* placed in the column captioned *HM* for hazardous material. *Courtesy of Shell Chemical Company.*

Table 3.32
Shipping Paper Identification

Transportation Mode	Shipping Paper Name	Location of Papers	Party Responsible
Air	Air Bill	Cockpit	Pilot
Highway	Bill of Lading	Vehicle Cab	Driver
Rail	Waybill/ Consist	Engine or Caboose	Conductor
Water	Dangerous Cargo Manifest	Bridge or Pilothouse	Captain or Master

to check the appropriate locations. In trucks and airplanes, these papers are placed near the driver or pilot. On ships and barges, the papers are placed on the bridge or in the pilothouse of a controlling tugboat. On trains, the waybills (each car's cargo lists), wheel reports, and/or consists (also called *wheels*) (entire train's cargo lists) may be placed in the engine, caboose, or both. During pre-incident surveys, the location of the papers for a specific rail line can be determined. **Appendix E** provides a summary of shipping paper requirements from the U.S. Coast Guard.

Transborder shipments between the U.S. and Mexico are accompanied by shipping documents in both English and Spanish. To satisfy the emergency response information requirements in the U.S. or Mexico, a shipper may attach a copy of the appropriate guide page from the current *ERG* to the shipping papers. The information must be provided in Spanish when the material is shipped to Mexico and in English when shipped to the U.S. so that emergency responders in each country will be able to understand the appropriate initial response procedures in the event of a hazardous material release. **Table 3.34, p. 206** shows the format of Mexico's emergency sheet for the transport of hazardous materials and wastes required by NOM-005-SCT2-1994.

Presently many of the domestic shipping descriptions and exceptions identified in the HMR §172.101 Hazardous Materials Table are not authorized for use in Mexico (for example, descriptions preceded by a *D*). North American (NA) identification numbers are not authorized for use in Mexico.

Table 3.33
Shipping Paper Required Information

Information	Regulation (Title 49 *CFR*)
Shipper's name and address	
Receiver's name and address	
Proper shipping names of materials	172.202(a)(1)
Hazard class of materials	172.202(a)(2)
Identification number (UN/NA number)	172.202(a)(3)
Packing group (in Roman numerals)	172.202(a)(4)
Gross weight or volume of material shipped	172.202(a)(5)
First-listed order of hazardous materials on the shipping papers	172.201(a)(1)(i)
X placed before the shipping name in a column captioned *HM* for hazardous material (*X* may be replaced with *RQ* when the hazardous materal is considered a reportable quantity)	172.201(a)(1)(iii)
Emergency response telephone number	172.201(d)

Material Safety Data Sheets

[NFPA 472: 4.2.1(10)(a –b), 5.2.2 (2), 5.2.2(3)]
A *material safety data sheet (MSDS)* is a detailed information bulletin prepared by the manufacturer or importer of a chemical that describes or gives the following information:

1. Company Name and Address
 	
    • Manufacturer   • Importer
    • Consumer   • Distributor
    • Generator
 	
2. Shipper's Emergency Phone and
    Fax Numbers
	3. Product or Residue
	    Commercial Name:
	
	Chemical Name:
		6. Carrier Company
		
		7. Emergency Phone and Fax

	4. Class	
	5. UN No. of Material	

| 8. Physical State | 9. Physical and
    Chemical Properties | 10. Report to National Emergency System and Hazardous Materials
     Specific Authorities: Federal Highway Police, Fire Department, Red
     Cross, etc. |

11. Personal Protection Equipment

In Case of Accident
- Stop engine
- Set signals in danger zone
- Keep unnecessary people away; out of the danger zone

12. Risks
 	
    If this happens
	13. Actions
	
	    Do this

14. Intoxication/Exposure	15.
16. Pollution	17.
18. Medical Information	19.
20. Spills/Leakages	21.
22. Fire/Explosion	23.
24. Name	Signature Position Phone

25. This sheet must be on an easily accessible place to be used in case of emergency and must be filled in its entirety.

- Hazardous ingredients
- Physical and chemical properties (including fire and explosion hazard data)
- Physical and health hazards
- Routes of exposure
- Precautions for safe handling and use
- Emergency and first-aid procedures
- Control measures for the product

MSDSs are often the best sources of detailed information about a particular material to which first responders have access. First responders can acquire an MSDS from the manufacturer of the material, the supplier, the shipper, an emergency response center such as CHEMTREC®, or the facility hazard communication plan. MSDSs are sometimes attached to shipping papers and containers as well. Both OSHA and Canadian regulations have requirements on MSDS contents. ANSI has developed a format that both countries recommend following. GHS uses a Safety Data Sheet (SDS) that is the equivalent of an MSDS.

OSHA Requirements

[NFPA 472: 5.2.2(3)(a–j)]

OSHA specifies the information that must be provided by law on an MSDS, but it does not prescribe the precise format for an MSDS. A nonmandatory MSDS form that meets HCS requirements has been issued and can be used as is or expanded as needed. First responders will find that many MSDSs follow this voluntary format. Presently, MSDSs must be written in English for use in the U.S. and are required to include the following information:

- *Top — Chemical identity*
  - Chemical and common name(s) must be provided for single chemical substances
  - Identity on the MSDS must be cross-referenced to the identity found on the label

- *Section I — Manufacturer's Information and Chemical Identity*
  - Manufacturer's name and address
  - Emergency telephone number
  - Date prepared

- *Section II — Hazardous Ingredients*
  - Chemical and common names of hazardous components
  - Permissible exposure limits (PELs) and other recommended exposure limits

- *Section III — Physical and Chemical Characteristics*
  - Boiling point
  - Vapor pressure
  - Vapor density
  - Specific gravity
  - Melting point
  - Evaporation rate
  - Solubility in water
  - Physical appearance and odor

- *Section IV — Fire and Explosion Hazard Data*
  - Flash point
  - Flammability limits (lower explosive limit [LEL], upper explosive limit [UEL])
  - Extinguishing media
  - Special fire-fighting procedures
  - Unusual fire and explosion hazards

- *Section V — Reactivity (Instability) Data*
  - Stability (stable/unstable conditions to avoid)
  - Incompatibility (materials to avoid)
  - Hazardous decomposition or byproducts
  - Hazardous polymerization (may or may not occur, conditions to avoid)

- *Section VI — Health Hazard Data*
  - Routes of entry (inhalation, skin, ingestion)
  - Health hazards (acute and chronic)
  - Carcinogenicity
  - Signs and symptoms of exposure
  - Medical conditions generally aggravated by exposure
  - Emergency and first-aid procedures.

- **Section VII — Precautions for Safe Handling and Use**
  - Steps to be taken in case of a release or spill
  - Waste disposal method
  - Precautions to be taken in handling or storage, and other precautions.
- **Section VIII — Control Measures**
  - Engineering controls such as ventilation, safe handling procedures, and personal protective equipment
  - Work/hygienic practices

Canadian Requirements

In Canada, the information mandated for MSDSs is specified in the Controlled Products Regulations. All materials covered by WHMIS must be accompanied by an MSDS. Canadian MSDSs are available in both English and French. Nine items must be disclosed on Canadian MSDSs as listed in **Table 3.35.**

ANSI Recommended Format

While the voluntary OSHA form ensures that the minimum required elements are provided on a MSDS, OSHA encourages supplemental information be provided as well. ANSI standard Z400.1, "Hazardous Industrial Chemicals – Material Safety Data Sheets – Preparation," specifies 16 different sections for an MSDS. OSHA now recommends that the ANSI format be used, although this format is not presently mandated.

Canadian regulatory authorities accept the ANSI 16-heading format if all the information required by the Controlled Products Regulations is included. Other organizations prescribing the 16-section MSDS format include the International Labour Organization (ILO), European Union (EU, formerly the European Communities, EC), and ISO. The ANSI standard MSDS sections are as follows:

1: Substance Identity and Company Contact Information
2: Chemical Composition and Components
3: Hazard Identification
4: First Aid Measures
5: Fire-Fighting Measures
6: Accidental Release Measures
7: Handling and Storage
8: Exposure Controls and Personal Protection
9: Physical and Chemical Properties
10: Stability and Reactivity
11: Toxicological Information
12: Ecological Information
13: Disposal Considerations
14: Transport Information
15: Regulatory Information
16: Other Information

 The MSDS provided for 1,2-butylene oxide was written to meet ANSI standards. See Scenario Table 2, p. 105, in Part 1 of this chapter.

GHS Safety Data Sheets

The GHS for Hazard Classification and Communication sets forth recommendations for minimum information to be provided on a Safety Data Sheet (SDS), the GHS equivalent of an MSDS. SDSs include essentially the same information as recommended by ANSI for an MSDS, with some minor differences such as the order in which they are presented. Identification information on a GHS SDS references the GHS product identifier and GHS classification as well as incorporates GHS label elements in addition to other information.

Emergency Response Guidebook

[NFPA 472: 4.4.1(10), 4.2.3, 4.2.3(1)]
[ODP Awareness Level I.c., I.d.]

The current *ERG* was developed jointly by TC, DOT, the Secretaría de Comunicaciones y Transportes (SCT) of Mexico, and Argentina's response center for use by firefighters, law enforcement, and other emergency services personnel who may be the first to arrive at the scene of a transportation incident involving dangerous goods/hazardous materials **(Figure 3.78, p. 211).** This book is updated on a

Table 3.35
Information Disclosed on a Canadian MSDS

Item	Category	Information
1	Hazardous Ingredients	• Information required by Subparagraphs 13(a)(i) to (iv) of the Act • CAS registry number and product identification number • LC_{50} (species and route) • LD_{50} (species and route)
2	Preparation Information	• Name and phone of the group, department or party responsible for the preparation of the material safety data sheet • Date of preparation of the material safety data sheet
3	Product Information	• Manufacturer's Information, name, street address, city, province, postal code, and emergency telephone number • Supplier identifier, the supplier's street address, city, province, postal code, and emergency telephone number • Product identifier • Product use
4	Physical Data	• Physical state (that is, gas, liquid, or solid) • Odour and appearance • Odour threshold • Specific gravity • Vapour pressure • Vapour density • Evaporation rate • Boiling point • Freezing point • pH • Coefficient of water/oil distribution
5	Fire or Explosion Hazard	• Conditions of flammability • Means of extinction • Flash point and method of determination • Upper flammable limit • Lower flammable limit • Autoignition temperature • Hazardous combustion products • Explosion data—sensitivity to mechanical impact • Explosion data—sensitivity to static discharge
6	Reactivity Data	• Conditions under which the product is chemically unstable • Name of any substance or class of substance with which the product is incompatible • Conditions of reactivity • Hazardous decomposition products

Continued

Table 3.35 (continued)
Information Disclosed on a Canadian MSDS

Item	Category	Information
7	Toxicological Properties	• Route of entry, including skin contact, skin absorption, eye contact, inhalation, and ingestion
		• Effects of acute exposure to product
		• Effects of chronic exposure to product
		• Exposure limits
		• Irritancy of product
		• Sensitization to product
		• Carcinogenicity
		• Reproductive toxicity
		• Teratogenicity
		• Mutagenicity
		• Name of toxicologically synergistic products
8	Preventative Measures	• Personal protective equipment to be used
		• Specific engineering controls to be used
		• Procedures to be followed in case of leak or spill
		• Waste disposal
		• Handling procedure and equipment
		• Storage requirements
		• Special shipping information
9	First Aid Measures	Specific first aid measures

regular basis. Always refer to the current edition to ensure up-to-date information.

The *ERG* is primarily a guide to aid first responders in quickly identifying the specific or generic hazards of materials involved in an emergency incident and protecting themselves and the general public during the initial response phase of the incident. For the purposes of the guidebook, the *initial response phase* is that period following arrival at the scene of an incident during which first responders confirm the presence of and/or identifies dangerous goods/hazardous materials, initiates protective action, secures the area, and requests the assistance of other qualified personnel. This phase is *not* the period in which first responders gather information on the physical or chemical properties of the dangerous goods/hazardous materials.

The guidebook assists responders in making initial decisions upon arrival at the scene of a hazardous materials incident. The *ERG* does not address all possible circumstances that may be associated with a dangerous goods/hazardous materials incident. It is primarily designed for use at a dangerous goods/hazardous materials incident occurring on a highway or railroad. There may be limited value in its application at fixed-facility locations.

The *ERG* incorporates dangerous goods lists from the most recent *UN Recommendations* as well as from other international and national regulations. Explosives are not listed individually by either proper shipping name or ID Number. They do, however, appear under the general heading *Explosives* on the first page of the ID Number index (yellow-bordered pages) and alphabetically in the Name of Material index (blue-bordered pages). Also, the letter *P* following the Guide number in the yellow-bordered and blue-bordered pages identifies those materials that present a ploymerization hazard under certain conditions — for example, acrolein, inhibited, Guide No. 131P.

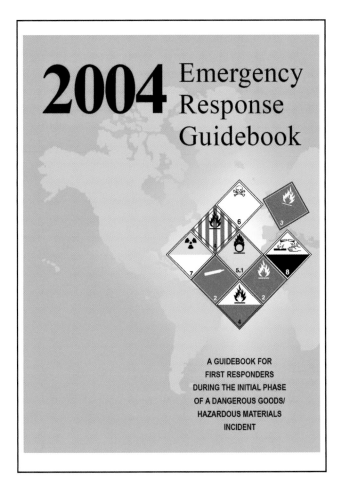

Figure 3.78 The current *Emergency Response Guidebook* *(ERG)* was developed by the U.S. DOT, Transport Canada (TC), Mexico's Secretariat of Transport and Communications (SCT), and Argentina's response center.

First responders at the scene of a dangerous goods/hazardous materials incident should seek additional specific information about any material in question as soon as possible. The information received by contacting the appropriate emergency response agency, calling the emergency response number on the shipping document, or consulting the information on or accompanying the shipping document may be more specific and accurate than the guidebook in providing guidance for the materials involved.

BECOME FAMILIAR WITH THE ERG BEFORE USING IT DURING AN EMERGENCY! In the U.S., first responders must be trained regarding the use of this guidebook according to the requirements of OSHA in 29 *CFR* 1910.120 and regulations issued by EPA in 40 *CFR* Part 311. The sections that follow give details of the information contained in the colored pages of the *ERG*.

ID Number Index (Yellow Pages)

The yellow-bordered pages of the *ERG* provide an index list of hazardous materials in numerical order of ID number. This index quickly identifies the Guide to consult for the ID Number/material involved. This list displays the four-digit UN/NA ID number of the material followed by its assigned emergency response Guide and the material's name **(Figure 3.79, p. 212).**

The purpose of the yellow section in the *ERG* is to enable first responders to quickly identify the Guide (orange-bordered pages) to consult for the ID number of the substance involved. The letters *UN* or *NA* often precede the four-digit ID number on a container or shipping paper. However, for the purpose of the *ERG*, the distinction is not necessary and the letters are ignored. If a material in the yellow or blue index is highlighted, it means that it releases gases that are toxic inhalation hazard (TIH) materials (see information box, p. 216). These materials require the application of additional emergency response distances.

Material Name Index (Blue Pages)

The blue-bordered pages of the *ERG* provide an index of dangerous goods in alphabetical order of material name so that the first responder can quickly identify the Guide to consult for the name of the material involved. This list displays the name of the material followed by its assigned emergency response Guide and four-digit ID number **(Figure 3.80, p. 212).**

 Lt. Adams used the blue pages to look up 1,2-butylene oxide. The entry for 1,2-butylene oxide lists Guide 127 in the orange section.

Initial Action Guides (Orange Pages)

[NFPA 472: 4.2.3(2), 4.4.1(4)(a–b), 4.4.1(5)]

The orange-bordered section of the book is the most important because it provides first responders with safety recommendations and general hazards information. It comprises a total of 62 individual guides presented in a two-page format.

Figure 3.79 When provided with the four-digit UN identification number, first responders can quickly identify a material using the yellow-bordered pages of the *ERG*. For example, the number *1090* on a placard would identify the material as *acetone* and refer responders to Guide No. 127 for response information.

ID No.	Guide No.	Name of Material	ID No.	Guide No.	Name of Material
1075	115	Isobutane mixture	1089	129	Acetaldehyde
1075	115	Isobutylene	1090	127	Acetone
1075	115	Liquefied petroleum gas	1091	127	Acetone oils
1075	115	LPG	1092	131P	Acrolein, inhibited
1075	115	Petroleum gases, liquefied	1093	131P	Acrylonitrile, inhibited
1075	115	Propane	1098	131	Allyl alcohol
1075	115	Propane mixture	1099	131	Allyl bromide
1075	115	Propylene	1100	131	Allyl chloride
1076	125	CG	1104	129	Amyl acetates
1076	125	Diphosgene	1105	129	Amyl alcohols
1076	125	DP	1105	129	Pentanols
1076	125	Phosgene	1106	132	Amylamines
1077	115	Propylene	1107	129	Amyl chloride
1078	126	Dispersant gas, n.o.s.	1108	127	n-Amylene
1078	126	Refrigerant gas, n.o.s.	1108	127	1-Pentene
1079	125	Sulfur dioxide	1109	129	Amyl formates
1079	125	Sulfur dioxide, liquefied	1110	127	n-Amyl methyl ketone
1079	125	Sulphur dioxide	1110	127	Amyl methyl ketone

Figure 3.80 When provided with the name of a hazardous material, first responders can quickly identify a material using the blue-bordered pages of the *ERG*. For example, the name *sulphuric acid* refers responders to Guide No. 137.

Name of Material	Guide No.	ID No.	Name of Material	Guide No.	ID No.
Sulphur dioxide, liquefied	125	1079	Tear gas substance, solid, n.o.s.	159	1693
Sulphur hexafluoride	126	1080	Tellurium compound, n.o.s.	151	3284
Sulphuric acid	137	1830	Tellurium hexafluoride	125	2195
Sulphuric acid, fuming	137	1831	Terpene hydrocarbons, n.o.s.	128	2319
Sulphuric acid, fuming, with less than 30% free Sulphur trioxide	137	1831	Terpinolene	128	2541
Sulphuric acid, fuming, with not less than 30% free Sulphur trioxide	137	1831	Tetrabromoethane	159	2504
			1,1,2,2-Tetrachloroethane	151	1702
Sulphuric acid, spent	137	1832	Tetrachloroethane	151	1702
Sulphuric acid, with more than 51% acid	137	1830	Tetrachloroethylene	160	1897
Sulphuric acid, with not more than 51% acid	157	2796	Tetraethyl dithiopyrophosphate	153	1704
Sulphuric acid and Hydrofluoric acid mixtures	157	1786	Tetraethyl dithiopyrophosphate, mixture, dry or liquid	153	1704
Sulphurous acid	154	1833	Tetraethyl dithiopyrophosphate and gases, in solution	123	1703
Sulphur tetrafluoride	125	2418	Tetraethyl dithiopyrophosphate and gases, mixtures	123	1703
Sulphur trioxide	137	1829	Tetraethyl dithiopyrophosphate and gases, mixtures, or in solution (LC50 more than 200 ppm but not more than 5000	123	1703
Sulphur trioxide, inhibited	137	1829			

The left-hand page provides safety-related information, whereas the right-hand page provides emergency response guidance and activities for fire situations, spill or leak incidents, and first aid. Each Guide is designed to cover a group of materials that possesses similar chemical and toxicological characteristics. The Guide title identifies the general hazards of the dangerous goods covered. For example, Guide 124 is entitled "Gases – Toxic and/or Corrosive – Oxidizing" **(Figure 3.81a).**

Each Guide is divided into three main sections: The first section (*Potential Hazards*) describes potential hazards that the material may display in terms of fire/explosion and health effects upon exposure. The highest potential is listed first. Emergency responders consult this section first, which allows them to make decisions regarding the protection of the emergency response team as well as the surrounding population.

The second section (*Public Safety*) outlines suggested public safety measures based on the situation. It provides general information regarding immediate isolation of the incident site and recommended type of protective clothing and respiratory protection **(Figure 3.81b, p. 214).** This section also lists suggested evacuation distances for small and large spills and for fire situations (fragmentation hazard). When the material is one highlighted in the yellow-bordered and blue-bordered pages, this section also directs the reader to consult the tables on the green-bordered pages listing TIH materials and water-reactive materials.

The third section (*Emergency Response*) covers emergency response areas, including precautions for incidents involving fire, spills or leaks, and first aid. Several recommendations are listed under each of these areas to further assist the responder in the decision-making process. The information on first aid is general guidance before seeking medical care.

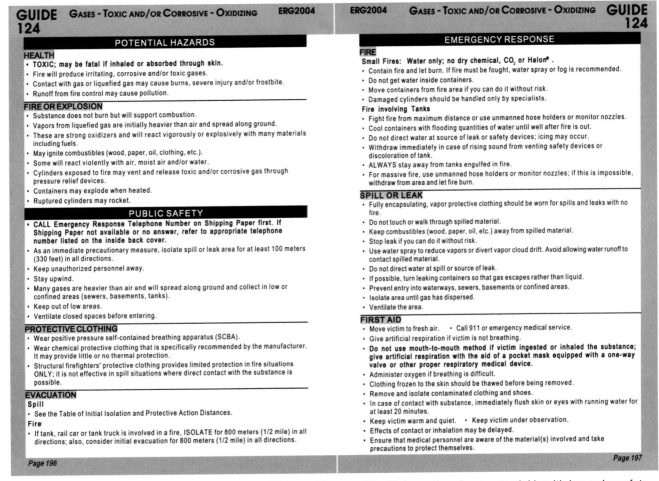

Figure 3.81a The orange-bordered pages of the *ERG* provide a wealth of information about potential health hazards, safety recommendations, and general response guidelines for the material involved.

POTENTIAL HAZARDS

HEALTH

- TOXIC; may be fatal if inhaled or absorbed through skin.
- Fire will produce irritating, corrosive and/or toxic gases.
- Contact with gas or liquefied gas may cause burns, severe injury and/or frostbite.
- Runoff from fire control may cause pollution.

FIRE OR EXPLOSION

- Substance does not burn but will support combustion.
- Vapors from liquefied gas are initially heavier than air and spread along ground.
- These are strong oxidizers and will react vigorously or explosively with many materials including fuels.
- May ignite combustibles (wood, paper, oil, clothing, etc.).
- Some will react violently with air, moist air and/or water.
- Cylinders exposed to fire may vent and release toxic and/or corrosive gas through pressure relief devices.
- Containers may explode when heated.
- Ruptured cylinders may rocket.

PUBLIC SAFETY

- CALL Emergency Response Telephone Number on Shipping Paper first. If Shipping Paper not available or no answer, refer to appropriate telephone number listed on the inside back cover.
- As an immediate precautionary measure, isolate spill or leak area for at least 100 meters (330 feet) in all directions.
- Keep unauthorized personnel away.
- Stay upwind.
- Many gases are heavier than air and will spread along ground and collect in low or confined areas (sewers, basements, tanks).
- Keep out of low areas.
- Ventilate closed spaces before entering.

PROTECTIVE CLOTHING

- Wear positive pressure self-contained breathing apparatus (SCBA).
- Wear chemical protective clothing that is specifically recommended by the manufacturer. It may provide little or no thermal protection.
- Structural firefighters' protective clothing provides limited protection in fire situations ONLY; it is not effective in spill situations where direct contact with the substance is possible.

EVACUATION

Spill

- See the Table of Initial Isolation and Protective Action Distances.

Fire

- If tank, rail car or tank truck is involved in a fire, ISOLATE for 800 meters (1/2 mile) in all directions; also, consider initial evacuation for 800 meters (1/2 mile) in all directions.

EMERGENCY RESPONSE

FIRE

Small Fires: Water only; no dry chemical, CO₂ or Halon®.

- Contain fire and let burn. If fire must be fought, water spray or fog is recommended.
- Do not get water inside containers.
- Move containers from fire area if you can do it without risk.
- Damaged cylinders should be handled only by specialists.

Fire involving Tanks

- Fight fire from maximum distance or use unmanned hose holders or monitor nozzles.
- Cool containers with flooding quantities of water until well after fire is out.
- Do not direct water at source of leak or safety devices; icing may occur.
- Withdraw immediately in case of rising sound from venting safety devices or discoloration of tank.
- ALWAYS stay away from tanks engulfed in fire.
- For massive fire, use unmanned hose holders or monitor nozzles; if this is impossible, withdraw from area and let fire burn.

SPILL OR LEAK

- Fully encapsulating, vapor protective clothing should be worn for spills and leaks with no fire.
- Do not touch or walk through spilled material.
- Keep combustibles (wood, paper, oil, etc.) away from spilled material.
- Stop leak if you can do it without risk.
- Use water spray to reduce vapors or divert vapor cloud drift. Avoid allowing water runoff to contact spilled material.
- Do not direct water at spill or source of leak.
- If possible, turn leaking containers so that gas escapes rather than liquid.
- Prevent entry into waterways, sewers, basements or confined areas.
- Isolate area until gas has dispersed.
- Ventilate the area.

FIRST AID

- Move victim to fresh air.   • Call 911 or emergency medical service.
- Give artificial respiration if victim is not breathing.
- **Do not use mouth-to-mouth method if victim ingested or inhaled the substance; give artificial respiration with the aid of a pocket mask equipped with a one-way valve or other proper respiratory medical device.**
- Administer oxygen if breathing is difficult.
- Clothing frozen to the skin should be thawed before being removed.
- Remove and isolate contaminated clothing and shoes.
- In case of contact with substance, immediately flush skin or eyes with running water for at least 20 minutes.
- Keep victim warm and quiet.   • Keep victim under observation.
- Effects of contact or inhalation may be delayed.
- Ensure that medical personnel are aware of the material(s) involved and take precautions to protect themselves.

Figure 3.81b The *Public Safety* section of a material's orange-bordered guide provides information about personal protective equipment.

Guide 127 informed Lt. Adams that 1,2-butylene oxide was a flammable liquid with potential inhalation or contact health effects. Based on the information provided, she was able to establish an initial isolation distance as soon as responders arrived on the scene. She also knew what PPE was required, and the guide provided her a list of actions to take in case of a leak or spill.

These materials are highlighted for easy identification in both numeric (yellow-bordered pages) and alphabetic (blue-bordered pages) *ERG* indexes. The table provides isolation and protective action distances for both small (approximately 53 gallons [200 L] or less) and large spills (more than 53 gallons [200 L]).

Table of Initial Isolation and Protective Action Distances (Green Pages)

[NFPA 472: 4.4.1(4 (c), 4.4.1(7), 4.4.1(9)(a, b)]

This section contains a table that lists (by ID number) toxic inhalation hazard materials — including certain chemical warfare agents, and water-reactive materials that produce toxic gases upon contact with water. The table provides two different types of recommended safe distances: *initial isolation distances* and *protective action distances*.

ERG Spill Sizes

[NFPA 472: 4.4.1(8)]

The *ERG* identifies small spills as approximately 53 gallons (200 L) or less, while large spills involve quantities more than that. For practical purposes, that means any spill involving a single small package, small cylinder, or 55-gallon (208 L) drum would be classified as a *small spill*. A *large spill* would involve multiple packages, large packages, tank trucks, railcars, one-ton cylinders, or similar large containers.

The list is further subdivided into daytime and nighttime situations. This division is necessary because atmospheric conditions significantly affect the size of a chemically hazardous area, and differences can be generally associated with typical daytime and nighttime conditions. The warmer, more active atmosphere normal during the day disperses chemical contaminants more readily than the cooler, calmer conditions common at night. Therefore, during the day, lower toxic concentrations may be spread over a larger area than at night, when higher concentrations may exist in a smaller area. The quantity of material spilled or released and the area affected are both important, but the single most critical factor is the concentration of the contaminant in the air.

The *initial isolation distance* is a distance within which all persons are considered for evacuation in all directions from the actual spill/leak source. It is a distance (radius) that defines a circle (initial isolation zone) within which persons may be exposed to dangerous concentrations upwind of the source and may be exposed to life-threatening concentrations downwind of the source. For example, in the case of compressed gas, toxic, n.o.s. (not otherwise specified), ID No. 1955, Inhalation Hazard Zone A, the isolation distance for small spills is 1,411 feet (430 m), representing an

evacuation circle of 2,821 feet (860 m) in diameter (see explanations in information box, p. 216).

For the same material, the protective action distance is 2.6 miles (4.2 km) for a daytime incident and 5.2 miles (8.4 km) for a nighttime incident. *Protective action distances* represent downwind distances from a spill/leak source within which protective actions should be implemented **(Figure 3.82)**. *Protective actions* are those steps taken to preserve the health and safety of emergency responders and the public. People in this area could be evacuated and/or sheltered in-place (directed to stay inside until danger passes). See Protective Actions section in Chapter 5, Strategic Goals and Tactical Objectives. For more information, consult the current *ERG*.

Inventory Records and Facility Documents

The HCS requires U.S. employers to maintain Chemical Inventory Lists (CILs) of all their hazardous substances **(Figure 3.83, p. 217)**. Because CILs usually contain information about the locations of materials within a facility, they can be useful tools in identifying containers that may have damaged or missing labels or markings (such as a label or marking made illegible because of fire damage). Several other documents and records may provide information about hazardous materials at a facility such as the following:

TABLE OF INITIAL ISOLATION AND PROTECTIVE ACTION DISTANCES

| ID No. | NAME OF MATERIAL | SMALL SPILLS (From a small package or small leak from a large package) | | | | LARGE SPILLS (From a large package or from many small packages) | | | |
| | | First ISOLATE in all Directions | | Then PROTECT persons Downwind during- | | First ISOLATE in all Directions | | Then PROTECT persons Downwind during- | |
		Meters	(Feet)	DAY Kilometers (Miles)	NIGHT Kilometers (Miles)	Meters	(Feet)	DAY Kilometers (Miles)	NIGHT Kilometers (Miles)
1953 1953	Liquefied gas, flammable, poisonous, n.o.s. Liquefied gas, flammable, poisonous, n.o.s. (Inhalation Hazard Zone A)	120 m	(400 ft)	1.2 km (0.8 mi)	5.1 km (3.2 mi)	1000 m	(3000 ft)	8.7 km (5.4 mi)	11.0+ km (7.0+ mi)
1953	Liquefied gas, flammable, poisonous, n.o.s. (Inhalation Hazard Zone B)	30 m	(100 ft)	0.2 km (0.2 mi)	1.2 km (0.8 mi)	420 m	(1400 ft)	4.0 km (2.5 mi)	10.8 km (6.7 mi)
1953	Liquefied gas, flammable, poisonous, n.o.s. (Inhalation Hazard Zone C)	30 m	(100 ft)	0.2 km (0.1 mi)	0.8 km (0.5 mi)	240 m	(800 ft)	2.4 km (1.5 mi)	6.4 km (4.0 mi)
1953	Liquefied gas, flammable, poisonous, n.o.s. (Inhalation Hazard Zone D)	30 m	(100 ft)	0.1 km (0.1 mi)	0.2 km (0.1 mi)	90 m	(300 ft)	0.8 km (0.5 mi)	2.4 km (1.5 mi)
1953 1953	Liquefied gas, flammable, toxic, n.o.s. Liquefied gas, flammable, toxic, n.o.s. (Inhalation Hazard Zone A)	120 m	(400 ft)	1.2 km (0.8 mi)	5.1 km (3.2 mi)	1000 m	(3000 ft)	8.7 km (5.4 mi)	11.0+ km (7.0+ mi)
1953	Liquefied gas, flammable, toxic, n.o.s. (Inhalation Hazard Zone B)	30 m	(100 ft)	0.2 km (0.2 mi)	1.2 km (0.8 mi)	420 m	(1400 ft)	4.0 km (2.5 mi)	10.8 km (6.7 mi)
1953	Liquefied gas, flammable, toxic, n.o.s. (Inhalation Hazard Zone C)	30 m	(100 ft)	0.2 km (0.1 mi)	0.8 km (0.5 mi)	240 m	(800 ft)	2.4 km (1.5 mi)	6.4 km (4.0 mi)
1953	Liquefied gas, flammable, toxic, n.o.s. (Inhalation Hazard Zone D)	30 m	(100 ft)	0.1 km (0.1 mi)	0.2 km (0.1 mi)	90 m	(300 ft)	0.8 km (0.5 mi)	2.4 km (1.5 mi)
1955 1955	Compressed gas, poisonous, n.o.s. Compressed gas, poisonous, n.o.s. (Inhalation Hazard Zone A)	600 m	(2000 ft)	5.9 km (3.7 mi)	11.0+ km (7.0+ mi)	1000 m	(3000 ft)	11.0 km (7.0+ mi)	11.0+ km (7.0+ mi)

Figure 3.82 The green-bordered Table of Initial Isolation and Protective Action Distances provides the downwind distances (from spill and leak sources) within which protective actions (such as evacuation) should be implemented. These distances vary depending on the size of the spill and whether it is day or night.

What is a TIH Material? What is a Hazard Zone?

A *toxic inhalation hazard (TIH)* material is a liquid or a gas known to be so toxic to humans as to pose a hazard to health during transportation or (in the absence of adequate data on human toxicity) is presumed to be toxic to humans because it has a lethal concentration value (LC_{50}) of not more than 5,000 ppm when tested on laboratory animals.

Even though the term *zone* is used, the hazard zones do not represent an actual area or distance. All distances listed in the green-bordered pages are calculated using mathematical models for each TIH material. Zone A is more toxic than Zone D. Hazard zone assignments follow.

- *Hazard Zone A* — LC_{50} of less than or equal to 200 ppm
- *Hazard Zone B* — LC_{50} greater than 200 ppm and less than or equal to 1,000 ppm
- *Hazard Zone C* — LC_{50} greater than 1,000 ppm and less than or equal to 3,000 ppm
- *Hazard Zone D* — LC_{50} greater than 3,000 ppm and less than or equal to 5,000 ppm

Isolation or evacuation distances are shown in the Guides (orange-bordered pages) and in the Table of Initial Isolation and Protective Action Distances (green-bordered pages). These distances may confuse users not thoroughly familiar with the *ERG*.

Some Guides refer to non-TIH materials only (40 Guides) and some refer to both TIH and non-TIH materials (22 Guides). A Guide refers to both TIH and non-TIH materials only when the following sentences appear under the title *EVACUATION* and then *Spill*: *See the Table of Initial Isolation and Protective Ac-tion Distances for highlighted substances. For non-highlighted substances, increase, in the downwind direction, as necessary, the isolation distance shown under "PUBLIC SAFETY."* If these sentences do not appear, then this particular guide refers to non-TIH materials only.

When dealing with a TIH material (highlighted entries in the index lists), the isolation and evacuation distances are found directly in the green-bordered pages. The orange-bordered Guide pages also remind the user to refer to the green-bordered pages for evacuation-specific information involving highlighted materials.

When dealing with a non-TIH material and the Guide refers to both TIH and non-TIH materials, an immediate isolation distance is provided under the heading *PUBLIC SAFETY*. It applies to the non-TIH materials only. In addition, for evacuation purposes, the Guide informs the user under the title *EVACUATION* and then *Spill* to increase (for nonhighlighted substances) in the downwind direction, if necessary, the immediate isolation distance listed under *PUBLIC SAFETY*.

For example, Guide 124, Gases – Toxic and/or Corrosive – Oxidizing, instructs the user as follows: *Isolate spill or leak area immediately for at least 100 to 200 meters (328 to 656 feet) in all directions.* In case of a large spill, the isolation area could be expanded from 328 feet (100 meters) to a distance deemed safe by the on-scene incident commander (IC) and emergency responders.

When dealing with a non-TIH material and the Guide refers only to non-TIH material, the immediate isolation and evacuation distances are specified as actual distances in the Guide (orange-bordered pages) and are not referenced in the green-bordered pages.

- Shipping and receiving documents
- Inventory records
- Risk management and hazardous communication plans
- Chemical inventory reports (known as *Tier II reports*)

Clue 6
Senses

[NFPA 472: 4.2.1(11), 4.2.1(12)]

Vision is definitely the safest of the five senses to use in the detection of a hazardous material. While it may be perfectly safe to observe an overturned cargo tank from a distance through binoculars, emergency responders have to come into close or actual physical contact with a hazardous material (or its mists, vapors, dusts, or fumes, and the like) in order to hear a release, smell it, taste it, or feel it. While many products release odors well below IDLH levels (levels immediately dangerous to life or health), there is a good chance that if first responders at Awareness and Operational Levels are this close to a hazardous material, they are *too* close for safety's sake. However, any smells, tastes, or symptoms reported by victims and witnesses may prove to be helpful.

OSU ENVIRONMENTAL HEALTH & SAFETY
Hazard Communications
Chemical Inventory

Dept: ____
Invntry Supv: ____
Campus Addr: ____ Phone #: ____
Building Name: ____
Building Number: ____
Date of Inventory: ____

Act Count	Max Amt	Chemical Name	Common Name	Container Size	Type	PS	CAS Number	Manufacturer	N.F.P.A. Rating H	F	R	S	Location Room #	MSDS? Yes	No

Figure 3.83 Chemical inventory lists (CILs) can be useful when making pre-incident surveys as well as determining what materials may be involved during an emergency.

WARNING
Deliberately using the human senses to detect the presence of hazardous materials is both unreliable and unsafe. *It could kill you!*

First responders must be aware of visual/physical chemical indicators that provide tangible evidence of the presence of hazardous materials. Unusual noises (such as the hiss of a gas escaping a valve at high pressure) may also alert first responders to the presence of hazards. Some hazardous materials have odorants added to them in order to aid in detection; for example, the distinct odor normally associated with natural gas (an odorless gas) is actually caused by mercaptan, an additive. Responders also need to recognize physical symptoms of chemical exposure to the public and emergency responders.

Without seeing the material itself, responders can begin to deduce the potential of an incident by observing the presence of the following equipment:

- Loading/unloading facilities
- Forklifts
- Dollies and hand trucks
- Booms
- A-frames
- Ramps
- Assorted riggings
- Loading docks
- Fume hood vents or chemical exhaust stacks
- Spray rigs

Direct visible evidence that physical and/or chemical actions and reactions are taking place include such items as the following:

- Spreading vapor cloud or smoke
- Unusual colored smoke
- Flames
- Gloves melting
- Changes in vegetation

- Container deterioration
- Containers bulging
- Sick humans
- Dead or dying birds, animals, insects, or fish
- Discoloration of valves or piping

Physical Action Evidence

Physical actions are processes that do not change the elemental composition of the materials involved. One example is a liquefied, compressed material changing to a gas as it escapes from a vessel. The resulting white vapor cloud is another physical change, which is the condensation of moisture in the air by the expanding material. Several indications of a physical action are as follows:

- Rainbow sheen on water surfaces
- Wavy vapors over a volatile liquid
- Frost or ice buildup near a leak
- Containers deformed by the force of an accident
- Activated pressure-relief devices
- Pinging or popping of heat-exposed vessels

Chemical Reaction Evidence

Chemical reactions convert one substance to another. There is much visual and sensory evidence of chemical reactions:

- Exothermic heat
- Unusual or unexpected temperature drop (cold)
- Extraordinary fire conditions
- Peeling or discoloration of a container's finish **(Figure 3.84)**
- Spattering or boiling of unheated materials
- Distinctively colored vapor clouds
- Smoking or self-igniting materials
- Unexpected deterioration of equipment
- Peculiar smells
- Unexplained changes in ordinary materials
- Symptoms of chemical exposure

Figure 3.84 Peeling or discoloration of a container's finish may provide visual evidence of a chemical reaction. In this case, oxidization of the metal (rust) may be damaging the integrity of this pressure cylinder.

Chemical Exposure Physical Symptoms

Watch for the onset of any physical symptoms of chemical exposure. Symptoms can occur separately or in clusters, depending on the chemical. Be alert for the following symptoms of chemical exposure in humans:

- *Changes in respiration* — Difficult breathing, increase or decrease in respiration rate, tightness of the chest, irritation of the nose and throat, and/or respiratory arrest
- *Changes in level of consciousness* — Dizziness, lightheadedness, drowsiness, confusion, fainting, and/or unconsciousness
- *Abdominal distress* — Nausea, vomiting, and/or cramping
- *Changes in activity level* — Fatigue, weakness, stupor, hyperactivity, restlessness, anxiety, giddiness, and/or faulty judgment
- *Visual disturbances* — Double vision, blurred vision, cloudy vision, burning of the eyes, and/or dilated or constricted pupils
- *Skin changes* — Burning sensations, reddening, paleness, fever, and/or chills
- *Changes in excretion or thirst* — Uncontrolled tears, profuse sweating, mucus flowing from the nose, diarrhea, frequent urination, bloody stool, and/or intense thirst
- *Pain* — Headache, muscle ache, stomachache, chest pain, and/or localized pain at sites of substance contact

Clue 7
Monitoring and Detection Devices

[NFPA 472: 5.2.4(3)]

Monitoring and detection devices can be useful in determining the presence of hazardous materials as well as the concentration(s) present. As with the senses, effectively using the monitoring and detection devices discussed in this section requires actual contact with the hazardous material (or its mists, dusts, vapors, or fumes) in order to measure it. Therefore, with some exceptions, monitoring exceeds the scope of actions permitted to first responders at the Awareness Level. In some situations (such as our scenario), Operational-Level personnel may be allowed to use monitors, provided they have appropriate personal protective equipment and training. However, many facilities may have fixed detectors on their premises that can provide information to anyone present, and there are some devices such as combustible gas indicators (CGIs) with which all first responders should be familiar.

Combustible Gas Indicator

CGIs are used to detect the concentration of combustible gases and vapors in the air. Typically they measure the percentage of the LEL, percent of gas by volume, or ppm of the material in air. They are designed to sound an alarm if hazardous or potentially hazardous concentrations are found (often set to sound at the equivalent of 10 percent LEL or higher).

Two-, Three-, and Four-Gas Monitors

CGI sensors are often combined with other common gas sensors — such as those that detect oxygen, carbon monoxide, or hydrogen sulfide — to form monitors that can detect two, three, or four gases, depending on the combination of sensors. A four-gas monitor would simultaneously check for combustible gases, oxygen concentrations (both high and low), carbon monoxide levels, and hydrogen sulfide levels (**Figure 3.85**). Single sensor meters (also called *oxygen meters*) may also be found for oxygen, carbon monoxide, and hydrogen sulfide. Typically, an alarm is sounded when hazardous or potentially hazardous levels are detected.

Figure 3.85 Four-gas monitors such as those pictured simultaneously check for combustible gases, oxygen, carbon monoxide, and hydrogen sulfide. The white circles on the back of the monitors are the actual sensors.

Firefighters Linder and George used a four-gas CGI to determine if the maintenance workers correctly identified the extent of the release. If they had measured a significant increase in flammables (above 10 percent LEL) while doing reconnaissance outside the anticipated hazard area, they would have known that the initial isolation area needed to be expanded.

Other Monitoring/Detection Devices

While CGIs and multigas monitors are probably the most common monitoring and detection devices that first responders will encounter, a host of other monitoring/detection devices are available. With recent concerns of terrorist attacks, new devices are being developed, and the following list is certainly not all-inclusive:

- *Photoionization detectors (PID)* — Generally, used to detect the concentrations of many organic and some inorganic gases and vapors at the same time; make good general survey instruments and are particularly useful when chemical hazards are unidentified or undetermined

- *Specific chemical monitors* — Usually fixed devices used to sound an alarm when the presence of a specific chemical is detected. Carbon monoxide monitors are especially common (**Figure 3.86, p. 220**), but one can also find monitors that detect chlorine, hydrogen sulfide, ammonia, ethylene oxide, and hydrogen cyanide.

Figure 3.86 This carbon monoxide monitor is small enough to be worn on protective clothing.

- *Indicator papers and pH meters* — *Details*:
  - Indicator papers change colors to indicate the presence of specific hazards such as oxidizers, hydrogen sulfide, and peroxides. Similar papers are now being used to detect the presence of biohazards such as anthrax. Indicator papers change color to indicate the pH of acids or alkalines. See Chapter 2, Hazardous Materials Properties and Hazards.
  - Meters may also measure pH.

- *Detector tubes* — Detect a variety of gases and vapors; can be chemical specific or colorimetric; are most useful if a particular chemical is suspected — as opposed to trying to identify a complete unknown **(Figure 3.87)**

- *Radiation monitors* — Detect levels of alpha, beta, or gamma radiation by collecting and counting the number of ions present; readings are provided in cpm (counts per minute), mR/hr (milliroentgens per hour), or rem 1/hr (roentgens one per hour) (see Chapter 2, Hazardous Materials Properties and Hazards) **(Figure 3.88)**

- *Personal dosimeters* — Generally worn as badges that passively measure an individual's exposure to a particular chemical or radiation **(Figure 3.89)**

- *Other badges* — Include organic vapor badges (or film strips), mercury badges, and formaldehyde badges or strips used to measure individual exposure to certain chemicals

Figure 3.87 Detector tubes can confirm the suspected identity of a chemical.

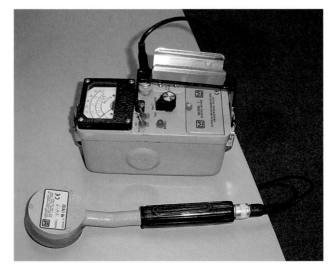

Figure 3.88 Radiation survey meter example. A radiation survey meter using a Geiger tube is often called a *Geiger counter*.

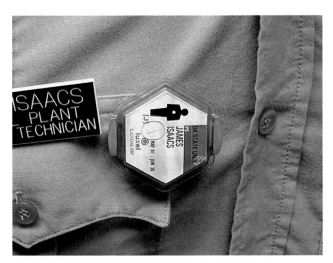

Figure 3.89 Personal dosimeters are generally worn as badges that passively measure an individual's exposure to radiation.

Figure 3.90 Improper use of monitoring devices (such as sticking it in a coat pocket) can lead to false (and potentially life-threatening) readings.

Don't Be a . . .

. . . canary in a coal mine. CGIs, specific chemical monitors, and multiple gas monitors are designed to alert you to the presence of hazardous or potentially hazardous atmospheres. If a monitor sounds an alarm (or the canary dies), heed the warning!

It is very important to use the monitoring device properly. Improper use can lead to false (and potentially life-threatening) readings **(Figure 3.90)**. You must understand how to correctly interpret the information it is giving you as well. Know the limitations of the instrument you are using. Many devices have a wide range of error. For example, colorimetric tubes have a 30-percent error margin. You must know the shelf life of some components and/or devices. Also, the instruments need to be calibrated to produce reliable results. Filters, sensors, and other components may need to be replaced periodically for the instrument to work properly. And finally: Do *not* use a monitoring device without appropriate training and instruction!

If the four-gas CGI that Firefighters Linder and George were using on their reconnaissance mission had sounded an alarm, they would have moved to a safe area immediately.

Part 3
Summary

[NFPA 472: 4.2.2(1)]

First responders at the Awareness and Operational Levels must be able to identify the presence of hazardous materials at emergency incidents. By paying attention to and using the seven clues to the presence of hazardous materials — occupancy; container shape; transportation placards, labels, and markings; other markings and colors; written resources; senses; and monitoring and detection devices — first responders can take the first steps towards successful mitigation of a hazardous material incident.

However, responders need to be aware that making a correct identification may be difficult despite knowledge and recognition of these clues. Fires or explosions can destroy shipping papers, labels, and other markings. Shipments may contain mixed loads or quantities of materials so small that placards are not required. Facilities may not be in compliance with regulations requiring MSDSs, and mistakes can be made in labeling and placarding. For that matter, responders may be unable to get close enough to the material or container to make an accurate identification. For these and other reasons, responders must always be prepared to face the unexpected and deal with the unknown.

Part Two

Incident Problem-Solving Process

Chapter 4

Incident Management Elements

This chapter provides information that will assist the reader in meeting the following first responder competencies from NFPA 472, *Professional Competence of Responders to Hazardous Materials Incidents,* 2002 Edition. The numbers are noted directly in the text under the section titles where they are addressed.

NFPA 472

Chapter 4 — Competencies for the First Responder at the Awareness Level

4.4.1 Initiating Protective Actions. Given examples of facility and transportation hazardous materials incidents, the local emergency response plan, the organization's standard operating procedures, and the current edition of the Emergency Response Guidebook, first responders at the awareness level shall be able to identify the actions to be taken to protect themselves and others and to control access to the scene and shall also meet the following requirements:

(1) Identify the location of both the local emergency response plan and the organization's standard operating procedures.

Chapter 5 — Competencies for the First Responder at the Operational Level

5.1.2.1 The first responder at the operational level shall be able to perform the following tasks:

(4) Evaluate the progress of the actions taken to ensure that the response objectives are being met safely, effectively, and efficiently by completing the following tasks:

(a) Evaluate the status of the defensive actions taken in accomplishing the response objectives

(b) Communicate the status of the planned response

5.2.1 Surveying the Hazardous Materials Incident. Given examples of both facility and transportation scenarios involving hazardous materials, the first responder at the operational level shall survey the incident to identify the containers and materials involved, determine whether hazardous materials have been released, and evaluate the surrounding conditions and also shall meet the requirements in 5.2.1.1 through 5.2.1.6.

5.2.1.4 The first responder at the operational level shall identify and list the surrounding conditions that should be noted by the first responders when surveying hazardous materials incidents.

5.2.1.5 The first responder at the operational level shall give examples of ways to verify information obtained from the survey of a hazardous materials incident.

5.2.3 Predicting the Behavior of a Material and its Container. Given an incident involving a single hazardous material, the first responder at the operational level shall predict the likely behavior of the material and its container and also shall meet the following requirements:

(1) Given two examples of scenarios involving known hazardous materials, interpret the hazard and response information obtained from the current edition of the *Emergency Response Guidebook;* MSDS; CHEMTREC/CANUTEC/SETIQ; local, state, and federal authorities; and shipper/manufacturer contacts as follows:

(a) Match the following chemical and physical properties with their significance and impact on the behavior of the container and/or its contents:

    i. Boiling point

    ii. Chemical reactivity

    iii. Corrosivity (pH)

    iv. Flammable (explosive) range (LEL and UEL)

    v. Flash point

    vi. Ignition (autoignition) temperature

    vii. Physical state (solid, liquid, gas)

    viii. Specific gravity

    ix. Toxic products of combustion

    x. Vapor density

    xi. Vapor pressure

    xii. Water solubility

    xiii. Radiation (ionizing and non-ionizing)

(b) Identify the differences between the following pairs of terms:

    i. Exposure and hazard

    ii. Exposure and contamination

    iii. Contamination and secondary contamination

    iv. Radioactive material exposure (internal and external) and radioactive contamination

(2) Identify three types of stress that could cause a container system to release its contents.

(3) Identify five ways in which containers can breach.

(4) Identify four ways in which containers can release their contents.

(5) Identify at least four dispersion patterns that can be created upon release of a hazardous material.

(6) Identify the three general time frames for predicting the length of time that exposures can be in contact with hazardous materials in an endangered area.

(7) Identify the health and physical hazards that could cause harm.

5.2.4 Estimating the Potential Harm. The first responder at the operational level shall estimate the potential harm within the endangered area at a hazardous materials incident and also shall meet the following requirements:

(1) Identify a resource for determining the size of an endangered area of a hazardous materials incident.

(4) Given the concentrations of the released material, identify the factors for determining the extent of physical, health, and safety hazards within the endangered area of a hazardous materials incident.

5.3.1 Describing Response Objectives for Hazardous Materials Incidents. Given at least two scenarios involving hazardous materials incidents (one facility and one transportation), the first responder at the operational level shall describe the first responder's response objectives for each problem and also shall meet the following requirements:

(2) Given an analysis of a hazardous materials incident, describe the steps for determining defensive response objectives.

5.4.1 Establishing and Enforcing Scene Control Procedures. Given scenarios for facility and/or transportation hazardous materials incidents, the first responder at the operational level shall identify how to establish and enforce scene control including control zones, emergency decontamination, and communications and shall meet the following requirements:

(6) Identify the items to be considered in a safety briefing prior to allowing personnel to work at the following:

(a) Hazardous materials incident

(b) Hazardous materials incident involving criminal or terrorist activities

5.4.2 Initiating the Incident Management System. Given simulated facility and/or transportation hazardous materials incidents, the first responder at the operational level shall initiate the incident management system specified in the local emergency response plan and the organization's standard operating procedures and shall meet the following related requirements:

(1) Identify the role of the first responder at the operational level during hazardous materials incidents as specified in the local emergency response plan and the organization's standard operating procedures.

(2) Identify the levels of hazardous materials incidents as defined in the local emergency response plan.

(3) Identify the purpose, need, benefits, and elements of an incident management system at hazardous materials incidents.

(4) Identify the considerations for determining the location of the command post for a hazardous materials incident.

(5) Identify the procedures for requesting additional resources at a hazardous materials incident.

(6) Identify the authority and responsibilities of the safety officer.

5.4.3 Using Personal Protective Equipment. The first responder at the operational level shall demonstrate the ability to don, work in, and doff the personal protective equipment provided by the authority having jurisdiction, and shall meet the following related requirements:

(1) Identify the importance of the buddy system in implementing the planned defensive options.

(2) Identify the importance of the backup personnel in implementing the planned defensive options.

(3) Identify the safety precautions to be observed when approaching and working at hazardous materials incidents.

5.5.1 Evaluating the Status of Defensive Actions. Given simulated facility and/or transportation hazardous materials incidents, the first responder at the operational level shall evaluate the status of the defensive actions taken in accomplishing the response objectives and shall meet the following related requirements:

(1) Identify the considerations for evaluating whether defensive options are effective in accomplishing the objectives.

(2) Describe the circumstances under which it would be prudent to withdraw from a hazardous materials incident.

5.5.2 Communicating the Status of the Planned Response. The first responder at the operational level shall communicate the status of the planned response to the incident commander and other response personnel and shall meet the following related requirements:

(1) Identify the methods for communicating the status of the planned response to the incident commander through the normal chain of command.

(2) Identify the methods for immediate notification of the incident commander and other response personnel about critical emergency conditions at the incident.

A.5.4.2(6) The hazardous materials safety officer should meet all the competencies for the responder at the level of operations being performed.

A hazardous materials branch safety officer is an individual who directs the safety of operations within the hot and warm zones. A hazardous materials branch safety officer should be designated specifically at all hazardous material incidents (29 CFR 1910.120). The hazardous materials safety officer has the following responsibilities:

(1) Obtains a briefing from the incident commander or incident safety officer and the hazardous materials branch safety officer

(2) Participates in the preparation of and monitors the implementation of the incident safety considerations (including medical monitoring of entry team personnel before and after entry)

(3) Advises the incident commander/sector officer of deviations from the incident safety considerations and of any dangerous situations

(4) Alters, suspends, or terminates any activity that is judged to be unsafe

Reprinted with permission from NFPA 472, *Standard on Professional Competence of Responders to Hazardous Materials Incidents,* Copyright © 2002, National Fire Protection Association, Quincy, MA 00269. This reprinted material is not the complete and official position of the National Fire Protection Association on the referenced subject, which is represented only by the standard in its entirety.

Emergency Responder Guidelines

This chapter provides information that will assist the reader in meeting the following first responder guidelines for fire service and law enforcement from the Office for Domestic Preparedness (ODP) *Emergency Responder Guidelines,* 2002 Edition. The numbers are noted directly in the text under the section titles where they are addressed.

ODP Emergency Responder Guidelines

Fire Service and Law Enforcement

Awareness Level for Events Involving Weapons of Mass Destruction

III. **Know and follow self-protection measures for WMD events and hazardous materials events.** The responder should:

    d. Understand the role of the first responder as well as other levels of response in the department's emergency response plan.

    e. Be familiar with his/her agency's emergency response plan and procedures. Understand the individual officers' role in those procedures

V. **Know and follow agency/organization's scene security and control procedures for WMD and hazardous material events.** The responder should:

    b. Be familiar with his/her agency's incident command procedures.

VI. **Possess and know how to properly use equipment to contact dispatcher or higher authorities to report information collected at the scene and to request additional assistance or emergency response personnel.** The responder should:

    a. Know how to use communications equipment, including a two-way radio or cellular phone to contact the dispatcher or higher authorities to apprise them of the situation at the scene and to request additional assistance and personnel to properly deal with the event.

    c. Know when to request additional help and follow the fire department's emergency response plan procedures for establishing incident command.

    d. Know how to notify the communications center or dispatcher and to assess the degree of hazard to obtain appropriate additional resources.

Performance Level for Events Involving Weapons of Mass Destruction

II. **Know the Incident Command System and be able to follow Unified Command System procedures for integration and implementation of each system. Know how the systems integrate and support the incident. Be familiar with the overall operation of the two command systems and be able to assist in implementation of the Unified Command System if needed.** The responder should:

    a. Know how to implement initial site management procedures following the department's incident command system and emergency response plan. Such procedures include establishing communications with the dispatcher or command center, setting up the control zones for the scene, locating the command post, and forwarding any intelligence that has been collected on the scene.

    b. Be able to implement the Incident Command System component of the department's emergency response plan for a potential WMD event.

    e. Understand the purpose and function of the Unified Command System. Know department procedures for assisting in implementation of the Unified Command System on the scene of a potential WMD event.

    i. Know how to develop an Incident Action Plan in coordination with the on-scene incident commander. Ensure that the Incident Action Plan is consistent with the department's emergency response plan.

Chapter 4
Incident Management Elements

A hazardous materials incident is one of many problems that emergency responders are called upon to solve. Incident resolution is achieved through incident management elements such as setting priorities, implementing a management structure, and following a problem-solving process. In our sample haz mat incident scenario, the process of solving the problem (a spill of butylene oxide) went smoothly and safely. However, if vital incident management elements were not in place and used properly, the scenario could have had a very different ending.

Haz mat incidents are challenging enough without adding confusion, indecisiveness, and a lack of coordination and communication on the part of first responders. First responders must bring order to the incident, and it is their responsibility to begin managing the incident. ***Mistakes made in the initial response to the incident can make the difference between solving the problem and becoming part of it.***

All fire and emergency services organizations need to have predetermined guidelines or procedures for how to manage incidents involving hazardous materials. These guidelines include incident management elements that (if put into use properly) will enable first responders to manage haz mat emergencies effectively and safely. In those cases where haz mat incidents progress very slowly, first responders may be tempted to take shortcuts to speed the process, or they may be pressured into moving more quickly by local businesses or other officials. It is very important that first responders continue to follow their predetermined incident management elements to avoid taking shortcuts that may result in adverse consequences.

In general, predetermined guidelines or procedures for how to manage a haz mat incident contain the following incident management elements:

- *Priorities*
  - Life safety
  - Incident stabilization
  - Protection of property and the environment

- *Management structure*
  - Command system (National Fire Service Incident Management System/FIRESCOPE Incident Command System/National Incident Management System [IMS/ICS/NIMS])
  - Predetermined procedures and guidelines such as emergency response plans, standard operating procedures (SOPs), standard operating guidelines (SOGs), or operating instructions (OIs [military]) that outline operational procedures regarding communications, equipment, personnel, resources, mutual aid, and other needs

- *Problem-solving process*
  - Analyzing the incident through scene analysis, information gathering, and/or size-up to try to understand and identify the problem(s) and assess hazards and risks
  - Planning the response by determining specific strategic goals
  - Implementing the response using tactical objectives and assignment of tasks
  - Evaluating progress (feedback loop)

This chapter focuses on these incident management elements. In-depth details relating to strategies and tactics are covered in Chapter 5, Strategic Goals and Tactical Objectives.

Incident Priorities

There are three incident priorities for all haz mat incidents (which are the same for all emergency services organizations — law enforcement, fire, emergency medical services [EMS], or other). The three priorities for haz mat incidents (in order) are as follows:

- Life safety
- Incident stabilization
- Protection of property and the environment

All decisions during the problem-solving process must be made with these priorities in mind. The first priority is the safety of emergency responders and civilians because if responders do not protect themselves first, they cannot protect the public. Life safety must be a consideration from the moment an incident is reported until its termination — from the response to the scene until the ride back to the station. A dead, injured, or unexpectedly contaminated first responder becomes part of the problem, *not* the solution.

If there is no immediate threat to either responders or civilians, the next consideration is stabilizing the incident. When the first two priorities are satisfied, the conservation or protection of property and the environment can be addressed. Stabilizing the incident can minimize environmental and property damage. If the situation calls for it, these priorities can be changed, but generally, first responders need to consider them in the order presented.

Decisions weighing the life safety of responders versus the life safety of the public must be based upon a careful risk/benefit analysis. Adopting a policy of cautious assessment before taking action is vital. Consider the following variables:

- Risk to rescuers
- Ability of rescuers to protect themselves
- Probability of rescue
- Difficulty of rescue
- Capabilities and resources of on-scene forces
- Possibilities of explosions or sudden material releases
- Available escape routes and safe havens
- Constraints of time and distance

Specific information about rescue actions Awareness and Operational Level responders can take is contained in Chapter 5, Strategic Goals and Tactical Objectives, in the Rescue section.

When Lt. Adams analyzed the incident at Ace Trucking, she prioritized the problems she identified according to life safety, incident stabilization, and protection of property and the environment (see Scenario Table 1). Even before taking any other actions, she ensured the life safety of her fellow responders and herself by approaching the incident from uphill and upwind and positioning Engine 1 in a safe location.

Management Structure

Without order, there could be chaos at any emergency incident. Incident management elements form the framework for a control and coordination structure that enables emergency personnel to turn chaos into order and effectively manage any emergency incident. Incident management systems and standard operating procedures (or the equivalent) provide a predetermined set of procedures to follow at every haz mat incident. When used correctly, these tried-and-true management tools enable first responders to quickly establish control of haz mat incidents. The following sections provide information on incident command/management systems and their elements, establishment and transfer of command, unified command, haz mat positions within a management system, and predetermined procedures (standard operating procedures).

Incident Command or Management Systems

[NFPA 472: 5.4.2, 5.4.2(3), 5.1.2.1(3)(b)] [ODP Awareness V.b., V.I.c.] [ODP Operations II.a.]

Perhaps the most crucial aspect of controlling any incident (including haz mat incidents) is the implementation and use of an incident management or command system **(Figure 4.1)**. An *incident management system* is a management framework used to organize emergency incidents (see information box, p. 228). Using an incident management system provides the following advantages:

Figure 4.1 Implementation of an incident management system is a crucial aspect of controlling any emergency incident. *Courtesy of Chad Love.*

- ***Common terminology*** — Names of organizational elements, resources, and facilities are consistent. All organizations must use common terminology in order to understand the situation and act accordingly.

- ***Modular organization*** — The management system is built from the top down, with branches/sections added as needed according to the size and complexity of the incident. It must have the ability to increase or decrease in size as the incident changes.

- ***Integrated communication*** — In many areas, law enforcement, fire, and EMS personnel are on different frequencies and in some cases have different dispatch/telecommunication centers. For the management system to function correctly, all of the emergency service organizations involved in the incident must be able to communicate with each other.

- ***Unified command structure*** — All of the individuals or emergency service organizations that have jurisdictional responsibility are represented within the command structure **(Figure 4.2, p. 230)**. However, while many organizations may be a part of a unified command, only one person manages the incident.

- ***Consolidated action plans*** — Action plans are developed with input from all organizations/agencies involved, coordinating all functions.

- ***Manageable span of control*** — The management system enables an effective supervisory span of control at each level of the organization, which is determined by the ability of supervisors to monitor and effectively communicate with the personnel assigned to them. The optimum number of subordinates under any position is five. The span of control could be two to seven, depending on the complexity of the operation.

NFPA 1561, *Standard on Emergency Services Incident Management System* (2002), requires that all emergency services organizations (including law enforcement organizations, fire departments, fire brigades, EMS, and other support organizations such as the American Red Cross) adopt an incident management system to manage all emergency incidents. Details of the incident management system must be incorporated into the organization's SOPs (see Predetermined Procedures and Emergency Response Plans section).

In the U.S., Occupational Safety and Health Administration (OSHA) regulations (29 *CFR* 1910.120, *Hazardous Waste Site Operations and Emergency Response [HAZWOPER]*) mandate implementation of an incident command system as part of the requirements for emergency response to hazardous materials incidents.

Figure 4.2 Many organizations may be part of a unified command.

What's the Difference Among IMS, ICS, FGC, and NIMS?

In the early 1970s, a system was developed in California to address the resource management needs associated with large-scale wildland fires. This system eventually became known as the California FIRESCOPE *Incident Command System (ICS).*

During the same period, another incident management system, *Fire Ground Command (FGC),* was developed by the Phoenix (Arizona) Fire Department. The FGC system also lent itself very well to managing the different events to which most fire departments respond.

In order to address inconsistencies between these two early incident management systems, the National Fire Service Incident Management System Consortium was formed in 1991. The Consortium merged the two systems into the *National Fire Service Incident Management System (IMS)* in 1993.

In February 2003, the U.S. Department of Homeland Security (DHS) issued a directive to create a *National Incident Management System (NIMS).* NIMS was approved in March 2004. The Incident Command System (ICS) portion of the overall plan is very similar in structure to the existing incident management systems. By law, all agencies must show that they are in compliance with NIMS in order to receive future federal funding. Furthermore, legislation requires that NIMS ICS be used on all incidents that involve a federal response or for which federal reimbursement will be sought. Thus, jurisdictions may use existing incident management systems in their daily responses; however, they must be prepared to follow NIMS ICS should the incident expand beyond the use of local resources.

Because most hazardous materials incidents will not expand beyond the local level, this chapter describes incident management systems in a generic sense. The information is generally applicable regardless of which of the incident management systems is used by the jurisdiction (FIRESCOPE ICS, IMS, FGC, NIMS ICS). In the rare cases that a haz mat incident does elevate to the level dictated by the NIMS legislation, minor changes will be required by agencies using the other incident management systems. For details on the differences between NIMS ICS and the other systems, see Appendix L.

Be a Team Player!

Regardless of what type of incident management system is used by your organization, you must understand your role and responsibilities (as a first responder) within the command structure. Freelancing or taking action on your own without consent or knowledge of the incident commander (IC) is unacceptable and potentially very dangerous.

The need for an integrated and cooperative incident management system cannot be overemphasized. The next few sections provide a brief explanation of the common elements found in most model incident management systems.

Elements of an Incident Management System

Emergency situations can be as simple as a small combustible liquid fire or as complex as a terrorist attack of massive proportions. Depending on both the nature and the scope of the incident, different levels of incident management are needed. The incident management structure should be only as large as necessary to handle the incident safely and efficiently.

To understand an incident management structure, first responders need to know the major elements/functions within any incident management system: Command, Operations, Planning, Logistics, and Finance/Administration. Additionally, within these functions are organizational levels that divide/define various responsibilities. For example, during the early stages of large-scale or complex incidents, the Command organization may need to be expanded into *Sections*. The four Sections correspond with the major functional roles of Operations, Planning, Logistics, and Finance/Administration. Other elements include staging areas, resources, and incident plans.

Sections may have *Branches*, an organizational level having functional/geographic responsibility for major segments of incidents (for example, an Air Operations Branch under the Operations Section). On the tactical leve, *Divisions*, *Groups*, or *Sectors* are used to assemble companies and/or resources for a common purpose. *Divisions* represent geographic operations (such as the Roof Division), and *Groups* represent functional operations (such as the Air Support Group under the Air Operations Branch under the Operations Section). The term *Sector* is generic and can be used for both geographic and functional operations when operating using FGC or the National Fire Service IMS. Sectors are not recognized as a management unit in NIMS, NIIMS, or FIRESCOPE ICS.

Figure 4.3, p. 232, provides the full command structure common to all incident management systems for a major incident requiring maximum resources. Most incidents, including our incident

scenario, do not require implementation of this full structure. Small incidents may simply have an incident commmander (IC) and one or two tactical level Groups/Divisions/Sectors to carry out tasks.

At the initial stage of incident management, Lt. Adams was responsible for all incident management functions not otherwise staffed. Not only was she the IC, she was also responsible for operations, planning, logistics, finance/administration, and safety until she staffed the positions or transferred responsibility for those functions to someone else. She established an incident management organization appropriate to the needs of the incident. At this phase in the incident management development, Lt. Adams is fulfilling the responsibilities of the following incident management roles:

- *IC*
  - Taking command
  - Establishing incident priorities (determine incident objectives)
  - Developing appropriate incident management structure
  - Requesting additional resources
  - Assessing overall incident safety needs
- *Operations* — Assigning tactical functions
- *Planning*
  - Determining initial action plan
  - Assessing overall situation
  - Determining resource needs
- *Logistics* — Requesting additional resources
- *Finance/Administration* — Taking no action at this point, but being aware that emergency response agencies can seek reimbursement for response costs; if needed, initiating a cost-tracking system (depending on agency predetermined procedures)

Command

Command is the function of directing, ordering, and controlling resources by virtue of explicit legal, agency, or delegated authority. It is important that lines of authority be clear to all involved. Lawful commands by those in authority need to be followed immediately and without question. The basic configuration of the Command organization includes the following three levels:

Incident Management Organizational Structure

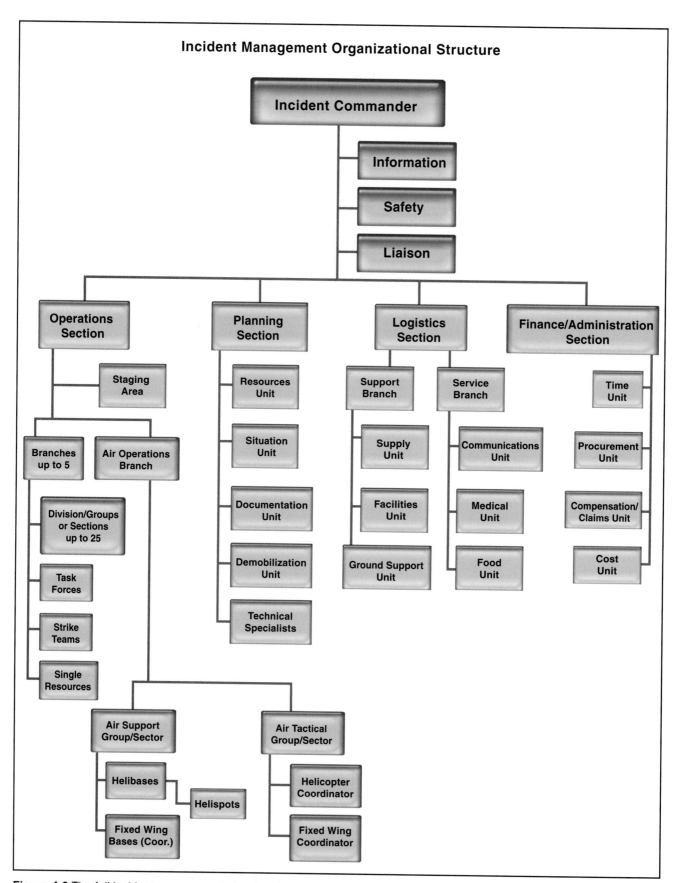

Figure 4.3 The full incident management structure for a major incident requiring maximum resources.

- *Strategic level* — Entails the overall direction and goals of the incident

- *Tactical level* — Identifies the objectives that the tactical-level supervisor/officer must achieve to meet the strategic goals

- *Task level* — Describes the specific tasks needed to meet tactical-level requirements, and assigns these tasks to operational units, companies, or individuals

The person in overall command of an incident is the IC, who establishes the Command Post (CP) and is ultimately responsible for all incident activities, including the development and implementation of a strategic plan. This process may include making a number of critical decisions and being responsible for the results of those decisions. The IC has the authority both to call resources to the incident and release them from it. Additional duties and responsibilities of the IC are discussed in the next section.

If the size and complexity of the incident requires, the IC may delegate authority to the following Command Staff positions:

- *Safety Officer* (OSHA mandates the appointment of a safety officer at haz mat incidents)

- *Liaison Officer*

- *Public Information Officer*

At the beginning of our incident scenario, Lt. Adams determined the initial strategy and tactics and supervised the crews doing the tasks **(Figure 4.4)**. By the time Lt. Adams transferred command to Battalion Chief Arasim, the incident management organization had expanded to include additional resources **(Figure 4.5)**.

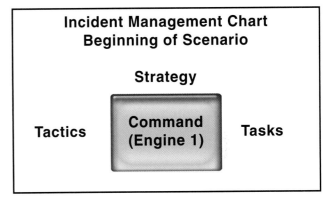

Figure 4.4 At the initial stage of incident management, (see Scenario Diagram 2, p. 102) Lt. Adams determined the initial strategy and tactics and supervised the crews doing tasks. She was responsible for all functions not otherwise staffed.

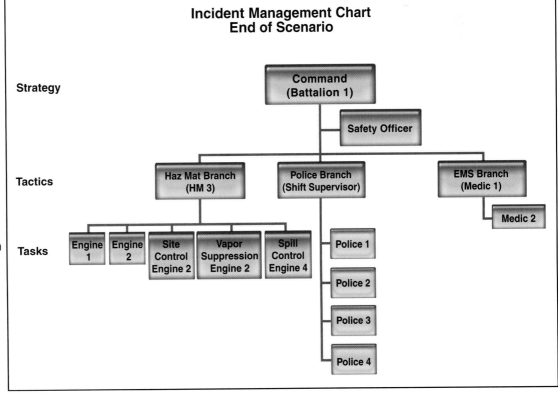

Figure 4.5 The organization had expanded to include additional resources by the time Command was transferred to Battalion Chief Arasim (see Scenario Diagram 4, p. 109).

Incident commander. *[OSHA 29 CFR 1910.120 (q)(3)]* The *IC* is the officer at the top of an incident chain of command and in overall charge of the incident. The IC is ultimately responsible for everything that takes place at the emergency scene and primarily responsible for formulating the incident action plan (IAP) (plan for managing the emergency) and coordinating and directing all incident resources to implement the plan and meet its goals and objectives. No aggressive plan should be undertaken unless sufficient information is available to make logical decisions and the safe coordination of operations can be accomplished. The IC must make it known to the telecommunicator and other responders when Command is assumed or transferred. ICs at haz mat incidents have specific responsibilities in addition to standard IC functions. The IC does not have to actually perform or supervise each function but may choose to delegate them to others. The IC is required to perform the following functions at haz mat incidents:

- Establish the site safety (also called *scene safety*) plan

- Implement a site security and control plan to limit the number of personnel operating in the control zones (see Chapter 5, Strategic Goals and Tactical Objectives)

- Designate a safety officer

- Identify the materials or conditions involved in the incident

- Implement appropriate emergency operations

- Ensure that all emergency responders (not just those of their own organizations) wear appropriate personal protective equipment (PPE) in restricted zones

- Establish a decontamination plan and operation

- Implement postincident emergency response procedures (incident termination)

Safety officer. *[NFPA 472: 5.4.1(6)(a–b), 5.4.2(6), A.5.4.2 (6)(1–4)] [OSHA 29 CFR 1910.120 (q)(3)(vii & viii)]* The *Safety Officer* is responsible for monitoring and identifying hazardous and unsafe situations and developing measures for ensuring personnel safety **(Figure 4.6)**. Although the Safety Officer may exercise emergency authority to stop or prevent unsafe acts when immediate action is required, the officer generally chooses to correct them through the regular line of authority. Many unsafe acts or conditions are addressed in the IAP (see Incident Action Plan section). The Safety Officer must be trained to the level of operations conducted at the incident and is required to perform the following duties:

- Obtain a briefing from the IC.

- Review IAPs (see Incident Action Plan section) for safety issues.

- Identify hazardous situations at the incident scene.

- Participate in the preparation and monitoring of incident safety considerations, including medical monitoring of entry team personnel before and after entry.

HAZWOPER IC Requirements

According to OSHA regulations (29 *CFR* 1910.120, *HAZWOPER*), any emergency responder expected to perform as an IC must be trained to fulfill the obligations of the position at the level of response the responder is providing (Operational Level, minimum), which includes the ability to perform the following duties:

- Analyze a hazardous substance incident to determine the magnitude of the response problem.

- Plan and implement an appropriate response plan within the capabilities of available personnel and equipment.

- Implement a response to favorably change the outcome of an incident in a manner consistent with the local emergency response plan and the organization's predetermined procedures.

- Evaluate the progress of the emergency response to ensure that the response objectives are being met safely, effectively, and efficiently.

- Adjust the response plan to the conditions of the response and notify higher levels of response when required by changes to the response plan.

Appendix F, Hazardous Materials Incident Commander Checklist, provides a sample checklist designed to ensure compliance with *HAZWOPER*.

Figure 4.6 The safety officer monitors the scene for unsafe conditions.

- Maintain communications with the IC, and advise the IC of deviations from the incident safety considerations and of any dangerous situations.

- Alter, suspend, or terminate any activity that is judged to be unsafe.

At hazardous waste cleanup sites and other nonemergency operations involving hazardous materials, OSHA *HAZWOPER* and the Canadian Ministry of Labour require appointment of a *Site Safety and Health Supervisor* whose duty is to oversee onsite safety and health issues. These individuals must have training specific to the safety of haz mat incidents.

The Safety Officer also needs to ensure that safety briefings are conducted for entry team personnel before entry. Safety briefings include information about the status of the incident (based on the preliminary evaluation and subsequent up-

dates), the hazards identified, a description of the site, the tasks to be performed, the expected duration of the tasks, the PPE requirements, monitoring requirements, notification of identified risks, and any other pertinent information. At incidents involving potential criminal or terrorist activities, the safety briefing should also cover the following items:

- Being alert for secondary devices

- Not touching or moving any suspicious-looking articles (bags, boxes, briefcases, soda cans, and the like)

- Not touching or entering any damp, wet, or oily areas

- Wearing full protective clothing, including self-contained breathing apparatus (SCBA)

- Limiting the number of personnel entering the crime scene

- Documenting all actions

- Not picking up or taking *any* souvenirs

- Photographing or videotaping anything suspicious

- Not destroying any possible evidence

  Seeking professional crime-scene assistance

Command post. *[NFPA 472: 5.4.2(4)]* *[ODP Operations II.a.]* Establishing a *Command Post (CP)* to which informa-tion flows and from which orders are issued is vital to a smooth operation. The IC must be accessible (either directly or indirectly) and a CP ensures this accessibility. A CP can be a predetermined location at a facility, a conveniently located building, or a radio-equipped vehicle located in a safe area **(Figure 4.7, p. 236)**. Ideally, the CP is located where the IC can observe the scene, although such a location is not absolutely necessary. The location of the CP is relayed to the telecommunicator/dispatcher and responding fire companies. A CP needs to be readily identifiable. One common identifier is a green flashing light. Other methods include pennants, signs, and flags.

Operations Section

The *Operations Section* is responsible for the direct management of all incident tactical activities, the tactical priorities, and the safety and welfare of

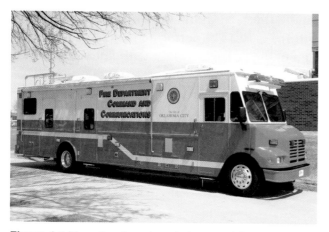

Figure 4.7 Many fire departments have mobile command posts; however, a command post can also be a predetermined location at a facility, a conveniently located building, or any radio-equipped vehicle located in a safe area.

personnel working in the Operations Section. The *Operations Section Chief* reports directly to the IC and is responsible for managing all operations that directly affect the primary mission of eliminating a problem incident. The Operations Section Chief directs the tactical operations to meet the strategic goals developed by the IC.

Planning Section

The *Planning Section* is responsible for gathering, assimilating, analyzing, and processing information needed for effective decision-making. Information management is a full-time task at large incidents. The Planning Section serves as the IC's *clearinghouse* for incidents, which allows the IC's staff to provide information instead of having to deal with dozens of information sources. Command uses the information compiled by the Planning position to develop strategic goals and contingency plans. Specific units under Planning include the *Resources Unit, Situation Unit, Documentation Unit, Demobilization Unit,* and any technical specialists whose services are required.

Logistics Section

The *Logistics Section* is the support mechanism for the organization. It provides services and support systems to all the organizational components involved in the incident including facilities, transportation needs, supplies, equipment, maintenance, fueling supplies, meals, communications, and responder medical services (**Figure 4.8**). Two

Figure 4.8 The IMS Logistics Section is responsible for providing supplies, equipment, and services for an incident (such as sand for diking and tankers to remove contaminated runoff water). *Courtesy of Chad Love.*

branches are within Logistics: Support Branch and Service Branch. The *Service Branch* includes medical, communications, and food services. The *Support Branch* includes supplies, facilities, and ground support (vehicle services).

Finance/Administration Section

The *Finance/Administration Section* is established on incidents when agencies involved have a specific need for financial services. Not all agencies require the establishment of a separate Finance/Administration Section. In some cases (such as cost analysis), that position could be established as a Technical Specialist in the Planning Section. Specific units under the Finance/Administration Section include the *Time Unit*, *Procurement Unit*, *Compensation Claims Unit*, and *Cost Unit*.

Staging Area

The *staging area* is where personnel and equipment awaiting assignment to the incident are held. This practice keeps the responders and their equipment a short distance from the scene until they are needed and minimizes confusion at the scene. The staging area needs to be located at an isolated spot in a safe area where occupants cannot interfere with ongoing operations. A safe direction of travel to the staging area should be broadcast to all resources responding to the incident.

Resources

Resources are all personnel, equipment, and major pieces of apparatus on scene or en route on which status is maintained. Resources may be individual companies, task forces, strike teams, or other specialized units. Resources are considered to be *available* when they have checked in at the incident and are not currently committed to an assignment. The status of these resources must be tracked so that they can be assigned when and where they are needed without delay.

Incident Action Plan

The *incident action plan (IAP)* is the plan for managing the emergency. A plan needs to be formulated for *every* incident. The IAP identifies the strategic goals and tactical objectives that must be achieved to eliminate the problem. See Planning the Response/Setting Strategic Goals: Incident Action Plans section for more details.

Incident Command Establishment and Transfer

[ODP Operations II.b.]

When using any incident management system, one directive is clear: The first person on the scene or the ranking individual of the first company on the scene assumes command of the incident. ***The IC must have incident management training and be at the hazardous materials Operational Level.*** That individual maintains command until a higher ranking or more extensively trained responder arrives on the scene and assumes command. Before command is transferred, the person accepting it must be capable of assuming command (that is, have the necessary qualifications) and be willing to accept it. If the transfer cannot take place face to face, it can be accomplished over the radio, but *command can only be transferred to someone who is on scene.* As an incident grows larger, command may be transferred several times before the situation is brought under control. A smooth and efficient transfer of command contributes greatly to bringing an incident to a timely and successful conclusion.

The person relinquishing command must provide the person assuming command with as clear a picture of the situation as possible. This update can be accomplished by giving a *situation status report:* an updated version of the incident evaluation performed on arrival. The person assuming command acknowledges receipt of the information by repeating it back to the other person. If the reiteration is accurate, the recipient is ready to accept control of and responsibility for the management of the incident. The former IC can then be reassigned to an operating unit or retained at the CP as an aide or as a member of the Command Staff.

In most cases there is only ***ONE*** IC, except in a multijurisdictional incident when a unified command is appropriate. A multijurisdictional incident involves services (fire, law enforcement, EMS, and the like) from one city but beyond the jurisdiction of one organization/agency. The chain of command must be clearly defined, especially when a unified command is used. Although there may be several members of a unified command team, one designated person issues all orders through the chain of command to avoid the confusion caused by conflicting orders.

When command is transferred, the former IC must announce the change to avoid any possible confusion caused by others hearing a different voice acknowledging messages and issuing orders. If all involved follow the chain of command and use correct radio protocols, they will not call anyone by name, rank, or job title, so it does not matter who answers their radio messages. Because the early stages of an emergency can be chaotic, anything done to reduce confusion is desirable. Announcing a transfer of command is one way of accomplishing that objective.

When a complex emergency occurs, command may be transferred several times as the organization grows. It is important that transitions are as smooth and as efficient as possible.

Unified Command

[ODP Operations II.e.]

Control of an incident involving multiple agencies with overlapping authority and responsibility is accomplished through the use of unified command. The concept of *unified command* simply means that all agencies that have a jurisdictional responsibility at a multijurisdictional incident contribute to the process by taking the following actions:

- Determine overall incident objectives.
- Select strategies.
- Accomplish joint planning for tactical activities.

- Ensure integrated tactical operations.
- Use all assigned resources effectively.

Proactive organizations identify target hazards in their areas of jurisdiction and also identify any other agencies with authority and responsibility for those target hazards. Ideally, those agencies meet, identify differences in agency incident management practices, and establish a *memorandum of understanding for unified command:* a written agreement defining roles and responsibilities within a unified command structure. It is signed by the lead officials of the agencies and becomes policy governing the personnel within those agencies.

Controlling hazardous material incidents may require the coordinated efforts of several agencies/organizations such as the following:

- Fire service
- Law enforcement
- EMS
- Private concerns
  — Material's manufacturer
  — Material's shipper
  — Facility manager
- Government agencies (local, state/provincial, federal) with mandated interests in health and environmental issues
- Privately contracted cleanup and salvage companies
- Specialized emergency response groups, organizations, and technical support groups
- Utilities and public works

To avoid jurisdictional and command disputes, identify the specific agency/organization responsible for handling and coordinating response activities before an incident happens. Know what mutual aid contracts do and do not cover. Pre-incident coordination should be done at the local level so that jurisdictional disputes can be avoided. The responsible or *lead* agency can then begin documenting the identities and capabilities of nearby support sources. Proper planning and preparation lead to safe and successful responses to a hazardous material incident. The occurrence of a serious haz mat incident is not the time to discover that a neighboring fire department or industry cannot provide desperately needed equipment, personnel, or technical expertise. When emergency services organizations work together to develop their haz mat pre-incident surveys, they can meet the following objectives:

- Share vital resource information.

- Develop rapport among participating emergency services organizations.

- Identify and pool needed resources.

Haz Mat Positions Within an Incident Management System

Incident management systems provide an organizational structure for necessary supervision and control of the essential functions required at virtually all hazardous materials incidents. These positions are at the Technician Level, but Awareness and Operational Level responders need to be familiar with them **(Figure 4.9)**. Standard positions commonly used at hazardous materials incidents are as follows:

- *Hazardous Materials Group/Sector Supervisor* — Directs the primary tactical functions

- *Entry Leader* — Supervises all companies and personnel operating in the hazardous area, with the responsibility to direct all tactics and control the positions and functions of all personnel in the hazardous area

- *Decontamination Leader* — Supervises operations in the scene-control zone where decontamination is conducted, and ensures that all rescued citizens, response personnel, equipment, and the like have been decontaminated before leaving the incident

- *Site Access Control Leader* — Controls all movement of personnel and equipment between the control zones (see Chapter 5, Strategic Goals and Tactical Objectives), and is responsible for isolating the control zones and ensuring proper routes; also has the responsibility for the control, care, and movement of people before they are decontaminated; may appoint a Safe Refuge Area Manager

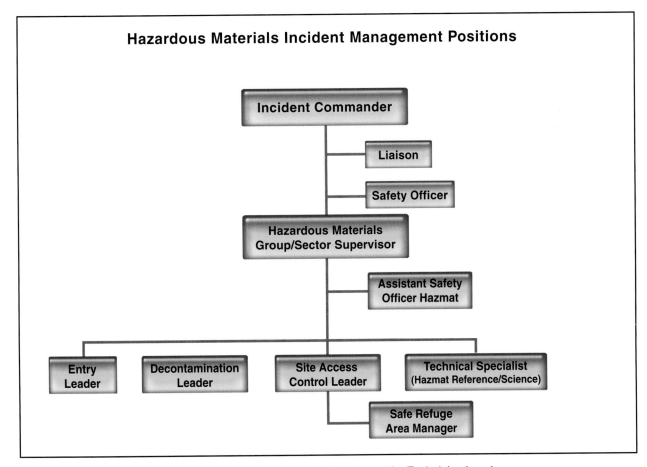

Figure 4.9 Hazardous materials incident management positions are at the Technician Level.

- *Assistant Safety Officer (Hazardous Materials)* — Is responsible for the overall safety of assigned personnel within the Hazardous Materials Group/Sector, and reports directly to the Safety Officer; must be appointed at hazardous materials incidents and have the requisite knowledge to function as the Assistant Safety Officer at a haz mat incident

- *Technical Specialist (Hazardous Materials Reference/Science Technical Specialist)* — Is responsible for providing technical information and assistance to the Hazardous Materials Group/Sector and the Planning Section using various sources such as computer databases, technical journals, public and private technical information agencies, facility representatives, and product specialists

- *Safe Refuge Area Manager* — Is responsible for evaluating and prioritizing victims for treatment, collecting information from the victims, and preventing the spread of contamination by these victims; also recommended that this person have an EMS background

The functional positions of the Hazardous Materials Group/Sector (Entry Leader, Decontamination Leader, and Site Access Control Leader) require a high degree of control and close supervision. The Hazardous Materials Group/Sector Supervisor manages the functional responsibilities, which includes all tactical operations carried out in the hazardous area.

All rescue operations come under the direction of the Hazardous Materials Group/Sector Supervisor. In addition to the primary functions, the Hazardous Materials Group/Sector Supervisor works with an Assistant Safety Officer who is trained in hazardous materials and must be present at the hazardous site. The Hazardous Materials Group/Sector Supervisor may also supervise one or more Technical Specialists. Evacuation and all other tactical objectives that are outside the scene-control zones are not responsibilities of the Hazardous Materials Group/Sector Supervisor. These tactical operations as well as many other hazardous materials related functions are managed by regular incident management positions.

Predetermined Procedures and Emergency Response Plans

[NFPA 472: 4.4.1(1), 5.4.2(1)] [ODP Awareness Level III.d., III.e.]

Many emergency services organizations have predetermined procedures for nearly every conceivable type of emergency that can occur. These plans are known as the organization's *SOPs, SOGs,* or *OIs.* Additionally, OSHA 29 *CFR* 1910.120(q)(2) requires emergency response organizations in the U.S. to develop emergency response plans that must cover the following elements:

- Pre-emergency planning and coordination with outside parties

- Personnel roles, lines of authority, training, and communication

- Emergency recognition and prevention

- Safe distances and places of refuge

- Site security and control

- Evacuation routes and procedures

- Decontamination

- Emergency medical treatment and first aid

- Emergency alerting and response procedures

- Critiques of response and follow up

- PPE and emergency response equipment

Combined, these predetermined plans and procedures or guidelines provide a standard set of actions that form the core of every hazardous material incident plan, and they need to comply with any procedures set forth in the local emergency response plan (see Appendix C, Emergency Response Plans). The procedures may vary considerably in different localities, but the principles are usually the same. However, they must incorporate specific regulatory requirements such as those required by OSHA. Predetermined procedures must be written and their use required in order for them to be effective. Individuals must be trained in their use and disciplined when they do not follow the procedures.

Even though there are obvious variations in haz mat incidents, they all have some similarities. These similarities are the basis for predetermined actions. The IC knows the predetermined procedures and can base a plan of action upon them. Procedures have a built-in flexibility that allows, with reasonable justification, adjustments when unforeseen circumstances occur. The first units that reach the scene usually initiate the predetermined actions. They do not replace size-up, decisions based on professional judgment, evaluation, or Command. In addition, there may be several predetermined procedures from which to choose, depending on incident severity, location, and the ability of first-in units to achieve control.

Following predetermined procedures and the provisions of the emergency response plan reduces chaos on the haz mat scene. All resources can be used in a coordinated effort to rescue victims, stabilize the incident, and protect the environment and property. Operational procedures that are standardized, clearly written, and mandated to each department/organization member establish accountability and increase command and control effectiveness. When first responders are trained properly in predetermined procedures, confusion is lessened. They understand their duties and require a minimum of direction.

These predetermined procedures also help prevent duplication of effort and uncoordinated operations because all positions are assigned and

covered. The assumption and transfer of command, communications procedures, and tactical procedures are other areas that must be covered by predetermined procedures. Applying these procedures to communications, levels of incidents, and safety procedures are described in the sections that follow. Appendix B, Sample Standard Operating Guideline, provides an example of operational guidelines for hazardous materials response.

Communications

[NFPA 472: 5.5.2(1), 5.5.2, 5.5.2(2), 5.1.2.1(4)(b), 5.4.2(5), 5.1.2.1(3)(a)] [ODP Awareness Level VI.a., VI.c., VI.d.] [ODP Operations II.a., II.c.]

Departmental/organizational predetermined procedures usually cover methods of communication (both externally and internally) at incidents, whether by radio, cell phone, hand-light signals, or hand signals. Traditionally, two-way radios are the primary means of communication; however, advances in technology have made a variety of communication tools available to emergency responders **(Figure 4.10)**. First responders must be able to communicate the need for assistance through their department/organization's communications equipment. Some of these communications might

Figure 4.10 Advances in technology have improved the number of ways emergency responders can communicate at incidents.

be requests for additional personnel or special equipment or to notify others at the incident of any apparent hazards. Several procedures and guidelines for using communications equipment correctly are as follows:

- **Radio procedures** — Communication protocols, priority transmission methods, and terminology:
  - Use simple English (*clear text*) as required under NFPA 1561.
  - Transmit *only essential information* when sending information and orders.
  - Use appropriate channels to communicate with both the IC and the telecommunicator.
  - Use appropriate number of channels for the size and complexity of the incident:
    - Routine, day-to-day incidents are usually handled on a single channel.
    - Large incidents may require using several channels to allow for clear and timely exchanges of information.
    - Separate channels may be needed for Command, entry, decontamination, research support, tactical, and support functions.

- **Requesting additional help** — Additional units, specialized equipment, alarm signals, and what to do when they are received:
  - Know what types of additional help are available.
  - Identify these items in the local emergency response plan.

- **Emergency radio traffic** — Distress messages sent to telecommunicators at telecommunications centers (who are better equipped than on-scene personnel to hear weak signals from portable and mobile radios) and urgent messages for additional resources or to relay detailed instructions:
  - Make the urgency clear to the telecommunicator.
  - Wait while the telecommunicator gives an attention tone (if used in that system), advises all other units to stand by, and advises the caller to proceed with the emergency message.

- Resume normal or routine radio traffic when the emergency communication is complete after the telecommunicator notifies all units to do so.

- **Evacuation signals** — Broadcasts pulling all emergency personnel from a hazardous area because conditions have deteriorated beyond the point of safety; similar to emergency traffic procedures:
  - Broadcast a radio message ordering evacuation.
  - Sound audible warning devices (sirens and air horns) on the apparatus at the incident scene for an extended time period (works well outside small structures).
  - Broadcast the message several times.

External communications. An external communication system facilitates communication between onsite and offsite personnel, which may be necessary to coordinate an emergency response while maintaining contact with essential offsite personnel and technical experts. The primary means of external communications are cell phone, telephone, and radio, but other technologies may enable use of computers (e-mail, digital messaging for pagers, etc.) and other devices. Predetermined procedures may also address external communications with the media and public.

Internal communications. Information regarding the incident is received and shared among emergency responders once they arrive on the scene. Examples of internal communications are as follows:

- Alerting team members to emergencies
- Passing along safety information
- Communicating changes in the action plan
- Maintaining site control

Verbal communication at a site can be impeded by onsite background noise and the use of PPE. For example, speech transmission through a respirator can be poor, and protective hoods and respirator airflow can impair hearing. Often for effective internal communication, commands must be prearranged. In addition, audio or visual cues can help convey messages. The most important thing is that signals must be agreed upon in advance.

Both primary and backup systems of communication are recommended, particularly when developing a set of signals for use only during emergencies. All communication devices used in a potentially explosive atmosphere must be intrinsically safe and not capable of sparking; check them daily to ensure that they are operating. Several examples of internal communication devices are as follows:

- Radios
- Cell phones
- Pagers
- Noisemakers
  — Bells
  — Compressed-air horns
  — Megaphones
  — Sirens
  — Whistles
- Visual signals
  — Flags
  — Flares or smoke bombs
  — Hand signals
  — Lights
  — Signal boards
  — Whole body movements

Telecommunicator roles. Haz mat incidents compose a very small portion of overall emergency calls handled by telecommunicators. For this reason, telecommunicators require special training to ensure that they recognize the significance of the call and act accordingly. Telecommunicators must be trained to obtain as much information as possible regarding a reported incident. They should ask questions of callers that help determine whether a hazardous material may be involved and, if so, what the material is. It is best if the telecommunicator has a prepared list of questions to ask. This list helps determine the nature of an incident. The telecommunicator must also be cognizant of the local emergency response plan (LERP), the fire and emergency services organization's predetermined procedures, and special procedures for making haz mat incident notifications and information requests.

If a haz mat incident is in progress, either the telecommunicator or the first responder should initiate the organization's predetermined procedure for this type of incident. Depending on the capabilities of local emergency forces and the requirements of the LERP, this initial response may be no more than that normally dispatched to conduct an investigation of unknown trouble. Where resources are available, specialized personnel and equipment may be sent immediately. Telecommunicators must be prepared to change the response whenever additional information warrants such a change. They must be prepared to take the following actions:

- Establish internal or external clear-line communications with technical advisors.
- Notify mutual aid agencies.
- Activate other prescribed departmental/ organizational procedures.
- Advise next-in-line supervisors and chief officers of the incident.

Telecommunicators must relay all available information to responding units, and each unit responds with reports to the telecommunicator. Telecommunicators must not filter, edit, delete, or change the information that they receive. They must relay all information as promptly and accurately as possible. The amount of information requested and transmitted between command, tactical, and support units during these incidents may seriously strain the abilities of single-channel, single-operator dispatching systems. Ideally, telecommunicators relaying information between units should have no other assignments in order to avoid confusion and loss of information.

In addition, it is desirable for all units operating at a haz mat incident to switch to a radio frequency that is separate from radio frequencies used for normal daily operations. The telecommunicators and on-scene personnel must communicate all pertinent information regarding the incident to the IC who states clearly all directives to on-scene personnel and confirms with personnel that orders are understood.

Whenever possible, on-scene command personnel should talk directly to technical advisors. However, when direct communications with technical advisors are not possible, the telecommunicator must perform the function of liaison between technical advisors and on-scene personnel. Telecommunicators need to gather as much information about the nature of the incident as possible before contacting technical sources. The Canadian Transport Emergency Centre (CANUTEC) and Chemical Transportation Emergency Center of the American Chemistry Council (CHEMTREC®) are examples of highly useful services with which telecommunicators may communicate. While these organizations primarily provide immediate information on material properties, their hazards, and suggested control techniques, they also serve an equally important role as a communications link with other technical support resources.

Levels of Incidents
[NFPA 472: 5.4.2(2)]

First responders must understand that hazardous material incidents are different from other types of emergencies. They must also understand who needs to get involved in an incident and why. This understanding comes through the knowledge of the organization's predetermined procedures and emergency response plans. These documents dictate how resources, depending on the level of risk, are devoted to incidents.

Most models used for determining the level of a hazardous material incident define three levels of response graduating from Level I (least serious) to Level III (most serious). By defining the levels of response, an increasing level of involvement and necessary resources can be identified based on the severity of the incident.

In addition to this system of determining the levels of hazardous materials incidents, NFPA defines three levels of response in NFPA 471, *Recommended Practice for Responding to Hazardous Materials Incidents* (2002). **Table 4.1** is primarily used to determine the level of incident in planning a response or training exercise. The application of this information is basically the same as that for the three levels previously mentioned. Four criteria for one model used to determine the level of a haz mat incident are as follows:

- Extent of municipal, county/parish/borough, state/provincial, and federal involvement (or potential involvement)
- Level of technical expertise required at the scene
- Extent of evacuation of civilians
- Extent of injuries or deaths

Level I. This type of incident is within the capabilities of the fire or emergency services organization or other first responders having jurisdiction. A Level I incident is the least serious and the easiest to handle. It may pose a serious threat to life or property, although this situation is not usually the case. Evacuation (if required) is limited to the immediate area of the incident. The following are examples of Level I incidents:

- Small amount of gasoline or diesel fuel spilled from an automobile
- Leak from domestic natural gas line on the consumer side of the meter
- Broken containers of consumer commodities such as paint, thinners, bleach, swimming pool chemicals, and fertilizers (owner or proprietor is responsible for cleanup and disposal)

Level II. This type of incident is beyond the capabilities of the first responders on the scene and may be beyond the capabilities of the first response agency/organization having jurisdiction. Level II incidents require the services of a formal haz mat response team. A properly trained and equipped response team could be expected to perform the following tasks:

- Use chemical protective clothing.
- Dike and confine within the contaminated areas.
- Perform plugging and patching activities (**Figure 4.11, p. 246**).
- Sample and test unknown substances (**Figure 4.12, p. 246**).
- Perform various levels of decontamination.

The following are examples of Level II incidents:

- Spill or leak requiring large-scale evacuation

Table 4.1
Planning Guide for Determining Incident Levels for Response and Training

Incident Conditions	Incident Level		
	One	Two	Three
Product identifications	Placard not required, NFPA 0 or 1 all categories, all Class 9 and ORM-D	DOT placarded, NFPA 2 for any categories, PCBs without fire, EPA regulated waste	Class 2, Division 2.3 – poisonous gases, Class 1, Division 1.1 and 1.2 – explosives, organic peroxide, flammable solid, materials dangerous when wet, chlorine, fluorine, anhydrous ammonia, radioactive materials, NFPA 3 and 4 for any categories including special hazards, PCBs and fire, DOT inhalation hazard, EPA extremely hazardous substances, and cryogenics
Container size	Small [e.g., pail, drums, cylinders except 910-kg (1-ton), packages, bags]	Medium [e.g., 910-kg (1-ton) cylinders, portable containers, nurse tanks, multiple small packages]	Large (e.g., tank cars, tank trucks, stationary tanks, hopper cars/trucks, multiple medium containers)
Fire/Explosion potential	Low	Medium	High
Leak severity	No release or small release contained or confined with readily available resources	Release may not be controllable without special resources	Release may not be controllable even with special resources
Life safety	No life-threatening situation from materials involved	Localized area, limited evacuation area	Large area, mass evacuation area
Environmental impact (potential)	Minimal	Moderate	Severe
Container integrity	Not damaged	Damaged but able to contain the contents to allow handling or transfer of product	Damaged to such an extent that catastrophic rupture is possible

Reprinted with permission from NFPA 471-2002 *Responding to Hazardous Materials Incidents,* Copyright © 2002, National Fire Protection Association, Quincy, MA. This reprinted material is not the complete and official position of the NFPA on the referenced subject, which is represented only by the standard in its entirety.

- Any major accident, spillage, or overflow of flammable liquids **(Figure 4.13, p. 246)**
- Spill or leak of unfamiliar or unknown chemicals
- Accident involving extremely hazardous substances
- Rupture of an underground pipeline
- Fire that is posing a boiling liquid expanding valor explosion (BLEVE) threat in a storage tank

Level III. This type of incident requires resources from state/provincial agencies, federal agencies, and/or private industry and also requires unified command. A Level III incident is the most serious of all hazardous material incidents. A large-scale evacuation may be required. Most likely, the incident will not be concluded by any one agency. Successful handling of the incident requires a collective effort from several of the following resources/procedures.

Figure 4.11 Level II incidents require the services of a hazardous materials response team to perform activities such as plugging and patching. *Courtesy of Steve Hendrix.*

Figure 4.12 Sampling and testing should be conducted by technicians. *Courtesy of Sherry Arasim.*

Figure 4.13 A leaking tanker is an example of a Level II incident. *Courtesy of Chris E. Mickal.*

- Specialists from industry and governmental agencies

- Sophisticated sampling and monitoring equipment

- Specialized leak and spill control techniques

- Decontamination on a large scale

The following are examples of Level III incidents:

- Incidents that require an evacuation extending across jurisdictional boundaries

- Incidents beyond the capabilities of the local hazardous material response team

- Incidents that activate (in part or in whole) the federal response plan

---

As soon as Lt. Adams found that the incident involved a 300-gallon (757 L) intermediate bulk container (IBC) of 1,2-butylene oxide and had found the chemical's information in the *Emergency Response Guidebook (ERG),* she notified dispatch to upgrade the incident to Level II. This action was taken even before arriving on the scene, because she knew that a single engine would not have the resources to effectively manage the situation, and the services of a haz mat team would be required to fully mitigate the release.

Safety Procedures

Predetermined procedures must include the use of safety procedures. Accountability of all personnel at a haz mat incident is critical, and first responders must be familiar with the department/organization's system for tracking and identifying all personnel working at an incident. Additionally, all personnel working in hazardous areas at haz mat incidents must be working as part of a team or buddy system. OSHA and the Canadian Ministry of Labour require the use of buddy systems and backup personnel at haz mat incidents.

Accountability systems/tracking resources. One of the most important functions of an incident management system is to provide a means of tracking all personnel and equipment assigned to the incident. Most units responding to an incident arrive fully staffed and ready to be assigned an operational objective; other personnel may have to be formed into units at the scene. To handle these and other differences in the resources available, the IAP must contain a tracking and accountability system that has the following elements:

- Procedure for checking in at the scene

- Way of identifying and tracking the location of each unit and all personnel on scene

- Procedure for releasing people, equipment, and apparatus no longer needed

Because accountability systems are such an important aspect of safety, the incident safety officer is responsible for ensuring that the system is in place and that all members are in compliance. The incident safety officer must have the authority to enforce the use of the system and correct any violations. Working through the IC, the incident safety officer may enforce the accountability system and alter tactical operations until all personnel are accounted for.

Accountability systems are especially important for haz mat incidents where multiple agencies/organizations may be responding, all of which may have different levels of PPE and training. The agency/organization in command is responsible for tracking all responders (not just their own).

Buddy systems and backup personnel. [NFPA 472: 5.4.3(1), 5.4.3(2)] [OSHA 29 CFR 1910.120(q)(3)(v–vi)] Use of buddy systems and backup personnel are mandated by NFPA and OSHA at haz mat incidents. A *buddy system* is a system of organizing personnel into workgroups in such a manner that each member has a *buddy* or partner, so that nobody is working alone **(Figure 4.14, p. 248).** The purpose of the buddy system is to provide rapid help in the event of an emergency. In addition to using the buddy system, backup personnel shall be standing by with equipment ready to provide assistance or rescue if needed. Qualified basic life support personnel (as a minimum) shall also be standing by with medical equipment and transportation capability. Any haz mat team working within the hazardous area must have at least two members. The minimum number of personnel necessary for performing tasks in the hazardous area is four — two working in the area itself and two standing by as backup.

Figure 4.14 Personnel operating in or near the hazard area should always be working with a buddy, never alone. *Courtesy of Phil Linder.*

Problem-Solving Process

Incident priorities, an incident management system, and predetermined procedures provide a management structure for first responders. But the incident still needs mitigation (actions taken to lessen the harm or hostile nature of an incident). The problem must be solved through a process of problem-solving and decision-making. While not all first responders are in a command position responsible for planning an appropriate response to a haz mat emergency, it is important for them to understand the incident management process. The most common haz mat management processes contain the elements of the following basic four-step problem-solving formula developed by George Polya, a former professor of mathematics at Stanford University:

Incident Problem-Solving Process Models

Many haz mat incident management process models are in use that provide first responders a series of steps or actions to take at every haz mat emergency. Some of the better known systems are as follows:

- *GEDAPER* by David Lesak:

 G — Gather information

 E — Estimate potential course and harm

 D — Determine strategic goals

 A — Assess tactical options and resources

 P — Plan of action implementation

 E — Evaluate operations

 R — Review the process

- *DECIDE* by Ludwig Benner

 D — Detect the presence of hazardous materials

 E — Estimate likely harm without intervention

 C — Choose response objectives

 I — Identify action options

 D — Do best option

 E — Evaluate progress

- *APIE* by the International Association of Fire Fighters (IAFF)

 A — Analyze

 P — Plan

 I — Implement

 E — Evaluate (and repeat)

- *IFSTA* by International Fire Service Training Association (IFSTA)

 I — Identify the nature of the problem

 F — Formulate objectives based on available information

 S — Select the desired alternatives from the available options

 T — Take appropriate action

 A — Analyze outcomes continually

Gregory G. Noll, Michael S. Hildebrand, and James G. Yvorra developed the Eight Step Incident Management Process©, which is a tactical decision-making model that focuses on haz mat incident safe operating practices.* The eight steps are as follows:

1. Site management and control
2. Identify the problem
3. Hazards and risk evaluation
4. Select personal protective clothing and equipment
5. Information management and resource coordination
6. Implement response objectives
7. Decontamination
8. Terminate the incident

---

* See *Hazardous Materials: Managing the Incident,* 3rd edition, by Gregory G. Noll, Michael S. Hildebrand, and James G. Yvorra, 2004, distributed by Fire Protection Publications.

Step 1: Understand the problem.

Step 2: Devise a plan.

Step 3: Carry out the plan.

Step 4: Look back.

While there are many problem-solving and decision-making models, this particular four-step problem-solving process by Polya has been widely adapted for use in any problem-solving or decision-making situation (see sidebar, left). Other models may have more steps, but most will contain the four common elements: (1) an information gathering or input stage; (2) a processing, analysis, and/or planning stage; (3) an implementation or output stage; and (4) a review or evaluation stage. In the case of haz mat incidents, it must be understood that problem-solving and decision-making are fluid processes, and a first responder's understanding of a problem (and consequent plans to address it) may change as more information becomes available and/or conditions change.

The basic four-step formula for problem solving is roughly analogous to the division of required first responder competency tasks in NFPA 472, *Standard for Professional Competence of Responders to Hazardous Materials Incidents* (2002), and the *APIE* haz mat incident management model (**Table 4.2, p. 250**). It is also the basis for the National Fire Service IMS hazardous materials incident planning process. For those reasons, when discussing haz mat incident management, this manual references the four-step process rather than *GEDAPER, DECIDE, IFSTA,* or the Eight Step Incident Management Process©.

Analyzing the Incident/ Understanding the Problem

[NFPA 472: 5.2.1, 5.2.1.4, 5.2.1.5, 5.2.3(1), 5.2.4(4), 5.1.2.1(1), 5.1.2.1(1)(a)]

It is impossible to solve a problem without enough information to understand it. For example, first responders cannot fully mitigate a haz mat incident if they don't know what material is involved. For that matter, they can't take appropriate steps to protect themselves or others if they don't know that hazardous materials are involved in the first place.

Within the framework of incident priorities, an incident management system, and predetermined procedures, understanding the problem becomes

the first step in managing (or solving the problem of) any emergency incident. Understanding the problem (including all of its subproblems or multiple elements) enables first responders to form an overall plan of action (see safety alert, p. 251).

In the case of hazardous materials incidents, one of the key pieces of information needed to begin understanding the problem is the identity of the hazardous material. Responders must first survey the scene to detect the presence of hazardous materials, and they must then correctly identify them. This detection/identification process can be done by paying attention to the seven clues to the presence of hazardous materials as discussed in Chapter 3, Hazardous Materials Identification. The information gathered must then be correctly interpreted and verified by emergency response agencies, shippers, and/or other resources that can confirm handling procedures, product identity, and appropriate response information. These resources assist the first responder in estimating the size of the endangered area (by using the *ERG's* recommended isolation distances) and the potential harm posed by the material.

However, the identity of the hazardous material is just one piece of the information needed. Many factors may have an effect on the situation — everything from wind direction, topography, land use, and the presence of victims to concerns such as equipment access and available response personnel. The initial survey should include the answers to the following questions:

- Where is the incident scene in relation to population and environmental and property exposures?
- Is the incident scene inside a building or outside?
- What are the hazardous materials?
- What hazard classes are involved?
- What quantities are involved?
- What concentrations are involved?
- How could the material react?
- Is it a liquid or solid spill or a gas release?
- Is something burning?
- What kind of container holds the material?

Table 4.2
Four-Step Problem Solving Process

Four-Step Problem-Solving Process	APIE Model	NFPA 472 Competencies
Understand the problem. • State the question(s) • Compare to similar problems, past experiences, and training situations • Identify elements and subproblems • Consider known and unknown factors and conditions • Recognize patterns • Utilize drawings and written resources • Conduct size-up and risk/hazard analysis • Identify goal(s)	**A**nalyze	Analyzing the incident
Devise a plan. • Break it into subproblems (by addressing these, it may be possible to solve the entire problem) • Consider methods used during similar problems, past experiences, and training situations • Outline a potential solution (including solutions to subproblems) • Develop strategies to achieve goal(s)/solution(s)	**P**lan	Planning the response
Carry out the plan. • Relate tasks to known and unknown conditions • Check validity of each step/tactic • Define steps in relation to the whole • Use tactics to implement strategies	**I**mplement	Implementing the planned response
Look back. • Evaluate effectiveness of approach • Process and provide feedback • Confirm results • Assess usefulness of solution for solving other problems	**E**valuate	Evaluating progress

- What is the condition of the container?

- How much time has elapsed since the incident began?

- What personnel, equipment, and extinguishing agents are available?

- Is there private fire protection or other help available?

- What effect can the weather have?

- Are there nearby lakes, ponds, streams or other bodies of water?

- Are there overhead wires, underground pipelines, or other utilities?

- Where are the nearest storm and sewer drains?

- What has already been done?

All of these factors and others can affect the problem. The first responder must also be able to make reasonable determinations as to the amount or level of hazard present and the risks associated with dealing with the incident. This information is gathered during the incident scene analysis or *size-up* and then analyzed through a hazard and risk assessment model such as the General Hazardous Materials Behavior Model (a useful tool in hazard and risk assessment). The General Hazardous Materials Behavior Model enables first responders to predict the behavior of hazardous materials.

Understand the Problem!

Understanding what is happening (and what has happened) at an emergency incident is not a linear process. Unfortunately, there is not a checklist of *All the Things You Need to Know Right Now* that you can follow, check off all that apply, and subsequently act upon them. Every incident is going to be different. You may be bombarded with visual, audible, and sometimes conflicting information; yet you must be able to make sense of what you are given in order to understand the situation. Skillful ICs are able to quickly identify relevant information and analyze it in order to form a clear picture of the incident.

The process of gathering information and analyzing it is usually done intuitively and, in emergencies, very quickly. However, there are techniques that can be used to assist in understanding a problem. Some of these (in no particular order) are as follows:

- *State the relevant question(s)* — Questions to ask are *who, what, when, where, why,* and *how*.

- *Identify elements and subproblems* — Most haz mat incidents have multiple elements or subproblems (normally just called *problems;* the *subproblem* distinction is given for this section only). These subproblems can be anything from how to isolate the perimeter with only two people to identifying the hazards presented by the material itself. However, by identifying and addressing the subproblems, you can sometimes piece together a solution to the bigger problem.

- *Consider known and unknown factors and conditions* — What you don't know about an incident can be just as important (and potentially deadly) as what you do know.

- *Use drawings and written resources* — Preplans and written resources providing information about the material involved can greatly assist your understanding of the problem. For example, once a material is identified, the *ERG* can provide you with a wealth of information that you can use, ranging from recommended isolation distances to a list of potential hazards (or subproblems).

- *Recognize patterns* — Terrorists have established a pattern of using secondary explosive devices to wound and kill emergency responders. Pattern recognition clues you to the possible problem of secondary devices at terrorist incidents. Over time, other patterns involving haz mat incidents may become apparent.

- *Compare to similar problems, past experiences, and training situations* — Basically, by cueing in to the similarities between a new situation and past experiences, you can make rapid decisions based on what you know was successful in the past.

- *Identify goal(s)* — Stating what you want to accomplish assists you in understanding the parts of the problem that need to be addressed in order to achieve those goals.

Lt. Adams started analyzing the incident en route to the scene. By checking the pre-incident survey, she gathered much valuable information she needed in order to understand the problem (such as the layout of Ace Trucking and potential access difficulties). Having been given the name of the chemical involved in the incident in advance, she was able to understand the hazards (and many of the potential subproblems) presented by 1,2-butylene oxide (such as its flammability).

Once provided with the information gathered through size-up — actual incident conditions, location of evacuated employees, existence of two missing maintenance workers — Lt. Adams was able to quickly identify the additional subproblems presented by the incident. Her understanding of the overall problem (release of butylene oxide) divided into subproblems (flammable gas hazard, missing workers, and the like) coupled with the initial isolation distances provided in the *ERG* enabled Lt. Adams to quickly devise an effective incident action plan. Implementation of her plan began with task assignments.

Scene Analysis: Size-up/Hazard and Risk Assessment

[NFPA 472: 5.2.1.4]

Size-up is the assessment of incident conditions and recognition of cues indicating problems and potential problems presented by an incident. It is the mental process of considering all available factors that will affect an incident during the course of the operation. The information gained from the size-up is used to determine the strategy and tactics that are applied to the incident during the planning and implementation stages. *Hazard and risk assessment* is part of the size-up process, focusing particularly on the dangers, hazards, and risks presented by the incident. (See the safety alert, p. 254, for the distinction between hazard and risk.)

As with a structure fire, haz mat size-up must consider all six sides of the incident (Alpha, Bravo, Charlie, Delta, and the top and bottom) **(Figure 4.15)**. Haz mat size-up is frequently complicated by limited information. The IC's view of the incident may be limited by the size of the hazard area or location of the release (that is, inside a vehicle or structure). In addition, limited or conflicting

information regarding the product or products involved is possible. Initial assessment is based on anticipated conditions and updated as additional information becomes available.

Risk Assessment Is for Everyone!

[NFPA 472: 5.4.3(3)]

It's important to realize that size-up/hazard and risk assessment isn't something that's done solely by the IC upon arrival at the scene — it's a continuing process, and all first responders need to be aware of the situation around them. Furthermore, they are responsible for reporting this information to the IC through appropriate channels. Conditions can change rapidly and responders must be continually alert **(Figure 4.16, p. 254)**. When a cloud of green gas starts drifting in your direction because the wind direction has changed unexpectedly, you need to notice it, react to it accordingly, and then report it!

Hazard and risk assessment is a continual evaluation. It starts with pre-incident planning, extends through the receipt of an alarm, and continues throughout the course of an incident. The first IC who arrives on the scene conducts an extensive hazard assessment, and repeats this process as the incident continues. Much information needed for hazard and risk assessment can be obtained at the time the incident is reported:

- Number and type of injuries
- Occupancy type
- Type of incident
- Product and container information if available
- Location of the incident
- Equipment and resources responding
- Time of day
- Weather
- Other important information

By taking the following actions, first responders can gather additional information relating to size-up:

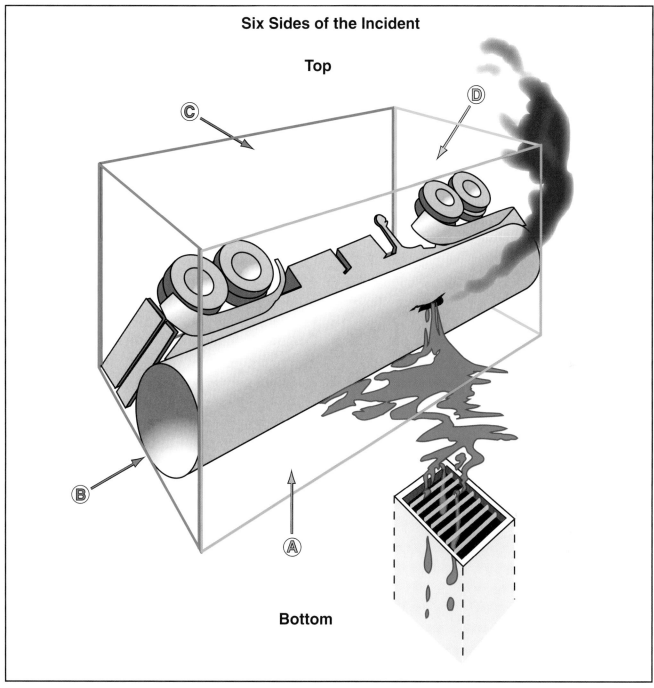

Figure 4.15 Hazardous materials size-up must consider all six sides of an incident (Alpha, Bravo, Charlie, Delta, and the top and bottom). Always remember that hazardous vapors and gases rise or sink depending on their vapor density.

- Review pre-incident surveys and sketches.
- Review topography maps and utility plans (for drains/sewers, rivers, streams, and the like).
- Note arrival time of other responding units.
- Note exposure types and distances.
- Review hydrant and water supply conditions.
- Consider scene access conditions.
- Consider resource staging areas.
- Make preliminary plans for apparatus placement at the scene.
- Secure any additional information from the telecommunicator.
- Decide if and what additional units are needed.

Once on the scene, the final pieces of the hazard and risk assessment are added to the information made available before arrival. In some cases, industrial fire brigades or on-site safety personnel can provide specific, detailed information. With this combined information, a formal plan of action may be decided upon and implemented. Evaluate the following conditions at the incident scene:

- Unusual signs (smoke, fire, explosions, leaking material, vapor clouds, and the like)

- Life hazards

- Product(s) involved

- Container types

- Amount of product involved

- Product travel or path of fire

- Actions already taken by people on the scene

Figure 4.16 First responders must continually monitor their situation. For example, this firefighter needs to be alert to any change in wind direction. *Courtesy of Chad Love.*

What Is the Difference Between Hazard and Risk?

The *physical and health hazards* associated with hazardous materials were discussed in the TRACEMP (thermal, radiological, asphyxiation, chemical, etiological, mechanical, and psychological) sections of Chapter 2, Hazardous Materials Properties and Hazards. An important part of the hazard assessment, then, is determining which of these hazards are present at the haz mat scene. Also discussed were the numerous resources available for identifying materials and their associated hazards in Chapter 3, Hazardous Materials Identification. Of course, there may be other hazards present at a scene that have nothing to do with the hazardous material itself. Traffic hazards or electrical hazards are examples of dangers that need to be considered during the hazard assessment as well.

Risk, on the other hand, deals more with probabilities — the probability of getting hurt or injured or suffering damage, harm, or loss because of the hazards present. Assessing the risk at a haz mat incident is a matter of determining the *ifs* of a situation: *If I do this, then this might happen. If this happens, then this will follow. If I don't do this, then this could occur.* Once you know the hazards (or potential hazards), it is a matter of estimating how likely it is that harm or loss will actually occur. Needless to say,

assessing risk is often more difficult than assessing the hazards themselves. Experience and knowledge are valuable assets in the ability to quickly predict future events. ICs who are skillful at estimating the course of an incident (and its potential harm) are better able to conduct a risk-benefit analysis and choose a wise plan of action in which the benefits outweigh the potential risks.

IFSTA Principles of Risk Management

1. Activities that present a significant risk to the safety of members shall be limited to situations where there is a potential to save endangered lives.

2. Activities that are routinely employed to protect property shall be recognized as inherent risks to the safety of members, and actions shall be taken to reduce or avoid these risks.

3. No risk to the safety of members shall be acceptable when there is no possibility to save lives or property.

Key Points

- Team integrity is vital to safety and must always be emphasized.

- No property is worth the life of a member.

- Members should not be committed to interior offensive fire-fighting operations in abandoned or derelict structures that are known or reasonably believed to be unoccupied.

General Hazardous Materials Behavior Model

[NFPA 472 5.2.3, 5.1.2.1(c), 5.1.2.1(d)]

An important element of hazard and risk assessment is predicting how a hazardous material is likely to behave in any given situation. Ludwig Benner developed an excellent working definition of hazardous materials: *Hazardous materials are things that can escape from their containers and hurt or harm the things that they touch.* The general premise of the General Hazardous Materials Behavior Model (sometimes referred to as the *General Emergency Behavior Model* or *GEBMO*) is based on this definition. Hazardous materials incidents have the following common elements:

- Material or materials presenting hazards to people, the environment, or property

- Container or containers that have failed or have the potential to fail

- Exposure or potential exposure to people, the environment, and/or property

GEBMO helps first responders predict the course of an incident, thereby enabling them to limit the effects of a hazardous material. *GEBMO* is basically a defensive-mode action that is concerned with potential haz mat emergencies involving containers. First responders must calmly assess the situation at hand and then identify the appropriate response depending on answers to the following questions:

- How long will the harmful exposure exist?

- What has stressed or is stressing the container?

- How will the stressed container and its material behave?

- What are the harmful effects of the container materials?

The application of information gained through answering these questions helps responders develop a strategy for mitigating the incident. If it is not possible to make all predictions required to analyze the incident, then further assistance is needed. This assistance may be sought from the manufacturer, shipper and consignee, carrier, or other agencies involved with hazardous materials.

The events in a hazardous materials incident follow a general pattern or model. As with many other types of events, prediction may be based on past experience. In hazardous materials incidents the sequence shown in the chart generally occurs. This sequence is elaborated in the paragraphs that follow.

General Hazardous Materials Behavior Model

- ***Stress*** — If a container is stressed beyond its design strength, it fails or breaches.

- ***Breach*** — The way in which a container breaches is based on the material of which it is constructed, type of stress that it is exposed to, and pressure inside the container at the time that it fails. A breach or failure of the container may be partial (as in a puncture) or total (as in disintegration). A breached container releases its contents.

- ***Release*** — When a container is breached or fails, its contents, stored energy, and pieces of the container may release. A release always involves the product and may (depending on the product, container, and incident conditions) involve the release of energy and container parts. The released product disperses.

- ***Dispersion/Engulfment*** — When released, the product inside the container, any stored energy, and the container disperse. The patterns of dispersion are based on the laws of chemistry, physics, and the characteristics of the product.

- ***Exposure/Contact*** — Anything (such as persons, the environment, or property) that is in the area of the release is exposed.

- ***Harm*** — Depending on the container, product, and energy involved, exposures may be harmed.

Stress. *[NFPA 472: 5.2.3(2)]* Container stress is stimulus causing *strain* (excessive tension or compression), *pressure* (force applied at right angles to a surface), or *deformity* (distortion by torque or twisting). According to U.S. Department of Transportation (DOT) records, almost one-fourth of all reported haz mat incidents are caused by container failure. One or all three of the stressors listed may come into play at each haz mat incident. For instance, heat (thermal stress) can initiate or speed a chemical reaction while weakening a container and increasing internal pressure. Similarly, a mechanical blow can initiate a violent chemical reaction in an unstable chemical while simultaneously damaging the container.

When evaluating container stress, consider the type of container, the type and amount of stress, and its potential duration. Container stress may involve a single factor or several stressors acting on the container simultaneously. The factors placing stress on a container may be readily visible such as a collision or a fire impinging on a container surface. In other cases, container stress cannot be directly observed and must be predicted based on conditions or other indirect indicators. If the container has already failed, think about other containers that may be exposed, and evaluate the affect of product contact. Preventing container failure may require reducing or eliminating the stress. Common stressors are as follows:

- ***Thermal*** — Excessive heat or cold causing intolerable expansion, contraction, weakening (loss of temper), or consumption of the container and its parts; thermal stress may also simultaneously increase internal pressure and reduce container shell integrity, resulting in sudden failure. Thermal stress may result from the heating or cooling of the container. Clues may include observation of flame impingement on the container, operation of a relief device, or changing environmental conditions (increased temperature) **(Figure 4.17)**.

- ***Chemical*** — Uncontrolled reactions/interactions of contents in the container and the container itself, resulting in a sudden or long-term deterioration of the container. Reactions involving two chemicals placed into the same container can cause excessive heat

Figure 4.17 Thermal stress may cause container failure. *Courtesy of Chad Love.*

and/or pressure, also resulting in container failure. Chemical stress may be the result of corrosive action or other chemical attack on an incompatible container material. Clues may include visible corrosion or other degradation of container surfaces. However, the interior of a container may experience chemical stress with no visible indication from the exterior.

- ***Mechanical*** — Physical application of energy resulting in container/attachment damage; mechanical application may change the shape of the container (crushing), reduce the thickness of the container surface (abrading or scoring), crack or produce gouges, unfasten or disengage valves and piping, or penetrate the container wall. Common causes may include collision, impact, or internal overpressure. Clues may include physical damage, the mechanism of injury (forces placed on the container), or operation of relief devices.

Breach. *[NFPA 472: 5.2.3(3)]* When a container is stressed beyond its limits of recovery (its design strength or ability to hold contents), it opens or breaches and releases its contents. Different container types breach in different ways. Containers can be pressurized as well as nonpressurized. A breach is dependent upon the type of container and the stress applied. The extent of a breach or failure varies with container construction and the type of stress to which it is subjected. First responders should try to visualize how the container would be damaged by the stress that is being (or has been) applied. The nature of a breach is a major factor in planning offensive product control operations. Several types of breaches are as follows:

- *Disintegration* — Container suffers a general loss of integrity such as a glass bottle shattering or a grenade exploding. This type of breach occurs in containers that are made of a brittle material (or that have been made more brittle by some form of stress).

- *Runaway cracking* — Crack develops in a container as a result of some type of damage, which continues to grow rapidly, breaking the container into two or more relatively large pieces. This type of breach is associated with closed containers such as drums, tank cars, or cylinders. Runaway linear cracking is commonly associated with BLEVEs.

Figure 4.18 Given enough force at a point of impact, containers such as this barrel can be punctured.

- *Attachments (closures) open or break* — Attachments (such as pressure-relief devices, discharge valves, or other related equipment) fail, open, or break off when subjected to stress, leading to a total failure of a container. When evaluating an attachment failure, first responders should consider the entire system and the effect of failure at a given point.

- *Puncture* — Mechanical stress coming into contact with a container causes a puncture **(Figure 4.18)**. Examples: forklifts puncturing drums and couplers puncturing a rail tank car.

- *Split or tear* — Welded seam on a tank or drum fails or a seam on a bag of fertilizer rips. Mechanical or thermal stressors may cause splits or tears **(Figure 4.19)**.

- *Metal reduction* — Corrosive action of an acid on steel causes metal reduction on a container.

Release. [NFPA 472: 5.2.3(4)] When a container fails, three things may release: the product, energy, and the container (whole or in pieces). Consider a compressed-gas cylinder containing chlorine. If the cylinder suffers an attachment failure at the valve due to mechanical stress, the product (a toxic, corrosive oxidizer) is released along with a substantial amount of energy (because of stored pressure) and rapid acceleration of the valve and/or cylinder in the opposite direction from the release. Depending on the situation, this release can occur quickly or over an extended time period. Generally, when a great amount of

Figure 4.19 This cargo tank has been torn open.

chemical/mechanical energy is stored, a more rapid release of the material (causing a greater risk to first responders) is possible. Releases are classified based on how fast they occur as follows:

- *Detonation* — Instantaneous and explosive release of stored chemical energy of a hazardous material. The results of this release include fragmentation, disintegration, or shattering of the container; extreme overpressure; and considerable heat release. The duration of a detonation can be measured in hundredths or thousandths of a second. An example would be detonation of a high explosive.

- *Violent rupture* — Immediate release of chemical or mechanical energy caused by runaway cracks. The results are ballistic behavior of the container and its contents and/or localized projection of container pieces/parts and hazardous material such as with a BLEVE. Violent ruptures occur within a timeframe of 1 second or less.

- *Rapid relief* — Fast release of a pressurized hazardous material through properly operating safety devices caused by damaged valves, piping, or attachments or holes in the container **(Figure 4.20)**. This action may occur in a period of several seconds to several minutes.

- *Spill/leak* — Slow release of a hazardous material under atmospheric or head pressure through holes, rips, tears, or usual openings/attachments can occur in a period of several minutes to several days.

When evaluating release potential, remember the total amount of product in the container. A valve blowout causes a rapid release. If this size breach occurs in a 150-pound (68 kg) cylinder, the product remaining quickly releases. If this same type of release occurs in a ton container, cargo tank, or railcar, the release occurs over a longer period of time and may have a substantially greater effect.

Dispersion/engulfment. *[NFPA 472: 5.2.3(5), 5.2.4(1)]* In the *GEBMO*, the *dispersion* of material is sometimes referred to as *engulfment*. Dispersion of the product, energy, and container components depends on the type of release as well as physical and chemical laws. The product may release in the form of a solid, liquid,

Figure 4.20 The venting of this liquefied petroleum gas (LPG) tank is an example of *rapid relief*.

or gas/vapor. Mechanical, thermal, or chemical energy and ionizing radiation may also be released. The path of product, energy, and container travel depends on its form and physical characteristics. Based on product characteristics and environmental conditions (such as weather and terrain), the pattern of dispersion may be predicted. Once a container has been compromised, the hazardous material will be distributed over the surrounding area according to five factors:

- Physical/chemical properties
- Prevailing weather conditions
- Local topography
- Duration of the release
- Control efforts of responders

The shape and size of the pattern also depends on how the material emerges from its container — whether the release is an instantaneous *puff,* a continuous plume, or a sporadic fluctuation. The outline of the dispersing hazardous material, sometimes called its *footprint,* can be described in a number of ways. Dispersion patterns are as follows:

- *Hemispheric* — Semicircular or dome-shaped pattern of airborne hazardous material that is still partially in contact with the ground or water **(Figure 4.21)**. Hemispherical dispersion generally results from a rapid release of energy (detonation, deflagration, violent rupture, etc.). *Other dispersion elements:*

  — Energy generally travels outward in all directions from the point of release.

  — Dispersion of energy is affected by terrain and cloud cover. Solid cloud cover can reflect the detonation shock wave, increasing the explosion impact.

  — Energy release may propel the hazardous material and container parts; however, this dispersion may not be hemispherical. Large container parts generally (but not always) travel in line with the long axis of the container.

- *Cloud* — Ball-shaped pattern of the airborne hazardous material where the material has collectively risen above the ground or water **(Figure 4.22, p. 260)**. Gases, vapors, and finely divided solids that are released quickly (puff release) can disperse in cloud form when wind conditions are minimal. Terrain and/or wind effects can transform a cloud into a plume.

- *Plume* — Irregularly shaped pattern of an airborne hazardous material where wind and/ or topography influence the downrange course from the point of release **(Figure 4.23, p. 260)**. Dispersion of a plume (generally composed of gases and vapors) is affected by vapor density and terrain (particularly if vapor density is greater than 1) as well as wind speed and direction. **Figure 4.24, p. 261,** provides several general *rules of thumb* regarding plume modeling behavior in urban environments as described in the U.S. Department of Energy/Los Alamos National Laboratory publication, *Emergency Responders' "Rules of Thumb" for Air Toxics Releases in Urban Environments,* by Michael J. Brown and Gerald E. Streit. Other dispersion elements include the following:

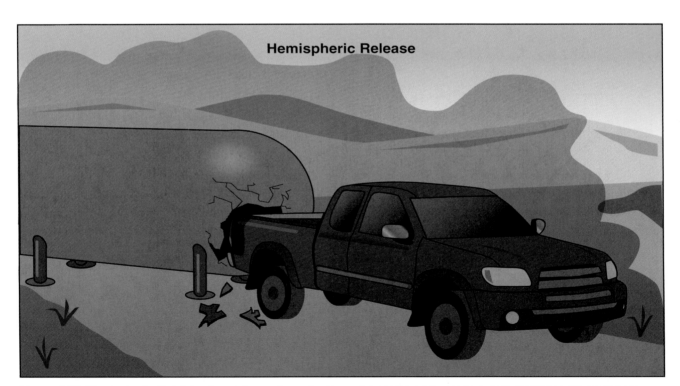

Figure 4.21 *Hemispheric*: Semicircular or dome-shaped pattern of an airborne hazardous material that is still partially in contact with the ground or water.

Figure 4.22 *Cloud:* Ball-shaped pattern of an airborne hazardous material where the material has collectively risen above the ground or water.

Figure 4.23 *Plume*: Irregularly shaped pattern of an airborne hazardous material where wind and/or topography influence the downrange course from the point of release.

"Rules of Thumb" For Air Toxics Releases in Urban Environments

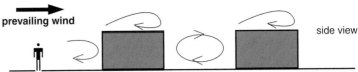

APPARENT WIND ANOMALIES
The locally-measured wind may not match the large-scale wind due to building-induced circulations.

"my judgement of wind direction may be opposite to the prevailing wind direction"

Lesson: because of the complicated flows that develop around buildings, a measurement of wind made at ground-level may not be indicative of the upper-level prevailing wind. Evacuation zones far downwind must be determined by the larger-scale plume transport which follows the prevailing wind, not the local wind.

AGENT TRAPPING IN VORTICES
For winds nearly face-on to the building wall, concentrations of hazardous material can build-up in between buildings and take a relatively long time to flush out.

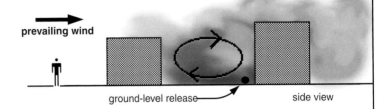

ground-level release   side view

Lesson: air contaminants can become trapped between buildings in slow moving vortices, thus taking longer to flush out with clean air. In most cases, wider buildings and narrower streets will trap the pollutant longer.

AGENT ENTRAPMENT
Recessed entryways or architectural alcoves may trap and hold air contaminants for some time after the plume has passed by.

ground-level release

Lesson: even after clearly determining that the main portion of the plume has disappeared, be aware that some of the air contaminant may have collected in alcoves and other zones of stagnation.

ON-AXIS CHANNELING EFFECTS
For winds parallel to the street, the plume can become contained within the street canyon; however, the plume can travel up side streets.

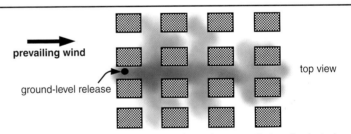

ground-level release

Lesson: after determining that the prevailing wind direction is parallel to the street containing the release, be aware that contaminated air is likely to travel several blocks in each direction along side streets.

OFF-AXIS CHANNELING EFFECTS
The plume can get channeled by streets near the source and end-up traveling off the prevailing wind direction axis.

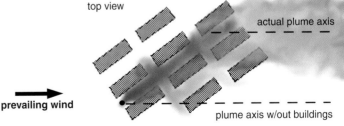

top view

actual plume axis

prevailing wind

plume axis w/out buildings

Lesson: for determining larger-scale evacuation zones, be aware that the plume initially may be transported in a direction off-angle from the prevailing wind. Once the plume gets dispersed above the buildings, it will then travel with the prevailing wind, but the plume's center axis will be offset from the release point.

Figure 4.24 Responders should be aware of these *rules of thumb* regarding plume modeling behavior in urban environments. *Courtesy of Los Alamos National Laboratory. (continued)*

"Rules of Thumb" For Air Toxics
Releases in Urban Environments

EDDY TRANSPORT OF AGENT

The air contaminant can move short distances against the prevailing wind direction in recirculation zones along the sides and top of the building.

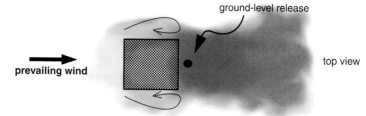

Lesson: even if the source is determined to be downwind of you, be careful at locations near the building upstream of the source, as the plume can travel short distances in the opposite direction to the prevailing wind.

LARGE-SCALE WIND VARIABILITY

The prevailing wind switches direction occasionally, so that the upwind safe zone may now be downwind.

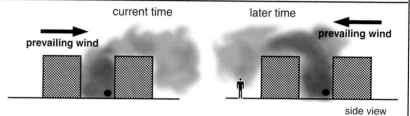

Lesson: the prevailing wind is not fixed and under some circumstances can change direction quickly; thus, monitor the prevailing wind direction so that safe zones can be maintained.

SMALL-SCALE WIND VARIABILITY

The local wind can switch direction very rapidly, so that the plume may switch from one side of the building to the other in a matter of seconds.

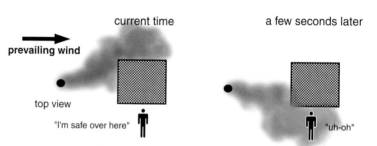

Lesson: due to the turbulent nature of the wind, it is very common for a plume to bounce from one side of the building to the other; hence, don't assume that you are safe on one side of the building just because the plume is currently on the other side.

AGENT DEPOSITION

After the plume has left the area of release, the ground and building surfaces may still be contaminated due to deposition of the toxic agent.

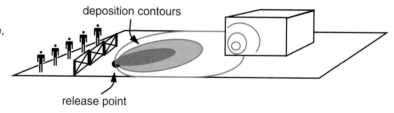

Lesson: because the contaminant may stick to surfaces, touching surfaces in the vicinity of the release point is not recommended until decontamination is complete.

INDOOR EFFECTS

When the plume is passing over, it is probably safer to remain indoors. After the plume has passed by, it may be safer to move outdoors.

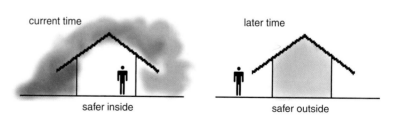

Lesson: for an outdoor release, modeling studies show that concentrations can initially be lower indoors, but then later the concentrations become lower outside. These relationships, however, depend upon the details of the building ventilation.

Figure 4.24 (Continued)

— When all of the material is released at one time (puff release), the concentration of gas or vapor in the cloud or plume decreases over time.

— In an ongoing release, concentration increases over time until the leak is stopped or all of the product has been exhausted; then it decreases.

• *Cone* — Triangular-shaped pattern of a hazardous material with a point source at the breach and a wide base downrange (**Figure 4.25**). An energy release may be directed (based on the nature of the breach) and may project solid, liquid, or gaseous material in a three-dimensional cone-shaped dispersion. Examples: Container failures in a BLEVE or a pressurized liquid or gas release.

• *Stream* — Surface-following pattern of liquid hazardous material that is affected by gravity and topographical contours (**Figure 4.26, p. 264**). Liquid releases flow downslope whenever there is a gradient away from the point of release.

• *Pool* — Three-dimensional (including depth), slow-flowing liquid dispersion. Liquids assume the shape of their container and pool in low areas (**Figure 4.27, p. 264**). As the liquid level rises above the confinement provided by the terrain, the substance flows outward from the point of release. If there is a significant gradient or confinement due to terrain, this flow forms a stream.

• *Irregular* — Irregular or indiscriminate deposit of a hazardous material (such as that carried by contaminated responders) (**Figure 4.28, p. 265**).

Some facilities' pre-incident surveys may contain plume dispersion models that can be used to estimate the size of an endangered area in the event of a release. Computer software such as *CAMEO* (Computer-Aided Management of Emergency Operations), *ALOHA* (Area Locations of Hazardous Atmospheres), and *HPAC* (Hazard Prediction and Assessment Capability) can also assist in the prediction of plume dispersion patterns. Of course, first responders should always consult the *ERG* for isolation and evacuation distances.

Figure 4.25 *Cone*: Triangular-shaped pattern of a hazardous material with a point source at the breach and a wide base downrange.

Figure 4.26 *Stream*: Surface-following pattern of a liquid hazardous material affected by gravity and topographical contours.

Figure 4.27 *Pool*: Liquids assume the shape of their container and accumulate in low areas.

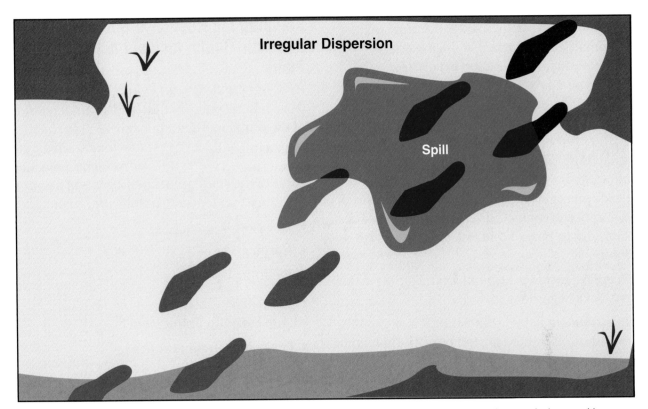

Irregular Dispersion

Spill

Figure 4.28 *Irregular*: Irregular or indiscriminate deposit of a hazardous material (such as that carried around by contaminated responders).

Dispersion of Solids

Solids in the form of dusts, powders, or small particles may also have dispersion patterns. In many cases, the simplest dispersion pattern of a released solid could best be described as a *pile* **(Figure 4.29)**. When the material is spilled or released from its container, it forms a pile. This pile can then be dispersed by wind, a moving liquid, or contact with a moving object (such as a forklift driving through the spill).

For example, a release of a pesticide powder could be picked up by the wind and dispersed in the form of a plume. Depending on the properties (such as solubility) of the solid, if it spills into a stream or sewer system (or is washed away by a hose stream), it could be carried along and dispersed by the movement of the liquid in the *stream* dispersion pattern. Some dusts, powders, and particles can remain suspended in the air for hours or days such as in a *cloud.* An example of the latter would be microscopic asbestos fibers that can remain airborne for very long periods of time.

While *pile* is not normally included in the *GEBMO*, it is important for first responders to remember that hazardous materials also come in solid form, and that potential dispersion of the solid(s) is an important consideration in planning an appropriate response.

Release of Solids: Pile

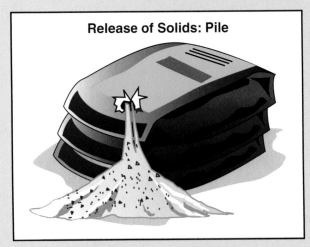

Figure 4.29 Dispersion of a released solid can sometimes be described as a *pile.*

Exposure/contact. *[NFPA 472: 5.2.3(6)]* As a container is breached, it releases its materials and impinges upon exposures: people, the environment, and property. Some hazardous materials may present a threat to one specific exposure type (such as marine pollutants that threaten fish and other marine plants and animals) and others present a threat to all types. In evaluating the severity of exposures, consider the hazards presented, concentration of the material, and duration of contact. Several types of exposures to consider in hazard and risk assessment are as follows:

- ***People*** — Includes responders and others in the path of a hazardous material.

- ***Environment*** — Includes the air, water, ground, and life forms other than humans. The potential effect on the environment varies with the location in which the product is released as well as its characteristics.

- ***Property*** — Things threatened directly by the product or the energy liberated at the time of release (as with exposure to the heat from a burning product).

Contacts (impingements) are associated with the following general timeframes:

- ***Immediate*** — Milliseconds, seconds; examples: deflagration, explosion, or detonation

- ***Short-term*** — Minutes, hours; example: gas or vapor cloud

- ***Medium-term*** — Days, weeks, months; example: lingering pesticide

- ***Long-term*** — Years, generations; example: permanent radioactive source

Harm. *[NFPA 472 5.2.3 (7)]* Injury or damage caused by exposure to a hazardous material. According to NFPA, the health and physical hazards that could cause harm in a hazardous materials incident are thermal, mechanical, poisonous, corrosive, asphyxiation, radiation, and etiologic (see Chapter 2, Hazardous Materials Properties and Hazards).

Planning the Response/Setting Strategic Goals: Incident Action Plans

[NFPA 472: 5.3.1(2), 5.1.2.1 (2)(a), 5.1.2.1(2)]

Once first responders have a basic understanding of the problem, they can begin to plan their solution to the problem by establishing strategic goals (sometimes referred to as *response objectives*). Some of the standard strategic goals of hazardous materials incidents are as follows:

- Isolation

- Notification

- Identification

- Protection

- Spill control/confinement

- Leak control/containment

- Fire control

- Recovery/termination

While those listed are some of the common strategic goals of haz mat incidents, ICs can set whatever goals they deem appropriate, using whatever terms they prefer **(Figure 4.30)**. For example, *rescue* might be considered an important strategic goal at one incident but not at another. If conditions at an incident change suddenly, *getting the heck out of Dodge* might become a strategic goal that springs to the top of the priority list.

Figure 4.30 Incident Commanders set whatever goals they deem appropriate.

Strategic goals are prioritized depending on available resources and the particulars of the incident. Some of these goals may not be needed if the hazard is not present at the incident. For example, if the material involved is nonflammable, fire control may not be an issue. Some goals may require the use of specialized resources (such as chemical protective clothing or specific absorbent materials) that are not yet available and therefore must be postponed. Others may require the use of so many of the available resources that the ability to complete other goals in an expedient timeframe might be compromised. Strategic goals must be selected based on the following criteria:

- Their ability to be achieved
- Their ability to prevent further injuries and/or deaths
- Their ability to minimize environmental and property damage within the constraints of safety, time, equipment, and personnel

Strategies are divided into three options that relate to modes of operation: defensive, offensive, and nonintervention. A *defensive strategy* provides confinement of the hazard to a given area by performing diking, damming, or diverting actions. An *offensive strategy* includes actions to control the incident such as plugging a leak (**Figure 4.31**). A *nonintervention strategy* allows the incident to run its course on its own. Modes of operation are covered in more detail in the next section.

Regardless of the strategy, the IC must maintain contact with the officers and crew implementing this decision and constantly reevaluate the situation. If crews cannot achieve the objective, the IC must reassess the situation and prepare an alternate plan.

Strategy cannot evolve properly unless first responders have done their planning before arriving on the scene. The process depends on information first responders receive from the pre-incident survey and other sources on the way to the incident. This information must be correct and current to produce accurate decisions. Strategy also involves a number of the following activities that cannot be performed until first responders arrive at the incident and assess the situation:

- Setting and achieving immediate goals and objectives
- Knowing or estimating the resources required for the situation
- Managing personnel, equipment, and resources to solve the problem

Making the right strategic decision at a haz mat incident is critical because of the variety of things that can occur. Poorly developed decision-making processes can lead to greater problems (**Figure 4.32**). The elements of setting strategic goals include determining modes of operation, developing IAPs, and considering

Figure 4.32 Little margin may exist for error at hazardous materials incidents. Poor decisions often lead to greater problems.

Figure 4.31 Plugging a leak is an offensive strategy.

safety procedures. Specific strategies and tactics are discussed in more detail in Chapter 5, Strategic Goals and Tactical Objectives.

Determining Modes of Operation

When considering strategies, the IC determines the mode of operation (nonintervention, defensive, or offensive). The safety of first responders is the uppermost consideration in selecting a mode of operation. The mode of operation may change during the course of an incident. For example, first-arriving responders may be restricted to a nonintervention or defensive mode. After the arrival of the haz mat team, the IC may switch to offensive mode and initiate offensive tactics. Selection of the strategic mode is based on the risk to responders, their level of training, and the balance between the resources required and those that are available. The following three incident- based elements affect the selection of strategic mode, and the IC must always have a clear picture of them as the IAP is developed:

- *Value* — Related directly to the incident priorities of life safety, incident stabilization, and property conservation. Value is stated in terms of *yes* or *no* — either there is value (*yes*) or there is no value (*no*). Once value has been determined with a *yes,* the degree of value can be assessed. If a civilian life hazard (savable victim or victims) exists, the value is high. If no civilian life hazard exists but environmental harm may be prevented or property may be saved, the value is somewhat less. If no civilian life hazard exists and responder actions will have little affect on environmental or property protection, there is no value. In the absence of value, a nonintervention or defensive strategy is indicated.

- *Time* — Possible limited window of opportunity exists to intervene before an incident escalates dramatically (such as cooling of a liquefied gas container exposed to direct flame impingement on its vapor space); estimated time during which offensive operations may be initiated. In other cases, the reaction and response times of Technician-Level responders may be the driving factor in selecting the strategic mode for incident operations.

- *Size* — Most frequently driven by the need to conduct protective action (evacuation or protec-

tion in place) concurrently with incident control operations. Resource requirements are driven by tactical requirements. In most cases (with the exception of fires involving hazardous materials), fire flow is not the descriptor of *size.*

Nonintervention operations. *[NFPA 472: 5.5.1.2]* Operations in which the responders take no direct actions on the actual problem **(Figure 4.33)**. Not taking any action is the only safe strategy in many types of incidents and the best strategy in certain types of incidents when mitigation is failing or otherwise impossible. An example of a situation for nonintervention is a pressure vessel that cannot be adequately cooled because it is exposed to fire. In such incidents, responders should evacuate personnel in the area and withdraw to a safe distance. The nonintervention mode is selected when one or more of the following circumstances exist:

- The facility or LERP calls for it based on a pre-incident evaluation of the hazards present at the site.

- The situation is clearly beyond the capabilities of responders.

- Explosions are imminent.

- Serious container damage threatens a massive release.

In such nonintervention situations, first responders should take the following actions:

- Withdraw to a safe distance.

- Report scene conditions to telecommunications center.

Figure 4.33 Nonintervention operations are used when attacking the incident poses more risk than benefit.

- Initiate an incident management system.
- Call for additional resources as needed.
- Isolate the hazard area and deny entry.
- Commence evacuation where needed.

Defensive operations. *[NFPA 472: 5.1.2.1(2)(b)]* Operations in which responders seek to confine the emergency to a given area without directly contacting the hazardous materials involved **(Figure 4.34)**. See Chapter 5, Strategic Goals and Tactical Objectives, for more information on defensive options. The defensive mode is selected when one of the following circumstances exists:

- The facility or LERP calls for it based on a pre-incident evaluation of the hazards present at the site.
- Responders have the training and equipment necessary to confine the incident to the area of origin.

In defensive operations, Awareness-Level first responders should take the following nonintervention actions:

- Report scene conditions to telecommunications center.
- Initiate an incident management system.
- Call for additional resources as needed.
- Isolate the hazard area and deny entry.
- Establish and indicate zone boundaries (see Chapter 5, Strategic Goals and Tactical Objectives).
- Commence evacuation where needed.
- Control ignition sources.

In defensive operations, the Operational-Level first responder may take the following additional actions:

- Use appropriate defensive control tactics.
- Protect exposures.
- Perform rescues when safe and appropriate.
- Evaluate and report incident progress.
- Perform emergency decontamination procedures.

Figure 4.34 First responders should avoid direct contact with hazardous materials during defensive operations. *Courtesy of Chad Love.*

Offensive operations. Operations where responders take aggressive, direct action on the material, container, or process equipment involved in the incident. These operations may result in contact with the material and therefore require responders to wear appropriate chemical-protective clothing and respiratory protection. Offensive operations are beyond the scope of responsibilities for first responders and are conducted by more highly trained hazardous materials personnel (with the exception of those responders trained to deal with gasoline, diesel fuel, natural gas, and liquefied petroleum gas incidents).

What Does This Mean to You?

As an Awareness-Level responder, you are limited to *Nonintervention Operations.*

As an Operational-Level responder, you are limited to *Defensive Operations* with the exceptions (operations involving gasoline, diesel fuel, natural gas, and liquefied petroleum gas) detailed in Chapter 1, Hazardous Materials Regulations, Definitions, and Statistics.

Technician-Level responders handle *Offensive Operations* at haz mat incidents that involve products other than gasoline, diesel fuel, natural gas, and liquefied petroleum gas.

Developing Incident Action Plans
[ODP Operations II.i.]

IAPs are critical to the rapid, effective control of emergency operations. An IAP is a well-thought-out, organized course of events developed to address all phases of incident control within a specified time. The timeframe specified is one that allows the least negative action to continue. Written IAPs may not be necessary for short-term, routine operations; however, large-scale or complex incidents require the creation and maintenance of a written plan for each operational period.

Action planning starts with identifying the strategy to achieve a solution to the confronted problems. Strategy is broad in nature and defines *what* has to be done. Once the strategy has been defined, the Command Staff needs to select the tactics (the *how, where,* and *when*) to achieve the strategy. Tactics are measurable in both time and performance. An IAP also provides for necessary support resources such as water supply, utility control, SCBA cylinder filling, and the like.

The IAP essentially ties the entire problem-solving process together by stating what the analysis has found, what the plan is, and how it shall be implemented. Once the plan is established and resources are committed, it is necessary to assess its effectiveness. Information must be gathered and analyzed so that necessary modifications may be made to improve the plan if necessary. This step is part of a continuous size-up process. Elements of an IAP include the following:

- Strategies/incident objectives
- Current situation summary
- Resource assignment and needs
- Accomplishments
- Hazard statement
- Risk assessment
- Safety plan and message
- Protective measures
- Current and projected weather conditions
- Status of injuries
- Communications plan
- Medical plan

All incident personnel must function according to the IAP. Company officers or sector officers should follow predetermined procedures, and every action should be directed toward achieving the goals and objectives specified in the plan.

For practical purposes, all first responders should be familiar with the concept of IAPs and site safety plans because they have a direct effect on actions taken at the emergency incident scene. A first responder assuming the role of IC or incident safety officer needs to be familiar with emergency response plans and the many different types of pre-incident plans for the area.

How Many Plans Do I Need?

At various times throughout this manual, we refer to different types of plans: *pre-incident survey* (sometimes called *pre-incident plan* or *preplan*), *emergency action plan*, *site safety and health plan*, *emergency response plan*, *site safety and control plan*, *integrated contingency plan*, *incident action plan (IAP)*, *local emergency response plan (LERP)*, and others. Numerous U.S. state and federal laws require the development of both facility response plans and community emergency plans, and the different names for these plans can be confusing. **Table 4.3** summarizes many of these plans.

Plan/Predetermined Procedures or Guidelines*	Developed	Authority	Who Needs to Know?
Table 4.3			
How Many Plans Do I Need?			
SOPs/SOGs/OIs	By the agency or department before an incident	Agency or Department	First Responders at Awareness and Operational Levels
Pre-Incident Survey/Plan	By the surveying/planning agency or department before an incident	None	First Responders at Awareness and Operational Levels
Local Emergency Response Plan	By the Local Emergency Planning Committee (LEPC) before an incident	U.S. Environmental Protection Agency (EPA)	First Responders at Awareness and Operational Levels
Incident Action Plan	By the Incident Commander (IC) at the scene of an incident	Incident Management System (IMS)	First Responders at Awareness and Operational Levels
Site Safety and Health Plan	Usually by the Site Safety and Health Supervisor at the scene of hazardous waste sites	Title 29 *CFR* 1910.120, *Hazardous Waste Operations and Emergency Response (HAZWOPER)*	Everyone working at the hazardous waste site
Emergency Response Plan	Part of the Site Safety and Health Plan at the scene of hazardous waste sites	Title 29 *CFR* 1910.120, *Hazardous Waste Operations and Emergency Response (HAZWOPER)*	Everyone working at the hazardous waste site
Site Safety and Control Plan	Part of the Emergency Response Plan (which is part of the Site Safety and Health Plan) at the scene of hazardous waste sites	Title 29 *CFR* 1910.120, *Hazardous Waste Operations and Emergency Response (HAZWOPER)*	Everyone working at the hazardous waste site
Emergency Response Plan	By employers whose employees are engaged in emergency response no matter where it occurs	Title 29 *CFR* 1910.120, *Hazardous Waste Operations and Emergency Response (HAZWOPER)*	First Responders at Awareness and Operational Levels
Emergency Action Plan	By the facility employer before an emergency	U.S. Occupational Safety and Health Administration (OSHA)	All employees at the facility
Integrated Contingency Plan	By the facility employer before an emergency	Designed to meet the requirements of the required plans of EPA, Department of Transportation (DOT), and OSHA	All employees at the facility

* This table is just a sample of plans that first responders may encounter. There may be other plans on a national, state, or local level with which first responders may need to be familiar.

Lt. Adams assigned Firefighter Miller to be the Incident Safety Officer. In that capacity, Firefighter Miller began to prepare the site safety and control plan for the incident.

Considering Safety Procedures

[NFPA 472: 5.4.3.3]

Figure 4.35 Emergency responders should always work as part of a team.

A number of safety-related concerns exist involving personnel, procedures, and precautions that an IC should consider before committing to action at hazardous material incidents. Consider the answers to the following questions:

- Are all emergency responders (law enforcement, fire, EMS, public works, and the like) working as members of a team **(Figure 4.35)**? See buddy systems and backup personnel paragraphs under Safety Procedures section for more information.

- Have all emergency responders been adequately briefed on the IAP and the hazards of the situation? Each responder needs to be aware of the following aspects of the response:
  - Immediate goal
  - Who performs which task
  - Operation completion time
  - How to call for help
  - Escape route
  - Material's effects
  - Signs/symptoms of exposure
  - PPE appropriate to the assignment, including capability and permeation rates

- Can reconnaissance be made visually?

- Can approach be made from upwind/uphill/upstream?

- Can contact with the material be avoided?

- Can the vapor cloud, mist, dust, or smoke spread?

- Is the risk worth the benefit?

In addition to the safety responsibilities of the IC and/or the safety officer, responders must be able to recognize a number of threats to their own safety. To accomplish this task, first responders must respect the material, note the surroundings, observe the container, and eliminate ignition sources if the material is flammable. The brief site safety and control plan needs to cover all pertinent safety considerations.

Implementing the Plan: Tactics and Tasks

[NFPA 472: 5.1.2.1(3)]

After strategic goals have been selected and the IAP formulated, the IC can begin to implement the plan. Strategic goals are achieved through tactics (or tactical objectives). Strategies and tactics are accomplished or conducted by performing specific tasks. **Figure 4.36** illustrates the relationship between priorities, strategic goals, tactics, tasks, and the incident management system level normally associated with each.

Tactics follow their respective strategies in that they can be nonintervening, offensive, or defensive in nature. Tactics related to controlling chemical releases basically fall into two categories: confinement (spill control) and containment (leak control), with the majority of defensive control options being related to confinement. The tactics related to confinement and containment are discussed in Chapter 5, Strategic Goals and Tactical Objectives, which also discusses tactics related to other strategic goals. Other tactics may include such things as establishing scene-control zones, calling for additional resources, wearing appropriate PPE, conducting decontamination, and extinguishing fires.

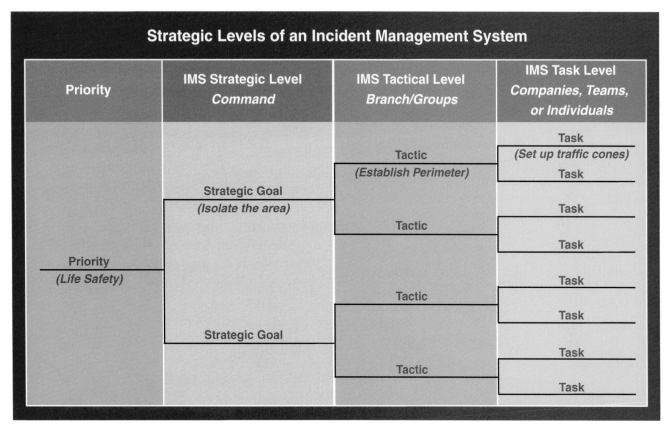

Figure 4.36 The relationship between priorities, strategic goals, tactics, tasks, and the incident management system level normally associated with each.

Lt. Adams determined that her first strategic goal was to isolate the incident spill in order to protect the life safety of the public and emergency responders. The tactic she chose to achieve this goal was to establish an initial isolation zone. By first using the *ERG* to determine the size of the initial isolation zone and then setting that size as an initial boundary, this tactic was accomplished.

Evaluating Progress/Looking Back

[NFPA 472: 5.5.1, 5.5.1(1), 5.1.2.1(4)(a), 5.1.2.1 (4), 5.1.2.1(4)(b)]

The final aspect of the problem-solving process is *looking back* or evaluating progress. If an IAP is effective, the IC should receive favorable progress reports from tactical and/or task supervisors and the incident should begin to stabilize. If, on the other hand, mitigation efforts are failing or the situation is getting worse (or more intense), the plan must be reevaluated and very possibly revised. The plan must also be reevaluated as new information becomes available and circumstances change. If the initial plan isn't working, it must be changed either by selecting new strategies or by changing the tactics used to achieve them. In accordance with predetermined communication procedures, it is important for first responders to communicate the status of the planned response and the progress of their actions to the IC.

Summary

Emergency response to haz mat incidents must be conducted within a certain management framework and structure to ensure successful mitigation of the incident. Every response must be conducted with these priorities in mind: life safety, incident stabilization, and protection of property and the environment. Furthermore, an incident management system must be implemented at all incidents, and operations must be guided by emergency response plans and predetermined procedures that specify communication procedures and other important predetermined actions. Incidents that involve a federal response require NIMS ICS to be implemented as the incident management system for those incidents.

With the management framework in place, responders can focus on the problem-solving process itself. First, they must analyze the incident to understand the problem by successfully identifying the material, conducting size-up and hazard/risk assessment, and predicting the behavior of the hazardous material and the containers involved. Second, based on the understanding they have gained from analyzing the incident, they must plan an appropriate response by setting strategic goals, determining the mode(s) of operation, and developing the IAP. Third, once a plan is in place, it must be implemented by choosing tactics and assigning tasks. Finally, the progress of the response must be evaluated by determining if mitigation efforts are succeeding and the incident is stabilizing. If they are not, the plan must be reevaluated and changed or altered accordingly.

Figure 4.37 provides a summary of these incident management elements. While not all responders are responsible for every aspect of managing the incident (for example, the IC will be deciding the specific strategic goals and objectives), everyone must be conscious of their role or roles in the greater scheme of things. For example, Awareness-Level responders need to be aware that they operate primarily in the nonintervention mode, and all responders need to be aware that hazard and risk assessment is not just for ICs.

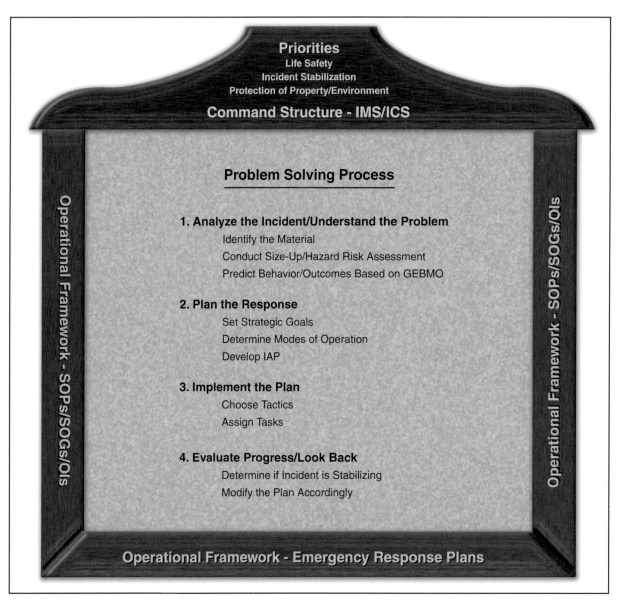

Figure 4.37 Emergency response plans and predetermined procedures (such as SOPs/SOGs/OIs) form the framework for other incident management elements.

Part Two

Incident Problem-Solving Process

Chapter 5

Strategic Goals and Tactical Objectives

First Responder Competencies

This chapter provides information that will assist the reader in meeting the following first responder competencies from NFPA 472, *Professional Competence of Responders to Hazardous Materials Incidents,* 2002 Edition. The numbers are noted directly in the text under the section titles where they are addressed.

NFPA 472

Chapter 4 Competencies for the First Responder at the Awareness Level

4.4.1 Initiating Protective Actions. Given examples of facility and transportation hazardous materials incidents, the local emergency response plan, the organization's standard operating procedures, and the current edition of the Emergency Response Guidebook, first responders at the awareness level shall be able to identify the actions to be taken to protect themselves and others and to control access to the scene and shall also meet the following requirements:

(3) Identify the following basic precautions to be taken to protect themselves and others in a hazardous materials incident:

    (a) Identify the precautions necessary when providing emergency medical care to victims of hazardous materials incidents.

(6) First responders at the awareness level shall identify the definitions for each of the following protective actions:

    (a) Isolation of the hazard area and denial of entry

    (b) Evacuation

    (c) Sheltering in-place protection

(7) First responders at the awareness level shall identify the shapes of recommended initial isolation and protective action zones.

(11) First responders at the awareness level shall identify the techniques used to isolate the hazard area and deny entry to unauthorized persons at hazardous materials incidents.

4.4.2 Initiating the Notification Process. Given either a facility or transportation scenario involving hazardous materials, regardless of the presence of criminal or terrorist activities, the first responder at the awareness level shall identify the initial notifications to be made and how to make them, consistent with the local emergency response plan or the organization's standard operating procedures.

Chapter 5 Competencies for the First Responder at the Operational Level

5.1.2.1 The first responder at the operational level shall be able to perform the following tasks:

(2) Plan an initial response within the capabilities and competencies of available personnel, personal protective equipment, and control equipment by completing the following tasks:

    (b) Describe the defensive options available for a given response objective

(3) Implement the planned response to favorably change the outcomes consistent with the local emergency response plan and the organization's standard operating procedures by completing the following tasks:

    (a) Establish and enforce scene control procedures including control zones, emergency decontamination, and communications

    (d) Perform defensive control functions identified in the plan of action

5.2.2 Collecting Hazard and Response Information. Given known hazardous materials, the first responder at the operational level shall collect hazard and response information using MSDS; CHEMTREC/CANUTEC/SETIQ; local, state, and federal authorities; and contacts with the shipper/manufacturer and also shall meet the following requirements:

(7) Identify the procedure for contacting local, state, and federal authorities as specified in the local emergency response plan (ERP) or the organization's standard operating procedures.

5.2.4 Estimating the Potential Harm. The first responder at the operational level shall estimate the potential harm within the endangered area at a hazardous materials incident and also shall meet the following requirements:

(1) Identify a resource for determining the size of an endangered area of a hazardous materials incident.

(2) Given the dimensions of the endangered area and the surrounding conditions at a hazardous materials incident, estimate the number and type of exposures within that endangered area.

5.3.1 Describing Response Objectives for Hazardous Materials Incidents. Given at least two scenarios involving hazardous materials incidents (one facility and one transportation), the first responder at the operational level shall describe the first responder's response objectives for each problem and also shall meet the following requirements:

(1) Given an analysis of a hazardous materials problem and the exposures already lost, identify the steps for determining the number of exposures that could be saved by the first responder with the resources provided by the authority having jurisdiction and operating in a defensive fashion.

(3) Describe how to assess the risk to a responder for each hazard class in rescuing injured persons at a hazardous materials incident.

5.3.2   Identifying Defensive Options. Given simulated facility and transportation hazardous materials problems, the first responder at the operational level shall identify the defensive options for each response objective and shall meet the following requirements:

(1) Identify the defensive options to accomplish a given response objective.

(2) Identify the purpose for, and the procedures, equipment, and safety precautions used with, each of the following control techniques:

(a) Absorption

(b) Dike, dam, diversion, retention

(c) Dilution

(d) Remote valve shutoff

(e) Vapor dispersion

(f) Vapor suppression

5.4.1   Establishing and Enforcing Scene Control Procedures. Given scenarios for facility and/or transportation hazardous materials incidents, the first responder at the operational level shall identify how to establish and enforce scene control including control zones, emergency decontamination, and communications and shall meet the following requirements:

(1) Identify the procedures for establishing scene control through control zones.

(2) Identify the criteria for determining the locations of the control zones at hazardous materials incidents.

(3) Identify the basic techniques for the following protective actions at hazardous materials incidents:

(a) Evacuation

(b) Sheltering in-place protection

5.4.4   Performing Defensive Control Actions. Given a plan of action for a hazardous materials incident within their capabilities, the first responder at the operational level shall demonstrate defensive control actions set out in the plan and shall meet the following related requirements:

(1) Using the type of fire-fighting foam or vapor suppressing agent and foam equipment furnished by the authority having jurisdiction, demonstrate the effective application of the fire-fighting foam(s) or vapor suppressing agent(s) on a spill or fire involving hazardous materials.

(2) Identify the characteristics and applicability of the following foams:

(a) Protein

(b) Fluoroprotein

(c) Special purpose

i. Polar solvent alcohol-resistant concentrates

ii. Hazardous materials concentrates

(d) Aqueous film-forming foam (AFFF)

(e) High expansion

(3) Given the required tools and equipment, demonstrate how to perform the following defensive control activities:

(a) Absorption

(b) Damming

(c) Diking

(d) Dilution

(e) Diversion

(f) Retention

(g) Vapor dispersion

(h) Vapor suppression

(4) Identify the location and describe the use of the mechanical, hydraulic, and air emergency remote shutoff devices as found on cargo tanks.

(5) Describe the objectives and dangers of search and rescue missions at hazardous materials incidents.

Emergency Responder Guidelines

This chapter provides information that will assist the reader in meeting the following first responder guidelines for fire service and law enforcement from the Office for Domestic Preparedness (ODP) *Emergency Responder Guidelines,* 2002 Edition. The numbers are noted directly in the text under the section titles where they are addressed.

ODP Emergency Responder Guidelines

Fire Service and Law Enforcement

Awareness Level for Events Involving Weapons of Mass Destruction

V. **Know and follow agency/organization's scene security and control procedures for WMD and hazardous material events.** The responder should:

a. Understand his/her agency/organization's site security and scene control procedures for awareness level trained personnel. Follow these procedures for ensuring scene security and for keeping unauthorized persons away from the scene and adjacent hazardous areas. Such procedures include cordoning off the area to prevent anyone from inadvertently entering the scene. Maintain scene security and control until a higher authority arrives at the scene.

d. Know and follow his/her agency's procedures for isolating the danger area. Know how to deal with contaminated victims until a higher authority arrives.

Performance Level for Events Involving Weapons of Mass Destruction

II. **Know the Incident Command System and be able to follow Unified Command System procedures for integration and implementation of each system. Know how the systems integrate and support the incident. Be familiar with the overall operation of the two command systems and be able to assist in implementation of the Unified Command System if needed.** The responder should:

a. Know how to implement initial site management procedures following the department's incident command system and emergency response plan. Such procedures include establishing communications with the dispatcher or command center, setting up the control zones for the scene, locating the command post, and forwarding any intelligence that has been collected on the scene.

f. Be able to assist in a critique of the actions taken during the complete response to a WMD event. Assist in documenting lessons learned from the critique as they pertain to fire service response activities.

g. Understand the importance of and know how termination documentation for a WMD event is to be conducted related to fire service activities on the scene.

III. **Know and follow self-protection measures and rescue and evacuation procedures for WMD events.** The responder should:

d. Know the protective measures that will be needed to protect victims and others on the scene of a potential WMD event.

e. Know the department's and the on-scene incident commander's plan for evacuation of persons (including casualties) from the hazard area of a potential WMD event.

f. Be able to assist in rescuing and in moving victims of a potential WMD event to a safe area for triage and treatment by emergency medical responders.

[NFPA 472: 5.3.1, 5.3.2, 5.4.1]

As part of the problem-solving process, incident commanders (ICs) must select the strategic goals and the tactical objectives used to mitigate a haz mat incident. As discussed in Chapter 4, Incident Management Elements, *strategic goals* are broad statements of what must be done to resolve the incident, while *tactical objectives* are the specific operations that must be done in order to accomplish those goals. This chapter discusses some of the standard defensive control tactics used to accomplish the following strategic goals:

- Isolation
- Notification
- Identification
- Protection
- Confinement/spill control
- Containment/leak control
- Fire control
- Recovery and termination

The goal of *identification* was discussed in Chapter 3, Hazardous Materials Identification, and is not addressed further. The goals listed are very broad strategy categories, and mitigation of an actual incident may require a variety of specific strategies (not given in the list) based on the problems presented at the scene. **Appendix G,** Typical Haz Mat Problems with Potential Mitigating Strategies and Tactics, provides a table with examples of common problems presented at haz mat incidents with more narrowly defined strategies and tactics. See Chapter 8, Incident-Specific Strategies and Tactics, for incident-specific strategies and tactics based on the U.S. Department of Transportation (DOT) hazard classes.

Other Strategic Goal Systems/Models

There are several strategic goal systems/models used by emergency responders. For example, there are different systems for fire fighting as well as for haz mat incidents.

REVAS: Traditional fire-fighting goal system/model

- **R**escue
- **E**xposures
- **V**entilation
- **A**ttack
- **S**alvage

RECEO-VS: Fire-fighting priority system/model by Lloyd Layman

- **R**escue
- **E**xposure
- **C**onfinement
- **E**xtinguishment
- **O**verhaul
- **V**entilation
- **S**alvage

IFSTA Haz Mat Strategic Goals (as identified in Hazardous Materials for First Responders, 2nd Edition)

- Rescue
- Exposure Protection
- Fire Extinguishment
- Confinement
- Containment
- Recovery

Isolation

[NFPA 472: 4.4.1, 4.4.1(3), 5.1.2.1(3)(a)] [ODP Awareness V.a., V.d.] [ODP Operations II.a.]

Isolation is one of the primary strategic goals at a haz mat incident and one of the most important means by which first responders can ensure the safety of themselves and others. Separating people from the potential source of harm is a good way to protect the life safety of all involved. *Isolation* involves physically securing and maintaining the emergency scene by establishing perimeters and protective action zones and denying entry to un-authorized persons. The process continues with either evacuation or shelter in place (sometimes called *protection in place*) of people located within the protective action zone. The process of controlling the scene concludes with the establishment of hazard-control zones.

Scene Perimeters

[NFPA 472: 4.4.1(6)(a), 5.4.1(1), 5.4.1(2)]

Physical control of the scene begins by isolating the site using an isolation perimeter, removing people who are within this perimeter, and denying entry of unauthorized persons. The process continues by determining the initial isolation distance and establishing initial isolation zones and protective action zones.

Isolation Perimeter

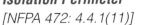

[NFPA 472: 4.4.1(11)]

The *isolation perimeter* (sometimes called the *outer perimeter*) is the boundary established to prevent access by the public and unauthorized persons. It may be established even before the hazardous material is positively identified. If an incident is inside a building, the isolation perimeter might be set at the outside entrances, accomplished by posting personnel to deny entry. If the incident is outside, the perimeter might be set at the surrounding intersections with response vehicles or law enforcement officers diverting traffic and pedestrians. Traffic cones or banner tape can also designate isolation perimeters **(Figure 5.1)**. Some people disregard these measures. Without emergency responders guarding the perimeter, it

Figure 5.1 In addition to putting up barricades, barrier tape, or traffic cones, posting a guard is the best way to ensure that civilians do not cross the isolation perimeter into hazardous areas.

cannot be assured that civilians won't go into the area even though it is clearly marked.

The isolation perimeter can be expanded or reduced as needed. For example, in some cases, the initial isolation perimeter established by first responders is expanded outward as additional help arrives. Law enforcement officers are often used to establish and maintain isolation perimeters. Once hazard-control zones are established, the isolation perimeter is generally the boundary between the public and the cold (safe) zone (see Hazard-Control Zones section).

 The initial isolation perimeter established at the scenario incident was the fence surrounding Ace Trucking, with access being controlled at each of the two entrances. As additional resources arrived, the perimeter was expanded to the closest intersections on either side.

Initial Isolation Distance and Initial Isolation Zone

[NFPA 474: 4.4.1(7)]

The *initial isolation distance* is a distance within which all persons should be considered for evacuation in all directions from an actual hazardous materials spill/leak source, according to the *Emergency Response Guidebook (ERG)*. The *initial isolation zone* is a circular zone (with a radius equivalent to the initial isolation distance) within which persons may be exposed to dangerous concentrations upwind of the source and life-threatening concentrations downwind of the source.

The process for establishing an initial isolation distance is discussed in the *ERG*. It contains a protective-action distances table in the back part of the book (green-bordered pages that apply to *highlighted* chemicals). In order to use this information, first responders must have already identified the material involved in the incident and found its name or ID number in either the yellow- or blue-bordered pages of the *ERG*. As discussed in Chapter 3, Hazardous Materials Identification, those sections contain names of some chemicals that are highlighted in color and others that are not. The chemical names that are highlighted were selected for inclusion in the Table of Initial Isolation and Protective Action Distances because of the chemical's poison/inhalation hazards. The orange-bordered pages in the *ERG* provide recommended isolation and evacuation distances for nonhighlighted chemicals.

NOTE: If hazardous materials are on fire or have been leaking for longer than 30 minutes, this *ERG* table does not apply. Seek more detailed information on the involved material on the appropriate orange-bordered page in the *ERG*.

In addition to determining the material involved in the incident, first responders must also determine the amount of material involved in the incident. The Table of Initial Isolation and Protective Action Distances gives parameters for establishing isolation and protective-action distances. These distances are based on whether the spill is small or large. According to the *ERG*, a *small spill* is one that involves a single, small package (up to a 55-gallon [208 L] drum), small cylinder, or small leak from a large package. A *large spill* is one that involves a spill from a large package or multiple spills from many small packages.

The smallest isolation distance given for any chemical in the table is 100 feet (30 m) (**Figure 5.2**). When first responders have determined the initial isolation distance for a particular chemical, all people within that distance of the spill should be directed to move in a crosswind direction away from the spill until they are outside the isolation distance (**Figure 5.3**). Some of the recommended isolation distances in the orange-bordered pages may be less than 100 feet (30 m).

The initial isolation distance recommended for 1,2-butylene oxide in the *ERG* is 80 to 160 feet (25 m to 49 m). When firefighters Linder and George were sent on reconnaissance, they stayed outside the anticipated radius of the initial isolation zone.

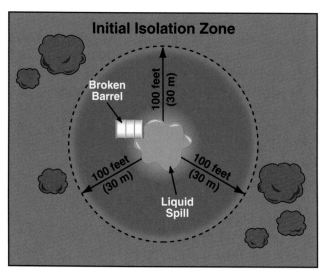

Figure 5.2 The smallest initial isolation distance for any chemical listed in the green-bordered pages of the *ERG* is 100 feet (30 m).

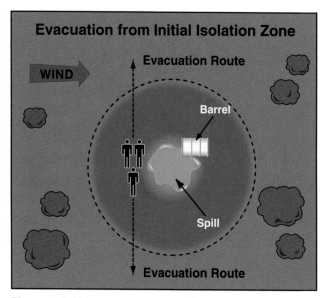

Figure 5.3 Whenever possible, evacuate in a crosswind direction, which is especially important when a person is downwind of the spill or leak.

Protective Action Zone

The *protective action zone* is the area immediately adjacent to and downwind from the initial isolation zone. This area is in imminent danger of being contaminated by airborne vapors within 30 minutes of material release **(Figure 5.4)**.

Hazard-Control Zones

Hazard-control zones provide the rigid scene control needed at haz mat incidents to protect responders from interference by unauthorized persons, help regulate movement of first responders within the zones, and minimize contamination. These control zones are not necessarily static and can be adjusted as the incident changes. Zones divide the levels of hazard of an incident, and what a zone is called generally depicts this level. NFPA 472, *Standard for Professional Competence of Responders to Hazardous Materials Incidents* (2002), refers to the zones as hot, warm, and cold **(Figure 5.5)**.

U.S. Occupational Safety and Health Administration (OSHA) and the U.S. Environmental Protection Agency (EPA) refer to these zones collectively as *site work zones*. They are sometimes called *scene-control zones* as well.

Hot

The *hot zone* (also called *exclusion zone*) is an area surrounding an incident that is contaminated or has the potential to become contaminated by a released material. This area is exposed to the gases, vapors, mists, dusts, or runoff of the hazardous material. It is generally the same as the isolation distance and could include the protective-action area. The hot zone may or may not correspond to the initial isolation zone. The zone extends far enough to prevent people outside the zone from suffering ill effects from the released material. Work performed inside the hot zone is often limited to haz mat technicians.

> **WARNING**
>
> First responders at the Awareness Level do not operate in the hot zone. Responders at the Operational Level must have proper training and appropriate personal protective equipment (PPE) to support work being done inside the hot zone.

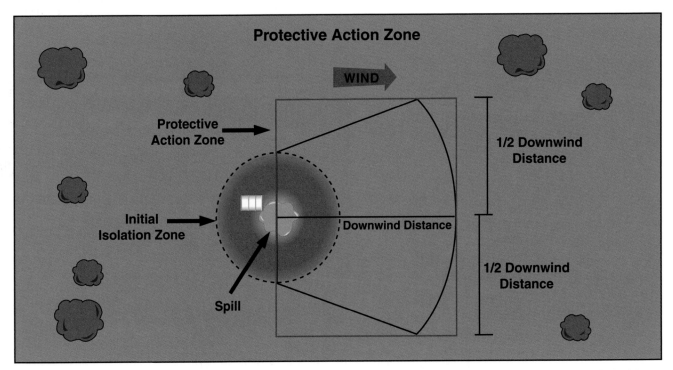

Figure 5.4 The protective action zone is the area in imminent danger of being contaminated by airborne vapors within 30 minutes of the release.

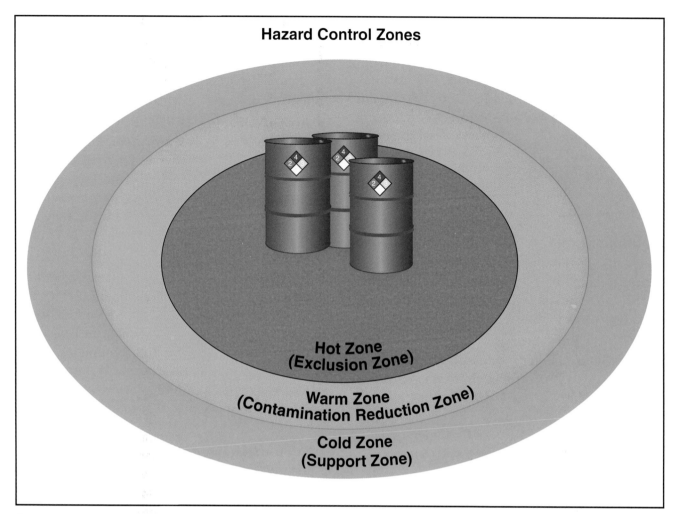

Hazard Control Zones

Hot Zone
(Exclusion Zone)

Warm Zone
(Contamination Reduction Zone)

Cold Zone
(Support Zone)

Figure 5.5 Hazard-control zones divide the levels of hazard at an incident into hot, warm, and cold zones, with the hot zone indicating the highest degree of danger.

Truck 1 was assigned the task of establishing the hot-zone boundary as the exterior walls of the warehouse and 160 feet (49 m) from the exterior of the building on Side Bravo adjacent to the loading dock. The exterior walls of the building defined the hot zone on Sides Alpha, Charlie, and Delta. Captain Hendrix assigned the truck's firefighters to deploy cones on Side Bravo to establish a 160-foot (49 m) radius hot zone.

Warm

The *warm zone* (also called *contamination reduction zone* or *corridor*) is an area abutting the hot zone and extending to the cold zone (see following section) **(Figure 5.6).** It is considered safe for workers to enter without special protective clothing (until decontamination [decon] starts), unless they are assigned a task requiring increased protection. The warm zone is used as a buffer between the hot

and cold zones and is the place to decontaminate personnel and equipment exiting the hot zone. Decontamination usually takes place within a corridor (decon corridor) located in the warm zone.

Figure 5.6 Decontamination takes place in the warm zone. *Courtesy of Joan Hepler.*

Cold

The *cold zone* (also called *support zone*) encompasses the warm zone and is used to carry out all other support functions of the incident or haz mat operations. Workers in the cold zone are not required to wear personal protective clothing because the zone is considered safe. The command post (CP), staging area, donning/doffing area, backup teams, research teams, and triage/treatment/rehabilitation (rehab) areas are located within the cold zone.

Isolation Summary

As always, terminology may differ from organization to organization, but the following terms provide a summary of the commonly used zones and areas likely to be established at haz mat incidents:

- *Isolation perimeter* — Outer boundary of an incident that is controlled to prevent entrance by the public or unauthorized persons

- *Initial isolation distance* — Distance within which all persons should be considered for evacuation in all directions from the actual spill/leak source (*ERG* term)

- *Initial isolation zone* — Circular zone (with a radius equivalent to the initial isolation distance) within which persons may be exposed to dangerous concentrations upwind of the source and may be exposed to life-threatening concentrations downwind of the source (*ERG* term)

- *Protective action distance* — Downwind distance for which protective actions should be considered (*ERG* term)

- *Protective action zone* — Area immediately adjacent to and downwind from the initial isolation zone, which is in imminent danger of being contaminated by airborne vapors within 30 minutes of material release (*ERG* term); see the *ERG* green-bordered pages where the boundaries of this area are given in units of tenths of miles (kilometers)

- *Hazard-control zones* — Zones dividing the levels of hazard of an incident (hot, warm, or cold), with the hot zone representing the highest degree of hazard; U.S. EPA/OSHA term: *site work zones;* also called *scene-control zones*

- *Decontamination zone* — Area located in the warm zone where contaminated clothing, people, and equipment can be cleaned or secured; see Chapter 7, Contamination and Decontamination

- *Area of safe refuge* — Primarily an area serving as a safe place to wait for evacuation assistance in the event of fire when building elevators are normally inaccessible; used in the haz mat world as a safe location (or locations) where evacuated persons are directed to gather while potential emergencies are assessed, decisions are made, and mitigating activities are begun

- *Staging area* — Area where personnel and equipment awaiting assignment to the incident are held (which keeps responders and equipment out of the way and safe until needed), minimizing confusion and freelancing at the scene; located at an isolated spot in the cold zone where occupants cannot interfere with ongoing operations (Incident Management System [IMS] term)

- *Rehabilitation area (rehab area)* — Safe location where emergency personnel can rest, sit or lie down, have food and drink, and have medical conditions evaluated; located in the cold zone

- *Triage/treatment area* — Area where victims of an incident are brought for medical assessment (triage) and stabilization (treatment); located in the cold zone unless a patient is contaminated, then it would have to be the warm zone

NOTE: Triage and treatment is delegated to first responders who are trained and equipped to provide medical aid as required in NFPA 473, *Standard for Competencies for EMS Personnel Responding to Hazardous Materials Incidents* (2002).

The size, nature, and scope of an incident determine which of these zones and areas are needed. Predetermined procedures help identify which zones and areas to establish under what circumstances. Responders involved in transporting victims from decon to triage/treatment areas need to protect themselves in case contaminated victims have not been thoroughly decontaminated.

Notification

[NFPA 472: 4.4.2, 5.2.2(7)]

Various aspects of notification and communication such as verbal reports, predetermined procedures, internal and external communications, and how to request additional help at an incident have already been discussed in this manual. It is very important for first responders to understand their role in the notification process. However, predetermined procedures such as standard operating procedures (SOPs) and the emergency response plan should define them.

For Awareness-Level responders, notification may be as simple as dialing 9-1-1 to report an incident and get additional help dispatched (**Figure 5.7**). Fixed-facility responders may have their own internal procedures to follow such as calling for an internal fire brigade or haz mat response team.

Figure 5.7 Contacting the telecommunicator to request additional help may be all that is necessary to meet the strategic goal of notification.

For Operational-Level responders, the strategic goal of notification may include such items as incident-level identification and public emergency information/notification. Predetermined procedures should also identify procedures for contacting and notifying the appropriate local, state, and federal authorities.

Notification Example

When the amount of a hazardous substance release or oil spill exceeds established reporting quantities in the U.S., by law the federal government's National Response Center (NRC) must be notified. Once a report is made, the NRC immediately notifies a predesignated EPA or U.S. Coast Guard (USCG) On-Scene Coordinator (OSC), based on the location of the spill. The OSC may then determine that local action is sufficient and no additional federal action is required. If the incident is large or complex, the federal OSC may remain on the scene to monitor the response and advise on the deployment of personnel and equipment. However, the federal OSC takes command of the response in any one of the following situations:

- When the party responsible for the chemical release or oil spill is unknown or not cooperative

- When the OSC determines that the spill or release is beyond the capacity of company, local, or state responders to manage

- For oil spills, when the incident is determined to present a substantial threat to public health or welfare due to the size or character of the spill.

Protection

Protection is the overall goal of ensuring the safety of responders and the public. Protection goals also include rescue and measures taken to protect property and the environment. Protection goals are accomplished through such tactics as the following:

- Use and wear appropriate PPE (see Chapter 6, Personal Protective Equipment).

- Use decontamination procedures (see Chapter 7, Contamination and Decontamination).

- Provide emergency medical care and first aid.
- Conduct preentry medical monitoring.
- Conduct preentry briefings.
- Conduct safety assessments.
- Take any other measures to protect the public, particularly evacuation and shelter in place.

Rescue

[NFPA 472: 5.3.1(3), 5.4.4(5)]

Due to the defensive nature of Awareness- and Operational-Level actions, rescue can be a difficult strategy to implement for first responders, particularly in the initial stages of a response. Search and rescue attempts should be made within the framework of the incident action plan with appropriate PPE, backup personnel, and other safety considerations in place.

The safety of emergency personnel is the IC's first priority. When a rescue is too dangerous, the proper decision may be to protect the victims in place. This rule may directly conflict with the fire-fighting strategic priority of *rescue first* as well as with many responders' natural desire to help victims as quickly as possible. However, because of the dangers presented by hazardous materials, responders who rush to the rescue often require the need for rescue themselves.

Fight the Urge!

Never *rush* to conduct a rescue without proper PPE, planning, and coordination under the direction of the IC!

The IC makes decisions about rescue based on a variety of factors at the incident, including a risk-benefit analysis that weighs the possible benefits of taking certain actions versus the potential negative outcomes that might result. See the safety alert, Exceptions to the Rule, p. 288, in the Operational-Level Actions section for more information. The following factors affect the ability of personnel to perform a rescue:

- Nature of the hazardous material and incident severity

- Availability of appropriate PPE
- Availability of monitoring equipment
- Number of victims and their conditions
- Time needed (including a safety margin) to complete a rescue
- Tools, equipment, and other devices needed to affect the rescue

Awareness-Level Actions

[NFPA 472: 4.4.1(3)(a)] [ODP Awareness III.c., V.d.]

Because Awareness-Level responders should *never* come in contact with a hazardous material, they are essentially prohibited from physically touching or moving a victim who is either contaminated (or potentially contaminated) or located within the initial isolation zone, warm zone, or hot zone. Awareness-Level responders' rescue actions are limited to telling people what to do and/or where to go. Thus, these responders can take the following actions from a distance:

- Direct people to an area of safe refuge or evacuation point located in a safe place that is upwind and uphill of the hazard area.
- Instruct victims to move to an area that is less dangerous before moving them to an area that offers complete safety.
- Direct contaminated or potentially contaminated victims to an isolation point, safe refuge area, safety shower, eyewash facility, or decontamination area **(Figure 5.8, p. 288).**
- Give directions to a large number of people for mass decontamination.

If there are injured victims at the scene, Awareness-Level responders must also be aware of the potential dangers of contamination and the need to decontaminate as part of the treatment process (see Chapter 7, Contamination and Decontamination).

Operational-Level Actions

[ODP Operations III.f.]

Like Awareness-Level responders, Operational-Level responders may instruct people on what to do and where to go, plus they may assist with searches in the warm zone and decontamination

Assessing Rescue Risks

Responders can begin to assess the following *risks** of conducting a rescue at a hazardous materials incident based on the DOT hazard classes of the material:

- *Class 1 Risk:* Explosives that may involve thermal injury, due to the heat generated by the detonation, mechanical injury from the shock, blast overpressure, fragmentation, shrapnel, or structural damage, and chemical injuries from associated contamination. During a rescue, contact with the blood or other bodily fluids from the victim may result in etiological harm. Because burning depletes oxygen, asphyxiation should always be a consideration.

- *Class 2 Risk:* Gases that are stored in containers that may be under pressure can rupture violently and, depending upon their contents, could create a thermal, asphyxiant, chemical, or mechanical hazard. Cryogenic materials (Class 2.2), such as liquid oxygen, may cause thermal harm because of its extremely cold temperature. Asphyxiation is always a concern with chemical vapors in a confined space because chemical reactions may deplete oxygen or create gases that displace oxygen such as carbon dioxide (CO_2).

- *Class 3 Risk:* Flammable liquids that could also disseminate shrapnel caused by a forceful explosion, resulting in thermal hazards from heat and fire as well as associated chemical and mechanical injuries.

- *Class 4 Risk:* Flammable solids, spontaneously combustible materials, and dangerous when wet materials that could cause thermal harm from heat and flammability. Mechanical harm could occur as some materials react spontaneously creating slip, trip, and fall hazards, while other water reactive, toxic, and/or corrosive materials can cause chemical harm.

- *Class 5 Risk:* Oxidizers and organic peroxides that can create thermal, chemical, and mechanical harm, because they supply oxygen to support combustion and are sensitive to heat, shock, friction and contamination.

- *Class 6 Risk:* Toxic/poisonous materials and infectious substances that cause chemical harm due to toxicity by inhalation, ingestion, and skin and eye contact. Etiological harm can come from either disease-causing organisms or toxins derived from living organisms. Because these products may be flammable, thermal injuries are a potential hazard.

- *Class 7 Risk:* Radioactive material that may cause thermal harm as well as radiological harm from alpha, beta, and neutron particles, and gamma rays, although depending upon the proximity of the responder to the source and the cumulative dose rate, delayed effects would most likely occur. Radiological substances should not be overlooked as chemical hazards. For Class 7 (radioactive) material, a great deal of information regarding risk to response personnel can be obtained by determining the type of package present. Excepted, industrial, and Type A packages contain non-life-endangering amounts of radioactive material. Type B packages may contain life-endangering amounts of radioactive material; however, life-endangering conditions would only exist if the contents of a Type B package are released or if package shielding fails. Type B packages are designed to withstand severe accident conditions.

- *Class 8 Risk:* Corrosive materials that have chemical and thermal hazards associated with the disintegration of contacted tissues and the recognition that chemical reactions create heat, especially if the material is fuming and/or water reactive. Corrosive chemicals, like strong acids, can weaken structural elements, causing the potential for mechanical harm.

- *Class 9 Risk:* Miscellaneous dangerous goods incidents that would be agent and situation specific but could encompass a multitude of potential hazards.

---

*Reprinted with permission of the *Hazardous Materials Response Handbook,* 4th Edition, Copyright © 2002, National Fire Protection Association, Quincy, MA 02269.

procedures. Because they may be allowed to do reconnaissance and take other actions within the warm zone, Operational-Level responders may also perform the following actions with appropriate PPE for the hazardous material:

- Conduct searches during reconnaissance or defensive activities.

- Conduct searches on the edge of the hot zone.

- Direct victims to the decontamination area (for example, eyewash stations or showers).

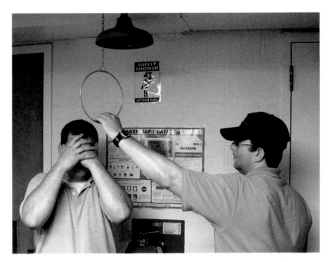

Figure 5.8 First responders can direct contaminated or potentially contaminated victims to safety showers, areas of safe refuge, or decontamination areas.

- Assist with decontamination while not coming into contact with the hazardous material itself.
- Assist with the identification of victims.
- Give instructions to a large number of people for mass decontamination.

Firefighters Linder and George (reconnaissance group) assisted the two maintenance workers to the emergency decon area set up by Firefighter Miller. If the maintenance workers had been incapacitated inside the warehouse (inside the initial isolation zone) rather than being conscious and alert on the loading dock, the firefighters' actions would have been limited to notifying the IC of the victims' location. Also note that the contaminated victim was instructed to wash himself, rather than having the responders do it for him.

Exposure Protection

[NFPA 472: 5.2.4(2), 5.3.1, 5.3.1(1)]

Exposure protection is a defensive control tactic. Most firefighters should be familiar with the concept of protecting exposures in fire situations, usually in terms of protecting property that is exposed to a fire in order to keep it from spreading. However, at the haz mat scene, the same concept is expanded to include the following:

- Protecting people
- Protecting the environment

Exceptions to the Rule

This book emphasizes the difference between defensive and offensive operations, repeating the basic rule that Awareness- and Operational-Level responders should *not* enter the hot zone or come into physical contact with hazardous materials (except in those cases where they are trained to do so in regards to certain petroleum products). When it comes to rescue operations, however, a risk-benefit analysis may determine that it is acceptable to conduct a rescue despite these usual restrictions.

For example, conducting a rescue in the hot zone might be appropriate *if* the following conditions are met:

- The product is positively identified.
- Responders have appropriate PPE to protect from any possible hazards presented.
- The risk to responders is minimal.
- A life can be saved or serious injury prevented.

In these cases, the IC may decide that it is appropriate to take action and conduct a rescue before haz mat technicians arrive. However, this is a decision that only the IC should make and only after a serious risk/benefit assessment has been conducted.

Responders should be aware that the reason the offensive/defensive distinction is drawn and emphasized in this manual is because too many first responders get into trouble and become victims themselves. If ever in doubt, play it safe.

- Protecting property not yet directly involved in but threatened by an expanding incident (including closed containers and piping)

This list can include protecting exposures from fires involving hazardous materials but also protecting the environment from the harmful effects of hazardous materials that are *not* burning. For example, diking a storm drain is a tactic that protects the environment from being exposed to (and harmed by) potentially toxic materials (**Figure 5.9**).

Operational-level personnel should be able to size up a haz mat incident and estimate the number and type of exposures involved. By using the *ERG* and other sources (for example, *General Emergency*

Figure 5.9 Diking a storm drain is a defensive tactic that protects the environment.

Behavior Model [*GEBMO*] or plume-modeling software if available), they should be able to predict or attempt to predict where the hazardous material may be going given its physical state of matter (liquid, gas, or solid) and the physical conditions present (night or day, wind or no wind, indoors or outdoors, and the like) at the incident. Once the size of the endangered area has been estimated, they should be able to predict the potential exposures, including the number of people in the area, the buildings/property, and the environmental concerns (such as sewer drains, streams, lakes, ponds, wells, and the like).

Following the understanding of the potential area affected and number of exposures, Operational-Level responders should be able to determine a number of strategic goals and tactical objectives (response options or objectives) that could be used to begin stabilizing the incident. Decisions on which options to use should be based on such factors as availability of resources and a risk/benefit analysis as discussed in Chapter 4, Incident Management Elements.

Protecting People

The most important exposure consideration is the threat to life, which is true regardless of whether the haz mat incident involves a fire. Life safety must be preserved not only during the initial stages of an incident but over the complete cycle of the incident. Ideally, the best way to protect lives that may be exposed to hazardous materials is to evacuate the people to a place of safety. Another option is to shelter in place. However, if the primary threat is fire, or potential fire, evacuation becomes the obvious choice.

Protecting the Environment

Environmental damage is also an important concern. The air, surface water, wildlife, water table, and land surrounding an incident may be seriously affected by released materials. Water used during fire-control activities may potentially become contaminated. The nonbiodegradable nature of many materials means that the consequences of contamination may take years for the full effect to be realized. The result of contamination may also require large sums of money to repair. All released materials and runoff need to be confined and held until their effect on the environment can be determined.

Protecting Property

The property risk is similar to that created by other fire hazards except that the threatening material may not always be readily evident. Flammable and toxic gases, mists, and vapors can contaminate and pose an ignition threat with no visible signs. Protective actions must be tailored to the material, its properties, and any reactions to the proposed protective medium. ICs have appropriately *written off* property when operations were potentially risky. Lives or the environment must not be unduly compromised to save property.

Protective Actions

[NFPA 472: 4.4.1, 5.4.1(3)] [ODP Operations III.d.]

Once the protective action zone has been determined, first responders must act to protect or preserve the health and safety of those people within the zone as well as emergency responders who are on the scene. The options for protective action are evacuation, shelter in place, or a combination of both. The IC selects the best option (or combination of options) based on factors that include but are not limited to the following:

- Material considerations
  - Toxicity
  - Quantity
  - Rate of release
  - Type of release and dispersion
  - Possibility of controlling and/or stopping the release
  - Direction of spread
- Environmental conditions
  - Wind direction
  - Wind velocity
  - Temperature
  - Humidity
  - Precipitation
  - Tides and currents
  - Topography
- Population at risk
  - Population density
  - Proximity
  - Warning/notification systems
  - Method of transport
  - Ability to control and/or stop the release
  - Special needs

Evacuation

[NFPA 472: 4.4.1(6)(b), 5.4.1(3)(a)] [ODP Operations III.e.]

Evacuate means to move all people from a threatened area to a safer place. To perform an evacuation, there must be enough time to warn people, for them to get ready, and for them to leave the area. Generally, if there is enough time for evacuation, it is the best protective action. First responders should begin evacuating people nearby, downwind, or crosswind of the incident within the distance recommended by the *ERG*. Even after people move the recommended distances, they are not completely safe from harm. Do not permit evacuees to congregate at these *safe* distances. Send them by a specific route to a designated place (or *area of safe refuge*) upwind/uphill/upstream of the incident so that they do not have to move again, even if the wind shifts.

The number of responders needed to perform an evacuation varies with the size of the area and number of people to evacuate. Evacuation can be a labor-intensive operation, so it is important to assign enough personnel resources to an incident to conduct it. Evacuation and traffic-control activities on the downwind side could cause responders and evacuees to become contaminated and, consequently, need decontamination. Responders may also need to wear PPE to safely conduct the evacuation. Evacuation plans (including casualties) for likely terrorist targets such as stadiums and other public gathering places should be made in advance as part of the local emergency response plan. See Chapter 9, Terrorist and Other Criminal Activities.

Shelter in Place

[NFPA 472: 4.4.1(6)(c), 5.4.1(3)(b)]

Shelter in place means to direct people to go quickly inside a building and remain inside until danger passes. It may be determined that shelter in place is the preferred option over evacuation. The decision to shelter in place may be guided by the following factors:

- The population is unable to initiate evacuation because of health care, detention, or educational occupancies.
- The material is spreading too rapidly to allow time for evacuation.
- The material is too toxic to risk any exposure.
- Vapors are heavier than air, and people are in a high-rise structure.

When protecting people inside a structure, direct them to close all doors and windows and turn off all heating, ventilating, and air-conditioning (HVAC) systems. Shelter in place may not be the best option if vapors or gases are explosive, it will take a long time for the vapors or gases to clear the area, or the building cannot be closed tightly. Vehicles are not as effective as buildings for shelter in place, but they can offer temporary protection if windows are closed and the ventilation system is turned off. Whether using evacuation or shelter in place, the public needs to be informed as early as possible and receive additional instructions and information throughout the course of an emergency. Shelter in place may be more effective if public education has been done ahead of time through emergency planning.

First responders should also pay attention to the condition of surrounding buildings before ordering sheltering in place. For example, some areas may have old and dilapidated structures without air-conditioning or with openings between floorboards. Sheltering in place might not provide sufficient protection in such cases, making evacuation the better option.

Spill Control/Confinement

[NFPA 472: 5.3.2, 5.3.2(1), 5.3.2(2), 5.1.2.1(2)(b), 5.1.2.1(3)(d), 5.4.4, 5.4.4(3)]

In order to understand the principles behind spill control/confinement, it is useful to return to the information in the General Hazardous Materials Behavior Model section (Chapter 4, Incident Management Elements). Container stress can result in a breach (rupture). When the container is breached, it may release its contents. The released material then disperses according to its chemical and physical properties, topography, prevailing weather conditions, and the amount and duration of the release. Depending on its hazardous properties, the material can then harm whatever it contacts.

The strategic goal of spill control involves controlling the product that has already been released from its container. In other words, *spill control* minimizes the amount of contact the product makes with people, property, and the environment by limiting or *confining* the dispersion and/or reducing the amount of harm caused by contact with the material **(Figure 5.10, p. 292)**. Tactics and tasks relating to spill control are determined by the material involved and type of dispersion but are usually less related to the specific type of container or breach than leak-control procedures. Spill-control and confinement actions are generally defensive in nature.

The main priority of spill control is confinement and the prevention of further contamination or contact with the hazardous material. However, some spill-control tactics such as neutralization and dispersion minimize the amount of harm caused by contact with the material. Responders trained to the Operational Level may perform spill-control activities as long as they do not come in contact with the product or have appropriate training and PPE for the specific substance such as flammable liquids. In the latter case, they still limit their contact with the material as much as possible. Spill control is a defensive operation with the most important issue being the safety of the responders performing these actions.

Spills may involve gases, liquids, or solids, and the product involved may be released into the air (as a vapor or gas), into water, and/or onto a surface such as the ground or a bench top. The type of dispersion determines the defensive measure(s) needed to control it. For example, in the event of a flammable liquid spill, first responders must address not only the liquid spreading on the ground, but the vapors being released into the air as well. If the spill pours into a sanitary sewer system or stream, responders need to address the contamination of the water, too.

Spill Control/Confinement

Figure 5.10 Spill control is aimed at confining the material that has been (or is being) released from a container. Damming, diking, and vapor suppression are examples of spill control measures that minimize the amount of contact the product makes with people, property, and the environment.

Confinement Tactics

Hazardous materials may be confined by building dams or dikes near the source, catching the material in another container, or directing (diverting) the flow to a remote location for collection. Generally, the fire apparatus carries the following necessary tools:

- Shovels for building earthen dams
- Salvage covers for making catch basins
- Charged hoselines for creating diversion channels

Before using the equipment to confine spilled materials, ICs need to seek advice from technical sources to determine if the spilled materials will adversely affect the equipment. Large or rapidly spreading spills may require the use of heavy construction-type equipment, floating confinement booms, or special sewer and storm drain plugs.

Confinement is not restricted to controlling liquids. Dusts, vapors, and gases can also be confined. A protective covering consisting of a fine spray of water, a layer of earth, plastic sheets, or a salvage cover can keep dusts from blowing about at incidents. Foam blankets can be used on liquids to reduce the release of vapors. Strategically placed fire streams can direct gases, or allow the water to absorb them. Check reference sources for the proper procedures for confining gases. The material type, rate of release, speed of spread, number of personnel available, tools and equipment needed, weather, and topography dictate confinement efforts.

Confinement of a spilled material is often performed initially to protect exposures, and then leak containment is started (see Leak Control/Containment section). Both processes may be started simultaneously if personnel and equipment are available. Most containment efforts include establishing a confinement area in the event that a patch or plug fails. First responders who are properly trained, are outfitted with appropriate PPE, and have the equipment to carry out these measures may take defensive control measures.

Operational-Level responders are expected to take protective actions but not to physically stop the release unless it can be done from a safe location by closing a remote shutoff valve (see Leak Control/Containment section). The following defensive confinement actions are discussed in the following sections:

- Absorption
- Adsorption
- Blanketing/covering
- Dam, dike, diversion, and retention
- Vapor suppression

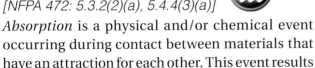

CAUTION

Confinement actions are undertaken only if first responders are reasonably ensured that they will not come in contact with or be exposed to the hazardous material.

Absorption
[NFPA 472: 5.3.2(2)(a), 5.4.4(3)(a)]

Absorption is a physical and/or chemical event occurring during contact between materials that have an attraction for each other. This event results

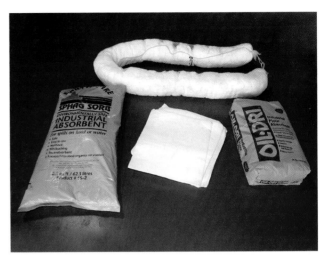

Figure 5.11 Many different materials are used as absorbents.

in one material being retained in the other. The bulk of the material being absorbed enters the cell structure of the absorbing medium. An example of absorption is soaking an axe head in water to make the handle swell. Some of the materials typically used as absorbents are sawdust, clays, charcoal, and polyolefin-type fibers **(Figure 5.11).** The absorbent is spread directly onto the hazardous material or in a location where the material is expected to flow. After use, absorbents must be treated and disposed of as hazardous materials themselves because they retain the properties of the materials they absorb.

Adsorption

Adsorption is different from absorption in that the molecules of the hazardous material physically adhere to the *ad*sorbent material rather than being *sucked* into the inner spaces of an *ab*sorbent material. Adsorbents tend to not swell like absorbents, and they are often organic-based materials such as activated charcoal or carbon. Adsorbents are primarily used to control shallow liquid spills. It is important to make sure that the adsorbent used is compatible with the spilled material in order to avoid potentially dangerous reactions. According to NFPA 471, *Recommended Practice for Responding to Hazardous Materials Incidents* (2002), the principle characteristics of the adsorption process* are as follows:

- *The sorbent surface, unlike absorbents, is rigid and no volume increase occurs.*

- *The adsorption process is often accompanied by heat of adsorption whereas absorption is not.*

- *Adsorption occurs only with activated surfaces, e.g., activated carbon, alumina, etc.*

---

* Reprinted with permission from NFPA 471, *Recommended Practice for Responding to Hazardous Materials Incidents*, Copyright © 2002, National Fire Protection Association, Quincy, MA 00269. This reprinted material is not the complete and official position of the National Fire Protection Association on the referenced subject, which is represented only by the standard in its entirety.

Adsorption or Absorption?

Simply put, hazardous materials *attach* to adsorptive materials and *soak* into absorptive materials.

Blanketing/Covering

As the title implies, this spill-control measure involves blanketing or covering the surface of the spill to prevent dispersion of materials such as powders or dusts. Blanketing or covering of solids can be done with tarps, plastic sheeting, salvage covers, or other materials (including foam), but consideration must be given to compatibility between the material being covered and the material covering it. Covering may also be done as a form of temporary mitigation for radioactive and biological substances.

Blanketing of liquids is essentially the same as vapor suppression (see Vapor Suppression section), because it primarily uses an appropriate aqueous (water) foam agent to cover the surface of the spill. Operational-Level responders may or may not be allowed to perform blanketing/covering actions, depending on the hazards of the material, the nature of the incident, and the distance from which they must operate to ensure their safety.

Dike, Dam, Diversion, and Retention

[NFPA 472: 5.3.2(2)(b), 5.4.4(3)(b), 5.4.4(3)(c), 5.4.4(3)(d), 5.4.4(3)(e), 5.4.4(3)(f)]

Diking, damming, diverting, and retaining are ways to confine a hazardous material. These actions are taken to control the flow of liquid hazardous materials away from the point of discharge. Responders can use available earthen materials or materials carried on their response vehicles to construct curbs that direct or divert the flow away from gutters, drains, storm sewers, flood-control channels, and outfalls (**Figure 5.12**). In some cases, it may be desirable to direct the flow into certain locations in order to capture and retain the material for later pickup and disposal. Dams may be built that permit surface water or runoff to pass over the dam while holding back the hazardous material. Any construction materials that contact the spilled material must be properly disposed of.

Figure 5.12 These responders are building an overflow dam to trap a hazardous material that has a specific gravity greater than 1. The water will flow out the pipes at the top while the heavier hazardous material will be trapped behind the barrier. *Courtesy of Rich Mahaney.*

Lt. Hartin's crew constructed a circle dike around the storm drain located outside the hot zone in order to keep any of the leaking 1,2-butylene oxide and/or runoff from entering it.

Vapor Suppression

[NFPA 472: 5.3.2(2)(f), 5.4.4(3)(h)]

Vapor suppression is the action taken to reduce the emission of vapors at a haz mat spill. Fire-fighting foams are effective on spills of flammable and combustible liquids if the foam concentrate is compatible with the material **(Figure 5.13)**. Water-miscible (capable of being mixed) materials such as alcohols, esters, and ketones destroy regular fire-fighting foams and require an alcohol-resistant foam agent. In general, the required application rate for applying foam to control an unignited liquid spill is substantially less than that required to extinguish a spill fire.

Figure 5.13 Fire-fighting foams may be used to suppress hazardous vapors at haz mat incidents. *Courtesy of Chad Love.*

Knowing that foam would be the best option for vapor suppression and/or extinguishment of 1,2-butylene oxide, Ace Command directed Engine 2 to deploy a foam line. Lt. Allen and Firefighter Jirka extended a 2½-inch (65 mm) hoseline to the access door of the warehouse, and Driver/Operator Wright then supplied this hoseline with a 3-percent aqueous film forming foam (AFFF) (commonly pronounced *A-triple-F*) solution using an alcohol-type concentrate (AFFF-ATC).

What Type of Foam Concentrate Should Be Used?

The orange section of the current *ERG* provides information on what type of foam to use. For polar/water-miscible liquids, it recommends alcohol-resistant foam. For nonpolar/water-immiscible liquids, it recommends regular foam **(Figure 5.14)**.

ERG2000 **FLAMMABLE LIQUIDS (POLAR/WATER-MISCIBLE)** **GUIDE 127**

EMERGENCY RESPONSE

FIRE
CAUTION: All these products have a very low flash point: Use of water spray when fighting fire may be inefficient.

Small Fires
• Dry chemical, CO$_2$, water spray or alcohol-resistant foam.

Large Fires
• Water spray, fog or alcohol-resistant foam.
• Use water spray or fog; do not use straight streams.
• Move containers from fire area if you can do it without risk.

Fire involving Tanks or Car/Trailer Loads
• Fight fire from maximum distance or use unmanned hose holders or monitor nozzles.
• Cool containers with flooding quantities of water until well after fire is out.
• Withdraw immediately in case of rising sound from venting safety devices or discoloration of tank.
• ALWAYS stay away from tanks engulfed in fire.
• For massive fire, use unmanned hose holders or monitor nozzles; if this is impossible, withdraw from area and let fire burn.

SPILL OR LEAK
• ELIMINATE all ignition sources (no smoking, flares, sparks or flames in immediate area).
• All equipment used when handling the product must be grounded.
• Do not touch or walk through spilled material.
• Stop leak if you can do it without risk.

Figure 5.14 The orange-bordered pages of the *ERG* provide information on what type of foam to use. Alcohol-resistant foams should be used on polar/water-miscible liquids. Regular foam may be used on spills of nonpolar/water-immiscible liquids.

Foam concentrates vary in their finished-foam quality and, therefore, their effectiveness for suppressing vapors. Foam quality is measured in terms of its 25-percent-drainage time and its expansion ratio. *Drainage time* is the time required for one-fourth (25 percent or quarter) of the total liquid solution to drain from the foam. *Expansion ratio* is the volume of finished foam that results from a unit volume of foam solution.

Long drainage times result in long-lasting foam blankets. The greater the expansion ratio is, the thicker the foam blanket that can be developed in a given period of time. All Class B foam concentrates

(see Fire Control section), except the special foams made for acid and alkaline spills, may be used for both fire fighting and vapor suppression. Air-aspirating nozzles produce a larger expansion ratio than do water fog nozzles.

First responders must exercise care when applying any of the foams onto a spill. All foams (except fluoroprotein types) should not be plunged directly into the spill but applied onto the ground at the edge of the spill and rolled gently onto the material **(Figure 5.15)**. If the spill surrounds some type of obstacle, the foam can be banked off the obstacle **(Figure 5.16)**. Another foam application method is the rainfall method. Foam is sprayed into the air over the target area in a fog pattern. The tiny foam droplets *rain* down over the spill. As the foam bubbles burst, the foam bleeds together to form a film over the fuel. When possible, first responders should use air-aspirating nozzles for vapor suppression rather than water fog nozzles.

Selection of the proper foam concentrate for vapor suppression is important. Because finished foam is composed principally of water, it should

Figure 5.15 The roll-on method of foam application is performed by directing the foam stream at the front edge of the spill.

Figure 5.16 The bank-down method of foam application relies on a vertical surface from which to deflect the foam stream.

not be used to cover water-reactive materials. Some fuels destroy foam bubbles, so a foam concentrate must be selected that is compatible with the liquid as mentioned earlier. Other points to consider when using foam for vapor suppression are as follows:

- Water destroys and washes away foam blankets; do not use water streams in conjunction with the application of foam.

- A material must be below its boiling point; foam cannot seal vapors of boiling liquids.

- If the film that precedes the foam blanket is not visible (such as with AFFF blankets), the foam blanket may be unreliable. Reapply aerated foam periodically until the spill is completely covered.

First responders must be trained in the techniques of vapor suppression. Training for extinguishment of flammable liquid fires does not necessarily qualify a first responder to mitigate vapors produced by haz mat spills. More information on foam application is contained in the Fire Control section.

Other Spill Control Tactics

Rather than attempting to confine the dispersion, some defensive spill control tactics are aimed at reducing the amount of harm caused by the material by diluting the concentration or changing its physical and/or chemical properties. These tactics include the following:

- Ventilation
- Vapor dispersion
- Dispersion
- Dilution
- Dissolution

This section also discusses *neutralization,* which is considered an offensive containment tactic by many experts. However, neutralization is aimed at reducing or eliminating the chemical hazard of the material rather than physically containing it. The tactics of dilution, neutralization, and dissolution are used only infrequently at haz mat incidents and under very specific circumstances.

Ventilation

Ventilation involves controlling the movement of air by natural or mechanical means. Ventilation is used to remove and/or disperse harmful airborne particles, vapors, or gases when spills occur inside structures. The same ventilation techniques used for smoke removal can be used for haz mat incidents (see IFSTA's **Essentials of Fire Fighting** manual). When conducting negative-pressure ventilation, fans and other ventilators must be compatible with the atmosphere where they are being operated. Equipment must be *explosion proof* in a flammable atmosphere **(Figure 5.17).** When choosing the type of ventilation to use, remember that positive-pressure ventilation is usually more effective than negative-pressure ventilation when it comes to removing atmospheric contaminants. Some experts consider ventilation to be a type of vapor dispersion.

Ace Command decided to set up positive-pressure ventilation to assist in dispersing the vapors inside the warehouse. Because the wind was blowing from S.E. to N.W., a ventilation fan was set up on the S.E. side of the building, enabling natural ventilation to assist the mechanical ventilation.

Figure 5.17 Fans and other ventilators must be compatible with the atmosphere. Using a *nonexplosion proof* fan in a flammable or explosive atmosphere could cause a fire or explosion.

Vapor Dispersion
[NFPA 472: 5.3.2(2)(e), 5.4.4(3)(g)]

Vapor dispersion is the action taken to direct or influence the course of airborne hazardous materials. Pressurized streams of water from hoselines or unattended master streams may be used to help disperse vapors **(Figure 5.18)**. These streams create turbulence, which increases the rate of mixing with air and reduces the concentration of the hazardous material. After using hoselines for vapor dispersion, it is necessary for first responders to confine and analyze runoff water for possible contamination.

Dispersion

Dispersion (as opposed to *vapor dispersion*) involves breaking up or dispersing a hazardous material that has spilled on a solid or liquid surface. Both chemical and biological agents have been used for this purpose, usually on hydrocarbon spills such as oceanic crude oil. Dispersion often has the unfortunate effect of spreading the material over a wide area, however, and the process itself

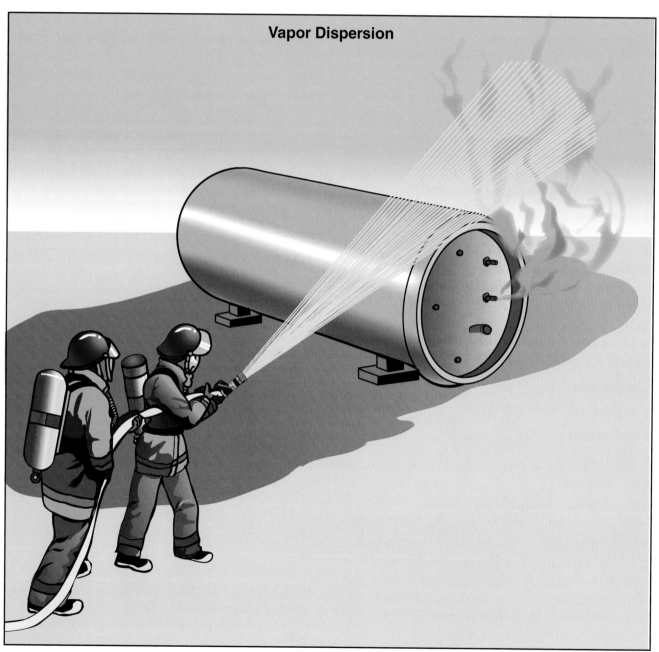

Vapor Dispersion

Figure 5.18 Vapor dispersion actions using pressurized water streams can prevent toxic gases or vapors from moving downwind, but contaminated runoff water from this procedure can create its own problems.

may cause additional problems. Because of these problems, the use of dispersants may require the approval of government authorities.

Dilution

[NFPA 472: 5.3.2(2)(c)]

Dilution is the application of water to a water-soluble material to reduce the hazard. Dilution of liquid materials rarely has practical applications at haz mat incidents in terms of spill control; dilution is often used during decontamination operations. The amount of water needed to reach an effective dilution increases overall volume and creates a runoff problem. This situation is especially true of slightly water-soluble liquids. Dilution may be useful when very small amounts of corrosive material are involved such as in a minor accident in a laboratory, but even then, it is generally considered for use only after other methods have been rejected.

Dissolution

The process of dissolving a gas in water is called *dissolution*. This tactic can only be used on water-soluble gases such as anhydrous ammonia or chlorine and is generally conducted by applying a fog stream to a breach in a container or directly onto the spill. Ideally, the escaping gas then passes through the water and dissolves. When considering this option, first responders must remember that it may create additional problems with contaminated runoff water and other issues. For example, using water spray at a chlorine incident to bring the vapors to the ground may have the beneficial effect of reducing or eliminating a toxic plume, but it may also create hydrochloric acid on the ground with all the complications associated with that chemical.

Neutralization

Some hazardous materials may be neutralized to minimize the amount of harm they do upon contact. Usually, *neutralization* involves raising or lowering the pH of corrosive materials to render them *neutral* (pH 7). However, the term can be applied to any chemical reaction that reduces the hazard of the material. Neutralization is a difficult process; for example, adding too much of a neutralizer can cause a pH shift in the opposite direction.

Neutralization should only be conducted (with few exceptions) under the direction of individuals with considerable expertise in this area. Neutralization is usually *not* an effective option for spills over 100 gallons (379 L). An Operational-Level responder might be allowed to conduct neutralization in cases where a very small amount of material is involved such as putting lime on a small spill of battery acid.

Spill Control Summary

Table 5.1, p. 300, provides a summary of the spill control tactics that can be used on different types of releases and their resulting dispersions. It also provides an example of a task related to one of the appropriate tactics.

NFPA 472 specifically identifies the following actions as defensive control tactics that Operational-Level emergency responders can take:

- Absorption
- Dike, dam, diversion, and retention
- Dilution
- Remote valve shutoff (see Leak Control/ Containment section)
- Vapor dispersion
- Vapor suppression

Leak Control/ Containment

[NFPA 472: 5.3.2(1), 5.3.2(2)(d), 5.4.4(4)]

A *leak* involves the physical breach in a container through which product is escaping. The goal of *leak control* is to stop or limit *the escape* or to *contain* the release either in its original container or by transferring it to a new one **(Figure 5.19, p. 301).** The type of container involved, the type of breach, and properties of the material determine tactics and tasks relating to leak control. Leak control and containment are generally considered offensive actions. Offensive actions are not attempted by personnel trained below the Technician Level with two exceptions: The first is turning off a remote valve **(Figure 5.20, p. 301).** The second involves situations dealing with gasoline, diesel, liquefied petroleum gas (LPG), and natural gas fuels. With

Table 5.1
Spill Control Tactics Used According to Type of Release

Type of Release	Type of Dispersion	Spill Control Tactics	Task Example
Liquid: Airborne Vapor	Hemispheric, cloud, plume, or cone	• Vapor Suppression • Ventilation • Vapor Dispersion • Dissolution	Cover spill with vapor suppressing foam (Vapor Suppression)
Liquid: Surface	Stream	• Diking • Diversion • Retention • Adsorption • Absorption	Dig a ditch to divert a spill away from a stream (Diversion)
Liquid: Surface	Pool	• Absorption • Adsorption (for shallow spills) • Neutralization	Cover spill with an absorbent pillow (Absorption)
Liquid: Surface	Irregular	• Dilution • Absorption • Neutralization	Spray slightly contaminated surfaces with water (Dilution)
Liquid: Waterborne Contamination	Stream or pool	• Damming • Diversion • Retention • Absorption • Dispersion	Place absorbent booms across a river (Absorption)
Solid: Airborne Particles	Hemispheric, cloud, plume, or cone	• Particle Dispersion/ Ventilation • Particle Suppression (wetting material) • Blanketing/Covering	Set up ventilation fans (Particle Dispersion/Ventilation)
Solid: Surface	Pile	• Blanketing/Covering • Vacuuming	Cover spilled material with a tarp or salvage cover (Blanketing/Covering)
Solid: Surface	Irregular	• Blanketing/Covering • Dilution • Dissolution	Spray scattered sprinkles of corrosive powders or dusts with water (Dilution)
Gas: Airborne Gas	Hemispheric, cloud, plume, or cone	• Ventilation • Vapor Dispersion • Dissolution	Spray leaking cylinder with fog stream (Dissolution)

these fuels, Operational-Level responders can take offensive actions provided they have appropriate training, procedures, equipment, and PPE.

Leak control dictates that personnel enter the hot zone, which puts them at great risk. The IC must remember that the level of training and equipment provided to personnel are limiting factors in performing leak control. A list of leak control/ containment tactics follows; however, the scope of this book does not include discussing each of them (except for remote valve shutoff activation):

• Remote valve shutoff activation (control of release)
• Patching/plugging
• Overpacking
• Product transfer
• Crimping

Figure 5.19 Leak control is aimed at containing the material to prevent further release by such tactics as plugging, patching, and/or overpacking.

Figure 5.20 Operational-Level responders may stop the flow of hazardous materials by operating remote shut-off valves.

- Valve actuation
- Vacuuming
- Pressure isolation and reduction
- Solidification

In some situations it may be safe and acceptable for Operational-Level responders to operate emergency remote shutoff valves on cargo tank trucks. The locations and types of remote shutoff valves vary depending on the truck (**Figures 5.21 a and b, p. 302**).

Piping systems and pipelines carrying hazardous materials may have remote shutoff or control valves that can be operated to stop the flow of product to the incident area without entering the hot zone. For example, by closing remote valves feeding a broken natural gas line, the flow of gas to the break can be stopped. A significant amount of product may release for some time before the flow stops. In most cases, onsite maintenance personnel or local utility workers know where these valves are located and can be given the authority and responsibility for closing them under the direction of the IC. However, Operational-Level first responders who are trained and authorized to operate shutoff valves at their facilities in the event of emergency may do so in accordance with their SOPs.

Figures 5.21 a and b Locations and types of remote shutoff valves on cargo tank trucks vary, depending on the truck. (*Left*) Shutoff valve on a nonpressure liquid tank. (*Right*) Shutoff valve on a corrosive liquid tank.

Fire Control

Fire control is the strategy of minimizing the damage, harm, and effect of fire at a haz mat incident. Typical fire-control tactics include the following:

- Controlled burn
- Exposure protection
- Withdrawal
- Extinguishment

Obviously, if a fire is present in addition to a release (spill or leak), the incident is considerably more complicated. Based on risk and hazard assessment, a decision must be made whether to extinguish the fire (*extinguishment*), and if so, how. If the products of combustion are less of a hazard than the leaking chemical, the best course of action may be to protect exposures (*exposure protection*) and let the fire burn until the fuel is consumed (*controlled burn*). If there is a threat of boiling liquid expanding vapor explosion (BLEVE) or other explosion or if the resources needed to control the incident are unavailable, *withdrawal* may be the safest (and best) tactical option **(Figure 5.22).**

The location of an incident also influences the decision on attempting extinguishment. If the location is in a rural area that is sparsely populated, the decision to let a fire consume the fuel is much easier than if it is in the central business district

Figure 5.22 Withdrawing at least half a mile (0.8 km) may be the safest (and best) tactical option if there is a threat of BLEVE.

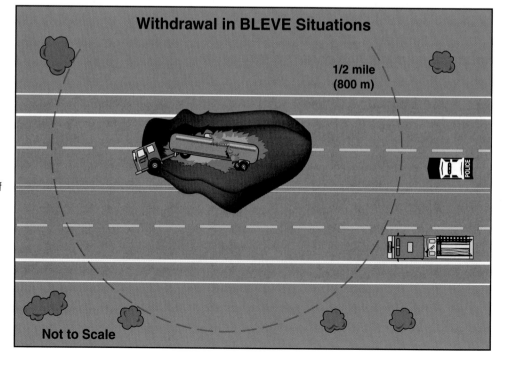

Withdrawal in BLEVE Situations

1/2 mile
(800 m)

POLICE

Not to Scale

of a major city. First responders must weigh all options and choose the course that presents the least risk to response personnel and the general public. The potential for harm is always more important than convenience. In some circumstances, if the identity of the material(s) is not known, it may be better to let the material burn and concentrate on protecting life and surrounding property.

The following sections discuss the tactics of controlled burn, exposure protection, withdrawal, and extinguishment. The Foam Operations/Principles section also details the special hazards of closed containers and foam principles in extinguishment and vapor suppression and provides more information about the use of foam at haz mat incidents.

Controlled Burn

A controlled burn is a nonintervention control tactic. When personnel or environmental risks are determined to be too great for extinguishment, the practice of letting hazardous materials burn until

Natural Gas Fires

It is generally best to let a natural gas fire consume the fuel unless responders can stop the flow of gas by closing a valve at some distant point outside the hot zone. Even after closing a distant valve, some gas is still in the line(s). Use fog streams to keep the area cooled and let the fire consume the fuel **(Figure 5.23)**.

Incidents may exist where it is necessary to extinguish a gas fire in order to access a valve to turn off the flow. Use large amounts of water fog to cool the area, and use dry chemical or CO_2 extinguishers to extinguish the fire. Extinguishing the fire without stopping the flow of gas is dangerous because gas and air may form an explosive mixture. If the surrounding area is still hot, it may provide an ignition source and cause an explosion. An explosion may cause more injuries and more property damage than the original fire.

Figure 5.23 Before extinguishing a pipeline fire, turn off the fuel flow by closing the closest control valve upstream of the incident. Leave the valves downstream open to drain the remaining product from the line.

they are consumed is an appropriate option. This process is particularly useful when dealing with pesticides and flammable liquids when the fire temperature is hot enough to destroy the product. Personnel can let the fire burn freely to destroy as much of the material as possible, but they must be aware of the possibility of downwind contamination from smoke. Protecting exposures during a controlled burn can also be a problem because of the time it takes for fuel consumption.

First responders should extinguish burning spills and leaks completely only when the flow of materials has been or can be immediately controlled. When shutoffs cannot be accomplished immediately, hoselines and other portable equipment can be used to decrease the intensity of a fire while permitting controlled burning at the leak site.

Exposure Protection (Fire)

When hazardous materials incidents involve fire, consideration must be given to protecting exposures. Typical exposures include nearby buildings, structures, or other containers of hazardous materials. Because containers of hazardous materials are often stored close to each other at fixed facilities, it may be extremely important to protect other containers by cooling them or, in some cases, actually remove them from the scene if possible **(Figure 5.24)**.

When containers or tanks of flammable liquids or gases are exposed to flame impingement, apply solid streams (500 to 1,000 gallons/minute or gpm [1 893 L/min to 3 785 L/min] or more) from their maximum effective reach in order to prevent a BLEVE. This cooling can best be achieved on tanks by lobbing a stream along its top so that water runs down both sides. This water stream cools the tank's vapor space. Also cool steel supports under tanks to prevent their collapse.

Fires burning around relief valves or piping should not be extinguished unless turning off the supply can stop the leaking product. An increase in the intensity of sounds or fire issuing from a relief valve may indicate that rupture of the vessel is imminent. Do not assume that relief valves are sufficient to safely relieve excess pressures under severe

Figure 5.24 Protect exposures by cooling them with water, or remove them entirely when it is safe to do so (such as moving pallets of flammable liquids away from a fire with a forklift).

fire conditions. The rupture of both large and small flammable liquid vessels that have been subjected to flame impingement has killed responders.

Withdrawal

Withdrawal from the scene may become a last resort if an incident rapidly deteriorates or a threat of explosion, BLEVE, or mass fire exists. Withdrawing may also become necessary when the resources needed to control the incident are overwhelmed or unavailable.

Extinguishment

When a haz mat incident involves a fire, the tactical priority may be fire extinguishment: an offensive control tactic. In some cases (such as fire around a leaking gasoline tanker), it may be necessary to extinguish the fire before containing the material. In other cases (such as a pressurized natural gas fire), it is the containment of the gas (turning off the supply) that actually extinguishes the fire.

The practice of fire and emergency services organizations has always been to attack fires aggressively. However, this approach may not be the best one when a fire involves a hazardous material. The IC should always carefully evaluate the situation before committing personnel to fire suppression. When the IC considers it safe and appropriate to begin fire suppression, sufficient fire-suppression capabilities must be available to attack the fire and to protect each exposure. Extinguishing methods include the use of fire/fog streams, extinguishers, or foam.

Water Fire Streams

First responders applying water fire streams must avoid making the situation worse. Fire streams can dramatically increase the size and intensity of a fire. Increased size adds to the runoff from a spill. When extinguishing agents are applied to burning tanks, they could overflow and threaten adjacent containers. Runoff from fire streams applied to hazardous materials needs to be confined until it can be analyzed.

Solid water streams cause powders and other materials to spread about in an uncontrolled manner. Solid streams directed into burning liquids splash the burning materials and may spread the fire. When operating at a fixed facility, first responders should know in advance how much water they have available for fire fighting. At a transportation incident, the volume of water needed to safely attack a fire may not be available. The best option in this situation may be to *back off and protect the exposures.*

Fog streams from unattended monitors or even large-volume hoselines that are secured in place can be effective in knocking down or suppressing vapors. However, monitors/hoselines need to have a continuous supply of water. Through the use of fog streams, water may also dissipate flammable vapors. Fog streams aid in dilution and dispersion, and these streams can control (to a small degree) the movement of vapors to a desired location. Be aware that mist falling back to the ground from this action is now contaminated and must be managed.

Runoff management may be done by diking or damming well in front of runoff materials. Care must be taken to keep personnel out of danger from contamination or contact with the materials. Pits may be dug also to contain runoff. With some chemicals, diluting the runoff water in a pit may reduce the hazard to a more manageable level. Sometimes it is desirable to knock down the vapors from a product that is water-reactive. Under these circumstances, care must be taken to not let the water splash onto the material. Set up monitors well in front of the material and be aware of changes in the wind direction or speed.

Water from hoselines can be used to move Class B fuels (burning or not) to areas where they can safely burn or where ignition sources are more easily controlled. Fuels must never be flushed down drains or sewers. Use appropriate fog patterns for protection from radiant heat and to prevent *plunging* the stream into the burning liquid, which causes increased production of flammable vapors and greatly increases fire intensity. Move the stream slowly from side to side, and *sweep* the fuel or fire to the desired location. Care must be taken to keep the leading edge of the fog pattern in contact with the fuel surface or else the fire may run underneath the stream and flash back around the attack crew.

When small leaks occur, apply a solid stream directly to the container opening to hold the escaping liquid back. The pressure of the stream must exceed that of the leaking material in order for this procedure to work properly. Care must be taken to not overflow the container.

Portable Extinguishers

Halon-alternative agents, CO_2, and dry chemicals are effective on many flammable and combustible liquids. The limiting factor is the method of application. Generally, these agents come in handheld extinguishers that require responders to get within a few feet (meters) of the fire. With most hazardous materials, that distance is too close for first responders at the Operational Level. Handheld equipment is meant for first-aid fire fighting and small fires.

Some industrial facilities have special extinguishers on wheels or vehicles containing dry chemical or CO_2. Many large fire and emergency services organizations also have this equipment. These extinguisher types are better able to fight large fires. Fires involving combustible metals usually require *dry powder* extinguishers (do *not* confuse with dry chemical; they are not the same).

Foam Fire Streams

Finished foam can be very effective for suppressing vapors and extinguishing many flammable liquids. Some materials such as alcohols and amines are water-soluble and dissolve ordinary foam. Check the foam concentrate supplier and the container label for the uses and limitations of a particular foam concentrate. The use of foam on materials that are water-reactive may not be desirable. The reaction may be so great that it outweighs the benefits of using foam. If attacking a fire with foam, be sure to have enough foam at the scene before beginning the attack. Starting without enough concentrate to finish the job may cause the fire to rekindle and destroy the foam blanket already applied. See Foam Operations/Principles section for more information.

Foam Operations/ Principles

[NFPA 472: 5.4.4(1), 5.4.4]

Extinguishment of flammable and combustible liquid haz mat fires requires properly applied foam in adequate quantities. All first responders must be knowledgeable in the principles of foam, the different types of foam concentrate, foam proportioning, application rates, and how to assemble a foam fire stream system.

All foam concentrates in use today are of the mechanical type; that is, they must be proportioned (mixed with water) and aerated (mixed with air) before they can be used. These mechanical foam concentrates are divided into two general categories: those intended for use on Class A fuels (ordinary combustibles) and those for use on Class B fuels (flammable and combustible liquids). Foam concentrates must match the fuel to which they are applied to be effective. Class A foam concentrates are not designed to extinguish Class B fires. For that reason, this section will focus primarily on Class B foams.

First responders must also be aware that there are significant differences in Class B foam concentrates. For example, concentrates designed solely for hydrocarbon fires (such as regular fluoroprotein and regular AFFF) will not extinguish polar solvent (alcohol-type fuel) fires regardless of the concentration at which they are used. However, foam concentrates that are intended for polar solvents may be used on hydrocarbon fires. The *ERG* provides guidance on when alcohol-resistant foam should be used for a particular material.

CAUTION

Failure to match the proper foam concentrate with the fuel may result in an unsuccessful extinguishing attempt and could endanger fire and emergency services responders.

Foam extinguishes and/or prevents fire by the following methods (**Figure 5.25**):

- *Separating* — Creates a barrier between the fuel and burning vapors

- *Cooling* — Lowers the temperature of the fuel and adjacent surfaces

- *Suppressing* (sometimes referred to as *smothering*) — Prevents the release of additional flammable vapors, access to oxygen in the at-

How Foam Works

Separates
Smothers
Cools

Suppresses

Figure 5.25 Foam prevents ignition and extinguishes fire by cooling, smothering, separating, and suppressing vapors.

mosphere, and therefore reduces the possibility of ignition or reignition

More detailed information about using Class B foam at incidents involving flammable and combustible liquid spills is provided in the IFSTA manual, **Principles of Foam Fire Fighting,** 2nd edition, but a general summary of important information is provided in the following sections.

How Foam Is Generated

Before discussing the foam-making process, it is important to understand the following terms **(Figure 5.26)**:

- *Foam concentrate* — Liquid found in a foam storage container before the introduction of water, typically found as 1-, 3-, or 6-percent concentrates
- *Foam solution* — Mixture in the proper ratio of foam concentrate and water before the introduction of air
- *Foam proportioner* — Device that mixes foam concentrate in the proper ratio with water
- *Finished foam* — Completed product after air is introduced into the foam solution and after it leaves the nozzle or aerator

Four elements are necessary to produce high-quality foam: foam concentrate, water, air, and mechanical agitation. These elements must be blended in the correct ratios. Removing any element results in either no foam or poor-quality foam **(Figure 5.27, p. 308)**. Finished foam is produced in two stages. First, water is mixed with foam liquid concentrate to form a foam solution (proportioning stage). Second, the foam solution passes through the piping or hose to a foam nozzle or sprinkler that aerates the foam solution to form finished foam (aeration stage). Aeration produces an adequate amount of foam bubbles to form an effective foam

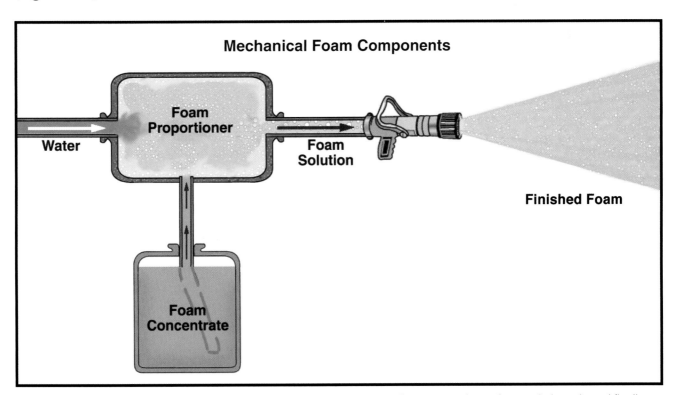

Mechanical Foam Components

Water

Foam Proportioner

Foam Solution

Finished Foam

Foam Concentrate

Figure 5.26 The foam-making process includes water, foam concentrate, foam proportioner, foam solution, air, and finally finished foam.

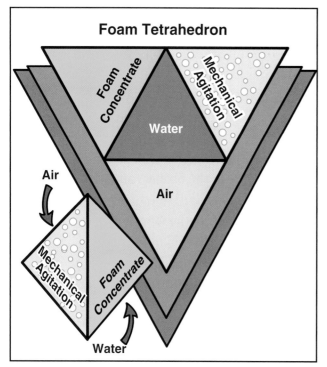

Foam Tetrahedron

Figure 5.27 Four elements are necessary to produce high-quality foam: foam concentrate, water, air, and mechanical agitation.

Figure 5.28 Foam containers are marked for proportioning ratio and the intended hazard type. *Courtesy of Kidde Fire Fighting.*

blanket. Proper aeration also produces uniform-sized bubbles that form a long lasting blanket. A good foam blanket maintains an effective cover over a fuel.

Proportioners and foam nozzles or sprinklers are engineered to work together. Using a foam proportioner that is not hydraulically matched to the foam nozzle or sprinkler (even if the two are made by the same manufacturer) can result in either unsatisfactory foam or no foam. Numerous appliances are available for making and applying foam. A number of these are discussed later in this section.

Specific Foam Concentrates

[NFPA 472: 5.4.4(2)]
Class B foam concentrates are manufactured from either a synthetic or protein base. Protein-based foam concentrates are derived from animal protein. Synthetic foam concentrates are made from mixtures of fluorosurfactants. Some foam concentrates are made from a combination of synthetic and protein bases.

Regular protein foam. *[NFPA 472: 5.4.4(2)(a)]* The use of regular protein foam concentrates started before World War II. These foams are virtually nonexistent in today's municipal, industrial, or military fire service. Although rare, regular protein foam concentrate may still be found in some fixed fire-suppression systems. However, modern derivatives such as film forming fluoroprotein (FFFP) foam and AFFF are in service worldwide. Regular protein foam concentrate is derived from naturally occurring sources of protein such as hoof, horn, or feather meal. The protein meal is hydrolyzed in the presence of lime and converted to a protein liquid. Other components such as foam stabilizers, corrosion inhibitors, antimicrobial agents, and freezing-point depressants are then added **(Figure 5.28).**

Regular protein foam generally has very good heat stability, but it is not as mobile or fluid on the fuel surface as synthetic-based foam concentrates or modern fluoroprotein derivatives. Regular protein foam concentrate is very susceptible to fuel pickup; consequently, care should be taken to minimize submergence through plunging of the foam stream into the fuel. Regular protein foam concentrates have the following characteristics:

- Available in 3- and 6-percent concentrations
- Excellent water-retention capabilities
- High heat resistance
- Performance affected by freezing and thawing
- Stores at temperatures ranging from 35 to 120°F (2°C to 49°C)
- Compounded for freeze protection using a non-flammable antifreeze solution
- Not compatible with dry-chemical extinguishing agents
- Only used on hydrocarbon fuels

Fluoroprotein foam. *[NFPA 472: 5.4.4(2)(b)]* Fluoroprotein foam concentrate, a combination protein-based and synthetic-based foam concentrate, is derived from protein foam concentrates to which fluorochemical surfactants are added. The fluorochemical surfactants are similar to those developed for AFFF concentrates (described later) but are used in much lower concentrations. The addition of these chemicals produces finished foam that flows across fuel surfaces rapidly. Because of these surfactants, fluoroprotein foam concentrates are oleophobic (oil shedding) and well suited for subsurface injection: a process by which foam solution is pumped into the bottom of a burning petroleum tank and then floats to the top to form a fire-extinguishing foam blanket (**Figure 5.29**). Fluoroprotein foam concentrates have the following characteristics:

- Available in 3- and 6-percent concentrations
- Stores at temperatures ranging from 35 to 120°F (2°C to 49°C); however, can be freeze-protected with nonflammable antifreeze solution
- Performance not affected by freezing and thawing
- Premixable for short periods of time (based on the manufacturer's recommendations)

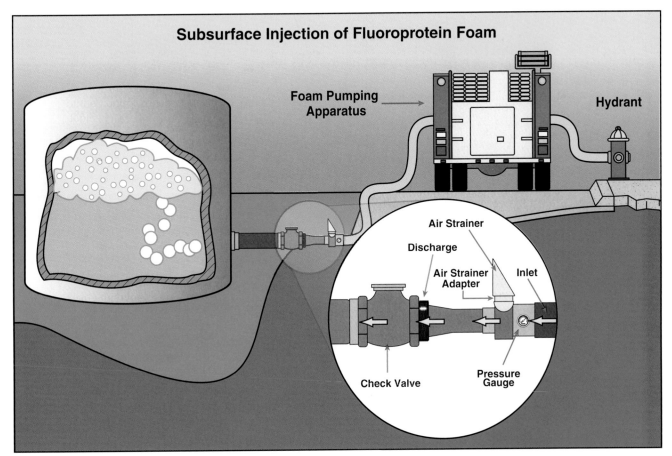

Figure 5.29 Fluoroprotein foam is very effective for subsurface injection into flammable liquid storage tanks. This illustration shows the method generally used for this application.

- Maintains rather low viscosity at low temperatures

- Compatible with simultaneous application of dry-chemical extinguishing agents

- Delivered through air-aspirating equipment

- Suitable for use on gasoline that has been blended with oxygen additives

Fluoroprotein foam concentrates can be formulated to be alcohol-resistant by adding ammonia salts that are suspended in organic solvents. Alcohol-resistant fluoroprotein foam concentrate maintains its alcohol-resistive properties for about 15 minutes. Alcohol-resistant fluoroprotein foam concentrates have a very high degree of heat resistance and water retention.

Film forming fluoroprotein foam. FFFP foam concentrate is based on fluoroprotein foam technology with AFFF concentrate capabilities. This FFFP foam concentrate incorporates the benefits of AFFF concentrate for fast fire knockdown and the benefits of fluoroprotein foam concentrate for long-lasting heat resistance. FFFP foams have the following characteristics:

- Available in 3- and 6-percent concentrations

- Stores at temperatures ranging from 35 to 120°F (2°C to 49°C) with fair low-temperature viscosity

- Stores premixed in portable fire extinguishers and fire apparatus water tanks (Refer to the manufacturer for long-term storage recommendations.)

- Compatible with simultaneous application of dry-chemical fire-fighting agents

- Performance not affected by freezing and thawing

- Uses either freshwater or saltwater

FFFP foam concentrate is available in an alcohol-resistant formulation. Alcohol-resistant FFFP foam concentrate has all the fire-fighting capabilities of regular FFFP foam concentrate, including some of the following advantages:

- ***Multipurpose*** — Can be used on polar solvent fuels at 6-percent and on hydrocarbon fuels at 3-percent concentrations (New concentrates that can be used at 3-percent concentrations on either type of fuel are also available.)

- ***Storage*** — Can be stored at temperatures ranging from 35 to 120°F (2°C to 49°C)

- ***Premixable*** — Can be mixed into a solution and stored ready for use

- ***Subsurface injection*** — Can be used for subsurface injection applications

- ***Plunge into fuel*** — Can be plunged into the fuel during application

Aqueous film forming foam. *[NFPA 472: 5.4.4(2)(d)]* With the introduction of high-expansion detergent-based foam, the U.S. Navy became interested in using that technology to improve their flammable liquid fire-fighting capabilities on aircraft carriers. The resulting research work was called *Project Light Water*. The 3M Company later trademarked the term *Light Water*™. The U.S. Navy discovered that when a fluorinated surfactant was added to detergent foam concentrates, the water that drained from the foam blanket actually floated on jet fuel spills. This film is known as an *aqueous film* (**Figure 5.30**). In order to identify the class of foam concentrate providing a film, the NFPA foam committee introduced the term *aqueous film forming foam (AFFF) concentrate*. AFFF is the most commonly used foam concentrate today.

AFFF concentrate is completely synthetic. It consists of fluorochemical and hydrocarbon surfactants combined with high boiling point solvents and water. Fluorochemical surfactants reduce the surface tension of water to a degree less than the surface tension of the hydrocarbon so that a thin aqueous film can spread across the fuel. AFFF has the following characteristics:

- Available in 1-, 3-, and 6-percent concentrations for use with either freshwater or saltwater

- Premixable in portable fire extinguishers and apparatus water tanks

- Stores at temperatures ranging from 25 to 120°F (-5°C to 49°C) (Freezing and thawing do not adversely affect AFFF concentrates, but consult the manufacturer for details.)

- Freeze-protective with a nonflammable antifreeze solution

- Good low-temperature viscosity

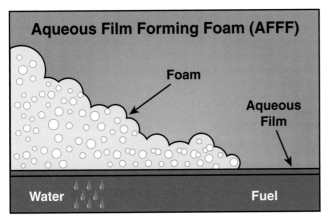

Aqueous Film Forming Foam (AFFF)

Foam

Aqueous Film

Water   Fuel

Figure 5.30 The film of aqueous film forming foam (AFFF) floats on the surface of a fuel, spreading ahead of the foam blanket.

- Suitable for subsurface injection
- Fair penetrating capabilities in baled storage fuels or high surface-tension fuels such as treated wood
- Compatible with dry-chemical extinguishing agents
- Rather fast draining (Reapply AFFF finished foam often to maintain hot-spill security.)
- Film-forming characteristics adversely affected by fuels in excess of 140°F (60°C)
- Oxygen additives (mandated by EPA) in blended gasoline can adversely affect film-forming characteristics; solvent-based performance additives in reformulated gasoline can also hamper AFFF's performance

When AFFF (as well as the previously mentioned FFFP) finished foam is applied to a hydrocarbon fire, the following three things occur:

- An air/vapor-excluding film is released ahead of the foam blanket.
- The fast-moving foam blanket then moves across the fuel's surface and around objects, adding further insulation.
- As the aerated (7:1 to 20:1) foam blanket continues to drain its water, more film is released. This gives AFFF finished foam the ability to *heal* areas where the foam blanket has been disturbed.

Alcohol-resistant AFFF. *[NFPA 472: 5.4.4 (2)(c), 5.4.4(2)(c)(i), 5.4.4(2)(c)(ii)]* Another class of AFFF concentrates is composed of alcohol-resistant concentrates (AR-

AFFF). They are available from most foam manufacturers. On most polar solvents, alcohol-resistant AFFF concentrates are used at 3- or 6-percent (3:97 or 6:94 water/concentrate ratios) use concentrations, depending on the particular brand selected. Stronger polar solvents require application rates that are higher than those required for weaker solvents or hydrocarbons. Alcohol-resistant AFFF solutions can also be used on hydrocarbon fires at 3-percent (3:97 ratio) proportions.

Concentrates designed to be proportioned at 3 percent on hydrocarbon fuels and 6 percent (6:94 ratio) on polar solvent fuels are commonly referred to as *3 by 6* concentrates. Concentrates proportioned at 3 percent on both types of fuels are called *3 by 3* concentrates. Recently developed AR-AFFF concentrates are available in 1-by-3-percent formulations: Use at 1 percent (1:99) for hydrocarbon spills that are 1 inch (25 mm) or less in depth and 3 percent (3:97) for hydrocarbon spills that are more than 1 inch (25 mm) in depth or polar solvents.

When alcohol-resistant AFFF concentrates are applied to polar solvent fuels, they create a membrane rather than a film over the fuel. This membrane separates the water in the foam blanket from the attack of the solvent. Apply alcohol-resistant AFFF finished foam gently to the fuel so that the membrane can form first. Do not plunge alcohol-resistant AFFF finished foam into a polar fuel **(Figure 5.31)**.

Alcohol-resistant AFFF may be used in subsurface injection applications on certain light hydrocarbons such as gasoline, kerosene, and

Figure 5.31 Never plunge alcohol-resistant AFFF into the surface of a polar solvent fuel. Instead, spray it over the top of the fuel in a rain-down method.

jet propulsion fuels. AR-AFFF concentrate is not designed for premix applications.

High-expansion foam. *[NFPA 472: 5.4.4(2)(e)]* High-expansion foam concentrates are special-purpose foam concentrates that are similar to Class A foams. Because they have a low-water content, they minimize water damage. Their low-water content is also useful when runoff is undesirable. Using high-expansion finished foam outside is generally not recommended because the slightest breeze may remove the foam blanket in sheets and reexpose the hazard to stray ignition sources. High-expansion foam concentrates have the following three basic applications:

- Concealed spaces such as shipboard compartments, basements, coal mines, and other subterranean spaces
- Fixed-extinguishing systems for specific industrial uses such as rolled or bulk paper storage
- Class A fire applications (slow draining)

High-expansion foam concentrates have the following characteristics:

- Stores at temperatures ranging from 35 to 120°F (2°C to 49°C)
- Not affected by freezing and thawing
- Poor heat resistance because air-to-water ratio is very high
- Expansion ratios of 200:1 to 1,000:1 for high-expansion uses and 20:1 to 200:1 for medium-expansion uses (Whether the finished foam is used in either a medium- or high-expansion capacity is determined by the type of application device.)

Emulsifiers. Emulsifiers are foam concentrates that are used with either Class A or Class B fires. Unlike finished foam that blankets the fuel, an emulsifier is designed to mix with the fuel, breaking it into small droplets and encapsulating them. The resulting emulsion is rendered nonflammable **(Figure 5.32)**. However, the following drawbacks exist when using emulsifiers:

- Emulsifiers should only be used with fuels that are 1 inch (25 m) or less in depth. When the fuel is deeper, it is almost impossible to mix the emulsifier thoroughly with the fuel.

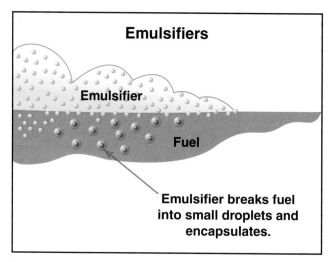

Figure 5.32 Emulsifiers are designed to mix with a fuel, breaking it into small droplets and encapsulating them. The resulting emulsion is not flammable.

- Once the emulsifier is thoroughly mixed with the fuel, it renders the fuel unsalvageable.
- Emulsifiers do not work effectively with water-soluble or water-miscible fuels because an emulsion cannot be formed between the concentrate and the fuel.
- Emulsifiers can have a negative effect on fish, aquatic life, and bodies of water. When emulsifiers are used for Class A fires and Class B spills, the effects of run-off must be taken into consideration.

Proportioning

Class B finished foam may be proportioned into the fire stream via a fixed system, an apparatus-mounted system, or portable foam proportioning equipment. Foam may be applied either with standard fog nozzles (AFFF and FFFP concentrates) or air-aspirating foam nozzles (all types).

Today's Class B foam concentrates are mixed in proportions from 1 to 6 percent (1:99 or 6:94 ratio of water to concentrate). The proper proportion for any particular concentrate is listed on the outside of the foam concentrate container. Some multipurpose foam concentrates designed for use on both hydrocarbon and polar solvent fuels can be used at different concentrations, depending on which one of the two fuels they are used. These concentrates are normally used at a 3-percent rate (3:97 ratio) on hydrocarbons and a 6-percent rate (6:94 ratio) on polar solvents. New multipurpose foam concentrates may be used at 3-percent concentrations regardless on which type of fuel they are used. High-expansion foam concentrates are typically used between 1- and 2.5-percent concentrations. In addition, 1-percent AR foam concentrates are available for use on hydrocarbon spill fires using foam cannons or handheld nozzles.

Application Rates

[NFPA 472: 5.4.4(1)]

The dynamics of ignited fuels causes them to consume finished foam as it is applied. Therefore, the rate at which finished foam is applied must exceed its rate of consumption. For example, when employing AFFF, FFFP foam, or AR-AFFF solution on a hydrocarbon spill fire, the discharge rate should equal 10 percent of the area of a spill. Thus if a spill measures 1,000 square feet (93 m²), the solution application rate is 200 gpm (379 L/min). This rate varies with fuel type, fuel depth, finished foam type, and method of foam application (**Figure 5.33**). For example, fires involving polar solvent fuels generally require a higher rate of application and an alcohol-resistant foam concentrate. Once the fire is extinguished, finished foam consumption is only affected by the latent heat of the fuel, weather conditions, and finished foam's natural drainage rate.

Unignited liquid spills do not require the same application rates as ignited liquid spills because radiant heat, open flame, and thermal drafts do not break down the finished foam as they would under fire conditions. For unignited spills, a lower application rate may be satisfactory. Foam is reapplied when the one-fourth (25 percent or quarter) lifetime limit of the foam has been reached or

Figure 5.33 Foam application rates are determined by the fuel type, fuel depth, foam type, and application method. Flammable liquid fires such as this simulated shipboard fire may require more than one attack line flowing foam.

when vapor-measuring equipment shows that the vapors being emitted from the spill are in the lower flammable range. The instructions on the foam concentrate container lists what the one-fourth (25 percent or quarter) lifetime for that particular concentrate is. If the spill does ignite, prepare to flow at least the minimum application rate for fire conditions.

First responders must remember that enough foam concentrate must be on hand before operations are initiated. **Table 5.2** provides a summary of foam concentrate characteristics and application techniques.

Foam Fire Stream System Assembly

[NFPA 472: 5.4.4(1)]

To provide a foam fire stream, the first responder or apparatus driver/operator must be able to correctly assemble the components of the system. The following procedure describes the steps for placing a foam line in service using an in-line eductor proportioner:

Step 1: Select the proper foam concentrate for the burning fuel involved and make sure that enough of it is available to extinguish the fire and to reapply as required.

Step 2: Check the eductor and nozzle to make sure that they are hydraulically compatible (rated for same flow).

Step 3: Check to see that the foam concentration listed on the foam container matches the eductor percentage rating. If the eductor is adjustable, set it to the proper concentration setting.

Step 4: Attach the eductor to a hose capable of efficiently flowing the rated capacity of the eductor and nozzle. *Details:*

— Avoid kinks in the hose.

— Make sure that the ball valve gates are completely open if the eductor is attached directly to a pump discharge outlet. In addition, avoid connections to discharge elbows because any condition that causes water turbulence adversely affects the operation of the eductor.

Step 5: Attach the attack hoseline and desired nozzle to the discharge end of the eductor. The length of the hose should not exceed the manufacturer's recommendations.

Step 6: Open enough pails of foam concentrate to handle the task. Place them at the eductor so that the operation can be carried out without interruption in the flow of concentrate.

Step 7: Place the eductor suction hose into the concentrate. Make sure that the bottom of the concentrate is no more than 6 feet (1.8 m) below the eductor.

Step 8: Increase the water supply pressure to that required for the eductor. Consult the manufacturer's recommendations for the specific eductor. Foam should now be flowing.

Recovery and Termination

Normally, the last strategic goals for the proper management of a hazardous materials emergency are the recovery and termination efforts. It is important to remember that there is a distinct difference between these functions. *Recovery* deals with returning the incident scene and responders to a pre-incident level of readiness. *Termination* involves documenting the incident and using this information to evaluate the response. This evaluation leads to an improvement of future response capabilities based upon problems that were identified during the original incident.

Recovery

The major goals of the recovery phase are as follows:

- Return the operational area to a safe condition.

- Debrief personnel before they leave the scene.

- Return the equipment and personnel of all involved agencies to the condition they were in before the incident.

On-scene Recovery

On-scene recovery efforts are directed toward returning the scene to a safe condition. These activities may require the coordinated effort of

Table 5.2
Foam Concentrate Characteristics/Application Techniques

Type	Characteristics	Storage Range	Application Rate	Application Techniques	Primary Uses
Protein Foam (3% and 6%)	• Protein based • Low expansion • Good reignition (burnback) resistance • Excellent water retention • High heat resistance and stability • Performance can be affected by freezing and thawing • Can freeze protect with antifreeze • Not as mobile or fluid on fuel surface as other low-expansion foams	35–120°F (2°C to 49°C)	0.16 gpm/ft² (6.5 L/min/m²)	• Indirect foam stream; do not mix fuel with foam • Avoid agitating fuel during application; static spark ignition of volatile hydrocarbons can result from plunging and turbulence • Use alcohol-resistant type within seconds of proportioning • Not compatible with dry chemical extinguishing agents	• Class B fires involving hydrocarbons • Protecting flammable and combustible liquids where they are stored, transported, and processed
Fluoroprotein Foam (3% and 6%)	• Protein and synthetic based; derived from protein foam • Fuel shedding • Long-term vapor suppression • Good water retention • Excellent, long-lasting heat resistance • Performance not affected by freezing and thawing • Maintains low viscosity at low temperatures • Can freeze protect with antifreeze • Use either freshwater or saltwater • Nontoxic and biodegradable after dilution • Good mobility and fluidity on fuel surface • Premixable for short periods of time	35–120°F (2°C to 49°C)	0.16 gpm/ft² (6.5 L/min/m²)	• Direct plunge technique • Subsurface injection • Compatible with simultaneous application of dry chemical extinguishing agents • Deliver through air-aspirating equipment	• Hydrocarbon vapor suppression • Subsurface application to hydrocarbon fuel storage tanks • Extinguishing in-depth crude petroleum or other hydrocarbon fuel fires
Film Forming Fluoroprotein Foam (FFFP) (3% and 6%)	• Protein based; fortified with additional surfactants that reduce the burnback characteristics of other protein-based foams • Fuel shedding • Develops a fast-healing, continuous-floating film on hydrocarbon fuel surfaces • Excellent, long-lasting heat resistance	35–120°F (2°C to 49°C)	**Ignited Hydrocarbon Fuel:** 0.10 gpm/ft² (4.1 L/min/m²) **Polar Solvent Fuel:** 0.24 gpm/ft² (9.8 L/min/m²)	• Cover entire fuel surface • May apply with dry chemical agents • May apply with spray nozzles • Subsurface injection • Can plunge into fuel during application	• Suppressing vapors in unignited spills of hazardous liquids • Extinguishing fires in hydrocarbon fuels

Continued

Type	Characteristics	Storage Range	Application Rate	Application Techniques	Primary Uses
FFFP (continued)	• Good low-temperature viscosity • Fast fire knockdown • Affected by freezing and thawing • Use either freshwater or saltwater • Can store premixed • Can freeze protect with antifreeze • Use alcohol-resistant type on polar solvents at 6% solution and on hydrocarbon fuels at 3% solution • Nontoxic and biodegradable after dilution				
Aqueous Film Forming Foam (AFFF) (1%, 3%, and 6%)	• Synthetic based • Good penetrating capabilities • Spreads vapor-sealing film over and floats on hydrocarbon fuels • Can use nonaerating nozzles • Performance may be adversely affected by freezing and storing • Has good low-temperature viscosity • Can freeze protect with antifreeze • Use either freshwater or saltwater • Can premix	25–120°F (-4°F to 49°C)	0.10 gpm/ft^2 (4.1 L/min/m^2)	• May apply directly onto fuel surface • May apply indirectly by bouncing it off a wall and allowing it to float onto fuel surface • Subsurface injection • May apply with dry chemical agents	• Controlling and extinguishing Class B fires • Handling land or sea crash rescues involving spills • Extinguishing most transportation-related fires • Wetting and penetrating Class A fuels • Securing unignited hydrocarbon spills
Alcohol-Resistant AFFF (3% and 6%)	• Polymer has been added to AFFF concentrate • Multipurpose: Use on both polar solvents and hydrocarbon fuels (use on polar solvents at 6% solution and on hydrocarbon fuels at 3% solution) • Forms a membrane on polar solvent fuels that prevents destruction of the foam blanket • Forms same aqueous film on hydrocarbon fuels as AFFF • Fast flame knockdown	25–120°F (-4°C to 49°C) (May become viscous at temperatures under 50°F [10°C])	**_Ignited Hydrocarbon Fuel:_** 0.10 gpm/ft^2 (4.1 L/min/m^2) **_Polar Solvent Fuel:_** 0.24 gpm/ft^2 (9.8 L/min/m^2)	• Apply directly but gently onto fuel surface • May apply indirectly by bouncing it off a wall and allowing it to float onto fuel surface • Subsurface injection	Fires or spills of both hydrocarbon and polar solvent fuels

Continued

Type	Characteristics	Storage Range	Application Rate	Application Techniques	Primary Uses
AR-AFFF *(continued)*	• Good burnback resistance on both fuels • Not easily premixed				
High-Expansion Foam	• Synthetic detergent based • Special-purpose, low water content • High air-to-solution ratios: 200:1 to 1,000:1 • Performance not affected by freezing and thawing • Poor heat resistance • Prolonged contact with galvanized or raw steel may attack these surfaces	27–110°F (-3°C to 43°C)	Sufficient to quickly cover the fuel or fill the space	• Gentle application; do not mix foam with fuel • Cover entire fuel surface • Usually fills entire space in confined space incidents	• Extinguishing Class A and some Class B fires • Flooding confined spaces • Volumetrically displacing vapor, heat, and smoke • Reducing vaporization from liquefied natural gas spills • Extinguishing pesticide fires • Suppressing fuming acid vapors • Suppressing vapors in coal mines and other subterranean spaces and concealed spaces in basements • Extinguishing agent in fixed extinguishing systems • Not recommended for outdoor use
Class A Foam	• Synthetic • Wetting agent that reduces surface tension of water and allows it to soak into combustible materials • Rapid extinguishment with less water use than other foams • Use regular water stream equipment • Can premix with water • Mildly corrosive • Requires lower percentage of concentration (0.2 to 1.0) than other foams • Outstanding insulating qualities • Good penetrating capabilities	25–120°F (-4°C to 49°C) (Concentrate is subject to freezing but can be thawed and used if freezing occurs)	Same as the minimum critical flow rate for plain water on similar Class A Fuels; flow rates are not reduced when using Class A foam	• Can propel with compressed-air systems • Can apply with conventional nozzles	Extinguishing Class A combustibles only

numerous agencies, technical experts, and contractors. Generally, fire and emergency services organizations do not conduct remedial cleanup actions unless those actions are absolutely necessary to eliminate conditions that present an imminent threat to public health and safety. If such imminent threats do not exist, contracted remediation firms under the oversight of local, state/provincial, and federal environmental regulators generally provide for these cleanup activities. In these situations, the fire and emergency services organization may also provide control and safety oversight according to local SOPs.

Operations such as product transfer and vehicle/container removal may require the continued involvement of hazardous materials responders trained to a higher level than Operational. The complexity and potential for reescalation of the incident dictate this need. During these operations, it is important that the IC develop a joint effort between regulators, contractors, and emergency response forces for the purpose of ensuring the safety of all personnel. As long as the IC is in control, the IC and safety officer are responsible for ensuring the safety of personnel on the scene. The organization's emergency response plan needs to define the role of the IC during this stage of the incident. There is also a need to develop a transition plan to return the scene to the property's responsible party, regardless of whether the property is public or private. Often fire/haz mat responders leave the scene with law enforcement or public works personnel in charge, and these personnel may not really know what needs to be done.

On-scene Debriefing

On-scene debriefing, conducted in the form of a group discussion, gathers information from all operating personnel, including law enforcement, public works, and EMS responders. During the debriefing stage, obtain the following information *from* responders:

- Important observations
- Actions taken
- Timeline of those actions

In addition, one very important step in this process is to provide information to personnel concerning the signs and symptoms of overexposure to the hazardous materials, which is referred to as the *hazardous communication briefing* (required by OSHA in the U.S.). It is extremely important that this debriefing process be thoroughly documented. Each person attending must receive and understand the instructions and *sign* a document stating those facts. The information provided *to* responders before they leave the scene includes the following:

- Identity of material involved
- Potential adverse effects of exposure to the material
- Actions to be taken for further decontamination
- Signs and symptoms of an exposure
- Mechanism by which a responder can obtain medical evaluation and treatment
- Exposure documentation procedures

Operational Recovery

Operational recovery involves those actions necessary to return the resource forces to a level of pre-incident readiness. These actions involve the release of units, resupply of materials and equipment, decontamination of equipment and PPE, and preliminary actions necessary for obtaining financial restitution.

The financial effect of hazardous materials emergencies can be far greater than any other activity conducted by the fire and emergency services. Normally, a fire and emergency services organization's revenues obtained from taxes or subscriber fees are calculated based upon the equipment and personnel needs necessary to conduct fire-suppression and other emergency activities. It is recommended that communities have in place the necessary ordinances to allow for the recovery of costs incurred from such emergencies. In addition, the proper documentation of costs through the use of forms such as the *Unit Log* and other tracking mechanisms is a vital part of this process.

Termination

[ODP Operations II.g.]

The *termination* phase involves two procedural actions: critiques and after-action analysis. Analysis includes study of all postincident reports and critiques. In order to conclude an incident, the IC must ensure that all strategic goals have been accomplished and the requirements of laws have been met.

Critiques

[ODP Operations II.f.]

One of the most overlooked processes required for properly responding to hazardous materials emergencies is that of the postincident critique. OSHA Title 29 *CFR* 1910.120 mandates that incidents be critiqued for the purposes of identifying operational deficiencies and learning from mistakes. As with all critiques performed by the fire and emergency services, hazardous materials incident critiques need to occur as soon as possible after the incident and involve all responders, including law enforcement, public works, and EMS responders. As with other administrative and emergency-response functions, the critique is documented to identify those in attendance as well as any operational deficiencies that were identified.

The complexity of the critique process is determined by the complexity of the incident. This process could range from on-scene critiques or debriefings for minor incidents that involved a limited number of personnel to a series of critique meetings to facilitate the attendance of multiple response organizations. Regardless of the form of critique used, documentation is extremely important.

After-Action Analysis

The *after-action analysis* process compiles the information obtained from the debriefings, postincident reports, and critiques to identify trends regarding operational strengths and weaknesses. Once trends have been identified, recommendations for improvements are made. These recommendations may be made in the following categories:

- Operational weaknesses
- Training needs
- Necessary procedural changes
- Required additional resources

Also included in the after-action analysis is the completion of necessary reporting procedures required to document personal exposures, equipment exposures, incident reports, and staff analysis reports. After-action analysis forms the basis for improved response. Therefore, any recommendations for change or improvement are benchmarked for further consideration. Schedule follow-up activities to ensure successful implementation.

Summary

In order to mitigate an incident successfully, the IC must determine the strategic goals and tactical objectives that will begin to stabilize the incident and bring it to a successful conclusion with the least amount of harm and damage. The resources available, a risk/benefit analysis, and other factors that are specific to the individual problems presented by the incident largely determine these goals and objectives. Several strategic goals applicable to most haz mat incidents are discussed in this chapter. Goals range from isolation to protective actions to incident control to recovery and termination.

Frequently, as first emergency responders to arrive at the scene of an incident, Awareness-Level and Operational-Level personnel are responsible for isolating the incident, notifying the proper authorities, identifying the material(s) involved, and initiating protective actions such as evacuation. It is likely that Operational-Level personnel will be more involved in rescue, spill control, and fire control. To a lesser degree, they may also be involved in leak control and recovery/termination efforts, but usually in a supporting role (although all personnel may be involved in postincident critiques and on-scene debriefings).

Part Two

Incident Problem-Solving Process

Chapter 6

Personal Protective Equipment

First Responder Competencies

This chapter provides information that will assist the reader in meeting the following first responder competencies from NFPA 472, *Professional Competence of Responders to Hazardous Materials Incidents,* 2002 Edition. The numbers are noted directly in the text under the section titles where they are addressed.

NFPA 472

Chapter 4   Competencies for the First Responder at the Awareness Level

4.4.1   Initiating Protective Actions. Given examples of facility and transportation hazardous materials incidents, the local emergency response plan, the organization's standard operating procedures, and the current edition of the *Emergency Response Guidebook,* first responders at the awareness level shall be able to identify the actions to be taken to protect themselves and others and to control access to the scene and shall also meet the following requirements:

(5) Given the name of a hazardous material, identify the recommended personal protective equipment from the following list:

(a) Street clothing and work uniforms

(b) Structural fire-fighting protective clothing

(c) Positive pressure self-contained breathing apparatus

(d) Chemical-protective clothing and equipment

Chapter 5   Competencies for the First Responder at the Operational Level

5.1.2.1 The first responder at the operational level shall be able to perform the following tasks:

(2) Plan an initial response within the capabilities and competencies of available personnel, personal protective equipment, and control equipment by completing the following tasks:

(c) Determine whether the personal protective equipment provided is appropriate for implementing each defensive option

(3) Implement the planned response to favorably change the outcomes consistent with the local emergency response plan and the organization's standard operating procedures by completing the following tasks:

(c) Don, work in, and doff personal protective equipment provided by the authority having jurisdiction

5.3.3   Determining Appropriateness of Personal Protective Equipment. Given the name of the hazardous material involved and the anticipated type of exposure, the first responder at the operational level shall determine whether available personal protective equipment is appropriate for implementing a defensive option and also shall meet the following requirements:

(1) Identify the respiratory protection required for a given defensive option and the following:

(a) Identify the three types of respiratory protection and the advantages and limitations presented by the use of each at hazardous materials incidents.

(b) Identify the required physical capabilities and limitations of personnel working in positive pressure self-contained breathing apparatus.

(2) Identify the personal protective clothing required for a given defensive option and the following:

(a) Identify skin contact hazards encountered at hazardous materials incidents.

(b) Identify the purpose, advantages, and limitations of the following levels of protective clothing at hazardous materials incidents:

    i.   Structural fire-fighting protective clothing

    ii. High temperature-protective clothing

    iii. Chemical-protective clothing

    iv. Liquid splash-protective clothing

    v.   Vapor-protective clothing

5.4.3   Using Personal Protective Equipment. The first responder at the operational level shall demonstrate the ability to don, work in, and doff the personal protective equipment provided by the authority having jurisdiction, and shall meet the following related requirements:

(4) Identify the symptoms of heat and cold stress.

(5) Identify the physical capabilities required for, and the limitations of, personnel working in the personal protective equipment as provided by the authority having jurisdiction.

(6) Match the function of the operational components of the positive pressure self-contained breathing apparatus provided to the hazardous materials responder with the name of the component.

(7) Identify the procedures for cleaning, disinfecting, and inspecting respiratory protective equipment.

(8) Identify the procedures for donning, working in, and doffing positive pressure self-contained breathing apparatus.

(9) Demonstrate donning, working in, and doffing positive pressure self-contained breathing apparatus.

Emergency Responder Guidelines

This chapter provides information that will assist the reader in meeting the following first responder guidelines for fire service and law enforcement from the Office for Domestic Preparedness (ODP) *Emergency Responder Guidelines,* 2002 Edition. The numbers are noted directly in the text under the section titles where they are addressed.

ODP Emergency Responder Guidelines

Fire Service and Law Enforcement

Awareness Level for Events Involving Weapons of Mass Destruction

III. **Know and follow self-protection measures for WMD events and hazardous materials events.** The responder should:

    b. Know how to use, inspect, and properly maintain the personal protective equipment issued to the officer. Understand the limitations of this equipment in protecting someone exposed to WMD agents or hazardous materials.

Performance Level for Events Involving Weapons of Mass Destruction

III. **Know and follow self-protection measures and rescue and evacuation procedures for WMD events.** The responder should:

    a. Know how and when to use appropriate personal protective equipment (PPE) issued by the department to work in the warm zone on the scene of a potential WMD event. Fully understand the limitations of the PPE. Follow departmental policy for use, inspection, and maintenance of PPE.

    b. Understand the hazards and risks associated with wearing chemical protective clothing and other protective clothing at a potential WMD event. Understand and follow the rehabilitation steps to help responders reduce the level of heat stress. Know what other precautions to take to protect responders on the scene.

    c. Know how to determine the appropriate PPE for protecting responders who will be entering the warm zone on the scene of a potential WMD event.

Chapter 6
Personal Protective Equipment

[NFPA 472: 5.1.2.1(3)(c)] [ODP Awareness III.b.][ODP Operations III.a.]

Personnel responding to a hazardous material incident must be protected from the hazards at the scene by personal protective equipment (PPE). Typical PPE consists of respiratory equipment (self-contained breathing apparatus [SCBA]) and either structural fire-fighting, high-temperature, or chemical-protective clothing (CPC). An ensemble of appropriate PPE protects the skin, eyes, face, hands, feet, body, head, and respiratory system. Structural fire-fighting and high-temperature protective clothing offer very limited protection against chemical hazards. CPC offers protection against hazardous materials, but its use requires training above the first responder Awareness Level. All first responders, however, need to be aware of the types of CPC available and understand that they have limitations.

Design, certification, and testing requirements of PPE are found in the following NFPA standards:

- NFPA 1971, *Standard on Protective Ensemble for Structural Fire Fighting* (2000)

- NFPA 1981, *Standard on Open-Circuit Self-Contained Breathing Apparatus for Fire and Emergency Services* (2002)

- NFPA 1991, *Standard on Vapor-Protective Ensembles for Hazardous Materials Emergencies* (2000)

- NFPA 1992, *Standard on Liquid Splash-Protective Ensembles and Clothing for Hazardous Materials Emergencies* (2000)

- NFPA 1994, *Standard on Protective Ensembles for Chemical/Biological Terrorism Incidents* (2001)

- NFPA 1999, *Standard on Protective Clothing for Emergency Medical Operations* (2003)

For U.S. requirements, additional information can be found in Occupational Safety and Health Administration (OSHA) regulations 29 *CFR* 1910.132, *Personal Protective Equipment*, and 29 *CFR* 1910.134 *Respiratory Protection*. For detailed information about respiratory protection, see the IFSTA manual, **Respiratory Protection for Fire and Emergency Services.**

In general terms, PPE can refer to anything from safety glasses and hard hats to SCBA and vapor-protective ensembles. This chapter primarily focuses on PPE as identified by NFPA 472, *Standard for Professional Competence of Responders to Hazardous Materials Incidents* (2002), specifically, *protective clothing* and *respiratory protection*, the two basic components of PPE needed to protect the individual from chemical-entry routes **(Figure 6.1, p. 326).**

The U.S. Environmental Protection Agency (EPA) and OSHA standards regarding PPE are discussed in this chapter. The U.S. Department of Homeland Security (DHS) has adopted standards for PPE to protect first responders against chemical, biological, radiological, nuclear, and explosive (CBRNE) threats. The National Institute for Occupational Safety and Health (NIOSH) and NFPA developed these standards, and they are also described. Also included in this chapter are sections on protective clothing and respiratory protection types and PPE ensembles and classifications. In addition, the chapter discusses PPE selection, use, care, and inspection. Information about climate concerns and health issues from temperature extremes is also included.

PPE Guards the Routes of Entry

Respiratory Protection Protects Against Inhalation and Ingestion

Protective Clothing Protects Against Skin Contact

Figure 6.1 Protective clothing and respiratory protection prevent exposure to hazardous chemicals by protecting the routes of entry.

Personal Protective Clothing Types

[NFPA 472: 5.3.3, 5.3.3(2), 5.3.3(2)(a), 5.3.3(2)(b)]

Protective clothing must be worn whenever a wearer faces potential hazards arising from chemical exposure. Typical protective clothing used at haz mat incidents is designed to protect the wearer from heat and hazardous materials contacting the skin or eyes. Skin contact with hazardous materials can cause a variety of symptoms, including chemical burns, allergic reactions and rashes, and absorption of toxic materials into the body. No single combination or ensemble of protective equipment, including respiratory protection, can protect against all hazards. First responders — particularly those at the Operational Level — must be concerned with safety when choosing and using protective clothing. For example, it is extremely important to realize that fumes and vapors of many hazardous chemicals can easily penetrate fire-fighting turnout coats and pants.

Several types of personal protective clothing are available. NFPA 472 identifies the following three types of protective clothing:

- Structural fire-fighting protective clothing
- High-temperature protective clothing
- Chemical-protective clothing (CPC)
  — Liquid-splash protective clothing
  — Vapor-protective clothing

Structural Fire-Fighting Protective Clothing

[NFPA 472: 4.4.1(5)(b), 5.3.3(2)(b)(i)]
Structural fire-fighting protective clothing gives a person protection from heat, moisture, and the ordinary hazards associated with structural fire fighting. It includes a helmet, coat, pants, boots, gloves, personal alert safety system (PASS) device, and a hood to cover parts of the head not protected by the helmet and facepiece.

Structural fire-fighting clothing and SCBA provide limited protection against hazardous materials. The multiple layers of the coat and pants may provide short-term exposure protection from some materials; however, to avoid harmful exposures, first responders must recognize the limitations of this level of protection. Structural fire-fighting clothing is neither corrosive-resistant nor vapor-tight. Any liquids can soak through, acids and bases can dissolve or deteriorate the outer layers, and gases can penetrate the garment. Gaps in structural fire-fighting clothing occur at the neck, wrists, waist, and the point where the pants and boots overlap. First responders must know about the fabrics used in structural fire-fighting protective clothing and how hazardous materials can affect them.

Besides knowing what can deteriorate or destroy protective clothing, first responders should be alert for hazardous materials that *permeate* (pass through at the molecular level) and remain in the protective equipment. Chemicals absorbed into the equipment can subject the wearer to repeated exposure or to a later reaction with another chemical. In addition, the rubber or neoprene in boots, gloves, kneepads, and SCBA facepieces can become permeated by chemicals and rendered

unsafe for use. It may be necessary to discard any equipment exposed to permeating types of chemicals.

First responders must *never* clean turnout clothing at their homes, in an organization's laundry facilities that are not designed for washing PPE, at public laundries, or anyplace where they might mix with other clothing. Because of its ability to absorb chemicals, structural fire-fighting turnout clothing must always be cleaned in a dedicated area, away from other clothing. Structural turnout clothing should *not* be worn into sleeping or eating areas of fire stations because of potential contamination.

Wear structural fire-fighting protective clothing only when the chance of physical contact from splashes is unlikely and the total atmospheric concentrations do *not* contain high levels of chemicals that are toxic via skin contact (**Figure 6.2**). Struc-

Figure 6.2 While structural fire-fighting protective clothing may provide limited protection against many hazardous chemicals, liquids can still soak through to come in contact with skin, acids and bases can dissolve or deteriorate the outer layers, and gases can penetrate the material. *Courtesy of Bob Parker.*

tural fire-fighting protective clothing is commonly used at hazardous materials incidents when the following conditions are met:

- Contact with splashes of extremely hazardous materials is unlikely.

- Total atmospheric concentrations do not contain high levels of chemicals that are toxic to the skin, and there are no adverse effects from chemical exposure to small areas of unprotected skin.

- There is a chance of fire or there is a fire (for example, a flammable liquid fire), and this type of protection is appropriate.

High-Temperature Protective Clothing

[NFPA 472: 5.3.3(2)(b)(ii)]

Another type of special protective clothing that first responders may encounter is high-temperature clothing. This clothing is designed to protect the wearer from short-term high-temperature exposures in situations where heat levels exceed the capabilities of standard fire-fighting protective clothing. This type of clothing is usually of limited use in dealing with chemical hazards. Two basic types of high-temperature clothing that are available are as follows:

- *Proximity suits* — Permit close approach to fires for rescue, fire-suppression, and property-conservation activities such as in aircraft rescue and fire fighting or other fire-fighting operations involving flammable liquids. Such suits provide greater heat protection than standard structural fire-fighting protective clothing.

- *Fire-entry suits* — Allow a person to work in total flame environments for short periods of time; provide short-duration and close-proximity protection at radiant heat temperatures as high as 2,000°F (1 093°C). Each suit has a specific use and is not interchangeable. Fire-entry suits are not designed to protect the wearer against chemical hazards.

Several limitations to high-temperature protective clothing are as follows:

- Contributes to heat stress by not allowing the body to release excess heat

- Is bulky

- Limits wearer's vision

- Limits wearer's mobility

- Limits communication

- Requires frequent and extensive training for efficient and safe use

- Is expensive to purchase

Chemical-Protective Clothing

[NFPA 472: 4.4.1(5)(d), 5.3.3(2)(b)(iii)]

The purpose of CPC and equipment is to shield or isolate individuals from the chemical, physical, and biological hazards that may be encountered during hazardous materials operations. As listed earlier, NFPA 472 recognizes two types of CPC: liquid-splash protective clothing and vapor-protective clothing.

CPC is made from a variety of different materials, none of which protects against all types of chemicals **(Figure 6.3)**. Each material provides

Figure 6.3 No one type of chemical-protective clothing will protect against all hazardous materials. For example, these responders may be protected against many chemical splashes and most alpha and beta radiation, but they are not protected against gamma radiation.

protection against certain chemicals or products, but only limited or no protection against others. The manufacturer of a particular suit must provide a list of chemicals for which the suit is effective. Selection of appropriate CPC depends on the specific chemical and on the specific tasks to be performed by the wearer.

CPC may be purchased as a single or multipiece garment, depending on the manufacturer's design. The clothing may be *encapsulating* (designed to completely cover the responder including the respiratory equipment), or *nonencapsulating* (designed to provide protection in conjunction with the wearer's respiratory protection, attached or detachable hood, gloves, and boots). More information on these combinations is provided in the PPE Ensembles, Classifications, and Selection section.

CPC is designed to afford the wearer a known degree of protection from a known type, concentration, and length of exposure to a hazardous material, but only if it is fitted properly and worn correctly. Improperly worn equipment can expose and endanger the wearer. One factor first responders should remember during the selection process is that most protective clothing is designed to be impermeable to moisture, thus limiting the transfer of heat from the body through natural evaporation. This concern is particularly important in hot environments and when strenuous tasks cause such garments to increase the likelihood of heat injury (see Climate Concerns and Health Issues section). Other factors include the garment's degradation, permeation, and penetration abilities and its service life. A written management program regarding selection and use of CPC is recommended. Regardless of the type of CPC worn at an incident, it must be decontaminated before storage or disposal.

Permeation, Degradation, and Penetration

The effectiveness of CPC can be reduced by three actions: permeation, degradation, and penetration. These are also characteristics that must be considered when choosing and using protective ensembles (see PPE Ensembles, Classifications, and Selection section).

Operations Requiring Use of Chemical-Protective Clothing (CPC)

Without regard to the level of training required to perform them, OSHA identifies the following emergency response operations that may require the use of CPC:

- *Site survey* — Initial investigation of a hazardous materials incident, usually characterized by a large degree of uncertainty that mandates the highest levels of protection.

- *Rescue* — Entering a hazardous environment for the purpose of removing an exposure victim. Special consideration must be given to how the selected protective clothing may affect the ability of the wearer to perform rescue and handle the contamination and decontamination of the victim.

- *Spill mitigation* — Entering a hazardous environment to prevent a potential spill or reduce the hazards from an existing spill (for example, applying a chlorine kit on a railroad tank car). Protective clothing must accommodate required tasks without sacrificing adequate protection.

- *Emergency monitoring* — Outfitting personnel in protective clothing for the primary purpose of observing a hazardous materials incident without entry into the spill site; may apply to monitoring contract activity for spill cleanup.

- *Decontamination* — Applying decontamination procedures to personnel or equipment leaving the site; in general, requires a lower level of protective clothing.

- *Evacuation* — Evacuating people downwind of a scene when potential for hazardous material exposure exists.

If first responders at the Operational Level are involved in any of these activities, consideration must be given to what type of protective equipment is necessary, given the known and/or unknown hazards present at the scene.

Permeation. Process that occurs when a chemical passes through a fabric on a molecular level. In most cases, there is no visible evidence of chemicals permeating a material. The rate at which a compound permeates CPC depends on factors such as the chemical properties of the compound, nature of the protective barrier in the CPC, and concentration of the chemical on the surface of the CPC (**Figure 6.4**). Most CPC manufacturers provide charts on breakthrough time (time it takes for a chemical to permeate the material of a protective suit) for a wide range of chemical compounds. Permeation data also includes information about the permeation rate or the speed at which the chemical moves through the CPC material after it breaks through.

Chemical degradation. Process that occurs when the characteristics of a material are altered through contact with chemical substances. Examples include cracking, brittleness, and other changes in the structural characteristics of the garment (**Figure 6.5**). The most common observations of material degradation are discoloration, swelling, loss of physical strength, or deterioration.

Penetration. Process that occurs when a hazardous material enters an opening or a puncture in a protective material. Rips, tears, and cuts in protective materials — as well as unsealed seams, buttonholes, and zippers — are considered penetration failures. Often such openings are the result of faulty manufacture or problems with the inherent design of the suit (**Figure 6.6**).

Service Life

Service life is another issue for CPC. Protective clothing may be labeled as *reusable* (multiuse) for repeated use, *limited use* (not disposable), or *disposable* for one-time use. For example, a Saranex/Tyvek® garment may be designed to be a coverall (covering the wearer's torso, arms, and legs) intended for liquid-splash protection and single use. Other suits are designed to be reused multiple times. The distinctions between these types of clothing are both vague and complicated. Disposable clothing is generally lightweight and inexpensive. Reusable clothing is often more rugged and costly. Nevertheless, extensive contamination of any garment may require its removal from service. The key assumption in this determination is the reliability of the garment following exposure.

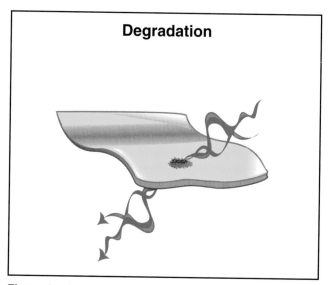

Figure 6.5 An acid eating away the outer layers of structural fire-fighting protective clothing is an example of chemical degradation.

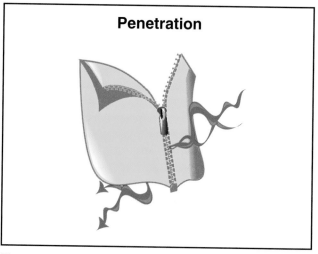

Figure 6.6 Chemicals can penetrate PPE through gaps, tears, punctures, or other openings.

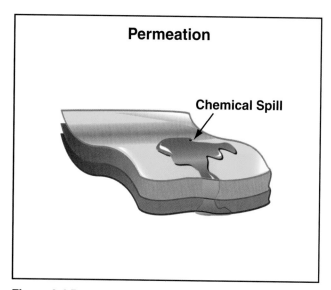

Figure 6.4 Permeation occurs when a chemical passes through a fabric or material on a molecular level. This process often goes unnoticed.

All types require decontamination when the wearer leaves a contaminated area. However, reusable suits must receive extra decontamination measures to ensure they are *clean* for the next user. Chapter 7, Contamination and Decontamination, provides more information about contamination and decontamination of CPC.

Written Management Program

All emergency responders and organizations who routinely select and use CPC should establish a written Chemical-Protective Clothing Management Program. In the U.S., this program must reference Title 29 *CFR* 1910.120, *Hazardous Waste Operations and Emergency Response.* A written management program includes policy statements, procedures, and guidelines. Copies must be made available to all personnel who may use CPC in the course of their duties or job. Technical data on clothing, maintenance manuals, relevant regulations, and other essential information must also be made available.

The two basic objectives of any management program are protecting the wearer from safety and health hazards and to preventing injury to the wearer from incorrect use or malfunction of the CPC. To accomplish these goals, a comprehensive CPC management program includes the following elements:

- Hazard identification
- Medical monitoring
- Environmental surveillance
- Selection, care, testing, and maintenance
- Training

Responsibility for selecting appropriate protective clothing is vested in a specific individual, such as a safety officer or industrial hygienist, who is trained in both chemical hazards and protective-clothing use. Only chemical-protective suits labeled as compliant with the appropriate performance requirements should be used. In cases where the chemical hazards are known in advance or are encountered routinely, clothing selection can be predetermined; that is, specific clothing items are designated for specific chemical operations without the opportunity for individual selection of other clothing items. All clothing and equipment manufacturers provide decision trees to relate information about chemical hazards to protection levels and performance needed.

Liquid-Splash Protective Clothing
[NFPA 472: 5.3.3(2)(b)(iv)]

Primarily *liquid-splash protective clothing* is designed to protect users from chemical liquid splashes but not against chemical vapors or gases. NFPA 1992 sets the minimum design criteria for this type of clothing. Liquid-splash protective clothing can be encapsulating or nonencapsulating **(Figure 6.7)**.

An *encapsulating* suit is a single, one-piece garment that protects against splashes or, in the case of vapor-protective encapsulating suits, also against vapors and gases (see Vapor-Protective Clothing section). Boots and gloves are sometimes separate, or attached and replaceable. Two primary limitations to fully encapsulating suits are as follows:

Figure 6.7 Liquid-splash protective clothing may be nonencapsulated (*left*) or encapsulated (*right*). Most commonly it is nonencapsulated.

- Impairs worker mobility, vision, and communication
- Traps body heat necessitating a cooling vest, particularly when SCBA is also worn

A *nonencapsulating* suit commonly consists of a one-piece coverall, but sometimes is composed of individual pieces such as a jacket, hood, pants, or bib overalls. Gaps between pant cuffs and boots and between gloves and sleeves are usually taped closed. Several limitations to nonencapsulating suits include the following:

- Protects against splashes and dusts but not against gases and vapors
- Does not provide full body coverage: parts of head and neck are often exposed
- Traps body heat and contributes to heat stress

One limitation common to both encapsulating and nonencapsulating liquid-splash protective clothing is that such clothing is not resistant to heat or flame exposure. The material of liquid-splash protective clothing is made from the same types of material used for vapor-protective suits (see following section). Liquid-splash protective clothing must be tested for penetration resistance to the following chemicals listed in NFPA 1992 Section 5-1.3, Protective Garment Requirements:

- Acetone
- Acetonitrile
- Ethyl acetate
- Hexane
- 50 percent w/w sodium hydroxide
- 93.1 percent w/w sulfuric acid
- Tetrahydrofuran

This list is representative of the chemicals that are the worst penetration hazards most commonly encountered by responders. Most manufacturers test their materials against far more chemicals than the minimum required.

When used as part of a protective ensemble, liquid-splash protective ensembles may use an SCBA, an airline (supplied-air respirator [SAR]), or a full-face, air-purifying, canister-equipped respirator. This type of protective clothing is a component of EPA Level B chemical protection ensembles. Class 3 ensembles described in NFPA 1994 also use liquid-splash protective clothing (see PPE for CBRNE Events).

Vapor-Protective Clothing
[NFPA 472: 5.3.3(2)(b)(v)]

Vapor-protective clothing is designed to protect the wearer against chemical vapors or gases and offers a greater level of protection than liquid-splash protective clothing **(Figure 6.8)**. NFPA 1991 gives requirements for a minimum level of protection for response personnel facing exposure to specified chemicals. This standard sets performance requirements for vapor-tight totally encapsulating chemical-protective (TECP) suits and includes rigid chemical- and flame-resistance tests and a permeation test against 21 challenge chemicals. NFPA 1991 also includes standards for performance tests in simulated conditions.

Figure 6.8 Vapor-protective clothing provides the highest degree of protection against hazardous materials. *Courtesy of the Illinois Fire Service Institute.*

Vapor-protective ensembles must be worn with positive-pressure SCBA or combination SCBA/SAR. These suits are primarily used as part of an EPA Level A protective ensemble (see PPE Ensembles, Classifications, and Selection), providing the greatest degree of protection against respiratory, eye, or skin damage from hazardous vapors, gases, particulates, sudden splash, immersion, or contact with hazardous materials. Vapor-protective ensembles are also components of Class 1 and Class 2 ensembles to be used at chemical and biological terrorist incidents as specified in NFPA 1994 (see PPE for CBRNE Events) **(Figure 6.9)**. Several limitations to vapor-protective suits are as follows:

- Does not protect the user against all chemical hazards

- Impairs mobility, vision, and communication

- Does not allow body heat to escape, so can contribute to heat stress, which may require the use of a cooling vest

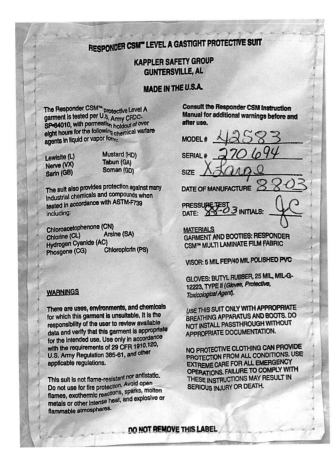

Figure 6.9 Vapor-protective ensembles that are designed to be used at chemical and biological terrorist incidents will be labeled accordingly. *Courtesy of Rich Mahaney.*

Vapor-protective ensembles are made from a variety of special materials. No single combination of protective equipment and clothing is capable of protecting a person against all hazards. NFPA 1991 requires, as a minimum, that the suit be certified to provide minimum protection from the chemicals listed in Section 5-2.1, Suit Requirements.

> ### WARNING
> First responders at the Awareness Level *do not* have sufficient training to operate in conditions requiring the use of vapor-protective ensembles.

Vapor-protective suit materials are tested for permeation resistance against the following chemicals:

- Acetone
- Acetonitrile
- Anhydrous ammonia (gas)
- 1,3-Butadiene (gas)
- Carbon disulfide
- Chlorine (gas)
- Dichloromethane
- Diethyl amine
- Dimethyl formamide
- Ethyl acetate
- Ethylene oxide (gas)
- Hexane
- Hydrogen chloride (gas)
- Methanol
- Methyl chloride (gas)
- Nitrobenzene
- Sodium hydroxide
- Sulfuric acid
- Tetrachloroethylene
- Tetrahydrofuran
- Toluene

Respiratory Protection Types, Limitations, and Programs

[NFPA 472: 5.3.3(1), 5.3.3(2)]

Respiratory protection is a primary concern to first responders because one of the major routes of exposure to hazardous substances is inhalation. Irritants, asphyxiants, poisons, toxins, and other health hazards discussed in Chapter 2, Hazardous Materials Properties and Hazards, are respiratory hazards that first responders may encounter during an incident. Protective breathing equipment protects the body from inhaling these products. However, each type of respiratory protection equipment is limited in its capabilities. The two basic types of protective breathing equipment used by first responders at haz mat incidents are as follows:

- Atmosphere-supplying respirators
  - Closed circuit SCBA
  - Open circuit SCBA
  - Combination SCBA
  - Supplied-air respirator (SAR)
- Air-purifying respirators (APRs)
  - Particulate removing
  - Vapor and gas removing
  - Combination particulate and vapor-and-gas-removing

The following sections discuss the two groups of respiratory protection listed, describe supplied-air hoods being marketed for use in hospitals and emergency rooms, explain respiratory equipment limitations, and describe respiratory protection programs and facepiece fit-testing requirements.

Atmosphere-Supplying Respirators

[NFPA 472: 5.4.3(8–9)]

A respirator that provides air from a source other than the surrounding atmosphere is called an *atmosphere-supplying respirator*. First responders are probably most familiar with SCBA, but they may also encounter and use SARs, depending on availability and the circumstances at the incident **(Figure 6.10)**.

NIOSH classifies SCBA as either *closed-circuit* or *open-circuit*. Three types of SCBA are currently being manufactured in closed- or open-circuit designs: demand, pressure-demand, or positive-pressure. SCBA may also be either a high- or low-pressure type. However, only use of positive-pressure open-circuit or closed-circuit SCBA is allowed at incidents where personnel are exposed to hazardous materials; therefore, only these types will be discussed in this manual. **Appendix H** contains donning and doffing procedures for SCBA respirators.

NFPA Classifications of Respiratory Equipment

The NFPA and the IFSTA manual, **Respiratory Protection for Fire and Emergency Services**, categorize respiratory equipment into the following three groups (that differ slightly from those listed in this manual):

- Positive pressure self-contained breathing apparatus (SCBA)
- Supplied-air respirator (SAR)
- Air-purifying respirator (APR)

In this manual, SCBAs and SARs are both classified as atmosphere-supplying respirators as opposed to air-purifying types.

Figure 6.10 SCBA is considered the minimum respiratory protection for first responders in atmospheres where the conditions and potential hazards are unknown and/or unquantified. *Courtesy of Joan Hepler.*

Positive-Pressure SCBA

[NFPA 472: 4.4.1(5)(c)]

SCBA is an atmosphere-supplying respirator for which the user carries the breathing-air supply. The unit consists of a facepiece, pressure regulator, compressed air cylinder, harness assembly, and end-of-service-time indicators (also known as *low-air supply* or *low-pressure alarms*).

NIOSH and Mine Safety and Health Administration (MSHA) must certify all SCBA for immediately dangerous to life or health (IDLH) use. SCBA that is not NIOSH/MSHA certified must not be used. The apparatus must also meet the design and testing criteria of NFPA 1981 in jurisdictions that have adopted that standard by law or ordinance. In addition, American National Standards Institute (ANSI) standards for eye protection apply to the facepiece lens design and testing.

The mixing of SCBA components manufactured by various companies is also prohibited. The practice of mixing components may void both the NIOSH approval and the third-party certification required for NFPA compliance. SCBA are tested and certified as complete systems consisting of facepiece, pressure regulator, harness assembly, air cylinder, and end-of-service-time indicator alarm device(s). NFPA 1981 now sets requirements for heads-up displays (HUDs) that provide the SCBA user with the following information:

- Breathing air supply status
- Alerts that notify users when the breathing air supply is at 50 percent of capacity
- For battery-powered HUDs, a low-battery alert that signals when the charge is reduced to the level at which the HUD can operate only for 2 more hours

In contrast to a demand (or negative-pressure) unit, positive-pressure SCBA maintains air pressure inside the facepiece slightly higher than normal atmospheric pressure outside. This design affords the SCBA wearer the highest level of protection against airborne contaminants because any facepiece leakage generally forces air outward and pushes contaminants away. However, this action is not the case for negative-pressure apparatus that may allow contaminants to enter the facemask if it is not properly sealed.

The advantages of using SCBA-type respiratory protection are independence and maneuverability; however, several disadvantages are as follows:

- Weight of the units
- Limited air-supply duration
- Change in profile that may hinder mobility because of the configuration of the harness assembly and the location of the air cylinder
- Limited vision caused by facepiece fogging
- Limited communications if the facepiece is not equipped with a microphone or speaking diaphragm

Closed-Circuit SCBA

Closed-circuit SCBA are sometimes used for haz mat incidents because they have air supply durations that exceed those of open-circuit SCBA. These SCBA (also known as *rebreathers*) recycle the wearer's exhaled gases and contain a small cylinder of oxygen to supplement the exhaled air. Exhaled carbon dioxide is removed and oxygen content is restored, using compressed or liquid oxygen or an oxygen-generating solid.

Closed-circuit SCBA usually weigh less than open-circuit SCBA. One of the disadvantages of the closed-circuit system is that once the system is turned on, the process cannot be stopped **(Figure 6.11, p. 336)**.

Open-Circuit SCBA

[NFPA 472: 5.4.3(6)]

The most common SCBA is the open-circuit, positive-pressure type. In this type, replacement breathing air is supplied under positive pressure to the wearer through the facepiece from a compressed breathing-air cylinder. Open-circuit SCBA exhausts the exhaled air into the atmosphere. Because minute amounts of oil may be present in the valves or regulator, creating an explosion hazard when they are mixed with oxygen, the use of compressed oxygen in a system designed for breathing air is prohibited **(Figure 6.12, p. 336).**

Supplied-Air Respirator

The SAR or airline respirator is an atmosphere-supplying respirator where the user does not carry the breathing air source. The apparatus

Figure 6.11 Although not used for fire-fighting operations, closed-circuit SCBA may be used at long-duration hazardous materials incidents.

usually consists of a facepiece, a belt- or facepiece-mounted regulator, a voice communications system, up to 300 feet (91 m) of air supply hose, an emergency escape pack or emergency breathing support system (EBSS), and a breathing air source (either cylinders mounted on a cart or a portable breathing-air compressor) **(Figure 6.13).** Because of the potential for damage to the air-supply hose, the EBSS provides enough air, usually 5, 10, or 15 minutes' worth, for the user to escape a hazardous atmosphere. SAR apparatus are not certified for fire-fighting operations because of the potential damage to the airline from heat, fire, or debris.

NIOSH classifies SARs as Type C respirators. Type C respirators are further divided into two approved types: One type consists of a regulator and facepiece only, while the second consists of a regulator, facepiece, and EBSS. This second type may also be referred to as a SAR with escape (egress) capabilities. It is used in confined-space environments, IDLH environments, or potential IDLH environments. SARs used at haz mat incidents must provide positive pressure to the facepiece.

SAR apparatus have the advantage of reducing physical stress to the wearer by removing the weight of the SCBA. The air supply line is a limi-

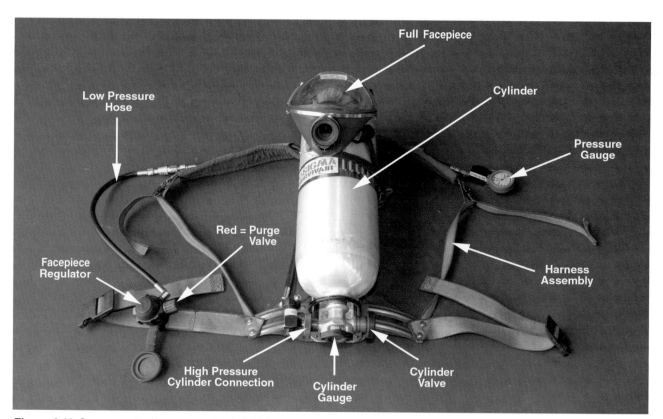

Figure 6.12 Components of an open-circuit SCBA.

Figure 6.13 A complete supplied-air respirator (SAR) consists of the air-supply cart, manifold, air-supply hose, regulator, facepiece, and emergency breathing support system (EBSS).

tation because of the potential for mechanical or heat damage. In addition, the length of the airline (no more than 300 feet [91 m] from the air source) restricts mobility. Other limitations are the same as those for SCBA: restricted vision and communications.

Air-Purifying Respirators

APRs contain an air-purifying filter, canister, or cartridge that removes specific contaminants found in ambient air as it passes through the air-purifying element. Based on what cartridge, canister, or filter is being used, these purifying elements are generally divided into the three following types:

- Particulate-removing APRs
- Vapor-and-gas-removing APRs
- Combination particulate-removing and vapor-and-gas-removing APRs

APRs may be powered (PAPRs) or nonpowered. APRs do not supply oxygen or air from a separate source, and they protect only against specific contaminants at or below certain concentrations. Combination filters combine particulate-removing elements with vapor-and-gas-removing elements in the same cartridge or canister.

Respirators with air-purifying filters may have either full facepieces that provide a complete seal to the face and protect the eyes, nose, and mouth or half facepieces that provide a complete seal to the face and protect the nose and mouth (**Figures 6.14 a and b**). Disposable filters, canisters, or cartridges

Figures 6.14 a and b (a) Half-facepiece air-purifying respirators (APRs) are designed to protect against specific inhalation hazards, but they do not protect against chemicals that can be absorbed through the skin or eyes (*top*). *Courtesy of Federal Emergency Management Agency (FEMA) News Photo.* (b) Full-facepiece APRs provide greater protection for the face and eyes (*bottom*).

are mounted on one or both sides of the facepiece. Canister or cartridge respirators pass the air through a filter, sorbent, catalyst, or combination of these items to remove specific contaminants from the air. The air can enter the system either from the external atmosphere through the filter or sorbent or when the user's exhalation combines with a catalyst to provide breathable air.

As with CPC, no single canister, filter, or cartridge protects against all chemical hazards. Therefore, responders must know the hazards present in the atmosphere in order to select the appropriate canister, filter, or cartridge. Responders should be able to answer the following questions before deciding to use APRs for protection at a haz mat incident:

- What is the hazard?
- Is the hazard a vapor or a gas?
- Is the hazard a particle or dust?
- Is there some combination of dust and vapors present?
- What concentrations are present?

Furthermore, first responders should know that APRs do *not* protect against oxygen-deficient or oxygen-enriched atmospheres. The three primary limitations of an APR are as follows:

- Limited life of its filters and canisters
- Need for constant monitoring of the contaminated atmosphere
- Need for a normal oxygen content of the atmosphere before use

Particulate-Removing Filters

Particulate filters protect the user from particulates (including airborne diseases) in the air. These filters may be used with half facepiece masks or full facepiece masks. Eye protection must be provided when the full facepiece mask is not worn.

In the U.S., particulate-removing filters are classified by their level of effectiveness and regulated by Title 42 (Public Health) *CFR* 84, *Approval of Respiratory Protection Devices*. They are divided into nine classes, three levels of filtration (95, 99, and 99.97 percents), and three categories of filter degradation. The following three categories of filter degradation indicate the use limitations of the filter:

WARNING

Do *not* wear APRs during emergency operations where unknown atmospheric conditions exist. Wear APRs only in controlled atmospheres where the hazards present are completely understood and at least 19.5 percent oxygen is present. SCBA must be worn during emergency operations.

Take the following precautions before using APRs or PAPRs:

- Know what chemicals/air contaminants are in the air.
- Know how much of the chemicals/air contaminants are in the air.
- Ensure that the oxygen level is between 19.5 and 23.5 percent.
- Ensure that atmospheric hazards are below IDLH conditions.

- *N* — not resistant to oil
- *R* — resistant to oil
- *P* — used when oil or nonoil lubricants are present

Particulate filters can also be described as absolute and nonabsolute. *Absolute* filters use screening to remove particles from the air; that is, they exclude the particles that are larger than the filter's pores. However, most respirator filters are *nonabsolute* filters, which means they contain pores larger than the particles to be removed. Absolute and nonabsolute filters use combinations of interception capture, sedimentation capture, inertial impaction capture, diffusion capture, and electrostatic capture to remove particles.

In the fire and emergency services, particulate-removing filters are used primarily at emergency medical incidents, but they may also be used to protect against toxic dusts, mists, metal fumes, asbestos, and similar hazards. High-efficiency particulate air (HEPA) filters used for medical emergencies must be 99.97 percent efficient, while 95 and 99 percent effective filters may be used depending on the health risk hazard **(Figure 6.15).**

Figure 6.15 Medical response units may be equipped with particle masks in addition to APR units.

Figure 6.16 Particle masks are classified as particulate-removing air-purifying filters, but they will not protect against very small particulates such as asbestos. *Courtesy of Federal Emergency Management Agency (FEMA) News Photo.*

Particle masks (also known as *dust masks*) are also classified as particulate-removing air-purifying filters **(Figure 6.16).** These disposable masks protect the respiratory system from large-sized particulates and are worn when working with particulate-producing tools such as paint sprayers or sanding equipment. Dust masks provide very limited protection and should not be used to protect against chemical hazards or small particles such as asbestos fibers.

Vapor- and Gas-Removing Filters

As the name implies, vapor-and-gas-removing cartridges and canisters are designed to protect against specific vapors and gases. They typically use some kind of sorbent material to remove the targeted vapor or gas from the air (see sidebar). Individual cartridges and canisters are usually designed to protect against related groups of chemicals such as *organic vapors* or *acid gases.* Many manufacturers color-code their canisters and

Figure 6.17 APR canisters, filters, and cartridges are usually color coded to indicate what hazards they are designed to protect against.

cartridges so it is easy to see what contaminant(s) the canister or cartridge is designed to protect against **(Figure 6.17).** Manufacturers also provide information about contaminant concentration limitations.

Air-Purifying Terms

Catalyst

A *catalyst* is a substance that influences the rate of chemical reaction between or among other substances. A catalyst used in respirator cartridges and canisters is Hopcalite®, a mixture of porous granules of manganese and copper oxides that speeds the reaction between toxic carbon monoxide and oxygen to form carbon dioxide.

Sorbent

A *sorbent* is a material, compound, or system that holds by adsorption or absorption. *Adsorption* retains the contaminant molecule on the surface of the sorbent granule by physical attraction. The intensity of the attraction varies with the type of sorbent and contaminant. Adsorption by physical attraction holds the adsorbed molecules weakly. When chemical forces are involved in the process (chemisorption), the bonds holding the molecules to the sorbent granules are much stronger and can be broken only with great difficulty. An *absorbent* is a solid or liquid that absorbs other substances. A characteristic common to all adsorbents is a large specific surface area, up to 1,500 m^2/g of sorbent. Activated charcoal is the most common adsorbent and is used primarily to remove organic vapors, although it does have some capacity for adsorbing acid gases.

Powered Air-Purifying Respirator

The PAPR uses a blower to pass contaminated air through a product that removes the contaminants and supplies the purified air to the facepiece (**Figure 6.18**). Several types of PAPRs are available. Some units are supplied with a small blower and are battery operated. The small size allows users to wear one on their belts. Other units have a stationary blower (usually mounted on a vehicle) that is connected by a long, flexible tube to the respirator facepiece.

Supplied-Air Hood

Powered- and supplied-air hoods provide loose fitting, lightweight respiratory protection that can be worn with glasses, facial hair, and beards (**Figure 6.19**). Hospitals, emergency rooms, and other fire and emergency services organizations use these hoods as an alternative to other respirators, in part, because they require no fit testing and are simple to use.

Figure 6.18 A blower forces ambient air through the filter canister and into the facepiece of this powered air-purifying respirator (PAPR).

Protective Breathing Equipment Limitations

To operate effectively, first responders must be aware of the limitations of protective breathing equipment. These include limitations of the wearer, the equipment, and the air supply.

Wearer

[NFPA 472: 5.3.3(1)(b), 5.4.3(5)]

The following physical, medical, and mental limitations affect first responders' ability to use respiration protection equipment effectively:

- *Physical condition* — The wearer must be in good physical condition in order to maximize the work that can be performed and to stretch the air supply as far as possible.

- *Agility* — Wearing a protective breathing apparatus with an air cylinder or backpack restricts wearers' movements and affects their balance. Good agility can overcome these obstacles.

- *Facial features* — The shape and contour of the face affect the wearer's ability to get a good facepiece-to-face seal. Fit testing must be performed to ensure that facepieces fit properly.

Figure 6.19 Supplied-air hoods are gaining in popularity because they are simple to use and require no fit testing.

- **Neurological functioning** — Good motor coordination is necessary for operating effectively in protective breathing equipment.

- **Mental soundness** — First responders must be of sound mind to handle emergency situations that may arise.

- **Muscular/skeletal condition** — First responders must have the physical strength and size required to perform necessary tasks while wearing protective breathing equipment.

- **Cardiovascular conditioning** — Poor cardiovascular conditioning can result in heart attacks, strokes, or other related problems during strenuous activity.

- **Respiratory functioning** — Proper respiratory functioning maximizes the wearer's operation time while wearing respiratory protection.

- **Training in equipment use** — First responders must be knowledgeable in every aspect of protective breathing apparatus use.

- **Self-confidence** — First responders' belief in their abilities has an extremely positive overall effect on the actions that are performed.

- **Emotional stability** — The ability to maintain control in an excited or high-stress environment reduces the chances of making a serious mistake.

Do not assign a task requiring use of respirators and other PPE unless the individual is physically able to do the work. Review the wearer's medical history and require a physical examination to determine the individual's capabilities. The medical doctor who completes the physical exam to determine fitness for duty for respirator use has the authority to deem the individual fit or unfit. Responders are at risk when wearing a respirator if they have any of the following diseases or conditions:

- Asthma

- Emphysema

- Chronic lung disease

- Psychological problems or symptoms including claustrophobia

- Physical deformities or abnormalities of the face

- Medical condition requiring medication usage

- Intolerance to increased heart rate, which can be produced by heat stress

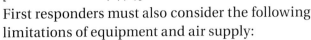

Equipment
[NFPA 472: 5.3.3(1)(a)]

First responders must also consider the following limitations of equipment and air supply:

- **Limited visibility** — Facepieces reduce peripheral vision, and facepiece fogging can reduce overall vision.

- **Decreased ability to communicate** — Facepieces hinder voice communication.

- **Increased weight** — Depending on the model, the protective breathing equipment can add 25 to 35 pounds (11 kg to 16 kg) of weight to the emergency responder.

- **Decreased mobility** — The increase in weight and splinting effect of the harness straps reduce the wearer's mobility.

- **Inadequate oxygen levels** — APRs cannot be worn in IDLH or oxygen-deficient atmospheres.

- **Chemical specific** — APRs can only be used to protect against certain chemicals. The specific type of cartridge depends on the chemical the wearer is exposed to.

Air Supply
[NFPA 472: 5.3.3(1)(a)]

Open- and closed-circuit SCBA have maximum air-supply durations that limit the amount of time a first responder has to perform the tasks at hand. Some of the limitations affecting air supply include the following:

- **Physical condition of user** — If the wearer is in poor physical condition, the air supply is depleted faster.

- **Degree of physical exertion** — The harder that wearers exert themselves, the faster the air supply is depleted.

- **Emotional stability** — Persons who become excited increase their respirations and use air faster.

- *Condition of equipment* — Minor leaks and poor adjustment of regulators can result in excess air loss.

- *Cylinder pressure before use* — If the cylinder is not filled to capacity, the amount of working time is reduced proportionately.

- *Training and experience* — Poorly trained and inexperienced personnel use air at a fast rate.

Respiratory Protection Programs and Fit Testing

A written policy covering the proper use of all respiratory protection equipment is required by NFPA 1500, *Standard on Fire Department Occupational Safety and Health Program* (2002); NFPA 1582, *Standard on Comprehensive Occupational Medical Program for Fire Departments* (2003); and OSHA 29 *CFR* 1910.134. Individual facepiece fit testing and medical testing is required of all employees who are going to use respiratory protection equipment. For more information on respiratory protection programs and fit testing, see the IFSTA **Respiratory Protection for Fire and Emergency Services** manual.

Respiratory Protection Program

Like all operating procedures and policies, a respiratory protection program must be defined in a written document that is reviewed periodically and revised as necessary. A respiratory protection policy requires the following elements in the written program:

- Selection criteria for respirators

- Inspection criteria

- Proper-use procedures

- Individual facepiece fit testing for employees

- Maintenance program

- Training program

- Air-quality testing program

- Medical evaluation and certification for those wearing respirators

- Procedures for regularly evaluating program effectiveness

Facepiece Fit Testing

Fit testing helps to ensure a full and complete seal of the mask to the face. Testing must be done before allowing any employee to use the mask in a hazardous atmosphere **(Figure 6.20)**. The requirement for a proper fit prohibits the wearing of any facial hair such as beards or sideburns that would interfere with a complete seal of the facepiece on the wearer. Specific steps in the fit-testing process are found in the IFSTA **Respiratory Protection for Fire and Emergency Services** manual and OSHA 29 *CFR* 1910.134. Medical clearance is required before fit testing.

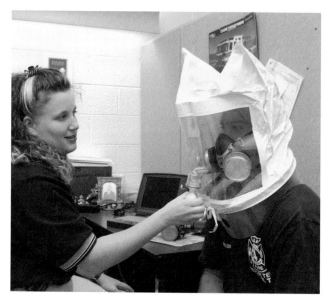

Figure 6.20 Facepiece fit testing must be performed before a responder is allowed to use the mask in a hazardous or potentially hazardous atmosphere.

Medical Testing

Medical requirements for personnel using respiratory protection must be included in the written respiratory protection policy. Both NFPA and OSHA require that all personnel who use respirators have a medical evaluation. General guidelines for these evaluations can be found in NFPA 1582. The initial medical evaluation, which usually takes place when an individual is hired, provides a baseline for all future evaluations. Thereafter, annual evaluations are performed on each employee. An employee's medical records are confidential, and the organization's physician may release only a pass/fail result of the pulmonary fitness test.

What Does This Mean to You?

The minimum requirement for respiratory protection at hazardous materials incidents (emergency operations until concentrations have been determined) is positive-pressure SCBA. Therefore, the minimum respiratory protection for first responders at the Operational Level is positive-pressure SCBA in atmospheres where the conditions and potential hazards are unknown and/or unquantified. APRs and PAPRs can only be used under the following conditions:

- Air contaminant(s)/hazards are known.
- Concentration(s) of the contaminant(s)/hazards are known.
- The oxygen level is between 19.5 and 23.5 percent.
- The atmosphere is below IDLH conditions.

Awareness-Level responders should not be close enough to the hazardous material to require respiratory protection.

PPE for Chemical, Biological, Radiological, Nuclear, and Explosive Events

[ODP Operations III.c.]

Because of the potentially extreme hazards associated with CBRNE materials likely to be used in terrorist attacks (such as military nerve agents), DHS has adopted standards developed by NIOSH or NFPA for personal protective equipment to protect first responders against these hazards. NIOSH also certifies SCBA and recommends ways to select and use protective clothing and respirators for protection against biological agents for emergency responders including law enforcement and EMS personnel. These standards are described as follows:

- ***NIOSH Chemical, Biological, Radiological and Nuclear (CBRN) Standard for Open-Circuit Self-Contained Breathing Apparatus (SCBA) (December 2001)*** — This standard establishes performance and design requirements to certify SCBA for use in CBRN exposures by first responders. The standard employs a three-tier certification program:

— The first two tiers of the program ensure the SCBA meets current minimum NIOSH requirements and enhanced requirements of NFPA 1981, including greater flow, improved breathing resistance, environmental stresses, communications, and vision.

— The third tier incorporates special testing conducted by NIOSH to identify the hazard a first responder is likely to encounter at a terrorist event and to define levels of respiratory protection required for the first responder.

- ***NIOSH Standard for Chemical, Biological, Radiological, and Nuclear (CBRN) Full Facepiece Air-Purifying Respirator (APR) (April 2003)*** — This standard specifies minimum requirements to determine the effectiveness of full-facepiece APRs (commonly referred to as *gas masks*) used during entry into CBRN atmospheres that are not IDLH. Atmospheres that are above IDLH concentrations require the use of SCBA.

- ***NIOSH Standard for Chemical, Biological, Radiological, and Nuclear (CBRN) Air-Purifying Escape Respirator and CBRN Self-Contained Escape Respirator (October 2003)*** — This standard specifies minimum requirements to determine the effectiveness of escape respirators that address CBRN materials identified as inhalation hazards from possible terrorist events for use by the general working population. Escape respirators (also known as *escape hoods*) come in two types.

— In the first type, called an *air-purifying escape respirator,* a filter canister is mounted on the hood. The user breathes outside air through the canister, which filters out harmful contaminants before the air is inhaled.

— The second type, called a *self-contained escape respirator,* consists of a hood with a tightly fitting neckpiece and a contained source of breathing air. The hood provides a barrier against contaminated outside air, and the user breathes air from the attached source.

- ***NFPA 1951, Standard on Protective Ensemble for USAR Operations (2001)*** — Urban search and rescue (USAR) operations in urban and other nonwilderness locations are complex incidents requiring specially trained personnel and special equipment to complete the mission.

— This standard establishes minimum requirements for garments, head protection, gloves, and footwear for fire and emergency services personnel operating at technical rescue incidents involving building or structural collapse, vehicle/person extrication, confined-space entry, trench/cave-in rescue, rope rescue, and similar incidents.

— The requirements of the standard address the design, performance, testing, and certification of these ensembles and ensemble elements to protect against physical, environmental, thermal, chemical-splash, and bloodborne hazards associated with USAR operations.

- **NFPA 1981, Standard on Open-Circuit Self-Contained Breathing Apparatus for Fire and Emergency Services (2002)** — This document specifies the minimum requirements for the design, performance, testing, and certification of SCBA for fire and emergency services personnel.

- **NFPA 1991, Standard on Vapor-Protective Ensembles for Hazardous Materials Emergencies (2000)** — This standard specifies minimum requirements for the design, performance, testing, and certification of elements of vapor-protective ensembles:

— For emergency responders responding to hazardous materials incidents and chemical or biological terrorism incidents and for protection from specified chemical-vapor, liquid-splash, and particulate exposures.

— Also provides additional optional requirements for protection from chemical and biological agents that could be released during a terrorism incident, chemical flash-fire protection, liquefied gas protection, and combined chemical flash-fire and liquefied-gas protection.

- **NFPA 1994, Standard on Protective Ensembles for Chemical/Biological Terrorism Incidents (2001)** — This standard establishes minimum requirements for ensembles and ensemble elements for fire and emergency services personnel exposed to victims and agents during assessment, extrication, rescue, triage, and treatment operations at chemical and biological terrorism incidents.

— The requirements address the design, performance, testing, documentation, and certification of these protective ensembles that provide protection for fire and emergency services personnel from terrorism agents, including dual-use industrial chemicals, chemical-terrorism agents, or biological-terrorism agents.

— The standard establishes three levels of protective ensembles (Class 1, Class 2, and Class 3 ensembles [see sidebar]) that could be selected for protection of fire and emergency services personnel based on what the incident risk analysis indicates is necessary protection for the intended operations.

- **NFPA 1999, Standard on Protective Clothing for Emergency Medical Operations (2003)** — This standard establishes minimum performance requirements for ensembles and ensemble elements to protect first responders from contact with blood- and body-fluid-borne pathogens when providing victim or patient care during emergency medical operations. This standard specifies minimum documentation, design, performance, testing, and certification requirements for new single-use and new multiple-use emergency medical clothing used by fire and emergency services personnel during emergency medical services (EMS) operations. These items include the following:

— *Garments:* both full and partial, upper and lower torso protection

— *Three types of gloves:* (1) examination gloves for patient care, (2) work gloves for situations that pose higher physical hazards such as extrication, and (3) cleaning gloves for handling and cleaning contaminated EMS equipment

— *Footwear*

— *Face protection*

EMS PPE must provide blood- and body-fluid pathogen barrier protection to whatever parts of the body they cover. While no partial protection is allowed for the EMS PPE item, the items might be configured to cover only part of the upper or lower torso such as arms with sleeve protectors, torso front with apron-styled garments, and face with faceshields.

NIOSH Certification of SCBA

In April, 2000, NIOSH entered into a *Memorandum of Understanding* with the National Institute of Standards and Technology (NIST), OSHA, and NFPA to jointly develop a certification program for SCBA used in emergency response to terrorist attacks. Working with the U.S. Army Soldier and Biological Chemical Command (SBCCOM), they developed a new set of respiratory protection standards and test procedures for SCBA used in situations involving weapons of mass destruction. Under this voluntary program, NIOSH issues a special approval and label identifying the SCBA as appropriate for use against chemical, biological, radiological, and nuclear agents. The SCBA certified under this program must meet the following minimum requirements:

- Approval under NIOSH 42 *CFR* 84, Subpart H
- Compliance with NFPA 1981
- Special tests under NIOSH 42 *CFR* 84.63(c):
  — Chemical Agent Permeation and Penetration Resistance Against Distilled Sulfur Mustard (HD [military designation]) and Sarin (GB [military designation])
  — Laboratory Respirator Protection Level (LRPL)

NIOSH maintains and disseminates an approval list for the SCBAs approved under this program.

NFPA 1994: PPE Ensemble Classifications

NFPA 1994 establishes performance requirements for three classes of PPE ensembles that are used in situations involving chemical or biological terrorism agents. Unlike EPA levels that describe widely different combinations of PPE (from work uniforms to vapor-protective clothing), the NFPA 1994 classes apply very specifically to the different performance standards of chemical (and biological) protective clothing.

The ensembles for all three classes must be designed to protect the wearer's upper and lower torso, head, hands, and feet; ensemble elements must include protective garments, protective gloves, and protective footwear. Ensembles can be either encapsulating or nonencapsulating and must accommodate appropriate respiratory protection.

Each ensemble (or component) bears a label describing the class to which it belongs and the circumstance for which it is designed to be used. According to NFPA 1994, manufacturers must provide a variety of information with liquid-splash protective clothing items or ensembles, including safety considerations, PPE limitations, storage practices, recommended inspection procedures, directions for use, storage life, and care and maintenance instructions.

Class 1

Class 1 ensembles provide the highest degree of protection. They are designed to protect responders at chemical/biological terrorism incidents in the following situations:

- Whenever the identity or concentration of the vapor or liquid agent is undetermined or in question
- When vapor protection is needed
- Anytime liquid contact is expected and no direct skin contact can be permitted because exposure may present a serious health threat such as death or incapacitation (as with chemical nerve agents)

Class 2

Class 2 ensembles are designed to protect responders at chemical/biological terrorism incidents in the following situations:

- To provide necessary sufficient vapor protection for the intended operation
- When direct contact with liquid droplets is likely
- When victims are not ambulatory but are showing signs or symptoms of exposure

Class 3

Class 3 ensembles are designed to protect responders at chemical/biological terrorism incidents in the following situations:

- To provide necessary sufficient liquid protection for the intended operation
- When direct contact with liquid droplets is likely
- When victims are impaired but ambulatory

This list is entitled "CBRN (Chemical, Biological, Radiological, and Nuclear agents) SCBA (Self-Contained Breathing Apparatus)" and contains the name of the approval holder, model, component parts, accessories, and rated duration. This list is maintained as a separate category within the NIOSH Certified Equipment List.

NIOSH authorizes the use of an additional approval label on apparatus that demonstrate compliance to the CBRN criteria. This label is placed in a visible location on the SCBA backplate (for example, on the upper corner or in the area of the cylinder neck). The addition of this label provides visible and easy identification of equipment for its appropriate use. A sample label is shown:

CBRN Agent Approved

See Instructions for Required Component
Part Numbers, Accessories, and Additional
Cautions and Limitations of Use

NIOSH Recommendations for Protective Clothing and Respirators

The approach to any potentially hazardous atmosphere (including biological hazards) must be made with a plan that includes an assessment of hazard and exposure potential, respiratory protection needs, entry conditions, exit routes, and decontamination strategies. Any plan involving a biological hazard should be based on relevant infectious disease or biological safety recommendations by the Centers for Disease Control and Prevention (CDC) and other expert groups, including emergency first responders, law enforcement officers, and public health officials. The need for decontamination and treatment of all first responders with antibiotics or other medications should be decided in consultation with local public health authorities.

The *Interim Statement* (October, 2001) is based on current understanding of the potential threats and existing recommendations issued for biological aerosols. CDC makes this judgment because of the following facts:

- Biological weapons may expose people to bacteria, viruses, or toxins as fine airborne particles. Depending upon the particular type of agent, biological agents are infectious through one or more of the following mechanisms of exposure:

  — Inhalation (with infection through respiratory mucosa or lung tissues)

  — Ingestion

  — Contact with the mucous membranes of the eyes or nasal tissues

  — Penetration of the skin through open cuts (even very small cuts and abrasions of which people might be unaware)

  Organic airborne particles share the same physical characteristics in air or on surfaces as inorganic particles from hazardous dusts. This fact has been demonstrated in military research on biological weapons and in civilian research to control the spread of infection in hospitals.

- Because biological weapons are particles, they will not penetrate the materials of properly assembled and fitted respirators or protective clothing.

- Existing recommendations for protecting workers from biological hazards require the use of half-mask or full facepiece APRs with particulate filter efficiencies ranging from N95 (for hazards such as pulmonary tuberculosis) to P100 (for hazards such as hantavirus) as a minimum level of protection.

- Some devices used for intentional biological terrorism may have the capacity to disseminate large quantities of biological materials in aerosols.

- Emergency first responders typically use SCBA respirators with full facepieces operated in the most protective, positive-pressure (pressure demand) mode during emergency responses. This type of SCBA provides the highest level of protection against airborne hazards when properly fitted to the user's face and properly used. *Details:*

  — NIOSH respirator policies state that under those conditions, SCBA reduces the user's exposure to a hazard by a factor of at least

10,000. This reduction is true whether the hazard is from airborne particles, a chemical vapor, or a gas.

— SCBA respirators are used when hazards and airborne concentrations are either unknown or expected to be high. Respirators providing lower levels of protection are generally allowed once conditions are understood and exposures are determined to be at lower levels.

When using respiratory protection, the type of respirator is selected on the basis of the hazard and its airborne concentration. For a biological agent, the air concentration of infectious particles depends upon the method used to release the agent. Current data suggest that the SCBA that first responders currently use for entry into potentially hazardous atmospheres provides responders with respiratory protection against biological exposures associated with a suspected act of biological terrorism.

Protective clothing, including gloves and booties, also may be required for the response to a suspected act of biological terrorism. Protective clothing may be needed to prevent skin exposures and/or contamination of other clothing. The type of protective clothing needed depends upon the type of agent, concentration, and route of exposure.

The interim recommendations for PPE, including respiratory protection and protective clothing, are based upon the anticipated level of exposure risk associated with different response situations such as the following:

• Responders should use a NIOSH-approved, pressure-demand SCBA in conjunction with a Level A protective suit when responding to a suspected biological incident where any of the following information is unknown or the event is uncontrolled:
— Type(s) of airborne agent(s)
— Dissemination method
— If dissemination via an aerosol-generating device is still occurring or has stopped; there is no information on the duration of dissemination or what the exposure concentration might be

• Responders may use a Level B protective suit with an exposed or enclosed NIOSH-approved pressure-demand SCBA when the situation can be defined in the following situations:
— Suspected biological aerosol is no longer being generated
— Other conditions may present a splash hazard

• Responders may use a full facepiece respirator with a P100 filter or a PAPR with HEPA filters when it can be determined that the situations are as follows:
— An aerosol-generating device was not used to create high airborne concentration
— Dissemination was by a letter or package that can be easily bagged

These types of respirators reduce the user's exposure by a factor of 50 if the user has been properly fit tested.

Care should be taken when bagging letters and packages to minimize creating a puff of air that could spread pathogens. It is best to avoid large bags and to work very slowly and carefully when placing objects in bags. Disposable hooded coveralls, gloves, and foot coverings also should be used. NIOSH recommends against wearing standard firefighter turnout gear into potentially contaminated areas when responding to reports involving biological agents.

Decontamination of protective equipment and clothing is an important precaution to make sure that any particles that might have settled on the outside of protective equipment are removed before doffing gear. Decontamination sequences currently used for hazardous material emergencies should be used as appropriate for the level of protection employed. Equipment can be decontaminated using soap and water, and 0.5 percent hypochlorite solution (one part household bleach to 10 parts water) can be used as appropriate or if gear had any visible contamination. Note that bleach may damage some types of firefighter turnout gear (one reason why it should not be used for biological-agent response actions). After doffing gear, response workers should shower using large quantities of soap and water.

Source: NIOSH *Interim Statement,* Publication 2002-109, October, 2001.

Protective Ensembles for Law Enforcement and EMS Personnel

A 1999 assessment conducted by the U.S. Army SBCCOM concluded that law enforcement and EMS personnel can be equipped with an effective low-cost clothing ensemble when responding to incidents of chemical-warfare terrorism. An ensemble consisting of a high-quality respirator, butyl rubber gloves, and a commercial chemical overgarment (elastic wrists and hood closures with built-in boots) will provide some liquid-droplet and vapor protection to the responder. This level of protection would only be used by personnel working on the perimeter (cold zone only) of an incident. It might also provide some protection in the area around the cold/warm zone boundary (where responders might be assisting with the evacuation or decontamination process). However, it must be emphasized that this clothing ensemble is *NOT* adequate protection for patrol officers in areas where significant levels of chemical warfare agent vapor concentration might be present such as in the hot zone.

PPE Ensembles, Classifications, and Selection

[NFPA 472: 5.1.2.1(2)(c)]

The approach in selecting PPE must encompass an *ensemble* of clothing and equipment items that are easily integrated to provide both an appropriate level of protection and still allow one to perform activities involving hazardous materials such as chemicals **(Figure 6.21)**. For example, simple protective clothing such as gloves and a work uniform in combination with a faceshield (or safety goggles) may be sufficient to prevent chemical exposure to certain chemical solids or etiological agents (such as bloodborne pathogens). At the other end of the spectrum, the use of vapor-protective, TECP suits combined with positive-pressure SCBA is considered the minimum level of protection necessary when dealing with vapors, gases, or particulates of material that are harmful to skin or capable of being absorbed through the skin.

Figure 6.21 A PPE ensemble must be appropriate for the activities to be performed as well as the hazards present. PAPRs, as shown in this photo, should only be used in controlled atmospheres where the hazards present are completely understood and at least 19.5 percent oxygen is present.

The following list of components may form the chemical-protective ensemble:

- Protective clothing (suits, coveralls, hoods, gloves, and boots)
- Respiratory equipment (SCBA, combination SCBA/SAR, and APR)
- Cooling system (ice vest, air circulation, and water circulation)
- Communications device
- Head protection
- Eye protection
- Ear protection
- Inner garment
- Outer protection (overgloves, overboots, and flashcover)

Factors that affect the selection of ensemble components include the following:

- Consider how each item accommodates the integration of other ensemble components. Some ensemble components may be incompatible due to how they are worn; for example, some SCBAs may not fit within a particular chemical-protective suit or allow acceptable mobility when worn.

- Consider the ease of interfacing ensemble components without sacrificing required task performance; for example, a poorly fitting overglove can reduce wearer dexterity. Performance issues range from the need to climb ladders to the potential need of law enforcement or military personnel to fire weapons during terrorist attacks.

- Consider limiting the number of equipment items to reduce donning time and complexity; for example, some communications devices are built into SCBAs, which are NIOSH certified as a unit.

While the EPA has established a set of chemical-protective PPE ensembles providing certain levels of protection that are commonly used by fire and emergency service organizations, other organizations such as law enforcement, industrial responders, and the military may have their own standard operating procedures (SOPs) or equivalent procedures guiding the choice and use of appropriate combinations of PPE. A special weapons attack team (SWAT) may be equipped with a far different PPE ensemble than a firefighter, haz mat technician, or environmental cleanup person responding to the same terrorist incident.

EPA Levels of Protection
[29 CFR 1910.120(q)(6)(ii)(B)]

The EPA has established the following levels of protective equipment: Level A, Level B, Level C, and Level D (**Figures 6.22, 6.23, 6.24,** and **6.25**). NIOSH, OSHA, and the U.S. Coast Guard (USCG) also recognize these levels. They can be used as the starting point for ensemble creation; however, each ensemble must be tailored to the specific situation in order to provide the most appropriate level of protection.

Selecting protective clothing and equipment by how they are designed or configured alone is not sufficient to ensure adequate protection at haz mat

Figure 6.22 The EPA Level A ensemble consists of a fully encapsulating vapor-protective suit worn over an SCBA. *Courtesy of Kenneth Baum.*

Figure 6.23 The EPA Level B ensemble consists of a liquid-splash protective suit and SCBA. *Courtesy of Kenneth Baum.*

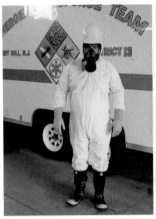

Figure 6.24 The EPA Level C ensemble consists of a liquid-splash protective suit and air-purifying respirator. *Courtesy of Kenneth Baum.*

Figure 6.25 The EPA Level D ensemble consists of work uniforms, street clothing, or coveralls. *Courtesy of Kenneth Baum.*

incidents. Just having the right components to form an ensemble is not enough. First responders must understand that the EPA levels of protection do not define or specify what performance (for example, vapor protection or liquid-splash protection) the selected clothing or equipment must offer, and they do not mirror the performance requirements of NFPA 1991 and 1992.

Level A

The Level A ensemble provides the highest level of protection against vapors, gases, mists, and particles for the respiratory tract, eyes, and skin.

Operational-Level responders are generally not allowed to operate in situations requiring Level A protection. However, Operational-Level personnel must be appropriately trained to wear Level A PPE if they are required to wear it. The elements of Level A ensembles are as follows:

- **Components** — Ensemble requirements from NFPA 471, *Recommended Practice for Responding to Hazardous Materials Incidents* (2002),* are as follows:

  — Positive-pressure, full facepiece, SCBA, or positive-pressure airline respirator with escape SCBA approved by NIOSH

  — Vapor-protective suits: TECP suits constructed of protective-clothing materials that meet the following criteria:

    ○ Cover the wearer's torso, head, arms, and legs

    ○ Include boots and gloves that may either be an integral part of the suit or separate and tightly attached

    ○ Enclose the wearer completely by itself or in combination with the wearer's respiratory equipment, gloves, and boots

    ○ Provide equivalent chemical-resistance protection for all components of a TECP suit (such as relief valves, seams, and closure assemblies)

    ○ Meet the requirements in NFPA 1991.

  — Coveralls (optional)

  — Long underwear (optional)

  — Chemical-resistant outer gloves

  — Chemical-resistant inner gloves

  — Chemical-resistant boots with steel toe and shank

  — Hard hat (under suit) (optional)

  — Disposable protective suit, gloves, and boots (can be worn over totally encapsulating suit, depending on suit construction)

  — Two-way radios (worn inside encapsulating suit)

- **Protection Provided** — Highest available level of respiratory, skin, and eye protection from solid, liquid, and gaseous chemicals.

- **Use** — Ensembles are used in the following situations:

  — Chemical hazards are unknown or unidentified.

  — Chemical(s) have been identified and have high level of hazards to respiratory system, skin, and eyes.

  — Site operations and work functions involve a high potential for splash, immersion, or exposure to unexpected vapors, gases, or particulates of material that are harmful to skin or capable of being absorbed through intact skin.

  — Substances are present with known or suspected skin toxicity or carcinogenicity.

  — Operations that are conducted in confined or poorly ventilated areas.

Level B

Level B protection requires a garment that includes an SCBA or a supplied-air respirator and provides protection against splashes from a hazardous chemical. This ensemble is worn when the highest level of respiratory protection is necessary but a lesser level of skin protection is needed. A Level B ensemble provides liquid-splash protection, but little or no protection against chemical vapors or gases to the skin. Level B CPC may be encapsulating or nonencapsulating. The elements of Level B ensembles are as follows:

- **Components** — Ensemble requirements from NFPA 471* are as follows:

  — Positive-pressure, full facepiece, SCBA, or positive-pressure airline respirator with escape SCBA approved by NIOSH

  — Hooded chemical-resistant clothing that meets the requirements of NFPA 1992 (overalls and long-sleeved jacket, coveralls, one- or two-piece chemical-splash suit, and disposable chemical-resistant overalls)

  — Coveralls (optional)

  — Chemical-resistant outer gloves

  — Chemical-resistant inner gloves

  — Chemical-resistant boots with steel toe and shank

— Disposable chemical-resistant outer boot covers (optional)

— Hard hat (outside or on top of nonencapsulating suits or under encapsulating suits)

— Two-way radios (worn inside encapsulating suit or outside nonencapsulating suit)

— Faceshield (optional)

- **Protection Provided** — Ensembles provide the same level of respiratory protection as Level A but have less skin protection. Ensembles provide liquid-splash protection, but no protection against chemical vapors or gases.

- **Use** — Ensembles are used in the following situations:

— Type and atmospheric concentration of substances have been identified and require a high level of respiratory protection but less skin protection.

— Atmosphere contains less than 19.5 percent oxygen or move than 23.5 percent oxygen.

— Presence of incompletely identified vapors or gases is indicated by a direct-reading organic vapor-detection instrument, but the vapors and gases are known not to contain high levels of chemicals harmful to skin or capable of being absorbed through intact skin.

— Presence of liquids or particulates is indicated, but they are known not to contain high levels of chemicals harmful to skin or capable of being absorbed through intact skin.

Level C

Level C protection differs from Level B in the area of equipment needed for respiratory protection. Level C is composed of a splash-protecting garment and an air-purifying device (APR or PAPR). Level C protection includes any of the various types of APRs. Emergency response personnel would not use this level of protection unless the specific material is known, it has been measured, and this protection level is approved by the incident commander (IC) after all qualifying conditions for APRs and PAPRs have been met (that is, the product is known, an appropriate filter is available, the atmospheric oxygen concentration is between 19 to 23.5 percent, and the atmosphere is not IDLH).

Periodic air monitoring is required when using this level of PPE. The elements of Level C ensembles are as follows:

- **Components** — Ensemble requirements from NFPA 471* are as follows:

— Full-face or half-mask APRs, NIOSH approved

— Hooded chemical-resistant clothing (overalls, two-piece chemical-splash suit, and disposable chemical-resistant overalls)

— Coveralls (optional)

— Chemical-resistant outer gloves

— Chemical-resistant inner gloves

— Chemical-resistant boots with steel toe and shank

— Disposable, chemical-resistant outer boot covers (optional)

— Hard hat

— Escape mask (optional)

— Two-way radios (worn under outside protective clothing)

— Face shield (optional)

- **Protection Provided** — Ensembles provide the same level of skin protection as Level B but have a lower level of respiratory protection. Ensembles provide liquid-splash protection but no protection from chemical vapors or gases on the skin.

- **Use** — Ensembles are used in the following situations:

— Atmospheric contaminants, liquid splashes, or other direct contact will not adversely affect exposed skin or be absorbed through any exposed skin.

— Types of air contaminants have been identified, concentrations have been measured, and an APR is available that can remove the contaminants.

— All criteria for the use of APRs are met.

— Atmospheric concentration of chemicals does not exceed IDLH levels. The atmosphere must contain between 19.5 and 23.5 percent oxygen.

Level D

[NFPA 472: 4.4.1(5)(a)]

Level D ensembles consist of typical work uniforms, street clothing, or coveralls. This PPE level is used for nuisance contamination only. Level D protection can be worn only when no atmospheric hazards exist. The elements of Level D ensembles are as follows:

- **Components** — Ensemble requirements from NFPA 471* are as follows:
  - Coveralls
  - Gloves (optional)
  - Chemical-resistant boots/shoes with steel toe and shank
  - Disposable, chemical-resistant outer boot covers (optional)
  - Safety glasses or chemical-splash goggles
  - Hard hat
  - Escape device in case of accidental release and the need to immediately *escape* the area (optional)
  - Faceshield (optional)
- **Protection Provided** — Ensembles provide no respiratory protection and minimal skin protection.
- **Use** — Ensembles may not be worn in the hot zone and are not acceptable for haz mat emergency response above the Awareness Level. Level D ensembles are used when both of the following conditions exist:
  - Atmosphere contains no hazard.
  - Work functions preclude splashes, immersion, or the potential for unexpected inhalation of or contact with hazardous levels of any chemicals.

---

*Reprinted with permission from NFPA 471-2002 *Responding to Hazardous Materials Incidents*, Coypright © 2002, National Fire Protection Association, Quincy, MA. This reprinted material is not the complete and official position of the NFPA on the referenced subject, which is represented only by the standard in its entirety.

PPE Selection Factors

Many available sources can be consulted for determining which type and what level of PPE to use at haz mat incidents. First-arriving responders often rely upon information in the *Emergency Response Guidebook (ERG)* to determine the minimum type of protection required for defensive operations. This information is found in the *ERG* on the orange-bordered Guide pages.

The *ERG* recommendation for 1-2 butylene oxide (orange Guide 127) is: *Wear positive-pressure self-contained breathing apparatus (SCBA). Structural firefighter's protective clothing will only provide limited protection.* Selection of the PPE for offensive operations is a complex matter and should be performed only by technically qualified personnel.

There are some things that first responders need to know and remember in the selection process. For example, the use of PPE itself can create significant wearer hazards such as heat stress and physical and psychological stress, in addition to impaired vision, mobility, and communication. In general, the higher the level of PPE is, the greater the associated risks. For any given situation, select equipment and clothing that provide an adequate level of protection. Overprotection as well as underprotection can be hazardous and should be avoided.

Many factors affect the selection of PPE ensembles at haz mat incidents. First responders trained to Awareness and Operational Levels will not make the decisions about which PPE is worn by haz mat technicians entering the hot zone, but it is nevertheless important for them to understand the selection process. General selection factors that need to be considered are as follows:

- **Chemical hazards** — Chemicals present a variety of hazards such as toxicity, corrosiveness, flammability, reactivity, and oxygen deficiency. Depending on the chemicals present, any combination of hazards may exist.
- **Physical environment** — Exposure to hazardous materials or chemicals can happen anywhere under various conditions. The choice of ensemble components must account for varied conditions:

- Industrial settings, on the highways, or in residential areas

- Exposure may occur either indoors or outdoors

- Environments may be extremely hot, extremely cold, or moderate

- Exposure sites may be relatively uncluttered or rugged (which presents a number of physical hazards)

- Incident resolution activities may involve entering confined spaces, lifting heavy items, climbing ladders, or crawling on the ground.

- *Exposure Duration*—The protective qualities of ensemble components may be limited by a variety of factors, including exposure levels, material chemical resistance, and air supply. The decision for determining how long to use an ensemble must be made by assuming the worst-case exposure so that safety margins can be added to increase the protection available to personnel.

- *Available Protective clothing or equipment* — An array of different clothing or equipment should be available to personnel to meet all intended applications. Reliance on one particular clothing type or equipment item may severely limit a facility's ability to handle a broad range of hazardous materials or chemical exposures. In its acquisition of equipment and protective clothing, the responsible authority should attempt to provide a high degree of flexibility while choosing protective clothing and equipment that is easily integrated and provides protection against each conceivable hazard.

Protective clothing selection factors include the following:

- *Clothing design* — Manufacturers sell clothing in a variety of styles and configurations. Design considerations include the following:
  - Clothing configuration
  - Seam and closure construction
  - Components and options
  - Sizes
  - Ease of donning and doffing
  - Clothing construction

- Accommodation of other selected ensemble equipment
- Comfort
- Restriction of mobility

- *Material chemical resistance* — The chosen material(s) must resist permeation, degradation, and penetration by the respective chemicals. Mixtures of chemicals can be significantly more aggressive towards protective clothing materials than any single chemical alone. One permeating chemical may pull another with it through the material. Other situations may involve unidentified substances. *Details:*

  - Very little test data are available for chemical mixtures. If clothing must be used without test data, clothing that demonstrates the best chemical resistance against the widest range of chemicals should be chosen.

  - In cases of chemical mixtures and unknowns, serious consideration must be given to selecting protective clothing.

- *Physical properties* — Clothing materials may offer wide ranges of physical qualities in terms of strength, resistance to physical hazards, and operation in extreme environmental conditions. Comprehensive performance standards (such as those from NFPA) set specific limits on these material properties, but only for limited applications such as emergency response. Users may also need to ask manufacturers the following questions:

  - Does the material have sufficient strength to withstand the physical strength of the tasks at hand?

  - Will the material resist tears, punctures, cuts, and abrasions?

  - Will the material withstand repeated use after contamination and decontamination?

  - Is the material flexible or pliable enough to allow users to perform needed tasks?

  - Will the material maintain its protective integrity and flexibility under hot and cold extremes?

  - Is the material flame-resistant or self-extinguishing (if these hazards are present)?

— Are garment seams in the clothing constructed so they provide the same physical integrity as the garment material?

- **Ease of decontamination** — The degree of difficulty in decontaminating protective clothing may dictate whether disposable clothing, reusable clothing, or a combination of both is used.

- **Cost** — Protective clothing end users must endeavor to obtain the broadest array of protective equipment they can buy with available resources to meet their specific applications.

PPE Care and Inspection

[ODP Awareness Level III.b.]
[ODP Operations III.a.]

When wearing protective clothing and equipment, the user must take all necessary steps to ensure that the protective ensemble performs as expected. During emergencies is not the right time to discover discrepancies in the protective clothing or respiratory protection. Following a standard program for inspection, proper storage, maintenance, and cleaning along with realizing PPE limitations is the best way to avoid hazardous materials or chemical exposure during emergency response.

Inspection Procedures

All PPE and respiratory protection equipment must be inspected on a routine basis. Inspection schedules should be written down as part of an organization's predetermined procedures. An effective CPC inspection program features the following five different inspections:

- Inspection and operational testing of equipment received new from the factory or distributor

- Inspection of equipment when it is selected for a particular hazardous material or chemical operation

- Inspection of equipment after use or training and before maintenance

- Periodic inspection of stored equipment

- Periodic inspection when a question arises concerning the appropriateness of selected equipment or when problems with similar equipment are discovered

Each inspection covers different areas with varying degrees of depth. Personnel responsible for clothing inspection should follow manufacturers' directions; many vendors provide detailed inspection procedures. The generic inspection checklist given in **Table 6.1** may serve as an initial guide for developing more extensive procedures.

Records must be kept of all inspection procedures. Assign individual identification numbers to all reusable pieces of equipment (many clothing and equipment items may already have serial numbers), and maintain records by that number. Periodic review of these records can provide an indication of protective clothing or equipment that requires excessive maintenance and can also serve to identify clothing or equipment that is susceptible to failure. At a minimum, record the following information at each inspection:

- Clothing or equipment item identification number

- Date of inspection

- Person making the inspection

- Results of the inspection

- Any unusual conditions noted

Respiratory equipment is initially inspected when it is purchased. Once the equipment is placed into service, the organization's personnel perform periodic inspections. Operational inspections of respiratory protection equipment occur after each use, daily or weekly, monthly, and annually. The organization must define the frequency and type of inspection in the respiratory protection policy.

Self-Contained Breathing Apparatus
[NFPA 472: 5.4.3(7)]

NFPA 1852, *Standard on Selection, Care, and Maintenance of Open-Circuit Self-Contained Breathing Apparatus (SCBA),* list the following components of an SCBA that need to be inspected with the inspection requirements for each:

- **Facepiece** — Inspect for the following conditions:

  — Deterioration, pliability, and tackiness of the facepiece skirt; cracks, tears, and holes in the skirt; dirt

Table 6.1
Sample PPE Checklist

Clothing

Before Use:

☐ Determine that the clothing material is correct for the specified task at hand.

Visually inspect for the following:

☐ Imperfect seams
☐ Nonuniform coatings
☐ Tears
☐ Malfunctioning closures
☐ Pinholes (hold up to light)

Flex product:

☐ Observe for cracks
☐ Observe for other signs or shelf deterioration

If the product has been used previously, inspect inside and out for signs of chemical attack. Note the following conditions:

☐ Discoloration
☐ Swelling
☐ Stiffness

During the work task, periodically inspect for the following:

☐ Evidence of chemical attack such as discoloration, swelling, stiffening, and softening. Keep in mind, however, that chemical permeation can occur without any visible effects.
☐ Closure failure
☐ Tears
☐ Punctures
☐ Seam discontinuities

Chemical Protective Gloves

Before Use:

☐ Pressurize glove to check for pinholes. Either blow into glove, and then roll gauntlet towards fingers, or inflate glove and hold under water. In either case, no air should escape.

Vapor Protective Suits

Before Use:

☐ Check the operation of pressure relief valves
☐ Inspect the fitting of wrists, ankles, and neck
☐ Check faceshield (if so equipped) for the following:
    ☐ cracks
    ☐ crazing
    ☐ fogginess

— Breaks, wear, or loss of elasticity in head-harness buckles, straps, and webbing

— Full extension of head-harness straps

— Holes, cracks, scratches, and heat damage to the lens and a proper seal with the facepiece material **(Figure 6.26)**

— Cleanliness and proper operation of valve seat, springs, and covers for the exhalation valve where present

— Proper operation of or damage to regulator connection(s)

— Damage to and cleanliness of the speaking diaphragm where present

— Operation of inhalation valve on the nosecup

• *Backframe and harness assembly* — Inspect for the following conditions:

— Cuts, tears, abrasion, heat damage, and chemical-related damage

— Proper operation of buckles, fasteners, and adjustments

— Damage to and proper operation of the cylinder retention system (cylinder should be securely attached to the backframe)

— Full extension of harness straps

• *Cylinder assembly* — Inspect for the following conditions:

— Current hydrostatic test date on the cylinder **(Figure 6.27)**

— Damage to the cylinder pressure gauge

— Cracks, dents, weakened areas, indications of heat damage, and indications of chemical damage in the cylinder body

— Cuts, gouges, loose composite materials, and the absence of resin in the composite portion of the cylinder

— Damage to cylinder valve outlet sealing surface and threads

— Damage to and proper alignment, serviceability, and secure attachment of valve hand wheel

— Debris in and cleanliness of burst disc outlet area

— Cylinder fully charged to within 90 percent of rated capacity

— Cylinder's original manufacturer date; check to ensure that the cylinder's service life has not expired

• *Hose* — Inspect for the following conditions:

— Cuts, abrasions, bubbling, cracks, and heat or chemical damage

— Visual signs of damage to external fittings

— Tight connections with regulator, cylinder, and facepiece fittings

— Condition of protective sleeves

Figure 6.26 When inspecting the SCBA facepiece, check for damage or separation of the facepiece lens and the facepiece material.

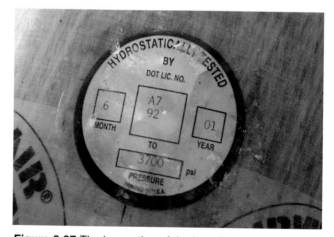

Figure 6.27 The inspection of the breathing-air cylinder includes checking to make certain that the hydrostatic test date is visible and current. If there is any doubt, the cylinder must be removed from service and tested.

- *End-of-service-time indicator(s)* — Inspect for the following conditions:
  - Damage to, cleanliness, and secure attachment of the alarm and mounting hardware
  - Proper activation at 20 to 25 percent of the rated cylinder pressure
- *Regulator* — Inspect for the following conditions:
  - Damage to and proper operation of regulator controls where present
  - Visual damage to pressure relief devices
  - Damage to housing and components
  - Any unusual sounds such as whistling, chattering, clicking, or rattling during test operation
  - Proper function of regulator and bypass during test operation
- *Pressure indicator* — Inspect for the following conditions:
  - Damage
  - Cylinder pressure gauge and the remote gauge read within 10 percent of each other **(Figure 6.28)**

Accessories such as communications devices that are attached to the SCBA are inspected for wear, damage, security, cleanliness, and proper operation. Quick-fill male and female connections,

Figure 6.28 The air-pressure indicators on the regulator and the breathing-air cylinder must be inspected with pressure on the system. The two gauges should register within 10 percent of each other.

voice amplifiers, and the like should be maintained in accordance with manufacturer guidelines. The low-pressure alarm should sound once when the unit is initially pressurized. During inspection, the dual alarm should be checked as well. Personal alert safety system (PASS) devices that are integrated into the SCBA system are inspected for the following conditions:

- Wear and damage
- Secure attachment of covers and compartments
- Proper operation of all modes
- Operation of the low-battery warning signal

After each component of the system is inspected, the entire SCBA is checked for pressure retention by closing all regulator valves, opening the cylinder valve to pressurize the SCBA, and then closing the cylinder valve. The SCBA shall hold the system pressure (according to the manufacturer's specifications) after the cylinder valve is closed. Following the pressure check, the system pressure is released. The unit is then cleaned, placed in service or storage, or submitted for repairs depending on the outcome of the inspections.

Supplied-Air Respirator

The components of the SAR system that need to be inspected are as follows:

- Facepiece
- Harness assembly
- Air source
- Hose
- End-of-service-time indicator(s)
- Regulator
- Accessories
- EBSS **(Figure 6.29, p. 358)**

In addition to the inspection steps used for the SCBA, combination SCBA/SAR units should be inspected for the condition and operation of the airline connection and control valve. SAR units equipped with EBSS should follow the same outline as the SCBA with the following addition: SCBA/SAR units that are intended for use with fully encapsulating hazardous materials suits must include the inspection of the air supply line fittings on the suit.

Figure 6.29 All components of the EBSS attached to an SAR must be inspected, including the valves, hoses, cylinder, harness, and regulator connections shown in this photo.

Air-Purifying Respirator

Visual inspections provide assurance that an APR is ready to be placed into service and will provide its designed level of protection. The inspection process recommended by NIOSH for APRs includes the following components:

- *Facepiece* — Inspect for the following conditions:

  — Excessive dirt

  — Cracks, tears, holes, or distortion from improper storage

  — Inflexibility (stretch and massage the material to restore flexibility)

  — Cracked or badly scratched lenses in facepieces (**Figure 6.30**)

  — Incorrectly mounted lens or broken or missing mounting clips

  — Cracked or broken air-purifying element holders, badly worn threads, or missing gaskets

- *Head straps or head harness* — Inspect for the following conditions:

  — Breaks

  — Loss of elasticity

Figure 6.30 Facepiece lenses should be inspected for physical, chemical, or heat damage that may obscure the user's vision.

  — Broken or malfunctioning buckles and attachments

  — Excessively worn serration on the head harness buckle that might permit slippage

- *Exhalation valve* — Inspect for the following conditions:

  — Debris in and around the valve seat

  — Cracks, tears, or distortions in the valve material

  — Improper insertion of the valve body in the facepiece

  — Cracks, breaks, or chips in the valve body, particularly in the sealing surface

  — Missing or defective valve cover

  — Improper installation of the valve in the valve body

- *Egress or escape unit* — Inspect the breathing-air cylinder following the items listed under Self-Contained Breathing Apparatus section given earlier.

- *Air-purifying element* — Inspect for the following conditions:

  — Incorrect cartridge, canister, or filter for the assigned hazard

  — Incorrect installation, loose connections, missing or worn gaskets, or cross-threading in the holder

  — Expired shelf-life date on the cartridge or filter

— Cracks or dents in the outside case of filter, cartridge, or canister

— Evidence of prior use of sorbent cartridge or canister (indicated by absence of sealing material, tape, or foil over the inlet)

- *Corrugated breathing tube* (if part of APR) — Inspect for the following conditions:

— Broken or missing end connectors, gaskets, or *O*-rings

— Missing or loose hose clamps

— Deterioration (determined by stretching the tube and looking for cracks)

- *Front- or back-mounted gas mask harness*

— Inspect for the following conditions:

— Damage or wear to the canister holder that may prevent its being held securely in place

— Broken harness straps or fastenings

— Cleanliness

— Absorbent type and condition

Filters intended for the removal of gases and vapors may be equipped with NIOSH-approved end-of-service-life indicators (ESLIs). These ESLIs warn the user that the sorbent is approaching saturation and is no longer effective. The remaining usefulness of the filter should be determined and the filter replaced as needed. For filters without ESLIs, a sorbent change schedule must be established. This schedule is based on the manufacturer's recommendation for filter use. The manufacturer may also provide information about the chemical hazard the filter is designed to protect against.

Storage

PPE must be stored properly to prevent damage or malfunction from exposure to dust, moisture, sunlight, damaging chemicals, extreme temperatures (hot and cold), and impact. Procedures are needed for both initial receipt of equipment and after use or exposure of that equipment. Many manufacturers specify recommended procedures for storing their products. Follow these procedures to avoid equipment failure resulting from improper storage.

Some specific guidelines for general storage of CPC (whether new or potentially contaminated) include the following:

Potentially Contaminated CPC

- Store potentially contaminated clothing in an area separate from street clothing or unused protective clothing.

- Store potentially contaminated clothing in a well-ventilated area with good airflow around each item if possible.

New or Decontaminated CPC

- Store different types and materials of clothing and gloves separately to prevent issuing the wrong material by mistake (for example, many glove materials are black and cannot be identified by appearance alone).

- Fold or hang protective clothing in accordance with manufacturer instructions.

- Store clothing out of direct sunlight in a place where temperature and humidity can be controlled.

Maintenance
[NFPA 472: 5.4.3(7)]

Manufacturers frequently restrict the sale of certain protective-suit parts to individuals or groups who are specially trained, equipped, or authorized by the manufacturer to purchase them. Adopt explicit procedures to ensure that only those individuals who have specialized training and equipment perform the appropriate level of maintenance. Personnel should *never* attempt to repair equipment without checking with the person who is responsible for CPC maintenance. Many manufacturers also indicate which repairs, if performed in the field, void the warranty of their products. All repairs made must be documented on the records for the specific clothing along with appropriate inspection results.

The care, cleaning, and maintenance schedules of respiratory protection equipment should be based on the manufacturer's recommendation, NFPA standards, or OSHA requirements. The minimum requirements are as follows:

- Clean respiratory protection equipment as needed during the daily/weekly inspections at the beginning of the work period.

- Inspect, clean, and disinfect respiratory protection equipment following use before placing it back into service **(Figure 6.31, p. 360)**.

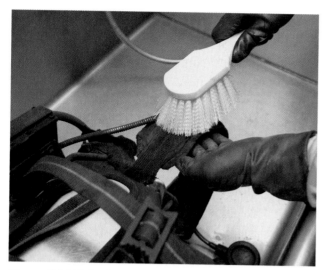

Figure 6.31 Following use, respiratory protection equipment (such as this SCBA backpack harness) should be cleaned to remove dirt, grime, and contaminants. Personnel should wear protective gloves and other garments to protect themselves from exposure to unknown contaminants.

- Clean respiratory protection equipment units that are used infrequently during the weekly inspection when required. Clean units before placing them in storage. Clean as needed when units are removed from storage.

Part of the postincident care and cleaning process is to replace used filters, cartridges, and canisters. Because these items may have been contaminated with hazardous materials, certain protocols must be followed. Follow the manufacturer's recommendations along with the authority's policy.

The processes of disinfecting, cleaning, and drying SCBA facepieces are extremely important. If facepieces are not cleaned properly, they can spread infection through the eyes, nose, and mouth of the wearer. Disinfecting and cleaning facepieces must follow the manufacturer's recommendation and the guidelines found in the current edition of NFPA 1852 or other applicable respiratory protection standards. The written protocols for cleaning and disinfecting SCBA facepieces must designate the areas for cleaning and disinfecting and methods for maintaining them. This cleaning and disinfecting must *never* be done in kitchens or bathrooms.

Designated Cleaning and Disinfecting Areas

OSHA 29 *CFR* 1910.1030, *Bloodborne Pathogens;* NFPA 1500; and 1581, *Standard on Fire Department Infection Control Program* (2000), require separate areas be designated for cleaning and disinfecting PPE **(Figure 6.32).** One designated area is for the cleaning of equipment and protective clothing. The other area is for disinfecting emergency medical

Generic Cleaning Procedures for Respiratory Protection Equipment

The methods used for cleaning and disinfecting respiratory protection equipment must not cause damage to the equipment or harm to the user. Generic cleaning steps are as follows:

Step 1: Remove filters, cartridges, or canisters. Disassemble the facepiece to the extent instructed by the manufacturer. Discard or repair defective parts.

Step 2: Wash components in warm (maximum 110°F [43°C]) water with a mild detergent or with a cleaner recommended by the manufacturer. Use a stiff bristle (not wire) brush to facilitate the removal of dirt or grime.

Step 3: Rinse components *thoroughly* in clean, warm, preferably running water. Drain.

NOTE: The importance of thorough rinsing cannot be overemphasized. Detergent or disinfectant residue that dries on facepieces may cause dermatitis. In addition, some disinfectants may cause deterioration of rubber parts or corrosion of metal parts if they are not completely removed.

Step 4: Immerse respirator components in one of the disinfectants listed for at least 2 minutes if the cleaner does not contain a disinfecting agent:

- Hypochlorite solution (50 ppm chlorine)
- Aqueous solution of iodine (50 ppm)
- Other disinfectants approved by the manufacturer that are equally potent

Step 5: Repeat *Step 3* if *Step 4* was implemented.

Step 6: Air-dry or hand-dry components with a clean, lint-free cloth.

Step 7: Reassemble the facepiece, and replace the filtering elements.

Step 8: Test the respirator to verify that all components work properly.

Figure 6.32 This well-lighted respiratory protection equipment cleaning area includes two sinks, shelves, drain boards, and storage for cleaning supplies.

and other equipment/clothing. Cleaning materials such as scrub brushes, disinfectant solutions, soaps, and sponges are stored in these two areas within easy reach of sinks.

To prevent further exposure or contamination, personnel performing decontamination and disinfection procedures must wear chemical goggles, aprons, and vinyl medical gloves. Provide a written protocol for disinfecting and cleaning of protective clothing, medical equipment, and fire-fighting tools and apparatus. Post this protocol in the disinfecting area and include it in the health and safety training for all personnel. The health and safety officer or infection control officer must ensure that all personnel wear proper clothing when they are involved in cleaning or disinfecting activities. Allow equipment that has been cleaned or disinfected to drain into the sink and not onto the floor. This precaution prevents the possibility of tracking contaminated water into living and working areas and also prevents slipping hazards. Provide well-ventilated drying areas for clothing and equipment.

In addition to the cleaning and disinfecting sinks, locate an eyewash stand and disinfecting shower within the work area **(Figure 6.33).** In the event of a corrosive liquids spill, the area must be available to an injured person to reduce potential injuries by flushing the contact area or diluting the corrosive liquid. The eyewash stand and disinfecting shower must have proper drainage

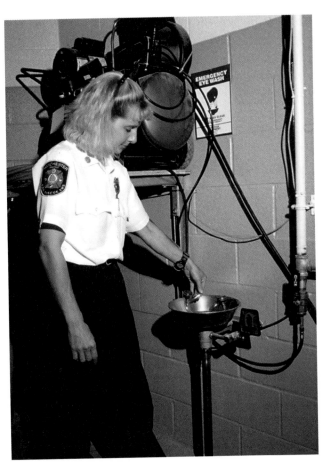

Figure 6.33 Eyewash stands must be provided in work areas where corrosive liquids are used or stored.

and not leak onto the floor where contaminants could create a slipping hazard or track into the living quarters.

Cleaning Area

The designated cleaning area must be equipped with proper ventilation, lighting, and drainage facilities. Drainage must be connected to sanitary sewer systems or septic tanks and located away from kitchens, sleeping and living quarters, bathrooms, offices or other working areas, and designated disinfecting areas. Personal protective clothing, fire-fighting equipment, and portable equipment are cleaned in this area. The immediate cleaning of contaminated clothing and equipment prevents the potential contamination of other personnel or other portions of the facility.

Disinfecting Area

The designated disinfecting area is primarily intended for the disinfecting of medical equipment exposed to bloodborne pathogens. It is designated for disinfecting only and is *not* used for the cleaning of mops, other materials used for general cleaning, or equipment and clothing that have not been contaminated by blood or other body fluids. Equip the area with a stainless steel, two-bay utility sink with hot- and cold-water services, nonporous rack shelving, adequate drainage, proper lighting, and proper ventilation. Immediate disinfecting of contaminated medical equipment reduces the possibility of exposure to bloodborne pathogens by other personnel.

Climate Concerns and Health Issues

[NFPA 472: 5.4.3(4)] [ODP Operations III.b.]
Wearing personal protective equipment protects an individual from a hostile climate: both heat and cold extremes. The body functions efficiently in a narrow temperature range. The core temperature of an individual is the deep temperature of the body — not the skin or extremities temperature. The body can sustain a small fluctuation of 2 degrees below and 3 degrees above the normal core temperature of 99.7°F (37.6°C) or normal oral temperature of 98.6°F (37°C). When this range is exceeded, serious health threats exists. Prolonged exposure to freezing temperatures can also result in serious health problems.

Most types of PPE inhibit the body's ability to disperse heat, which is magnified because a first responder is usually performing strenuous work while wearing the equipment. Take preventive measures to reduce the effects of any temperature extreme. Medical monitoring of responders is required when they are at risk because of environmental hazards

Heat Disorders

Wearing PPE or other special full-body protective clothing puts the wearer at considerable risk of developing heat stress. It is important for first responders to understand the effects of heat stress. This stress can result in health effects ranging from transient heat fatigue to serious illness (heat stroke) or death. Heat stress is caused by a number of interacting factors, including the following:

- Climate conditions
- Type of protective ensemble worn
- Work activity required
- Individual characteristics of the responder

When selecting CPC and respiratory equipment, carefully evaluate each item's benefits and its potential to increase the risk of heat stress. For example, if a lighter, less insulating suit can be worn without a sacrifice in protection, choose it. Because the incidence of heat stress depends on a variety of factors, monitor all personnel wearing full-body chemical-protective ensembles (see Medical Monitoring section).

First responders need to be aware of several heat disorders, including heat stroke (the most serious), heat exhaustion, heat cramps, heat rashes, and heat fatigue. In addition, they should know how to prevent the effects of heat exposure.

Heat Stroke

Heat stroke occurs when the body's system of temperature regulation fails and body temperature rises to critical levels. This condition is caused by a combination of highly variable factors, and its occurrence is difficult to predict. **Heat stroke is a serious medical emergency and requires immediate medical treatment and transport to a medical care facility.** The primary signs and symptoms of heat stroke are as follows:

- Confusion
- Irrational behavior
- Loss of consciousness
- Convulsions
- Lack of sweating (usually)
- Hot, dry skin
- Abnormally high body temperature (for example, a rectal temperature of 105.8°F [41°C])

When the body's temperature becomes too high, it causes death. The elevated metabolic temperatures caused by a combination of workload and environmental heat load, both of which contribute to heat stroke, are also highly variable and difficult to predict. If a first responder shows signs of possible heat stroke, obtain professional medical treatment immediately.

Heat Exhaustion

The signs and symptoms of heat exhaustion are headache, nausea, vertigo, weakness, thirst, and giddiness. Heat exhaustion responds readily to prompt treatment. However, do not dismiss heat exhaustion lightly for several reasons: (1) The fainting associated with heat exhaustion can be dangerous because the victim may be operating machinery or controlling an operation that should not be left unattended; moreover, the victim may be injured when fainting. (2) The signs and symptoms seen in heat exhaustion are similar to those of heat stroke. Untreated heat exhaustion can lead to heat stroke.

Heat Cramps

Performing hard physical labor in a hot environment usually causes heat cramps. These cramps have been attributed to an electrolyte imbalance caused by sweating. It is important to understand that cramps can be caused by both too much and too little salt. Cramps appear to be caused by the lack of water replenishment. Because sweat is a hypotonic solution (±0.3 percent sodium chlorine [NaCl]), excess salt can build in the body if the water lost through sweating is not replaced. Thirst is not reliable as a guide to the need for water; instead, water must be taken every 15 to 20 minutes in hot climates.

Under extreme conditions, such as working for 6 to 8 hours in heavy protective gear, a loss of sodium may occur. Recent studies have shown that drinking commercially available carbohydrate-electrolyte replacement liquids is effective in minimizing environmental disturbances during recovery.

Heat Rashes

Heat rashes are the most common problem in hot work environments. Prickly heat is manifested as red papules and usually appears in areas where clothing is restrictive. As sweating increases, these papules give rise to a prickling sensation. Prickly heat occurs in skin that is persistently wetted by unevaporated sweat. Heat-rash papules may become infected if they are not treated. Heat rashes generally disappear when the affected individual returns to a cool environment.

Heat Fatigue

A factor that predisposes an individual to heat fatigue is lack of acclimatization. The use of a program of acclimatization and training for work in hot climates is advisable. The signs and symptoms of heat fatigue include impaired performance of skilled sensorimotor, mental, or vigilance jobs. There is no treatment for heat fatigue except to remove the heat stress before a more serious heat-related condition develops.

Heat-Exposure Prevention

Responders wearing protective clothing need to be monitored for effects of heat exposure. Methods to prevent and/or reduce the effects of heat exposure include the following:

- **Fluid consumption** — Use water or commercial body-fluid-replenishment drink mixes to prevent dehydration. First responders should drink generous amounts of fluids both before and during operations. Drinking 7 ounces (200 ml) of fluid every 15 to 20 minutes is better than drinking large quantities once an hour. Balanced diets normally provide enough salts to avoid cramping problems. *Details:*
  - Before working, drinking chilled water is good.
  - After a work period in protective clothing and an increase in core temperature, drinking room-temperature water is better. It is not as severe a shock to the body.

- **Body ventilation** — Wear long cotton undergarments or similar types of clothing to provide natural body ventilation.

- **Body cooling** — Provide mobile showers and misting facilities to reduce the body temperature and cool protective clothing. Wearing cooling vests beneath CPC can also help cooling (**Figure 6.34, p. 364**).

- **Rest areas** — Provide shaded and air-conditioned areas for resting.

- **Work rotation** — Rotate responders exposed to extreme temperatures or those performing difficult tasks frequently.

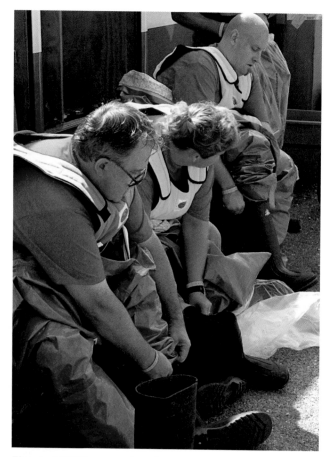

Figure 6.34 The use of cooling vests can help prevent heat illness when wearing chemical-protective clothing.

- *Proper liquids* — Avoid liquids such as alcohol, coffee, and caffeinated drinks (or minimize their intake) before working. These beverages can contribute to dehydration and heat stress.
- *Physical fitness* — Encourage responders to maintain good physical fitness.

Cold Disorders

Cold temperatures caused by weather and/or other conditions such as exposure to cryogenic liquids are also environmental factors that must be considered when selecting PPE. Prolonged exposure to freezing temperatures can result in health problems as serious as trench foot, frostbite, and hypothermia. Protection from the cold must be a priority when conditions warrant.

An individual gains body heat from food and muscular activity and loses it through convection, conduction, radiation, and sweating to maintain a constant body temperature. When body temperature drops even a few degrees below its normal oral temperature of 98.6°F (37°C), the blood vessels constrict, decreasing peripheral blood flow to reduce heat loss from the surface of the skin. Shivering generates heat by increasing the body's metabolic rate. If you suspect someone may have hypothermia, look for the actions ending in the suffix -*umbles* — *stumbles, mumbles, fumbles,* and *grumbles*. These actions show that cold is affecting how well a person's muscles and nerves work.

The four primary enironmental conditions that cause cold-related stress are low temperatures, high/cool winds, dampness, and cold water. Wind chill, a combination of temperature and velocity, is a crucial factor to evaluate when working outside. For example, when the actual air temperature of the wind is 40°F (4.4°C) and its velocity is 35 mph (56 kmph), the exposed skin experiences conditions equivalent to the still-air temperature of 11°F (-12°C). A dangerous situation of rapid heat loss may arise for any individual exposed to high winds and cold temperatures. The major risk factors for cold-related stresses are as follows:

- Wearing inadequate or wet clothing that increases the effects of cold on the body
- Taking certain drugs or medications such as alcohol, nicotine, caffeine, and other medications that inhibit the body's response to the cold or impairs judgment
- Having a cold or certain diseases such as diabetes, heart conditions, vascular problems, and thyroid problems that may make a person more susceptible to winter elements
- Being male may increase risk to cold-related stresses (men seem to experience far greater death rates due to cold exposure than women, perhaps due to inherent risk-taking activities, body-fat composition, or other environmental differences)
- Becoming exhausted or immobilized, especially due to injury or entrapment, that speeds the effects of cold weather
- Being elderly increases one's vulnerability to the effects of harsh winter weather

CPC in Cold Climates

The use of CPC in cold climates can cause harm because it is not designed to provide thermal protection from the cold. CPC is *not* what to wear to shovel snow from a driveway. Warm clothing, gloves, foot protection, and head protection must be added to the CPC ensemble for cold temperatures.

Hypothermia

General hypothermia occurs when body temperature falls to a level where normal muscular and cerebral functions are impaired. While hypothermia is generally associated with freezing temperatures, it may occur in any climate where a person's body temperature falls below normal. For instance, hypothermia is common among the elderly who live in cold houses. Symptoms and treatment are as follows:

- *Initial symptoms* — When core body temperature decreases to around 95°F (35°C):
  - Shivering
  - Inability to do complex motor functions
  - Lethargy
  - Mild confusion

- *Moderate symptoms* — When body temperature continues to fall:
  - State of dazed consciousness
  - Fails to complete even simple motor functions
  - Slurred speech
  - Irrational behavior

- *Severe symptoms* — When body temperature falls below 90°F (32.2°C):
  - Hibernation state: slowing heart rate, blood flow, and breathing
  - Unconsciousness and full heart failure

- *Treatment*
  - Conserve remaining body heat (specific measures vary depending upon severity and setting: field or hospital).
    - Obtain shelter.
    - Remove wet clothing.
    - Add layers of dry clothing/blankets.
    - Use a prewarmed sleeping bag.
  - Provide additional heat sources.
  - Handle person very carefully because of the increased irritability of the cold heart.
  - Seek medical assistance.
  - Employ external rewarming techniques when medical treatment is significantly delayed:
    - Provide body-to-body contact (for example, place the person in a prewarmed sleeping bag with a person of normal body temperature).
    - Apply chemical heat packs or insulated hot water bottles (place in armpits, neck, chest, and groin areas to person lying down).
    - Give warm fluids orally, but avoid beverages containing alcohol or caffeine.

Trench Foot

Trench foot is caused by long, continuous exposure to a wet, cold environment or actual immersion in water. Symptoms and treatment are as follows:

- *Symptoms*
  - Tingling and/or itching sensation
  - Burning sensation
  - Pain
  - Swelling, sometimes forming blisters in more extreme cases

- *Treatment*
  - Move individual to a warm, dry area.
  - Wash and dry the affected tissue carefully.
  - Rewarm foot and elevate slightly.
  - Seek medical assistance as soon as possible.

Frostbite

Frostbite occurs when the skin tissue actually freezes, causing ice crystals to form between cells and draw water from them, which leads to cellular dehydration. Ears, fingers, toes, cheeks, and noses are primarily affected. Although this situation typically occurs at temperatures below 30°F (-1.1°C), wind-chill effects can cause frostbite at above-freezing temperatures. Symptoms and treatment are as follows:

- *Symptoms*
  - Uncomfortable sensations of coldness initially
  - Tingling, stinging, or aching feeling of the exposed area followed by numbness
  - Areas appearing white and cold to the touch (varies depending on whether rewarming has occurred)
  - Exposed areas becoming numb, painless, and hard to the touch (caused by freezing of deeper tissues such as muscles, tendons, and the like)
- *Treatment*
  - Seek medical assistance immediately.
  - Treat any existing hypothermia first (See Hypothermia section).
  - Cover frostbitten parts with dry, sterile gauze or soft, clean cloth bandages.
  - Do not massage frostbitten tissue because massage sometimes causes greater injury. Severe cases may require hospitalization and even amputation of affected tissue.
  - Take measures to prevent further cold injury.
  - Consult with a licensed health-care professional for training on rewarming techniques if formal medical treatment is delayed.

Medical Monitoring

NFPA 471 requires ongoing medical monitoring of responders who may be at risk because of environmental hazards (heat/cold stresses) as well as potential exposure to hazardous materials. Medical monitoring is conducted before responders wearing chemical liquid-splash or vapor-protective clothing enter the warm and hot zones as well as after leaving these zones **(Figure 6.35)**. The evaluation will check such things as vital signs, hydration, skin, mental status, and medical history. A postmedical monitoring follow-up is also required. OSHA Title 29 *CFR* 1910.120, *Hazardous Waste Operations and Emergency Response (HAZWOPER)* also has medical monitoring and surveillance requirements.

Summary

No single combination of protective equipment and clothing is capable of protecting against all

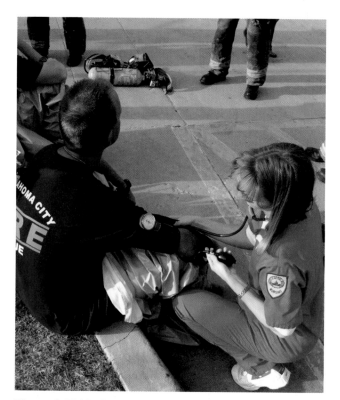

Figure 6.35 Medical monitoring should be conducted before responders wearing chemical liquid-splash or vapor-protective clothing enter the warm and hot zones as well as after they leave those zones.

hazards. Thus, first responders must use care and caution when selecting appropriate PPE for the incident. They must also be aware that the use of PPE can itself create significant worker hazards such as heat stress, physical and psychological stress, and impaired vision, mobility, and communication. In general, the higher the level of PPE protection is, the greater the associated risks.

The *ERG* provides recommendations on PPE and represents a good place to start looking for information about what PPE is appropriate given the chemical(s) involved in an incident. Overprotection can be as hazardous as underprotection and should be avoided. Personnel must receive training in how to use the PPE they are expected to wear. The two basic objectives of any PPE program is to protect the wearer from safety and health hazards and prevent injury to the wearer from incorrect use and/or malfunction of the PPE. To accomplish these goals, a comprehensive PPE program includes the following: hazard identification; medical monitoring; environmental surveillance; selection, use, maintenance, and decontamination of PPE; and training.

Part Two

Incident Problem-Solving Process

Chapter 7

Contamination and Decontamination

This chapter provides information that will assist the reader in meeting the following first responder competencies from NFPA 472, *Professional Competence of Responders to Hazardous Materials Incidents,* 2002 Edition. The numbers are noted directly in the text under the section titles where they are addressed.

NFPA 472

Chapter 5   Competencies for the First Responder at the Operational Level

5.1.2.1   The first responder at the operational level shall be able to perform the following tasks:

(2) Plan an initial response within the capabilities and competencies of available personnel, personal protective equipment, and control equipment by completing the following tasks:

   (d) Identify the emergency decontamination procedures

(3) Implement the planned response to favorably change the outcomes consistent with the local emergency response plan and the organization's standard operating procedures by completing the following tasks:

   (a) Establish and enforce scene control procedures including control zones, emergency decontamination, and communications

5.2.3   Predicting the Behavior of a Material and its Container. Given an incident involving a single hazardous material, the first responder at the operational level shall predict the likely behavior of the material and its container and also shall meet the following requirements:

(1) Given two examples of scenarios involving known hazardous materials, interpret the hazard and response information obtained from the current edition of the *Emergency Response Guidebook*; MSDS; CHEMTREC/CANUTEC/SETIQ; local, state, and federal authorities; and shipper/manufacturer contacts as follows:

   (b) Identify the differences between the following pairs of terms:

      i. Exposure and hazard

      ii. Exposure and contamination

      iii. Contamination and secondary contamination

5.3.4   Identifying Emergency Decontamination Procedures. The first responder at the operational level shall identify emergency decontamination procedures and shall meet the following requirements:

(1) Identify ways that personnel, personal protective equipment, apparatus, tools, and equipment become contaminated.

(2) Describe how the potential for secondary contamination determines the need for emergency decontamination procedures.

(3) Identify the purpose of emergency decontamination procedures at hazardous materials incidents.

(4) Identify the advantages and limitations of emergency decontamination procedures.

(5) Describe the procedure listed in the local emergency response plan or the organization's standard operating procedures for decontamination of a large number of people exposed to hazardous materials.

(6) Describe procedures, such as those listed in the local emergency response plan or the organization's standard operating procedures, to preserve evidence at hazardous materials incidents involving suspected criminal or terrorist acts.

5.4.1   Establishing and Enforcing Scene Control Procedures. Given scenarios for facility and/or transportation hazardous materials incidents, the first responder at the operational level shall identify how to establish and enforce scene control including control zones, emergency decontamination, and communications and shall meet the following requirements:

(4) Identify the considerations associated with locating emergency decontamination areas.

(5) Demonstrate the ability to perform emergency decontamination.

Emergency Responder Guidelines

This chapter provides information that will assist the reader in meeting the following first responder guidelines for fire service and law enforcement from the Office for Domestic Preparedness (ODP) *Emergency Responder Guidelines,* 2002 Edition. The numbers are noted directly in the text under the section titles where they are addressed.

ODP Emergency Responder Guidelines

Fire Service and Law Enforcement

Performance Level for Events Involving Weapons of Mass Destruction

III. **Know and follow self-protection measures and rescue and evacuation procedures for WMD events.** The responder should:

    h. Know how to implement appropriate decontamination procedures for victims, responders, mass casualties, and equipment. Understand the importance of proper decontamination of equipment that will be reused.

IV. **Know and follow procedures for working at the scene of a potential WMD event.** The responder should:

    c. Know how to implement appropriate on-the-scene decontamination procedures for protection of victims, the public, emergency responders, and others that may have been contaminated by agents or materials from a potential WMD event.

    d. Know how to implement basic life support procedures for protection and treatment of victims and others at the scene.

    e. Know how to implement procedures and measures for minimizing the spread of contamination of hazardous agents or materials to other locations and persons.

Chapter 7
Contamination and Decontamination

[NFPA 472: 5.3.4]

Contamination is the transfer of a hazardous material to persons, equipment, and the environment in greater than acceptable quantities. *Decontamination* (commonly referred to as *decon)* or *contamination reduction* is the process of removing hazardous materials to prevent the spread of contaminants beyond a specific area and reduce contamination to levels that are no longer harmful. Decontamination is performed when a victim, responder, animal, or equipment leaves the hot zone **(Figure 7.1)**. Everyone and everything in the hot zone is subject to contact with the hazardous material and can become contaminated. Because of this potential, anything that goes into the hot zone passes through a decon area when leaving the zone.

First responders need to understand how people, equipment, and the environment become contaminated. First responders at the Operational Level must be able to assist in decontamination operations, which include selecting a decon site, setting up the site, and performing both basic and emergency decon.

Because decon procedures, terminology, and other details may differ greatly from organization to organization, first responders should know their organization's predetermined decon procedures. This book primarily uses the decon terminology found in NFPA 471, *Recommended Practice for Responding to Hazardous Materials Incidents* (2002), and NFPA 472, *Standard for Professional Competence of Responders to Hazardous Materials Incidents* (2002). This chapter discusses contamination types, decontamination methods and types, and how to implement decontamination procedures.

Figure 7.1 Even animals that have entered the hot zone must be decontaminated.

Contamination

[NFPA 472: 5.3.4(1)]

Anytime hazardous materials are present at an emergency, it is possible that responders, their tools and equipment, and the public may become contaminated. Furthermore, there is a risk that contamination will spread beyond the point of initial contact. In other words, those individuals who were initially contaminated can then spread contamination wherever they go. Contamination is sometimes categorized as *primary* or *secondary* depending on how and where it occurs. Other categories include *surface* and *permeation* contaminations.

Primary (or Direct)

Primary or direct contamination (often simply referred to as *contamination*) occurs in the hot zone because of direct contact with a hazardous material. *Primary contamination* is the direct transfer of a hazardous material to persons, animals, equipment, and the environment. Victims or first responders exposed to a hazardous material — and emergency response personnel directly involved with offensive mitigation and control efforts within the hot zone — are very likely to become contaminated.

Ideally, first responders will recognize the presence or locations of hazardous materials in order to avoid primary contamination. However, they must be aware that walking into a liquid fuel spill, walking through a vapor cloud, or touching the material might contaminate them. Tools used by haz mat technicians to tighten a leaking valve or to plug a leak may become contaminated (**Figure 7.2**). Even vehicles can be contaminated if driven through contamination in the hot zone. Coming into contact with hazardous materials' dusts, particles, fumes, vapors, and mists along with runoff water can contaminate first responders and the environment. Smoke and other products of combustion are also sources of contamination. Law enforcement and other traffic-control personnel can become contaminated downwind of an incident if they come into contact with the hazardous material (pass through a plume or cloud) as it disperses. The environment becomes contaminated when materials soak into the ground or flow into storm drains and waterways.

Obviously, the easiest way to avoid contamination is to prevent or avoid contact with the hazardous material. For example, using remote sampling

What Is the Difference Between Contamination and Exposure?

[NFPA 472: 5.2.3(1)(b)(i–iii)]

A person who has been exposed to a hazardous material has not necessarily been contaminated by it. According to NFPA:*

Contamination is the process of transferring a hazardous material from its source to people, animals, the environment, or equipment, which may act as a carrier.

Exposure is the process by which people, animals, the environment, and equipment are subjected to or actually come in contact with a hazardous material.

It's a fine distinction, but, essentially, in the case of first responders (or other living organisms), exposure implies that individuals have been in a situation where the hazardous material had the potential to contact or enter their bodies (or has actually entered their bodies) by one or more routes of entry.

An example: If you smell perfume, you have been exposed to it because some of the perfume molecules have entered your nose in order to be smelled (*exposure route = inhalation*). However, you are not likely to carry the perfume (or its smell) around unless you have actually been contaminated by the perfume, which implies that you got enough of the material on you so that it physically remains there.

Chemical-protective clothing (CPC) is designed to protect a person from exposure to chemicals, but in the process of doing so, it (and the person, in the sense that the person is wearing the clothing) may become contaminated. Just because the CPC has become contaminated does not mean that the person has been exposed to the material. When a person is exposed to a chemical or other product, it is the *hazard* of the material (or the harm it can do) based on the nature of the exposure (amount inhaled, duration of exposure, and the like) that determines how it may ultimately affect a person's health.

---

* Reprinted with permission from NFPA 472, *Standard on Professional Competence of Responders to Hazardous Materials Incidents,* Copyright © 2002, National Fire Protection Association, Quincy, MA 00269. This reprinted material is not the complete and official position of the National Fire Protection Association on the referenced subject, which is represented only by the standard in its entirety.

Figure 7.2 Tools and equipment (including weapons carried by law enforcement personnel) used in the hot zone will need to be decontaminated. *Courtesy of Steve Hendrix.*

Figure 7.3 If decontamination is not conducted, secondary contamination can be spread well beyond the initial hot zone. *Courtesy of Steve Hendrix.*

devices, personal protective equipment (PPE), and confinement and containment techniques will minimize contact. First responders must have good situational awareness in order to avoid stepping in hazardous materials or contacting them accidentally with tools or equipment.

Secondary

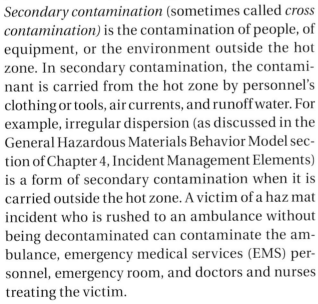

[NFPA 472: 5.3.4(2)]

Secondary contamination (sometimes called *cross contamination*) is the contamination of people, of equipment, or the environment outside the hot zone. In secondary contamination, the contaminant is carried from the hot zone by personnel's clothing or tools, air currents, and runoff water. For example, irregular dispersion (as discussed in the General Hazardous Materials Behavior Model section of Chapter 4, Incident Management Elements) is a form of secondary contamination when it is carried outside the hot zone. A victim of a haz mat incident who is rushed to an ambulance without being decontaminated can contaminate the ambulance, emergency medical services (EMS) personnel, emergency room, and doctors and nurses treating the victim.

If personnel are not decontaminated before leaving the hot zone, they can contaminate whomever and whatever they touch thereafter **(Figure 7.3)**. For example, their tools are a source of second-

ary contamination when laid on the ground in the cold zone or running board of fire apparatus. Both emergency decontamination and technical decontamination, discussed later in the chapter, prevent secondary contamination.

Surface and Permeation

As the name implies, *surface contamination* is limited to the surface of a material. This type of contamination doesn't penetrate, permeate, or soak into materials. For example, dry solids (chemical powders or dusts) are unlikely to contaminate anything except the outer surfaces they contact.

However, chemicals can also *permeate* or penetrate below the surface of a material, particularly if chemicals are liquids or gases and the material they are contacting is porous. As discussed in Chapter 6, Personal Protective Equipment, CPC is designed to prevent permeation contamination, but no one type of material is impervious to all chemicals.

In many cases, surface contamination will be easy to see and remove (see the dust; wash it off). In other cases, even though it may not be visible, it must be assumed that surfaces are contaminated. Contaminates that have permeated a material may be more difficult (or even impossible) to detect and remove. For this reason, responders must be aware of what the contaminant is and how likely it is to permeate a given material. Some examples are as follows:

- Powders are not as likely to permeate a material as a liquid.

- Wood handles on tools are more likely to be permeated by chemicals than metal handles.

- Cotton is more likely to be permeated by chemicals than rubber.

- Certain types of chemicals permeate certain types of CPC more rapidly than others.

Decontamination (Contamination Reduction)

[NFPA 472: 5.1.2.1(2)(d), 5.1.2.1(3)(a)]
[ODP Operations III.h., IV.e.]

As mentioned earlier, decontamination is performed to remove contaminants from PPE, tools, equipment, and anything else that has been contaminated. Realistically, since removing *all* contaminants may be impossible in many cases, decontamination is done simply to reduce contamination to a level that is no longer harmful (contamination reduction) **(Figure 7.4)**. Such decon is done to prevent harmful exposures and reduce or eliminate the spread of contaminants outside the hot zone.

Decon minimizes the chance of secondary contamination of people, animals, equipment, and the environment. It is an important function at all haz mat incidents. Operational-Level responders are often called upon to assist with decon procedures. A variety of factors determine whether the decontamination process is a relatively simple matter or an extremely complicated, technical one.

Figure 7.4 The purpose of decontamination is to reduce contamination to a safe level. *Courtesy of Chris Mickal.*

Decontamination Terminology

The process of decontamination can be categorized in the following ways:

- *Type* — Emergency, gross, technical (formal), secondary, definitive, buddy, or self

- *Method* — Wet or dry, physical, or chemical

- *People* — Patient decon and mass decon *versus* decon of response personnel

Operational-Level responders are primarily concerned with gross, emergency, and technical decon (according to the definitions used in this book). However, decon terminology differs greatly from region to region, so responders should be aware that these terms may be used differently in different areas. Some basic definitions for various types of decontamination are as follows:

- *Gross decon* — Quickly removing the worst surface contamination, usually by rinsing with water from handheld hoselines, emergency showers, or other water sources. This type is sometimes called *emergency decon*. However, some experts differentiate between *gross decon* and *emergency decon* in the following ways:

  — Gross decon takes place only within a decon corridor.

  — Emergency decon is done wherever necessary.

For purposes of this book, gross decon is performed on the following people in the following situations:

  — Entry team personnel before technical decon

  — Victims during emergency decon

  — Persons requiring mass decon

- *Emergency decon* — Removing contamination on individuals in potentially life-threatening situations with or without the formal establishment of a decontamination corridor. Emergency decon can consist of anything from simply removing contaminated clothing to flushing a person with water from a safety shower or hoseline. Emergency decon is a type of gross decon.

- *Technical (formal) decon* — Using chemical or physical methods to thoroughly remove contaminants from responders (primarily entry team personnel) and their equipment. It may also be used on incident victims in non-life-threatening situations. Technical decon is usually conducted within a formal decon line

Decontamination Terminology (continued)

or corridor following gross decon. The type and scope of technical decon is determined by the contaminants involved at the incident. The terms *technical decon* and *formal decon* are sometimes used interchangeably. Methods of technical decon are discussed later in the chapter but include the following:

- Absorption
- Adsorption
- Chemical degradation
- Dilution
- Disinfection
- Neutralization
- Sanitizing
- Sterilization
- Solidification
- Vacuuming
- Washing

- *Mass decon* — Conducting gross decontamination of multiple people at one time. Mass decon may be conducted with or without a formal decon corridor or line and usually involves removing clothing and flushing contaminated individuals with large quantities of water from low-pressure hoselines or other water sources **(Figure 7.5)**.

- *Secondary decon* — Taking a shower after having completed a technical decon process.

- *Definitive decon* — Decontaminating further after technical decon. Definitive decon may involve sampling and/or lab testing and is conducted by hospital staff or other experts.

- *Patient decon* — Decontaminating injured patients or victims.

- *Buddy decon* — Performing decontamination between entry team personnel (or others), making it easier to rinse difficult-to-reach areas such as the back and backs of legs and knees **(Figure 7.6)**.

- *Self decon* — Conducting emergency decontamination on oneself; usually by rinsing with water or using a blotting/absorption method.

Figure 7.5 First responders at the Operational Level may conduct mass decon at incidents involving large numbers of contaminated or potentially contaminated victims. *Courtesy of Steve Hendrix.*

Figure 7.6 Using buddies or additional personnel in the decon corridor makes it easier to rinse difficult-to-reach areas such as the back and backs of legs and knees. *Courtesy of Chris Mickal.*

The decon situation in the scenario was a fairly simple one, with Operational-Level responders under the direction of the incident commander (IC) setting up a simple decon station to assist the two maintenance workers who had been exposed — and potentially contaminated — by the hazardous material.

However, decon operations can be quite complicated, depending on the size of the incident, chemical or chemicals involved, weather (washing off contaminants with a hose stream may not be a viable option in subzero temperatures), personnel available, and a variety of other factors. Personnel, apparatus, tools, and equipment must be decontaminated anytime contamination is suspected. Regardless of the many variables that may be encountered at the incident, the basic principles of any decontamination operation are easy to summarize: (1) Get it off, (2) Keep it off, and (3) Contain it (prevent secondary contamination).

Because decontamination occurs in the warm zone to prevent the spread of hot-zone contaminants to the cold zone, many organizations refer to the warm zone as the *contamination reduction zone* (see Chapter 5, Strategic Goals and Tactical Objectives). The idea is to provide a decontamination corridor that runs from the hot zone to the cold zone through which contaminated individuals must pass (**Figure 7.7**).

In some cases, multiple decon stations are set up within the corridor so that contaminants may be removed in a progressive order (**Figure 7.8**). At each

station or stop along the way, more contaminant is removed. At other times (such as in the scenario), only a single station is needed. In either case, by the time the individual reaches the cold zone, the contamination has been reduced to safe levels or has been entirely eliminated. No entry into the hot zone should be permitted until a decontamination plan has been formulated — except when a rescue can be made and emergency decontamination can be conducted.

However, theory is sometimes challenged in the face of reality. For example, in the March 19, 1995, sarin attack in a Tokyo subway, hundreds of contaminated victims took themselves to hospitals even before emergency responders arrived. These victims spread secondary contamination wherever they went, including directly into hospital

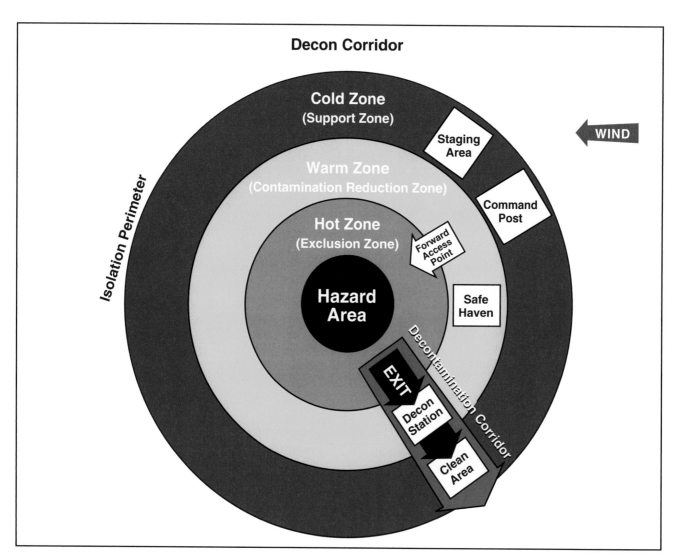

Figure 7.7 The decon corridor runs from the hot zone, through the warm zone, and into the cold zone.

Figure 7.8 Multiple stations enable progressive removal of contaminants.

Operations Plus

In most cases, decon operations are directed by individuals with Technician-Level training or above. Operational-Level responders will not come into direct contact with the material; thus, the decisions as to what type and methods of decon to use are made by technicians or other technical resources. However, OSHA 29 *CFR* 1910.120, *Hazardous Waste Operations and Emergency Response*, allows Operational-Level first responders to receive additional training in order to perform a specific function or fill a position such as decon officer. An Operational-Level responder who has been properly trained may be appointed decon officer with applicable responsibilities.

emergency rooms where many hospital staff in turn became ill. It took some time before any sort of contamination/decontamination control could be established with authority and effectiveness. On the opposite end of the scale, a small chemical spill in a laboratory or industrial site may require a trip to a safety shower but not necessarily require the establishment of a decontamination corridor.

One of the important roles of first responders is to direct victims to a safe location to await decontamination and prevent victims from leaving the scene. This action prevents situations such as the Tokyo sarin incident in which the deadly chemical was spread well beyond the initial incident area. If responders are aware that people have or may have left the scene, they should notify hospitals and poison control centers of the possibility that contaminated individuals might be seeking assistance. Even a short warning may give enough time for medical facilities to minimize contamination problems. Operational-Level first responders also need to be able to select an appropriate site to perform both emergency/gross decontamination and technical decontamination procedures.

Decontamination Methods

Before allowing personnel to enter the hot zone, the IC or decon officer must determine the type and method of decon to use and then make the appropriate preparations according to the decon plan. The decon plan must be part of the total incident action plan, and the decon officer must communicate the plan to the haz mat supervisor, entry team leader, safety officer, entry team personnel, and other personnel.

Decontamination methods can be divided into the four broad categories mentioned earlier: Wet or dry methods and physical or chemical methods. Decontamination methods vary in their effectiveness for removing different substances. What works to remove one type of contaminant may not work well for another. Many factors may play a part in the selection decision. For example, a mixture of hypochlorite and water may be much more effective at decontaminating mustard agents than plain water, but it is critical to remove mustard agents as quickly as possible to minimize exposure. If hypochlorite is not immediately available (or not enough is immediately available) to mix a water/hypochlorite solution for decon, then flushing with plain water may be the best (and only) immediate option (see Chapter 9, Terrorist and Other Criminal Activities, Chemical Agent Incidents section).

Often, flushing the contaminated surface with water is effective at removing the harmful substance or sufficiently diluting it to a safe level. This reason is why flushing with water is usually used for gross and emergency decon. Technical decon frequently washes with water and some sort of soap, detergent, or chemical solution.

It is important to continually assess the effectiveness of any decontamination operation. If monitoring determines that the selected method is not working, a different technique must be tried. Before initiating decontamination, the answers to the following questions should be considered:

- Is it safe to conduct decon?
- What are the alternatives?
- Are there adequate resources to conduct the operation? If not, can additional resources be obtained in a timely fashion?

Wet and Dry

As their names imply, wet and dry methods are categorized by whether they use water or other solutions as part of the decon process. Wet methods usually involve washing the contaminated surface with solutions (see **Table 7.1**) or flushing with a hose stream or safety shower, whereas dry methods such as scraping, brushing, and absorption do not.

Wet methods usually necessitate the collection of runoff water in wading pools or other liquid-retaining devices **(Figure 7.9)**. Collected or containerized water may need to be analyzed for treatment and disposal. In some cases, wet methods may be difficult or impractical to use due to environmental or weather conditions.

Dry methods may be as simple as removing contaminated clothing and putting it into a 55-

Figure 7.9 Wading pools or other containment basins should be used to collect contaminated runoff. *Courtesy of Rich Mahaney.*

Table 7.1
Sample Decontamination Solutions

Solution	Sample Uses
Solution containing 5% sodium carbonate and 5% trisodium phosphate	Inorganic acids, PCBs, solvents such as toluene
Solution containing 10% calcium hypochlorite	Heavy metals, pesticides, cyanides
Solution containing 5% trisodium phosphate, which can be used as a general-purpose rinse	PBBs, PCBs, solvents, and organic compounds such as trichlorethylene and toluene
Dilute solution of hydrochloric acid (HCL): 1 pint (0.5 L) of concentrated HCL to 10 gallons (38 L) of water, stirred with a wood or plastic implement	Inorganic bases, alkali, and caustics wastes

gallon (208 L) storage bag or allowing an aerosol to evaporate. Other dry methods include vacuuming a powder or dust from a contaminated surface or using sticky tape (or a sticky pad) to clean or wipe off contamination. Dry methods have the advantage of not creating large amounts of contaminated liquid runoff (although absorption can result in a greater amount of contaminated material in general), and they may be accomplished through the systematic removal of disposable PPE while avoiding contact with any contaminants.

Physical and Chemical

Physical methods of decontamination remove the contaminant from a contaminated person without changing the material chemically (although with wet methods it may be diluted). The contaminant is then contained for disposal. Examples of physical decontamination methods include absorption, adsorption, brushing and scraping, dilution, evaporation, isolation and disposal, washing, and vacuuming.

Chemical methods are used to make the contaminant less harmful by changing it through some kind of chemical process. For example, using bleach to sanitize tools and equipment that have been exposed to potentially harmful etiological agents is a form of chemical decontamination because the organisms are actually killed by the bleach. Examples of chemical methods include chemical degradation, sanitization, disinfection, sterilization, neutralization, and solidification.

Decontamination Types and Procedures

[ODP Operations IV.D, IV.C.]

Many different types of decontamination exist. The names and definitions for these types may vary greatly. First responders at the Operational Level may perform gross/emergency decontamination. However, given appropriate training, they may also play active roles in the decon corridor during nonemergency, technical decon procedures. For this reason, this section provides details on gross and emergency decon and gives a very basic set of procedures for technical decon. Also provided are sample procedures for patient and mass decon. Other types of decon are addressed in the IFSTA

Hazardous Materials for Technicians manual (publication expected in 2005). First responders at the Operational Level also need to be familiar with their organization's decon procedures because they may differ from the examples presented in this book.

Gross

Gross decontamination is aimed at getting the worst contaminate parts off the victim quickly, usually by flushing with water from a hose stream, safety shower, or other water source. As mentioned earlier, gross decon is performed on entry team personnel before technical decon, victims during emergency decon, and persons requiring mass decon.

Emergency

[NFPA 472: 5.3.4(3), 5.4.1(4), 5.4.1(5)]

The goal of *emergency decontamination* is to remove the threatening contaminant from the victim as quickly as possible — there is no regard for the environment or property **(Figure 7.10, p. 380)**. Emergency decon may be necessary for both victims and rescuers. If either is contaminated, individuals are stripped of their clothing and washed quickly. Victims may need immediate medical treatment, so they cannot wait for a formal decontamination corridor to be established. The following situations are examples of instances where emergency decontamination is needed:

- Failure of protective clothing
- Accidental contamination of first responders
- Heat illness or other injury suffered by emergency workers in the hot zone
- Immediate medical attention required for other victims

Emergency decontamination could be considered a *quick fix,* which is a definite limitation. Removal of all contaminants may not occur, and a more thorough decontamination must follow. Emergency decontamination can definitely harm the environment. However, the advantage of eradicating a life-threatening situation far outweighs any negative effects that may result.

There are times when what appears to be a *normal* incident really involves hazardous materials. First responders may become contaminated before

Figure 7.10 Emergency decon is conducted whenever and wherever necessary. The object is to get the contamination off as quickly as possible. *Courtesy of Judy Halmich.*

they realize what the situation really is. When this situation occurs, first responders need to withdraw immediately. They need to remove their turnout clothing and get emergency decon even if there is no apparent contamination evidence. These responders should remain isolated until someone with the proper expertise can ensure that they have been adequately decontaminated.

Emergency Decontamination: Advantages and Limitations

[NFPA 472: 5.3.4(4)]

Advantages:
- Requires minimal equipment (usually just a water source such as a hoseline)
- Reduces contamination quickly
- Does *not* require a formal contamination reduction corridor or decon process

Limitations:
- Does *not* always totally decontaminate the victim
- Creates contaminated runoff that can harm the environment and other exposures

Decontamination procedures may differ depending on the circumstances and hazards present at the scene. However, a basic set of emergency decontamination procedures is as follows:

Step 1: Remove the victim from the contaminated area.

Step 2: Wash immediately any exposed body parts with flooding quantities of water.

Step 3: Remove victim's clothing and/or PPE rapidly — if possible, cutting from the top down in a manner that minimizes the spread of contaminants.

Step 4: Perform a quick cycle of head-to-toe rinse, wash, and rinse.

Step 5: Transfer the victim to treatment personnel for assessment, first aid, and medical treatment.

Step 6: Ensure that ambulance and hospital personnel are told about the contaminant involved.

Technical (Formal)

Technical decontamination uses chemical or physical methods to thoroughly remove contaminants from responders (primarily entry team personnel) and their equipment. It may also be used on incident victims in non-life-threatening situations. Technical decon is usually conducted within a formal decon line or corridor after gross decon. The type and scope of technical decon is determined by the contaminants involved at the incident. Technical decon may use the following techniques:

- **Absorption** — Process of picking up liquid contaminants with absorbents. Some examples of absorbents used in decon are soil, diatomaceous earth, baking powder, ashes, activated carbon, vermiculite, or other commercially available materials. Most absorbents are inexpensive and readily available. They work extremely well on flat surfaces. Some of their disadvantages are as follows:

  — They do not alter the hazardous material.

  — They have limited use on protective clothing and vertical surfaces.

  — Their disposal may be a problem.

- **Adsorption** — Process in which a hazardous liquid interacts with (or is bound to) the surface of a sorbent material (such as activated charcoal).

- **Brushing and scraping** — Process of removing large particles of contaminant or contaminated materials such as mud from boots or other PPE. Generally, brushing and scraping alone is not sufficient decontamination. This technique is used before other types of decon.

- **Chemical degradation** — Process of using another material to change the chemical structure of a hazardous material. For example, household liquid bleach is commonly used to neutralize spills of etiological agents. The interaction of the bleach with the agent almost instantaneously kills the dangerous germs and makes the material safer to handle. Several of the following materials are commonly used to chemically degrade a hazardous material (also see Table 7.1 for decon solutions):

  — Household bleach (sodium hypochlorite)

  — Isopropyl alcohol

  — Hydrated lime (calcium oxide)

  — Household drain cleaner (sodium hydroxide)

  — Baking soda (sodium bicarbonate)

  — Liquid detergents

Chemical degradation can reduce cleanup costs and the risk posed to the first responder. Some of the disadvantages of the process are as follows:

  — Takes time to determine the right chemical to use (which should be approved by a chemist) and set up the process.

  — Can be harmful to first responders if the process creates heat and toxic vapors. For this reason, chemical degradation is rarely used on people who have been contaminated.

- **Dilution** — Process of using water to flush contaminates from contaminated victims or objects and diluting water-soluble hazardous materials to safe levels. Dilution is advantageous because of the accessibility, speed, and economy of using water. However, there are disadvantages as well. Depending on the material, water may cause a reaction and create even more serious problems. Additionally, runoff water from the process is still contaminated and must be confined and then disposed of properly.

- **Neutralization** — Process of changing the pH of a corrosive, raising or lowering it towards 7 (neutral) on the pH scale.

- **Sanitization, disinfection, or sterilization** — Processes that render etiological contaminates harmless:

  — *Sanitization:* Reduces the number of microorganisms to a safe level (such as by washing hands with soap and water).

  — *Disinfection:* Kills most of the microorganisms present. In a decon setting, disinfection may be accomplished by a variety of chemical or antiseptic products. Most first responders are familiar with the disinfection procedures used to kill bloodborne pathogens such as wiping contaminated surfaces with a bleach solution.

  — *Sterilization:* Kills all microorganisms present. Sterilization is normally accomplished with chemicals, steam, heat, or radiation. While sterilization of tools and equipment may be necessary before they are returned to service, this process is usually impossible or impractical to do in most onsite decon situations. Such equipment will normally be disinfected on the scene and then sterilized later.

- *Solidification* — Process that takes a hazardous liquid and treats it chemically so that it turns into a solid.

- *Vacuuming* — Process using high efficiency particulate air (HEPA) filter vacuum cleaners to vacuum solid materials such as fibers, dusts, powders, and particulates from surfaces. Regular vacuums are not used for this purpose because their filters are not fine enough to catch all of the material.

- *Washing* — Process similar to dilution in that they are both wet methods of decontamination. However, washing also involves using prepared solutions such as solvents, soap, and/or detergents mixed with water in order to make the contaminant more water-soluble before rinsing with plain water **(Figure 7.11)**. The difference is similar to simply rinsing a dirty dinner dish in the sink *versus* washing it with a dishwashing

Figure 7.11 Washing involves using water mixed with some other prepared solution or detergent (such as soap).

Sandia Foam/Decon Foam 100

The U.S. Sandia National Laboratories has developed a foam that is safe for people and can be used for decontamination of biochemical agents. The foam was used during the U.S. 2001 anthrax attacks to decontaminate media and congressional offices.

Sandia foam begins neutralizing both chemical and biological agents in minutes. Because it is not harmful to people, it can be dispensed on the disaster scene immediately, even before casualties are evacuated.

In laboratory tests at Sandia, the foam destroyed simulants of the most worrisome chemical agents (Nerve Agent VX, mustard gas, and soman) and killed a simulant of anthrax — the toughest known biological agent. Against the anthrax simulant, the foam achieved what the researchers called a *7-log kill* — after 1 hour only one anthrax spore out of 10 million was still alive.

International law prohibits the Sandia researchers from possessing real chemical or biological agents, but they have taken samples of the foam to the Illinois Institute of Technology in Chicago where the foam was tested against actual Nerve Agent VX, mustard gas, and soman. In those tests the foam neutralized

half the remaining chemical agent molecules every 2 to 10 minutes, depending on the agent. For most chemical agents, the contamination remaining after 1 hour of exposure to the foam was insignificant. The foam neutralizes viral particles in minutes as well.

The foam — a cocktail of ordinary substances found in common household products — neutralizes chemical agents in much the same way a detergent lifts away an oily spot from a stained shirt. Its surfactants (like those in hair conditioner) and mild oxidizing substances (like those in toothpaste) begin to chemically digest the chemical agent, seeking out the phosphate or sulfide bonds holding the molecules together and chopping the molecules into nontoxic pieces.

The foam expands to about 100 times its liquid volume through a special nozzle that draws air into the spray. The foam fills spaces and automatically seeks contact with chemical or biological agents in crevices and other hiding places or in the air for airborne agents. In several hours, it collapses back to its compact liquid state and, in theory, is benign enough following a biochemical incident to be washed down the drain like dish soap.

Source: Information Courtesy of Sandia National Laboratories

liquid. In some cases the former may be sufficient, in others the latter may be necessary. Washing is an advantageous method of decontamination because of the accessibility, speed, and economy of using water and soap. As with the dilution process, runoff water from washing must be contained and disposed of properly.

While the following techniques are not always considered technical decon techniques, first responders should also be familiar with them:

- *Evaporation* — Some hazardous materials evaporate quickly and completely. In some instances, effective decontamination can be accomplished by simply waiting long enough for the materials to evaporate. Evaporation is generally not a technique used during emergency operations. However, it can be used on tools and equipment when extending exposure time is not a safety issue.

- *Isolation and disposal* — This process isolates the contaminated items (such as clothing, tools, or equipment) by collecting them in some fashion and then disposing of them in accordance with applicable regulations and laws **(Figure 7.12)**. All equipment that cannot be decontaminated properly must be disposed of correctly. All spent solutions and wash water must be collected and disposed of properly. Disposing of equipment may be easier than decontaminating it; however, disposal can be very costly in circumstances where large quantities of equipment have been exposed to a material.

Figure 7.12 Contaminated clothing, tools, and equipment are sometimes isolated for disposal rather than being decontaminated.

First responders must know what to do when assigned to a decontamination corridor or line. They should be briefed before being assigned. Technical decon corridors vary in the number of stations, depending on the needs of the situation. Corridors may be set up for wet methods or dry methods. **Figure 7.13, p. 384,** provides a sample technical decon corridor layout with decon steps as advocated by the U.S. Agency for Toxic Substances and Disease Registry (ATSDR). **Table 7.2, p. 385,** is a sample technical decon checklist.

Mass

[NFPA 472: 5.3.4(5)]

Mass decontamination is the process of conducting gross decontamination of multiple people at one time in emergency situations. Mass decon may be conducted with or without a formal decon corridor or line. Mass decon is initiated where the number of victims and time constraints do not allow the establishment of an in-depth decontamination process. It is a gross decon process that uses large volumes of low-pressure water to reduce the level of contamination. Ideally, a soap-and-water solution or universal decontamination solution would be more effective; however, availability of such solutions in sufficient quantities cannot always be ensured.

Extensive research into mass decon operations at terrorist incidents involving chemical warfare agents has been conducted by the U.S. Army's Soldier and Biological Chemical Command (SBCCOM). The resulting guidelines are available through documents on the Internet and the supplemental CD provided with this book. While these guidelines were written with chemical warfare incidents in mind, they can be applied to any haz mat incident.

Mass decon needs to be established quickly to reduce the harm being done to victims by contaminants. While a more formal process is being set up, initial operations include removing victims' clothing and flushing them with water from handheld hose lines or master streams supplied from fire apparatus **(Figure 7.14, p. 386)**. **Figure 7.15, p. 386,** provides an example of a mass decon schematic.

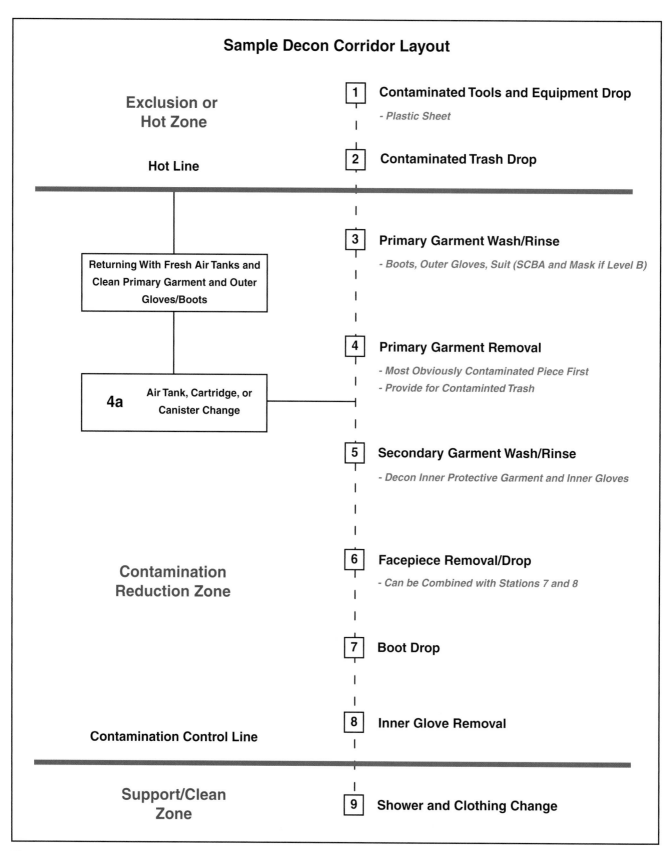

Sample Decon Corridor Layout

Exclusion or Hot Zone

Hot Line

1 **Contaminated Tools and Equipment Drop**
- *Plastic Sheet*

2 **Contaminated Trash Drop**

Returning With Fresh Air Tanks and Clean Primary Garment and Outer Gloves/Boots

3 **Primary Garment Wash/Rinse**
- *Boots, Outer Gloves, Suit (SCBA and Mask if Level B)*

4 **Primary Garment Removal**
- *Most Obviously Contaminated Piece First*
- *Provide for Contaminted Trash*

4a **Air Tank, Cartridge, or Canister Change**

5 **Secondary Garment Wash/Rinse**
- *Decon Inner Protective Garment and Inner Gloves*

Contamination Reduction Zone

6 **Facepiece Removal/Drop**
- *Can be Combined with Stations 7 and 8*

7 **Boot Drop**

8 **Inner Glove Removal**

Contamination Control Line

Support/Clean Zone

9 **Shower and Clothing Change**

Figure 7.13 A sample nine-step technical (or formal) decon corridor layout. The number of stations varies depending on the needs of the incident. *Original source courtesy of the U.S. Agency for Toxic Substances and Disease Registry (ATSDR).*

Table 7.2
Sample Decon Checklist

Date: _____   **Location:** _____

- ☐ Initial briefing from the team leader
- ☐ Incident profile
- ☐ Decon solution and method
- ☐ PPE

Personnel Assignments

Decon Officer

[ ] Identified by vest

- ☐ All personnel monitored by Medical Branch

Decon Site Selection Criteria

- ☐ Decon is located in Warm Zone at exit from Hot Zone
- ☐ Decon area located uphill/upwind from Hot Zone
- ☐ Decon area level or sloped toward Hot Zone
- ☐ Water supply available

Decon Site Setup

- ☐ Area clearly marked with traffic cones and barrier tape to be secure against unauthorized entry
- ☐ Entry and exit points marked
- ☐ Emergency corridor established and clearly marked
- ☐ Runoff contained (tarp, plastic sheeting, dikes)
- ☐ Gross decon shower(s) setup
- ☐ Water supply established
- ☐ Containment basins and pools arranged in proper order
- ☐ Disposal containers in place for PPE and equipment drop
- ☐ Decon solutions mixed
- ☐ Brushes, hand sprayers, hoses and equipment in place
- ☐ Tool drop set up
- ☐ Spare SCBA cylinders available
- ☐ Relief personnel available

Branch Officers Briefing

- ☐ Preparation of branch status report
- ☐ Evaluation of branch readiness for mitigation plan

Entry/Decon Operations

- ☐ Decon and entry personnel briefed on hazards
- ☐ Emergency procedures and hand signals reviewed and understood
- ☐ Decon and entry personnel briefed on decon procedures
- ☐ Decon corridor complete
- ☐ Decon personnel on air
- ☐ Monitored for adequate relief personnel

Termination

- ☐ Disposable/contaminated materials isolated, bagged, and containerized
- ☐ All containers sealed, marked, and isolated
- ☐ All team equipment cleaned and accounted for

Source: Department of Fire Services, Office of Public Safety, Commonwealth of Massachusetts.

Figure 7.14 Many different ways are available to conduct mass decon, but flushing with water from handheld hose lines or apparatus master streams can usually be accomplished quickly. *Courtesy of Steve Hendrix.*

Emergency responders should not overlook existing facilities when identifying means for rapid decontamination methods. For example, although water damage to a facility might result, the necessity of saving victims' lives would justify the activation of overhead fire sprinklers for use as showers. Similarly, having victims wade and wash in water sources such as public fountains, chlorinated swimming pools, swimming areas, and the like provides an effective, high-volume decontamination technique.

Many new innovations and products have been developed to assist in mass decon, from decon trailers and portable tents (that help alleviate privacy concerns) to portable water heaters and tagging and bagging systems **(Figure 7.16)**. Emergency responders should be familiar with the equipment and resources available as well as the mass decon procedures used by their agency.

Patient

[NFPA 472: 5.2.4(6)]

Patient decontamination is necessary whenever victims have been contaminated yet need medical attention. Patient decon uses essentially the same techniques as gross, emergency, or technical decon, depending on the circumstances of the incident. Patient decon, however, gives special consideration

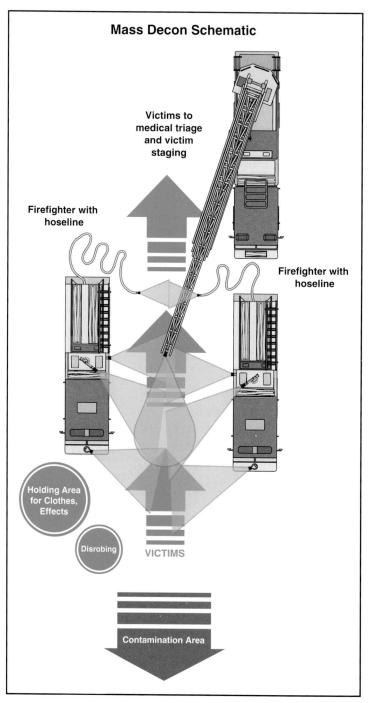

Mass Decon Schematic

Victims to medical triage and victim staging

Firefighter with hoseline

Firefighter with hoseline

Holding Area for Clothes, Effects

Disrobing

VICTIMS

Contamination Area

Figure 7.15 A sample mass decon schematic using handheld hoselines and master streams. *Original source courtesy of the U.S. Army Soldier and Biological Chemical Command (SBCCOM).*

Figure 7.16 Many new innovations and products have been developed to assist in decon operations. Decon tents and trailers can help alleviate some privacy concerns.

Figure 7.17 A system of rollers can be used to push nonambulatory patients through the decon corridor.

to the injuries and medical conditions of the victims. For example, an incident involving a large number of incapacitated victims may require additional resources for the decon corridor since nonambulatory victims will not be able to walk through the decon line (**Figure 7.17**).

To determine victim priority during patient decon, responders must consider factors related both to medical triage and decontamination. For maximum effectiveness, it is recommended that patients be divided into two groups: ambulatory and nonambulatory.

The patient decon steps in the following paragraphs are based upon a model originally provided by the U.S. National Disaster Medical System (NDMS) Office of Emergency Preparedness with separate sections provided for ambulatory and nonambulatory patients. First responders must be familiar with the procedures used by their departments/organizations because they may differ from those provided here.

Ambulatory patients. Victims who are able to understand directions, talk, and walk unassisted are considered ambulatory, and they should be directed to a gathering area where they can be prioritized for decontamination in the warm zone. Most ambulatory victims are triaged as *minimal* unless severe signs or symptoms are present. Several of the following factors determine the highest priority for ambulatory patients:

- Casualties closest to the point of release
- Casualties reporting exposure to the hazardous material
- Casualties with evidence of contamination on their clothing or skin
- Casualties with serious medical symptoms (such as shortness of breath or chest tightness)
- Casualties with conventional injuries (broken bones, open wounds, and the like)

Ambulatory patients may be decontaminated using the following procedures:

Step 1: Direct patients by voice, public-address (PA) system amplification, and/or hand signals to the gross decontamination area just inside the hot zone but away from the high-risk area.

Step 2: Direct patients to remove their clothing down to their underwear.

Step 3: Place the patient's clothing in trash barrels whenever possible, separating valuable personal effects (wallets, rings, watches, identification, and the like) into clear plastic bags, and placing the patient's name or a unique identifying number (triage tag, ticket, etc.) on the bags whenever possible.

Step 4: Vacuum, brush, or wipe all particulate matter off the contaminated patients.

Step 5: Have patients close their mouths and eyes.

Step 6: Using handheld sprayers containing tepid water and/or a diluted bleach solution, rinse the patient from head to toe for 1 minute.

Step 7: Direct patients to proceed to the cold zone.

Nonambulatory patients. Nonambulatory patients are victims who are unconscious, unresponsive, or unable to move unassisted. These patients may be more seriously injured than ambulatory patients. They will remain in place while further prioritization for decontamination occurs. It is recommended that prioritization of patients for decontamination be done using medical triage systems such as START (Simple Triage and Rapid Treatment/Transport). **Figure 7.18** provides four START Categories as provided

START Medical Triage System

START Category	Decon Priority	Classic Observations	Chemical Agent Observations
IMMEDIATE Red Tag	1	Respiration is present only after repositioning the airway. Applies to victims with respiratory rate >30. Capillary refill delayed more than 2 seconds. Signifacantly altered level of consciousness.	• Serious signs/symptoms • Known liquid agent contamination
DELAYED Yellow Tag	2	Victim displaying injuries that can be controlled/treated for a limited time in the field.	• Moderate to minimal signs/symptoms • Known or suspected liquid agent contamination • Known aerosol contamination • Close to point of release
MINOR Green Tag	3	Ambulatory, with or without minor traumatic injuries that do not require immediate or significant treatment.	• Minimal signs/symptoms • No known or suspected exposure to liquid, aerosol, or vapor
DECEASED/ EXPECTANT Black Tag	4	No spontaneous effective respiration present after an attempt to reposition the airway.	• Very serious signs/symptoms • Grossly contaminated with liquid nerve agent • Unresponsive to autoinjections

Figure 7.18 While the example provided here was designed for chemical warfare agent incidents, responders can adapt these four START categories to triage patients at many haz mat incidents. Courtesy of the U.S. Army Soldier and Biological Chemical Command (SBCCOM).

in the SBCCOM "Guidelines for Mass Casualty Decontamination During a Terrorist Chemical Agent Incident."

Nonambulatory patients may be decontaminated using the following procedures:

Step 1: Remove the person from the high-risk area in the quickest way possible and carry the patient (preferably on a Stokes stretcher or Reeves backboard) to the edge of the hot zone bordering the warm zone.

Step 2: Remove the patient's clothing, cutting it off as necessary, down to the underwear.

Step 3: Place the patient's clothes in a trash barrel, separating personal effects into clear plastic bags, and placing the patient's name or a unique identifying number on the bags whenever possible.

Step 4: Vacuum, brush, or wipe off all particulate matter from the patient.

Step 5: Close the patient's mouth and pinch the nose shut if the patient cannot do so.

Step 6: Using the handheld sprayer or hoseline, rinse the patient with tepid water for 1 minute, beginning with the face and airway and proceeding to open wounds. Follow by head-to-toe rinsing in a systematic fashion.

Step 7: Ensure that the armpits, genitalia, and the back are rinsed.

Step 8: Rinse the backboard before transferring the patient to the cold zone, unless switching to clean basin.

Step 9: Apply a C-collar as soon as possible if a C-spine injury is suspected and a collar is available.

Step 10: Determine whether secondary decontamination will be done. If not, carry the patient into a decontamination alley to be quickly dried, covered, wrapped in an enclosing blanket, and then carried to the cold zone on a backboard.

Step 11: Scan the patient with detection equipment and report the results to the treatment team if a radiologic agent is involved.

Step 12: Transfer the patient to properly protected cold-zone personnel who will perform indicated patient care.

Figure 7.19 provides an example of a decon corridor layout for patient decon as described in the SBCCOM "Guidelines for Mass Casualty

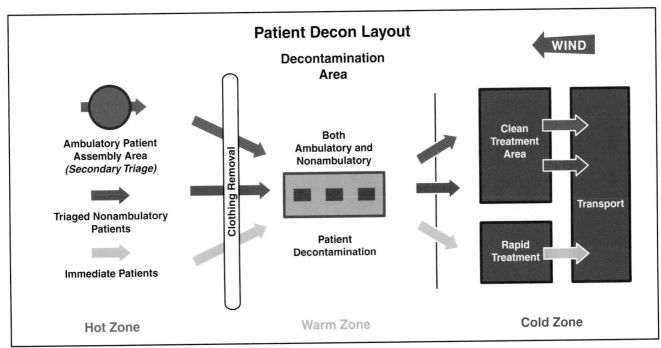

Figure 7.19 A sample schematic for moving ambulatory and nonambulatory patients through decon. *Original source courtesy of the U.S. Army Soldier and Biological Chemical Command (SBCCOM).*

Decontamination During a Terrorist Chemical Agent Incident."

Decontamination Implementation

Many things must be considered when implementing decontamination. An appropriate site must be selected, the number of stations and setup of the decon corridor or line during technical decon must be decided, methods for collecting evidence must be determined, and termination procedures must be followed.

Site Selection

[NFPA 472: 5.4.1(4)]

The following factors are considered when choosing a decontamination site:

- *Accessibility* — The site must be away from the hazards, but adjacent to the hot zone so that persons exiting the hot zone can step directly into the decontamination corridor. An adjacent site eliminates the chance of contaminating clean areas. It also puts the decontamination site as close as possible to the actual incident. Time is a major consideration in the selection of a site. The less time it takes personnel to get to and from the hot zone, the longer personnel can work. Four crucial time periods are as follows:

  — Travel time in the hot zone

  — Time allotted to work in the hot zone

  — Travel time back to the decontamination site

  — Decontamination time

- *Terrain and surface material* — The decontamination site ideally slopes toward the hot zone; thus, anything that may accidentally get released in the decontamination corridor would drain toward or into the contaminated hot zone. If the site slopes away from the hot zone, contaminants could flow into a clean area and spread contamination. Finding the perfect topography is not always possible, and first responders may have to place some type of barrier to ensure confinement of an unintentional release (**Figure 7.20**). *Details:*

  — Diking around the site prevents accidental contamination escaping.

  — It is best if the site has a hard, nonporous surface to prevent ground contamination.

  — When a hard-surfaced driveway, parking lot, or street is not accessible, some type of impervious covering may be used to cover the ground. Salvage covers or plastic sheeting will prevent contaminated water from soaking into the earth.

  — Use covers or sheeting to form the decontamination corridor regardless of whether the surface is porous (**Figure 7.21**).

Figure 7.20 Technical (formal) decon corridors should provide secondary confinement to prevent unintentional release of contaminated runoff in case of spillage and splashing. In this example, a simple wooden frame is used. *Courtesy of Joan Hepler.*

Figure 7.21 Tarps, plastic sheeting, or salvage covers should be used for flooring even when the decon corridor is set up on a hard surface such as concrete or asphalt.

- **Lighting (and electrical supply)** — The decontamination corridor should have adequate lighting to help reduce the potential for injury to personnel in the area. Selecting a decontamination site illuminated by streetlights, floodlights, or other type of permanent lighting reduces the need for portable lighting. If permanent lighting is unavailable or inadequate, portable lighting will be required. Ideally, the decontamination site will have a ready source of electricity for portable lighting (as well as heaters, water heaters, and other needs). However, if such a source is not available, portable generators will be needed.

- **Drains and waterways** — Locating a decontamination site near storm and sewer drains, creeks, ponds, ditches, and other waterways should be avoided. If this situation is not possible, a dike can be constructed to protect the sewer opening, or a dike may be constructed between the site and a nearby waterway. Protect all environmentally sensitive areas.

- **Water supply** — Water must be available at the decontamination site. This situation is probably not a problem for most fire and emergency services organizations. Fire apparatus carry water on board, or an apparatus can easily hook to fire hydrants. Water is more of a concern for private emergency response groups and cleanup companies that are working without the assistance of a fire and emergency services organization. They may not have the ability to provide adequate amounts of water to the scene. *Basic materials:*

  — Water and detergent are most commonly used for decontamination. They dilute and remove most hazardous materials.

  — Some jurisdictions use other solutions that degrade the contaminant. The use of such solutions, however, normally takes place in a formal decontamination setting and requires a higher level of training than an Operational-Level first responder.

- **Weather** — The decontamination site needs to be upwind of the hot zone to help prevent the spread of airborne contaminants into clean areas. If the decontamination site is improperly located downwind, wind currents will blow mists, vapors, powders, and dusts toward first responders. Ideally, during cold weather, the site should be protected from blowing winds, especially near the end of the corridor. Certainly victims should be shielded from cold winds when they are removing protective clothing. *Solutions:*

  — Set up a portable decontamination shelter or tent **(Figure 7.22)**.

  — Set up decontamination trailers at the scene.

  — Use a remote building such as a fire station away from the site. This practice extends travel time and may not be practical.

Figure 7.22 Decon shelters, tents, and trailers provide protection from the elements during cool or cold weather.

Decontamination Corridor

Establish the decontamination corridor before performing any work in the hot zone. First responders are often involved with setting up and working in the decontamination corridor. The types of decontamination corridors vary as to the numbers of sections or steps used in the decontamination process. Corridors can be straightforward and require only a few steps, or they can be more complex and require a handful of sections and a dozen or more steps. First responders must understand the process and be trained in setting up the type of decontamination required by different materials. Some factors to consider are as follows:

- **Ensure privacy** — Decon tents or decon trailers allow more privacy for individuals going through the decon corridor. Decon officers and ICs need to be particularly sensitive to the needs of women being asked to remove their clothing in front of men (regardless of whether they are other victims or emergency responders). Lawsuits have resulted from situations in which women have felt uncomfortable or even humiliated while going through decon. Providing a private, restricted area such as a tent or trailer in which to conduct decon may prevent similar litigation. Use female responders to assist whenever possible when decontaminating women.

• ***Bag and tag contaminated clothing/effects*** — Various methods can be used. Place clothing and/or personal effects in bags into trash barrels. Label the bags whenever possible. Separate personal effects (wallets, rings, watches, identification cards, and the like) into clear plastic bags clearly marked with the person's name or a unique identifying number (triage tag, ticket, and the like). These items may need to be decontaminated before being returned. Have some sort of system in place to label or mark all personal effects so that they can be returned to their proper owners after the incident without confusion. Commercial *tagging systems* may be used for this purpose or multiple-part plastic hospital identification bracelets for example.

The decontamination corridor may be identified with barrier tape, safety cones, or other items that are visually recognizable (**Figure 7.23**). Coverings such as a salvage covers or plastic sheeting may also be used to form the corridor. Aside from delineating the corridor and providing privacy, protective covering ensures against environmental harm if contaminated rinse water splashes from a containment basin. Containment basins can be constructed of salvage covers and fire hose or ladders (**Figure 7.24**). Some organizations use wading pools or portable drafting tanks as containment basins. Also needed at the site are recovery drums or other types of containers and plastic bags for stowing contaminated tools and PPE. A low-volume, low-pressure hoseline such as a garden hose or booster hoseline is ideal for decontamination (**Figure 7.25**). Pump pressure at idling speed is adequate and minimizes splashing.

How first responders are protected when working in the decontamination area depend on the hazards of the material. Standard firefighter personal protective clothing and self-contained breathing apparatus (SCBA) may be adequate. In some cases, CPC may be necessary. Often, those conducting decon are dressed in an ensemble classified one level below that of the entry team (see Chapter 6, Personal Protective Equipment). Thus, if the entry team is dressed in an Environmental Protection Agency (EPA) Level A ensemble, the decon team is dressed in Level B. In either case, chemical gloves are necessary; fire-fighting gloves should not be

Figure 7.23 The decon corridor should be visually identifiable. This may be accomplished by using barrier tape or safety cones. *Courtesy of Rich Mahaney.*

Figure 7.24 Containment basins can be constructed of salvage covers and fire hose or ladders.

Figure 7.25 Garden hoses are ideal for providing low-volume, low-pressure spray for decontamination operations. *Courtesy of Joan Hepler.*

used in decontamination procedures. Because there is a possibility that first responders in decontamination operations will become contaminated themselves, they need to pass through decontamination before leaving the corridor.

Evidence Collection (Crime Scenes)

It is important for first responders to remember that haz mat incidents may also be crime scenes. The scene of a chemical weapon terrorist attack is a good example. In these situations, emergency responders need to remember that any actions they take (moving victims, spraying water for emergency decon, and the like) may physically alter crime-scene evidence. While life safety must always be the top priority, responders at

crime scenes need to minimize the amount of disturbance they do. If possible, take notes or pictures documenting where victims were located and how the scene looked upon arrival (before anything was disturbed).

Dead victims at crime scenes may contain evidence on or in their bodies, but they still need to go through a decon process before transport to the medical examiner. Personal effects removed during decon become crime-scene evidence and must be handled accordingly. More detailed information about haz mat operations at crime scenes is in Chapter 9, Terrorist and Other Criminal Activities.

Termination

According to NFPA 471, a debriefing needs to be held for those involved in the incident as soon as practical. Provide exposed persons with as much information as possible about the delayed health effects of the hazardous materials involved in the incident. Schedule follow-up examinations with medical personnel if necessary. The individual's personal physician and employer need to maintain exposure records for future reference.

Summary

Any time hazardous materials are involved in an incident, contamination becomes a concern. Contamination with hazardous materials can lead to exposure, which can in turn cause harm, depending on the hazards of the material and the nature of the exposure. Decontamination is conducted to prevent the spread of contaminants from the hot zone to other areas, and it is done to reduce the level of contamination to levels that are not harmful.

Emergency responders at the Awareness Level need to be aware of the potential need to decontaminate victims at haz mat incidents, and responders at the Operational Level need to understand the different decon types and techniques that may be used. Additionally, Operational-Level responders may be called upon to assist in decon operations such as selecting an appropriate site, helping in the decon corridor, or performing emergency decon on victims or other emergency responders.

Chapter 8

Incident-Specific
Strategies and Tactics

First Responder Competencies

This chapter provides information that will assist the reader in meeting the following first responder competencies from NFPA 472, *Professional Competence of Responders to Hazardous Materials Incidents,* 2002 Edition. The numbers are noted directly in the text under the section titles where they are addressed.

NFPA 472

Chapter 5   Competencies for the First Responder at the Operational Level

5.4.4   Performing Defensive Control Actions. Given a plan of action for a hazardous materials incident within their capabilities, the first responder at the operational level shall demonstrate defensive control actions set out in the plan and shall meet the following related requirements:

(6) Describe methods for controlling the spread of contamination to limit impacts of radioactive materials.

Reprinted with permission from NFPA 472, *Standard on Professional Competence of Responders to Hazardous Materials Incidents,* Copyright © 2002, National Fire Protection Association, Quincy, MA 00269. This reprinted material is not the complete and official position of the National Fire Protection Association on the referenced subject, which is represented only by the standard in its entirety.

Chapter 8
Incident-Specific Strategies and Tactics

The single factor that most affects all areas of a haz mat incident response is the hazardous material itself. The properties of the material, the extent of the release, and the condition of the container dictate what control techniques are necessary. Emergency response agencies/organizations must have plans for dealing with incidents involving each of the basic hazard classes they may encounter. Each first responder must be thoroughly familiar with these plans and capable of implementing them or operating within them should the need arise. **Table 8.1, p. 398,** provides a summary of general actions that first responders (either Awareness or Operational Level) should always take at any hazardous materials incident. At all haz mat incidents, first responders must assume the following responsibilities:

- Follow the incident priorities: (1) life safety, (2) incident stabilization, and (3) protection of property and the environment.

- Establish an incident management or command system and follow applicable predetermined procedures.

- Try to solve the problem(s) given the resources and circumstances available. Call for additional help, isolate and deny entry, conduct hazard and risk assessment, evacuate or shelter in place, and the like.

To review from Chapter 3, Hazardous Materials Identification, the United Nations (UN)/U.S. Department of Transportation (DOT) hazard classes are as follows:

- Explosives (Class 1)
- Gases (Class 2)

- Flammable and combustible liquids (Class 3)
- Flammable solids, spontaneously combustible materials, and dangerous-when-wet materials (Class 4)
- Oxidizers and organic peroxides (Class 5)
- Poison (toxic), poison inhalation hazard, infectious substance (Class 6)
- Radioactive materials (Class 7)
- Corrosive materials (Class 8)
- Miscellaneous hazardous materials (Class 9)

This chapter contains information on basic control measures for incidents involving each of the UN/DOT hazard classes, with the exception of Class 9, miscellaneous hazardous materials. While these classes are basically applied to transportation emergencies, the information in this chapter is also relevant to emergencies at fixed facilities.

Explosives (Class 1)

Explosive materials are used in military applications, mining, logging, construction, demolition operations, and terrorism incidents. Terrorist incidents are discussed in greater detail in Chapter 9, Terrorism and Other Criminal Activities. Explosives in their normal storage and transport states are relatively stable materials that can be handled safely. Most explosives (except for old or damaged explosives) will not detonate during proper handling. However, explosives must be protected from open flame, excessive heat, friction, impact, electrical shock, and chemical contamination.

Table 8.1
First Responder General Actions at
Hazardous Materials Incidents

Level*	General Actions
Awareness	Consider wind direction and terrain — stay upwind, uphill, and upstream if possible.
	Implement the Incident Management System (IMS).
	Use the *Emergency Response Guidebook* (*ERG*) or other resources to identify the material.
	Isolate and evacuate the area according to *ERG* guidelines, deny entry, and keep unauthorized personnel away.
	Call for additional assistance as necessary.
	Avoid physical contact with the material even when wearing personal protective equipment (PPE).
	Wear appropriate PPE if available (if not, withdraw to a safe area).
	Eliminate ignition sources when unknown, flammable, or combustible materials are involved.
Operational	Protect exposures when fire is involved.
	Wear full protective clothing, self-contained breathing apparatus (SCBA), or other respiratory protection when operating in or near the danger zone.
	Conduct rescues as safe and appropriate.

* NOTE: Actions taken by Awareness-Level responders also apply to Operational-Level responders

Explosives, particularly dynamite, may detonate during routine handling if they have been stored for many years and have started to decompose or if they misfire during use. Decomposition is indicated by either a crystallized residue on the explosive or evidence that internal contents are leaking through the exterior container. Explosives in this condition are very motion-sensitive and require careful handling. Only properly trained personnel such as bomb-disposal technicians should handle, neutralize, or remove damaged or decomposed explosives.

The first responder may encounter explosives that have been used as threats in deliberate acts of incendiarism or bombings or any of the previously listed normal uses. Policies and procedures should coordinate the responsibilities and activities of all personnel who have active roles at these incidents. Detailed pre-incident plans should be prepared for any facilities that use or store explosives on a regular basis within the response organization's jurisdiction. Explosives package types and emergencies are discussed in the sections that follow.

Explosives Package Types

Explosives are packaged in numerous configurations and quantities. Dynamite is packaged in various-sized paper or fiberboard cartridges (**Figures 8.1 and 8.2**). A *cartridge* is a case that contains an explosive charge for blasting. Small cartridges are packed in fiberboard boxes for shipment. Large cartridges are packed in heavy-

Figure 8.1 Examples of dynamites. *Courtesy of the U.S. Bureau of Alcohol, Tobacco, Firearms and Explosives and the Oklahoma Highway Patrol Bomb Squad.*

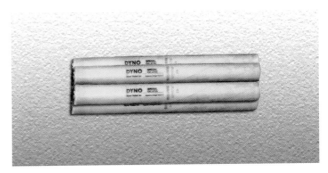

Figure 8.2 Ammonia gelatin dynamite. *Courtesy of the U.S. Bureau of Alcohol, Tobacco, Firearms and Explosives and the Oklahoma Highway Patrol Bomb Squad.*

walled, spiral-wound fiberboard tubes. DOT specifications *do not* require large cartridges to be packed in fiberboard boxes for shipment. Large cartridges may be shipped as single cartridges or taped together to form bundles. Examples of other package types are as follows:

- Emulsions, slurries, and water gels are packaged in plastic tubes or paper cartridges (**Figure 8.3**).

- Detonators (fuse blasting caps and electric blasting caps) are packed in fiberboard cartons that are placed in a fiberboard case (similar to a dynamite box) for shipment. The detonating cord is generally packaged on a spool that is shipped in a fiberboard case.

- Black powder and smokeless powder for small arms ammunition are often packaged in 1-pound (0.45 kg) metal cans and shipped in fiberboard cases (**Figure 8.4**). Each case usually holds 50 cans. Black powder is also shipped in large metal kegs or in plastic bags that are stored in fiberboard cases.

- Some blasting agents, such as ammonium nitrate and fuel oil, are packaged in multiwalled paper bags similar to cement sacks (**Figure 8.5, p. 400**). The bags contain moisture-resistant plastic liners and usually have closures that are sewn together.

- A number of explosive materials — principally blasting agents such as ammonium nitrate, fuel oil, certain emulsions, slurries, and water gels — are shipped in bulk in special cargo trucks.

Explosives (No Fire) Emergencies

The immediate concern at an incident involving explosives without any involvement with fire is to withdraw and protect life safety. The primary objectives are to isolate the area, deny entry, and evacuate. Visually inspect the load from a safe

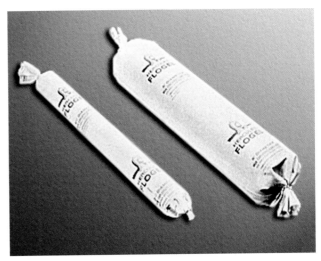

Figure 8.3 Water gels and slurries are often packaged in plastic tubes. *Courtesy of the U.S. Bureau of Alcohol, Tobacco, Firearms and Explosives and the Oklahoma Highway Patrol Bomb Squad.*

Figure 8.4 Metal cans of black powder. *Courtesy of the U.S. Bureau of Alcohol, Tobacco, Firearms and Explosives and the Oklahoma Highway Patrol Bomb Squad.*

Figure 8.5 Multiwalled paper bag containing ammonium nitrate and fuel oil. *Courtesy of the U.S. Bureau of Alcohol, Tobacco, Firearms and Explosives and the Oklahoma Highway Patrol Bomb Squad.*

Figure 8.6 First responders must exercise extreme caution whenever explosives such as these pictured here are involved in an incident.

distance, and seek assistance from technical experts such as a bomb squad. Fire can cause explosives to detonate, so it is important to eliminate ignition sources. **Table 8.2** presents common actions taken by first responders when confronted with an emergency involving explosives that are not on fire or immediately threatened by fire.

Explosives on Fire (or Threatened by Fire) Emergencies

The immediate concerns at an incident involving explosives on fire or threatened by fire are to withdraw and protect life safety. The primary objectives are to isolate the area, deny entry, and evacuate. If fire directly involves a cargo or storage area containing explosives, first responders must exercise extreme caution **(Figure 8.6)**. Fire can cause the explosives to detonate. Such incidents call for immediate withdrawal from the area by all civilians and first responders. For most explosives the *Emergency Response Guidebook (ERG)* recommends that all civilians and first responders travel a distance of 1 mile (1 609 m) in any direction away from the area.

> **WARNING**
> The Institute of Makers of Explosives and DOT recommend that first responders *not* make an attack on fires involving explosives. Instead, they should withdraw and let the fire burn.

The destructive power of a blast is radiated equally in all directions. This force dissipates as it meets an obstacle and gradually decreases in strength and intensity over distance. Certainly, the best option is to put maximum distance between first responders and the explosive material. Lacking this option, responders need to identify a strong barrier such as a large earthen bank or berm behind which to seek cover.

> **WARNING**
> First responders should *never* handle explosive devices.

When a fire is external (outside) and does *not* involve a cargo or storage area containing explosives, first responders should attack and extinguish the fire quickly. The fire must be extinguished before it progresses into an area where explosives are stored. Large-volume fire

Table 8.2
First Responder Actions at Explosives
(No Fire) Incidents

Level*	Strategic Goal	Actions (Tactics)
	Isolation	Isolate and evacuate the area according to *ERG* guidelines.
		Move people out of the line of sight of the scene and away from windows and doorways; reroute bystanders and traffic as the situation warrants.
	Identification	Review the vehicle's shipping papers, and confirm this information with the driver/operator.
		Visually inspect the load from a safe distance for evidence of damage, spills, or leaks.
	Fire Control	Eliminate ignition sources.
	Notification/Identification	Consult the appropriate technical specialists through the emergency contact telephone number listed on the shipping documents.
	Fire Control	Ground all equipment used when handling the product.
	Protection	Protect the cargo from contamination and shock.
	Recovery/Termination	Have the responsible party make the necessary contacts for transfer or disposal of the load. Assist with cleanup and/or disposal of explosives **ONLY** under the supervision of a qualified specialist.

Level	Actions to Avoid
	Do not touch explosive materials or their containers.
	Do not operate radio transmitters within 330 feet (100 m) of electric detonators (according to the *ERG*).

* **NOTE:** Actions taken by Awareness-Level responders also apply to Operational-Level responders

streams are desirable to ensure rapid knockdown of the fire. Direct fire streams with care to avoid the possibility of shocking, dislodging, or mixing the nearby explosives. Confine runoff water until it can be determined that the water is free of contaminants damaging to the environment. Explosives that have been exposed to heat and/flames may be extremely sensitive to heat, shock, pressure, friction, or movement.

The precautions to take when explosives are not involved in fire (calling for additional help, keeping unauthorized personnel away, avoiding exposure to the material, and the like) often apply to fire situations as well. The additional considerations and actions to take for incidents in which explosives are on fire or threatened by fire are presented in **Table 8.3, p. 402**.

If an explosive has detonated, it is primarily important for first responders to perform the following actions:

- Gain control of the scene.
- Isolate the area.
- Initiate rescue, perform triage, and/or treat survivors.
- Control fires that threaten remaining exposures.

Table 8.3
First Responder Actions at Explosives on
Fire (or Threatened by Fire) Incidents

Explosives on Fire

Level*	Strategic Goal	Actions (Tactics)
	Isolation	Isolate and evacuate the area according to *ERG* guidelines.
	Fire Control: Withdrawal	**Do not fight fire when fire reaches cargo or explosives!** Withdraw to a safe distance (according to *ERG* guidelines), and let the fire burn.

Level	Actions to Avoid
	Do not move, touch or shock explosives that have been exposed to heat.

Explosives Threatened by Fire

Level	Strategic Goal	Actions (Tactics)
	Isolation	Isolate and evacuate the area according to ERG guidelines.
	Fire Control: Extinguishment	Extinguish the fire quickly before it progresses into the area where explosives are stored or contained.
	Spill Control: Confinement	Confine runoff water.

Level	Actions to Avoid
	Do not move, touch, or shock explosives that have been exposed to heat.
	Avoid shocking, dislodging, or mixing nearby explosives with fire streams.

* **NOTE:** Actions taken by Awareness-Level responders also apply to Operational-Level responders

It may be necessary for first responders to support fixed fire-suppression systems such as automatic sprinklers or deluge systems or to assist occupants in escaping. Collect runoff water because the explosives or other materials could pose a long-term environmental threat. Personnel need to be conscious of explosives that may have been strewn about the area by the explosion but are not detonated. Further disturbance of these explosives may result in detonation.

Gases (Class 2)

Gases have a wide range of use in commercial, industrial, and residential settings. Gases are found universally in storage cylinders, large tanks, and distribution systems. In addition to the fire and explosion hazards posed by released flammable gases, any gas under pressure presents dangers to first responders. These dangers include the possible violent failure of the container due to overpressurization and release of the material. Additionally, gases can be corrosive and toxic, and some are oxidizers.

Gas Container Types

All compressed gases must be confined in special containers that are designed to withstand pressure. Generically, containers that hold compressed gases are referred to as *pressure vessels* (**Figures 8.7**). The pressure in these vessels may range anywhere from approximately 40 to 4,000 psi (276 kPa to 27 579 kPa) {2.76 bar to 276 bar}. There are many sizes and shapes of pressure vessels such as one-ton chlorine containers, breathing air cylinders on self-contained breathing apparatus (SCBA), acetylene bottles used on welding carts, portable fire extinguishers, and cylinders used in cascade systems.

Three basic types of containers used to handle compressed gases are pressure cylinders, pressure tanks, and pipelines. The difference between pressure cylinders and pressure tanks is a fine line. The designation of either tank or cylinder depends on which design criteria and regulations the container was built to meet. In previous years, containers that were small, portable, and contained high pressures were called *cylinders*. Large containers designed to be used in a fixed installation and typically containing low to moderate pressures were called *tanks*. Today, these distinctions no longer apply. The basic type descriptions are as follows:

- *Pressure cylinders* — These cylinders are manufactured in accordance with the requirements established by DOT and the Canadian Transport Commission (CTC), whose requirements are the same. A wide variety of gases are transported in cylinders, and these cylinders are considered the workhorses of the industry. Pressure cylinders have the following characteristics:
  - Range in size from the very small, handheld types to those with a maximum capacity of 1,000 pounds (454 kg)
  - Are usually transported in an upright position
  - Are often made of steel, but other materials such as aluminum or composites of aluminum and fiberglass or carbon fiber may also be used
  - Must have some type of pressure-relieving device (with a few exceptions: Many disposable cylinders and some containers for poison gases such as methyl bromide and hydrogen cyanide have no pressure-relieving devices)

- *Pressure tanks* — These tanks are constructed to comply with requirements set forth by the American Petroleum Institute (API) or the American

Figures 8.7 A spherical pressure vessel containing liquid nitrogen. *Courtesy of Rich Mahaney.*

Figure 8.8 Various modes are used to transport pressure tanks.

Society of Mechanical Engineers (ASME). Tanks are most commonly found in fixed facilities but may also be found on motor vehicles and railcars **(Figure 8.8)**. Tanks used in transportation are subject to additional criteria beyond API and ASME requirements. Pressure tanks have the following characteristics:

— Are often made of steel, but other materials such as aluminum or composites of aluminum and fiberglass or carbon fiber may also be used

— Must have some type of pressure-relieving device (with a few exceptions: Some containers for poison gases such as methyl bromide and hydrogen cyanide have no pressure-relieving devices)

• *Pipelines* — Pipelines carry compressed gases and are found in many forms. The most common type is the municipal natural gas distribution system. Other industrial gases such as oxygen, anhydrous ammonia, and hydrogen may be piped within or between facilities.

Gas Emergencies

Immediately upon arrival at incidents involving gases, first responders need to pursue answers to the following questions:

• What gas is involved?

• What is the type and size of container involved?

• Is there mechanical damage to a container?

• Is there a leak?

• Is there fire?

• Is there flame impingement on a container?

• What is the availability of water?

• Can the fuel supply valve be turned off safely?

Transportation emergencies that involve gases may include large highway tank trucks and rail tank cars. Accidents involving these vehicles can be very serious because of the quantity of gas involved and the locations in which the accidents occur. First responders must realize that their abilities to deal directly with this type of incident are limited. When there is a leak and/or fire, first responders need to call more highly trained personnel for assistance. Emergency personnel also commonly encounter leaks in municipal natural gas distribution systems. Most of the safety procedures described for transportation emergencies can also be applied to these incidents.

The sections that follow describe emergencies involving gases and the immediate concerns and primary objectives that need to be taken for each.

In most cases, the following general procedures are the best ones for first responders to follow in any gas emergency:

- Rely on the *ERG* for suggestions on evacuation distances.

- Determine wind direction and initiate evacuation downwind.

- Eliminate ignition sources, particularly when dealing with flammable gases.

- ***Do not*** allow anyone in or near the area until the arrival of specialists who have both the necessary technical knowledge and resources to handle the emergency.

- Set up unattended portable master stream nozzles to cool tanks and exposures (if there is a fire), and then have personnel withdraw to a safe distance.

- Execute any feasible rescues.

Nonflammable, Oxygen, and Poisonous Gas Leaks

The immediate concerns for these types of gas leak incidents are to protect life safety and exposures. The primary objective is to turn off the flow of gas if possible. The size of the container dictates how first responders react. Obviously, a small container can be quickly isolated. If it is leaking, it will not be a major problem unless a poison is involved. With proper personal protective equipment (PPE) and training, first responders may attempt to either roll or upright a cylinder to change a liquid leak situation into a gas leak situation.

When a gas is toxic such as chlorine or methyl bromide, a larger isolation area should be identified. Remember that Operational-Level responders do ***not*** have the proper PPE and are ***not*** allowed in the hot zone when dealing with toxic materials. Also remember that many materials become extremely brittle when in contact with refrigerated/cryogenic liquids and may break unexpectedly. **Tables 8.4 through 8.9** provide some basic actions

Table 8.4		
First Responder Actions at Nonflammable Gas Leak (No Fire) Incidents		
Level*	**Strategic Goal**	**Actions (Tactics)**
(icon)	Isolation	Isolate and evacuate the area according to *ERG* guidelines.
	Protection	Stay out of low areas. (Many gases are heavier than air and will collect in low-lying areas or confined spaces.)
(icon)	Spill Controll	Allow substances to evaporate as appropriate.
	Spill Control: Vapor Suppression	Use water spray to reduce vapors or divert vapor cloud drift, and prevent runoff water from contacting spilled material.
	Spill Control: Dike, Dam, Diversion	Prevent liquids/runoff water from entering waterways, sewers, basements, or confined areas.
	Spill Control: Ventilation	Ventilate the area, particularly enclosed spaces, before entry.
	Leak Control	Stop the leak by closing remote valve if it is safe to do so.
Level	**Actions to Avoid**	
(icon)	***Do not*** direct water at the source of the leak or safety devices because icing may occur.	

* **NOTE:** Actions taken by Awareness-Level responders also apply to Operational-Level responders

Table 8.5
First Responder Actions at Nonflammable Gas Leak
(Involving Fire) Incidents

Level*	Strategic Goal	Actions (Tactics)
	Isolation	Isolate and evacuate the area according to *ERG* guidelines.
	Protection	Move undamaged containers from fire area if it is safe to do (damaged containers should only be moved by specialists or technicians).
	Fire Control: Withdrawal	***STAY AWAY*** from tanks engulfed in fire.
	Fire Control: Extinguishment	Use extinguishing agent suitable for type of surrounding fire if tank is *not* engulfed.
	Fire Control	Fight fire from the maximum distance or use unattended hose streams.
	Fire Control: Exposure Protection	Cool containers with flooding quantities of water until well after the fire is extinguished.
	Fire Control: Withdrawal	Withdraw immediately in case of rising sound from venting safety devices or discoloration of tanks.
	Fire Control: Extinguishment/ Withdrawal	Use unattended hose streams for massive fires. If this action is *not* possible, withdraw from the area and let the fire burn.
	Fire Control: Exposure Protection	Protect exposures.

Level	Actions to Avoid
	Do not direct water at the source of the leak or safety devices because icing may occur.

* **NOTE:** Actions taken by Awareness-Level responders also apply to Operational-Level responders

that can be taken by first responders when dealing with nonflammable, oxidizing, and poisonous gas leak incidents.

Flammable Gas Leaks (No Fire)

The immediate concern at incidents involving flammable gas leaks not involving fire is to prevent ignition. The primary objective is to turn off the flow of gas. When working with a flammable gas leak, eliminate all ignition sources. If the gas is a liquefied petroleum gas (LPG) type, consider downwind ignition sources up to ½ mile (805 m) away because the vapors are heavier than air and can flash back great distances. Isolate the area until the incident is completely stabilized.

Locate the valves to see if the leak can be controlled. On residential natural gas systems, the valve is the petcock on or near the gas meter (**Figure 8.9**). Turn the petcock 90 degrees to stop the flow. If valves, valve stems, pressure-relief valves,

Table 8.6
First Responder Actions at Oxidizing
Gas Leak (No Fire) Incidents

Level*	Strategic Goal	Actions (Tactics)
	Isolation	Isolate and evacuate the area according to *ERG* guidelines.
	Fire Control	Keep combustible materials such as wood, paper, and oil away from spilled materials.
	Spill Control	Allow substance to evaporate as appropriate.
	Spill Control: Vapor Suppression	Use water spray to reduce vapors or divert vapor cloud drift, and prevent runoff water from contacting spilled material. **Do not** direct water at spill or leak source.
	Spill Control: Dike, Dam, Diversion	Prevent liquids/runoff from entering waterways, sewers, basements, or confined areas.
	Leak Control	Stop leak by closing remote valve if it is safe to do so.

* **NOTE:** Actions taken by Awareness-Level responders also apply to Operational-Level responders

Petcock

Figure 8.9 Turn the petcock 90 degrees to stop the flow of gas to leaks in residential natural gas systems.

or fusible plugs have been damaged or if the cylinder has been punctured, isolate the cylinder, move all civilians and personnel back, and eliminate all ignition sources. **Table 8.10, p. 411,** provides some basic actions that can be taken by first responders when dealing with flammable gas leaks in which there is no fire.

Flammable Gas Leaks Involving Fire or Flame Impingement

The immediate concern at a flammable gas leak incident involving fire or flame impingement is to protect exposed tanks by cooling. The primary objective is to turn off the flow of gas. Fire situations involving flammable gases are extremely serious. Ideally, the next objective is to direct large quantities of water onto all sides of the tank (or tanks) as quickly as possible. Water is used at a pressurized container fire for cooling the tank and reducing the internal vapor pressure — *not* for fire extinguishment.

**Table 8.7
First Responder Actions at Oxidizing Gas Leak
(Involving Fire) Incidents**

Level*	Strategic Goal	Actions (Tactics)
	Isolation	Isolate and evacuate the area according to *ERG guidelines*.
	Protection	Move undamaged containers from fire area if it is safe to do so. (Damaged containers should be moved only by specialists or technicians.)
	Fire Control: Withdrawal	**STAY AWAY from tanks engulfed in fire.**
	Fire Control: Extinguishment	Use extinguishing agent suitable for type of surrounding fire if tank is *not* engulfed in fire.
	Fire Control	Fight fire from maximum distance or use unattended hose streams.
	Fire Control: Exposure Protection	Cool containers with flooding quantities of water until well after fire is extinguished.
	Fire Control: Withdrawal	Withdraw immediately in case of rising sound from venting safety devices or discoloration of tanks.
	Fire Control: Extinguishment/Withdrawal	Use unattended hose streams for massive fires. If this action is is not possible, withdraw from the area and let the fire burn.
	Fire Control: Exposure Protection	Protect exposures.
Level	**Actions to Avoid**	
	Do not direct water at the source of the leak or safety devices because icing may occur.	

* **NOTE:** Actions taken by Awareness-Level responders also apply to Operational-Level responders

WARNING

Do not attack this type of emergency without a continuous water supply. There is no safe area around a tank with flame impingement. When rupturing, tanks can turn and travel great distances, break into many parts, and travel in any direction depending on conditions.

Lessons learned from historical review of LPG catastrophes provided the following facts:

- Large-capacity containers may fail violently within 10 to 20 minutes of direct-flame impingement. First responders must factor both the response time and the possible setup time for equipment when determining a course of action.

- Boiling liquid expanding vapor explosions (BLEVEs) of large-capacity containers typically create nonsurvivable fire conditions within

**Table 8.8
First Responder Actions at Poison Gas Leak
(No Fire) Incidents**

Level*	Strategic Goal	Actions (Tactics)
	Isolation	Isolate and evacuate the area according to *ERG* guidelines (consult Table of Initial Isolation and Protective Action Distances as applicable).
	Protection	Stay out of low areas. (Many gases are heavier than air and will collect in low-lying areas or confined spaces.)
	Protection	Keep water from getting inside containers and contacting spilled materials if possible/appropriate.
	Spill Control: Vapor Suppression	Use water spray to reduce vapors or divert vapor cloud drift, and prevent runoff water from contacting spilled material. ***Do not*** direct water at spill or source of leak.
	Spill Control: Dike, Dam, Diversion	Prevent liquids/runoff water from entering waterways, sewers, basements, or confined areas.
	Spill Control: Ventilation	Ventilate the area as appropriate.
	Leak Control	Stop leak by closing remote valve if it is safe to do so.

* NOTE: Actions taken by Awareness-Level responders also apply to Operational-Level responders

500 feet (152 m) and create severe tank shell fragmentation from 2,500 to 4,000 feet (762 m to 1 219 m).

● Unless cooling water in adequate and uninterrupted quantities can be applied on the exposed tank or container, rescue and evacuation activities need to be performed quickly followed by a total withdrawal from the area.

A flame impinging directly onto a tank shell quickly weakens the metal. Water must be directed onto the area being hit by the flame, especially if it is in the tank's vapor space. A minimum of 500 gpm (1 893 L/min) must be played on each large highway tank truck or rail tank car at the point of flame impingement (**Figure 8.10, p. 411**). An obvious sheen of water needs to be seen rolling down the tank shell to ensure that the water is not being converted to steam before it cools the tank. Streams must be directed from each side to maximize total coverage of the tank shell. First responders need to concentrate on the upper vapor space and allow water to flow down the sides. **Table 8.11, p. 412,** provides some basic actions that can be taken by first responders when dealing with flammable gas leaks threatened by or involved in fire.

Unfortunately, there are no absolute clues as to when a tank rupture might occur. However, some warning signals that indicate a situation is becoming worse are as follows:

● The pressure-relief device operates, indicating that pressure is building in the tank. Actions must be taken to reduce pressure.

WARNING
Never extinguish flames that come from a pressure-relief device. This action may allow flammable vapors to build in the area and reignite violently.

Table 8.9
First Responder Actions at Poison Gas Leak
(Involving Fire) Incidents

Level*	Strategic Goal	Actions (Tactics)
	Isolation	Isolate and evacuate the area according to *ERG* guidelines. (Consult Table of Initial Isolation and Protective Action Distances as applicable.)
	Protection	Keep water from getting inside containers and contacting spilled materials if possible/appropriate.
		Move undamaged containers from fire area if safe to do so. (Damaged containers should be moved only by specialists or technicians.)
	Fire Control: Withdrawal	***STAY AWAY* from tanks engulfed in fire.**
	Fire Control: Extinguishment	Use extinguishing agent suitable for type of surrounding fire if tank is *not* engulfed in fire.
	Fire Control	Fight fire from maximum distance or use unattended hose streams.
	Fire Control: Exposure Protection	Cool containers with flooding quantities of water until well after fire is extinguished.
	Fire Control: Withdrawal	Withdraw immediately in case of rising sound from venting safety devices or discoloration of tanks.
	Fire Control: Extinguishment/Withdrawal	Use unattended hose streams for massive fires. If this action is not possible, withdraw from the area and let the fire burn.
	Fire Control: Exposure Protection	Protect exposures.

Level	Actions to Avoid
	Do not direct water at the source of the leak or safety devices because icing may occur.

* **NOTE:** Actions taken by Awareness-Level responders also apply to Operational-Level responders

Table 8.10
First Responder Actions at Flammable Gas Leak
(No Fire) Incidents

Level*	Strategic Goal	Actions (Tactics)
	Isolation	Isolate and evacuate the area according to *ERG* guidelines.
	Fire Control	Eliminate all ignition sources.
	Protection	Stay out of low areas. (Many gases are heavier than air and will collect in low-lying areas or confined spaces.)
	Spill Control: Vapor Suppression and Confinement	Use water spray to reduce vapors or divert vapor cloud drift, and confine runoff water as appropriate.
	Spill Control: Confinement	Prevent vapors and/or runoff water from entering waterways, sewers, basements, or confined areas.
	Leak Control	Stop leak by closing remote valve if it is safe to do so.
	Fire Control	Ground all equipment used to handle the product/containers, use nonsparking tools, explosion-proof ventilation fans, etc.

Level	Actions to Avoid
	Do not direct water at the source of the leak or safety devices because icing may occur.

* **NOTE:** Actions taken by Awareness-Level responders also apply to Operational-Level responders

Figure 8.10 Play a minimum of 500 gpm (1 893 L/min) directly onto a flame-impinged tank.

- The pitch of the sound from the pressure-relief valve increases (becomes sharper) as the gas exits at a greater velocity, indicating a continuing increase in pressure.

- The size of the torch and the volume and pitch of sound from the pressure-relief valve continue to increase because of a greater volume of gas rushing out, indicating an increase in internal boiling and vapor production. If the fire or torch coming from the pressure in the tank is also increasing, on-scene cooling techniques are obviously inadequate.

- A pinging, popping, or snapping sound occurs, indicating that the metal has been softened by high heat and is stretching.

- Dry spots or visible steam appear on the tank surface, indicating insufficient cooling. If this situation occurs when water is applied, the tank shell is over 212°F (100°C) and more water is needed.

Level*	Strategic Goal	Actions (Tactics)
	Isolation	Isolate and evacuate area according to *ERG* guidelines.
	Fire Control: Withdrawal	***STAY AWAY* from tanks engulfed in fire.**
	Fire Control: Extinguishment	***Do not* extinguish a leaking gas fire unless the leak can be stopped.**
	Protection	Move undamaged containers from the fire area if it is safe to do so. (Damaged containers should be moved only by specialists or technicians).
	Fire Control: Exposure Protection	Cool containers with flooding quantities of water until well after fire is extinguished.
	Fire Control: Withdrawal	Withdraw immediately in case of rising sound from venting safety devices or discoloration of tanks.
	Fire Control: Extinguishment	Fight tank fires from maximum distance or use unattended hose streams.
	Fire Control: Extinguishment/ Withdrawal	Use unattended hose streams for massive fires. If this action is not possible, withdraw from the area and let the fire burn.
	Fire Control: Exposure Protection	Protect exposures.

Level	Actions to Avoid
	***Do not* direct water at the source of the leak or safety devices because icing may occur.**

* **NOTE:** Actions taken by Awareness-Level responders also apply to Operational-Level responders

- An impinging flame, usually in an isolated location, causes discoloration of the shell, indicating a weakening of the metal. The color of the tank turns from gray to an off-white, and small pieces of paint and metal flake off.

- A bulge or bubble appears on the tank shell, indicating a serious localized heating of the shell in the vapor space. The metal is softening and beginning to deform because of inadequate cooling of the shell.

Flammable and Combustible Liquids (Class 3)

Emergencies involving flammable and combustible liquids could involve large-capacity highway tank trucks, rail tank cars, industrial storage facilities or processes, or pipelines. Emergencies involving flammable liquid tanks tend to be more spectacular-looking than those involving gases; however, these tanks do not pose the same threats as pressurized vessels. Liquid tanks, as compared to gas tanks, are not as prone to BLEVE because the liquid tends to absorb the heat, preventing the buildup of pressure inside. If liquid levels are low or all the liquid is converted to a gas, a BLEVE may still occur. Flammable and combustible liquid container types and emergencies are covered in the sections that follow.

Flammable and Combustible Liquid Container Types

Flammable and combustible liquids can be found in a number of different containers such as metal cans, plastic (polyethylene) containers, pails, drums, tanks, and pipelines. First responders must be familiar with each of these containers and the specific hazards they pose. Containers are described as follows:

- *Metal cans* — These cans are the most common containers used for flammable and combustible liquids and are very popular for storing paint thinners, solvents, camping fuel, and motor fuels. They are commonly found in large numbers in paint and hardware stores, residential garages, variety stores, service stations, and wholesale outlets. When metal cans are shipped, they are usually packaged in cardboard boxes.

- *Safety cans* — These containers are designed to safely store gasoline or other flammable and combustible liquids that have been removed from their original packaging. Normally red in color, they may be made from plastic or metal, and they are equipped with self-closing lids. They are also designed to vent vapor pressure in the event of fire or overheating.

- *Pails* — The next size container is a pail, which is generally about 5 gallons (19 L) in size. The large-bulk demand for solvents and thinners necessitates the use of these popular containers (**Figure 8.11**). Pails are normally delivered on wood or plastic pallets, and it is common for containers to be placed on a pallet and stacked three or four high.

- *Drums* — Flammable and combustible liquids are commonly shipped in drums. Most drums are constructed of metal, but some plastic drums are used. Bulk oils, thinners, and a wide variety of cleaning solvents such as those used in automotive facilities are commonly transported and stored in drums.

- *Tanks* — DOT refers to tank trailers, tank trucks, and rail tank cars as *bulk containers*. Highway containers may be made of steel, stainless steel, or aluminum (the most extensively used). Most rail tanks are made of steel, although some aluminum, stainless steel, and nickel alloy cars are in service. DOT and CTC set the requirements for transportation tank design. The loading and unloading of these tanks varies:

Figure 8.11 Pails of flammable liquids.

— Loading or unloading of flammable and combustible liquid tanks is generally performed at the bottom of the tanks. Top-loading through manways on highway tank trucks is being phased out by the industry. All connections, fittings, and valves are now being placed underneath the tank (**Figure 8.12**). Most new highway tank trucks are equipped with vapor-recovery lines.

— Rail tank cars are usually top-loaded, and many are equipped with bottom unloading outlets.

• *Pipelines* — Pipelines transport large quantities of flammable and combustible liquids over long distances. Some pipelines are hundreds of miles (kilometers) long. They are primarily buried underground but may be exposed in some locations. Pipelines typically extend from one refinery or storage facility to another. Pumping stations are located in intermediate locations along the way (**Figure 8.13**).

DOT strictly forbids the use of glass containers for shipping flammable and combustible liquids. The practice of storing these substances in small glass containers is discouraged by fire-prevention bureaus, U.S. Occupational Safety and Health Administration (OSHA), and insurance companies. However, first responders need to realize that the private sector uses glass containers for storage of flammable and combustible liquids as well as for a variety of other chemicals. Additionally, these glass containers may not be properly labeled.

Flammable and Combustible Liquid Emergencies

The sections that follow describe the emergencies involving flammable liquids and the immediate concern and primary objective that need to be taken for each. The incidents described involve both those with no fire and those involving fire or flame impingement.

Flammable/Combustible Liquid Spills (No Fire)

The immediate concern at these incidents is to prevent ignition of the fuel. The primary objective is to stop the flow of fuel. If first responders can prevent the fuel from igniting, the incident will be

Figure 8.12 Connections, fittings, and valves of cargo tank trucks are placed underneath the tank. This example is from a nonpressure cargo tank.

Figure 8.13 A natural gas pumping station.

much easier to resolve. The vapors from flammable liquids are often two to three times heavier than air. They flow and sink like a liquid. Most of the time, vapors are invisible.

First responders must eliminate all ignition sources within the radius specified by the *ERG*. In those situations where there is a threat to life or exposures, first responders should apply a blanketing layer of foam to the liquid pool (**Figure 8.14**). This foam layer helps to suppress the amount of vapors emitted by the fuel. In addition, the area should be isolated and measures should be taken to evacuate all civilians beyond a specified perimeter.

When possible, leaking liquids should be channeled away from the incident scene and all exposures. If ignition does occur, the material can be allowed to burn under a controlled situation isolated away from on-scene activities. Street gutters, small drainage ditches, and dry creek beds may be used to channel the material to a

Figure 8.14 By applying a blanketing layer of finished foam, first responders can suppress dangerous vapors at flammable and combustible liquid spills.

collection point. First responders should dike storm drains or utility access holes along the collection route. If any measurable quantity of the substance has already poured into a storm-drain system, notify the appropriate departments and state/province agencies. These agencies should be identified *before* a release situation to allow for quick notification.

Material should be diked into a safe holding area at the collection point. A foam blanket is applied to the surface of the material in order to contain vapors and eliminate ignition at the collection point. Arrangements can be made later regarding removal and cleanup. The use of water must be restricted in order to minimize runoff problems.

Table 8.12 provides some basic actions that can be taken by first responders when dealing with flammable/combustible liquids that are not involved in fire. Remember that some flammable/combustible liquids may also be toxic and/or corrosive, and standard fire-fighting PPE may not provide sufficient protection when working with these materials.

Flammable/Combustible Liquid Spills Involving Fire or Flame Impingement

The immediate concern at this type of incident is to cool all exposures, including the tank itself. The primary objective is to stop the flow of fuel to enable extinguishment. First responders may

Table 8.12 First Responder Actions at Flammable/Combustible Liquid Spill (No Fire) Incidents		
Level*	**Strategic Goal**	**Actions (Tactics)**
	Isolation	Isolate and evacuate area according to *ERG* guidelines.
	Fire Control	Eliminate all ignition sources.
	Leak Control	Stop leak by closing remote valve if it is safe to do so.
	Spill Control: Vapor Suppression	Use appropriate vapor suppressing foam to reduce vapors.
	Fire Control	Ground all equipment used to handle the product/containers, use nonsparking tools, explosion-proof ventilation fans, etc.
	Spill Control: Confinement	Dike waterways, sewers, basements, or confined areas to prevent liquids from entering.
		Divert leaking liquids away from the incident scene and exposures.
		Dike and dam far ahead of the liquid for retention and later disposal.

* **NOTE:** Actions taken by Awareness-Level responders also apply to Operational-Level responders

not have the capability to successfully complete this objective. However, they can initiate basic tactics that, in time, will lead to accomplishing the objective.

First responders can control small flammable liquid fires using common fire-fighting equipment and Class B foam. Larger fires and spills take more planning, effort, personnel, equipment, and time. These will probably require expertise beyond the level of first responders. **Table 8.13** provides some basic actions that can be taken by first responders when dealing with flammable/combustible liquid spill fires.

Flammable Solids, Dangerous-When-Wet Materials, Etc. (Class 4)

Accidents involving flammable solids, spontaneously combustible materials, and materials that are dangerous when wet are relatively rare. When an accident does occur, these materials can prove to be difficult to handle. For the most part, extinguishment of Class 4 materials is *not* a primary objective for first responders. Actions of first responders are generally limited to securing the scene, establishing control zones and perimeters, evacuation, and calling for technical help. Because the immediate concerns of each Class 4 material may be different, the material container types and three divisions of emergencies are discussed separately.

Class 4 Material Container Types

A variety of containers are used for packaging Class 4 materials. Tubes, pails, steel and fiberboard drums, cardboard boxes, and bags are used for nonbulk packaging of the materials. These containers are either secured tightly to prevent contact of the material with moisture or filled with an inert medium that excludes air from the material. White phosphorous and sodium may be shipped in railroad tank cars, and other bulk materials (such as calcium carbide chips) may be shipped in metal totes.

Flammable Solid (Division 4.1) Emergencies

Metal powders (readily combustible solids that ignite by friction) and self-reactive materials that undergo a strong exothermal decomposition fall into the flammable-solid class division of Type 4 materials. Also included are explosives that are wetted to suppress the explosive properties. The following sections describe the emergencies involving flammable solid materials and the immediate concern and primary objective that should be taken for each.

Flammable Solid Spills (No Fire)

The immediate concern for these incidents is to prevent ignition of the material. The primary objective is to isolate and confine the material until it can be removed. Spills of solid flammable materials are not as difficult to confine as those of liquids and vapors. Solid materials do not spread like liquids and vapors do. However, when several different flammable solids are involved in a spill, the problem is more difficult than a single-material spill because the different materials may react with each other. Also, some flammable solids may be toxic and/or corrosive, requiring a higher level of PPE than structural fire-fighting gear. **Table 8.14, p. 418,** provides some basic actions that can be taken by first responders when dealing with flammable solids that are not involved fire.

Flammable Solid Spills Involving Fire or Flame Impingement

The immediate concern at these incidents is to cool exposures. The primary objective is to control the fire by extinguishment or by controlled burning. If a spill is on fire and large quantities are involved (such as materials from a cargo van or boxcar), the fire may be impossible to extinguish. Tremendous volumes of water are required to extinguish large quantities of flammable solids.

When the water supply is insufficient for extinguishment, use the water for exposure protection instead. First responders must then protect exposures until the fire consumes the fuel. When the

Table 8.13
First Responder Actions at Flammable/Combustible
Liquid Spill (Involving Fire) Incidents

Level*	Strategic Goal	Actions (Tactics)
	Isolation	Isolate and evacuate area according to *ERG* guidelines.
	Fire Control: Withdrawal	**STAY AWAY from tanks engulfed in fire.**
	Leak Control	Stop leaks by closing remote valve if it is safe to do so.
	Fire Control	Lay initial hoselines.
		Establish a continuous water supply of sufficient volume to control the incident.
	Fire Control: Exposure Protection	Cool containers with flooding quantities of water until well after fire is extinguished.
	Fire Control: Withdrawal	Withdraw immediately in case of rising sound from venting safety devices or discoloration of tank.
	Fire Control: Extinguishment	Fight tank fires from maximum distance or use unattended hose streams.
		Use unattended hose streams for massive fire. If this action is not possible, withdraw from the area and let the fire burn.
	Fire Control: Exposure Protection	Protect exposures.
	Spill Control: Confinement	Control (dam, dike, divert, and retain) flowing liquid material (including runoff) as appropriate.

Level	Actions to Avoid
+	Avoid use of straight streams. Use water spray, fog, or appropriate foam solutions; however, be aware that water spray alone may be inefficient/ineffective for fighting flammable liquid fires.

* **NOTE:** Actions taken by Awareness-Level responders also apply to Operational-Level responders

fire can be extinguished, confine the runoff water. It could contain residues that are harmful to the environment.

First responders need to wear full PPE and SCBA when they are close to these fires. The products of combustion from combustible solids are highly toxic. Some materials such as yellow and white phosphorous can explode and scatter flaming fragments over a wide area.

Class D dry powders are special powders used to extinguish small metal fires. They can be applied by spreading the powder onto the fire by hand, by scoop, by shovel, or with a portable extinguisher. First responders may attempt to

Level*	Strategic Goal	Actions (Tactics)
	Isolation	Isolate and evacuate area according to *ERG* guidelines.
	Fire Control	Eliminate all ignition sources.
	Spill Control: Confinement	Isolate and confine the material; prevent entry into waterways, sewers, basements, or other confined areas if possible.

* **NOTE:** Actions taken by Awareness-Level responders also apply to Operational-Level responders

extinguish metal fires with dry powder if it is safe to do so. *Do not* use the powder on reactive metals, on metals incompatible with the powder, or when first responders are untrained in its use. **Table 8.15** provides some basic actions that can be taken by first responders when dealing with flammable solids involved in fire or flame impingement.

Spontaneously Combustible Material (Division 4.2) Emergencies

Spontaneously combustible materials (also called *pyrophoric materials*) can ignite without an external ignition source after coming in contact with air. Spontaneously combustible materials can be either liquids or solids. The following sections describe the emergencies involving these materials and the immediate concern and primary objective of each.

Spontaneously Combustible Material Spills (No Fire)

The immediate concern at these incidents is to keep the material wet. The primary objectives are to isolate and confine the material until it can be removed. When the material is exposed to air following a spill or because of the slightest breach of a container, ignition could occur immediately or within 5 minutes. Employees who work with spontaneously combustible materials are trained to handle a release. A serious fire will occur if a person fails to respond properly to the material's release.

As with any hazardous materials incident, identifying the material involved is important in developing a plan of action. **Table 8.16, p. 420,** provides some basic actions that can be taken by first responders when dealing with spontaneously combustible materials that are not involved in fire. Pay close attention to PPE recommendations in the *ERG*. Additionally, obtain the answers to the following questions:

- Is the material pyrophoric?
- Are there other materials nearby that are water-reactive?
- What other chemicals are stored and how much?
- Can the area be isolated?
- Is everyone out of the area?

Spontaneously Combustible Material Spills Involving Fire or Flame Impingement

The immediate concern at these incidents is to protect exposures. The primary objective is to let the material burn until it is consumed. When large quantities of pyrophoric materials are involved, the situation becomes more serious. First responders cannot hope to bring incidents involving large quantities of pyrophoric materials to a quick conclusion. They *should not* attempt to extinguish the fire. Some spontaneously combustible materials react violently with water. **Table 8.17, p. 420,** provides some basic actions that

Table 8.15
First Responder Actions at Flammable Solid Spill
(Involving Fire or Flame Impingement) Incidents

Level*	Strategic Goal	Actions (Tactics)
(icon)	Isolation	Isolate and evacuate area according to *ERG* guidelines.
(icon)	Fire Control: Withdrawal	**STAY AWAY from tanks engulfed in fire.**
	Fire Control: Exposure Protection	Cool tank or containers with flooding quantities of water until well after fire is extinguished.
	Fire Control: Withdrawal	Withdraw immediately in case of rising sound from venting safety devices or discoloration of tank.
	Fire Control: Extinguishment	Use appropriate extinguishing agents (for example, a Class D fire extinguisher) to extinguish small quantities of burning flammable solids.
	Fire Control: Controlled Burn	Allow large quantities of flammable solids to burn (may be best option) because these fires may be difficult to extinguish.
	Fire Control: Extinguishment	Fight fire from the maximum distance or use unattended hose streams if extinguishment of large fires is attempted. Only attempt extinguishment if individuals have specialized training and the proper equipment.
	Fire Control: Exposure Protection	Protect exposures.
	Spill Control: Confinement	Dike, dam, divert, and retain any runoff water after fire-extinguishment activities.

* **NOTE:** Actions taken by Awareness-Level responders also apply to Operational-Level responders

can be taken by first responders when dealing with spontaneously combustible materials involved in fire or flame impingement.

Dangerous-When-Wet Material (Division 4.3) Emergencies

Some materials such as magnesium phosphide and trimethylchlorosilane become spontaneously flammable and/or emit flammable or toxic gas when they contact water. The following sections describe the emergencies involving materials that are dangerous when wet and the immediate concern and primary objective for each.

Dangerous-When-Wet Material Spills (No Fire)

The immediate concern at these incidents is to keep the material dry. The primary objectives are to isolate and confine the material until it can be removed. Dangerous quantities of flammable and toxic gases are produced when some water-reactive materials get wet. Ignition sources must be controlled. First responders must wear full PPE and SCBA to protect themselves against toxic gases. **Table 8.18, p. 421,** provides some basic actions that can be taken by first responders when dealing with dangerous-when-wet materials not involved in fire.

Table 8.16
First Responder Actions at Spontaneously Combustible Material Spill (No Fire) Incidents

Level*	Strategic Goal	Actions (Tactics)
	Isolation	Isolate and evacuate area according to *ERG* guidelines.
	Fire Control	Eliminate all ignition sources.
	Spill Control: Confinement	Prevent entry into waterways, sewers, basements, or confined areas.

* **NOTE:** Actions taken by Awareness-Level responders also apply to Operational-Level responders

Table 8.17
First Responder Actions at Spontaneously Combustible Material Spill (Involving Fire or Flame Impingement) Incidents

Level*	Strategic Goal	Actions (Tactics)
	Isolation	Isolate and evacuate area according to *ERG* guidelines.
	Fire Control: Withdrawal	***STAY AWAY* from tanks engulfed in fire.**
	Fire Control: Withdrawal/Control Burn	Withdraw and let the fire consume the fuel; usually is the best, safest option.
	Fire Control: Exposure Protection	Protect exposures.

* **NOTE:** Actions taken by Awareness-Level responders also apply to Operational-Level responders

Dangerous-When-Wet Material Spills Involving Fire or Flame Impingement

The immediate concern at these incidents is to protect exposures. The primary objective is to let the material burn until it is consumed. If a dangerous-when-wet material is on fire, ***do not*** attempt extinguishment with water. Instead, secure the area and allow the material to burn. First responders generally do not have the resources needed to extinguish the material. The best attack in this situation is *no* attack. **Table 8.19** provides some basic actions that

can be taken by first responders when dealing with dangerous-when-wet materials involved in fire or threatened by flame impingement.

Oxidizers and Organic Peroxides (Class 5)

Oxidizers (Division 5.1) such as perchloric acid contain oxygen in their molecular structure and easily release the oxygen when heated. Most oxidizers are noncombustible but accelerate the burning of combustible materials. When

Table 8.18
First Responder Actions at Dangerous-When-Wet
Material Spill (No Fire) Incidents

Level*	Strategic Goal	Actions (Tactics)
	Isolation	Isolate and evacuate area according to *ERG* guidelines.
	Fire Control	Eliminate all ignition sources.
		Keep combustibles (such as wood, paper, and oil) away.
	Fire Control	Prevent contact with water or wet materials (wet sand or wet earth) if possible to do in a defensive manner (see next item).
	Fire and Spill Control: Blanketing	Using *ERG* guidelines, cover small powder spills of noncorrosive water-reactive materials with a plastic sheet or tarp to minimize spread and keep powder dry.

* **NOTE:** Actions taken by Awareness-Level responders also apply to Operational-Level responders

Table 8.19
First Responder Actions at Dangerous-When-Wet Material Spill
(Involving Fire or Flame Impingement) Incidents

Level*	Strategic Goal	Actions (Tactics)
	Isolation	Isolate and evacuate area according to *ERG* guidelines.
	Fire Control: Withdrawal	***STAY AWAY*** **from tanks engulfed in fire.**
	Fire Control: Withdrawal/Control Burn	Usually, the best, safest option is to withdraw and let the fire consume the fuel.
	Fire Control: Exposure Protection	Protect exposures.

Level	Actions to Avoid
	DO NOT **use water or foam if fire control is attempted.**
	DO NOT **let water get inside containers when attempting to cool containers threatened/involved in fire with unattended fire streams.**

* **NOTE:** Actions taken by Awareness-Level responders also apply to Operational-Level responders

mixed with organic materials such as petroleum products, the mixture can ignite spontaneously. Prudence may dictate that first responders treat oxidizers as *close cousins* to explosives because of their tendency to be involved in explosive chemical reactions **(Figure 8.15)**.

Organic peroxides (Division 5.2) are organic derivatives of the inorganic compound hydrogen peroxide. Some organic peroxides are shock-sensitive, heat-sensitive, and even light-sensitive. Decomposition can be self-accelerating and result in an explosive pressure rupture of a container.

Class 5 material container types are discussed in the sections that follow. Emergencies involving oxidizers and organic peroxides are described along with the immediate concern and primary objective for each.

Class 5 Material Container Types

Packaging of oxidizers and organic peroxides covers a wide spectrum typical of hazardous materials **(Figure 8.16)**. A common package is the plastic-lined, multi-ply paper bag. Metal tins and fiberboard, plastic, and metal drums are also used for packaging oxidizers. Portable, stationary, and applicator tanks contain oxidizers that are made into slurry for agricultural use. Liquid or slurry oxi-

dizers are shipped in stainless-steel tank trucks. Dry-bulk tank trucks and railcars are used to move bulk loads of dry oxidizers.

Many organic peroxides are limited in the quantity that can be shipped. The containers range in size from a few ounces (milliliters) to 55-gallon (208 L) drums. Unlike similar containers used with other hazard class materials, the small organic peroxide containers are vented. Tank trucks may move some peroxides, but special permitting is usually required.

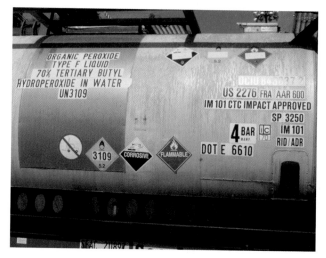

Figure 8.16 A tank car containing organic peroxides. These materials can be extremely dangerous. Some organic peroxides are shock-sensitive, heat-sensitive, and even light-sensitive. *Courtesy of Rich Mahaney.*

Figure 8.15 Because they accelerate combustion (sometimes explosively), incidents involving oxidizers such as with this liquid oxygen tank should be treated with extreme caution. In many cases withdrawal may be the best and safest option.

Oxidizer and Organic Peroxide Emergencies

Oxidizing materials are unpredictable; they can react suddenly, violently, and without warning to friction or heat. When first responders are unsure of what to do, they need to withdraw and do nothing. If first responders take a wrong action, it can quickly accelerate the seriousness of an oxidizer incident. Tactics must be well planned. If there is any doubt as to the success of an operation, responders must stop and reassess the situation.

The incident commander (IC) should never hesitate to order a total withdrawal when oxidizers are involved. The slightest hint of an incident worsening should initiate the withdrawal order. The following sections describe the emergencies involving oxidizers and organic peroxides and the immediate concern and primary objective for each.

Oxidizer Spills (No Fire)

The immediate concern at these incidents is to prevent ignition by isolating combustibles from the material. The primary objectives are to isolate and confine the material until it can be removed. First responders need to make every effort — in a safe manner — to prevent contact of the oxidizer with combustible materials. They should confine the spill by damming, diking, and diverting at a distance. They should remove nearby combustibles from the immediate area, touching and removing only adjacent materials.

In addition, first responders must take care to avoid walking into the oxidizing material when isolating the spill. Contaminants on the sole of a boot coming in contact with an oxidizer or the friction of stepping on the material can cause ignition, sometimes explosively. **Table 8.20** provides some basic actions that can be taken by first responders when dealing with oxidizers not involved in fire.

Oxidizer Spills Involving Fire

The immediate concern at these incidents is to protect exposures. The primary objective is to control the fire either by extinguishment or by controlled burning. Extinguishment of some oxidizer spills is within the capabilities of a fire and emergency services organization, but the fire generally requires large volumes of water. With a few exceptions, water is usually recommended for fire-fighting purposes, whereas foam is not. **Table 8.21, p. 424,** provides some basic actions that can be taken by first responders when dealing with oxidizer spills involved in fire.

Table 8.20 First Responder Actions at Oxidizer Spill (No Fire) Incidents		

Level*	Strategic Goal	Actions (Tactics)
	Isolation	Isolate and evacuate area according to *ERG* guidelines.
	Fire Control	Eliminate all ignition sources.
		Keep combustibles (wood, paper, oil, etc.) away.
	Protection	Withdraw if in doubt about actions to take.
	Spill Control: Confinement	Dam, dike, divert, or retain from a distance as appropriate and when safe.

* **NOTE:** Actions taken by Awareness-Level responders also apply to Operational-Level responders

Level*	Strategic Goal	Actions (Tactics)
	Isolation	Isolate and evacuate area according to *ERG* guidelines.
	Fire Control: Withdrawal	**STAY AWAY** from tanks engulfed in fire.
	Fire Control: Withdrawal/Control Burn	Withdraw and let the fire consume the fuel (best option in some cases).
	Fire Control	Flood the fire area with water from a safe distance if the decision is made to fight the fire. If the material is water-reactive, allow the material to burn.
	Fire Control: Exposure Protection	Cool tanks or containers with flooding quantities of water until well after fire is extinguished. **DO NOT** let water get inside containers when dealing with unstable oxidizers.
	Fire Control: Withdrawal	Withdraw immediately in case of rising sound from venting safety devices or discoloration of tank.
	Fire Control: Exposure Protection	Protect exposures.

* **NOTE:** Actions taken by Awareness-Level responders also apply to Operational-Level responders

Organic Peroxide Spills (No Fire)

Organic peroxides (such as hydrogen peroxide, benzoyl peroxide, and ethyl peroxide) are categorized as oxidizers, and, as with other oxidizers, the immediate concern is to prevent ignition by isolating combustibles from the material. The primary objectives are to isolate and confine the material until it can be removed.

Organic peroxides have some unique (and particularly hazardous) properties that first responders need to know. Organic peroxides tend to be very unstable and potentially explosive. They can be more volatile than other oxidizers, requiring a greater degree of caution on the part of first responders. Many organic peroxides will explode from heat, shock, friction, or contamination. They may easily ignite combustibles, and some spontaneously ignite when exposed to air. Containers may explode

when heated. Runoff water involving organic peroxides may create a fire or explosion hazard.

Some of these materials have a *maximum safe storage temperature (MSST)* or *control temperature*, below which they need to be kept in order to prevent spontaneous detonation. For that reason, they are often refrigerated. Obviously, in the event of a spill or container breach, the MSST of refrigerated materials may be exceeded, creating a very hazardous situation.

In rare cases, Technician-Level first responders may be able to keep the temperature low by using liquid nitrogen, dry ice, or ice. However, the most prudent action for first responders at the Awareness and Operational Levels is to withdraw to a safe distance and protect exposures. **Table 8.22** provides some basic actions that can be taken by first responders when dealing with organic peroxides not involved in fire.

Organic Peroxide Spills Involving Fire

Elevated temperatures decompose peroxides, and they become explosive. Involvement of these materials in a fire calls for isolation and withdrawal. Even attempting to get cooling water onto exposed containers of materials with a low MSST could be very dangerous. **Table 8.23** provides some basic actions that can be taken by first responders when dealing with organic peroxides involved in fire.

Poisonous Materials and Infectious Substances (Class 6)

Poisonous materials are those liquids and solids that are known to be toxic to humans or animals (Class 6, Division 6.1 materials). These materials include agricultural pesticides, cyanides, and even some exotic rocket fuels. An *infectious substance* (also called an *etiological agent)* is a microorganism (or its toxin) that causes human disease (Class 6, Division 6.2 materials). Examples of infectious substances are fluids or tissues infected with human immunodeficiency virus (HIV), rabies, and botulism. Descriptions of Class 6 Material Container Types and emergencies involving spills of poisonous materials and infectious substances are in the sections that follow.

Class 6 Material Container Types

Poisonous materials are packaged in all types of containers. They are shipped in bulk by intermodal portable tanks, tank trucks, railroad tank cars,

Table 8.22 First Responder Actions at Organic Peroxide Spill (No Fire) Incidents		
Level*	**Strategic Goal**	**Actions (Tactics)**
	Isolation	Isolate and evacuate area according to *ERG* guidelines.
	Fire Control	Eliminate all ignition sources.
		Keep combustibles (wood, paper, oil, etc.) away.
	Protection	Withdraw.

* **NOTE:** Actions taken by Awareness-Level responders also apply to Operational-Level responders

Table 8.23 First Responder Actions at Organic Peroxide Spill (Involving Fire) Incidents		
Level*	**Strategic Goal**	**Actions (Tactics)**
	Isolation	Isolate and evacuate area according to *ERG* guidelines.
	Fire Control Withdrawal/Control Burn	Withdraw and let the fire consume the fuel.
	Fire Control: Exposure Protection	Protect exposures.

* **NOTE:** Actions taken by Awareness-Level responders also apply to Operational-Level responders

barges, and marine tankers. Infectious substances are packaged in small vials that are measured in ounces (grams) and packed in strong containers for shipment **(Figure 8.17)**.

Poisonous Material Emergencies

The greatest danger associated with poisonous materials spills is the health threat. The following sections describe the incidents involving poisonous materials (either with fire or no fire) and the immediate concern and primary objective that need to be taken for each. Poisonous materials can harm first responders in any one of the following ways:

- Physical contact with the material
- Inhalation of vapors
- Inhalation of the material's products of combustion
- Contact with contaminated runoff water
- Contact with contaminated clothing

Poisonous Material Spills (No Fire)

The immediate concern at these incidents is to confine the spread of the material. The primary objectives are to stop the flow and isolate the area. Confine spills by diking from a safe distance or diverting the spill to a safe collection point. Protect storm and sewer drains, waterways, and other sensitive environmental areas. Confine solid materials by placing a salvage cover or plastic sheet over the spill, which will prevent the wind from scattering the material **(Figure 8.18)**.

Avoid contact with any poisonous material. More highly trained personnel must conduct most confinement and containment (stopping the flow) activities. **Table 8.24** provides some basic actions that can be taken by first responders when dealing with spilled poisonous materials that are not involved in fire.

Figure 8.18 When wind or other disturbances are concerns, confine spilled solids by placing a salvage cover or plastic sheet over them. Be sure that the material used is compatible with the solid.

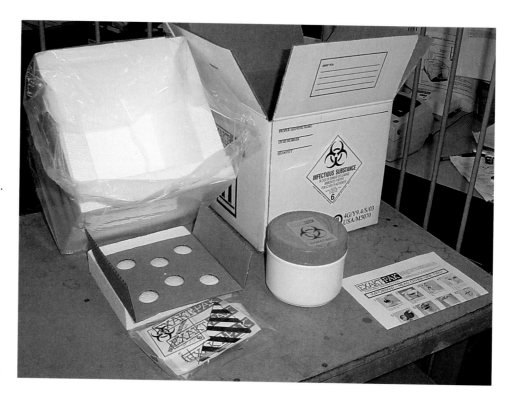

Figure 8.17 An infectious substance packaging system. Styrofoam and the external cardboard box protect the small internal container.

Table 8.24
First Responder Actions at Poisonous Material Spill
(No Fire) Incidents

Level*	Strategic Goal	Actions (Tactics)
	Isolation	Isolate and evacuate area according to *ERG* guidelines.
	Leak Control	Stop leak by closing remote valve if it is safe to do so.
	Spill Control: Blanketing	Cover spills of solids with tarps or plastic sheeting to prevent spreading.
	Spill Control: Confinement	Dike, dam, divert, and retain material as appropriate; prevent entry into waterways, sewers, basements, or other confined areas.

Level	Actions to Avoid
	Avoid getting water inside containers.

* **NOTE:** Actions taken by Awareness-Level responders also apply to Operational-Level responders

Poisonous Material Spills Involving Fire

The immediate concern at these incidents is to confine the spread of the material. The primary objectives are to stop the flow, isolate the area, and let the material burn. In some cases, doing nothing is the best approach for fires involving certain poisonous materials. Contaminated runoff water from fires involving certain poisonous materials (for example, pesticides) can be extremely damaging to the environment. An extremely hot fire destroys the toxic properties of some materials and reduces the cleanup effort.

When it is feasible to fight a fire, confine the runoff water for proper disposal. Wear PPE and SCBA because the products of combustion can be toxic. Poisonous material spill fires must be fought from upwind. **Table 8.25, p. 428,** provides some basic actions that can be taken by first responders when dealing with poisonous material spills that are involved in fire.

Infectious Substance Emergencies

Unless used as part of a terrorist incident, most infectious substances are found in and around hospitals, laboratories, and research centers. These incidents will be small because of the limited quantities used and shipped. Chapter 9, Terrorist and Other Criminal Activities, discusses biological hazards (including infectious substances) in the context of a terrorist attack. It also discusses biological hazards in much greater detail than found in this chapter.

Regulated medical wastes are included with infectious substances under DOT regulations. First responders need to recognize the biomedical symbol and the distinctive plastic bag used to contain the waste **(Figure 8.19, p. 429).** Medical wastes are found in hospitals, clinics, doctors' offices, and even some fire stations. Trucks transport medical wastes from these locations to disposal sites. First responders responding to incidents involving medical waste spills need to treat the waste as an infectious substance. They must also isolate the area, avoid handling the waste, and call for assistance.

Local health departments are often the regulating agency for medical waste. Above all, first responders must avoid contact with an infectious substance. The following sections describe the

Table 8.25
First Responder Actions at Poisonous Material Spill
(Involving Fire) Incidents

Level*	Strategic Goal	Actions (Tactics)
	Isolation	Isolate and evacuate area according to *ERG* guidelines.
	Fire Control: Withdrawal	**STAY AWAY from tanks engulfed in fire.**
	Fire Control: Withdrawal/Control Burn	Withdraw and let the fire burn, which in many cases is the best option.
	Fire Control	Follow *ERG*/expert guidance for the material involved if the decision is made to fight the fire.
	Fire Control: Exposure Protection	Cool tanks or containers with flooding quantities of water until well after fire is extinguished. **Do not** let water get inside containers.
	Spill Control: Confinement	Dike, dam, divert, and retain material and/or runoff water as appropriate.
	Fire Control: Withdrawal	Withdraw immediately in case of rising sound from venting safety devices or discoloration of tank.
	Fire Control: Exposure Protection	Protect exposures.

* **NOTE:** Actions taken by Awareness-Level responders also apply to Operational-Level responders

emergencies involving infectious substance spills (involving either no fire or fire) and the immediate concern and primary objective for each.

Infectious Substance Spills (No Fire)

The immediate concerns at these incidents are to protect life safety and confine the spread of the material. The primary objectives are to isolate the area and deny entry. Damage to an outer container does not necessarily mean the inner vial has been damaged **(Figure 8.20)**. However, first responders need to assume the worst. Treat the incident as if the vial is damaged and the infectious substance has been released. *Never* handle the container to see if a vial is broken.

An accepted way to treat infectious substance spill incidents is to cover the container with a liquid-bleach-saturated towel. Bleach kills most infectious substances if applied correctly. First responders must wear PPE and SCBA for protection during infectious substance spill incidents. Bystanders who may have had contact with the infectious substance(s) need to be isolated and given medical assistance immediately.

Advice on handling an infectious accident can be obtained from a local hospital, an emergency response center (see *ERG*), or the Centers for Disease Control and Prevention (CDC). **Table 8.26, p. 430,** provides some basic actions that can be taken by first responders when dealing with infectious substance spills that are not involved in fire or are not terrorist incidents.

Infectious Substance Spills Involving Fire

The immediate concerns at these incidents are to protect life safety and confine the spread of the material. The primary objectives are to isolate the area and let the material burn. When the incident

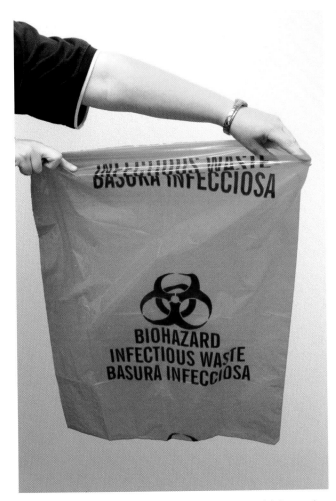

Figure 8.19 Red bags marked with the distinct biohazard symbol may contain infectious waste.

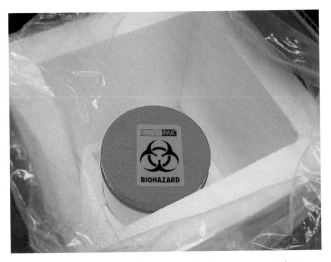

Figure 8.20 Even though damage to the outer container does not necessarily mean the inner vial has been damaged, emergency responders should treat incidents involving infectious substances packages as if the worst situation has occurred.

involves fire, protect exposures and let the fire consume the fuel. The heat of the flame destroys the infectious substance. **Table 8.27, p. 430,** provides some basic actions that can be taken by first responders when dealing with infectious substance spills that are on fire.

Radioactive Materials (Class 7)

As discussed in Chapter 3, Hazardous Materials Identification, *radioactive materials* are those that spontaneously emit ionizing radiation. Radioactive material packages are the strongest containers used to transport hazardous materials. For this reason, leakage of radioactive materials from containers is rare. This section discusses transportation incidents involving radioactive materials. Terrorist incidents involving radioactive materials (such as dirty bombs, nuclear events, etc.) are discussed in Chapter 9, Terrorist and Other Criminal Activities, along with the strategies and tactics for these potentially large-scale nuclear and radiological events.

Much of the information provided in the following packaging, transportation, and storage sections was adapted from the online training program, *Radiation Fundamentals for Emergency Responders,* as made available by the U.S. Department of Energy (DOE) and the Hanford (WA) Fire Department.

Radioactive Materials Packaging

Two primary categories of packaging for Class 7 radioactive material shipments are as follows:

- *Type A* — This packaging contains low-level commercial radioactive shipments. These containers include cardboard boxes, wooden crates, cylinders (for compressed radiological gases such as xenon), and metal drums. *Details:*

  — Measuring devices such as radiography instruments and soil-density meters contain radioactive materials and technically may be considered Type A packaging **(Figure 8.21, p. 430).**

  — Radiopharmaceuticals (medicines that contain a radioactive material used to diagnose or treat illnesses) are packaged in

Table 8.26
First Responder Actions at Infectious Substance Spill
(No Fire) Incidents

Level*	Strategic Goal	Actions (Tactics)
	Isolation	Isolate and evacuate area according to *ERG* guidelines.
	Protection/Control	Cover damaged packages or spilled substances (without touching them) with damp towels or rags, and keep them wet with liquid bleach or other disinfectant. ***Do not*** clean up or dispose of substances, except under supervision of a specialist.

* **NOTE:** Actions taken by Awareness-Level responders also apply to Operational-Level responders

Table 8.27
First Responder Actions at Infectious Substance Spill
(Involving Fire) Incidents

Level*	Strategic Goal	Actions (Tactics)
	Isolation	Isolate and evacuate area according to *ERG* guidelines.
	Fire Control: Control Burn	Allow the fire to burn and destroy the infectious substance.
	Fire Control: Exposure Protection	Protect exposures.

* **NOTE:** Actions taken by Awareness-Level responders also apply to Operational-Level responders

Figure 8.21 This density gauge is considered a Type A package. *Courtesy of Tom Clawson, Technical Resources Group, Inc.*

small quantities and generally limited to air transportation because of their short half-lives (degradation time).

- *Type B* — This packaging is stronger than Type A packaging and is used for more highly radioactive shipments. These containers include steel-reinforced concrete casks, lead pipe, and heavy-gauge metal drums. They can survive serious accidents and fire without release of the radioactive material. Type B containers are designed to carry the following:
  — Fissionable materials
  — High-grade raw materials
  — Nuclear fuels (both new and spent)
  — Highly radioactive metals

Radioactive Materials Transportation

Highways transport radioactive materials safely every day, and this mode is the most frequent transport method. Other modes include railways, airways, and waterways. Regulations covering these materials strictly control the types of radioactive materials that can be carried, their quantities, and their packaging. In addition, hazard communication standards help ensure that those who handle or come into contact with these materials—including emergency responders—will be able to identify the cargo and understand the hazards **(Figure 8.22).**

Trucks carry a wide variety of both low-level and high-level radioactive materials. Among other restrictions, carriers are required to follow the most direct interstate route, bypassing heavily populated areas when possible. However, containers used for shipping high-level radioactive materials are very strong, and releases are extremely rare.

Railways

Railway transport is the second most frequent method of transporting radioactive materials. Generally, trains carry material too large or heavy for highway transportation. Large volumes of low-level waste are commonly transported by rail. Rail accidents can be particularly dangerous for two reasons: First, extremely large quantities are involved; secondly, a serious accident can damage several railcars, resulting in combinations of hazardous materials.

The preferred method of shipping radioactive materials and waste is by *unit train,* which runs directly between its point of origin and destination. It receives priority right-of-way and expedited switching and does *not* receive or unload any additional cargo along the way. The radioactive loads are contained by a disposable liner and hard cover and carried in gondola cars **(Figure 8.23).**

Figure 8.23 Gondola cars loaded with radioactive material. *Courtesy of the U.S. Department of Energy Transportation Emergency Preparedness Program.*

Figure 8.22 Hazard communication standards help ensure that first responders will be able to identify radioactive materials when they are involved in highway accidents. *Courtesy of Tom Clawson, Technical Resources Group, Inc.*

Railcars placarded *RADIOACTIVE* cannot be placed next to a locomotive or an occupied caboose. A buffer car loaded with any nonradioactive material must be placed between a car carrying radioactive materials and a locomotive or caboose. Federal regulations require shippers and carriers to have emergency plans in place in case an accident involving a railcar occurs.

Airways

DOT strictly limits air shipments of radioactive materials. One exception is radiopharmaceuticals that are frequently short-lived, small, and lightweight. Often they must be delivered quickly to hospitals and medical laboratories, so air shipment is generally the best method. Air shipment of radioactive materials is not regulated by the *Code of Federal Regulations (CFR),* as are most other shipping methods. The International Atomic Energy Agency (IAEA) issues regulations for air transport. With the exception of nuclear weapons, large quantities of radioactive materials are rarely shipped by air. Military forces and their contract carriers are notable exceptions.

Waterways

Only a small percentage of radioactive materials are shipped by water, primarily because this type of transportation is slow and geographically limited. Materials that are occasionally transported via waterways include spent nuclear fuel coming into the U.S. from foreign research reactors, uranium metal, uranium hexafluoride, and low-level waste. When shipped by water, these materials are identified as *marine pollutants* and noted as such on manifests. The IAEA and the International Maritime Organization (IMO) govern international water transport of radioactive materials. DOT and the U.S. Nuclear Regulatory Commission (NRC) regulate transportation in U.S. waters. In addition, DOE has conducted extensive tests to ensure the safety of vessels carrying radioactive cargo. Shipments that exceed a certain level of radioactivity must be shipped exclusively on vessels hired specifically for that purpose.

Radioactive Materials Storage

When radioactive materials are depleted or lose their usefulness, they are considered waste and must be stored at a government-approved disposal facility. Each type of waste is sent to a disposal site that is appropriate for its characteristics.

High-Level Radioactive Waste

High-level radioactive waste results from the reprocessing of spent nuclear fuel in commercial or defense facilities. Reprocessing can recover the usable radioactive materials for research and defense programs. High-level waste is currently stored in underground tanks and vaults at government sites. Some of this waste is solidified in glass form, packaged in stainless steel canisters, and placed in heavily shielded casks for transport to a permanent geologic repository.

Spent Radioactive Fuel

Spent radioactive fuel results from processes at nuclear power plants or other reactors such as research reactors. After the usable fuel has been expended, highly radioactive fuel assemblies remain. The U.S. does not reprocess spent fuel from power plants but has reprocessed spent fuel from many types of reactors in the past. Spent fuel is shipped as a solid and packaged in casks for transport. Presently, spent fuel is stored in pools of water, aboveground vaults, or concrete casks onsite at reactor or commercial power plants. Spent fuel from DOE-owned reactors is stored where it is produced or at other DOE sites. Like high-level waste, spent fuel is eventually shipped to permanent geologic repositories. Under the Nuclear Waste Policy Act, DOE is responsible for transporting spent fuel from power plants as well as defense-related high-level radioactive waste to permanent repositories.

Transuranic Waste

Transuranic waste contains manufactured elements heavier than uranium (thus the name *trans* [or beyond] *uranic*), which results from defense production activities and includes contaminated protective clothing, tools, glassware, and equipment. Most transuranic waste is now stored at government sites throughout the U.S. Although most transuranic waste is no more radioactive than low-level waste, it is radioactive for a longer period of time (see following section). In the past, transuranic waste was shipped in railcars, but shipments to the Waste Isolation Pilot Plant (WIPP) in New Mexico are made by truck in a specially designed packaging called *TRUPACT-II* (**Figure 8.24**). WIPP disposes of transuranic waste in deep, geologically stable salt beds.

Low-Level Radioactive Waste

Low-level radioactive waste consists of contaminated rags, papers, filters, tools, equipment, and discarded protective clothing. It results from research, medical, and industrial processes that use radioactive materials. Commercial power plant operations and defense-related activities (including weapons disassembly and cleanup of production sites) also produce some low-level waste. Typically, low-level waste contains small amounts of short-lived radioactive material dispersed in large quantities of nonradioactive material. It is far less hazardous than high-level waste and is usually packaged in sturdy wooden or steel crates and steel drums for shipment to storage or disposal sites.

Low-level waste is sent to disposal sites licensed by NRC. Several commercial sites accept waste from producers of low-level waste, and some states have formed regional compacts to dispose of low-level waste when these facilities close. Sites have been established throughout the DOE complex for disposal of low-level waste produced by DOE.

Mixed Radioactive Waste

Mixed radioactive waste contains both hazardous chemical components and radioactive components. It is subject to the requirements of the Atomic Energy Act and the Resource Conservation and Recovery Act. Mixed waste is treated, packaged, and shipped offsite to DOE or commercial disposal sites by most DOE facilities that produce it. Envirocare of Utah, Inc. recently began accepting DOE mixed-waste shipments for disposal. The waste is encapsulated in melted recycled plastic and disposed of in an onsite landfill.

Uranium Mill Tailings

Uranium mill tailings are the residual wastes of milled ore that remain after the uranium has been recovered. The tailings are generated during the

Figure 8.24 Transuranic waste is shipped in a special packaging called *TRUPACT-II. Courtesy of Rich Mahaney.*

extraction of uranium from the ore as it is fed to the mill. They contain small amounts of naturally occurring radium that decays and emits a radioactive gas called *radon* (a known carcinogen). When radon gas is released into the atmosphere, it disperses harmlessly; however, radon gas might be dangerous if it is inhaled in high concentrations over a long period of time. Uranium mill tailings are transported to several disposal facilities specifically designed to accept them. When the disposal site reaches capacity, it is sealed to prevent dispersion of radon gas.

Radioactive Material Transportation Emergencies

[NFPA 472: 5.4.4(6)]

As discussed in Chapter 3, Hazardous Materials Identification, the three ways by which first responders can protect themselves against exposure to radiation are time, distance, and shielding. This protection is sometimes referred to as the *ALARA* (*As Low As Reasonably Achievable*) *method*. When first responders are exposed to radiation for short periods of time, they receive less exposure to the radiation. When first responders are farther from the source, the level of exposure is less (**Figure 8.25, p. 434**). Appropriate shielding also reduces the amount of exposure.

Relatively high levels of radioactivity do *not* necessarily preclude undertaking a rescue. First responders should be able to *get in, get the victim,*

Figure 8.25 The farther responders are from the source of radiation, the less the level of exposure. *Courtesy of Tom Clawson, Technical Resources Group, Inc.*

and get out without significant harm. Time is a significant factor as shown in the following equation:

Dose Rate × Exposure Time = Total Dose   (1)

Establishing control zones and conducting decontamination procedures can limit the spread of radioactive contamination. The following sections describe emergencies involving radioactive material spills (either involving no fire or fire) and the immediate concern and primary objective that need to be taken for each.

Radioactive Material Spills (No Fire)

The immediate concern at these incidents is to confine the spread of the material. The primary objectives are to isolate the area and deny entry. **Table 8.28** provides a list of actions for first responders to take when faced with a transportation incident involving radioactive material spills not involved in fire.

Radioactive Material Spills Involving Fire

The immediate concern at these incidents is to confine the spread of the material. The primary objective for a fire involving radioactive material spills is to extinguish the fire if it can be done without risk to responders. Responder actions are outlined in the *ERG*. Guides 161–166 are specific for response to a transportation incident involving radioactive materials involved in fire.

Technical help is definitely needed at incidents involving radioactive material spills. Remove nothing from the site until technicians have checked it for contamination. **Table 8.29** provides a list of actions for first responders to take when faced with transportation incidents involving radioactive material spills involved in fire.

Appendix I provides a series of flow charts designed for first responders at transportation accidents involving radiological materials. These flow charts were developed as part of the DOE's Transportation Emergency Preparedness Program (TEPP) and may serve as an excellent resource on how to respond appropriately to transportation incidents involving radioactive materials.

Corrosives (Class 8)

Corrosives are materials (either acids or bases) that corrode, degrade, or destroy human skin, aluminum, or steel. The terms *caustic* and *alkaline* are also used to refer to base materials. The pH of a material is used to determine whether it is an acid or a base. Acids have pH numbers of 1 through 6, and bases have pH numbers of 8 through 14. A pH of 7 is neutral. The sections that follow discuss container types and emergencies involving corrosive material spills (either involving fire or no fire).

Corrosives Container Types

Corrosives come in a wide variety of containers that range in size from glass/plastic bottles and carboys to plastic drums **(Figure 8.26).** Fiberboard drums and multilayered paper bags are used for acid materials and caustics in dry form. Wax bottles are used to store hydrofluoric acid because the acid also attacks glass. Intermodal portable tanks, tank trucks, railroad tank cars, barges, and pipelines are used to transport bulk shipments of corrosives.

Tanks that are smaller than those used for other types of liquids are used to transport corrosives because of the density of corrosives, which can weigh twice that of an equal volume of water. Maximum capacity for tank trucks is about 6,000 gallons (22 712 L) and about 24,000 gallons (90 850 L) for railroad tank cars.

Table 8.28
First Responder Actions at Radioactive Material Spill (No Fire) Incidents

Level*	Strategic Goal	Actions (Tactics)
	Isolation	Isolate and evacuate area according to *ERG* guidelines.
	Protection	Use time, distance, and shielding for protection.

* **NOTE:** Actions taken by Awareness-Level responders also apply to Operational-Level responders

Table 8.29
First Responder Actions at Radioactive Material Spill (Involving Fire) Incidents

Level*	Strategic Goal	Actions (Tactics)
	Isolation	Isolate and evacuate area according to *ERG* guidelines.
	Protection	Use time, distance, and shielding for protection.
	Fire Control: Extinguishment	Extinguish the fire according to normal procedures unless the material is corrosive or water-sensitive (such as uranium hexafluoride); in which case, ***do not*** use water or foam.
	Spill Control: Confinement	Dike, dam, divert, and retain runoff water from fire-extinguishment activities as appropriate.
	Fire Control: Exposure Protection	Protect exposures.

* **NOTE:** Actions taken by Awareness-Level responders also apply to Operational-Level responders

Figure 8.26 Packaging of corrosives varies widely. This tank contains sulfuric acid.

Corrosive Materials Emergencies

PPE is quite limited in protecting first responders from corrosives. Vapors can permeate PPE and irritate the skin, especially the damp areas of the body. Irritation can be severe and can cause skin damage. Incidents involving corrosives can be serious. The sections that follow describe the emergencies involving corrosive materials and the immediate concern and primary objective that need to be taken for each.

Corrosive Material Spills (No Fire)

The immediate concerns at these incidents are to confine the spread and *not* dilute the material. The primary objectives are to turn off the flow, isolate the area, and deny entry. First responders need to confine the spread of the material if confinement can be done without coming into contact with the material or its vapors. Keep corrosives from reaching organic materials or other corrosives. *Do not* use water because it only worsens the problem; water itself becomes corrosive after contact.

Dense vapor clouds are common with some corrosive spills, and controlling vapors is part of the confinement process. Foam streams may be used to reduce vapor production. Fog streams can be used to disperse or redirect vapors, but the water must *not* contact either the container or the spill.

First responders should cover the spill with salvage covers or plastic sheets to prevent wind currents from scattering solid corrosive materials. They should also keep corrosives from entering storm and sewer systems, creeks, canals, bayous, and rivers. Appropriate authorities should be notified if corrosives enter a waterway. Corrosives are environmentally damaging.

First responders should conduct emergency decontamination on victims who have come in contact with a corrosive. Victims should be directed to immediately remove their clothes, after which victims are thoroughly flushed with water. Medical personnel need to know the name of the corrosive so that proper treatment can be undertaken. **Table 8.30** provides some basic actions that can be taken by first responders when dealing with corrosive material spills that are not involved in fire.

Corrosive Material Spills Involving Fire

The immediate concerns at these incidents are to confine the spread of the material and protect exposures. The primary objectives are to turn off the flow, isolate the area, and deny entry. Some corrosives are flammable, and first responders need to consider ignition sources. Other corrosives are strong oxidizing agents and can ignite organic materials. If a spill is burning, the primary objective is to protect exposures — *not* to extinguish the fire. Water can worsen the situation.

Smoke from burning corrosives can be corrosive and should be avoided. Even with all exposed areas of the body covered, first responders can still be harmed. Smoke from burning corrosives (and especially the vapors) can permeate protective clothing. **Table 8.31, p. 438,** provides some basic actions that can be taken by first responders when dealing with corrosive material spills that are involved in fire.

Summary

At every hazardous materials incident, there are certain actions that all first responders should take. These actions include the following:

- Follow predetermined procedures for handling haz mat incidents.
- Approach the scene from upwind, uphill, and upstream if possible.
- Identify the material.
- Isolate and evacuate the area according to *ERG* or other guidelines.
- Eliminate ignition sources.
- Avoid contact with the material.

There are also guidelines that should be followed according to the materials involved. While the *ERG* describes actions that may be taken to mitigate incidents involving particular materials, some of those actions are aimed at Technician-Level responders and may be inappropriate for responders trained to Awareness and Operational Levels. First responders at Awareness and Operational Levels should be aware of what actions are appropriate for them given the different types of materials.

Level*	Strategic Goal	Actions (Tactics)
	Isolation	Isolate and evacuate area according to *ERG* guidelines.
	Leak Control	Stop leak by closing remote valve if it is safe to do so.
	Spill Control: Blanketing	Cover spills of solids with tarps or plastic sheeting to prevent spreading.
	Spill Control: Vapor Control	Use foam to reduce vapors when appropriate.
		Use fog streams to disperse or redirect vapors when appropriate. Take care to avoid mixing water with spilled materials.
	Spill Control: Confinement	Control and confine runoff water created by vapor-control activities.
		Dike, dam, divert, and retain material as appropriate; prevent entry into waterways, sewers, basements, or other confined areas; prevent contact with organic materials and other corrosives.

Level	Actions to Avoid
	Do not **let water get inside containers or contact spilled material.**

* **NOTE:** Actions taken by Awareness-Level responders also apply to Operational-Level responders

Level*	Strategic Goal	Actions (Tactics)
	Isolation	Isolate and evacuate area according to *ERG* guidelines.
	Fire Control: Withdrawal	**STAY AWAY from tanks engulfed in fire.**
	Fire Control: Withdrawal/Control Burn	Withdraw and let the fire burn, which in most cases is the best option; water can make the situation worse.
	Fire Control	Follow *ERG*/expert guidance for the material involved if the decision is made to fight the fire.
	Fire Control: Exposure Protection	Cool tanks or containers with flooding quantities of water until well after fire is extinguished. **Do not** let water get inside containers.
	Spill Control: Confinement	Dike, dam, divert, and retain material and/or runoff water as appropriate.
	Fire Control: Withdrawal	Withdraw immediately in case of rising sound from venting safety devices or discoloration of tank.
	Fire Control: Exposure Protection	Protect exposures.

* **NOTE:** Actions taken by Awareness-Level responders also apply to Operational-Level responders

Part Three

Special Topics

Chapter 9

Terrorist and Other Criminal Activities

This chapter provides information that will assist the reader in meeting the following first responder competencies from NFPA 472, *Professional Competence of Responders to Hazardous Materials Incidents*, 2002 Edition. The numbers are noted directly in the text under the section titles where they are addressed.

NFPA 472

Chapter 4   Competencies for the First Responder at the Awareness Level

4.2.1   Detecting the Presence of Hazardous Materials. Given various facility or transportation situations, or both, with and without hazardous materials present, the first responder at the awareness level shall identify those situations where hazardous materials are present and also shall meet the following requirements:

(13) Identify at least four types of locations that could become targets for criminal or terrorist activity using hazardous materials.

(14) Describe the difference between a chemical and a biological incident.

(15) Identify at least four indicators of possible criminal or terrorist activity involving chemical agents.

(16) Identify at least four indicators of possible criminal or terrorist activity involving biological agents.

4.4.1   Initiating Protective Actions. Given examples of facility and transportation hazardous materials incidents, the local emergency response plan, the organization's standard operating procedures, and the current edition of the Emergency Response Guidebook, first responders at the awareness level shall be able to identify the actions to be taken to protect themselves and others and to control access to the scene and shall also meet the following requirements:

(12) Identify at least four specific actions necessary when an incident is suspected to involve criminal or terrorist activity.

Chapter 5   Competencies for the First Responder at the Operational Level

5.2.1.6 The first responder at the operational level shall identify at least three additional hazards that could be associated with an incident involving criminal or terrorist activity.

5.2.2   Collecting Hazard and Response Information. Given known hazardous materials, the first responder at the operational level shall collect hazard and response information using MSDS; CHEMTREC/CANUTEC/SETIQ; local, state, and federal authorities; and contacts with the shipper/manufacturer and also shall meet the following requirements:

(6) Identify the type of assistance provided by local, state, and federal authorities with respect to criminal or terrorist activities involving hazardous materials.

5.2.3   Predicting the Behavior of a Material and its Container. Given an incident involving a single hazardous material, the first responder at the operational level shall predict the likely behavior of the material and its container and also shall meet the following requirements:

(9) Given the following types of warfare agents, identify the corresponding UN/DOT hazard class and division:

   (a) Nerve agents

   (b) Vesicants (blister agents)

   (c) Blood agents

   (d) Choking agents

   (e) Irritants (riot control agents)

   (f) Biological agents and toxins

5.3.4   Identifying Emergency Decontamination Procedures. The first responder at the operational level shall identify emergency decontamination procedures and shall meet the following requirements:

(6) Describe procedures, such as those listed in the local emergency response plan or the organization's standard operating procedures, to preserve evidence at hazardous materials incidents involving suspected criminal or terrorist acts.

Emergency Responder Guidelines

This chapter provides information that will assist the reader in meeting the following first responder guidelines for fire service and law enforcement from the Office for Domestic Preparedness (ODP) *Emergency Responder Guidelines,* 2002 Edition. The numbers are noted directly in the text under the section titles where they are addressed.

ODP Emergency Responder Guidelines

Fire Service and Law Enforcement

Awareness Level for Events Involving Weapons of Mass Destruction

II. **Know the protocols used to detect the potential presence of weapons of mass destruction (WMD) agents or materials.** The responder should:

   a. Understand what WMD agents or materials are and the risks associated with these materials in an emergency incident or event.

   b. Know the indicators and effects of WMD on individuals and property. Be able to recognize signs and symptoms common to initial victims of a WMD-related incident or event. Know the physical characteristics or properties of WMDX agents or materials that could be reported by victims or other persons at the scene.

   c. Be familiar with the potential use and means of delivery of WMD agents or materials.

   d. Know locations or properties that could become targets for persons using WMD agents or materials.

   e. Recognize unusual trends or characteristics that might indicate an incident or event involving WMD agents or materials.

III. **Know and follow self-protection measures for WMD events and hazardous materials events.** The responder should:

   a. Understand the hazards and risks to individuals and property associated with WMD agents and hazardous materials. Recognize the signs and symptoms of exposure to WMD agents and hazardous materials.

   f. Know what defensive measures to take during a WMD or hazardous materials incident or event to help ensure personal and community safety. These measures may include maximizing the distance between the officer and hot zone, using shielding such as solid walls for protection, minimizing person exposure to agents or materials that might be found in the warm zone or within the plume, and moving upgrade and upwind.

IV. **Know procedures for protecting a potential crime scene.** Whether or not a witness to the event, the responder should:

   a. Understand and implement procedures for protecting evidence and minimizing disturbance of the potential crime scene while protecting others. Understand the roles, responsibilities, and jurisdictions of Federal agencies related to a WMD event or incident.

   b. Recognize the importance of crime scene preservation and initiate measures to secure the scene.

   c. Protect physical evidence such as footprints, relevant containers, or wrapping paper, etc.

   d. Advise witnesses and bystanders who may have information to remain at the scene in a safe location until they have been interviewed and released. Be aware of people arriving or departing the scene. *Fire Service:* Understand what the hazards are and the risks associated with WMD agents and materials and hazardous materials as they related to human health and well-being. Have the basic knowledge of the hazards to humans and the common signs and symptoms of exposure to WMD agents and materials and hazardous materials. *Law Enforcement:* Note license plate numbers or other relevant data. Question the caller, witness(es), or victim(s) to obtain critical information regarding the incident or event.

V. **Know and follow agency/organization's scene security and control procedures for WMD and hazardous material events.** The responder should:

   c. Protect physical evidence such as footprints, relevant containers, or wrapping paper, etc.

   e. Recognize that the incident or event scene may be a crime scene and that evidence must be protected and undisturbed until a higher authority arrives and takes over.

VI. **Possess and know how to properly use equipment to contact dispatcher or higher authorities to report information collected at the scene and to request additional assistance or emergency response personnel.** The responder should:

   b. Understand how to accurately describe a WMD event and be aware of the available response assets within the affected jurisdiction(s) nearest the event location.

Performance Level for Events Involving Weapons of Mass Destruction

I. **Have successfully completed adequate and proper training at the awareness level for events involving hazardous materials, and for weapons of mass destruction (WMD) and other specialized training.** The responder should:

    b. Understand the terminology (including any glossary of WMD terms), classes of materials and agents, and toxicology of hazardous materials and WMD agents and materials.

    c. Be aware of any potential targets for possible attack by persons using WMD agents or materials. Know preplans to be used in his/her department's emergency response plan for these locations.

    d. Know how to collect and forward intelligence regarding potential terrorist/criminal actions involving possible WMD agents or materials. Be able to coordinate the gathering of such intelligence from a variety of sources and organizations that may be on the scene. Forward this information to the law enforcement manager or designee and the incident commander at the scene.

    e. Demonstrate skill and knowledge in preparing hazard and risk analysis of potential WMD targets in the local community. Know how to assess the potential for direct threats, as well as collateral damage effects.

    f. Participate in a joint training exercise or drill with other emergency response organizations that are expected to participate in responding to a potential WMD event in the local area.

    g. *Fire Service*: Recognize the special aspects of responding to a hazardous material or potential WMD event compared with more routine fire emergencies. Understand the special circumstances and properties of Haz Mat and WMD events compared with more routine fire emergencies.

II. **Know the Incident Command System and be able to follow Unified Command System procedures for integration and implementation of each system. Know how the systems integrate and support the incident. Be familiar with the overall operation of the two command systems and be able to assist in implementation of the Unified Command System if needed.** The responder should:

    d. Be familiar with the assets that could be made available from other local emergency response organizations. Understand and follow department's procedures for accessing these organizations for help with a potential WMD event.

    h. Know and follow departmental guidelines in dealing with the local media during a potential WMD event.

III. **Know and follow self-protection measures and rescue and evacuation procedures for WMD events.** The responder should:

    i. Know and follow departmental procedures and practices for requesting assistance from law enforcement in handling and securing unknown suspicious packages.

IV. **Know and follow procedures for working at the scene of a potential WMD event.** The responder should:

    a. *Fire Service:* Understand the importance of procedures in how to conduct a criminal investigation, such as a suspected arson incident, and in protecting possible crime scene evidence. *Law Enforcement:* Know how to conduct a criminal investigation, protect and collect possible crime scene evidence, and follow departmental procedures for chain of custody, documentation, and security measures to store crime scene evidence whether or not it is contaminated.

    b. Implement the department's emergency response plan scene security measures and procedures. These procedures include providing security for the command post and controlling or monitoring those entering and leaving the scene of a potential WMD event. *Fire Service:* Coordinate these activities with law enforcement.

    f. Be trained in how to recognize a potential terrorist incident. Be able to help identify the potential agents or materials that maybe present at a WMD event.

    g. Fully understand the role and jurisdiction of Federal agencies in a potential WMD event. Be able to coordinate and assist in the overall criminal investigation of the potential WMD event. *Law Enforcement:* Be aware of criminal laws, as well as privacy and security issues related to WMD events.

Chapter 9
Terrorist and Other Criminal Activities

Incidents involving terrorism and criminal activities are an increasing concern in many communities. Incidents involving terrorism and crime are different from other routine emergency incidents. These differences often bring about additional dangers to first responders, ranging from exposure to biological agents to encountering violent and armed individuals.

First responders must understand the role they play at incidents involving terrorism and criminal activities. They must know their limitations and realize when they cannot proceed. Because terrorist acts can have such devastating consequences, response to any act of terrorism requires coordination and cooperation among many different agencies. Both terrorist and criminal acts involve illegal activities, and the proper law-enforcement agencies must be involved.

This chapter defines terrorism and explores the different types of terrorist attacks. The chapter discusses other criminal activities such as illegal clandestine labs and dumps. It also includes information on operations at terrorist and criminal incidents.

Terrorism

Terrorists have the knowledge and the capability to strike anywhere in the world. Terrorists often target locations where civilians are present. Recent examples of terrorism include attacks on the U.S. World Trade Center in New York City, the Tokyo Subway nerve agent attack, and the Oklahoma City Murrah Federal Building bombing (**Figure 9.1, p. 444**). There have been smaller bombing incidents such as at the 1996 Olympics, which are not necessarily classed as terrorism events. The list most

likely will continue to grow. All societies, especially those that are free, are vulnerable to incidents involving terrorism. Many communities within a society contain some high-visibility targets. These targets often are situated along routes with high transportation and access potential. Many communities have manufacturing and testing facilities.

Terrorists are often difficult to stop, even when security precautions are taken. An act of terrorism can occur anywhere, at any minute, when least expected. No jurisdiction — urban, suburban, or rural — is totally immune from terrorist acts.

What Is Terrorism?

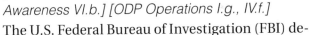

[NFPA 472: 5.2.1.6] [ODP Awareness VI.b.] [ODP Operations I.g., IV.f.]
The U.S. Federal Bureau of Investigation (FBI) defines terrorism as follows:

> *The unlawful use of force against persons or property to intimidate or coerce a government, the civilian population, or any segment thereof, in the furtherance of political or social objectives.*

This definition includes the following three elements:

- Terrorist activities are illegal and involve the use of force.
- Actions intend to intimidate or coerce.
- Actions are committed in support of political or social objectives.

Terrorism can be domestic or international. *Domestic* terrorism involves groups or individuals whose activities, conducted without foreign

Figure 9.1 Terrorists have the capability to strike anywhere in the world, and they often target civilians. *Courtesy of Federal Emergency Management Agency (FEMA) News Photo.*

influence, are directed at elements of a government or population. *International* terrorism involves activities committed by foreign-based groups or individuals who are either directed by countries or groups outside a country or whose activities transcend national boundaries.

The motives and methods of terrorist groups are evolving in ways that complicate prevention and counteraction activities and require the ability to shift resources quickly and with greater flexibility. These groups can strike at any time, anywhere, and they are spurred by seemingly unrelated events for which they judge an agency, group, or country blameworthy. They have a widening global reach and high degree of proficiency with sophisticated weapons and tactics **(Figure 9.2).**

Terrorist organizations intend their activities to have an emotional effect on the target audience, causing it to act in a manner that furthers the group's objectives. Terrorist operations can be categorized in terms of their associated goals. Some of these goals may be as follows:

- *Recognition* — The objective of these attacks is national and/or international attention for the group and its stated objectives. Terrorists groups often conduct attacks to gain recognition early in their life span. Groups often mount such attacks against highly visible symbols of state/province or national government control.

- *Coercion* — Groups intend coercion attacks to force individuals, organizations, or governments to act in a desired manner. Terrorists selectively target facilities with the intent of bringing increasing pressure on the targeted activity.

- *Intimidation* — Attacks designed primarily to intimidate are the means to prevent organizations or governments from acting in a defined manner. These attacks may also diminish the public's confidence in their government's ability to protect them.

- *Provocation* — These attacks aim to force government security forces to take repressive action against the general populace and generally are

Figure 9.2 The motives and methods of terrorist groups are evolving in ways that make prevention difficult. *Courtesy of Federal Emergency Management Agency (FEMA) News Photo.*

against critical infrastructures, popular or high-profile individuals, or important facilities. The goal of these attacks is to demonstrate the weakness of the legitimate government, thus causing an uncoordinated backlash.

In one sense, it makes no difference to first responders whether the incident is a terrorist act or not. They will still respond and be among the first on the scene. Naturally, the size and type of terrorist action are key factors in how a response is managed. However, it is important to note that an act of terrorism is essentially different from normal emergencies in that it is intended to cause damage, inflict harm, and kill **(Figure 9.3, p. 446).** The fire that starts in someone's home as a result of careless smoking did not occur with the intention to damage something, hurt someone, or kill someone. Exceptions, of course, are cases of arson, but most emergency incidents are not criminal in nature. Terrorists go to great lengths to make sure an event has the intended effect, even if it means destroying an entire building and killing all of its occupants.

The criminal component is the most important element separating a terrorist organization and its actions from a legitimate organization. However, any organization, legitimate or not, can resort to terrorist means to achieve its political or social agenda. Remember, too, that a terrorist can act alone.

At terrorist incidents, first responders may have to deal with circumstances far different from the usual structural fire, vehicle accident, or even hazardous materials incident. For example, terrorist events may involve large numbers of casualties or materials (such as radioactive materials) with which first responders have little experience.

Terrorists may also sequence events to inflict further harm on those whose job it is to respond to assist others. Some additional hazards in these situations include the following:

- Secondary events intended to incapacitate or delay emergency responders
- Armed resistance
- Use of weapons
- Booby traps
- Secondary contamination from handling patients

Potential Terrorist Targets
[NFPA 472: 4.2.1(13)] [ODP Awareness Level II.d.] [ODP Operations Level I.c., I.d., I.e., I.f.]

Just as some occupancies are more likely to contain hazardous materials than others, some are more likely to be terrorist targets than others. Obviously, when the goal is to kill as many people as possible, any place that has large public gatherings (such

Figure 9.3 Terrorist incidents are different from normal haz mat emergencies in that they are intended to kill, maim, and destroy.

as football stadiums, sports arenas, theaters, and shopping malls) might become potential targets. Terrorists might also target places with historical, economic, or symbolic significance such as local monuments, high-profile buildings, or bridges. First responders must be aware that any of the following are considered potential terrorist targets:

- Public assembly occupancies and locations
- Public buildings
- Mass transit systems
- Places with high economic significance
- Telecommunications facilities
- Places with historical or symbolic significance
- Military installations
- Airports
- Industrial facilities

The identification of possible terrorist targets is a critical step in local emergency response planning **(Figure 9.4).** First responders must be familiar with these locations from the local emergency response plans. Additionally, according to Office for

Figure 9.4 First responders need to identify likely terrorist targets in their areas and make plans for an organized response in case of attack. Joint training drills or exercises with other local emergency response organizations should be conducted to ensure an effective response.

Domestic Preparedness (ODP) guideline requirements, Operational-Level responders must be able to demonstrate skill and knowledge in preparing hazard and risk analyses of potential terrorist targets in their local communities. They must be able to identify those locations where a targeted attack has the potential to do the greatest harm and predict the consequences of such an attack. *Harm* should be defined in terms of the following concerns (and others that are similar):

- Killing or injuring persons
- Causing panic and/or disruption
- Damaging the economy
- Destroying property
- Demoralizing the community

Use this information in planning. Responders must become more vigilant to situations or occurrences that could indicate a potential terrorist incident. Responders should also participate in joint training exercises or drills with other emergency response organizations that would respond to terrorist incidents in their local area.

Terrorism is very similar to hazardous materials responses in that first responders must use basic indicators to identify potential incident types. The following are a few examples of situations (more are discussed later in this chapter) that can cue the responder to consider the possibility of terrorism:

- Report of two or more medical emergencies in public locations such as a shopping mall, transportation hub, mass transit system, office building, assembly occupancy, or other public buildings
- Unusually large number of people with similar signs and symptoms coming or being transported to physicians' offices or medical emergency rooms
- Reported explosion at a movie theater, department store, office building, government building, or a location with historical or symbolic significance

If criminal or terrorist activity is suspected at the scene of an incident, first responders must forward that information to the incident commander (IC) as quickly as possible. This information must be passed on to law-enforcement representatives

Figure 9.5 Law enforcement representatives must be informed immediately if criminal or terrorist activity is suspected at an incident. *Courtesy of Federal Emergency Management Agency (FEMA) News Photo.*

(Figure 9.5). Further information about operations at the scene of a terrorist or criminal incident is provided later in this chapter.

Types of Terrorist Attacks

[NFPA 472: 5.2.3 (9)] [ODP Awareness Level II.a., II.b., II.c., II.e., III.a.] [ODP Operations Level I.b., I.d., IV.f.]

Experts generally agree that there are five categories of terrorist incidents. In Chapter 6, Personal Protective Equipment, the abbreviation *CBRNE* was used for chemical, biological, radiological, nuclear, and explosive threats. The acronym *B-NICE* is a simple way to remember five similar categories:

- **B**iological
- **N**uclear
- **I**ncendiary
- **C**hemical
- **E**xplosive

Biological Attack

[NPFA 472: 4.2.1(16)]

The Centers for Disease Control and Prevention (CDC) defines *biological terrorism* as an intentional release of viruses, bacteria, or their toxins for the purpose of harming or killing citizens. In addition to aerosolization, food, water, or insects must be

Weapons of Mass Destruction

While this chapter discusses types of attacks based on the *B-NICE* acronym, you may hear different terms used to mean essentially the same thing. *Weapons of mass destruction (WMD)*, for example, is the *family name* for these types of weapons. You may also hear the terms *COBRA* (chemical, ordinance, biological, radiological agents), *CBRNE* (chemical, biological, radiological, nuclear, explosive) and *NBC* (nuclear, biological, chemical) as well as others.

According to the U.S. Government (*U.S. Code*)*, the term *weapon of mass destruction* means any weapon or device that is intended or has the capability to cause death or serious bodily injury to a significant number of people through the release, dissemination, or affect of one of the following means:

- Toxic or poisonous chemicals or their precursors
- A disease organism
- Radiation or radioactivity

Other parts of the *U.S. Code* also include certain explosive and incendiary devices in the definition.

*United States Code, Title 50, Chapter 40, Section 2302, and Title 18, Part I, Chapter 113B, Section 2332a.

considered as potential vehicles of transmission for biological weapons. First responders must be prepared to address various biological agents, including pathogens that are rarely seen in North America. They should also be aware of the possible indicators of biological attacks, the different types of biological agents, and the signs and symptoms of those biological agents most likely to be used as weapons. Four types of biological agents that first responders need to be concerned about are as follows:

- *Viral agents* — Viruses are the simplest types of microorganisms that can only replicate themselves in the living cells of their hosts. Viruses do not respond to antibiotics, making them an attractive weapon.

- *Bacterial agents* — Bacteria are microscopic, single-celled organisms. Most bacteria do not cause disease in people, but when they do, two

different mechanisms are possible: invading the tissues or producing poisons (toxins).

- *Rickettsias* — Rickettsias are specialized bacteria that live and multiply in the gastrointestinal tract of arthropod carriers (such as ticks and fleas). They are smaller than most bacteria, but larger than viruses. They have properties that are similar to both. Like bacteria, they are single-celled organisms with their own metabolisms, and they are susceptible to broad-spectrum antibiotics. However, like viruses, they only grow in living cells. Most rickettsias are spread only through the bite of infected arthropods and not through human contact.

- *Biological toxins* — Biological toxins are poisons produced by living organisms; however, the biological organism itself is usually not harmful to people. Some biological toxins have been manufactured synthetically and/or genetically altered in laboratories. They are similar to chemical agents in the way they are disseminated (and in their effectiveness) as biological weapons.

As the 2001 anthrax attacks in the U.S. demonstrated, an attack using a biological weapon may not be as immediately obvious as one using a bomb or industrial chemical. Generally, biological weapons agents do not cause immediate health effects. Most biological agents take hours, days, or weeks to make someone ill, depending on the incubation period of the agent. Because of this delay, the cause of illness may not be immediately evident, and the source of the attack may be difficult to trace.

In the beginning, patients may be few in number, with the number increasing when the disease continues to transmit from person to person (such as might happen with smallpox). The scope of the problem may not be evident for days or even weeks. However, certain biological toxins (such as saxitoxin, a neurotoxin produced by marine organisms) could potentially act more quickly (in minutes to hours).

Attack Indicators

Depending on the agent used and the scope of an incident, emergency medical services (EMS) responders and health-care personnel may be first to realize that there has been an attack. In some cases there may be reliable evidence to implicate terrorist activity such as a witness to an attack or the discovery of an appropriate delivery system (such as finding a contaminated bomb or rocket from which an infectious agent is subsequently isolated and identified). Terrorist activity may not be obviously evident, and first responders should be aware of the following examples of indicators of possible terrorist activity involving biological agents:

- *Unusual number of sick or dying people or animals (often of different species)* — Most biological weapons agents are capable of infecting/intoxicating a wide range of hosts. Any number of symptoms could occur. The time required before symptoms are observed depends on the agent used but may be days to weeks (**Figure 9.6**).

- *Multiple casualties with similar signs or symptoms* — Note reports from health-care facilities.

- *Dissemination of unscheduled or unusual spray* — Note especially when spraying occurs outdoors during darkness periods.

- *Abandoned spray devices* — Devices may have no distinct odors.

- *Illness type highly unusual for the geographic area* — For example, Venezuelan equine encephalitis in Europe is unusual.

- *Casualty distribution aligned with wind direction*

- *Lower attack rates among those working indoors than in those exposed outdoors* — Especially note areas with filtered-air or closed-ventilation systems.

Biological Agent Categories

[NFPA 472: 5.2.3(9)(f)]

Most biological agents and toxins fall under the United Nations/U.S. Department of Transportation (UN/DOT) Hazard Class 6.2. The CDC divides potential biological agents into three categories: A, B, and C. **Table 9.1, p. 450,** lists Category A agents that have the highest priority because they include organisms that pose a risk to national security in the following ways:

Figure 9.6 Dogs and other animals may be affected by a biological attack. Veterinarians may be the first to notice something unusual occurring. They should be alert to unusual numbers of sick animals or diseases appearing in areas where they are uncommon.

- Can be easily disseminated or transmitted person to person

- Cause high mortality and subsequently have a major public health effect

- Might cause public panic and social disruption

- Require special action for public-health preparedness

The CDC recommends that other less critical agents (Categories B and C) also receive attention for bioterrorism preparedness. These categories include new or emerging pathogens. **Table 9.2, p. 451,** gives the CDC's list of critical biological agents for Category B. A subset of Category B agents includes pathogens that are foodborne or waterborne. Category B agents include those that pose a risk in the following ways:

- Are moderately easy to disseminate

- Cause moderate morbidity and low mortality

- Require specific enhancements of CDC's diagnostic capacity and enhanced disease surveillance

Category C agents include emerging pathogens that could be engineered for mass dissemination in the future because they pose risks in the following ways:

Table 9.1
Category A* Biological Agents

Name	Biological Agent	Common Signs and Symptoms**
Smallpox	Virus *(Variola major)*	• Acute rash, fever, fatigue, head and back aches • Rash lesions start red and flat, but fill with pus after first week
Anthrax	Bacteria *(Bacillus anthracis)*	• **Inhalation anthrax:** Acute respiratory distress with fever. Initial symptoms may resemble a common cold. • **Intestinal anthrax:** Nausea, loss of appetite, vomiting, and fever followed by abdominal pain, vomiting of blood, and sever diarrhea. • **Cutaneous anthrax:** Skin infection begins as a raised itchy bump that resembles an insect bite but within 1 to 2 days develops into a vesicle and then a painless ulcer, usually 0.4 to 1 inch (10 mm to 30 mm) in diameter, with a characteristic black necrotic (dying) area in the center.
Plague	Bacteria *(Yersinia pestis)*	Acute respiratory distress, fever, weakness and headache
Botulism	Toxin from the bacteria *Clostridium botulinum*	**Neurological syndromes:** Double vision, blurred vision, drooping eyelids, slurred speech, difficulty swallowing, dry mouth, and muscle weakness
Tularemia	Bacteria *(Francisella tularensis)*	**Influenzalike illness:** Sudden fever, chills, headaches, muscle aches, joint pain, dry cough, progressive weakness, and sometimes pneumonia
Hemorrhagic Fever	Virus (for example, Ebola, Marburg, and Lassa)	• Specific signs and symptoms vary by the type of viral hemorrhagic fever (VHF), but initial signs and symptoms often include marked fever, fatigue, dizziness, muscle aches, loss of strength, and exhaustion. • Patients with severe cases of VHF often show signs of bleeding under the skin, in internal organs, or from body orifices such as the mouth, eyes, or ears. • Rash and red eyes may be seen in some patients infected with the Ebola virus.

* The highest-priority biological agents according to the Centers for Disease Control and Prevention (CDC).

** List of symptoms is *not* all-inclusive.

Table 9.2
Category B * Biological Agents

Name	Biological Agent	Common Signs and Symptoms**
Brucellosis	Bacteria *(Brucella melitensis, abortus, suis, and canis)*	Intermittent or irregular fever of variable duration, headache, weakness, profuse sweating, chills, weight loss, and generalized aching
Epsilon Toxin of *Clostridium Perfringens*	Toxin from the bacteria *Clostridium Perfringens* (a common cause of foodborne illness)	Intense abdominal pain (cramping and bloating) and diarrhea
Glanders	Bacteria *(Burkholderia mallei)*	• Symptoms depend upon the route of infection with the organism. • Types of infection include localized, pus-forming cutaneous infections, pulmonary infections, bloodstream infections, and chronic suppurative infections of the skin. • Generalized symptoms include fever, muscle aches, chest pain, muscle tightness, and headache. • Additional symptoms include excessive tearing of the eyes, light sensitivity, and diarrheal.
Melioidosis	Bacteria *(Burkholderia pseudomallei)*	• ***Acute, localized infection:*** Generally localized as a nodule resulting from inoculation through a break in the skin — Can produce fever and general muscle aches — May progress rapidly to infect the bloodstream • ***Pulmonary infection:*** Can produce a clinical picture of mild bronchitis to severe pneumonia — Onset is typically accompanied by high fever, headache, anorexia, and general muscle soreness. — Chest pain is common, but with a nonproductive or productive cough with normal sputum. • ***Acute bloodstream infection:*** Symptoms vary depending on the site of original infection, but generally include respiratory distress, severe headache, fever, diarrhea, development of pus-filled lesions on the skin, muscle tenderness, and disorientation.

Continued

Table 9.2 (continued)
Category B * Biological Agents

Name	Biological Agent	Common Signs and Symptoms**
Melioidosis *(continued)*		• ***Chronic suppurative infection:*** Infection that involves the organs of the body, typically including the joints, viscera, lymph nodes, skin, brain, liver, lung, bones, and spleen.
Psittacosis	Bacteria *(Chlamydia Psittaci)*	• Fever • Chills • Headache • Muscle aches • Dry cough
Q Fever	Bacteria (Rickettsia) *(Coxiella Burnetii)*	Only about one-half of those infected show signs of clinical illness; most acute cases begin with sudden onset of one or more of the following: • High fevers (up to 104–105°F) [40–40.5°C]; usually lasts for 1 to 2 weeks • Severe headache • General malaise • Myalgia • Confusion • Sore throat • Chills, sweats • Nonproductive cough • Nausea, vomiting • Diarrhea • Abdominal pain and chest pain • Weight loss can occur and persist for some time Thirty to fifty percent of patients with a symptomatic infection will develop pneumonia. Additionally, a majority of patients have abnormal results on liver function tests and some develop hepatitis.
Ricin Toxin	From *Ricinus Communis* (castor beans)	• ***Inhalation:*** Acute onset of fever, chest pain, and cough, progressing to severe respiratory distress • ***Ingestion:*** Nausea, vomiting, abdominal pain and cramping, diarrhea, gastrointestinal bleeding, low or no urinary output, dilation of the pupils, fever, thirst, sore throat, headache, vascular collapse, and shock

Continued

Table 9.2 (continued)
Category B * Biological Agents

Name	Biological Agent	Common Signs and Symptoms**
Staphylococcal Enterotoxin B (SEB)	Toxin from the bacteria *Staphylococcus Aureus* (common cause of foodborne illness)	• High fever (103–106°F) [39–41°C] and chills • Headache • Myalgia • Nonproductive cough
Typhus Fever	Bacteria (Rickettsia) *(Rickettsia Prowazekii)*	In general presents with features similar to a bad cold with fever, chills, headache, and muscle pains as well as body rash
Viral Encephalitis	Alphaviruses such as: • Venezuelan equine encephalitis (VEE) • Eastern equine encephalitis (EEE) • Western equine encephalitis (WEE)	• Fever, chills • Severe headache • Rigors • Photophobia • Muscle pain (especially in the legs and lower back) • Cough, sore throat • Vomiting
Food-Safety Threats	Bacteria such as: • *Salmonella* • *Escherichia Coli* 0157:H7 (sometimes called *E.* coli) • *Shigella*	• ***Salmonellosis:*** Diarrhea, fever, and abdominal cramps • ***E. coli:*** Often causes severe bloody diarrhea and abdominal cramps; sometimes causes nonbloody diarrhea or no symptoms • ***Shigellosis:*** Diarrhea (often bloody), fever, and stomach cramps
Water-Safety Threats	• ***Bacteria:*** *Vibrio Cholerae* (causes Asiatic or epidemic cholera) • ***Protozoa (single-celled organism):*** Cryptosporidium Parvum	• ***Cholera:*** Severe disease is characterized by profuse watery diarrhea, vomiting, and leg cramps; rapid loss of body fluids leads to dehydration and shock. • ***Cryptosporidiosis:*** If symptoms are present: — Intestinal cryptosporidiosis is characterized by severe watery diarrhea. — Pulmonary and tracheal cryptosporidiosis is associated with coughing and frequently a low-grade fever, often accompanied by severe intestinal distress.

* Less critical biological agents than Category A according to the Centers for Disease Control and Prevention (CDC).

** List of symptoms is *not* all-inclusive.

- Availability
- Ease of production and dissemination
- Potential for high morbidity and mortality and major health effect

Category C Agents are as follows:

- Nipah virus
- Hantaviruses
- Tickborne hemorrhagic fever viruses
- Tickborne encephalitis viruses
- Yellow fever virus
- Multidrug-resistant tuberculosis (*Mycobacterium tuberculosis*)

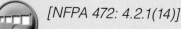

What's the Difference Between Chemical and Biological Incidents?

[NFPA 472: 4.2.1(14)]

According to NFPA 472, *Standard for Professional Competence of Responders to Hazardous Materials Incidents*, a *chemical incident* is characterized by a rapid onset of medical symptoms (minutes to hours) and can have observed features such as colored residue, dead foliage, pungent odor, and dead insect and animal life.

With *biological incidents*, the onset of symptoms usually requires days to weeks. Typically there are no characteristic features because biological agents are usually odorless and colorless. The area affected can be larger in biological incidents because of the movement of infected individuals between the time of infection and onset of symptoms. During that time, an infected person could transmit the disease to another person.

Nuclear/Radiological Attack

While it is still unlikely that most emergency first responders will ever face a terrorist incident involving nuclear or radiological materials, the threat is growing. Some terrorism experts believe it is only a matter of time before the U.S. is faced with its first nuclear/radiological attack. For that reason, first responders must be prepared for such a possibility.

Experts consider three scenarios to be most likely: First, there is the possibility of terrorists detonating a conventional explosive device incorporating nuclear materials (commonly known as *dirty bomb*). Second, there is the possibility of an attack on a source of nuclear materials such as detonating a truck bomb (large vehicle containing high quantities of explosives) in the vicinity of a nuclear power plant or radiological cargo in transport. Third, there is the possibility of terrorists actually detonating (or threatening to detonate) a nuclear bomb, improvised nuclear device (IND), or *suitcase bomb*. The latter scenario is probably the least likely because most terrorists do not have the means to build or acquire a nuclear bomb. However, there are growing concerns about the illicit availability of nuclear materials on the black market.

The sections that follow discuss the various types of nuclear/radiological bombs that terrorists might use. The information provided has been adapted from the "Weapons of Mass Destruction (WMD) Responder Operations Radiation/Nuclear Course" from the U.S. Department of Justice and other government sources.

Dirty Bomb

A *dirty bomb* or *radiological dispersal device (RDD)* spreads radioactive contamination over the widest possible area by detonating conventional high explosives wrapped with radioactive material. A dirty bomb does not produce a nuclear explosion. It destroys property and kills people in the immediate vicinity like any conventional bomb according to the strength of the initial blast. While a dirty bomb is likely to cause damage and a great deal of panic, it is unlikely to release lethal amounts of radiation.

The most significant effect of a dirty bomb, aside from the damage caused by the conventional explosion, would probably be the significant disruption of the area caused by evacuations (with associated economic costs) and potentially extreme costs associated with environmental cleanup. Radioactive particles (such as contaminated dust) can be carried long distances on a plume blown by the wind, creating a large area that might need to be isolated for decontamination (decon) of exposed surfaces (including the exteriors of buildings, vehicles, and the like) (**Figure 9.7**).

Phases of a Nuclear Incident

The "Manual of Protective Actions and Protective Action Guides" from the U.S. Environmental Protection Agency (EPA) defines three time phases that are generally accepted as being common to all nuclear incident sequences. First responders may hear these terms in reference to nuclear incidents:

- *Early phase* — Arbitrarily defined as the period beginning at the initiation of a radioactive release and extending to a few days later when deposition of airborne materials has ceased (also referred to as the *identification of the accident*). It also is the period when immediate decisions on protective actions are required. Decisions must be based primarily on predictions of radiological conditions in the environment. The early phase may last from hours to days. For purposes of dose projection (or prediction of doses), the time period is assumed to last 4 days.

- *Intermediate phase* — Arbitrarily defined as the period beginning after the source and releases have been brought under control and environmental measurements are available for use as a basis for decisions on protective actions. The phase extends until protective actions are completed. It may overlap with the early and late phases, and may last from weeks to many months. For purposes of dose projection, this phase is assumed to last 1 year. Relocation and decontamination (decon) are the principle protective actions for protection of the public during this phase.

- *Late phase* — The period beginning when recovery actions begin in order to reduce radiation levels in the environment to permit unrestricted, long-term use of property (also referred to as the *recovery* phase). The late phase ends when all recovery actions have been completed, and it may last from months to years.

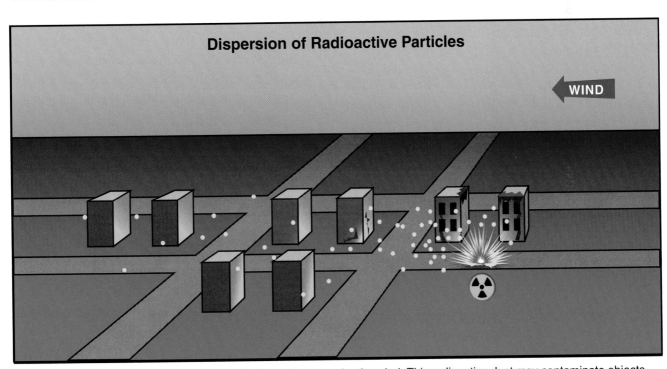

Figure 9.7 Radioactive particles can be carried long distances by the wind. This radioactive dust may contaminate objects far from the initial blast site.

A dirty bomb is the most likely radiological weapon to be used by terrorists because of the availability of materials to make one. Such radioactive materials are widely used at hospitals, research facilities, industrial sites, and construction sites. These radioactive materials are used for such purposes as diagnosing and treating illnesses, sterilizing equipment, and inspecting welding seams **(Figure 9.8, p. 456).** Weapons-grade radioactive material is not required for the design of a dirty bomb.

Atomic/Nuclear Device (Bomb)

The use of a nuclear or atomic device (bomb) by a terrorist would produce devastating effects, including thermal, blast overpressure, and radiation

Figure 9.8 Radioactive materials used in dirty bombs can be gathered from many sources, including instruments like this density gauge. *Courtesy of Tom Clawson, Technical Resources, Inc.*

Figure 9.9 Modern nuclear weapons are many times more destructive than the bombs dropped on Hiroshima and Nagasaki in World War II. *Courtesy of Federal Emergency Management Agency (FEMA) News Photo.*

contamination. It would also have a tremendous psychosocial effect. Most people living in the modern world are familiar with the destructive potential of nuclear bombs, but they may not be aware that the bombs dropped at the end of World War II on the Japanese cities of Hiroshima and Nagasaki were small (10 to 20 kiloton range) in comparison to many of today's nuclear devices **(Figure 9.9)**. The devices most likely to be used by terrorists would be in that range (explosive equivalent of 10,000 to 20,000 metric tons of trinitrotoluene or TNT). See **Appendix J** for a summary of the possible effects on a community from a terrorist attack using a nuclear bomb.

The activation of an atomic bomb or nuclear device would destroy a huge area in comparison to that of a conventional bomb, and it would overwhelm the emergency response effort in any community. Critical community infrastructures such as emergency services, public works services, communication systems, bridges, and roads would be affected.

Improvised Nuclear Device

INDs are designed to result in the formation of a nuclear-yield reaction (nuclear blast). These devices may be fabricated in a completely improvised manner or be a modification to a nuclear weapon. The use of INDs in the terrorist world is a growing concern. The ability to obtain fissile material is becoming a reality with illicit black-market opera-

tions. It is important for first responders to understand the destructive capabilities of such weapons and the effects they could have on society.

The destructive capability of INDs would depend on the explosive yield of the weapon and location of the detonation. While it is possible for the weapon to be substantial in yield, which would be the case with a tactical or strategic nuclear weapon, the likely scenario would be a low-yield *mininuke* of 5 kilotons (explosive equivalent of 5,000 metric tons of TNT) or less that could be easily concealed and transported.

In the case of a low-yield weapon, responders could expect damage similar to conventional high explosives (truck bombs) but on a much larger scale. Also, the spread of radiological fallout might create panic among the injured and the general public as well as providing substantial radiation exposure to first responders and rescue personnel attempting to extricate victims from damaged structures. The radiation released during a blast may injure large numbers of people who may show no symptoms for minutes to hours after the blast.

Suitcase Bomb

Both the U.S. and the former Soviet Union have made small, suitcase- or backpack-sized nuclear weapons. In 1998, Russian Army General Lebed said that one of his assignments was to account for over a hundred suitcase-sized nuclear weapons that the Soviet Union had manufactured during the 1970s and 80s. He also claimed that he had been unable to locate all of them. Unfortunately, it is impossible to tell with absolute certainty how many of these devices were actually made and may be missing. The serious concern, of course, is that one or more will fall into the hands of terrorists.

In the 1960s, the U.S. built a mininuclear device, the Special Atomic Demolition Munition (SADM). The device weighed 80 to 100 pounds (36 kg to 45 kg), was small enough to fit in a duffel bag or large case, and was designed for sabotage missions to destroy airfields, bridges, and dams. The Russian device, built for secret agents for the same sabotage purposes, had an explosive charge of about 1 kiloton (or 1,000 metric tons of TNT). For comparison, the damage caused by such a bomb could be expected to be approximately one-thirteenth of that of the bomb dropped on Hiroshima during World War II. A large section of a city could be devastated by the detonation of a 1-kiloton suitcase bomb.

Nuclear Power Plant Sabotage/Attack

Because of existing safety procedures, checks, and balances used at U.S. commercial nuclear power plants, it is unlikely that any sort of terrorist attack or assault would be successful at creating a nuclear explosion or major release. If an attack did somehow succeed, the role of first responders at such an incident would be established in the local emergency response plan, which applies to any type of incident involving nuclear power plants, terrorist attack, or other emergency. First responders in communities near nuclear power plants should be familiar with these plans and their role in any emergency involving such plants.

Incendiary Attack

An *incendiary device* is any mechanical, electrical, or chemical device used intentionally to initiate combustion and start a fire. Incendiary devices are sometimes categorized together with explosive devices (see Explosive Attack section). Trigger mechanisms usually consist of chemical, electrical, or mechanical elements that may be used singly or in combination. Incendiary materials burn with a hot flame for a designated period of time. The device's purpose is to set fire to other materials or

structures. Incendiary devices may be made and used by terrorists, arsonists, or anyone wanting to make a statement by starting a fire (such as a rioter throwing a Molotov cocktail during a political protest).

Incendiary devices may be simple or elaborate, and they come in all shapes and sizes. The type of device is limited only by a person's imagination and ingenuity. Incendiary devices can be as simple as a match applied to a piece of paper, but they are commonly considered to have three basic components: an igniter or fuse, a container or body, and an incendiary material or filler. The container can be glass, metal, plastic, or paper, depending on its desired use. A device containing solid chemical materials usually will be in a metal or other nonbreakable container. An incendiary device that uses a liquid accelerator usually will be in a breakable container such as glass.

Normally, incendiary devices are designed to produce enough heat and flame to cause combustible materials to burn once they reach their ignition temperature. Examples of easily made incendiary devices are as follows:

- Bottle, gasoline, rag, match (Molotov cocktail)
- Low flashpoint flammable liquid and a candle
- Match heads and sulfuric acid
- Road flare ignited by a model rocket fuse

The following is a list of other materials used to make incendiary devices:

- Flammable and combustible liquids
- Black powder and similar materials **(Figure 9.10, p. 458)**
- Flash powder
- Phosphorus (white phosphorus)
- Magnesium
- Thermite (powdered iron oxide and powdered aluminum)
- Chlorine tablets and granules
- Flammable gases (such as propane or butane)
- Oxidizers (in conjunction with other flammables)
- Pyrophoric materials
- Napalm

Figure 9.10 Black powder can be used in incendiary devices. *Courtesy of the U.S. Bureau of Alcohol, Tobacco, Firearms and Explosives and the Oklahoma Highway Patrol Bomb Squad.*

If an incendiary attack is suspected, first responders should be wary of secondary devices and always try to preserve evidence as appropriate to a crime scene (see Preserving Evidence section). First responders should be aware of the potential indicators of incendiary devices such as the following:

- Warning or threat of an attack

- Accelerant odors (gasoline smells and other similar odors)

- Multiple fires

- Incendiary device components (such as broken glass from a Molotov cocktail)

- Unexpectedly heavy burning or high temperatures

- Unusually fast burning fires

- Unusually colored smoke or flames

- Presence of propane or other flammable gas cylinders in unusual locations

Chemical Attack

[NFPA 472: 4.2.1(15), 5.2.3(9)]

A *chemical attack* is the deliberate release of a toxic gas, liquid, or solid that can poison people and the environment. Chemical warfare agents or toxic industrial materials (TIMs) may be used in a chemical attack. *Chemical warfare agents* are chemical substances that are intended for use in warfare or terrorist activities to kill, seriously injure, or seriously incapacitate people through their physiological effects. *TIMs* are particularly poisonous hazardous materials that are normally used for industrial purposes, but could be used by terrorists to deliberately kill, injure, or incapacitate people (see Toxic Industrial Materials section).

Unlike biological attacks, chemical attacks have effects that are usually noticed quickly, within minutes to hours. Chemical warfare agents attack the organs of the human body, preventing the organs from functioning normally. The results are usually disabling or fatal. TIMs used for terrorist purposes are chosen for maximum toxicity, dispersion, and hazard. Usually, the health effects of a chemical attack are acute. These materials may also kill animals, birds, insects, and, in some cases, plants and foliage. Chemical attacks may be characterized by rapid onset of medical symptoms and can have observed features such as colored residue, dead foliage, pungent odor, and dead insect and animal life. The following are some indicators of possible criminal or terrorist activity involving chemical agents:

- Presence of hazardous materials or laboratory equipment that is not relevant to the occupancy **(Figure 9.11)**

- Intentional release of hazardous materials

- Unexplained patterns of sudden onset of similar, nontraumatic illnesses or deaths (the pattern could be geographic, by employer, or associated with agent dissemination methods)

- Unexplained odors or tastes that are out of character with the surroundings

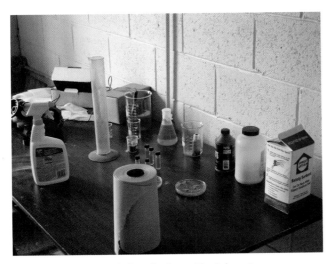

Figure 9.11 Unusual chemicals and/or laboratory equipment may be an indicator of possible criminal or terrorist activity involving chemical agents.

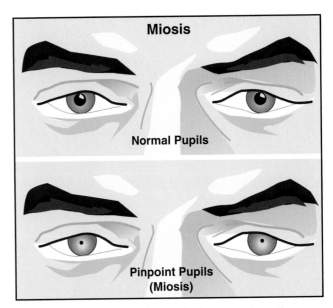

Figure 9.12 Miosis (pinpoint pupils) is a symptom of exposure to nerve agents.

- Multiple individuals exhibiting unexplained signs of skin, eye, or airway irritation

- Unexplained bomb or munitionlike material, especially if it contains a liquid

- Unexplained vapor clouds, mists, and plumes

- Multiple individuals exhibiting unexplained health problems such as nausea, vomiting, twitching, tightness in chest, sweating, pinpoint pupils (miosis), runny nose (rhinorrhea), disorientation, difficulty breathing, or convulsions. Some people teach remembering the problems with the acronym *SLUDGEM* as follows:

  — **S**alivation (drooling)

  — **L**acrimation (tearing)

  — **U**rination

  — **D**efecation

  — **G**astrointestinal upset/ aggravation (cramping)

  — **E**mesis (vomiting)

  — **M**iosis (pinpointed pupils) or **M**uscular twitching/ spasms **(Figure 9.12)**

- Unexplained deaths

- Trees, shrubs, bushes, food crops, and/or lawns that are dead (not just a patch of dead weeds), discolored, abnormal in appearance, or withered (not under drought conditions) **(Figure 9.13)**

- Surfaces exhibiting oily droplets or films and unexplained oily film on water surfaces

- Abnormal number of sick or dead birds, animals, and/or fish

- Unusual security, locks, bars on windows, covered windows, and barbed wire enclosures **(Figure 9.14, p. 460)**

Figure 9.13 Dead foliage can be caused by accidental or deliberate release of chemicals.

Figure 9.14 Unusual security measures such as barred windows can be a clue to criminal or terrorist activity.

As with most hazardous materials, there are different names and ways of categorizing chemical agents. Much of the information in this and the sections that follow was adapted from material provided by the U.S. Department of Justice, CDC, and other U.S. government resources. The following chemical-agent types are discussed:

- Nerve agents
- Blister agents (vesicants)
- Blood agents (cyanide agents)
- Choking agents (pulmonary or lung-damaging agents)
- Riot control agents (irritants)
- Toxic industrial materials (normal hazardous materials used for terrorist purposes)

Chemical Agents: Volatility and Persistence

Volatility refers to a substance's ability to become a vapor at a relatively low temperature. Essentially, volatile chemical agents have low boiling points at ordinary pressures and/or high vapor pressures at ordinary temperatures. The volatility of a chemical agent often determines how it is used.

Persistence refers to the length of time a chemical agent *stays around* and is effective. A persistent agent is one that usually remains effective in the open (at the point of dispersion) for a considerable period of time. Nonpersistent agents generally vaporize and disperse much more quickly. Persistency is directly related to the agent's vapor pressure.

A highly volatile (nonpersistent) substance poses a greater respiratory hazard than a less volatile (persistent) substance, but persistent substances generally continue to be a threat for a longer period of time. Terrain, wind speed, and temperature can have significant effects on an agent's persistency. Also, thickening agents can be added to nonpersistent agents to make them more persistent.

Nerve Agents

[NFPA 472: 5.2.3(9)(a)]

Nerve agents attack the nervous system by affecting the transmission of impulses and are the most toxic of the known chemical warfare agents. They are chemically similar to organophosphate pesticides. Nerve agents are stable, easily dispersed, highly toxic, and have rapid effects when absorbed both through the skin and respiratory system. Nerve agents can be manufactured by means of fairly simple chemical techniques. The raw materials are inexpensive but some may be difficult to acquire because of regulations restricting their sale and use. First responders should be familiar with the following nerve agents (military designations are provided in parentheses):

- *Tabun (GA)* — Usually low-volatility persistent chemical agent that is absorbed through skin contact or inhaled as a gas or aerosol
- *Sarin (GB)* — Usually volatile, nonpersistent chemical agent mainly inhaled

- *Soman (GD)* — Usually moderately volatile chemical agent that can be inhaled or absorbed through skin contact

- *Cyclohexyl sarin (GF)* — Low-volatility persistent chemical agent that is absorbed through skin contact and inhaled as a gas or aerosol

- *V-agent (VX)* — Low-volatility persistent chemical agent that can remain on material, equipment, and terrain for long periods; main route of entry is through the skin but also through inhalation of the substance as a gas or aerosol. First responders may also see reference to other *V*-agents including VE, VG, and VS, but the most common is VX.

Nerve agents in their pure states are colorless liquids. Their volatility varies widely. However, the *G*-agents tend to be nonpersistent (unless thickened with some other agent to increase their persistency), whereas the *V*-agents are persistent. For example, the consistency of VX is similar to motor oil. Its primary route of entry is through direct contact with the skin. GB is at the opposite extreme: an easily volatile liquid that is primarily an inhalation hazard. The volatilities of GD, GA, and GF are between those of GB and VX. **Table 9.3, p. 462,** gives the DOT Hazard Class, *ERG* guide number, and characteristics of common nerve agents. The paragraphs that follow discuss routes of entry and symptoms of exposure.

Routes of Entry. Nerve agents, either as a gas, aerosol, or liquid, enter the body through inhalation or through the skin. Poisoning may also occur through consumption of liquids or foods contaminated with nerve agents. The route of entry influences the symptoms developed and, to some extent, the sequence of the different symptoms. Generally, the poisoning works most rapidly when the agent is absorbed through the respiratory system rather than other routes because the lungs contain numerous blood vessels and the inhaled nerve agent can quickly diffuse into the blood circulation and thus reach target organs. Among these organs, the respiratory system is one of the most important. If a person is exposed to a high concentration of nerve agent, death may occur within a few minutes.

Poisoning works more slowly when the agent is absorbed through the skin. Since nerve agents are somewhat fat-soluble, they can easily penetrate the outer layers of the skin, but it takes longer for the poison to reach the deeper blood vessels. Consequently, the first symptoms do not occur until 20 to 30 minutes after the initial exposure, but subsequently the poisoning process may be rapid if the total dose of nerve agent is high.

Symptoms. When exposed to a low dose of nerve agent that is sufficient to cause minor poisoning, a victim experiences characteristic symptoms such as increased production of saliva, a runny nose, and a feeling of pressure on the chest. The pupil of the eye becomes contracted (miosis), which impairs night vision. In addition, the capacity of the eye to change focal length is reduced, and short-range vision deteriorates, causing the victim to feel pain when trying to focus on nearby objects. In fact, if the cause of an incident is unknown but it involves a large number of people with similar signs and symptoms (particularly pinpoint pupils and headaches), nerve agents may be suspected. Less specific symptoms are tiredness, slurred speech, hallucinations, and nausea.

Exposure to a somewhat higher dose leads to more dramatic developments, and symptoms are more pronounced. Changes to the respiratory system lead to difficulty in breathing and coughing. Discomfort in the gastrointestinal tract may develop into cramping and vomiting, and there may be involuntary discharge of urine and feces. There may also be excessive salivating, tearing, and sweating. If the poisoning is moderate, typical symptoms affecting the skeletal muscles may be muscular weakness, local tremors, or convulsions.

When exposed to a high dose of nerve agent, the muscular symptoms are more pronounced, and the victim may suffer convulsions and lose consciousness. The poisoning process may be so rapid that symptoms mentioned earlier may never have time to develop. Nerve agents affect the respiratory muscles causing muscular paralysis and also the respiratory center of the central nervous system. The combination of these two effects is the direct cause of death. Consequently, death caused by nerve agents is similar to death by suffocation.

Table 9.3
Nerve Agents: Characteristics

Nerve Agent (Symbol)	UN/DOT Hazard Class and *ERG* Guide	Descriptions	Symptoms (All Listed Agents)
Tabun (GA)	Hazard Class 6.1 *ERG* Guide No. 153	• Clear, colorless, and tasteless liquid • May have a slight fruit odor, but this feature cannot be relied upon to provide sufficient warning against toxic exposure • ***Probable Dispersion Method:*** Aerosolized liquid	***Low or moderate dose by inhalation, ingestion (swallowing), or skin absorption:*** Persons may experience some or all of the following symptoms within seconds to hours of exposure: • Runny nose • Watery eyes • Small, pinpoint pupils
Sarin (GB)	Hazard Class 6.1 *ERG* Guide No. 153	• Clear, colorless, tasteless, and odorless liquid in pure form • ***Probable Dispersion Method:*** Aerosolized liquid	• Eye pain • Blurred vision • Drooling and excessive sweating • Cough • Chest tightness
Soman (GD)	Hazard Class 6.1 *ERG* Guide No. 153	• Pure liquid is clear, colorless, and tasteless; discolors with aging to dark brown • May have a slight fruity or camphor odor, but this feature cannot be relied upon to provide sufficient warning against toxic exposure • ***Probable Dispersion Method:*** Aerosolized liquid	• Rapid breathing • Diarrhea • Increased urination • Confusion • Drowsiness • Weakness • Headache • Nausea, vomiting, and/or abdominal pain • Slow or fast heart rate • Abnormally low or high blood pressure
Cyclohexyl sarin (GF)	*ERG* Guide No. 153	• Clear, colorless, tasteless, and odorless liquid in pure form • Only slightly soluble in water • ***Probable Dispersion Method:*** Aerosolized liquid	***Skin contact:*** Even a tiny drop of nerve agent on the skin can cause sweating and muscle twitching where the agent touched the skin ***Large dose by any route:*** These additional health effects may result:

Continued

Table 9.3 (continued)
Nerve Agents: Characteristics

Nerve Agent (Symbol)	UN/DOT Hazard Class and *ERG* Guide	Descriptions	Symptoms (All Listed Agents)
V-Agent (VX)	Hazard Class 6.1 *ERG* Guide No. 153	• Clear, amber-colored odorless, oily liquid • Miscible with water and dissolves in all solvents • Least volatile nerve agent • Very slow to evaporate (about as slowly as motor oil) • Primarily a liquid exposure hazard, but if heated to very high temperatures, it can turn into small amounts of vapor (gas) • ***Probable Dispersion Method:*** Aerosolized liquid	• Loss of consciousness • Convulsions • Paralysis • Respiratory failure possibly leading to death ***Recovery Expectations:*** • Mild or moderately exposed people usually recover completely • Severely exposed people are not likely to survive • Unlike some organophosphate pesticides, nerve agents have *not* been associated with neurological problems lasting more than 1 to 2 weeks after the exposure

Source: Information on symptoms provided by the Centers for Disease Control and Prevention (CDC).

Blister Agents

[NFPA 472: 5.2.3 (9)(b)]

Blister agents (vesicants) burn and blister the skin or any other part of the body they contact. They act on the eyes, mucous membranes, lungs, skin and blood-forming organs **(Figure 9.15).** These agents damage the respiratory tract when inhaled and can cause vomiting and diarrhea when ingested. Blister agents are usually persistent and may be employed in the form of colorless gases and liquids. Blister agents are likely to produce casualties rather than fatalities, although exposure to such agents can be fatal. Blister agents can be categorized into the following groups:

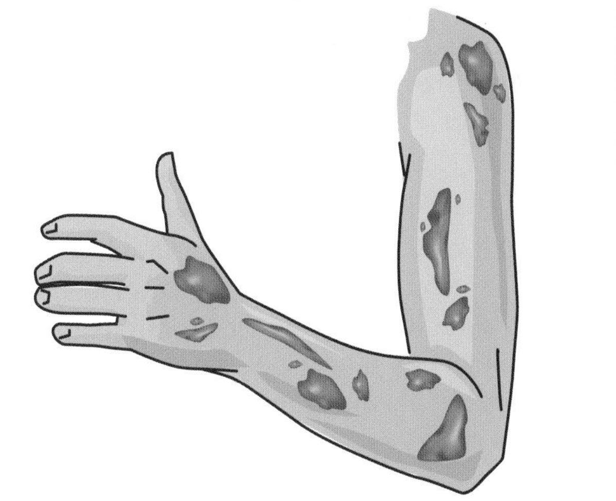

● *Mustard agents*
— Sulfur mustards (H, HD [also called *distilled mustard*], and HT)
— Nitrogen mustards (HN, HN-1, HN-2, and HN-3)

● *Arsenical vesicants*
— Lewisite (L, L-1, L-2, and L-3)

Figure 9.15 Blister agents cause blisters to form on the skin.

— Mustard/lewisite mixture (HL) (a mixture of lewisite [L] and distilled mustard [HD])
— Phenyldichloroarsine (PD)

● *Halogenated oximes* — Phosgene oxime (CX)

Mustard agents. At room temperature, mustard agents are liquid with low volatility. They are very stable during storage. Mustard agents can easily be dissolved in most organic solvents but have negligible solubility in water. Oxidants such as chloramines, however, react violently with mustard agents and form nonpoisonous oxidation products. Consequently, these substances are sometimes used for decon of mustard agents rather than water. The following agents are in the mustard group:

- *Sulfur mustards* — Sometimes smell like garlic, onions, or mustard; sometimes they have no odor. They can be a vapor (gaseous form of a liquid), an oily-textured liquid, or a solid. Sulfur mustards can be clear to yellow or brown colored when they are in liquid or solid form.

- *Nitrogen mustards* — Come in different forms that can smell fishy, musty, soapy, or fruity. They can be in the form of an oily-textured liquid, a vapor, or a solid. Nitrogen mustards are liquids at normal room temperature (70°F or 21°C). Nitrogen mustards can be clear, pale amber, or yellow colored when in liquid or solid form.

Arsenical vesicants. Arsenical vesicants are not as common or as stable as the sulfur or nitrogen mustards. They are colorless to brown-colored liquids. They are more volatile than mustards and have fruity to geranium-like odors. These types of vesicants are much more dangerous as liquids than as vapors. Absorption of either vapor or liquid through the skin in adequate dosage may lead to systemic intoxication or death.

Halogenated oximes. Phosgene oxime is a manufactured chemical that was developed as a potential chemical warfare agent, but its use on the battlefield has never been documented. It has a disagreeable penetrating odor. Pure phosgene oxime is a colorless, crystalline solid; the munitions grade compound is a yellowish-brown-colored liquid. Both the liquid and the solid can emit vapors at ambient temperatures.

Routes of entry and symptoms. Most blister agents are relatively persistent and are readily absorbed by all parts of the body. Poisoning may also occur through the consumption of liquids or foods contaminated with blister agents. These agents cause inflammation, blisters, and general destruction of tissues. In the form of gas or liquid, mustard agents attack the skin, eyes, lungs, and gastrointestinal tract. Internal organs, mainly blood-generating organs (such as bone marrow and spleen), may also be injured as a result of mustard agents being absorbed through the skin or lungs and transported into the body. If blisters are present on the skin, they are usually present internally as well. It may take several hours before blisters form. **Table 9.4** provides a summary of the DOT Hazard Class, ERG guide number, and characteristics of various blister agents.

Blood Agents
[NFPA 472: 5.2.3(9)(c)]

Blood agents (cyanide agents) are chemical asphyxiants because they interfere with oxygen utilization at the cellular level (see Chapter 2, Hazardous Materials Properties and Hazards, Asphyxiation section). The terms *blood agents* are sometimes used synonymously with *cyanogen agents,* but not all blood agents are cyanogens (for example, arsine is not). Neither are all cyanogens necessarily blood agents. Blood agents are sometimes categorized as TIMs because they also have industrial applications. **Table 9.5, p. 468,** provides the DOT Hazard Class, *ERG* guide number, and characteristics for types of blood agents. First responders should be familiar with the following blood agents:

- *Arsine (SA)* — Arsine gas is formed when arsenic comes in contact with an acid. It is a colorless, nonirritating toxic gas that has a mild garlic odor that can only be detected at levels higher than those necessary to cause poisoning. *Details:*

  — Arsine gas also has chronic health effects associated with exposure, namely kidney damage and neuropsychological problems such as memory loss and irritability.

  — Arsine gas is considered a nonpersistent hazard.

- *Hydrogen cyanide (AC)* — Hydrogen cyanide is a colorless, highly volatile liquid that is extremely flammable, highly soluble, and stable in water; gas/air mixtures may be explosive. The vapor is less dense than air and has a faint odor,

Table 9.4
Common Blister Agents: Characteristics

Blister Agent (Symbol)	UN/DOT Hazard Class and *ERG* Guide	Descriptions	Symptoms
Sulfur Mustard (H/HD)	Hazard Class 6.1 *ERG* Guide No. 153	• Can be clear to yellow or brown when in liquid or solid form • Sometimes smells like garlic, onions, or mustard; sometimes has no odor • Can be a vapor, an oily-textured liquid, or a solid • Vapors are heavier than air • *Probable Dispersion Method:* Aerosolized liquid	Symptoms include: • *Skin:* Redness and itching of the skin may occur 2 to 48 hours after exposure and change eventually to yellow blistering of the skin. • *Eyes:* Irritation, pain, swelling, and tearing may occur within 3 to 12 hours of a mild to moderate exposure. A severe exposure may cause symptoms within 1 to 2 hours and may include the symptoms of a mild or moderate exposure plus light sensitivity, severe pain, or blindness (lasting up to 10 days). • *Respiratory tract:* Runny nose, sneezing, hoarseness, bloody nose, sinus pain, shortness of breath, and cough within 12 to 24 hours of a mild exposure and within 2 to 4 hours of a severe exposure • *Digestive tract:* Abdominal pain, diarrhea, fever, nausea, and vomiting Other factors include: • Typically, signs and symptoms do not occur immediately. • Depending on the severity of the exposure, symptoms may not occur for 2 to 24 hours. • Some people are more sensitive than others. • Exposure is usually not fatal.

Continued

Table 9.4 (continued)
Common Blister Agents: Characteristics

Blister Agent (Symbol)	UN/DOT Hazard Class and *ERG* Guide	Descriptions	Symptoms
Nitrogen Mustard (HN)	Hazard Class 6.1 *ERG* Guide No. 153	• Comes in different forms that can smell fishy, musty, soapy, or fruity • Can be in the form of an oily-textured liquid, a vapor, or a solid • Is liquid at normal room temperature (70°F or 21°C) • Can be clear, pale amber, or yellow colored when in liquid or solid form • Vapors are heavier than air • ***Probable Dispersion Method:*** Aerosolized liquid	Symptoms include: • ***Skin:*** Redness usually develops within a few hours after exposure followed by blistering within 6 to 12 hours. • ***Eyes:*** Irritation, pain, swelling, and tearing may occur. High concentrations can cause burns and blindness. • ***Respiratory tract:*** Nose and sinus pain, cough, sore throat, and shortness of breath may occur within hours. Fluid in the lungs is uncommon. • ***Digestive tract:*** Abdominal pain, diarrhea, nausea, and vomiting • ***Brain:*** Tremors, incoordination, and seizures are possible following a large exposure. Other factors include: • Typically, signs and symptoms do not occur immediately. • Depending on the severity of the exposure, symptoms may not occur for several hours.
Lewisite (L)	Hazard Class 6.1 *ERG* Guide No. 153	• Colorless liquid in its pure form; can appear amber to black in its impure form • Has an odor like geraniums • Vapors are heavier than air • ***Probable Dispersion Method:*** Aerosolized liquid	Signs and symptoms occurring immediately following exposure include: • ***Skin:*** Pain and irritation within seconds to minutes; redness within 15 to 30 minutes followed by blister formation within several hours: — Blister begins small in the middle of red areas and then expands to cover the entire reddened area of skin. — Lesions (sores) heal much faster than lesions caused by other blistering agents (sulfur mustard and nitrogen mustards).

Continued

Table 9.4 (continued)
Common Blister Agents: Characteristics

Blister Agent (Symbol)	UN/DOT Hazard Class and *ERG* Guide	Descriptions	Symptoms
Lewisite (L) *(continued)*			— Discoloring of the skin that occurs later is much less noticeable • *Eyes*: Irritation, pain, swelling, and tearing may occur on contact • *Respiratory tract:* Runny nose, sneezing, hoarseness, bloody nose, sinus pain, shortness of breath, and cough • *Digestive tract:* Diarrhea, nausea, and vomiting • *Cardiovascular:* Lewisite shock or low blood pressure
Phosgene Oxime (CX)	*ERG* Guide No. 153	• Colorless in its solid form and yellowish-brown when liquid • Has a disagreeable, irritating odor • Vapors are heavier than air • *Probable Dispersion Method:* Aerosolized liquid	Signs and symptoms occur immediately following exposure: • *Skin:* Pain occurring within a few seconds, and blanching (whitening) of the skin surrounded by red rings occurring on the exposed areas within 30 seconds: — Within about 15 minutes, the skin develops hives — After 24 hours, the whitened areas of skin become brown and die, and a scab is then formed — Itching and pain may continue throughout the healing process • *Eyes:* Severe pain and irritation, tearing, and possibly temporary blindness • *Respiratory tract:* Immediate irritation to the upper respiratory tract, causing runny nose, hoarseness, and sinus pain • Absorption through the skin or inhalation may result in fluid in the lungs (pulmonary edema) with shortness of breath and cough

Source: Information on symptoms provided by the Centers for Disease Control and Prevention (CDC).

Table 9.5
Blood Agents: Characteristics

Blood Agent (Symbol)	UN/DOT Hazard Class and *ERG* Guide	Descriptions	Symptoms
Arsine (SA)	Hazard Class 2.3 *ERG* Guide No. 119	• Colorless, nonirritating toxic gas with a mild garlic odor that is detected only at levels higher than those necessary to cause poisoning • Is formed when arsenic comes in contact with an acid • ***Probable Dispersion Method:*** Vapor release	***Low or moderate dose by inhalation:*** Persons may experience some or all of the following symptoms within 2 to 24 hours of exposure: • Weakness • Fatigue • Headache • Drowsiness • Confusion • Shortness of breath • Rapid breathing • Nausea, vomiting, and/or abdominal pain • Red or dark urine • Yellow skin and eyes (jaundice) • Muscle cramps ***Large dose by any route:*** These additional health effects may result: • Loss of consciousness • Convulsions • Paralysis • Respiratory failure, possibly leading to death Other factors: • Showing these signs and symptoms does not necessarily mean that a person has been exposed • If people survive the initial exposure, chronic effects may include: — Kidney damage — Numbness and pain in the extremities — Neuropsychological symptoms such as memory loss, confusion, and irritability

Continued

Table 9.5 (continued)
Blood Agents: Characteristics

Blood Agent (Symbol)	UN/DOT Hazard Class and *ERG* Guide	Descriptions	Symptoms
Hydrogen cyanide (AC)	Hazard Class 6.1 *ERG* Guide No. 117	• Colorless gas or liquid • Characteristic bitter almond odor • Slightly lighter than air • Miscible • **Extremely flammable** • Explosive gas/air mixtures • Reacts violently with oxidants and hydrogen chloride in alcoholic mixtures, causing fire and explosion hazard • **Probable Dispersion Method:** Aerosolized liquid	May be absorbed through skin and eyes. Symptoms include: • ***Inhalation:*** Headache, dizziness, confusion, nausea, shortness of breath, convulsions, vomiting, weakness, anxiety, irregular heart beat, tightness in the chest, and unconsciousness. Effects may be delayed. • ***Skin:*** May be absorbed. See *Inhalation* for other symptoms. • ***Eyes:*** Redness; vapor is absorbed. See *Inhalation* for other symptoms. • ***Ingestion:*** Burning sensation. See *Inhalation* for other symptoms.
Cyanogen chloride (CK)	Hazard Class 2.3 *ERG* Guide No. 125	• Colorless gas • Pungent odor • Heavier than air • ***Probable Dispersion Method:*** Vapor release	Symptoms include: • ***Inhalation:*** Runny nose, sore throat, drowsiness, confusion, nausea, vomiting, cough, unconsciousness, edema with symptoms which may be delayed • ***Skin:*** Readily absorbed through intact skin, causing systemic effects without irritant effects on the skin; frostbite may occur on contact with liquid; liquid may be absorbed; redness and pain • ***Eyes:*** Frostbite on contact with liquid; redness, pain, and excess tears

Source: Information on symptoms provided by the Centers for Disease Control and Prevention (CDC).

somewhat like bitter almonds; although about 25 percent of the population is unable to smell it. *Details:*

— Because of its physical properties, the agent will not remain long in its liquid state, so decon may simply consist of allowing the material to evaporate.

— The agent represents a nonpersistent hazard.

- *Cyanogen chloride (CK)* — Cyanogen chloride is a colorless, highly volatile liquid that dissolves readily in organic solvents but is only slightly soluble in water. Its vapors are heavier than air. Cyanogen chloride has a pungent, biting odor. Normally, it is a nonpersistent hazard. The effects of exposure to cyanogen chloride are similar to hydrogen cyanide but with additional irritation to the eyes and mucous membranes.

Choking Agents

[NFPA 472: 5.2.3(9)(d)]

Choking agents are chemicals that attack the lungs causing tissue damage. For this reason they are sometimes called *pulmonary* or *lung-damaging agents*. Like blood agents, these chemicals also have industrial applications, and first responders may encounter them during normal haz mat incidents (as opposed to terrorist attacks). This section discusses phosgene (CG) and chlorine (CL) because of their prior use in wars and easy availability, but other chemicals such as diphosgene (DP), chloropicin (PS), ammonia, hydrogen chloride, phosphine, and elemental phosphorus may also be classified as choking agents. **Table 9.6** provides the DOT Hazard Class, *ERG* guide number, and characteristics of choking agents.

Phosgene. Phosgene is a colorless, nonflammable gas that has the odor of freshly cut hay. Its odor threshold is well above its permissible exposure limit, so it is already at a harmful concentration by the time someone smells it. It is used in the manufacture of dyestuffs, pesticides, plastics, pharmaceuticals, and other chemicals products. Phosgene was used as a chemical weapon for the first time in World War I, and it accounted for the majority of all chemical fatalities in that war.

Phosgene is a gas at room temperature but is sometimes stored as a liquid under pressure or refrigeration. Its boiling point is 47°F (8.2°C), making it an extremely volatile and nonpersistent agent. Its vapor density is much heavier than air; therefore, it may remain for long periods of time in trenches and other low-lying areas. Because of the agent's physical and chemical properties, it will not remain in its liquid form very long. Thus decon is usually not required except when the agent is used in very cold climates or when it has soaked clothing or skin.

Chlorine. Chlorine is one of the most commonly manufactured chemicals in the U.S. Chlorine was also used as a choking agent during World War I, but most people are more familiar with it because of its industrial uses **(Figure 9.16)**. Its most important use is as bleach in the manufacture of paper and cloth, but it is also used to make pesticides, rubber, and solvents. It is used in drinking water and swimming-pool water to kill harmful bacteria and as part of the sanitation process for industrial waste and sewage.

Chlorine gas is usually pressurized and cooled to a liquid state for storage and transportation. When liquid chlorine is released, it quickly turns into a gas that is heavier than air. Chlorine gas can be recognized by its pungent, irritating odor, which is like the odor of bleach. Chlorine gas is usually yellow-green in color. Chlorine itself is not flammable, but it can react explosively or form explosive compounds with other chemicals such as

Figure 9.16 Chlorine is a common choking agent.

Table 9.6
Choking Agents: Characteristics

Choking Agent (Symbol)	UN/DOT Hazard Class and *ERG* Guide	Descriptions	Symptoms
Phosgene (CG)	Hazard Class 2.3 *ERG* Guide No. 125	• Is a poisonous gas at room temperature • May appear colorless or as a white to pale yellow cloud • At low concentrations, has a pleasant odor of newly cut hay or green corn • At high concentrations, odor may be strong and unpleasant • Is nonflammable (not easily ignited and burned) but can cause flammable substances around it to burn • Gas is heavier than air • ***Probable Dispersion Method:*** Vapor release	***Exposure to dangerous-level concentrations:*** During or immediately after exposure, the following signs and symptoms may develop: • Coughing • Burning sensation in the throat and eyes • Watery eyes • Blurred vision • Difficulty breathing or shortness of breath • Nausea and vomiting • Skin contact can result in lesions similar to those from frostbite or burns ***Exposure to high concentrations:*** Person may develop fluid in the lungs (pulmonary edema) within 2 to 6 hours. ***Delayed effects:*** May not be apparent for up to 48 hours, even if a person feels better or appears well following removal from exposure. Monitor people who have been exposed for 48 hours. Delayed effects that can appear up to 48 hours include the following: • Difficulty breathing • Coughing up white to pink-tinged fluid (sign of pulmonary edema) • Low blood pressure • Heart failure Showing these signs or symptoms does not necessarily mean that a person has been exposed. ***Recovery Expectations:*** Most people who recover after an exposure make a complete recovery; however, chronic bronchitis and emphysema have been reported as an exposure result.

Continued

Table 9.6 (continued)
Choking Agents: Characteristics

Choking Agent (Symbol)	UN/DOT Hazard Class and *ERG* Guide	Descriptions	Symptoms
Chlorine (CL)	Hazard Class 2.3 *ERG* Guide No. 124	• Gas can be recognized by its pungent, irritating odor that smells like bleach • Gas is yellow-green in color • Is not flammable but can react explosively or form explosive compounds with other chemicals such as turpentine and ammonia • ***Probable Dispersion Method:*** Vapor release	***Dangerous-level concentrations:*** During or immediately after exposure, the following signs and symptoms may develop: • Coughing • Chest tightness • Burning sensation in the nose, throat, and eyes • Watery eyes • Blurred vision • Nausea and vomiting • Burning pain, redness, and blisters on the skin if exposed to gas • Skin injury similar to frostbite if exposed to liquid • Difficulty breathing or shortness of breath — May appear immediately if high concentrations of gas are inhaled — Symptom may be delayed if low concentrations of gas are inhaled • Fluid in the lungs (pulmonary edema) within 2 to 4 hours Showing these signs or symptoms does not necessarily mean that a person has been exposed. ***Recovery Expectations:*** • Long-term complications from exposure are not found in people who survive a sudden exposure unless they suffer complications such as pneumonia during therapy. • Chronic bronchitis may develop in people who develop pneumonia during therapy.

Source: Information on symptoms provided by the Centers for Disease Control and Prevention (CDC).

turpentine and ammonia. Because of its physical and chemical properties, the agent (like phosgene) does not remain in its liquid form very long. Thus decon is usually not required.

Riot Control Agents

[NFPA 472: 5.2.3(9)(e)]

Riot control agents (sometimes called *tear gas* or *irritating agents*) are chemical compounds that temporarily make people unable to function by causing immediate irritation to the eyes, mouth, throat, lungs, and skin. Several different compounds are considered riot control agents. All are solids and require dispersion in the form of aerosolized particles, usually released by pyrotechnics (such as with an exploding tear gas canister) or a propelled spray with the particles suspended in a liquid.

The extent of poisoning caused by riot control agents depends on the amount of agent to which a person is exposed, the location of the exposure (indoors versus outdoors), how the person was exposed, and the length of time the person was exposed. The effects of exposure to a riot control agent are usually short-lived (15 to 30 minutes) after the person has been removed from the source and decontaminated. While usually not lethal, riot control agents can cause asphyxiation under certain circumstances. They may also trigger asthma attacks and other respiratory problems. When dispersed, riot control agents are usually heavier than air.

Table 9.7, p. 474, provides the DOT Hazard Class, *ERG* guide number, and characteristics of common riot control agents. Because the symptoms of exposure are very similar for all the agents, they are listed only once. Irritant types are as follows:

- *Chlorobenzylidene malononitrile (CS or tear gas)* — Most commonly used irritant for riot control purposes

- *Chloroacetophenone (CN or mace)* — Also used in some countries for riot control purpose even though its toxicity is higher than that of CS

- *Chloropicrin (PS)* — Also used as a fumigant (substance that uses fumes to disinfect an area)

- *Bromobenzylcyanide (CA)*

- *Dibenzoxazepine (CR)* — New agent; pale yellow-colored crystalline solid

- *Oleoresin capiscum (OC or pepper spray)* — Often categorized as an irritant and riot control agent

- **Combinations of various agents**

Chlorobenzylidene malononitrile (CS or tear gas). CS is a white crystalline solid substance that is used as a riot control agent in many countries. It is also commonly used as a training agent for simulation of chemical warfare conditions and testing of respirators. The CS cloud is white at the point of release and for several seconds after release. Although it is a nonpersistent hazard, CS may stick to rough surfaces (such as clothing) from which it releases only slowly. At least 1 hour of aeration is necessary to cleanse CS from such materials after exposure. Exposure is associated with a pepper-like odor. Exposed persons should move to fresh air, face into the wind with eyes open and breathe deeply. Following exposure, clothing and individual equipment should be inspected for residue. If a residue is found, individuals should change and wash their clothing.

Chloroacetophenone (CN or mace). CN is a clear yellowish-brown-colored solid that is poorly soluble in water but dissolves in organic solvents. CN is a riot control agent still in use by police in some countries. The white smoke smells like apple blossoms. It acts very much like CS, and causes stimulation of sensory nerve endings.

Dibenzoxazepine (CR). CR is a pale yellow-colored crystalline solid that melts at 163°F (73°C). It has a pepper-like odor. It is similar in its effects to CS, but the minimum effective concentration is lower. CR differs from CS in that it is less toxic when inhaled, but CR skin effects are more pronounced. It is more persistent in the environment and on clothing.

Chloropicrin (PS). PS is an oily, colorless, insoluble liquid that causes tears and vomiting; it has an intense odor. PS was used as a chemical warfare agent during World War I and is now used both as a pesticide fumigant and a tear gas. It may also decompose violently if heated, and large volumes may be shock-sensitive.

Table 9.7
Riot Control Agents: Characteristics

Riot Control Agent (Symbol)	UN/DOT Hazard Class and *ERG* Guide	Descriptions	Symptoms (All Listed Agents)
Chlorobenzylidene malononitrile (CS)	Hazard Class 6.1 *ERG* Guide No. 159	• White crystalline solid • Pepper-like smell	***Immediately after exposure:*** People exposed may experience some or all of the following symptoms: • ***Eyes:*** Excessive tearing, burning, blurred vision, and redness • ***Nose:*** Runny nose, burning, and swelling • ***Mouth:*** Burning, irritation, difficulty swallowing, and drooling • ***Lungs:*** Chest tightness, coughing, choking sensation, noisy breathing (wheezing), and shortness of breath • ***Skin:*** Burns and rash • ***Other:*** Nausea and vomiting Long-lasting exposure or exposure to a large dose, especially in a closed setting, may cause severe effects such as the following: • Blindness • Glaucoma (serious eye condition that can lead to blindness) • Immediate death due to severe chemical burns to the throat and lungs • Respiratory failure possibly resulting in death Prolonged exposure, especially in an enclosed area, may lead to long-term effects such as the following: • Eye problems including scarring, glaucoma, and cataracts • May possibly cause breathing problems such as asthma ***Recovery Expectations:*** If symptoms go away soon after a person is removed from exposure, long-term health effects are unlikely to occur.
Chloroacetophenone (CN, mace)	Hazard Class 6.1 *ERG* Guide No. 153	• Clear yellowish brown solid • Poorly soluble in water, but dissolves in organic solvents • White smoke smells like apple blossoms	
Oleoresin Capsicum (OC, pepper spray)	Hazard Class 2.2 *ERG* Guide No. 159	• Oily liquid, typically sold as a spray mist • ***Probable Dispersion Method:*** Aerosol	
Dibenzoxazepine (CR)	Hazard Class 6.1 *ERG* Guide No. 159	• Pale yellow crystalline solid • Pepper-like odor • ***Probale Dispersion Method:*** Propelled	
Chloropicrin (PS)	Hazard Class 6.1	• Oily, colorless liquid • Intense odor • Violent decomposition when exposed to heat	

Source: Information on symptoms provided by the Centers for Disease Control and Prevention (CDC).

Oleoresin capsicum (OC or pepper spray). OC or pepper spray is an oily substance derived from chili peppers (*capsicum* is the scientific name for the genus of plants that includes chili peppers) **(Figure 9.17).** Pepper spray inflames the mucous membranes of the eyes, nose, and mouth, causing intense pain and discomfort. Depending on a variety of factors, the effects of a direct blast of pepper spray can last anywhere from 20 to 90 minutes. Although the effects of pepper spray are usually temporary, exposure has caused severe reactions resulting in death under some circumstances.

Figure 9.17 Pepper spray is a riot control agent derived from chili peppers.

Incapacitants and Vomiting Agents

In addition to tear gas, mace, pepper spray, and other irritants, the following agents are sometimes categorized as riot control agents:

- *Incapacitant*— Chemical agent that produces a temporary disabling condition that persists for hours to days after exposure has occurred (unlike that produced by most riot control agents). *Examples:*
  — Central nervous system (CNS) depressants (anticholinergics)
  — CNS stimulants (lysergic acid diethylamide or LSD)

- *Vomiting agent* — Agent that causes violent, uncontrollable sneezing, cough, nausea, vomiting and a general feeling of bodily discomfort. It is dispersed as an aerosol and produces its effects by inhalation or direct action on the eyes. *Principal agents:*
  — Diphenylchlorarsine (DA)
  — Diphenylaminearsine chloride (Adamsite or DM)
  — Diphenylcyanarsine (DC)

Toxic Industrial Materials

A TIM is an industrial chemical that is toxic at a certain concentration and is produced in quantities exceeding 30 tons (30.5 tonnes) per year at one production facility. TIMs are sometimes referred to as *toxic industrial chemicals* or *TICs*. TIMs are not as lethal as the highly toxic nerve agents, but because they are produced in very large quantities (multitons) and are readily available, they pose a far greater threat than chemical warfare agents. For example, sulfuric acid is not as lethal as a nerve agent, but it is easier to disseminate large quantities of sulfuric acid because large amounts of it are manufactured and transported everyday.

TIMs are divided into three hazard categories. **Table 9.8, p. 477,** lists them with respect to their hazard index ranking (high, medium, or low hazard) as provided in the "Summary of the Final Report of the International Task Force 25: Hazard from Industrial Chemicals," April 15, 1999. Definitions are as follows:

- *High hazard* — Indicates a widely produced, stored, or transported TIM that has high toxicity and is easily vaporized

- *Medium hazard* — Indicates a TIM that may rank high in some categories but is lower in others such as number of producers, physical state, or toxicity

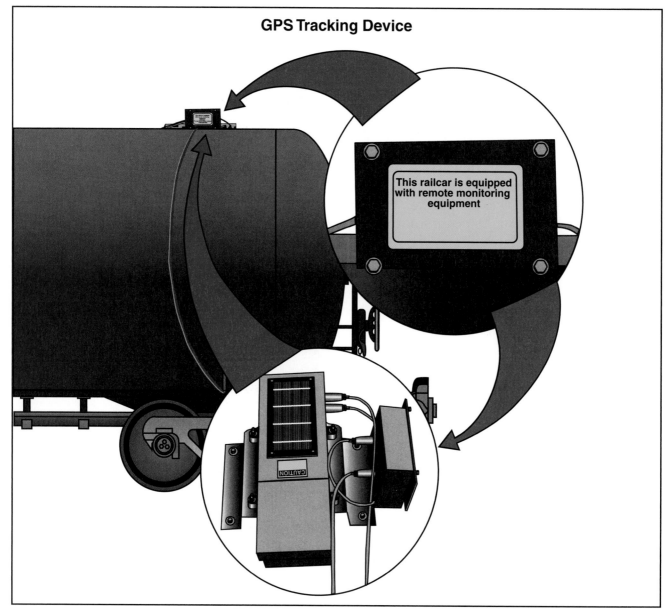

GPS Tracking Device

This railcar is equipped with remote monitoring equipment

CAUTION

Figure 9.18 Some transportation containers may now be tracked by Global Positioning System (GPS) devices.

• *Low hazard* — Indicates that this TIM is not likely to be a hazard unless specific operational factors indicate otherwise

It's Not a Bomb!

Because of the threat of terrorist attacks, some chemical manufacturers are now tracking transportation containers shipping toxic industrial materials (TIMs) and other toxic materials with GPS (global positioning system) devices. These devices may make a tank car or container look *wired*, but they are actually providing an additional degree of safety **(Figure 9.18).**

Because so many different chemicals are included in this table, signs, symptoms, and routes of exposure are not discussed. First responders should attempt to identify the material involved just as they would for any other hazardous materials incident. Follow predetermined procedures and the guidelines provided in the *ERG* when responding to emergencies involving TIMs.

Explosive Attack

Explosive devices can be anything from homemade pipe bombs to sophisticated military ordnance, but nonmilitary first responders are more likely to encounter improvised explosive devices (IEDs)

Table 9.8
Toxic Industrial Materials Listed by Hazard Index Ranking

High Hazard	Medium Hazard	Low Hazard
Ammonia	Acetonic cyanohydrin	Allyl isothiocyanate
Arsine	Acrolein	Arsenic trichloride
Boron trichloride	Acrylonitrile	Bromine
Boron trifluoride	Allyl alcohol	Bromine chloride
Carbon disulfide	Allylamine	Bromine pentafluoride
Chlorine	Allyl chlorocarbonate	Bromine trifluoride
Diborane	Boron tribromide	Carbonyl fluoride
Ethylene oxide	Carbon monoxide	Chlorine pentafluoride
Fluorine	Carbonyl sulfide	Chlorine trifluoride
Formaldehyde	Chloroacetone	Chloroacetaldehyde
Hydrogen bromide	Chloroacelonitrile	Chloroacetyl chloride
Hydrogen chloride	Chlorosulfonic acid	Crotonaldehyde
Hydrogen cyanide	Diketene	Cyanogen chloride
Hydrogen fluoride	1,2-Dimethylhydrazine	Dimethyl sulfate
Hydrogen sulfide	Ethylene dibromide	Diphenylmethane-4,4'-diisocyanate
Nitric acid, fuming	Hydrogen selenide	Ethyl chloroformate
Phosgene	Methanesulfonyl chloride	Ethyl chlorothioformate
Phosphorus trichloride	Methyl bromide	Ethyl phosphonothioic dichloride
Sulfur dioxide	Methyl chloroformate	Ethyl phosphonic dichloride
Sulfuric acid	Methyl chlorosilane	Ethyleneimine
Tungsten hexafluoride	Methyl hydrazine	Hexachlorocyclopentadiene
	Methyl isocyanate	Hydrogen iodide
	Methyl mercaptan	Iron pentacarbonyl
	Nitrogen dioxide	Isobutyl chloroformate
	Phosphine	Isopropyl chloroformate
	Phosphorus oxychloride	Isopropyl isocyanate
	Phosphorus pentafluoride	n-Butyl chloroformate
	Selenium hexafluoride	n-Butyl isocyanate
	Silicon tetrafluoride	Nitric oxide
	Stibine	n-Propyl chloroformate
	Sulfur trioxide	Parathion
	Sulfuryl chloride	Perchloromethyl mercaptan
	Sulfuryl fluoride	sec-Butyl chloroformate
	Tellurium hexafluoride	tert-Butyl isocyanate
	n-Octyl mercaptan	Tetraethyl lead
	Titanium tetrachloride	Tetraethyl pyrophosphate
	Trichloroacetyl chloride	Tetramethyl lead
	Trifluoroacetyl chloride	Toluene 2,4-diisocyanate
		Toluene 2,6-diisocyanate

Source: "Summary of the Final Report of the International Task Force 25: Hazard from Industrial Chemicals," April 15, 1999.

than military weapons. While most bombs made by criminals or terrorists are likely to be homemade or constructed in an improvised manner, they usually have one thing in common: they are designed to kill, maim, or destroy property. The truck bomb that exploded April 19, 1995, outside the Murrah Federal Building in Oklahoma City, killing 168 people and injuring many others, is testimony to the potential destructive power of such devices **(Figure 9.19).** Explosives in general may be classified in the following different ways:

- *Composition* — Explosive mixtures versus explosive compounds
- *Use* — Propellants, bursting explosives, blasting agents, pyrotechnic substances, and the like
- *Manufacture* — Commercial, military, or homemade
- *Susceptibility to initiation or sensitivity* — Primary explosives versus secondary explosives

Figure 9.19 Though often smaller than the truck bomb used to destroy the Murrah Federal Building in Oklahoma City, improvised explosive devices can be extremely powerful and devastating.

- *Chemical reaction* — Rate of decomposition/velocity of the explosion

First responders should understand the following commonly used classification system based on the chemical reaction or rate of decomposition:

- *High explosives* — Decompose extremely rapidly (almost instantaneously), which is normally called *detonation*. In other words, high explosives *detonate* (explode). Detonation velocities for high explosives range from 3,300 feet per second (fps) to 29,900 fps (1 006 mps to 9 114 mps) (faster than the speed of sound). Examples of commercially available high explosives include:
  — Plastic explosives
  — Nitroglycerin
  — TNT **(Figure 9.20)**
  — Blasting caps
  — Dynamite
  — Ammonium nitrate and fuel oil (ANFO) and other blasting agents

Figure 9.20 TNT is a high explosive and can be in liquid form.

- *Low explosives* — Decompose rapidly but do not produce an explosive effect unless they are confined; rather, they *deflagrate* (burn rapidly). An example is black powder. Low explosives confined in small spaces or containers are commonly used as propellants (bullets and fireworks). Unconfined low explosives may also be considered incendiary materials. Many experts do not separate incendiary devices/materials from explosives (see Incendiary Attack and Commercial/Military Explosives sections).

First responders may also encounter the following classifications based on the explosives' susceptibility to initiation (or sensitivity):

- *Primary explosives* — Easily initiated and highly sensitive to heat; usually used as detonators. Examples: lead azide, mercury fulminate, and lead styphnate.

- *Secondary explosives* — Designed to detonate only under specific circumstances; usually set off by activation energy provided by a primary explosive. They are less sensitive to initiating stimuli such as heat or flame. Example: TNT.

Propellants are sometimes included as a third category with primary and secondary explosives. Propellants are low explosives that deflagrate rather than explode (such as black powder). Many experts consider primary and secondary explosives to be subcategories of high explosives **(Figure 9.21)**.

As mentioned earlier, there are many different ways to categorize explosives. For example, black powder may be called a *low explosive*, a *propellant*, or an *incendiary material*. Blasting agents are high explosives that are sometimes separated from secondary explosives because they are extremely insensitive to detonators. Blasting agents such as ANFO require a booster to initiate detonation. Generally, *high* explosives have a bigger bang than *low* explosives, and *primary* explosives are more sensitive than *secondary* explosives.

Commercial/Military Explosives

Commercial and military explosives are normally used for such purposes as mining, demolition, excavation, construction, and military applications. Unfortunately, criminals and terrorists may also use them. Emergency response organizations should make note of commercial construction

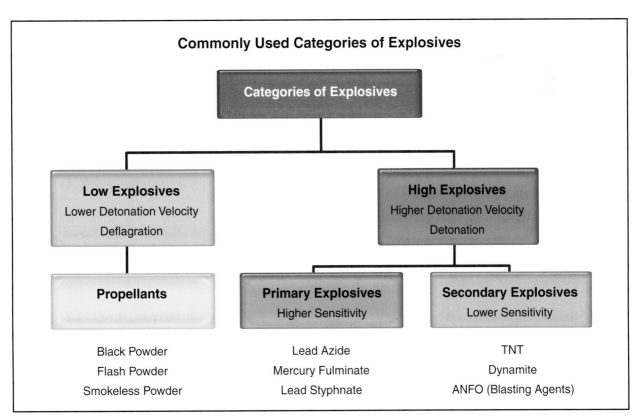

Figure 9.21 Commonly used categories of explosives.

sites in their area that may store or use commercial explosives. It is particularly important for law enforcement to notify fire and emergency services organizations if these explosives are ever stolen. **Appendix K** contains a comprehensive list of explosives as identified by the U.S. Bureau of Alcohol, Tobacco, Firearms and Explosives (ATF). An alphabetical list of commercial and military explosives and/or their explosive components is as follows:

- ***Ammonium nitrate*** — Common fertilizer that can be mixed with diesel fuel or oil to form an explosive mixture. Ammonium nitrate mixed with nitromethane was used in the 1995 Oklahoma City Murrah Federal Building bombing.

- ***Binary explosives*** — Composed of two different chemical components, one solid and one liquid. When separate, the two components are nonexplosive; however, when mixed, they become highly explosive **(Figure 9.22)**.

- ***Black powder*** — Mixture of potassium nitrate or sodium nitrate, sulfur, and charcoal.

- ***Composition C-4*** — Mixture of cyclotrimethylene-trinitramine/cyclonite (RDX), polyisabutylene, and fuel oil; commonly called a *plastic* explosive because of its pliability.

- ***Dynamite*** — Several types of dynamite may be divided into the following three categories:

  — *Granular:* Two types: Straight and ammonia granular. *Straight dynamite* is the oldest type; contains nitroglycerin and an absorbent mixture such as sawdust and sodium nitrate. *Ammonia-granular dynamite* is replacing straight dynamite in most modern uses because it is generally safer than straight dynamite. Most of its explosive energy is provided by ammonium nitrate rather than nitroglycerin **(Figure 9.23)**.

  — *Semigelatin:* Similar to ammonia-granular dynamites, but has a small amount of guncotton and (usually) additional nitroglycerin added to form a gel; often has somewhat higher detonation velocities than granular dynamites.

  — *Gelatin:* Two types: Straight and ammonia. *Straight gelatin* is composed of blasting gelatin, a stiff gel made of nitroglycerin mixed with other ingredients, including guncotton

Figure 9.22 Binary explosives are composed of two different chemical components that only become explosive when mixed. *Courtesy of the U.S. Bureau of Alcohol, Tobacco, Firearms and Explosives and the Oklahoma Highway Patrol Bomb Squad.*

Figure 9.23 Granular dynamite is composed of nitroglycerin or ammonium nitrate mixed with an absorbent material such as sawdust and sodium nitrate. *Courtesy of the U.S. Bureau of Alcohol, Tobacco, Firearms and Explosives and the Oklahoma Highway Patrol Bomb Squad.*

and sodium nitrate. Mixing ammonium nitrate and other ingredients to blasting gelatin makes *ammonia gelatin,* which is waterproof and used for underwater applications.

- ***Emulsion explosives*** — Made by suspending or mixing tiny, submicroscopic droplets of an oxidizer in a fuel such as mineral oil or fuel oil.

- ***Guncotton (nitrocellulose, nitrocotton)*** — Created by bathing cotton or purified wool cellulose in a mix of sulphuric and nitric acids. Once the soaked cotton is drained from the acid mixture, it is then boiled in water to remove the impurities. Finally, it is pulped and pressed into small slabs while still damp.

- ***High melting eXplosive (HMX)*** — Colorless solid that dissolves slightly in water (also known as *octogen* and *cyclotetramethylene-tetranitramine*). HMX explodes violently at high temperatures. Because of this property, it is used in various kinds of explosives, rocket fuels, and burster chargers. A small amount of HMX is also formed in making RDX.

- ***Pentaerythritol tetranitrate (PETN)*** — Very strong high explosive used primarily in booster and bursting charges of small caliber ammunition, in upper charges of detonators in some land mines and shells, and as the explosive core of primacord (explosive fuse); also used in blasting caps and sheet explosives.

- **Royal demolition eXplosive (RDX)** — White powder that is very explosive (also known as *cyclonite* or *hexogen*); chemical name is *1,3,5-trinitro-1,3,5-triazine*. RDX is usually mixed with other materials and used in detonation cord and blasting caps. RDX explosives can be pressed into rolls or flat sheets called *detasheet explosives*, which were involved in the 2001 Richard Reid *Shoe Bomber* case. RDX also forms the base of several military explosives including the following:
  — Composition A
  — Composition B
  — Composition C
  — HBX
  — H-6
  — Cyclotol

- **Semtex** — Highly malleable plastic explosive named after the Czech village, Semtin, where it is manufactured; primarily composed of RDX and PETN.

- **Smokeless Powders** — Explosive propellants designed to replace black powder. They leave a minimal amount of residue after activation (which is why they are called *smokeless*); have a nitrocellulose base, but may also contain nitroglycerin or nitroglycerin and nitroguanidine.

- **Triaminotrinitrobenzene (TATB)** — Heat-resistant, insensitive high explosive.

- **Tetryl** — Odorless, synthetic, yellow-colored, crystal-like solid (other names are *nitramine, tetralite, trinitrophenylmethylnitramine*, and *tetril*); was mostly used to make explosives during World Wars I and II; used as an explosive component of chemical bombs, demolition blocks, and cast-shaped charges.

- **Trinitrotoluene (TNT)** — Used in military shells, bombs, grenades, industrial uses, and underwater blasting (also called *triton, trotyl, trilite, trinol*, and *tritolo*). Unlike many other explosives that become more sensitive as they age, refined TNT is relatively stable and safe to store for long periods of time **(Figure 9.24)**. It is a component of many other explosives including the following:

  — Composition B
  — Amatol
  — Torpex
  — Pentolite
  — Tetrytol
  — Tritonal
  — Picratol
  — Ednatol
  — Water gels

- **Water gels/slurries** — Originally aqueous solutions composed of ammonium nitrate, TNT, and gelatinizing agents; more recent versions may contain aluminum powder and other metallic fuels.

Homemade Explosive Materials

Instructions on how to make many explosive materials are available on the Internet and in resources such as *The Anarchist Cookbook* **(Figure 9.25, p. 482)**. The cookbook, for example, provides

Figure 9.24 TNT is relatively stable and safe compared to some other explosives that deteriorate with age. *Courtesy of the U.S. Bureau of Alcohol, Tobacco, Firearms and Explosives and the Oklahoma Highway Patrol Bomb Squad.*

Figure 9.25 *The Anarchist Cookbook* provides instructions for making homemade explosives.

instructions on how to make nitroglycerin, mercury fulminate, blasting gelatin, dynamite, TNT, tetryl, picric acid, black powder, smokeless powder, nitrogen tri-iodide, and nitrogen trichloride (also called *chloride of azode, agene, chlorine nitride, trichloramine,* and *trichlorine nitride*). Picric acid, nitrogen trichloride, and nitrogen tri-iodide are not marketed as commercial explosives for blasting, mining, and the like but for laboratories and other industrial uses. They are potentially very unstable and sensitive explosive materials that could be used for criminal purposes.

Improvised Explosive Devices

These devices are categorized by their container (such as vehicle bombs) and the ways they are initiated. They are homemade, are usually constructed for a specific target, and can be contained in almost anything. IEDs (as well as other military and commercial explosive devices) usually have a firing train that consists of a fusing system, detonator, and main charge (explosive or incendiary). However, it is possible to have 2-, 3-, and 4-step firing trains (see **Figures 9.26 a–c**).

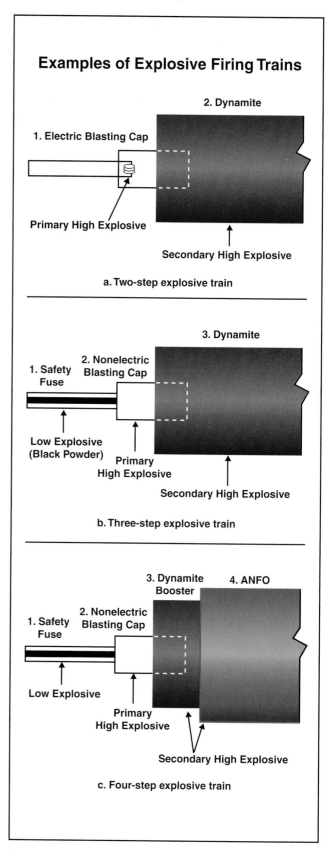

Examples of Explosive Firing Trains

a. Two-step explosive train

b. Three-step explosive train

c. Four-step explosive train

Figures 9.26 a–c Two-, three-, and four-step explosive firing trains. *Original source courtesy of the U.S. Environmental Protection Agency (EPA).*

Any switch that can turn something on or off can activate a device. Categories of fusing systems are as follows:

- **Timer activated** — Activated by a timer set to detonate (or arm) a device at a certain time; timer may be mechanical (such as kitchen timer, windup wristwatch, or pocket watch) or electronic (such as digital wristwatches, integrated circuit chips, or solid-state timers).

- **Victim activated** — Designed to detonate by pushing (pressure), pulling, moving, vibrating, tension releasing, or tilting the item; suicide bombers are usually *booby trapped* with victim-activated bombs.

- **Signal/command activated** — Triggered to detonate by a radio frequency signal, cell phone signal, or through a hidden wire from a remote location.

- **Environmentally activated** — Activated to detonate when there is a change in temperature, pressure, light, sound, or magnetic field. Any bomb that is ignited by a lit fuse (Molotov cocktail, fireworks, and the like) could be placed in this category.

There is no *stereotypical* bomb **(Figure 9.27).** The item must be carried or driven to where it will be placed, so concealment or masking of the device is usually necessary. Bomb types, based on the outer container, can include the following:

- **Vehicle bombs** — May contain many thousands of pounds (kilograms) of explosives that can cause massive destruction; are perhaps the most devastating of all IEDs. They can be easy to conceal, and the explosives can be placed anywhere in a vehicle but are often located in the trunk when small vehicles (such as passenger cars) are used. **Table 9.9, p. 484,** provides the ATF's recommended vehicle bomb explosion hazard and evacuation distances.

- **Pipe bombs** — Usually made of steel or polyvinyl chloride (PVC) pipe sections that are filled with explosives and capped or sealed on the ends **(Figure 9.28, p. 485).** Pipe bombs are often filled with slivered metal and/or gravel so that when detonated, they can throw shrapnel up to 300 feet (91 m) with lethal force. Explosive filler can get into the threads of the pipe making the device extremely sensitive to shock or friction.

Figure 9.27 Could it be a bomb? Yes! The look and packaging of improvised explosive devices is truly limited only by the imagination of the bomber.

- **Satchel, backpack, knapsack, briefcase, or box bombs** — Filled with explosives or an explosive device. These bombs come in any style, color, or size of carrying container (even as small as a cigarette pack).

- **Mail, package, or letter bombs** — Explosive device or material is concealed in a package or letter. Opening the package or letter usually triggers the bomb. The list of possible indicators of package or letter bombs is long **(Figure 9.29, p. 485).** Some of the most common indicators are as follows:

— Package or letter has no postage, noncancelled postage, or excessive postage. Normally a bomber does not want to mail a parcel over the postal counter and communicate with a window clerk face to face.

— Parcels may be unprofessionally wrapped with several combinations of tape to secure them and endorsed *Fragile — Handle With Care* or *Rush — Do Not Delay.*

— Sender is unknown, no return address is available, or the return address is fictitious.

— Addressee does not normally receive mail at that address.

— Mail may bear restricted endorsements such as *Personal* or *Private.* These endorsements are particularly important when addressees do not usually receive personal mail at their work locations.

Table 9.9
Vehicle Bomb Explosion Hazard and Evacuation Distances

Vehicle Profile	Vehicle Description	Maximum Explosives Capacity	Lethal Air Blast Range	Minimum Evacuation Distance	Falling Glass Hazard
	Compact Sedan	500 pounds (227 kg) [In trunk]	100 feet (30 m)	1,500 feet (457 m)	1,250 feet (381 m)
	Full Size Sedan	1,000 pounds (454 kg) [In trunk]	125 feet (38 m)	1,750 feet (533 m)	1,750 feet (533 m)
	Passenger Van or Cargo Van	4,000 pounds (1 814 kg)	200 feet (61 m)	2,750 feet (838 m)	2,750 feet (838 m)
	Small Box Van (14 ft [4 m] Box)	10,000 pounds (4 536 kg)	300 feet (91 m)	3,750 feet (1 143 m)	3,750 feet (1 143 m)
	Box Van or Water/Fuel Truck	30,000 pounds (13 608 kg)	450 feet (137 m)	6,500 feet (1 981 m)	6,500 feet (1 981 m)
	Semitrailer	60,000 pounds (27 216 kg)	600 feet (183 m)	7,000 feet (2 134 m)	7,000 feet (2 134 m)

Source: *U.S. Bureau of Alcohol, Tobacco, Firearms and Explosives (ATF).*

— Postmarks may show different locations than return addresses.

— Common words are misspelled on mail.

— Mail may display distorted handwriting, or the name and address may be prepared with homemade labels or cut-and-paste lettering.

— Package emits a peculiar or suspicious odor.

— Mail shows oily stains or discoloration.

— Letter or package seems heavy or bulky for its size and may have an irregular shape, soft spots, or bulges.

— Letter envelopes may feel rigid or appear uneven or lopsided.

— Mail may have protruding wires or aluminum foil.

— Package makes ticking, buzzing, or whirring noises.

— Unidentified person calls to ask if a letter or package was received.

• *Plastic bottle bombs* — Plastic pop bottles filled with a material (such as dry ice) that expands rapidly causing the container to explode.

• *Fireworks* — Legally obtained fireworks modified and/or combined to form more dangerous explosive devices.

• *M-devices* — Devices constructed of cardboard tubes (often red) filled with flash powder and sealed at both ends; are ignited by fuses. The most common are M-80s, which measure ⅝ × 1½ inches (16 mm by 25 mm). M-devices, while generally more dangerous than most fireworks, present more of a hazard as a potential incendiary than a destructive explosive (shock and fragmentation hazards are less than those from

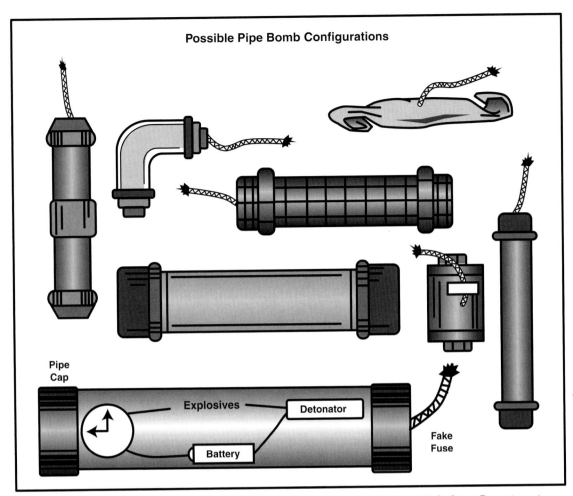

Figure 9.28 Typical pipe bomb configurations. *Original source courtesy of the U.S. State Department.*

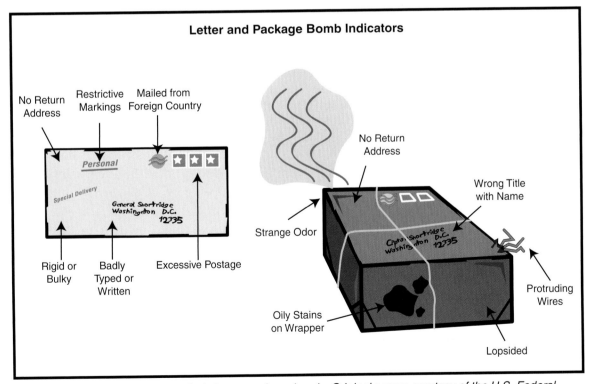

Figure 9.29 Possible indicators of a letter or package bomb. *Original source courtesy of the U.S. Federal Bureau of Investigation (FBI).*

a pipe or vehicle bomb). M-80s were available in the U.S. as commercial fireworks but were made illegal for safety reasons in 1966.

- *Carbon dioxide (CO₂) grenades* — Devices made by filling used CO_2 containers (such as those used to power pellet pistols) with an explosive powder; usually initiated by a fuse and can produce deadly shrapnel.

- *Tennis ball bombs* — Devices made by filling a tennis ball with an explosive mixture that ignites by a simple fuse.

- *Other existing objects* — Items that seem to have an ordinary purpose can be substituted or used as the bomb container. Examples: fire extinguishers, propane bottles, trash cans, gasoline cans, and books.

IEDs may be placed anywhere. Usually, bombers want to succeed without being detected or caught. The level of security and awareness of the public, security forces, employees, and the like determine where and how an IED is placed. Common areas where IEDs might be placed include the following:

- *Outside* — Trash cans, Dumpster® trash receptacles, mailboxes, bushes, storage areas, and parked vehicles; always approach Dumpster® fires cautiously.

- *Inside* — Mailrooms, restrooms, trash cans, planters, desk drawers or storage containers, false ceilings, utility closets, areas hidden by drapes or curtains, behind pictures, boiler rooms, or under stairwells. Notice recently repaired or patched segments of walls, floors, or ceilings. Remember to look at what is in plain view.

Other Criminal Activities

Terrorist attacks aren't the only criminal activities that may involve haz mat and result in emergencies. Illegal clandestine labs are an ever-increasing concern throughout the country. In some areas, they constitute a majority of haz mat related emergency response calls. Additionally, first responders may be called to the scene of some other type of illegal laboratory or even the scene of an illegal chemical dump. For example, barrels of unknown waste chemicals can be dumped beside roadways or on abandoned properties.

Illegal Clandestine Labs

Illegal clandestine labs are established to produce or manufacture illegal or controlled substances such as drugs, chemical warfare agents, explosives, or biological agents. Illegal clandestine labs can be found virtually anywhere. They may be located in abandoned buildings, hotel rooms, rural farms, urban apartments, rental storage units, or upscale residential neighborhoods. Illegal methamphetamine (meth) labs can be so portable that they have even been found in campgrounds, highway rest stops, and vehicles.

These labs can present numerous threats to first responders. In addition to the chemical, explosive, or etiological hazards present, responders may face armed resistance, booby traps, and/or other weapons when responding to emergencies at illegal labs. Many of the products used in clandestine labs are toxic, explosive, and/or highly flammable.

Drug Labs

It is estimated that a significant majority (80 to 90 percent) of all illegal clandestine drug labs are set up to produce meth. These labs may also make ecstasy, cocaine, phenyl-2-propanone (P2P), phencyclidine (PCP), heroine, LSD, amphetamines, and other illegal drugs. However, because meth labs represent the most common type of clandestine drug lab, this section primarily focuses on them.

Meth is easy to make and uses a variety of ingredients commercially available in local stores. Because of the increasing hazard of meth labs, some U.S. states have placed restrictions on the purchase of items used in making meth. The process of making meth is called *cooking*, and many different *recipes* or methods exist. Two of the most common are known as the *Red P* method and *Nazi/ Birch* method. The various recipes differ slightly in the process and the chemicals used, but all of them are potentially very dangerous because the chemicals are often highly flammable, corrosive and toxic (**Figures 9.30 a and b**). Meth labs present a danger to the meth cook, the community surrounding the lab, and emergency response personnel who discover the lab.

Flammability is perhaps the most serious hazard associated with meth labs, and many labs are discovered only after a fire or explosion has

Figures 9.30 a and b Meth lab products and equipment.

occurred. Some products used in making meth are highly corrosive acids or bases, while others are extremely toxic. One of the byproducts, phosphine gas, is sometimes classified as a chemical warfare choking agent. Some products are oxidizers. Meth production processes generate hydrogen chloride gas and hydrogen iodide gas. Meth lab locations may remain serious health and environmental hazards for years after the labs are removed unless they are properly decontaminated (often an extremely expensive process). A summary of the products commonly used in making meth and the hazards associated with them is provided in **Table 9.10, p. 488.**

Table 9.10
Methamphetamine Sources and Production Hazards

Chemical Name	Common Sources/Uses	Hazards	Production Role
Acetone	• Paint solvent • Nail polish remover	• Highly flammable • Vapor is irritating to eyes and mucous membranes • Inhalation may cause dizziness, narcosis, and coma • Liquid may do damage upon contact • Ingestion may cause gastric irritation, narcosis, and coma	• Pill extraction • Cleaning glassware • Cleaning finished methamphetamine (meth)
Anhydrous Ammonia	• Sold as fertilizer; also used as a refrigerant gas • Stolen from farms and other locations for illegal meth production • Often stored in propane tanks or fire extinguishers at illegal meth labs, which causes the fittings of the tank or extinguisher to turn blue (Figure 9.32, p. 491)	• Toxic • Corrosive • Flammable • Severe irritant; may cause severe eye damage, skin burns and blisters, chest pain, cessation of breathing, and death	Meth production process
Ethyl Alcohol/ Denatured Alcohol/ Ethanol/Grain Alcohol	• Sold as solvents • Is the alcohol found in beverages at greatly reduced concentrations	• Highly flammable • Toxic; may cause blindness or death if swallowed • Inhalation may affect central nervous system causing impaired thinking and coordination • Skin and respiratory tract irritant (may be absorbed through the skin) • May affect the liver, blood, kidneys, gastrointestinal tract, and reproductive system	• Used with sulfuric acid to produce ethyl ether (see Ethyl Ether/Ether entry) • Cleaning glassware

Continued

Table 9.10 (continued)
Methamphetamine Sources and Production Hazards

Chemical Name	Common Sources/Uses	Hazards	Production Role
Ephedrine	Over-the-counter cold and allergy medications	Harmful if swallowed in large quantities	Primary precursor for meth
Ethyl Ether/Ether	Starting fluids	• Highly flammable • Oxidizes readily in air to form unstable peroxides that may explode spontaneously • Vapors may cause drowsiness, dizziness, mental confusion, fainting, and unconscious at high concentrations	Separation of the meth base before the *salting-out* process begins, primarily in the *Nazi/Birch* method
Hydrochloric Acid/ Muriatic Acid (Other acids can be used as well, including sulfuric acid and phosphoric acid)	Commerical or industrial strength cleaners for driveways, pools, sinks, toilets, etc.	• Toxic; ingestion may cause death • Corrosive; contact with liquid or vapors may cause severe burns • Inhalation may cause coughing, choking, lung damage, pulmonary edema, and possible death • Reacts with metal to form explosive hydrogen gas	Production of water-soluble salts
Hydrogen Peroxide	• Common first aid supply • Used for chemical manufacturing, textile bleaching, food processing, and water purification	• Strong oxidizer • Eye irritant	Extrication of iodine crystals from Tincture of Iodine
Hypophosphorous Acid	Laboratory Chemical	• Corrosive • Toxic • Generates deadly phosphine gas during initial reaction	Source of phosphorous in *Red P* method

Continued

Table 9.10 (continued)
Methamphetamine Sources and Production Hazards

Chemical Name	Common Sources/Uses	Hazards	Production Role
Iodine	Tincture of iodine	• Toxic • Vapors irritating to respiratory tract and eyes • May irritate eyes and burn skin	• Meth production process • Can be mixed with hydrogen sulfide to make hydriodic acid (strong reducing agent) • Can be mixed with red phosphorus and water to form hydriodic acid
Isopropyl Alcohol	Rubbing Alcohol	• Flammable • Vapors in high concentrations may cause headache and dizziness • Liquid may cause severe eye damage	• Pill extraction • Cleaning finished meth
Lithium Metal	Lithium batteries	• Flammable solid • Water-reactive (reacts with water to form lithium hydroxide, which can burn the skin and eyes)	Reacts with anhydrous ammonia and ephedrine/pseudoephedrine in the *Nazi/Birch* method
Methyl Alcohol	HEET® Gas-Line Antifreeze and Water Remover	• Highly flammable • Vapors may cause headache, nausea, vomiting, and eye irritation • Vapors in high concentrations may cause dizziness, stupor, cramps, and digestive disturbances • Highly toxic when ingested	Pill extraction
Mineral Spirits/ Petroleum Distillate	• Lighter fluid • Paint thinner	• Flammable • Toxic when ingested • Vapors may cause dizziness • May affect central nervous system and kidneys	Separation of meth base before *salting-out* process begins

Continued

Table 9.10 (continued)
Methamphetamine Sources and Production Hazards

Chemical Name	Common Sources/Uses	Hazards	Production
Naphtha	Camping fuel for stoves and lanterns	• Highly flammable • Toxic when ingested • May affect the central nervous system • May cause irritation to the skin, eyes, and respiratory tract	• Separation of meth base before *salting-out* process begins • Cleaning preparation
Pseudoephedrine	Over-the-counter cold and allergy medications	Harmful if swallowed in large quantities	Production of meth (same as Ephedrine)
Red Phosphorous	Matches	• Flammable solid • Reacts with oxidizing agents, reducing agents, peroxides, and strong alkalis • When ignited, vapors are irritating to eyes and respiratory tract • Heating in a reaction or cooking process generates deadly phosphine gas • Can convert to white phosphorous (air reactive) when overheated	Mixed with iodine in the *Red P* method; serves as a catalyst by combining with elemental iodine to produce hydriodic acid (HI), which is used to reduce ephedrine or pseudoephedrine to meth
Sodium Hydroxide (Other alkaline materials may also be used such as sodium, calcium oxide, calcium carbonate, and potassium carbonate)	Drain openers	• Very corrosive; burns human skin and eyes • Generates heat when mixed with an acid or dissolved in water	After cooking, an alkaline product such as sodium hydroxide turns the very acidic mixture into a base
Sulfuric Acid	Drain openers	• Extremely corrosive • Inhalation of vapors may cause serious lung damage • Contact with eyes may cause blindness • Both ingestion and inhalation may be fatal	Creates the reaction in the salting phase; combines with salt to create hydrogen chloride gas, which is necessary for the *salting-out* phase

Continued

Table 9.10 (continued)
Methamphetamine Sources and Production Hazards

Chemical Name	Common Sources/Uses	Hazards	Production Role
Toluene	Solvent often used in automotive fuels	• Flammable • Vapors may cause burns or irritation of the respiratory tract, eyes, and mucous membranes • Inhalation may cause dizziness; severe exposure may cause pulmonary edema • May react with strong oxidizers	Separation of meth base before the *salting-out* process begins
Hydrogen Chloride		• Toxic • Corrosive • Eye irritant • Vapor or aerosol may produce inflammation and may cause ulceration of the nose, throat, and larynx	• Created by adding sulfuric acid to rock salt • Used to *salt out* meth from base solution
Phosphine Gas		• Very toxic by inhalation • Highly flammable; ignites spontaneously on contact with air and moisture, oxidizers, halogens, chlorine, and acids • May be fatal if inhaled, swallowed, or absorbed through skin • Contact causes burns to skin and eyes	• Byproduct • Produced when red phosphorous and iodine are combined during the cooking process
Hydrogen Iodide/ Hydriodic Acid Gas		• Highly toxic • Attacks mucous membranes and eyes	• Byproduct • Produced when red phosphorous and iodine are combined during the cooking process • Causes the reddish/orange staining commonly found on the walls, ceilings, and other surfaces of meth labs
Hydriodic Acid		• Corrosive • Causes burns if swallowed or comes in contact with skin	• Byproduct • Produced when red phosphorous and iodine are combined during the cooking process

People not wearing proper personal protective equipment (PPE) who enter a meth lab before it has been properly decontaminated and ventilated may experience headaches, nausea, dizziness, fatigue, shortness of breath, coughing, chest pain, lack of coordination, burns and even death. Risk of injury or toxicity from chemical exposure varies, depending on the toxic properties of the chemicals or byproducts, their quantity and form, their concentrations, the duration of exposure, and the route of exposure.

In addition to recognizing the types of chemicals typically found in meth labs, first responders should also be familiar with the types of equipment used in the process. They may expect to find the following items:

- **Condenser tubes** — Used to cool vapors produced during cooking **(Figure 9.31)**

- **Filters** — Coffee filters, cloth, and cheesecloth

- **Funnels/turkey basters** — Used to separate layers of liquids

- **Gas containers** — Propane bottles, fire extinguishers, self-contained underwater breathing apparatus (SCUBA) tanks, plastic drink bottles (often attached to some sort of tubing) **(Figure 9.32)**

Figure 9.31 Condenser tubes are used to cool vapors produced during the *cooking* phase of meth production.

Figure 9.32 Anhydrous ammonia will turn the brass fittings on propane cylinders and other containers blue.

- *Glassware* — Particularly Pyrex® or Visions® cookware, mason jars, and other laboratory glassware that can tolerate heating and violent chemical reactions

- *Heat sources* — Burners, hot plates, microwave ovens, and camp stoves (**Figure 9.33**)

- *Grinders* — Used to grind up ephedrine or pseudoephedrine tablets

- *pH papers* — Used to test the pH levels of the reactions

- *Tubing* — Glass, plastic, copper, or rubber

Other clues to the presence of meth labs in structures include the following:

- Windows covered with plastic or tinfoil

- Knowledge of renters who pay landlords in cash

- Unusual security systems or other devices

- Excessive trash

- Increased activity, especially at night

- Unusual structures

- Discoloration of structures, pavement, and soil

- Strong odor of solvents

- Smell of ammonia, starting fluid, or ether

- Iodine- or chemical-stained bathroom or kitchen fixtures (**Figure 9.34**)

Figure 9.34 Iodine is commonly used as part of the meth production process. Iodine can cause a yellow- to reddish-colored stain on walls, ceilings, or other fixtures in the area where the meth is being cooked.

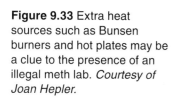

Figure 9.33 Extra heat sources such as Bunsen burners and hot plates may be a clue to the presence of an illegal meth lab. *Courtesy of Joan Hepler.*

It is estimated that for every pound (0.5 kg) of meth produced, 6 pounds (2.7 kg) of hazardous waste is generated. This waste may then be dumped in the regular residential trash, down the drain to the septic system, beside roadways, on vacant properties, and in streams or ponds/lakes. It may also be buried. Disposal of this waste is very expensive, and the cleanup process is potentially very dangerous. Many law enforcement departments have contracts with private hazardous materials waste disposal contractors to handle the cleanup and decon of seized illegal meth labs and dumps.

Chemical Agents Labs

Some chemical warfare agents are surprisingly easy to make. While the recipes may be easy to find, the actual materials necessary to make them may not be. Some ingredients may be common, but access to others is restricted. Chemical agent labs might be identified by the presence of military manuals, underground *cookbooks,* chemicals (such as organophosphate pesticides) that would not normally be used to make meth or other illegal drugs, and more sophisticated lab equipment that is necessary to conduct some of the chemical reactions needed to make the agents. Responders should be suspicious if a laboratory seems to have unusual equipment or chemicals.

Explosives Labs

Explosives labs may lack the glassware, tubing, Bunsen burners, chemical bottles, and other trappings traditionally associated with the term *laboratory.* For example, a work area in a garage used to assemble custom fireworks or pyrotechnics would be considered an explosives lab for purposes of this book. Generally, most explosive labs do not need to heat or cook any of their materials; however, a lab established to make explosive chemical mixtures might look more like a traditional industrial or university chemistry lab.

Obvious clues to the presence of an explosives lab might include literature on how to make bombs, significant quantities of fireworks, ammunition like shotgun shells, black powder, smokeless powder, blasting caps, commercial explosives, incendiary materials, or other chemicals on the ATF's explosive materials list (see Appendix K). Finding these items in conjunction with components that can be used to make IEDs (pipes, activation devices, empty fire extinguishers, propane containers, and the like) would give even more evidence of an explosives lab.

Biological Labs

Biological labs may look very similar to chemical agent or drug labs, but a trained and experienced person would see some significant differences. Biological labs are in the business of working with etiological agents; therefore, these labs are more likely to be equipped with petri dishes (used to grow biological organisms and materials), microscopes and glass slides (etiological agents are microscopic), autoclaves, and centrifuges. Generally, biological labs may also be cleaner than any other type of lab because keeping a sterile environment may be important to avoid contamination of samples. The presence of castor beans might also be a clue because castor beans are needed to make ricin **(Figure 9.35).**

Figure 9.35 Ricin is made from castor beans.

Illegal Dumps

Chemicals may be dumped illegally for a variety of reasons. In some cases, lawful disposal may be considered too expensive or complicated. In other cases, the materials may have been used in illegal clandestine labs or other illegal activities. Some chemical dumpsites may have been created years before any regulations prohibited such actions.

Discovery of an illegal dumpsite may or may not be considered an emergency, depending on the chemicals involved and where the site is located.

However, first responders are often the first persons called to the scene. Illegal dumps may be extremely expensive to clean up, and often require state/province and/or federal/national involvement. Frequently the following significant problems and hazards are associated with illegal dumps:

- *Unlabeled containers* — Chemicals may have been removed from their original containers or labels and identification information may have been deliberately removed **(Figure 9.36).**

- *Mixed chemicals* — Containers may have many different (and potentially incompatible chemicals) mixed together, making hazard and risk assessment extremely difficult.

- *Aged chemicals* — Many chemicals become unstable when subjected to age and weathering in outside climates.

- *Environmental contamination* — When chemicals are deliberately dumped in ponds, streams, rivers, and lakes, environmental contamination becomes a serious issue. Even if chemicals are not dumped in a body of water, leaking drums and other containers can pose a threat to groundwater sources.

Figure 9.36 Unlabeled containers are hazards found at illegal dumps. Responders may have no idea what potentially deadly mixtures of hazardous materials are present.

Special Operational Considerations at Terrorist or Criminal Incidents

[NFPA 472: 5.2.2(6)] [ODP Awareness III.f., IV.a, VI.b.] [ODP Operations Level I.d., II.d., II.h., IV.g., IV.b.]

The framework for a response to a terrorist or criminal incident is essentially the same as that used for a response to any other hazardous materials incident. However, because a crime is involved, law enforcement organizations must be notified and included in the response. Notifying law enforcement ensures that the proper state/province and federal/national agencies respond to the incident (such as the FBI who has jurisdiction over terrorist incidents in the U.S.). As with other hazardous materials incidents, responders must know what types of additional help are available in their areas (including those at the state/province and regional level such as regional response teams) and how to summon this help according to predetermined procedures. Responders must follow these same procedures for communicating with the media and the public during an incident.

> **WARNING**
> PPE used at WMD/CBRNE events should meet National Institute for Occupational Safety and Health (NIOSH) and NFPA certification for WMD/CBRNE hazards.

Terrorist and criminal incidents may differ because of their size, the number of casualties, their complexity, additional hazards such as booby traps or armed resistance, and their overall danger level. First responders must operate by the same basic principles they would for any other emergency such as the following:

- Follow the incident priorities of life safety, incident stabilization, and protection of property and the environment.

- Establish an incident command or management system and follow applicable predetermined procedures and the emergency response plan.

- Try to solve the incident problem(s) given the resources and circumstances available. When necessary, call for additional help, isolate and deny entry, conduct hazard and risk assessment, evacuate or shelter in place, and the like.

Chapter 8, Incident-Specific Strategies and Tactics, provided a list of actions to be taken by first responders at the scene of haz mat incidents. These actions should also be taken at emergencies involving terrorism and criminal activity. Once it is confirmed or even suspected that an incident involves terrorism or criminal activity, first responders at both the Awareness and Operational Levels must take some additional actions, including the following:

- *Notify authorities* — Communicate any suspicions of criminal or terrorist intent directly to the telecommunicator. Immediately notify law enforcement authorities, other emergency responders, and EMS personnel. It may be necessary to contact other local, state/provincial, or federal/national agencies and health or medical providers. Assume that any terrorist/criminal incident will eventually require unified command and response from many different agencies from all levels of government **(Figure 9.37).** Call for additional trained and equipped personnel immediately. When explosives are suspected, call

bomb technicians as soon as possible. In terrorist incidents, technical expertise is invaluable and must be summoned quickly.

- *Preserve crime scene evidence* — Realize the incident is a crime scene and coordinate with responding law enforcement officials. Document all initial observations and actions (see Evidence Preservation section).

- *Isolate exposed people and animals* — Ensure that exposed people and animals are properly isolated and decontaminated if possible in order to prevent the spread of secondary contamination. These measures are particularly important when dealing with deadly materials like WMD. Secondary contamination from handling victims/patients is always a concern when dealing with chemical, nuclear/radiological, and biological attacks.

- *Secure the scene* — Coordinate and implement with law enforcement personnel to secure the scene. Take additional security measures at terrorist incidents to ensure the protection and safety of the command post. Conduct careful monitoring of all persons entering or leaving the scene.

- *Take precautions against the possibility of secondary devices* — Always anticipate a secondary device at terrorist incidents, particularly those

Figure 9.37 The FBI has jurisdiction over terrorist incidents in the U.S.

involving explosives. Consider explosive or other hazardous devices being specifically placed to harm emergency response personnel or hinder emergency operations as a definite possibility at any terrorist incident. Address secondary devices both in the development of operational guidelines and during training.

- *Exercise caution concerning other potential hazards associated with terrorist and criminal activities* — Be alert for booby traps, armed resistance, use of weapons, and the like.

NFPA 472: Actions that Awareness-Level First Responders Must Take When Criminal or Terrorist Activity Is Suspected

[NFPA 472: 4.4.1(12)]

Actions are as follows:

- Take the appropriate actions to protect yourself and other responders.

- Communicate the suspicion during the notification process.

- Isolate potentially exposed people or animals.

- Document the initial observation.

- Attempt to preserve evidence while performing duties.

- Be alert for booby traps and/or explosive devices.

- Establish control zones and access control points.

- Prevent secondary contamination, including when handling patients.

Evidence Preservation

[NFPA 472: 5.3.4 (6)] [ODP Awareness IV.a., IV.b., IV.c., IV.d., V.c., V.e.] [ODP Operations IV.a.]

Incidents involving WMD or other illegal activities are crimes, and the locations where they occur are crime scenes **(Figure 9.38)**. It is important for first responders to preserve evidence so that investigators can identify and successfully prosecute guilty parties. The more the scene is disturbed, the more difficult it becomes for investigators to develop a clear and accurate picture of what actually occurred as well as gather accurate, acceptable information about the crime that can be used in court. Even seemingly irrelevant things (footprints, wrapping paper, containers, debris placement, victim locations, vehicles in the vicinity, location of witnesses and bystanders, and the like) can have tremendous significance to forensic experts and other law enforcement investigators.

Evidence can take many forms; it is not limited to pieces of a bomb or an incendiary device. Evidence can include everything from body fluids to tire tracks to cigarette butts **(Figure 9.39)**. The way debris are scattered can tell investigators about the force of an explosion **(Figure 9.40)**. Residue on debris can help identify what explosive materials were used. Clothing and jewelry removed from victims is considered evidence. At illegal clandestine labs, evidence may include such things as fingerprints, weapons, chemical containers, notes, letters, and papers. Evidence can be anything; therefore, responders must — to the degree possible — avoid disturbing a scene.

The preservation of life, of course, is more important than the preservation of evidence. However, even while conducting rescues and other vital operations, responders should do as much as possible to preserve the scene. By following preservation guidelines, first responders can minimize negative effects on the crime scene and greatly assist law enforcement officials in the criminal investigation. As soon as it is known or suspected that criminal or terrorist activity is involved at an incident, first responders should try to follow the following general rules to help preserve evidence and assist law enforcement:

- *DO NOT* touch anything unless it is necessary.

- Avoid disturbing areas not directly involved in rescue activities.

- Remember what the scene looked like upon first arrival as well as details about the progression of the incident. Note as many of the *W's* as possible: *who, what, when, where,* and *why.* If possible, pay attention to the following:

Figure 9.38 Terrorist incidents are crime scenes. Responders should take care to leave the scene as undisturbed as possible.

Figure 9.39 Responders should take measures to preserve evidence that could be disturbed easily such as placing a box over a footprint.

Figure 9.40 An example of evidence marked with tape and circled for better visibility.

— *Who* was present (including victims, people running from the scene, people acting suspiciously, bystanders, potential witnesses, and license plate numbers)

— *What* happened

— *When* important events occurred

— *Where* objects/people/animals were located

— *Why* events unfolded as they did

• Document observations as quickly as possible. While it may be quite some time before responders have the opportunity, the sooner information is written down, the more accurate it will probably be. This documentation may be used as evidence for legal proceedings.

- Take photographs and videos of the scene as soon as possible **(Figure 9.41)**.

- Remember and document when something was touched or moved. Document in the report where it was and where it was placed. Photograph the item before doing anything if possible.

- Minimize the number of people working in the area if possible. Establish travel routes that minimize disturbance.

- Leave fatalities and their surroundings undisturbed.

- Identify witnesses, victims, and the presence of evidence. Investigators will want to interview witnesses and victims as part of their investigations. These witnesses should be advised to remain at the scene in a safe location until they have been interviewed and released.

- Preserve potentially transient physical evidence (evidence present on victims or evidence that may be compromised by weather conditions such as chemical residue, body fluids, or footprints).

- Follow departmental procedures for establishing chain of custody, documentation, and security measures to store crime scene evidence.

Biological Attack Incidents

Before the recognition of and during a recognized disease outbreak caused by an act of biological terrorism, first responders may have had contact with patients who are infected by the biological agent. Most agents of bioterrorism are *not* transmitted from person to person; however, for agents such as smallpox and pneumonic plague, a first responder is at risk of acquiring infection from a patient. Many of the following people are potentially at risk due to occupational exposure during a biological terrorism attack:

- Traditional first responders (police, fire, and EMS personnel) who transport ill patients to medical facilities

- Health-care workers who care for patients in hospitals, residential facilities, outpatient settings, at home, or elsewhere

- Laboratory personnel handling clinical specimens

- Health department staff members who visit patients in or out of health-care facilities while conducting outbreak assessment or control measures

Figure 9.41 Take pictures of the scene as soon as possible, ideally before it becomes disturbed.

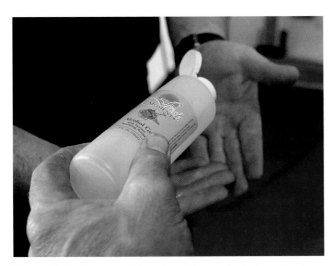

Figure 9.42 The use of hand sanitizers can help protect against biological agents.

To protect responders when the presence or nature of a bioterrorism agent is not known, all workers should adhere to universal precautions whenever they have contact with broken or moist skin, blood, or body fluids. These precautions include using disposable gloves, washing the hands immediately after removing gloves, and using disposable PPE and a face shield if any splashing is anticipated **(Figure 9.42).** Protective gear is changed between patients to prevent the worker from transmitting infection from patient to patient.

Once a specific agent is identified, additional precautions are applied based on the agent's mode of transmission, whether airborne, droplet, or contact. The local health department should be contacted for additional instructions for vaccinations, prophylactic antibiotic therapy, or other measures that may be appropriate for a given disease.

First responders and others involved in out-of-hospital patient transport will be in close proximity to patients during transport. They should comply with the infection-control guidelines described and take the following additional precautions:

- Operate the ambulance ventilation system on its highest setting, using outside air circulation to maximize air changes in the vehicle.

- Ensure that patients wear a surgical mask, disposable respirator (one without an exhalation valve) or, if needed for respiratory support, an

oxygen mask that does not exhaust to ambient air for diseases that are transmitted by respiratory transmission (droplet or aerosol).

- Know the different levels of worker respiratory protection that are required when transporting patients with different diseases.

When determining the need for decon in a biological setting, balance the risk that it poses to the patient against the benefits it could provide. Unless gross contamination is evident, decon is probably unwarranted. Instead, begin by removing clothes and placing them in a plastic bag pending agent identification. Taking a shower with soap and water should prevent illness. Where gross contamination is found, only those areas of the skin that have been grossly contaminated should be decontaminated. When the involved agent is unknown and could be either a chemical agent or biological agent, follow patient decon procedures for chemical agents (see Chemical Agent Incidents section).

Nuclear/Radiological Incidents

If a nuclear bomb has detonated, local first responders will probably be overwhelmed by the scale and scope of the disaster facing them. That fact does not mean that they cannot or should not take appropriate action. Outside assistance will undoubtedly be needed to successfully mitigate the incident. Communication, transportation, water supplies, and resources may be limited or nonexistent. The number of casualties and destruction may be overwhelming. When an organized response is possible, the same framework for any emergency response should be applied with special consideration given to nuclear/radiological hazards.

Response to a small radiological incident is more likely to be similar to the response to other emergency incidents. For example, a response to an attack on a shipment of radioactive materials would essentially be the same as that discussed in Chapter 8, Incident-Specific Strategies and Tactics, Radioactive Materials (Class 7) section, with additional consideration given to secondary devices and evidence preservation.

In the case of an attack with a dirty bomb, it may not be immediately evident that radiological materials are involved. **In this age of terrorism, emergency response agencies should include**

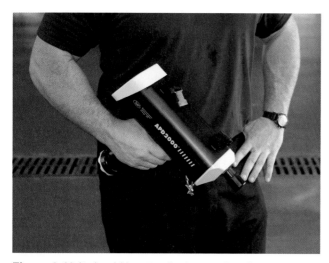

Figure 9.43 It should be standard procedure for responders to check for radiation at the scene of any explosion.

radiation monitoring as a normal part of response to any fire and/or explosion incident. The use of radiological monitoring equipment is the only sure way to confirm the presence of a radiological hazard **(Figure 9.43).**

When radiation or contamination is detected at the scene of a fire or explosion, first responders must act accordingly and modify their plan of action in response to this hazard. The scene must be treated as a hazardous materials incident, including consideration of wind and plume spread. The scale may be much smaller, but the same problems with radioactive dust and the need for protection will exist as with nuclear bomb incidents. The following are some considerations/actions to take during nuclear/radiological terrorist incidents:

● Use radiation and contamination survey instruments to determine radiation levels.

● Use the principles of time, distance, and shielding to protect against radiation exposure.

● Stay away from ground zero. Enter the surrounding area only to save lives. Radiation levels may be very high in these areas.

● Establish control zones like other incidents. If possible, do the following:

— Establish a perimeter based on radiation levels determined by monitoring.

— Remember that plumes of radioactive particles and dust can travel long distances when carried on the wind.

— Map the areas leading to the highest dose rates.

— Enter the high-dose rate areas only when necessary to save a life.

— Make these entries into high-dose rate areas as short as possible.

— Rotate the personnel who make entries into high-dose rate areas.

— Use time, distance, and shielding for protection.

● Isolate, evacuate, and/or shelter the public in place as appropriate.

● Wear respiratory protection to reduce the dose from inhalation of radioactive dust. Ideally, wear self-contained breathing apparatus (SCBA) or a respirator with a high-efficiency particulate air (HEPA) filter.

● Wear PPE. Standard firefighting gear or easily removed outer clothing is sufficient to protect from alpha and beta radiation, but it may not protect against other environmental hazards. Remember that none of the levels of PPE discussed in Chapter 6, Personal Protective Equipment, will protect against gamma or neutron radiation.

● Avoid skin contact with radioactive dust. Protect open wounds or abrasions from radioactive contamination by covering them.

● Do not eat, drink, chew, or smoke while exposed to potentially radioactive dust or smoke. When it is absolutely necessary to drink water, drink from a canteen or other closed container.

● Remember that physical injuries are more serious than radioactive contamination. Deal with life-threatening conventional injuries first.

● Decontaminate.

The types of contaminant, number of casualties, and types and quantity of equipment determine the type of decon operation to establish. Possible types of decon to use at nuclear/radiological incidents are as follows:

● *Wet decon* — Flush with large amounts of water; contain and control contaminated run-off.

● *Dry decon* — Remove clothing and/or remove contamination/dust with tape. Inhalation of contaminated particles is a major concern with dry decon, and personnel in the decon line must wear appropriate respiratory protection. Do not dry brush someone who is contaminated.

- *Secondary decon* — Follows dry decon.

Patients are not likely to die immediately from radiation exposure, so priority must be given to treating conventional, physical injuries. Hospitals must be prepared for the arrival of contaminated patients. As with a biological or chemical attack, many patients may transport themselves to local hospitals without being decontaminated at the scene.

Incendiary Incidents

[ODP Operations IV.a.]

Only specially trained personnel (such as bomb technicians and arson investigators) should handle incendiary devices discovered before ignition. Handling of such devices by inexperienced individuals can result in ignition and possible injury or death. After ignition, first responders should initiate actions appropriate to their training and the situation (calling for additional help, isolating the area, extinguishing any fire, and the like). Additionally, when it is suspected that an incendiary device started a fire, proper handling of potential evidence is critical for crime scene preservation.

Chemical Agent Incidents

Essentially, this entire book is dedicated to the purpose of educating first responders on how to appropriately respond to chemical incidents, including chemical attacks. Chemical warfare agents, particularly the nerve agents, are especially dangerous because they are specifically designed to kill people. If first responders rush in without taking appropriate precautions and wearing appropriate PPE, they may easily become victims themselves.

Other special considerations must be given to decon. Very little time is available to successfully conduct decon after skin contact with nerve agents and vesicants (perhaps 2 to 3 minutes at most). According to the report, *Guidelines for Mass Casualty Decontamination During a Terrorist Chemical Agent Incident*, prepared by the U.S.

Army Soldier and Biological Chemical Command (SBCCOM), the following general principles should guide emergency responders during a chemical agent incident:

- Expect at least a 5:1 ratio of unaffected to affected casualties.

- Decontaminate victims as soon as possible.

- Disrobe from head to toe to decontaminate successfully. The more clothing that can be removed, the better.

- Flush with water; generally this is the best mass decon method.

- Decontaminate emergency responders after a known exposure to liquid chemical agent as soon as possible to avoid serious effects.

The rapid physical removal of chemical agent from a victim is the single most important action associated with effective decon. Physical removal includes the following actions:

- Scrape or blot visible agent from the skin.

- Disrobe.

- Use adsorbents to soak up the agent.

- Flush or shower with large quantities of water **(Figure 9.44, p. 504).**

After a chemical agent attack, vapor or aerosol hazards may still be present for some time, especially if the agent was disseminated within an enclosed structure. Furthermore, potentially toxic levels of chemical agent vapor may be trapped inside clothes and could continue to affect people, even after they leave the incident site.

Since the most important aspect of decon is the timely and effective removal of the agent, the precise methods used to remove the agent are not nearly as important as the speed by which the agent is removed. From scientific literature showing the effectiveness of different types of solutions in preventing chemical effects and the widespread, ready availability of large quantities of water that can be rapidly used in decontaminating large numbers of people, the current thought is that mass decon can be most readily and effectively accomplished with a water shower system such as that detailed in Chapter 7, Contamination and Decontamination.

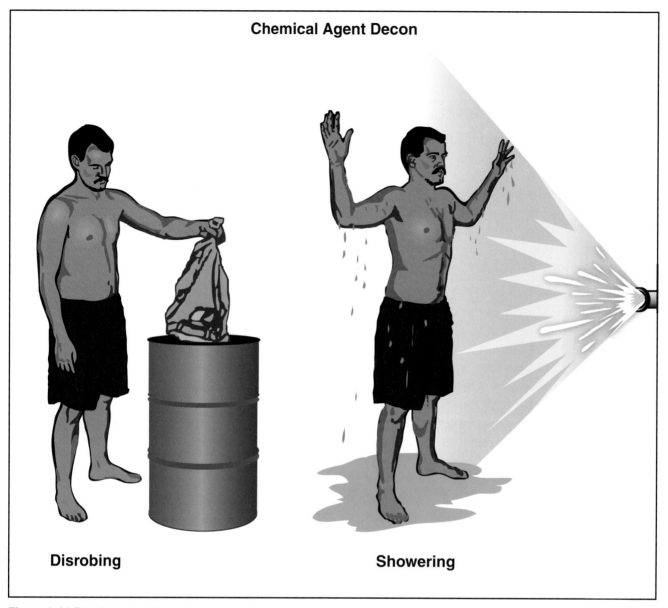

Chemical Agent Decon

Disrobing

Showering

Figure 9.44 Disrobing and showering are two of the most important elements of chemical agent decon.

Decon must be conducted as soon as possible to save lives **(Figure 9.45)**. Emergency responders should use resources that are immediately available and start as soon as possible. The most expedient approach may be to use currently available fire-fighting equipment to provide an emergency low-pressure deluge. The following forms of water-based decon may be considered:

- *Water alone* — Flushing or showering uses shear force and dilution to physically remove chemical agent from skin. Water alone is an excellent decon solution. The strongest recommendation is to rapidly use water, either with or without soap. The process should never be delayed to add soap or any other additive.

- *Soap and water* — By adding soap, a marginal improvement in results can be achieved by ionic degradation of the chemical agent. Soap aids in dissolving oily substances like mustard or blis-

Figure 9.45 First responders should direct victims to locations for mass decon as quickly as possible without causing panic. *Courtesy of Rich Mahaney.*

ter agent. Liquid soaps act quicker than solids and reduce the need for mechanical scrubbing. When scrubbing, potential victims should not abrade the skin. Disadvantages of soap:

— Need to have an adequate supply on hand

— Extra time may be spent using it

— May hydrate the skin, possibly increasing damage by blister agents

- *Bleach and water* — Bleach (sodium hypochlorite) and water solutions remove, hydrolyze, and neutralize most chemical agents. This approach is not recommended in a mass decon situation where speed is the paramount consideration for the following reasons:

— Commercial bleach must be diluted and applied with equipment not generally available to fire and emergency services responders.

— Skin contact time is excessive. Laboratory studies show that chemical agents and relatively nontoxic, aqueous decontaminants may need to be in contact with skin for durations longer than expected shower durations for significant reactions to occur.

— Laboratory studies suggest that bleach solutions at the 0.5 percent level may not be better than flushing with water alone.

— Medically, bleach solutions are not recommended for use near eyes or mucous membranes or those with abdominal, thoracic, or neural wounds.

Removing clothes and flushing or showering with water is the most expedient and the most practical method for mass casualty decon. Disrobing and showering meets all the purposes and principles of decon. Showering is recommended whenever liquid transfer from clothing to skin is suspected. Disrobing should occur before showering for chemical agents; however, the decision to require disrobing should be made by the IC based upon the situation. Wetting down casualties as they start to disrobe speeds the decon process and is recommended for decontaminating biological or radiological casualties. However, this process may cause the following unwanted results:

- Force chemical agents through the clothing if water pressure is too high

- Decrease the potential effectiveness of directly showering skin afforded by shear forces and dilution

- Relocate chemical agent within the actual showering area, thereby increasing the chance of contamination spread through personal contact and shower water runoff

The SBCCOM report recommends that victims remove clothing at least down to their undergarments before showering. Victims should be encouraged to remove as much clothing as possible, proceeding from head to toe. Victims unwilling to disrobe should shower clothed before leaving the decon area **(Figure 9.46)**. It is also recommended that emergency responders use a high volume of water delivered at a minimum of 60 psi (414 kPa) {4.14 bar} water pressure to ensure the showering process physically removes viscous agent. Standard household shower water pressures usually average between 60 to 90 psi (414 kPa to 620 kPa) {4.14 bar to 6.2 bar}. The actual showering time is an incident-specific decision but may be as long as 2 to 3 minutes per individual under ideal situations. When large numbers of potential casualties are involved and queued for decon, showering time may be significantly shortened. This time may also depend upon the volume of water available in the showering facilities.

In the course of decontaminating victims, first responders may inadvertently become contaminated. High-pressure, low-volume decon showers are recommended primarily for wet decon of emergency responders in Level A suits after a haz mat incident. This gross decon procedure forcibly removes the contaminant from the PPE worn by emergency responders while conserving water. Often a secondary wash and possibly a tertiary wash and rinse station are used. It is possible that high water pressure could force chemical agents through the victim's clothing onto the skin. The Occupational Safety and Health Administration (OSHA) standard for a chemical accident — high-volume, low-pressure — is the recommended method.

Explosives/Bomb Incidents

[ODP Operations III.i.]

As soon as it is determined that an explosive device is or was involved in an incident, first responders should request emergency assistance from bomb technicians and law enforcement **(Figure 9.47)**. When one device has been found or activated, secondary devices (specifically designed to kill and maim emergency responders) are also concerns. Emergency scenes involving bombs are also crime scenes. Agencies or individuals that may be called for this type of assistance should be identified in the local emergency response plan and may include the following:

• Local bomb technicians if available

• State Bureaus of Investigation (SBI)

• Explosives ordnance detachments (military)

Safety overrides all other concerns. First responders must take steps to identify and remove or mitigate safety hazards that may further threaten victims, bystanders, and public safety personnel. As with other haz mat incidents, first responders should act to evacuate the area, isolate, and deny entry. They must call for additional assistance as necessary. Hazard/risk assessments must include

Figure 9.46 Victims should be encouraged to remove as much clothing as possible. However, if they are unwilling to disrobe, they should shower clothed. *Courtesy of Rich Mahaney.*

Figure 9.47 Law enforcement personnel and bomb technicians should be contacted any time explosives are involved in an incident.

the consideration of possible secondary devices. It is also important for first responders to preserve evidence at bomb scenes (see Evidence Preservation section).

Don't Get Blown Up!

Some safety rules to keep in mind at incidents involving explosive devices are as follows:

- **NEVER touch or handle a suspected device, even if someone else already has.** Only certified, trained bomb technicians should touch, move, defuse, or otherwise handle explosive devices.

- **ALWAYS assume that there is more than one device present.** Secondary devices are often planted to target emergency responders.

- **Put a safe distance between you and any suspected devices.** Evacuate and deny entry.

- **DO NOT attempt to fight a fire if explosives are involved.** Isolate the area and protect exposures. The isolation distance depends on the conditions present and the type of materials. Prepare to isolate the area for distances up to at least 1 mile (1.6 km) in all directions.

- **Stay away from windows.** Shattering glass can be lethal in an explosion.

- **Stay low.**

- **Shield yourself.** Put a wall, response vehicle, tree, or other solid object between you and a bomb. Remember that other vehicles may contain secondary devices.

Illegal Clandestine Labs and Dumps

Illegal clandestine labs and dumps are both crime scenes and haz mat scenes, and first responders must act accordingly. Fire and EMS personnel must protect evidence, while law enforcement personnel must take measures to protect themselves from exposure to the hazards presented by the lab or dump involved. Because this situation is typically a law enforcement issue, that agency will be in charge of the incident. However, in some locations, a unified command may be used.

The type of lab and the hazards present determine the PPE needed for safe operation. Operations at a small explosives lab, for example, may not need respiratory equipment, whereas Level A suits may be needed at meth labs. A significant problem with meth labs is that, historically, their hazards have been underestimated. Biological labs will not usually present a respiratory hazard, but that situation may not always be the case. Caution is advised, particularly when dealing with unknown etiological agents.

Decon may be necessary for all personnel who enter the scene as well as for any patients and/or persons taken into custody. Law enforcement personnel must understand that their weapons need to be decontaminated. Fire and emergency services personnel must understand that it is not necessary to drop weapons into a bucket of soapy water. Weapons can undergo dry decon at a later time. Advance planning is needed to make operations at illegal clandestine lab incidents run smoothly.

If an illegal clandestine lab is involved in fire, it may be best to let it burn while protecting surrounding structures. As with pesticide storage facilities, the fire will destroy most of the toxic materials. If the fire is extinguished, attention must be given to the containment of highly toxic runoff. If the structure is saved, it must then be decontaminated from the remaining toxic materials.

Summary

Unfortunately, the likelihood that emergency responders will someday be called upon to respond to a terrorist or criminal incident is higher than ever before. Responders need to be vigilant, considering the possibility of terrorist or criminal involvement at every incident. For example, if an emergency is reported as an explosion, it is recommended that radiation monitoring be conducted in case a dirty bomb is involved. A fire at a single dwelling occupancy could involve a meth lab. An unusual number of unexplained illnesses could be caused by a biological attack.

Responders must be familiar with the indications of terrorist attack as well as the hazards associated with the materials used in illegal drug labs. Law enforcement responders must be aware of criminal laws as well as privacy and security issues related to terrorist events. Furthermore, they need to know how to protect themselves as well as preserve evidence. Identify likely terrorist targets. Finally, all agencies that might be involved in a terrorist attack should work together to conduct practice drills or training exercises in order to improved the response to a real emergency.

Appendix A
OSHA Plan States

OSHA State-Plan States and Non-state-Plan States

State-Plan States	Non-state-Plan States
Alaska	Alabama
Arizona	Arkansas
California	Colorado
Connecticut (state and local government employees only)	Delaware
Hawaii	District of Columbia
Indiana	Florida
Iowa	Georgia
Kentucky	Guam
Maryland	Idaho
Michigan	Illinois
Minnesota	Kansas
Nevada	Louisiana
New Mexico	Maine
New York (state and local government employees only)	Massachusetts
North Carolina	Mississippi
Oregon	Missouri
Puerto Rico	Montana
South Carolina	Nebraska
Tennessee	New Hampshire
Utah	New Jersey
Vermont	North Dakota
Virginia	Ohio
Virgin Islands	Oklahoma
Washington	Pennsylvania
Wyoming	Rhode Island
	South Dakota
	Texas
	West Virginia
	Wisconsin

Appendix B
Sample Standard Operating Guideline

TUALATIN VALLEY FIRE AND RESCUE
INCIDENT COMMAND MANUAL

SERIES 300X

OPERATIONAL GUIDELINE
HAZARDOUS MATERIALS RESPONSE

PURPOSE

To provide a standard by which companies trained to the "First Responder Operations" level respond to hazardous materials incidents.

DEFINITIONS

First Responder - Operations - A level of training for first responders to hazardous materials incidents, required by federal and state law; as defined in Oregon Administrative Rule (OAR) 437-01-100(q).

Full Protective Clothing - As it relates to hazardous materials response, full protective clothing means turnouts and SCBA.

On-Scene Commander - A level of training for Incident Commanders on hazardous materials incidents, required by federal and state law; as defined by OAR 437-01-100(q).

Responsible Party - Federal and state regulators assign responsibility for incident clean-up (and costs) to the party who is responsible for the hazardous materials incident (i.e., a fixed facility, transportation agent, etc.).

HMRT - Hazardous Materials Response Team.

Hazardous Materials Group Supervisor (HMRT Leader) - HazMat Group Supervisor reports to the Incident Commander (or Operations Section Chief, if staffed) and is responsible for hazardous materials tactical operations. The HazMat Group Supervisor position is staffed by the Hazardous Materials Response Team Leader.

*   Emergency Response Guidebook - North American Emergency Response Guidebook; formerly "DOT Emergency Response Guidebook".

PROCEDURES
I.   TRAINING REQUIREMENTS

A.   All response personnel must meet the training requirements for "First Responder – Operations" level.

B.   Incident Commanders on hazardous materials incidents must meet the training requirements for "On-Scene Commander".

II. INCIDENT COMMANDER

A. All incidents involving hazardous materials in a spill, release or fire, may require an Incident Commander trained to the "On-Scene Commander" level. All Battalion Chiefs and ICs on the Overhead Team are trained and required to maintain qualifications to the "On-Scene Commander" level.

B. The Incident Commander may call for a full or partial HMRT response if incident mitigation is beyond the training and capabilities of a company response. The IC may also call for technical assistance from the HMRT without a response to the incident site, if the situation warrants.

III. COMPANY FUNCTIONS

A. Companies will respond for the purpose of protecting nearby persons, property or the environment from a hazardous materials release.

B. Companies will respond in a *defensive* fashion without coming in contact with the release or taking actions to stop a release that would place them in danger of contact.

C. The primary function of the Operations level responder is to contain the release from a safe distance, keeping it from spreading and protect exposures. The basic functions are:
- isolate the hazard area and control access
- hazard and risk assessment
- basic control, containment and/or confinement procedures appropriate to the level of training and personal protective clothing and equipment.

D. Companies will not take any actions on hazardous materials incidents that cannot be safely performed in full protective clothing.

IV. HAZARDOUS MATERIALS RESPONSE AND OPERATIONS

A. While enroute to the scene:

1. Contact Fire Comm and obtain available information regarding:
   a. The nature of the incident, e.g., fixed facility, transportation related. etc.
   b. The type of product(s) involved, if known.
   c. The best direction for approaching the scene from upwind, upgrade and upstream.
   d. Who is on-scene that may have information on the nature of the incident.
   e. Any information on the incident conditions that may be known and can be provided while enroute to the incident scene.

* 2. The HazMat Team may be contacted via Fire Comm for technical assistance or response, as appropriate.

3. Approach the incident scene with caution.
   a. Approach the incident scene from upwind, upgrade, upstream or at a right angle to the wind direction and/or gradient.
   b. Consider escape routes. Be aware of situations that require entering areas with egress restrictions, such as fenced compounds.

        c.   Position vehicle/apparatus headed away from the incident scene at a safe distance.

B.   On Arrival

    1.   Establish Command and give size-up.

    2.   Establish a Unified Command if multiple agencies/jurisdictions are involved.

    3.   Ensure a qualified "On-Scene Commander" (i.e., Battalion Chief) is enroute to the scene.

    4.   Continuously evaluate need for HazMat Team technical assistance or response.

C.   Establish Safe Zone and Control Access

    1.   Determine the hazard area and establish the Hot Zone, Warm Zone and Cold Zone boundaries.
        a.   Based on initial observations, identify a safe distance for initial incident isolation to begin. Some recommendations include:
- Single drum, not leaking - minimum 150' in all directions
- Single drum, leaking - 500' in all directions
- Tank car or tank truck with BLEVE potential - half mile in all directions

        b.   Isolate and deny entry to:
- The general public
- Anyone not in proper protective clothing and equipment
- Anyone without a specific assignment

    2.   Establish the Command Post in the Cold Zone.

    3.   Identify and establish the Staging Area location in the Cold Zone.

    4.   Communicate the Zone information, Command Post and Staging Area locations to Fire Comm and incoming units.

    5.   Determine a safe approach for incoming units and direct them to locations at the Safe Zone Perimeter that will facilitate isolation of the incident, i.e., intersections to block and re-direct traffic, etc. All others should be directed to the Staging Area until assigned.

    6.   Request police assistance as needed to:
        a.   Handle Cold Zone Perimeter control to relieve fire units for incident mitigation.
        b.   Handle public evacuations.
        c.   Handle public notification for sheltering in place

    7.   While isolating the incident scene:
        a.   Treat all vapor clouds as being toxic and handle accordingly.
        b.   Do not walk into, through or touch any spilled materials.
        c.   Observe local on-site weather and wind conditions and adjust accordingly.
        d.   Position at a safe distance and utilize your binoculars!

*   D.   Attempt to Identify the Product.

       If the product is *known*, proceed to Section V and isolate in accordance with appropriate Emergency Response Guidebook recommendations. Record observations on the hazmat incident worksheet. (Provide the diagram to the incoming Battalion Chief or HazMat Response Team.)

       If the product is *unknown*, from a safe distance attempt to gather as much information as possible.

       Use Emergency Response Guide #111 isolation recommendations until the material is identified. Record observations on the hazmat incident worksheet.

1. Life Safety is the number one priority. Do not rush into the scene to effect a rescue without first identifying the hazards.

2. Attempt to identify outward warning signs that are indicators of the presence of hazardous materials. These include:
    a. Individuals that have collapsed or are vomiting inside the hazardous area (HMRT response).
    b. Any evidence of fire, as indicated by smoke, greatly increases all hazards.
    c. A loud roar of increasing pitch from a container's operating relief valve (HMRT response).
    d. Evidence of a leak, indicated by a hissing sound.
    e. Birds and insects falling out of the sky (HMRT response).

AND/OR

3. Attempt to identify the material(s) involved by using:
    a. Placards/labels
    b. Container markings
    c. Driver/operator provided information including shipping papers.

4. After determining product:
    a. Perform rescue, if needed, using safety guidelines related to that product.
    b. Re-evaluate distances for isolated area.

5. Communicate your observations to Fire Comm.

6. Anticipate shifting winds when establishing perimeters; consult with the weather service to obtain accurate forecasts of changes that might impact your incident scene and perimeters.

7. Eliminate ignition sources if flammable materials are involved. Remember that non-flammable materials, such as anhydrous ammonia are, in fact, flammable, so always identify if the product has a flammable range.

8. Request additional fire, law enforcement and public works resources, as needed, to secure the incident scene and maintain perimeter control.

*   9. If large dikes and dams need to be built to control spill, consider requisition for heavy equipment and/or assistance of public works resources.

E. Conduct a Risk/Benefit Analysis which includes asking the following questions in relation to the incident you are addressing:

1. What would the outcome be if we did absolutely nothing and allowed the incident to go through natural stabilization?

2. Once you have identified the outcomes of natural stabilization, the next question you should ask is "Can we change the outcomes of natural stabilization?"

3. If the answer to this question is "NO", then isolate the hazard area, deny entry, and protect exposures such as people, the environment and adjacent property/equipment.

4. If the answer to this question is "YES", then the next question to ask is "What is the cost of my intervention?"

IF THE INCIDENT COMMANDER DETERMINES DEFENSIVE OPERATIONS CAN STABILIZE/ CONTAIN THE INCIDENT *AND* IT CAN BE DONE IN FULL PROTECTIVE CLOTHING (TURNOUTS AND SCBA), THE IC SHALL CONDUCT OPERATIONS IN ACCORDANCE WITH THE "DEFENSIVE OPERATIONAL GUIDELINES".

V. DEFENSIVE OPERATIONAL GUIDELINES

A. Attempt to stop/slow/control leak using defensive techniques (such as turning off a valve, etc.).

B. If the leak cannot be stopped, utilize an appropriate containment procedure to prevent the material from flowing and increasing the exposed surface area (i.e., using dirt or absorbent).

VI. DECONTAMINATION: Perform field decontamination as directed by the Incident Commander and/or HazMat Response Team.

NOTE: *ALL CONTAMINATED PATIENTS MUST BE DECONTAMINATED OR PACKAGED FOR TRANSPORT IN A WAY TO PREVENT CONTAMINATION OF TRANSPORT UNITS AND HOSPITALS.*

VII. CLEAN-UP

A. If the incident is on a roadway or public access area, the Incident Commander must ensure that a public safety agency (coordinate with law enforcement officials, if available) remains on-scene to continue isolation procedures and standby until the clean-up company arrives.

B. If a responsible party is not on-scene and making arrangements for clean-up and disposal, contact the on-duty HMRT Team Leader for further instructions.

NOTE: *FIRE DEPARTMENT PERSONNEL SHALL NOT ENGAGE IN CLEAN-UP OPERATIONS. THE APPROPRIATE ROLE IS CONTAINMENT/ STABILIZATION. DO NOT TAKE HAZARDOUS MATERIALS FROM AN INCIDENT TO ANY FIRE DISTRICT FACILITY.*

VIII. CONDUCT TERMINATION PROCEDURES

A.   Prior to the demobilization and release of any equipment from the scene, conduct a debriefing of all response personnel (including cooperating agencies).

B.   An effective debriefing should:

       1.   Inform *all responders* exactly what hazardous materials were involved and the accompanying signs and symptoms of exposure.

       2.   Provide information for personal exposure records.

       3.   Identify equipment damage and unsafe conditions requiring immediate attention or isolation for further evaluation.

       4.   Conduct a post-incident analysis and critique. This may be done at the station.

HAZARDOUS MATERIALS RESPONSE
CHECKLIST

CHECKLIST USE

The checklist should be considered as a minimum requirement for this position. Users of this manual should feel free to augment this list as necessary. Note that some activities are one-time actions and others are on-going or repetitive for the duration of an incident.

____ While enroute to the scene, you may utilize the HazMat Team as a technical resource (contact via Fire Comm).

____ Approach incident cautiously, uphill, upwind, park headed away from incident, consider escape routes.

____ Establish Command.

____ Establish and maintain site access control. Establish initial Zones (Hot: min. of 150'; warm; cold). Establish Command Post and Staging locations.

____ Attempt to identify materials involved by using placards/labels, container markings, shipping papers and driver provided information. Use Guide #111 if spilled product is unknown.

____ Perform rescue only when the rescue operation can be done safely.

____ Request additional fire, law enforcement and public works resources as needed. Consider requisition for heavy equipment.

____ Conduct risk/benefit analysis.

____ If the Incident Commander determines defensive operations can stabilize/contain the incident, conduct defensive operations.
  • Attempt to stop/slow/control leak using defensive techniques (such as turning off a valve, etc.).
  • If the leak cannot be stopped, utilize an appropriate containment procedure to prevent the material from flowing and increasing the exposed surface area.

____ Perform field decontamination as directed by the Incident Commander.

____ Clean-Up
   If the incident is on a roadway or public access area, the Incident Commander must ensure that a public safety agency remains on-scene to continue isolation procedures and standby until the clean-up company arrives. If the responsible party is not on-scene and making arrangements for clean-up and disposal, contact the on-duty HMRT Team Leader for further instructions.

   NOTE: Fire Department personnel shall not engage in clean-up operations.

____ Prior to the demobilization and release of any equipment from the scene, conduct a debriefing of all response personnel (including cooperating agencies).

Appendix C
Emergency Response Plans

Title III of the Superfund Amendments and Re-authorization Act (commonly referred to as *SARA Title III*) of 1986 required jurisdictions in the U.S. to develop a local emergency response plan (LERP) for hazardous materials incidents. The LERP is developed by a local emergency planning committee (LEPC), which is composed of representatives from the following groups:

- Emergency response agencies
- Local and state agencies: government, emergency management, and transportation
- Health community
- The media
- Environmental groups
- Industry

When developing the LERP, the LEPC must address the following areas:

- Hazardous materials facilities and transportation routes
- Methods and procedures for handling hazardous materials incidents
- Methods of warning people at risk
- Hazardous materials equipment and information resources
- Evacuation plans
- Training of first responders
- Schedule for exercising the LERP

There is no legislation in Canada that is comparable to SARA Title III; however, local response agencies are required to develop plans that are similar to those used in the U.S. The Canadian plans are referred to as *emergency measures organization (EMO) plans.* These plans basically cover the same information that LERPs do in the U.S. For consistency in presentation, the term *LERP* is used throughout this appendix, and Canadian first responders should remember that this plan is the same as an EMO plan.

When the plan is complete, copies must be made available to all agencies and first responders. First responders must become familiar with the plan and its location. Because written copies of the actual plan are too bulky to be easily used at a response, first responders should carry a checklist of initial actions to take. First responders should thoroughly understand their organization's predetermined procedures.

The following sections of this appendix provide an expanded history of the Emergency Planning and Community Right-to-Know Act (EPCRA) (also known as *SARA Title III*) and the LEPC, a summary of EPCRA requirements (including the creation of emergency response plans), an explanation of emergency management planning, and risk management plans. All these elements tie into the concept of emergency response plans and how and why they are created.

History of SARA Title III and the LEPC

The National Response Team (NRT) was created in 1970 to assist in incidents involving chemical releases when the incident exceeded the capabilities of a region, when an incident affected two or more regions, or when an incident affected national security or presented a major hazard to a substantial number of people. In 1984, the NRT conducted a survey to access preparedness and response capabilities at the federal, state, and local levels. The survey revealed contingency plans were often poorly prepared or totally lacking. Training was limited, and first responders were frustrated by the low priority given to emergency response training. The survey found capacity varied greatly from state to state. Many states had limited amounts of response equipment. The survey also revealed some problems with equipment availability.

Soon after the survey was distributed, the question of preparedness took on increased importance as the disastrous consequences of chemical accidents were demonstrated by the accident in Bhopal, India, where a release of methyl isocyanate killed over 2,000 people and injured approximately 10,000. A subsequent release of aldicarb oxime in Institute, West Virginia, intensified concern in the U.S. This incident sent more than 100 people to the hospital and made Americans aware that such incidents can and do happen in the U.S.

A bill was drafted to establish planning districts, require reporting of certain toxic chemicals, and make information available to the public from facilities using, storing, and manufacturing chemicals in communities. The Comprehensive Environmental Response, Compensation, and Liability Act (CERCLA) (referred to as the *Superfund Act*) of 1980 was scheduled for reauthorization. This act addressed the problems of hazardous substance releases and provided the authority to clean up hazardous substance releases that affected any environmental media. It is often easier to add to a bill that is assured passage or add something to an existing law that is being reauthorized than to pass a new law. The new bill drafted to address the concerns noted in the NRT survey was known as the Emergency Planning and Community Right-to-Know Bill. The U.S. Congress enacted the EPCRA in 1986 by adding it to the CERCLA Reauthorization Act, and it became known as *SARA Title III* (it was the third article in the Act).

The EPCRA of 1986 was passed by Congress, signed by the President, and became effective on October 17, 1987. It required the governor of each state to appoint a State Emergency Response Commission (SERC). The SERC was required to designate planning districts in order to facilitate preparation and implementation of emergency plans. The governors were permitted to organize the planning districts anyway they desired. Some governors designated the entire state as the planning district; others designated a county as the local planning district. Some states allowed cities to become the planning district, cities within a county to form a district, and other combinations. The SERC was required to appoint members to a LEPC to develop the plan for the planning district.

EPCRA was an unfunded, mandated law that caused a financial hardship on many jurisdictions. The Act had two primary purposes: (1) Ensure that jurisdictions planned for chemical emergencies, including training, response, and exercising. (2) Provide public access to chemical information at facilities stored in their communities.

Some LEPCs have few members (below 10), and others have many (some reporting over 100). The Act required the SERC to appoint certain professional representatives from designated groups or organizations that include the following:

- Elected *state* officials
- Elected *local* officials
- Law enforcement
- Civil defense
- Firefighters or emergency responders
- First aid groups
- Health professionals
- Local environmental groups
- Hospital personnel
- Transportation personnel
- Broadcast and print media
- Community groups
- Owners and operators of facilities subject to the requirements

EPCRA Requirements

EPCRA has many requirements that affect LEPCs and emergency planning. Some of these requirements result in the creation of reports and other documents that can be used by emergency responders to plan for emergencies at the facilities in their areas. The following sections detail various sections of the law that directly affect emergency services.

Substance and Facilities Covered and Notification

Section 302 requires facilities to report chemicals on the Extremely Hazardous Substances (EHS) List if they exceed their threshold planning quantity (TPQ) (quantity in pounds that must be reported for planning purposes). These chemicals were chosen because of their extremely toxic properties. Originally 366 chemicals were on the EHS List, and this number varies from time to time, but it usually remains close to that original number. This list of chemicals and their TPQs are listed in Title 40 (Protection of Environment) *CFR* 355, *Emergency Planning and Notification*, Appendices A and B.

Comprehensive Emergency Response

Section 303 requires that the LEPC complete an emergency plan that must be reviewed at least once a year or more frequently if circumstance change in the community. It also requires the LEPC to evaluate the need for resources necessary to develop, implement, and exercise the emergency plan and make recommendations with respect to additional resources that may be required along with the means for providing additional resources. The emergency response plan must include the following nine provisions:

1. Identifications
   - Location of facilities reporting the TPQ of EHS
   - Routes likely to be used for transportation of EHS
   - Facilities contributing or subjected to additional risk because they are located close to these facilities

2. Methods and procedures to be followed by facility owners and operators and local emergency and medical personnel who respond to any release of such substances

3. Designation of a community emergency coordinator and facility emergency coordinators who shall make determinations necessary to implement the plan

4. Procedures providing reliable, effective, and timely notification by the facility emergency coordinators and the community emergency coordinator to persons designated in the emergency plan and the public that a release has occurred

5. Methods for determining the occurrence of a release and the area or population likely to be affected by such releases

6. Description of emergency equipment and facilities in the community and at each facility in the community subject to these requirements and an identification of the persons responsible for such equipment and facilities

7. Evacuation plans, including provisions for a precautionary evacuation and alternative traffic routes

8. Training programs, including schedules for training of local emergency response and medical personnel

9. Methods and schedules for exercising the emergency plans

Emergency Notification

CERCLA substances are hazardous substances listed under the Superfund hazardous waste cleanup regulations. The current list contains about 720 substances. Section 304 requires reporting of any release of reportable quantities (RQ) (listed on shipping papers) of CERCLA chemicals and EHS List chemicals to the LEPC with the following conditions:

1. Release must result in exposure to persons solely outside the site or sites on which a facility is located

2. Notification shall be given immediately after the release by the owner or operator of a facility to the community emergency coordinator

3. Release must also be reported to the SERC

4. Notification of chemical releases involving transportation can be made by dialing 9-1-1 (or the operator when 9-1-1 service does not exist)

Initial and follow-up notice of a RQ chemical release is required. Notification is not delayed even if the full extent of the release is not known. Initial reporting requirements are as follows:

- Chemical names or identity of any substance involved in a release

- Indication of whether the substance is on the CERCLA List or EHS List
- Estimate of the quantity of substance that was released into the environment
- Time and duration of release
- Medium or media into which the release occurred
- Any known or anticipated acute or chronic health risks associated with the emergency and advice regarding medical attention necessary for exposed individuals where appropriate
- Proper precautions to take as a result of the release, including evacuations
- Name and telephone number of the person to be contacted for further information

Emergency Training and Review of Emergency Systems

Section 305 requires federal, state, and local governments to provide training to emergency responders. The U.S. Occupational safety and Health Administration (OSHA) developed training requirements for the states that were under its authority. The U.S. Environmental Protection Agency (EPA) adopted the same regulations for the non-OSHA states.

Material Safety Data Sheets

Section 311 requires the owner or operator of any facility that is required to prepare or have available a material safety data sheet (MSDS) for a hazardous chemical under the Occupational Safety and Health Act of 1970 to submit a MSDS for each such chemical (or a list of such chemicals) to the LEPC, SERC, and the fire department with jurisdiction over the facility. It should be noted that not all LEPCs request or desire to have MSDSs because of the lack of storage space. The probability that someone will request a MSDS is remote, but LEPCs are required to furnish one to any person making a request.

Emergency and Hazardous Chemical Inventory Forms

Section 312 requires the owner or operator of any facility that is required to prepare or have available a MSDS for a hazardous chemical under OSHA to also prepare and submit an emergency and hazardous chemical inventory form to the LEPC, SERC, and fire department with jurisdiction over the facility. These chemicals are not included on a specific list, but are defined by the OSHA Hazard Communication Standard in Title 29 (Labor) *CFR* 1910.1200 as chemicals that represent a physical or health hazard. The inventory form may be a Tier I or Tier II report. Most reports are now Tier II reports because they contain more information than Tier I reports. Chemicals that must be reported on the Tier reports are those on the EHS List in excess of the TPQ and all OSHA chemicals in excess of 10,000 pounds (4 536 kg). Tier II reports must contain the following information:

- Chemical name or its common name as provided on the MSDS
- Estimate (in ranges) of the maximum amount of the hazardous chemical present at the facility at any time during the preceding calendar year
- Estimate (in ranges) of the average daily amount of the hazardous chemical present at the facility during the preceding year
- Brief description of the manner of storage of the hazardous chemical
- Indication of whether the owner elects to withhold location information of a specific hazardous chemical from disclosure to the public

Provision of Information to Health Professionals, Doctors, and Nurses

Section 323 requires an owner or operator of a facility covered under this act to provide the specific chemical identity (if known) of a hazardous chemical, extremely hazardous substance, or a toxic chemical to any health professional who requests such information in writing along with a written statement of need and confidentiality agreement. This procedure must be done anytime a health professional believes that the following situations apply:

- Information is needed for the purpose of diagnosis or treatment of an individual
- Individual or individuals being diagnosed or treated have been exposed to the chemical concerned

- Knowledge of the specific chemical identity of such chemical will assist in diagnosis or treatment

Emergency Management Planning

Emergency management has been known by many names in the past such as *civil defense, emergency preparedness,* and *disaster planning.* The organizational and operational concepts set forth in most emergency management plans are promulgated under the following authorities:

- *Federal*
  - Federal Civil Defense Act of 1950, P.L. 81-950 as amended
  - Disaster Relief Act of 1974, P.L. 93-288 as amended
  - Robert T. Stafford Disaster Relief and Emergency Assistance Act, P.L. 100–707
  - Emergency Management and Assistance, *Code of Federal Regulations (CFR)*, Title 44
  - Title III of the Superfund Amendments and Reauthorization Act of 1986 (SARA), P.L. 99-499 as amended
- *State*
  - State Disaster Act
  - Executive Order of the Governor
  - Attorney General Opinion(s)
- *Local*
  - Ordinances
  - Joint Resolutions

Most states require local jurisdictions to plan for disasters that could strike and affect their communities. The many major disasters that have occurred in recent years have increased the public interest in community planning. Contingency plans were written before the early 1980s, and plans were prepared for identified disasters. An *All-hazard Plan* is now in place in most jurisdictions.

Response Actions

After an emergency incident, the presiding official of a jurisdiction may declare a local state of disaster. The effect of the declaration is to activate the recovery and rehabilitation aspects of the emergency plan and authorize the furnishing of aid and assistance. When the emergency exceeds local government capability to respond, assistance will be requested from neighboring jurisdictions and/or the sate government.

Emergency management plans address the actions of many different departments/agencies during disasters. The major coordination effort differs from those emergencies handled on a daily basis by local fire, law enforcement, and medical services personnel. The plan attempts to be all-inclusive in combining the four phases of emergency management: mitigation, preparedness, response, and recovery.

The plan follows an all-hazard approach and acknowledges that most responsibilities and functions performed during an emergency are not hazard specific. Likewise, the plan accounts for activities before and after as well as during emergency operations. Consequently, all phases of emergency management are addressed as follows:

- *Mitigation* — Activities that eliminate or reduce the probability of a disaster occurring. Also included are those long-term activities that lessen the undesirable effect of unavoidable hazards.
- *Preparedness* — Activities that serve to develop the response capabilities needed in the event an emergency should arise. Planning and training are among the activities conducted under this phase.
- *Response* — Activities that provide the actual emergency services during a crisis. These activities help to reduce casualties and damage and speed recovery. Response activities include warning, evacuation, rescue, and other similar operations.
- *Recovery* — Period that is both a short-term and long-term process; also an opportune time to institute mitigation measures, particularly those related to the recent emergency. *Details:*
  - *Short-term operations:* Seek to restore vital services to the community and provide for the basic needs of the public.
  - *Long-term recovery:* Focuses on restoring the community to its normal, or improved, state of operation.

— Examples: Temporary housing and food, restoration of nonvital government services, and reconstruction of damaged areas.

Jurisdictions have emergency authority to implement provisions to protect the public during a disaster. They can usually declare a local state of disaster and implement the following measures:

- Wage, price, and rent controls; other economic stabilization measures
- Curfews, blockades, and limitations on utility usage
- Rules governing ingress and egress to and from the affected area
- Other security measures

Continuity of government is vital to a community. Emergency management plans provide for lines of succession for the governing body, emergency management, and jurisdictional departments. In order to provide normal government operations following a disaster, vital records must be protected, including legal documents as well as personal documents such as property deeds and tax records. The principal causes of damage to records are fire water, and wind.

Plan Sections

Most emergency management plans have three or more sections. Additional sections can be included to provide additional information.

Basic Plan

The *basic plan* lists the authority for the plan, purpose, situations, and assumptions. It also includes the concept of operations and provides the organization and assignment of responsibilities by listing the departments' assigned functions and primary responsibilities. Other parts or sections include the following:

- Direction and control section provides for the staffing and operations of the Emergency Operations Center (EOC) and the authority invested in the jurisdiction during a disaster.
- Increased readiness conditions section lists conditions and what actions should be taken during each. Conditions range from a level just above the readiness that is present in the jurisdiction

(such as the beginning of wildland fire season) to the highest level to signify that hazardous conditions are eminent (such as a wildland fire that is out of control, reaching the residential areas of the jurisdiction).

- Plan development, maintenance, and implementation section.

Annexes Section

Annexes state what the responsibilities and tasks are for the responding departments or agencies. A lead or responsible department is assigned to each Annex. Examples of Annexes that may be used are as follows:

- Warning
- Communications
- EOC direction and control
- Shelter/mass care
- Radiological protection
- Evacuation/sheltering in place
- Fire
- Law enforcement
- Health and medical
- Emergency public information
- Damage assessment
- Public works/engineering
- Facilities
- Resource management
- Human services
- Transportation
- Legal
- Rescue
- Hazard mitigation
- Hazardous materials
- Terrorism

Appendices Section

Appendices may be standard operating procedures, standard operating guidelines, or other information vital to an Annex. Examples of an appendix for a Hazardous Materials Annex might be as follows:

- Facilities and transportation routes
- Hazardous materials incident report
- Response personnel safety
- Personal protection of citizens
- Containment and clean-up
- Abbreviations and definitions
- Standard operations procedures
- Interjurisdictional response to hazardous material incidents

Risk Management Plans

In 1990, the amended Clean Air Act (CAA) established requirements for facilities to reduce the likelihood and severity of accidental chemical releases by requiring them to use hazard assessments, prevention programs, and emergency response planning. These requirements are implemented by the EPA's *Risk Management Program* regulations. Facilities that are covered by these regulations must summarize their risk management activities in Risk Management Plans (RMPs).

The RMP is primarily a series of data fields with numbers, words, and phrases, and *yes/no* answers to specific questions, but it is not like a contingency plan, even though it is called a *plan*. Emergency responders can use the information in the data fields to obtain information about the facility, the plans it has in place, the location of chemicals, levels of employee chemical training, and the facility's response capability. The RMP includes a brief description of the facility, its primary operations and processes, and the regulated substance(s) handled. The plan reviews the release scenarios from the offsite consequences analysis, general and chemical-specific release prevention activities, and the emergency response program.

The RMP regulation applies to processes at facilities that have any of 77 acutely toxic substances such as chlorine and ammonia and 63 highly flammable substances, including propane. Most of the acutely toxic regulated chemicals are also EHS under EPCRA Section 302. The flammable chemicals are all subject to reporting under EPCRA Sections 311 and 312. Each toxic regulated substance is assigned a TPQ under the RMP regulations that is generally higher than the TPQ for the same substance under EPCRA. The thresholds for toxic substances range from 500 to 20,000 pounds (227 to 9 072 kg). All flammable chemicals on the RMP list have a threshold quantity of 10,000 pounds (4 536 kg), the same as the threshold for these substances under EPCRA Sections 311 and 312. The TPQ under the RMP is determined by the maximum amount in a process, not the maximum quantity on site as it is under EPCRA.

The RMP requires the facility to develop a worst-case scenario that is defined as the release of the largest quantity of a substance from a vessel or process line failure. For most gases, the worst-case release scenario assumes the quantity is released in 10 minutes. Worst-case scenarios are also provided for other hazardous materials such as flammable liquids. This information may be very helpful to emergency responders.

A facility subject to regulation under the CAA must coordinate its response activities with the LEPC or local responders. A facility using its own employees to respond to releases must implement a full emergency response program that includes a plan, training, and plan review and updates. The facility must coordinate its plan with the LEPC plan. Facilities that do not have their own response team must coordinate with the LEPC concerning listed toxic chemicals and with the fire department about listed flammable chemicals. Local fire officials (in conjunction with building inspectors) can work with facilities to improve fire-prevention practices, including compliance with NFPA standards or other fire and related codes.

Summary

Sharing of the plans required by local fire codes (many of which have similar reporting requirements to SARA) as well as conducting pre-incident surveys can provide good information about the chemical hazards at fixed facilities in a community. This information (along with the information required by SARA Title III and on file with the LEPC) should provide initial assistance to emergency responders at the Awareness and Operational Level at an incident involving a chemical release or potential release. The local emergency management plan assists in providing information and procedures to follow when an incident goes beyond the resources and capabilities of the local jurisdiction.

Appendix D
UN Class Placards and Labels

Table D.1 provides the United Nations (UN) placards and labels required for the transportation of dangerous goods.

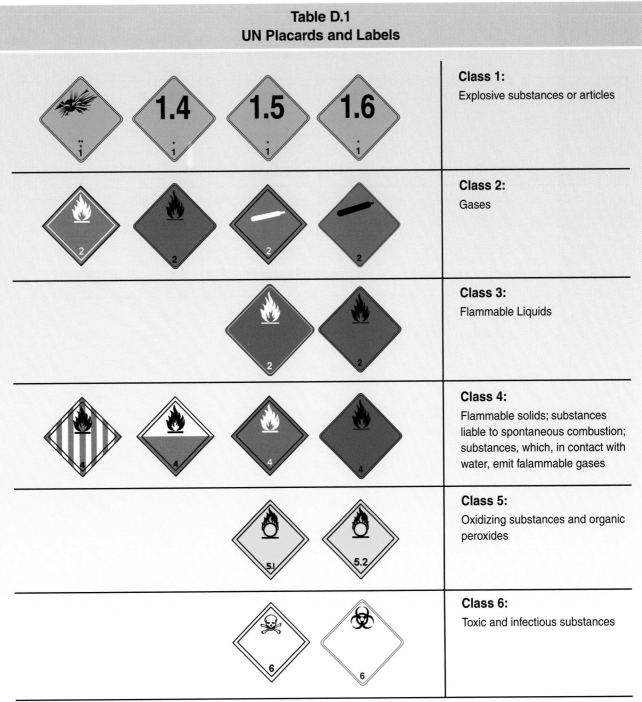

Table D.1 UN Placards and Labels	
	Class 1: Explosive substances or articles
	Class 2: Gases
	Class 3: Flammable Liquids
	Class 4: Flammable solids; substances liable to spontaneous combustion; substances, which, in contact with water, emit falammable gases
	Class 5: Oxidizing substances and organic peroxides
	Class 6: Toxic and infectious substances

Continued

Class 7:

Radioactive material

Class 8:

Corrosive substances

Class 9:

Miscellaneous dangerous substances and articles

Appendix E
Shipping Paper Requirements

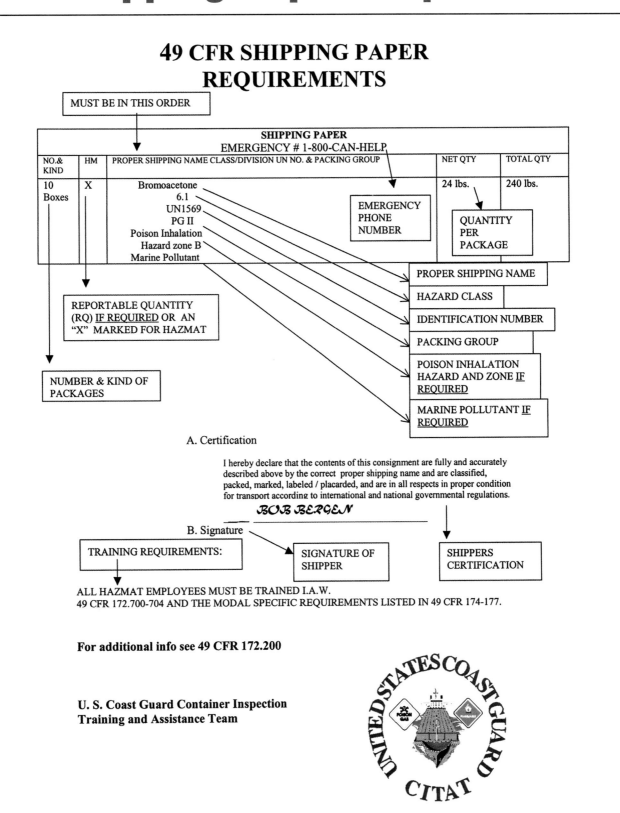

49 CFR SHIPPING PAPER REQUIREMENTS

MUST BE IN THIS ORDER

SHIPPING PAPER
EMERGENCY # 1-800-CAN-HELP

NO.& KIND	HM	PROPER SHIPPING NAME CLASS/DIVISION UN NO. & PACKING GROUP		NET QTY	TOTAL QTY
10 Boxes	X	Bromoacetone 6.1 UN1569 PG II Poison Inhalation Hazard zone B Marine Pollutant	EMERGENCY PHONE NUMBER	24 lbs.	240 lbs.

QUANTITY PER PACKAGE

REPORTABLE QUANTITY (RQ) IF REQUIRED OR AN "X" MARKED FOR HAZMAT

NUMBER & KIND OF PACKAGES

PROPER SHIPPING NAME

HAZARD CLASS

IDENTIFICATION NUMBER

PACKING GROUP

POISON INHALATION HAZARD AND ZONE IF REQUIRED

MARINE POLLUTANT IF REQUIRED

A. Certification

I hereby declare that the contents of this consignment are fully and accurately described above by the correct proper shipping name and are classified, packed, marked, labeled / placarded, and are in all respects in proper condition for transport according to international and national governmental regulations.

BOB BERGEN

B. Signature

TRAINING REQUIREMENTS:

SIGNATURE OF SHIPPER

SHIPPERS CERTIFICATION

ALL HAZMAT EMPLOYEES MUST BE TRAINED I.A.W.
49 CFR 172.700-704 AND THE MODAL SPECIFIC REQUIREMENTS LISTED IN 49 CFR 174-177.

For additional info see 49 CFR 172.200

**U. S. Coast Guard Container Inspection
Training and Assistance Team**

UNITED STATES COAST GUARD
CITAT

Appendix F
Hazardous Materials Incident Commander Checklist

☐ Establish Command
- *Consider Unified Command if appropriate*
- *Determine the need to staff Public Information Officer (PIO) position*

☐ Ensure appropriate notifications have been made
- *Haz mat response team to notify appropriate state and federal agencies*
- *Ensure notification to local affected agencies (city, public works, police, Cleanwater, etc.)*
- *Contact with "responsible party" if available*

☐ Ensure a site access control plan has been established
- *Limit and control site access*
- *Establish hot zone, warm zone, cold zone*

☐ Ensure use of appropriate personal protective equipment (PPE)
- *Approve use of appropriate PPE for ALL responders (including haz mat response team, fire, law enforcement, public works personnel)*

☐ Develop Action Plan (written is optimal)
- *Offensive or defensive operation*
- *Appropriate Operational/Technician Level actions*
- *Appropriate protective actions (evacuation or shelter in place)*
- *Appropriate decontamination procedures*
- *Coordination of all on-scene response agencies*
- *If fixed facility, coordinate with facility representative and/or emergency response team*

☐ Safety
- *Provide safety briefing for responders*
- *Ensure Safety Officer is trained to Technician Level*
- *Ensure medical surveillance of personnel in the hot zone*

☐ Ensure appropriate incident termination procedures are carried out
- *Provide ALL responders with information on signs/symptoms of exposure*
- *Provide information for personal exposure records*
- *Determine if any equipment/apparatus exposure occurred; identify follow-up actions if needed*
- *Ensure postincident analysis takes place*
- *Determine need for critical incident stress debriefing*
- *Identify any transition issues before transfer of command*
- *Transfer command to appropriate agency or company (get contact name/number)*

Typical Hazardous Materials Problems with Potential Mitigating Strategies and Tactics

Problem	Strategies	Tactics
Access: Access problems may be related to gaining access or denying access (to civilians or unprotected responders). Generally the first problem presented is limiting access to civilians and unprotected responders.	Isolate and deny entry	• Establish control zones (Hot and Cold) • Control traffic
Container Under Stress: The two types of container stress that responders can readily affect are generally thermal stress (heating) and mechanical stress (due to overpressure).	Ignore	Protect exposures (protective actions only)
	Cool	• Use master stream • Use hoseline
	Extinguish fire	• Remove fuel • Use master stream • Use hoseline • Use foam master stream
	Release pressure	• Transfer product • Release product to atmosphere • Vent and burn
Container Breach/Release: Active strategies to manage a breach/release generally require operations inside the hazard area (Hot Zone).	Ignore	Protect exposures (protective actions only)
	Contain	• Close valve(s) • Tighten attachments • Plug • Patch • Transfer product • Decontaminate (required for entry)

continued

Problem	Strategies	Tactics
Dispersion: Active strategies to control dispersion may be either offensive or defensive (depending on where they are performed). Dispersion control strategies are driven by the form of the material that has been (or is being) released.	Ignore	Protect exposures (protective actions only)
	Confine: Solid	Cover
	Confine: Liquid	• Adsorb or absorb • Dike (Circle or *V*-shape) • Divert • Retain • Dam (underflow or overflow) • Suppress vapor (foam)
	Confine: Energy	Shield
	Disperse: Gas	Disperse vapor (water fog or blower)
Fire: The fire problem includes a direct threat to life safety and exposures, potential to affect container integrity, and release of toxic products of combustion. However, in some cases (pesticides), fire may present less threat than fire-control operations.	Ignore	Protect exposures (protective actions only)
	Extinguish	• Use master stream • Use hoseline • Use foam master stream • Use foam hoseline • Use dry chemical • Use specialized extinguishing agent
Possible Victims: Possible victims may be reported (definitely a known imminent life threat) or inferred based on incident conditions. Victims removed from the hazard area (Hot Zone) may require decontamination.	Determine	Ask
	Notify	• Use public address system • Use telephone
	Locate	• Perform primary search/extraction • Perform decontamination • Perform secondary search
Visible/Known Victims: Victims may be visible or known to be inside the hazard area. These victims may (or may not) be able to rescue themselves. First responders must use care in assessing their capability to affect a rescue (due to limitations in personal protective equipment and training. Victims removed from the hazard area (Hot Zone) may require decontamination.	Rescue	• Rescue themselves • Move to safe refuge • Perform extraction • Perform decontamination

continued

Problem	Strategies	Tactics
Potential Life Exposure: Potential victims may become exposed due to dispersion (downhill or downwind). Responders must consider dispersion, time, and incident conditions in evaluating potential life exposure.	Protect in place	• Notify face to face • Notify by telephone • Notify media
	Evacuate	• Notify face to face • Notify by telephone • Notify media • Shelter • Control traffic • Perform security
Environmental/Property Exposure: Active strategies to minimize environmental/property damage are generally offensive in nature.	Ignore	Self-mitigate
	Control chemical	• Dilute • Neutralize
	Cool	• Use master stream • Use hoseline • Use foam master stream • Use foam hoseline

Appendix H
Donning and Doffing Procedures for SCBA Respirators

Fire and emergency services personnel must be able to don and doff self-contained breathing apparatus (SCBA) quickly and correctly. Several general methods of donning the SCBA backpack can be used, depending upon how the SCBA is stored. These methods include the following

- Over-the-head
- Regular or cross-arm coat
- Donning from a seat
- Side or rear mount
- Compartment or backup mount

The steps for donning differ with each method, but once the SCBA is on the body, the method of securing the unit is the same. Methods for donning the facepiece differ, depending upon the manufacturer and whether the regulator is harness-mounted or facepiece-mounted.

The procedures in this appendix are general in nature. Fire and emergency services personnel should be aware that there are different steps for donning different makes and models. Therefore, the instructions given in this appendix should be adapted to the specific type of SCBA used. Always follow the manufacturer's instructions when donning, doffing, and operating SCBA.

Donning the Open-Circuit SCBA

Because many fire and emergency services personnel prefer to don the SCBA backpack first and then the facepiece, procedures for donning the backpack are covered in this section. Methods for donning different types of facepieces are covered in the section that follows.

Donning the Backpack

The donning methods for the over-the-head, cross-armed coat, regular coat, seat mount, side or rear mount, and compartment or backup mount are described in the sections that follow.

Over-the-Head Method

SCBA stored in carrying cases must be stored ready to don. The backpack straps should be arranged so that they do not interfere with grasping the cylinder. The emergency responder should put on the protective hood, pull it back, button the turnout coat, and turn the collar up so that the shoulder straps do not hold the collar down. The procedures for donning a backpack using the over-the-head method are as follows:

Step 1: Check the unit.

a. Crouch or kneel at the end opposite the cylinder valve, regardless of whether the unit is in its case or on the ground.

b. Check the cylinder gauge to make sure that the air cylinder is full. Open the cylinder valve slowly and listen for the audible alarm as the system pressurizes. Then, open the cylinder valve fully. If the audible alarm does not sound, or if it sounds but does not stop, place the unit out of service by tagging it and notifying an officer or supervisor; use another unit.

c. Check the regulator gauge. Both the cylinder and regulator gauges should register within 10 percent of each other when the cylinder is pressurized to its rated capacity **(Figure H.1, p. 540)**. If increments are in other measurements, such as fractions or minutes, they should correspond. If the unit has a donning switch (for units with facepiece-mounted regulators), leave the cylinder valve open and the unit in the donning mode. If the unit is positive pressure only, refer to the manufacturer's instructions concerning the cylinder valve.

Step 2: Spread the harness straps out to their respective sides.

Step 3: Grasp the backplate or cylinder with both hands, one at each side **(Figure H.2)**. Make sure that the cylinder valve is pointed away from you. There should be no straps between the hands.

Step 4: Lift the cylinder, and let the regulator and harness hang freely **(Figure H.3)**.

Figure H.1 Pressure gauges on the regulator and cylinder should register within 10 percent of each other when the cylinder is fully pressurized.

Step 5: Stand and raise the cylinder overhead; let the elbows find their respective loosened harness shoulder strap loops **(Figure H.4)**. Keeping elbows close to the body, tuck the chin and grasp the shoulder straps as the SCBA begins to slide down the back. Let the straps slide through the hands as the backpack lowers into place.

Step 6: Lean forward to balance the cylinder on the back and partially tighten the shoulder straps by pulling them outward and downward **(Figure H.5)**.

NOTE: It is sometimes necessary to lean forward with a quick jumping motion to properly position the SCBA on the back while tightening the straps.

Step 7: Continue leaning forward on units equipped with chest straps, and then fasten the chest buckle if the unit has a chest strap.

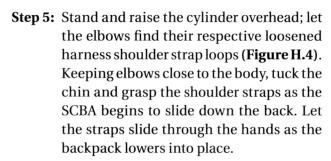

Figure H.2 With straps spread, grasp the cylinder through the shoulder straps, and lift it from the case.

Figure H.3 Lift the cylinder, allowing the regulator and harness to hang freely.

Figure H.4 Stand and raise the cylinder overhead, allowing the shoulder straps to fall outside the arms.

NOTE: Depending upon the emergency responder's physique, it may be more comfortable to fasten the chest buckle before tightening the shoulder straps.

Step 8: Fasten and adjust the waist strap until the unit fits snugly **(Figure H.6)**.

Step 9: Don the facepiece.

NOTE: This procedure is covered in the Donning the Facepiece section.

Figure H.5 Lean forward for balance and partially tighten the shoulder straps by pulling outward and downward.

Figure H.6 Fasten and adjust the waist strap. Readjust all other straps until the unit fits snugly.

WARNING

Some emergency services organizations have removed waist straps from SCBA. Without a waist strap fastened, the SCBA wearer suffers undue stress from side-to-side shifting of the unit and improper weight distribution of the unit. Even more important, removing waist straps permits the SCBA to be used in a nonapproved manner, which may violate NIOSH certification of the equipment and void the manufacturer's warranty.

Cross-Armed Coat Method

Self-contained breathing apparatus can be donned like a coat. The equipment should be arranged so that both shoulder straps can be grasped for lifting. Use the following steps:

Step 1: Check the unit.

    a. Crouch or kneel at the cylinder valve end of the unit, regardless of whether the unit is in its case or on the ground.

    b. Check the cylinder gauge to make sure that the air cylinder is full **(Figure H.7)**. Open the cylinder valve slowly and listen for the audible alarm as the system pressurizes. Then, open the cylinder valve fully. If the audible alarm does

Figure H.7 Always check the cylinder gauge before donning the SCBA. Open the valve fully before donning the unit.

not sound, or if it sounds but does not stop, place the unit out of service by tagging it and notifying an officer or supervisor; use another unit.

c. Check the regulator gauge. Both the cylinder and regulator gauges should register within 10 percent of each other when the cylinder is pressurized to its rated capacity. If increments are in other measurements, such as fractions or minutes, they should correspond. If the unit has a donning switch, leave the cylinder valve open and the unit in the donning mode. If the unit is positive pressure only, refer to the manufacturer's instructions concerning the cylinder valve.

Step 2: Spread the harness straps out to their respective sides. Cross the arms, left over right. Grasp the shoulder straps at the top of the harness, left hand holding the left strap and right hand holding the right strap (**Figure H.8**).

Step 3: Stand and lift the SCBA. Using both arms, swing the unit around the right shoulder, and raising the left arm, continue bringing the unit behind the head and onto the back. Both hands should still be grasping the shoulder straps high on the harness (**Figures H.9, H.10,** and **H.11**).

Step 4: Slide the hands down the straps to the shoulder strap buckles, maintaining a firm grip on the straps. The elbows should be between the straps and the backpack.

Step 5: Lean slightly forward to balance the cylinder on the back; tighten the shoulder straps by pulling them outward and downward.

NOTE: It is sometimes necessary to lean forward with a quick jumping motion to properly position the SCBA on the back while tightening the straps.

Step 6: Continue leaning forward, and fasten the chest buckle if the unit has a chest strap.

NOTE: It may be necessary to fasten the chest strap before completely tightening the shoulder straps.

Step 7: Fasten and adjust the waist strap until the unit fits snugly (**Figure H.12**).

Step 8: Recheck all straps to see that they are correctly adjusted.

Step 9: Don the facepiece.

NOTE: This procedure is covered in the Donning the Facepiece section.

Figure H.8 Kneel and grasp the shoulder straps with arms crossed, left over right.

Figure H.9 While rising to a standing position, lift the SCBA, keeping wrists together.

Figure H.10 Swing unit around the right shoulder, allowing wrists to separate.

Figure H.11 Guide unit onto back.

Figure H.12 Fasten the waist strap and adjust until snug.

Regular Coat Method

Self-contained breathing apparatus can be donned like a coat, putting one arm at a time through the shoulder strap loops. The unit should be arranged so that either shoulder strap can be grasped for lifting. Use the following steps:

Step 1: Check the unit.

    a. Crouch or kneel at the cylinder valve end of the unit, regardless of whether the unit is in its case or on the ground.

    b. Check the cylinder gauge to make sure that the air cylinder is full. Open the cylinder valve slowly and listen for the audible alarm as the system pressurizes. Then, open the cylinder valve fully. If the audible alarm does not sound, or if it sounds but does not stop, place the unit out of service by tagging and notifying an officer or supervisor; use another unit.

    c. Check the regulator gauge. Both the cylinder and regulator gauges should register within 10 percent of each other when the cylinder is pressurized to its rated capacity. If increments are in other measurements, such as fractions or minutes, they should correspond. If the unit has a donning switch, leave the cylinder valve open and the unit in the donning mode. If the unit is positive pressure only, refer to the manufacturer's instructions concerning the cylinder valve.

Step 2: Spread the straps out to their respective sides, and position the upper portion of the straps over the top of the backplate.

NOTE: By doing this, the straps are less likely to fall, and the arms can go through the straps with less difficulty.

NOTE: This procedure is written for those harnesses having the regulator attached to the left side of the harness. There are some SCBA that have the regulator mounted on the right. For these types, the right strap should be grasped with the right hand, and the backpack should be donned following the instructions in the next steps, but using directions opposite those indicated.

Step 3: Grasp the left strap with the left hand at the top of the harness. Grasp the lower portion of the same strap with the right hand (**Figure H.13**).

NOTE: When kneeling at the cylinder valve end, the left harness strap will be to the right hand.

Step 4: Lift the unit; swing it around the left shoulder and onto the back. Both hands should still be grasping the shoulder strap (**Figure H.14**).

Step 5: Continue to hold the strap with the left hand; release the right hand and insert the right arm between the right shoulder strap and the backpack frame.

Step 6: Lean slightly forward to balance the cylinder on the back; tighten the shoulder straps by pulling them outward and downward.

NOTE: It is sometimes necessary to lean forward with a quick jumping motion to properly position the SCBA on the back while tightening the straps.

Figure H.13 Grasp the top of the left shoulder strap with the left hand. Grasp the lower part of the same strap with the right hand.

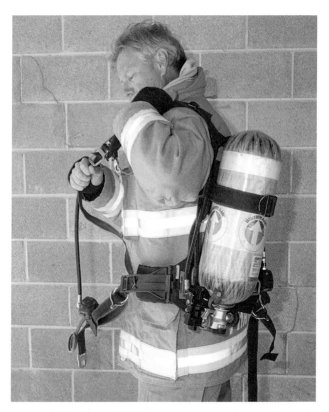

Figure H.14 Lift the SCBA by the straps and swing the unit around the left shoulder and onto the back while maintaining a firm grasp of the straps.

Step 7: Continue leaning forward, and fasten the chest buckle if the unit has a chest strap. Tighten the shoulder straps further if necessary.

Step 8: Fasten and adjust the waist strap until the unit fits snugly.

Step 9: Recheck all straps to see that they are correctly adjusted.

Step 10: Don the facepiece.

NOTE: This procedure is covered in the Donning the Facepiece section.

Seat Mount

Valuable time can be saved if the SCBA is mounted on the back of the emergency responder's seat in the vehicle **(Figure H.15)**. By having a seat mount, fire and emergency services personnel can don SCBA while en route to an incident. If the SCBA is not needed upon arrival, it can be removed quickly and remain mounted in its support.

Seat-mounting hardware comes in three main types: lever clamp, spring clamp, or flat hook. A drawstring or other quick-opening bag should enclose the facepiece to keep it clean and to protect it from dust and scratches.

Figure H.15 Seat-mounted SCBA are shown in the firefighting vehicle.

NOTE: Do not keep the facepiece hooked to the regulator during storage. These parts must be separate to check for proper facepiece seal.

Donning en route is done by inserting the arms through the straps while sitting with the seat belt on, then adjusting the straps for a snug fit **(Figures H.16** and **H.17)**.

Figure H.16 Donning en route, the firefighter inserts both arms through the straps and carefully connects the waist belt to avoid entanglement with the seat belt.

Figure H.17 The firefighter adjusts the straps as snugly as possible while seated. Upon leaving the apparatus, straps may be adjusted again as necessary.

The cylinder's position should match the proper wearing position for the emergency responder. The visible seat-mounted SCBA reminds and even encourages personnel to check the equipment more frequently. Because it is exposed, checks can be made more conveniently. Be sure to adjust the straps for a snug and comfortable fit when exiting the fire apparatus.

Side or Rear Mount

Although it does not permit donning en route, the side- or rear-mounted SCBA may be desirable. Time is saved because the steps needed to remove the equipment case from the fire apparatus, place it on the ground, open the case, and pick up the unit are eliminated. Current apparatus designs include mounting brackets inside weatherproof compartments (**Figure H.18**). However if the unit is mounted on the exterior of the apparatus, it will be exposed to weather and physical damage, in which case a canvas cover is desirable.

Figure H.18 In addition to storage for complete SCBA units, compartment brackets may also be used for storing spare breathing-air cylinders like the ones shown.

If the mounting height is correct, fire and emergency services personnel can don SCBA with little effort. Having the mount near the running boards or near the tailboard allows the emergency responder to don the equipment while sitting. The steps are essentially the same as those for seat-mounted SCBA.

Compartment or Backup Mount

SCBA stored in a closed compartment can be ready for rapid donning by using any number of mounts (**Figure H.19**). A mount on the inside of a compartment presents the same advantage, as does side-mounted equipment. Some compartment doors, however, may not allow an emergency responder to stand fully while donning SCBA. Other compartments may be too high for the emergency responder to don the SCBA properly.

Figure H.19 These SCBA are stored in a closed compartment. While providing good protection, this compartment may not be the correct height for proper donning.

Other compartment mounts feature a telescoping frame that holds the equipment out of the way inside the compartment when it is not needed (**Figure H.20**). One type of compartment mount telescopes outward, then upward or downward to proper height for quick donning.

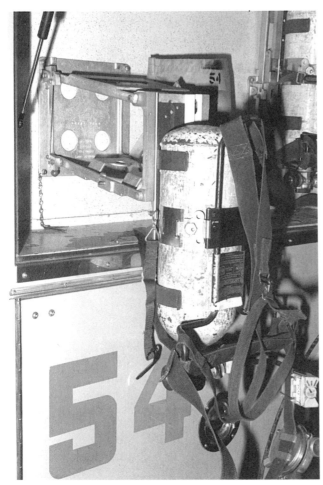

Figure H.20 A compartment mount featuring a telescoping frame to hold the equipment inside the compartment provides the proper height for donning.

The backup mount provides quick access to SCBA. Some high-mounted SCBA must be removed from the vehicle and donned using the over-the-head or coat method. The procedures for donning SCBA using the backup method, with slight variation for mounts from which the SCBA can be donned while seated, are as follows:

Step 1: Uncover the SCBA. Remove the facepiece and place it nearby.

Step 2: Check the unit.

    a. Open the cylinder valve slowly and listen for the audible alarm as the system pressurizes. Open the cylinder valve fully. If the audible alarm does not sound, or if it sounds but does not stop, place the unit out of service by tagging it and notifying an officer or supervisor; use another unit.

    b. Check the regulator gauge. Both the cylinder and regulator gauges should register within 10 percent of each other when the cylinder is pressurized to its rated capacity. If increments are in other measurements, such as fractions or minutes, they should correspond. If the unit has a donning switch, leave the cylinder valve open and the unit in the donning mode. If the unit is positive pressure only, refer to the manufacturer's instructions concerning the cylinder valve.

Step 3: Back up against the cylinder backplate, and place the arms through the harness straps (**Figure H.21**). While leaning slightly forward to balance the unit on the back, release the cylinder according to the kind of mounting device.

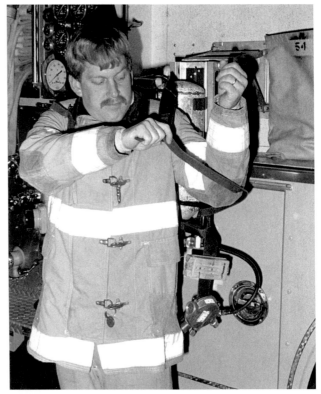

Figure H.21 Back up against the cylinder backplate, and place the arms through the harness straps.

Step 4: Step forward to clear the unit from the mount while fastening the chest buckle if the unit has a chest strap.

Step 5: Tighten the shoulder straps (**Figure H.22**).

Step 6: Fasten and adjust the waist strap until the unit fits snugly (**Figure H.23**).

Step 7: Don the facepiece.

> **NOTE:** Donning the facepiece is covered in the following section.

Figure H.22 With a slight jerk, pull the SCBA away from the bracket. Tighten the shoulder straps.

Figure H.23 Fasten and adjust the waist strap until the unit fits snugly.

Donning the Facepiece

The facepieces for most SCBA are donned similarly. One important difference in facepieces is the number of straps used to tighten the head harness (**Figure H.24**). Different models from the same manufacturer may have a different number of straps. Another important difference is the location of the regulator. The regulator may be attached to the facepiece or mounted on the waist belt. The shape and size of facepiece lenses may also differ. Despite these variations, the uses and donning procedures for facepieces are essentially the same.

WARNING

Interchanging facepieces or any other part of the SCBA from one manufacturer's equipment to another voids any warranty and NIOSH certification.

An SCBA facepiece cannot be worn loosely or it cannot seal against the face properly. An improper seal may permit toxic gases to enter the facepiece and be inhaled. Fire and emergency services personnel should not let long hair, sideburns, or mustaches interfere with the outer edges of the facepiece, thus preventing contact and a proper seal with the skin. OSHA and NFPA prohibit any facial hair, eyeglass frames, or other obstructions that might interfere with a complete seal.

An emergency responder should not rely solely on tightening facepiece straps to ensure proper

Figure H.24 Two types of head harnesses are depicted — a nylon mesh or hairnet model and a traditional style with five straps, sometimes referred to as a web-type harness.

facepiece fit. A facepiece tightened too much is uncomfortable and may cut off circulation to the face. Each emergency responder must be fitted with a facepiece that conforms properly to the face shape and size. For this reason, many SCBA are available with different-sized facepieces (**Figure H.25**). Nose cups, if used, must also properly fit the emergency responder.

Figure H.25 To meet the requirements for complete facepiece-to-face seal, manufacturers provide respiratory protection facepieces in a variety of sizes.

Harness-Mounted Regulator

The facepiece for an SCBA with a harness-mounted regulator has a low-pressure hose, or breathing tube, attached to the facepiece with clamps or threaded coupling nuts. The facepiece may be packed in a case or stored in a bag or coat pouch. Wherever it is stored, the straps should be left fully extended for donning ease and to keep the facepiece from becoming distorted. The procedures for donning a facepiece having a low-pressure hose are as follows:

Step 1: Pull the protective hood back and down so that the face opening is around the neck. Turn up the collar of the turnout coat.

Step 2: If the harness is a web-type, grasp the harness with the thumbs through the straps from the inside and spread the straps (**Figure H.26**).

Step 3: Push the top of the harness up the forehead to remove hair that may be present between the forehead and the sealing surface of the facepiece (**Figure H.27**).

Figure H.26 When donning a web-type head harness, grasp the harness with the thumbs through the straps from the inside and spread the straps.

Figure H.27 Push the top of the harness up the forehead to remove hair that may be present between the forehead and the sealing surface of the facepiece. The web is contacting the forehead.

Step 4: Center the chin in the chin cup and position the harness so that it is centered at the rear of the head (**Figure H.28**).

Step 5: Tighten the harness straps by pulling them evenly and simultaneously to the rear. Pulling the straps outward, to the sides, may damage them and prevents proper engagement with the adjusting buckles. Tighten the lower straps first, then the temple straps, and finally the top strap if there is one (**Figure H.29**).

Step 6: Check the facepiece seal. Exhale deeply, seal the end of the low-pressure hose with a bare hand, and inhale slowly (not deeply) (**Figure H.30**). Hold the breath for 10 seconds. This action allows the facepiece to collapse tightly against the face. If there is evidence of leaking, adjust or redon the facepiece.

NOTE: Inhaling very quickly temporarily seals any leak and gives a false sense of a proper seal.

Figure H.29 Tighten the straps evenly and simultaneously, starting with the lower straps.

Figure H.28 Center the chin in the chin cup and position the harness so that it is centered at the rear of the head.

Figure H.30 Use the negative-pressure test to check the facepiece seal by sealing the low-pressure hose and inhaling slowly and holding breath for 10 seconds.

Step 7: Check the exhalation valve. Inhale, seal the end of the low-pressure hose, and exhale. If the exhalation does not go through the exhalation valve, keep the low-pressure hose sealed, press the facepiece against the face, and exhale to free the valve. Use caution when exhaling against a sealed facepiece in order to prevent discomfort and possible damage to the inner ear from exhaling forcefully. If the exhalation valve does not become free, remove the facepiece and have it checked.

Figure H.31 Pull the protective hood into place, covering all exposed skin and being sure that vision is not obscured.

Step 8: Put on the helmet, first inserting the low-pressure hose through the helmet's chin strap. The helmet should rest on the shoulder until the SCBA is completely donned.

> **NOTE:** Helmets with straps that completely disconnect may be donned as a last step.

Step 9: Connect the low-pressure hose to the regulator. If the unit has a donning switch, turn it to the PRESSURE, USE, or ON position. If the unit does not have a donning switch, open the mainline valve.

Step 10: Check for positive pressure. Gently break the facepiece seal by inserting two fingers under the edge of the facepiece. Air should be felt moving past the fingers. If air movement is not felt, remove the unit and have it checked.

Figure H.32 Place the helmet on the head and ensure that the chin strap is under the chin and not tangled with the facepiece or hood.

Step 11: Pull the protective hood into place, making sure that all exposed skin is covered and that vision is not obscured (**Figure H.31**). Check to see that no portion of the hood is located between the facepiece and the face.

Step 12: Place the helmet on the head and tighten the chin strap (**Figures H.32** and **H.33**).

An alternative method is to wear the helmet while donning the SCBA. After donning the backpack, loosen the chin strap, allow the helmet to rest on the air cylinder or on the shoulder, and then don the facepiece. When the facepiece straps have been tightened and the hood is on, lift the helmet back onto the head and tighten the chin strap.

Figure H.33 Tighten the chin strap securely.

Facepiece-Mounted Regulator

Step 1: If using a protective hood, pull it back and down so that the face opening is around the neck. Turn up the collar of the turnout coat.

> **NOTE:** Depending upon the style of helmet used, it may be necessary to don the helmet now and allow it to rest on the shoulder.

Step 2: With the thumbs inserted through the straps, grasp the head harness and spread the webbing.

Step 3: Stabilize the facepiece with one hand, and use the other hand to remove hair that may be present between the forehead and the sealing surface of the facepiece.

Step 4: Center the chin in the chin cup and position the harness so that it is centered at the rear of the head.

Step 5: Tighten the harness straps by pulling them backward (not outward) evenly and simultaneously. Tighten the lower straps first, then the temple straps, and finally the top strap if there is one.

> **NOTE:** For two-strap harnesses, tighten the neck straps, and then stroke the harness firmly down the back of the head. Retighten the straps as necessary.

Step 6: Check the regulator to ensure that the gasket is in place around the regulator outlet port if the SCBA is so equipped.

Step 7: Attach the regulator to the facepiece (if separated from the facepiece) by positioning it firmly into the facepiece fitting. Lock it into place **(Figure H.34)**.

> **NOTE:** This procedure varies, depending upon the make of SCBA. Always follow the manufacturer's instructions.

Step 8: Check the facepiece seal. Make sure that the donning switch is in the DON position (positive pressure off). Inhale slowly (not deeply), and hold your breath for 10 seconds **(Figure H.35)**. The mask should draw up to the face. Listen for the sound of airflow. There should be no sound and no inward leakage through the exhalation valve or around the facepiece.

Figure H.34 If separated from the facepiece, attach regulator to the facepiece by positioning it firmly into the facepiece fitting and locking it in place.

Figure H.35 Use negative-pressure test to check the facepiece seal by inhaling slowly and holding breath for 10 seconds.

ALTERNATE METHOD: Another method for checking facepiece seal is to close the cylinder valve. Continue to breathe slowly until the mask collapses against the face, and hold the breath for 10 seconds. If the mask draws up to the face and no leaks are detected, reopen the cylinder valve. Adjust or redon the facepiece if there is evidence of leaking. If leakage persists, determine and correct the cause of the leakage. If unable to eliminate the leakage, obtain another facepiece and repeat the leak-check procedure. Use care with this method because it consumes some air.

Step 9: Check the exhalation valve. When exhaling during Step 8, make sure that the exhalation goes through the exhalation valve. If it does not, the valve may be stuck. To free it, press the facepiece against the sides of the face, and exhale to free the valve. Use caution when exhaling against a sealed facepiece in order to prevent discomfort and possible damage to the inner ear from exhaling forcefully. If the exhalation valve does not become free, remove the facepiece and have it checked.

Step 10: Check for positive pressure. Gently break the facepiece seal by inserting two fingers under the edge of the facepiece. Air should be felt moving past the fingers. If air movement is not felt, remove the unit and have it checked.

Step 11: Pull the protective hood into place, making sure that all exposed skin is covered and that vision is not obscured. Check to see that no portion of the hood is located between the facepiece and the face.

Step 12: Put the helmet back on the head and tighten the chin strap. Be sure to get the helmet strap under the chin.

NOTE: Helmets with a breakaway strap can be donned at this point.

ALTERNATE METHOD: An alternative method is to leave the helmet on while donning the backpack, then loosen the chin strap, and allow the helmet to rest on the air cylinder while donning the facepiece.

Doffing the Open-Circuit SCBA

Steps are given in the following sections for both types of open-circuit SCBA: those with harness-mounted regulators and those with facepiece-mounted regulators.

Harness-Mounted Regulator

When you are in a safe atmosphere, take the following steps to remove SCBA having a harness-mounted regulator:

Step 1: Close the mainline valve and disconnect the low-pressure hose from the regulator.

NOTE: If the unit has a donning switch, make sure that it is in the donning mode.

Step 2: Take off the helmet or loosen it and push it and the hood back off the head (Figure H.36).

Figure H.36 Remove or slide the helmet back off the head and pull off the protective hood.

Step 3: Loosen the facepiece harness strap buckles. Either rub them toward the face or lift the buckles slightly to loosen them and to disentangle them from the hair (**Figure H.37**). Take off the facepiece, extend the harness straps fully, and prepare it for inspection, cleaning, sanitizing, and storage.

Step 4: Unbuckle the waist belt and fully extend the adjustment (**Figure H.38**).

Step 5: Disconnect the chest buckle if the unit has a chest strap.

Step 6: Lean forward; release shoulder strap buckles and hold them open while fully extending the straps (**Figure H.39**).

Step 7: Grasp the shoulder straps firmly with the respective hands. Slip off the shoulder strap from the shoulder opposite the regulator, and remove the arm from the shoulder strap. Grasp the regulator with the free hand, allow the other strap to slide off the shoulder, and lower the SCBA to the ground (**Figures H.40** and **H.41**). Do not drop the regulator or allow it to strike anything.

Step 8: Close the cylinder valve and then relieve the excess pressure from the regulator. If the regulator has been removed from the facepiece, recouple it, hold the facepiece against the face, and breathe until the remaining pressure is depleted. Another method is to open the mainline valve and allow the excess pressure to vent (**Figure H.42**).

NOTE: Do not use the bypass valve to relieve excess pressure.

Step 9: Remove the facepiece from the regulator and extend the straps fully. Prepare the facepiece for inspection, cleaning, sanitizing, and storage.

Figure H.38 Unbuckle waist belt and fully extend it.

Figure H.39 Lean forward; release shoulder strap buckles and hold them open while extending the straps.

Figure H.37 Using the finger under the strap to maintain tension on the buckle, continue to rub the buckle using a scratching motion.

Figure H.40 Slip the shoulder strap from the shoulder opposite the regulator, and reach around to grasp the regulator with the free hand.

Figure H.41 Guide the SCBA to the ground while controlling the regulator.

Figure H.42 Open the mainline valve to depressurize the system.

Facepiece-Mounted Regulator

When you are in a safe atmosphere, take the following steps to remove SCBA having a facepiece-mounted regulator:

Step 1: Take off the helmet or loosen it and push it and the hood back off the head.

Step 2: Turn the positive pressure off if the unit has a donning switch or place it in donning mode.

Step 3: Disconnect the regulator from the facepiece, depending upon the make of SCBA and the manufacturer's instructions.

Step 4: Loosen the facepiece harness strap buckles. Either rub them toward the face or lift the buckles slightly to loosen them. Take off the facepiece and prepare it for inspection, cleaning, sanitizing, and storage. Extend the harness straps fully.

Step 5: Unbuckle the waist belt and fully extend the adjustment.

Step 6: Disconnect the chest buckle if the unit has a chest strap.

Step 7: Attach the regulator to the harness clip if the unit is so equipped, or control the regulator by holding it while performing the next steps.

Step 8: Lean forward; release shoulder strap buckles and hold them open while fully extending the straps.

Step 9: Grasp the shoulder straps firmly with the respective hands. Slip off the shoulder strap from the shoulder opposite the regulator, and remove the arm from the shoulder strap. Grasp the regulator with the free hand, allow the other strap to slide off the shoulder, and lower the SCBA to the ground. Do not drop the regulator or allow it to strike anything.

Step 10: Close the cylinder valve and breathe down the pressure from the regulator by holding the facepiece against the face and breathing until the pressure is depleted.

NOTE: Do not bleed off air by operating the bypass valve.

Appendix I
Radiological Materials Transportation Accidents: First Responder Response Flow Charts

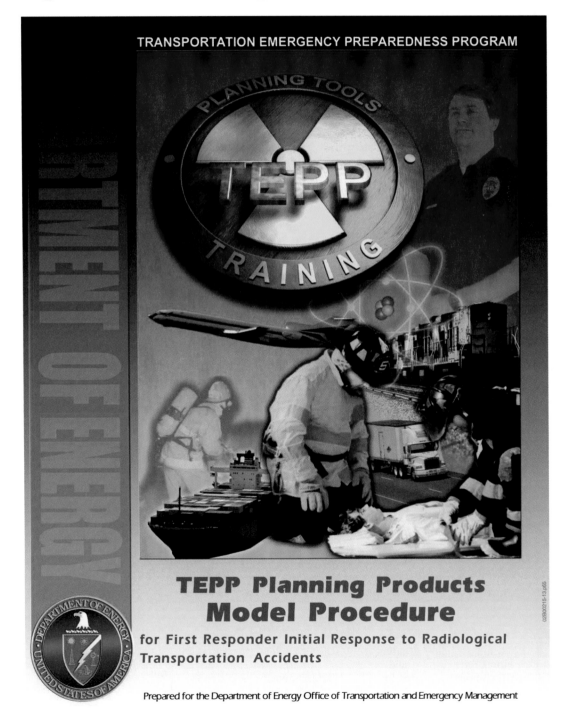

TRANSPORTATION EMERGENCY PREPAREDNESS PROGRAM

TEPP Planning Products
Model Procedure

for First Responder Initial Response to Radiological Transportation Accidents

Prepared for the Department of Energy Office of Transportation and Emergency Management

11.0 RESPONSE PROCEDURE

See the following First Response Flow Charts for Transportation Accidents Involving Radioactive Materials (Attachments 1 through 4).

RESPONSE FLOW CHART ATTACHMENT 1

Initial arrival on scene

Approach incident cautiously from upwind and upslope. Stay clear of all spills, vapors, fumes and smoke.

Perform scene "size up." Visually assess the accident from a distance. Try to identify the following:

- Spills, leaks, or fire
- Apparent hazardous properties of the cargo
- Victims
- Type of vehicle and containers involved
- Placards and markings
- Container/package damage
- Any person knowledgeable of the scene
- Shipping papers
- Runoff problems; work area hazards; exposure problems
- Entry point

Notify Emergency Communications Center of the situation and assume position of Incident Commander until relieved by higher authority.

Evaluate information and consult ERG to identify hazards and material involved. Follow guidelines in ERG until other assistance arrives.

Establish initial isolation zone 80 to 160 feet upwind of entry point. Establish lines of communication. Priorities for first responders include the following:

- Safety of response personnel
- Rescue of injured personnel
- Secure the incident scene
- Isolate the area and deny entry
- Ensure safety of people and environment
- Monitor radiation levels (if equipment is available)
- Restrict entry until Radiation Authority or radiological emergency response team arrives

Establish control zones: hot, warm, and cold, upwind and upslope from hazard area.

Don protective clothing and SCBA

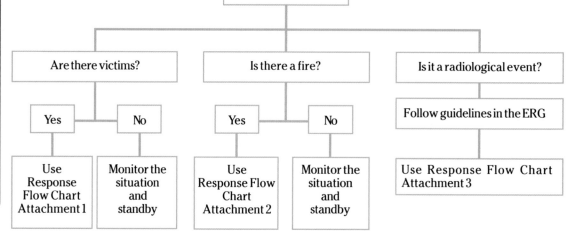

Are there victims?		Is there a fire?		Is it a radiological event?
Yes	No	Yes	No	Follow guidelines in the ERG
Use Response Flow Chart Attachment 1	Monitor the situation and standby	Use Response Flow Chart Attachment 2	Monitor the situation and standby	Use Response Flow Chart Attachment 3

4

Model Procedure for First Responder Initial Response
to Radiological Transportation Accidents

RESPONSE FLOW CHART ATTACHMENT 2

Accident involving victims

```
                          ┌──────────────────────┐
                          │       VICTIMS        │
                          └──────────────────────┘
```

Walking wounded or uninjured   **Non-walking wounded**

Detain walking wounded and uninjured persons who you suspect may have come in contact with radiological material and may be contaminated. Keep them in a treatment holding area within the controlled zone.

Assess and triage victims

Move victims to a treatment holding area within the controlled zone but away from the hazard area. Perform routine emergency care.

Assess and triage victims

Treat victims as if contaminated in the treatment area.

EMS personnel should:
- Use SCBA or particulate respirator (e.g., N95 mask)
- Wear Universal Precautions Personnel Protective Equipment
- Use disposable gloves

Patients should have:
- Oxygen mask (non-rebreather type) placed on their face to limit inhalation or ingestion of airborne contaminants
- Open wounds bandaged to prevent wound contamination
- Outer clothing cut away to remove majority of contamination

Transport

Yes   No

Notify receiving medical facility if possible

Reassess situation and take appropriate action to protect response personnel, victims, equipment, the public, and property based on any new information.

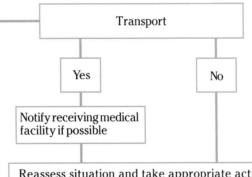

DEPARTMENT OF ENERGY

5

RESPONSE FLOW CHART ATTACHMENT 3

Accident involving a fire

```
                        FIRE
              ┌──────────┴──────────┐
        Small fires            Large fires
```

Small fires

Use:
- Dry chemical
- CO_2
- Water spray or regular foam

Large fires

Use:
- Water spray, fog, or regular foam
- Dike fire-control water for later disposal

If tanks or metal containers are present (Uranium Hexafluoride; UN 2977 or 2978):
- Cool containers with flooding amounts of water until well after the fire is out. If this is impossible, withdraw from area and let the fire burn.
- Do not use water or foam on material itself
- Always stay away from tanks engulfed in fire

Reassess situation and take appropriate action to protect response personnel, victims, equipment, the public, and property based on any new information.

6

Model Procedure for First Responder Initial Response
to Radiological Transportation Accidents

RESPONSE FLOW CHART ATTACHMENT 4

Accident involving radiological material

RADIOLOGICAL EVENT

- Call emergency response telephone number on the shipping papers. If shipping papers are unavailable or no answer, call appropriate number listed in the back of the ERG.

- Notify Radiation Authority of the accident situation and conditions.

- Priorities for rescue, life-saving, first aid, and control of fire and other hazards are higher than the priority for measuring radiation levels.

- Isolate spill or leak area at least 80 to 160 feet in all directions. Stay upwind. Keep unauthorized personnel away.

- Detain and/or isolate uninjured persons or equipment suspected to be contaminated.

- Delay decontamination and clean-up until instructions are received from Radiation Authority.

- Follow specific instructions in the ERG for evacuation, fire or explosion, spill or leak information, first aid, and health information.

Use *ERG Guide 163* as the guideline for first response actions and information if the situation is a known radiological event, but no other information is available about the material.

Reassess situation and take appropriate action to protect response personnel, victims, equipment, the public, and property based on any new information.

7

Possible Effects on a Community from a Nuclear Terrorist Attack

POSSIBLE EFFECTS ON A COMMUNITY FROM A NUCLEAR TERRORIST ATTACK

A 150-kiloton bomb constructed by terrorists is detonated in the heart of Manhattan, at the foot of the Empire State Building. The bomb goes off without warning at noontime. It is a clear spring day with a wind from the east.

T +1 Second

Blast Wave
At the end of the first second, the shock wave will have an overpressure of **20 pounds per square inch (psi)** at a distance of four tenths of a mile from ground zero. Even the most heavily reinforced steel and concrete buildings will be destroyed.

Casualties
This circle contains a daytime population of roughly 75,000. There will be no survivors. Those in the direct line of sight of the blast will be exposed to a thermal pulse in excess of 3,000 degrees Fahrenheit, causing instant death.

T + 4 Seconds

Blast Wave
An overpressure of at least **10 psi** extends out for one mile. The few buildings that remain standing on the outside edge of this ring will have their interiors destroyed. Though the thermal pulse is intense enough to ignite most materials, the shock wave will likely extinguish most fires in this ring.

Casualties
Almost all those outside and not in the direct line of sight of the blast will receive lung and ear drum injuries. The thermal pulse will kill those in direct line of sight instantly. Fatalities are estimated at 300,000 and an additional 100,000 non-fatal injuries.

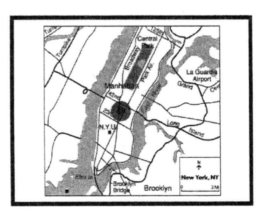

T + 6 Seconds

Blast Wave

In the next two seconds the shock wave moves out another half mile, extending the destruction out to a 1.5-mile radius. The overpressure has dropped to **5 psi** and covers an area of 4 square miles.

Casualties

This ring contains 500,000 people during the day. About 250,000 will be killed inside buildings by flying debris. The others will suffer varying degrees of injuries.

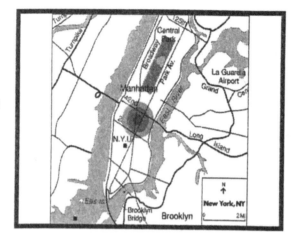

T + 10 Seconds

Blast Wave

This band extends out to a 2.5-mile radius and has an overpressure at the outside edge of **2 psi**. Structures will receive some damage, with buildings at the outer edge being almost undamaged.

Casualties

An estimated 235,000 people (15%) will be fatalities in this ring, with another 525,000 injured to varying degrees. No injuries will be due directly to the blast overpressure,

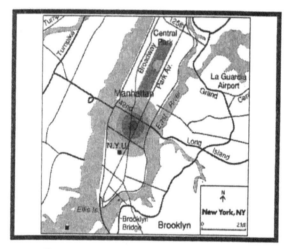

however the thermal pulse will still be sufficient to kill or incapacitate people not indoors. Darker clothing and skin will absorb more of the energy, producing severe burns.

T + 16 Seconds

Blast Wave

This band extends out for almost 4 miles and has an overpressure of **1 psi** at its outside edge. At the inner edge there will be light to moderate amounts of damage to un-reinforced brick and/or wood buildings.

Casualties

The affected population is estimated to be 500,000. Though this ring covers 30 square

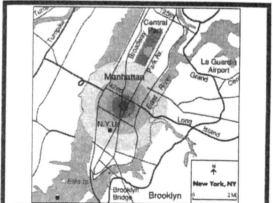

miles, there will be almost no additional fatalities and only 30,000 will receive injuries from the thermal pulse.

Long Term Fallout Pattern
Radioactive Fallout

A surface explosion will produce much more early fallout than a similarly sized airburst, where the fireball never touches the ground. The early fallout will drift back to earth on the easterly prevailing wind, creating an elliptical pattern stretching from ground zero out into New Jersey. Predicting levels of radiation is difficult and depends on many factors like bomb size, design, the ground surface, and soil type.

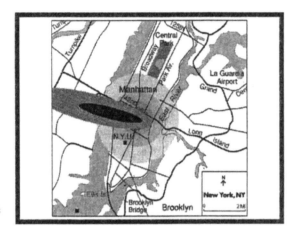

Distance from ground zero (mi)	Population	Fatalities	Injuries	Uninjured
0 - 0.4	75,000	75,000	0	0
0.4 - 1.0	400,000	300,000	100,000	0
1.0 - 1.5	500,000	220,000	220,000	60,000
1.5 - 2.5	1,500,000	235,000	525,000	740,000
2.5 - 4.0	500,000	0	30,000	470,000
Total	**2,975,000**	**830,000**	**875,000**	**1,270,000**

Computer Simulated Nuclear Blasts on Any Large U.S. City

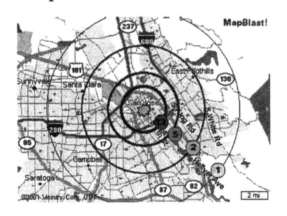

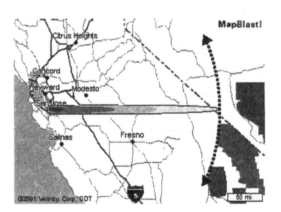

To create a similar example using any large city in the U.S., use the "Blast Mapper" on the PBS website at:http://www.pbs.org/wgbh/amex/bomb/sfeature/mapablast.html This site offers the choice of a 1 MT or 25 MT burst.

Fallout from Nuclear Weapons

A nuclear detonation at or near the ground surface produces highly radioactive fallout, or radioactive particulates that are combinations of the remains of the nuclear device, surface dust raised by the blast wave, vaporized earth and water raised by the fireball, and water condensed from moisture in the air. There will be large amounts of particles of less than 0.1 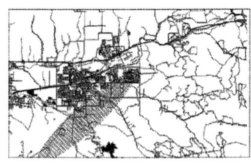 micrometer to several millimeters in diameter generated in a surface burst in addition to the very fine particles that contribute to worldwide fallout. The larger particles will not rise into the stratosphere but will settle to earth within about 24 hours as local fallout. Severe local fallout contamination can extend far beyond the blast and thermal effects, particularly in the case of high yield (Megaton yield) surface detonations. Prediction of fallout patterns on the ground is beyond the scope of this module. Computer software codes such as the HOTSPOT, RASCAL, ARAC and HPAC (Hazard Prediction and Assessment Capability) can generate fallout patterns based on weapon yield, altitude of burst, and current weather patterns.

Courtesy of the U.S. Department of Justice's "Emergency Response to Terrorism, Weapons of Mass Destruction (WMB) Responder Operations Radiation/Nuclear Course."

Appendix K
U.S. Bureau of Alcohol, Tobacco, Firearms and Explosives: List of Explosive Materials

A

Acetylides of heavy metals
Aluminum containing polymeric propellant
Aluminum ophorite explosive
Amatex
Amatol
Ammonal
Ammonium nitrate explosive mixtures (cap sensitive)
Ammonium nitrate explosive mixtures (non-cap sensitive)
Ammonium perchlorate having particle size less than 15 microns
Ammonium perchlorate composite propellant
Ammonium perchlorate explosive mixtures
Ammonium picrate [picrate of ammonia, Explosive D]
Ammonium salt lattice with isomorphously substituted inorganic salts
ANFO [ammonium nitrate-fuel oil]
Aromatic nitro-compound explosive mixtures
Azide explosives

B

Baranol
Baratol
BEAF [1, 2-bis (2, 2-difluoro-2-nitroacetoxyethane)]
Black powder
Black powder based explosive mixtures
Blasting agents, nitro-carbo-nitrates, including non-cap sensitive slurry and water gel explosives
Blasting caps
Blasting gelatin
Blasting powder
BTNEC [bis (trinitroethyl) carbonate]
BTNEN [bis (trinitroethyl) nitramine]
BTTN [1,2,4 butanetriol trinitrate]

Bulk salutes
Butyl tetryl

C

Calcium nitrate explosive mixture
Cellulose hexanitrate explosive mixture
Chlorate explosive mixtures
Composition A and variations
Composition B and variations
Composition C and variations
Copper acetylide
Cyanuric triazide
Cyclonite [RDX]
Cyclotetramethylenetetranitramine [HMX]
Cyclotol
Cyclotrimethylenetrinitramine [RDX]

D

DATB [diaminotrinitrobenzene]
DDNP [diazodinitrophenol]
DEGDN [diethyleneglycol dinitrate]
Detonating cord
Detonators
Dimethylol dimethyl methane dinitrate composition
Dinitroethyleneurea
Dinitroglycerine [glycerol dinitrate]
Dinitrophenol
Dinitrophenolates
Dinitrophenyl hydrazine
Dinitroresorcinol
Dinitrotoluene-sodium nitrate explosive mixtures
DIPAM [dipicramide; diaminohexanitrobiphenyl]
Dipicryl sulfone
Dipicrylamine
Display fireworks
DNPA [2,2-dinitropropyl acrylate]
DNPD [dinitropentano nitrile]
Dynamite

E

EDDN [ethylene diamine dinitrate]
EDNA [ethylenedinitramine]
Ednatol
EDNP [ethyl 4,4-dinitropentanoate]
EGDN [ethylene glycol dinitrate]
Erythritol tetranitrate explosives
Esters of nitro-substituted alcohols
Ethyl-tetryl
Explosive conitrates
Explosive gelatins
Explosive liquids
Explosive mixtures containing oxygenreleasing inorganic salts and hydrocarbons
Explosive mixtures containing oxygenreleasing inorganic salts and nitro bodies
Explosive mixtures containing oxygenreleasing inorganic salts and water insoluble fuels
Explosive mixtures containing oxygenreleasing inorganic salts and water soluble fuels
Explosive mixtures containing sensitized nitromethane
Explosive mixtures containing tetranitromethane (nitroform)
Explosive nitro compounds of aromatic hydrocarbons
Explosive organic nitrate mixtures
Explosive powders

F

Flash powder
Fulminate of mercury
Fulminate of silver
Fulminating gold
Fulminating mercury
Fulminating platinum
Fulminating silver

G

Gelatinized nitrocellulose
Gem-dinitro aliphatic explosive mixtures
Guanyl nitrosamino guanyl tetrazene
Guanyl nitrosamino guanylidene hydrazine
Guncotton

H

Heavy metal azides
Hexanite
Hexanitrodiphenylamine
Hexanitrostilbene

Hexogen [RDX]
Hexogene or octogene and a nitrated Nmethylaniline
Hexolites
HMTD [hexamethylenetriperoxidediamine]
HMX [cyclo-1,3,5,7-tetramethylene 2,4,6,8-tetranitramine; Octogen]
Hydrazinium nitrate/hydrazine/ aluminum explosive system
Hydrazoic acid

I

Igniter cord
Igniters
Initiating tube systems

K

KDNBF [potassium dinitrobenzofuroxane]

L

Lead azide
Lead mannite
Lead mononitroresorcinate
Lead picrate
Lead salts, explosive
Lead styphnate [styphnate of lead, lead trinitroresorcinate]
Liquid nitrated polyol and trimethylolethane
Liquid oxygen explosives

M

Magnesium ophorite explosives
Mannitol hexanitrate
MDNP [methyl 4,4-dinitropentanoate]
MEAN [monoethanolamine nitrate]
Mercuric fulminate
Mercury oxalate
Mercury tartrate
Metriol trinitrate
Minol-2 [40% TNT, 40% ammonium nitrate, 20% aluminum]
MMAN [monomethylamine nitrate]; methylamine nitrate
Mononitrotoluene-nitroglycerin mixture
Monopropellants

N

NIBTN [nitroisobutametriol trinitrate]
Nitrate explosive mixtures
Nitrate sensitized with gelled nitroparaffin

Nitrated carbohydrate explosive
Nitrated glucoside explosive
Nitrated polyhydric alcohol explosives
Nitric acid and a nitro aromatic compound
   explosive
Nitric acid and carboxylic fuel explosive
Nitric acid explosive mixtures
Nitro aromatic explosive mixtures
Nitro compounds of furane explosive mixtures
Nitrocellulose explosive
Nitroderivative of urea explosive mixture
Nitrogelatin explosive
Nitrogen trichloride
Nitrogen tri-iodide
Nitroglycerine [NG, RNG, nitro, glyceryl trinitrate,
   trinitroglycerine]
Nitroglycide
Nitroglycol [ethylene glycol dinitrate, EGDN]
Nitroguanidine explosives
Nitronium perchlorate propellant mixtures
Nitroparaffins Explosive Grade and ammonium
   nitrate mixtures
Nitrostarch
Nitro-substituted carboxylic acids
Nitrourea

O
Octogen [HMX]
Octol [75 percent HMX, 25 percent TNT]
Organic amine nitrates
Organic nitramines

P
PBX [plastic bonded explosives]
Pellet powder
Penthrinite composition
Pentolite
Perchlorate explosive mixtures
Peroxide based explosive mixtures
PETN [nitropentaerythrite, pentaerythrite
   tetranitrate, pentaerythritol tetranitrate]
Picramic acid and its salts
Picramide
Picrate explosives
Picrate of potassium explosive mixtures
Picratol
Picric acid (manufactured as an explosive)
Picryl chloride
Picryl fluoride
PLX [95% nitromethane, 5% ethylenediamine]

Polynitro aliphatic compounds
Polyolpolynitrate-nitrocellulose explosive gels
Potassium chlorate and lead sulfocyanate
   explosive
Potassium nitrate explosive mixtures
Potassium nitroaminotetrazole
Pyrotechnic compositions
PYX [2,6-bis(picrylamino)] 3,5- dinitropyridine

R
RDX [cyclonite, hexogen, T4, cyclo-1,3,5,-
   trimethylene-2,4,6,-trinitramine; hexahydro-
   1,3,5-trinitro-S-triazine]

S
Safety fuse
Salts of organic amino sulfonic acid explosive
   mixture
Salutes (bulk)
Silver acetylide
Silver azide
Silver fulminate
Silver oxalate explosive mixtures
Silver styphnate
Silver tartrate explosive mixtures
Silver tetrazene
Slurried explosive mixtures of water, inorganic
   oxidizing salt, gelling agent, fuel, and sensitizer
   (cap sensitive)
Smokeless powder
Sodatol
Sodium amatol
Sodium azide explosive mixture
Sodium dinitro-ortho-cresolate
Sodium nitrate explosive mixtures
Sodium nitrate-potassium nitrate explosive
   mixture
Sodium picramate
Special fireworks
Squibs
Styphnic acid explosives

T
Tacot [tetranitro-2,3,5,6-dibenzo- 1,3a,4,6a
   tetrazapentalene]
TATB [triaminotrinitrobenzene]
TATP [triacetonetriperoxide]
TEGDN [triethylene glycol dinitrate]
Tetranitrocarbazole
Tetrazene [tetracene, tetrazine, 1(5-tetrazolyl)-4-
   guanyl tetrazene hydrate]

Tetrazole explosives

Tetryl [2,4,6 tetranitro-N-methylaniline]

Tetrytol

Thickened inorganic oxidizer salt slurried explosive mixture

TMETN [trimethylolethane trinitrate]

TNEF [trinitroethyl formal]

TNEOC [trinitroethylorthocarbonate]

TNEOF [trinitroethylorthoformate]

TNT [trinitrotoluene, trotyl, trilite, triton]

Torpex

Tridite

Trimethylol ethyl methane trinitrate composition

Trimethylolthane trinitratenitrocellulose

Trimonite

Trinitroanisole

Trinitrobenzene

Trinitrobenzoic acid

Trinitrocresol

Trinitro-meta-cresol

Trinitronaphthalene

Appendix L
Upgrading Existing Incident Management Systems to NIMS ICS Compliancy

In Homeland Security Presidential Directive-5 (HSPD-5) released on February 28, 2003, President George W. Bush called on the Secretary of Homeland Security to develop a national incident management system to provide a consistent nationwide approach for federal, state, tribal, and local governments to work together to prepare for, prevent, respond to, and recover from domestic incidents, regardless of cause, size, or complexity.

On March 1, 2004, after close collaboration with state and local government officials and representatives from a wide range of public safety organizations, Homeland Security established the National Incident Management System (NIMS). It incorporates many existing best practices into a comprehensive national approach to domestic incident management, applicable at all jurisdictional levels and across all functional disciplines. One of those existing best practices is the use of the Incident Command System (ICS) to manage domestic incidents.

The requirements within NIMS were mandated to be adopted by all federal agencies and departments no later than October 1, 2004. These agencies were also mandated to make adoption of NIMS by state and local agencies a condition for federal preparedness assistance grants after that date. In the short term, state and local agencies need only to show compliance with the ICS portion of NIMS to be considered compliant and qualified for federal assistance grants. It will be a significant length of time before all the components of NIMS can be fully implemented.

The NIMS ICS system is virtually identical to the existing FIRESCOPE ICS, National Interagency Incident Management System (NIIMS ICS), and National Fire Service IMS systems. Agencies that are already adept in using the existing systems will only require minor modifications to their systems in order to be compliant with the basic structure of the NIMS ICS. Those changes are highlighted in the following sections. In addition to making minor changes to the basic ICS structure, agencies must also be basically familiar with some of the ICS components that will be called into play on major incidents. Those components are highlighted as well.

Primary Differences Between NIMS ICS and Existing Incident Management Systems

Within the basic structure of NIMS ICS and the existing incident management systems used throughout the United States, there are only three notable differences that need to be accounted for when adopting NIMS ICS. They are as follows:

1. *Renaming the Public Information Officer* — Existing incident management systems refer to this general staff position as simply the *Information Officer*. NIMS ICS adds the word *Public* to this position title.

2. *Eliminating the use of Sectors as an organizational tool* — Organizations that use the Fire Ground Command (FGC) or National Fire Service Incident Management System (IMS) may group resources that are deployed to a geographical area or for a specific function into tactical-level management units called *Sectors*. The term *Sectors* is not recognized by NIMS ICS. Rather, resources assembled for geographical assignments are referred to as *Divisions* and resources assigned for a specific function are referred to as *Groups* as they were in NIIMS and FIRESCOPE ICS.

3. ***Integrating the intelligence function into ICS*** — The traditional ICS organization has five major functions, including Command, Operations, Planning, Logistics, and Finance/Administration. In the NIMS ICS, a potential sixth functional area to cover the intelligence function can be established for gathering and sharing incident-related information and intelligence. It is highly unlikely that this function would be activated in most local-level hazardous materials incidents. It is more likely to be used in widespread incidents or those that have been identified as terrorist acts.

The intelligence function provides analysis and sharing of information and intelligence during an incident. Intelligence can include national security or classified information as well as such operational information as risk assessments, medical intelligence, weather information, structural designs of buildings, and toxic contaminant levels.

Traditionally, information and intelligence functions are located in the Planning Section. In exceptional situations, however, the IC may need to assign this role to other parts of the ICS organization. Under the NIMS ICS, the intelligence and information function may be assigned in one of the following ways:

- Within the Command Staff
- As a unit within the Planning Section
- As a branch within the Operations Section
- As a separate General Staff Section

A full chart showing the components of NIMS ICS is shown in **Figure L.1**.

Other Important Concepts Addressed by NIMS ICS

The use of an incident management system, such as NIMS ICS, has proven to be effective on all types of incidents. In extraordinary incidents such as the bombing of the Alfred P. Murrah building in Oklahoma City, the terrorist attacks of September 11, 2001, or a large-scale natural disaster, however, additional components beyond the standard ICS positions may be necessary to manage and control the incident. Situations that may require these additional components include the following:

- Multiple, concurrent incidents
- Incidents that are not site specific such as a large biological attack
- Incidents that are geographically dispersed
- Incidents that evolve over a long period of time

The following sections give a very brief overview of these components.

Unified Command

As previously discussed in the text of this manual, NIMS ICS provides specific guidelines for the use of Unified Command. Unified Command is established in two circumstances:

1. When there is more than one responding agency with responsibility for the incident
2. When the incident crosses jurisdictional boundaries

Under Unified Command, each of the responsible agencies designates a representative to participate as part of the Unified Command team. The Unified Command team works together to analyze intelligence information and establish a common set of objectives and strategies for a single incident action plan. Using a Unified Command does not change any of the other features of operating the ICS. It simply lets all those agencies or jurisdictions that have responsibility for an incident participate in the planning and management of the incident.

Area Command

Area Command may be established to coordinate multiple incidents that each have their own incident command structure or a large incident that crosses jurisdictional boundaries (**Figure L.2**). Area command may be particularly useful in bioterrorism or public health emergencies because they are not site specific, not immediately identifiable, and evolve over time. Area Command may be looked at as an *umbrella* command organization that serves to coordinate the resources and actions of multiple active incident command posts and structures.

In general, Area Command has the following responsibilities:

Incident Management Organizational Structure

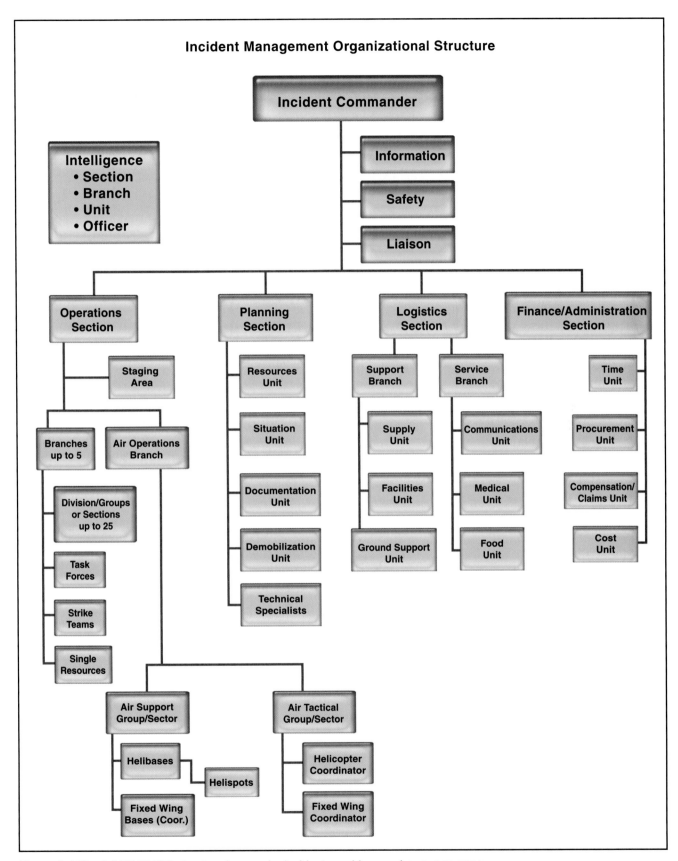

Figure L.1 The full NIMS ICS structure for a major incident requiring maximum resources.

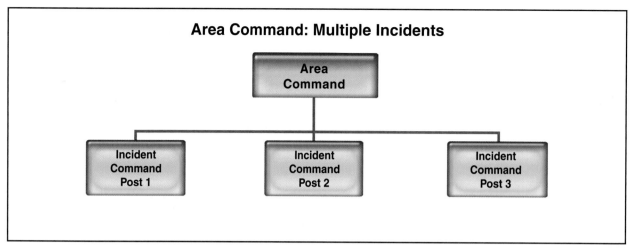

Figure L.2 Area Command may be responsible for overseeing multiple, individual incident command operational structures.

- Setting overall strategies and priorities
- Assigning critical resources according to the priorities
- Ensuring that incidents are run properly
- Ensuring that objectives are met
- Ensuring that strategies are followed

The command structure for an Area Command is very similar to that for a standard ICS structure. The Area Command may even be performed by a Uniformed Command structure when incidents are multijurisdictional or multiagency. The primary difference between an Area Command structure and a typical ICS structure is that there is no Operations Section in an Area Command structure. This is due to the fact that the Operations function is contained within each of the individual command structures being overseen by the Area Command. **Figure L.3** shows the structure of an Area Command.

Multiagency Coordination Systems

Multiagency coordination systems may be needed on large-scale incidents that require high-level resource or information management. Multiagency coordination systems are a combination of resources that are integrated into a common framework for coordinating and supporting domestic incident management activities. These resources may include facilities, equipment, personnel, procedures, and/or communications. Five primary functions of a multiagency coordination system are as follows:

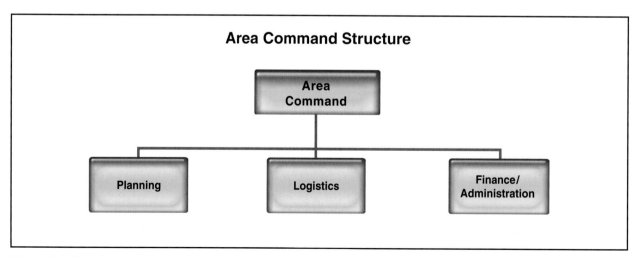

Figure L.3 Area Command is organized similarly to standard ICS structure, with the exception that there is no Operations Section under Area Command.

1. Support incident management policies and priorities.

2. Facilitate logistics support and resource tracking.

3. Make resource allocation decisions based on incident management priorities.

4. Coordinate incident-related information.

5. Coordinate interagency and intergovernmental issues regarding incident management policies, priorities, and strategies.

The implementation of a multiagency coordination system does not take tactical and operational responsibilities away from the incident commander.

There are two primary elements of multiagency coordination systems that can be implemented in large-scale incidents: *emergency operations centers* (EOCs) and *multiagency coordination entities*. EOCs are the locations from which the coordination of information and resources to support incident activities takes place. EOCs typically are established by entities of local or state government, and personnel representing multiple jurisdictions and functional disciplines may staff them. The organization and staffing of EOCs will vary, but in general should be designed to support the following functions:

- Coordination
- Communications
- Resource dispatching and tracking
- Information collection, analysis, and dissemination

Multiagency coordination entities consist of principle representatives from organizations that have direct incident management support or resource responsibilities. The multiagency coordination entities are used to facilitate incident management and policy coordination, and they are generally responsible for the following functions *during* an incident:

- Ensure that each agency is providing situation and resource status information.
- Establish priorities between incidents and/or Area Commands in concert with the Incident Command or Unified Command.

- Acquire and allocate resources required by incident management personnel.
- Coordinate and identify future resource requirements.
- Coordinate and resolve policy issues.
- Provide strategic direction.

Following the incident, the multiagency coordination entities are typically responsible for reviewing lessons learned from the incident and then ensuring that appropriate revisions to the following items are acted upon:

- Plans
- Procedures
- Communications
- Staffing
- Other capabilities necessary for improved incident management

Public Information

Public information is critical to domestic incident management for a number of reasons. One is that the incident commander must have a mechanism for gathering accurate information that may be helpful in managing the incident. Secondly, the response agencies need to ensure that accurate and appropriate information is transmitted to the public so that they are properly apprised of the situation and any actions that are required of them.

Under ICS, the public information officer (PIO) is a key member of the command staff who is charged with advising Command on all public information matters related to the incident. Duties include handling media and public inquiries, coordinating emergency public information and warnings, controlling rumors, monitoring media reports for accuracy, and disseminating timely and accurate information related to the incident.

One of the mechanisms available to the PIO on large incidents is to establish a joint information System (JIS). The JIS provides an organized, integrated, and coordinated mechanism for ensuring that decision makers and the public are fully informed throughout a domestic incident or other emergency. It includes plans, protocols, and structures used to provide information to the public during an emergency. Key elements of the JIS include interagency coordination and integration, developing and delivering coordinated messages, and support for decision makers.

One way to ensure that public information is coordinated in an efficient manner is to establish a joint information center (JIC). The JIC becomes a central, physical location from which information can be coordinated across various jurisdictions and agencies as well as between governmental partners, the private sector, and nongovernmental agencies. Incident commanders and multiagency coordination entities, working with the PIO, establish and oversee JICs and the process for coordinating and clearing public communications. The level of government at which the JIC is established will vary depending on the incident and local preferences and procedures. A single JIC location is preferable, but the JIS should be flexible enough

to accommodate multiple JICs should the situation dictate that. Regardless of local preferences, JICs have the following common characteristics:

- The JIC includes representatives of all players in managing the response. This may include jurisdictions, agencies, private entities, and nongovernmental organizations.

- Each JIC must have procedures and protocols for communicating and coordinating effectively with other JICs and with the appropriate components of the ICS organization.

The information in this Appendix was adapted from *IS700 NIMS Course Summary,* which (at the time of publication) can be found online at http:// training.fema.gov/EMIWeb/downloads/IS700-NIMS.pdf. More detailed information and on-line training on the NIMS ICS can be found at http:// training.fema.gov.

Glossary

A

Absorbent — Inert material or substance having no active properties that allows another substance to penetrate into the interior of its structure; can be used to pick up a liquid contaminant. An absorbent is commonly used in the abatement of hazardous materials spills. Examples are soil, diatomaceous earth, vermiculite, sand, and other commercially available products. *Also see* Contaminant.

Absorption — (1) Penetration of one substance into the structure of another such as the process of picking up a liquid contaminant with an absorbent. *Also see* Contaminant and Absorbent. (2) Passage of materials (such as toxins) through some body surface into body fluids and tissue. *Also see* Routes of Entry and Toxin.

ACGIH® — Abbreviation for American Conference of Governmental Industrial Hygienists®.

Acid — Compound containing hydrogen that reacts with water to produce hydrogen ions; a proton donor; a liquid compound with a pH less than 2. Acidic chemicals are corrosive. *Also see* Base and pH.

Activation Energy — Amount of energy that must be added to an atomic or molecular system to begin a reaction.

Acute — (1) Characterized by sharpness or severity; having rapid onset and a relatively short duration. (2) Single exposure (dose) or several repeated exposures to a substance within a short time period. *Also see* Chronic.

Acute Exposure Guideline Level — Airborne concentration of a substance at or above which it is predicted that the general population, including "susceptible" but excluding "hypersusceptible" individuals, could experience notable discomfort; established by the U.S. Environmental Protection Agency (EPA).

Acute Health Effects — Health effects that occur or develop rapidly after exposure to a substance. *Also see* Chronic Health Effects.

Aerator — Device for introducing air into dry bulk solids to improve flow ability.

Aerosol — Form of mist characterized by highly respirable, minute liquid particles. *Also see* Mist.

AFFF — Abbreviation for aqueous film forming foam.

Agency for Toxic Substances and Disease Registry (ATSDR) — Lead U.S. public health agency responsible for implementing the health-related provisions of the Comprehensive Environmental Response, Compensation, and Liability Act (CERCLA), and charged with assessing health hazards at specific hazardous waste sites, helping to prevent or reduce exposure and the illnesses that result, and increasing knowledge and understanding of the health effects that may result from exposure to hazardous substances.

Air Bill — Shipping document prepared from a bill of lading that accompanies each piece or each lot of air cargo. *Also see* Bill of Lading and Shipping Papers.

Airline Respirator — *See* Supplied-Air Respirator (SAR).

Air-Reactive Material — Substance that ignites when exposed to air at normal temperatures. Also called *pyrophoric*. *Also see* Reactive Material, Reactivity, and Water-Reactive Material.

Air Spring — Flexible, air-inflated chamber on a truck or trailer in which the air pressure is controlled and varied to support the load and absorb road shocks.

Alkali — Strong base. *Also see* Base, Acid, Caustic, and pH.

Allergen — Material that can cause an allergic reaction of the skin or respiratory system. Also called *sensitizer*.

Alpha Particle — Energetic, positively charged particles (helium nuclei) emitted from the nucleus during radioactive decay that rapidly lose energy when passing through matter. *Also see* Alpha Radiation, Beta Particle, and Gamma Ray.

Alpha Radiation — Consists of particles having a large mass and positive electrical charge; least penetrating of the three common forms of radiation. It is normally not considered dangerous to plants, animals, or people unless it gets into the body. *Also see* Beta Radiation, Radiation (2), and Gamma Radiation

Ambient Temperature — Temperature of the surrounding environment.

American Conference of Governmental Industrial Hygienists® (ACGIH) — Organization that promotes the free exchange of ideas and experiences and the development of standards and techniques in industrial health. *Also see* Biological Exposure Indices (BEI®).

Ammonium Nitrate and Fuel Oil (ANFO) — High explosive blasting agent made of common fertilizer mixed with diesel fuel or oil; requires a booster to initiate detonation. *Also see* High Explosive, Detonation, and Explosive (1).

ANFO — Abbreviation for Ammonium Nitrate and Fuel Oil.

Aqueous Film Forming Foam (AFFF) — Synthetic foam concentrate that (when combined with water) can form a complete vapor barrier over fuel spills and fires; highly effective extinguishing and blanketing agent on hydrocarbon fuels. *Also see* Foam Concentrate and Foam System.

Asphyxia — Suffocation.

Asphyxiant — Any substance that prevents oxygen from combining in sufficient quantities with the blood or from being used by body tissues. *Also see* Simple Asphyxiant and Chemical Asphyxiant.

Asphyxiation — Condition that causes death because of a deficient amount of oxygen and an excessive amount of carbon monoxide and/or other gases in the blood.

ATF — Abbreviation for U.S. Bureau of Alcohol, Tobacco, Firearms and Explosives.

Atmospheric Pressure — Force exerted by the atmosphere at the surface of the earth because of the weight of air. Atmospheric pressure at sea level is about 14.7 psi (101 kPa) {1.01 bar}. Atmospheric pressure increases as elevation decreases below sea level and decreases as elevation increases above sea level.

Atmospheric Stability — Degree to which vertical motion in the atmosphere is enhanced or suppressed. Vertical motions and smoke dispersion are enhanced in an unstable atmosphere. Stability suppresses vertical motion and limits smoke dispersion. *Also see* Inversion (1).

Atmospheric Storage Tank — Class of fixed facility storage tanks. Pressures range from 0 to 0.5 psi (0 to 3.4 kPa) {0 to 0.03 bar}. Sometimes called *nonpressure storage tank*. *Also see* Lifter Roof Storage Tank, Cone Roof Storage Tank, Floating Roof Storage Tank, Internal Floating Roof Tank, External Floating Roof Tank, Low-Pressure Storage Tank, Horizontal Storage Tank, and Pressure Storage Tank.

ATSDR — Abbreviation for Agency for Toxic Substances and Disease Registry.

Autoignition — Ignition that occurs when a substance in air, whether solid, liquid, or gaseous, is heated sufficiently to initiate or cause self-sustained combustion without an external ignition source. *Also see* Ignition, Autoignition Temperature, and Ignition Temperature.

Autoignition Temperature — Same as ignition temperature except that no external ignition source is required for ignition because the material itself has been heated to ignition temperature; temperature at which autoignition occurs through the spontaneous ignition of the gases or vapors emitted by a heated material. *Also see* Ignition Temperature, Autoignition, and Ignition.

Avulsion — Forcible separation or detachment; the tearing away of a body part.

Awareness Level — Lowest level of training established by the National Fire Protection Association for first responders at hazardous materials incidents. *Also see* Operational Level.

B

Bacteria — Microscopic, single-celled organisms. *Also see* Virus and Rickettsia.

Baffle — Intermediate partial bulkhead that reduces the surge effect in a partially loaded liquid tank.

Barge — Long, large vessel (usually flat-bottomed, self-propelled, or towed or pushed by another vessel) used for transporting goods on inland waterways. *Also see* Cargo Vessel.

Base — Corrosive water-soluble compound or substance containing group-forming hydroxide ions in water solution that reacts with an acid to form a salt; an alkaline (caustic) substance. *Also see* Acid, Alkali, Caustic, and pH.

Becquerel (Bq) — International System unit of measurement for radioactivity, indicating the number of nuclear decays/disintegrations a radioactive material undergoes in a certain period of time. *Also see* Radiation (2), Radioactive Material (RAM), and Curie (Ci).

BEI® — Abbreviation for Biological Exposure Indices.®

Beta Particle — Particle that is about 1/7,000th the size of an alpha particle but has more penetrating power; has a negative electrical charge. *Also see* Beta Radiation, Alpha Particle and Gamma Ray.

Beta Radiation — Type of radiation that can cause skin burns. *Also see* Alpha Radiation, Gamma Radiation, and Radiation (2).

Bill of Lading — Shipping paper used by the trucking industry (and others) indicating origin, destination, route, and product; placed in the cab of every truck tractor. This document establishes the terms of a contract between shippers and transportation companies; serves as a document of title, contract of carriage, and receipt for goods. *Also see* Shipping Papers and Lading.

Biochemical — Involving chemical reactions in living organisms.

Biological Attack — Intentional release of viruses, bacteria, or their toxins for the purpose of harming or killing citizens. *Also see* Terrorism.

Biological Exposure Indices (BEI®) — Guidance value recommended for assessing biological monitoring results that is established by the American Conference of Governmental Industrial Hygienists (ACGIH).

Biological Toxin — Poison produced by living organisms. *Also see* Toxin and Poison.

Blasting Cap — *See* Detonator.

Blast Pressure Wave — Shock wave created by rapidly expanding gases in an explosion.

BLEVE — Acronym for Boiling Liquid Expanding Vapor Explosion.

Blister Agent — Chemical warfare agent that burns and blisters the skin or any other part of the body it contacts. Also called *vesicant*. *Also see* Chemical Warfare Agent.

Blood Agent/Blood Poison — *See* Chemical Asphyxiant.

B-NICE — Acronym for Biological, Nuclear, Incendiary, Chemical, and Explosive.

Boiling Liquid Expanding Vapor Explosion (BLEVE) — Rapid vaporization of a liquid stored under pressure upon release to the atmosphere following major failure of its containing vessel; failure is the result of overpressurization caused by an external heat source, which causes the vessel to explode into two or more pieces when the temperature of the liquid is well above its boiling point at normal atmospheric pressure. *Also see* Boiling Point.

Boiling Point — Temperature of a substance when the vapor pressure exceeds atmospheric pressure. At this temperature, the rate of evaporation exceeds the rate of condensation. At this point, more liquid is turning into gas than gas is turning back into a liquid. *Also see* Physical Properties and Vapor Pressure.

Bq — Abbreviation for Becquerel.

Break Bulk Carrier — Ship designed with large holds to accommodate a wide range of products such as vehicles, pallets of metal bars, liquids in drums, or items in bags, boxes, and crates. *Also see* Cargo Vessel.

Bulk Cargo Carrier — Ship carrying either liquid or dry goods stowed loose in a hold and not enclosed in any container. *Also see* Cargo Vessel.

Bulk Container — Cargo tank container attached to a flatbed truck or rail flatcar used to transport materials in bulk. This container may carry liquids or gases. *Also see* Container (1).

Bulk Packaging — Packaging, other than a vessel or barge, including transport vehicle or freight container, in which hazardous materials are loaded with no intermediate form of containment and which has (a) a maximum capacity greater than 119 gallons (450 L) as a receptacle for a liquid, (b) maximum net mass greater than 882 pounds (400 kg) and a maximum capacity greater than 119 gallons (450 L) as a receptacle for a solid, or (c) water capacity greater than 1,000 pounds (454 kg) as a receptacle for a gas. Reference: Title 49 *CFR* 171.8. *Also see* Packaging (1) and Nonbulk Packaging.

Bumper — Structure designed to provide front- and rear-end protection of a vehicle.

Bureau of Alcohol, Tobacco, Firearms and Explosives (ATF) — Division of U.S. Department of Treasury that enforces federal laws and regulations relating to alcohol, tobacco, firearms, explosives, and arson.

C

California FIRESCOPE Incident Command System — *See* Incident Command System (ICS).

Canadian Nuclear Safety Commission — Agency responsible for regulating almost all uses of nuclear energy and nuclear materials in Canada.

Canadian Transport Emergency Centre (CANUTEC) — Canadian center that provides fire and emergency responders with 24-hour information for incidents involving hazardous materials; operated by Transport Canada, a department of the Canadian government. *Also see* Chemical Transportation Emergency Center (CHEMTREC®) and Emergency Transportation System for the Chemical Industry (SETIQ).

CANUTEC — Acronym for Canadian Transport Emergency Centre.

Capacity Indicator — Device installed on a tank to indicate capacity at a specific level.

Capacity Stencil — Number stenciled on the exterior of tank cars to indicated the volume of the tank.

Carboy — Cylindrical container of about 5 to 15 gallons (19 L to 57 L) capacity for corrosive or pure liquids; made of glass, plastic, or metal with a neck and sometimes a pouring tip; cushioned in a wooden box, wicker basket, or special drum. *Also see* Container (1).

Carcinogen — Cancer-producing substance.

Cargo Container — *See* Container (1).

Cargo Tank — *See* Cargo Tank Truck.

Cargo Tank Truck — Motor vehicle commonly used to transport hazardous materials via roadway. Also called *tank motor vehicle*, *tank truck*, and *cargo tank*. *Also see* Corrosive Liquid Tank, Cryogenic Liquid Tank, Dry Bulk Cargo Tank, High-Pressure Tank, Low-Pressure Chemical Tank, Compressed-Gas Tube Trailer, Nonpressure Liquid Tank, and Elevated Temperature Materials Carrier.

Cargo Vessel — Ship used to transport cargo (dry bulk, break bulk, roll-on/roll off, and container) via waterways. *Also see* Break Bulk Carrier, Bulk Cargo Carrier, Container Vessel, Roll-on/Roll-off Vessel, and Barge.

CAS Number — Number assigned by the American Chemical Society's Chemical Abstract Service that uniquely identifies a specific compound.

Caustic — Substance having the destructive properties of a base. *Also see* Base, Alkali, and Acid.

CBRNE — Abbreviation for Chemical, Biological, Radiological, Nuclear, and Explosive.

CERCLA — Abbreviation for Comprehensive Environmental Response, Compensation, and Liability Act.

CFR — Abbreviation for *Code of Federal Regulations.*

CGA — Abbreviation for Compressed Gas Association.

Chemical Asphyxiant — Substance that reacts to keep the body from being able to use oxygen. Also called *blood poison*, *blood agent*, or *cyanogen agent.*

Chemical Attack — Deliberate release of a toxic gas, liquid, or solid that can poison people and the environment. *Also see* Terrorism and Chemical Warfare Agent.

Chemical Carrier — Tank vessel that transports multiple specialty and chemical commodities. *Also see* Tanker.

Chemical Degradation — Process that occurs when the characteristics of a material are altered through contact with chemical substances.

Chemical Properties — Relating to the way a substance is able to change into other substances; reflect the ability to burn, react, explode, or produce toxic substances hazardous to people or the environment. *Also see* Physical Properties.

Chemical Protective Clothing (CPC) — Clothing designed to shield or isolate individuals from the chemical, physical, and biological hazards that may be encountered during operations involving hazardous materials. *Also see* Level A Protection, Special Protective Clothing (1), and Personal Protective Equipment (PPE).

Chemical Reaction — Any change in the composition of matter that involves a conversion of one substance into another.

Chemical Transportation Emergency Center (CHEMTREC®) — Center established by the American Chemistry Council that supplies 24-hour information for incidents involving hazardous materials. *Also see* Canadian Transport Emergency Centre (CANUTEC) and Emergency Transportation System for the Chemical Industry (SETIQ).

Chemical Warfare Agent — Chemical substances that are intended for use in warfare or terrorist activities to kill, seriously injury, or seriously incapacitate people through their physiological effects. *Also see* Chemical Attack, Choking Agent, Vomiting Agent, Blister Agent, and Nerve Agent.

CHEMTREC® — Acronym for Chemical Transportation Emergency Center.

Choking Agent — Chemical warfare agent that attacks the lungs causing tissue damage. *Also see* Chemical Warfare Agent.

Chronic — Marked by long duration; recurring over a period of time. *Also see* Acute.

Chronic Health Effects — Long-term effects from either a one-time or repeated exposure to a hazardous substance. *Also see* Acute Health Effects.

Ci — Abbreviation for Curie.

CIS — Abbreviation for Critical Incident Stress.

Class A Fire — Fire involving ordinary combustibles such as wood, paper, cloth, and the like.

Class A Foam Concentrate — Foam specially designed for use on Class A combustibles. *Also see* Foam Concentrate and Finished Foam.

Class B Fire — Fire involving flammable and combustible liquids and gases such as gasoline, kerosene, and propane.

Class B Foam Concentrate — Foam specially designed for use on ignited or unignited Class B flammable or combustible liquids. *Also see* Foam Concentrate and Finished Foam.

Cleanout Fitting — Fitting installed in the top of a tank to facilitate washing the tank's interior.

Cloud — Ball-shaped pattern of an airborne hazardous material where the material has collectively risen above the ground or water at a hazardous materials incident. *Also see* Cone, Hemispheric Release, and Plume.

Code of Federal Regulations (CFR) — Books or documents containing the specific United States regulations provided for by law; complete body of U.S. federal law.

Colorimetric Tube — Small tube that changes color when air that is contaminated with a particular substance is drawn through it. Also called *detector tube*.

Combination Packaging — Shipping container consisting of one or more inner packagings secured in a nonbulk outer packaging. *Also see* Packaging (1).

Combustible Gas Detector — Indicates the explosive levels of combustible gases.

Combustible Liquid — Liquid having a flash point at or above 100°F (37.8°C) and below 200°F (93.3°C). *Also see* Flammable Liquid.

Combustion — Exothermic chemical reaction that is a self-sustaining process of rapid oxidation of a fuel, which produces heat and light.

Composite Packaging — Single container made of two different types of material. *Also see* Packaging (1).

Compound — Substance consisting of two or more elements that have been united chemically.

Comprehensive Environmental Response, Compensation, and Liability Act (CERCLA) — U.S. law that created a tax on the chemical and petroleum industries and provided broad federal authority to respond directly to releases or threatened releases of hazardous substances that may endanger public health or the environment.

Compressed Gas — Gas that, at normal temperature, exists solely as a gas when pressurized in a container as opposed to a gas that becomes a liquid when stored under pressure. *Also see* Gas, Liquefied Compressed Gas, and Nonflammable Gas.

Compressed Gas Association (CGA) — Trade association that, among other things, writes standards pertaining to the use, storage, and transportation of compressed gases.

Compressed-Gas Tube Trailer — Cargo tank truck that carries gases under pressure; may be a large single container, an intermodal shipping unit, or several horizontal tubes. Also called *tube trailer. Also see* Cargo Tank Truck.

Concentration — (1) Quantity of a chemical material inhaled for purposes of measuring toxicity. (2) Percentage (mass or volume) of a material dissolved in water (or other solvent). *Also see* Lethal Concentration (LC_{50}) and Dose.

Condensation — Process of going from the gaseous to the liquid state.

Cone — Triangular-shaped pattern of an airborne hazardous material release with a point source at the breach and a wide base downrange. *Also see* Cloud, Hemispheric Release, and Plume.

Cone Roof Storage Tank — Fixed-site vertical atmospheric storage tank that has a cone-shaped pointed roof with weak roof-to-shell seams that are intended to break when excessive overpressure results inside; used to store flammable, combustible, and corrosive liquids. Also called *dome roof tank. Also see* Atmospheric Storage Tank.

Confinement — (1) Process of controlling the flow of a spill and capturing it at some specified location. (2) Operations required to prevent fire from extending from the area of origin to uninvolved areas or structures. *Also see* Containment.

Consignee — Person who is to receive a shipment.

Consist — Rail shipping paper that contains a list of cars in the train by order; indicates the cars that contain hazardous materials. Some railroads include information on emergency operations for the hazardous materials on board with the consist. Also called *train consist. Also see* Shipping Papers and Waybill.

Consumer Product Safety Commission (CPSC) — U.S. government agency charged with protecting the public from unreasonable risks of serious injury or death from more than 15,000 types of consumer products under the agency's jurisdic-

tion, including hazardous materials intended for consumer purchase and use.

Container — (1) Article of transport equipment that is (a) a permanent character and strong enough for repeated use; (b) specifically designed to facilitate the carriage of goods by one or more modes of transport without intermediate reloading; and (c) fitted with devices permitting its ready handling, particularly its transfer from one mode to another. The term does not include vehicles. Also called *freight container* and *cargo container.* (2) Boxes of standardized size used to transport cargo by truck or railcar when transported overland or by cargo vessels at sea. *Also see* Intermodal Container, Container Vessel, Refrigerated Intermodal Container, Bulk Container, Carboy, and Container Specification Number.

Container Specification Number — Shipping container number preceded by letters *DOT* that indicates the container has been built to U.S. federal specifications.

Container Vessel — Ship specially equipped to transport large freight containers in horizontal or, more commonly, vertical container cells; containers are usually loaded and unloaded by special cranes. *Also see* Cargo Vessel.

Containment — Act of stopping the further release of a material from its container. *Also see* Confinement.

Contaminant — Any foreign substance that compromises the purity of a given substance. *Also see* Contamination

Contamination — Condition of impurity resulting from a mixture or contact with foreign substance. *Also see* Decontamination, Surface Contamination, and Contaminant.

Control Agent — Material used to contain, confine, neutralize, or extinguish a hazardous material or its vapor.

Control Zones — *See* Hazard-Control Zones.

Convulsant — Poison that causes an exposed individual to have convulsions. *Also see* Poison.

Cooperating Agency — Agency supplying assistance other than direct fire suppression, rescue, support, or service functions to the incident control effort. Examples: American Red Cross, law enforcement agency, telephone company, and the like.

Corrosive — *See* Corrosive Material.

Corrosive Liquid Tank — Cargo tank truck that carries corrosive liquids, usually acids. *Also see* Cargo Tank Truck.

Corrosive Material — Gaseous, liquid, or solid material that can burn, irritate, or destroy human skin tissue and severely corrode steel. Also called *corrosive*. *Also see* Hazardous Material.

Covered Floating Roof Tank — *See* Internal Floating Roof Tank.

CPC — Abbreviation for Chemical Protective Clothing.

CPSC — Abbreviation for Consumer Product Safety Commission.

Critical Incident Stress (CIS) — Physical, mental, or emotional tension caused when persons have been exposed to a traumatic event where they have experienced, witnessed, or been confronted with an event or events that involve actual death, threatened death, serous injury, or threat of physical integrity of self or others. *Also see* Posttraumatic Stress Disorder (PTSD) and Stress (3).

Cross Contamination — *See* Secondary Contamination.

Crossover Line — Pipe installed in a bulk storage tank piping system that allows product unloading from either side of the tank.

Cryogen — Gas that is cooled to a very low temperature, usually below -130°F (-90°C), to change to a liquid. Also called *refrigerated liquid* and *cryogenic liquid*. *Also see* Cryogenic-Liquid Storage Tank and Cryogenic Liquid Tank.

Cryogenic Liquid — *See* Cryogen.

Cryogenic Liquid Storage Tank — Heavily insulated, vacuum-jacketed tanks used to store cryogenic liquids, equipped with safety-relief valves and rupture disks. *Also see* Cryogen.

Cryogenic Liquid Tank — Cargo tank truck that carries gases that have been liquefied by temperature reduction. *Also see* Cryogen and Cargo Tank Truck.

Curie (Ci) — English System unit of measurement for radioactivity, indicating the number of nuclear decays/disintegrations a radioactive ma-

terial undergoes in a certain period of time. *Also see* Becquerel, Radioactive Material (RAM), and Radiation (2).

Cyanogen Agent — *See* Chemical Asphyxiant.

D

Dangerous Cargo Manifest — Invoice of cargo used on ships containing a list of all hazardous materials on board and their location on the ship.

Dangerous Good — (1) Any product, substance, or organism included by its nature or by the regulation in any of the nine United Nations classifications of hazardous materials. (2) Term used to describe hazardous materials in Canada. (3) Term used in the U.S. and Canada for hazardous materials on board aircraft. *Also see* Hazardous Material (1).

Decon — Abbreviation for Decontamination.

Decontamination (Decon) — Process of removing a hazardous, foreign substance from a person, clothing, or area. *Also see* Contamination, Decontamination Corridor, Emergency Decontamination, Technical Decontamination, Definitive Decontamination, Gross Decontamination, Mass Decontamination, and Patient Decontamination.

Decontamination Corridor — Area where decontamination is conducted. *Also see* Decontamination.

Dedicated Railcar — Car set aside by the product manufacturer to transport a specific product. The name of the product is painted on the car.

Defensive Mode — *See* Defensive Strategy.

Defensive Operations — Operations in which responders seek to confine the emergency to a given area without directly contacting the hazardous materials involved. *Also see* Nonintervention Operations and Offensive Operations.

Defensive Strategy — Overall plan for incident control established by the Incident Commander (IC) that involves protection of exposures as opposed to aggressive, offensive intervention. *Also see* Nonintervention Strategy, Strategy, and Offensive Strategy.

Definitive Decontamination — Decontaminating further after technical decontamination; may involve sampling and/or lab testing and is usually conducted by hospital staff or other experts. *Also see* Decontamination and Technical Decontamination.

Degradation — *See* Chemical Degradation.

Dehydration — Process of removing water or other fluids.

Department of Defense (DOD) — Administrative body of the executive branch of the U.S. federal government that encompasses all branches of the U.S. military.

Department of Energy (DOE) — Administrative body of the executive branch of the U.S. federal government that manages national nuclear research and defense programs, including the storage of high-level nuclear waste.

Department of Homeland Security (DHS) — U.S. agency that has the missions of preventing terrorist attacks, reducing vulnerability to terrorism, and minimizing damage from potential attacks and natural disasters; includes the Federal Emergency Management Agency (FEMA), U.S. Coast Guard (USCG), and Office for Domestic Preparedness (ODP).

Department of Justice (DOJ) — Administrative body of the executive branch of the U.S. federal government that assigns primary responsibility for operational response to threats or acts of terrorism within U.S. territory to the Federal Bureau of Investigation (FBI). *Also see* Terrorism.

Department of Labor (DOL) — Administrative body of the executive branch of the U.S. federal government that is responsible for overseeing U.S. labor laws (labor policy, regulation, and enforcement).

Department of Transportation (DOT) — U.S. federal agency that regulates the transportation of hazardous materials; responsible for transportation policy, regulation, and enforcement.

Detector Tube — *See* Colorimetric Tube.

Detonation — Supersonic thermal decomposition that is accompanied by a shock wave in the decomposing material; high explosives decompose extremely rapidly (almost instantaneously). *Also see* High Explosive and Explosive (1 and 2).

Detonator — Device or small quantity of explosive used to trigger an explosion in explosives. Also called *blasting cap*. *Also see* Detonation.

DHS — Abbreviation for U.S. Department of Homeland Security.

Diatomaceous Earth — Light siliceous material consisting chiefly of the skeletons of minute unicellular algae; used especially as an absorbent or filter. Also called *diatomite*.

Diatomite — *See* Diatomaceous Earth.

Dilution — Application of water to a water-soluble material to reduce the hazard. *Also see* Water Solubility and Dissolution.

Dip Tube — Tube installed in a pressurized container from the top to the bottom to permit expelling the contents, liquid or solid, out the top of the container; for pressure unloading of product out the top of a tank.

Dirty Bomb — *See* Radiological Dispersal Device (RDD).

Dispersion — Act or process of being spread widely. *Also see* Engulf (1) and Vapor Dispersion.

Dissipate — To cause to spread out or spread thin to the point of vanishing.

Dissolution — Act or process of dissolving one thing into another; process of dissolving a gas in water. *Also see* Concentration (2) and Dilution.

DOD — Abbreviation for the U.S. Department of Defense.

DOE — Abbreviation for the U.S. Department of Energy.

DOJ — Abbreviation for the U.S. Department of Justice.

DOL — Abbreviation for the U.S. Department of Labor.

Dome Roof Tank — *See* Cone Roof Storage Tank.

Dose — Quantity of a chemical material ingested or absorbed through skin contact for purposes of measuring toxicity. *Also see* Lethal Dose (LD_{50}) and Concentration (1).

DOT — Abbreviation for the U.S. Department of Transportation.

Doubles — Truck combination consisting of a truck tractor and two semitrailers coupled together. Formerly called *double-trailer*.

Double-Trailer — *See* Doubles.

Dry Bulk Cargo Tank — Cargo tank truck that carries small, granulated, solid materials; generally does not carry hazardous materials but in some cases may carry fertilizers or plastic products that can burn and release toxic products of combustion. *Also see* Cargo Tank Truck.

Dust — Solid particle that is formed or generated from solid organic or inorganic materials by reducing its size through mechanical processes such as crushing, grinding, drilling, abrading, or blasting.

Dyspnea — Painful or difficult breathing; rapid, shallow respirations.

E

Element — Most simple substance that cannot be separated into more simple parts by ordinary means.

Elevated Temperature Material — Material that when offered for transportation or transported in bulk packaging is (a) in a liquid phase and at a temperature at or above 212°F (100°C), (b) intentionally heated at or above its liquid phase flash point of 100°F (38°C), or (c) in a solid phase and at a temperature at or above 464°F (240°C). *Also see* Flash Point, Bulk Packaging, and Elevated Temperature Materials Carrier.

Emergency Decontamination — Removing contamination on individuals in potentially life-threatening situations with or without the formal establishment of a decontamination corridor. *Also see* Decontamination and Decontamination Corridor.

Emergency Response Guidebook (ERG) — Guide developed jointly by Transport Canada (TC), U.S. Department of Transportation (DOT), and the Secretariat of Transport and Communications of Mexico (SCT) for use by firefighters, police, and other emergency services personnel who may be the first to arrive at the scene of a transportation incident involving dangerous goods. It is primarily a guide to aid first responders in quickly identify-ing the specific or generic hazards of the material involved and protecting themselves and the general public during the initial response phase.

Emergency Transportation System for the Chemical Industry (SETIQ) — Emergency response center for Mexico. *Also see* Canadian Transport Emergency Centre (CANUTEC) and Chemical Transportation Emergency Center (CHEMTREC®).

Emergency Valve — Self-closing tank outlet valve. *Also see* Emergency Valve Operator and Emergency Valve Remote Control.

Emergency Valve Operator — Device used to open and close emergency valves. *Also see* Emergency Valve and Emergency Valve Remote Control.

Emergency Valve Remote Control — Secondary means, remote from tank discharge openings, for operation in event of fire or other accident. *Also see* Emergency Valve Operator and Emergency Valve.

Emulsion — Insoluble liquid suspended in another liquid. *Also see* Insoluble.

Encapsulating — Completely enclosed or surrounded as in a capsule.

Engulf — (1) Dispersion of material as defined in the General Emergency Behavior Model (GEBMO). An engulfing event is when matter and/or energy disperses and forms a danger zone. (2) To flow over and enclose; in fire service context, it refers to being enclosed in flames. *Also see* Vapor Dispersion and Dispersion.

Environmental Protection Agency (EPA) — U.S. government agency that creates and enforces laws designed to protect the air, water, and soil from contamination; responsible for researching and setting national standards for a variety of environmental programs.

Environment Canada — Agency responsible for preserving and enhancing the quality of the natural environment (including water, air, and soil quality), conserving Canada's renewable resources, and coordinating environmental policies and programs for the federal government of Canada.

EPA — Abbreviation for the U.S. Environmental Protection Agency.

ERG — Abbreviation for *Emergency Response Guidebook*.

Etiological Agents — Living microorganisms, like germs, that can cause human disease; a biologically hazardous material.

Evacuation — Process of leaving or being removed from a potentially hazardous location. *Also see* Shelter in Place.

Evaporation — Process of a liquid turning into gas.

Excepted Packaging — Container used for transportation of materials that have very limited radioactivity. *Also see* Packaging (1), Type A Packaging, Type B Packaging, Industrial Packaging, and Strong, Tight Container.

Exothermal — Characterized by or formed with the evolution of heat.

Exothermic — Chemical reaction between two or more materials that changes the materials and produces heat, flames, and toxic smoke.

Explosive — (1) Any material or mixture that will undergo an extremely fast, self-propagation reaction when subjected to some form of energy. *Also see* High Explosive and Detonation. (2) Material capable of burning or bursting suddenly and violently. *Also see* Detonation and Low Explosive.

Explosive Device — *See* Incendiary Device.

Explosive Limit — *See* Flammable Limit.

Explosive Range — *See* Flammable Range.

Exposure — (1) Structure or separate part of the fireground to which a fire could spread. (2) People, properties, systems, or natural features that are or may be exposed to the harmful effects of a hazardous materials emergency.

External Floating Roof Tank — Fixed-site vertical storage tank that has no fixed roof but relies on a floating roof to protect the contents and prevent evaporation. Also called *open-top floating roof tank*. *Also see* Internal Floating Roof Tank and Floating Roof Storage Tank.

Extremely Hazardous Substance — Chemical determined by the Environmental Protection Agency (EPA) to be extremely hazardous to a community during an emergency spill or release as a result of its toxicity and physical/chemical properties. *Also see* Hazardous Substance.

F

FBI — Abbreviation for Federal Bureau of Investigation.

Federal Bureau of Investigation (FBI) — U.S. agency under the Department of Justice that investigates the theft of hazardous materials, collects evidence for crimes, and prosecutes criminal violation of federal hazardous materials laws and regulations; lead agency on terrorist incident scenes. *Also see* Terrorism.

Federal Emergency Management Agency (FEMA) — U.S. agency that is part of the Department of Homeland Security (DHS) and tasked with responding to, planning for, recovering from, and mitigating against disasters.

FEMA — Acronym for Federal Emergency Management Agency.

FIBC — Abbreviation for Flexible Intermediate Bulk Container.

Fiber — Solid particle whose length is several times greater than its diameter.

Fifth Wheel — Device used to connect a truck tractor to a semitrailer in order to permit articulation between the units. *Also see* Semitrailer.

Fill Opening — Opening on top of a tank used for filling the tank; usually incorporated in a manway cover.

Finished Foam — Extinguishing agent formed by mixing foam concentrate with water and aerating the solution for expansion. Also called *foam*. *Also see* Foam Blanket and Foam Concentrate.

Fire Point — Temperature at which a liquid fuel produces sufficient vapors to support combustion once the fuel is ignited; usually a few degrees above the flash point. *Also see* Flash Point.

Fire Tube — *See* Heating Tube.

Fissionable — Capable of splitting the atomic nucleus and releasing large amounts of energy.

Flame Impingement — Points at which flames contact the surface of a container or other structure.

Flammability — Fuel's susceptibility to ignition.

Flammable — Capable of burning and producing flames. *Also see* Nonflammable

Flammable Gas — Any material (except aerosols) that is a gas at 68°F (20°C) or less and that (a) is ignitable at 14.7 psi (101.3 kPa) when in a mixture of 13 percent or less by volume with air or (b) has a flammable range at 14.7 psi (101.3 kPa) by volume with air of at least 12 percent regardless of the lower limit. *Also see* Nonflammable Gas and Gas

Flammable Limit — Percentage of a substance in air that will burn once it is ignited. Most substances have an upper (too *rich*) and lower (too *lean*) flammable limit. Also called *explosive limit*. *Also see* Flammable Range, Upper Flammable Limit (UFL), and Lower Flammable Limit (LFL).

Flammable Liquid — Any liquid having a flash point below 100°F (37.8°C) and having a vapor pressure not exceeding 40 psi (276 kPa) {2.76 bar}. *Also see* Combustible Liquid and Polar Solvent Fuel.

Flammable Material — Substance that ignites easily and burns rapidly.

Flammable Range — Range between the upper flammable limit and lower flammable limit in which a substance can be ignited. Also called *explosive range*. *Also see* Flammable Limit.

Flammable Solid — Solid material (other than an explosive) that (a) is liable to cause a fire through friction or retained heat from manufacturing or processing or (b) ignites readily and then burns vigorously and persistently, creating a serious transportation hazard.

Flash Point — Minimum temperature at which a liquid gives off enough vapors to form an ignitable mixture with air near the surface of the liquid. *Also see* Fire Point.

Flexible Intermediate Bulk Container (FIBC) — *See* Intermediate Bulk Container (IBC).

Floating Roof Storage Tank — Atmospheric storage tank that stands vertically; is wider than it is tall. The roof floats on the surface of the liquid to eliminate the vapor space. *Also see* Atmospheric Storage Tank and Lifter Roof Storage Tank.

Foam — *See* Finished Foam.

Foam Blanket — Covering of finished foam applied over a burning surface to produce a smothering effect; can be used on unignited surfaces to prevent ignition. *Also see* Finished Foam and Foam Stability.

Foam Chamber — Foam delivery device that is mounted on storage tanks; applies foam onto the surface of the fuel in the tank.

Foam Concentrate — (1) Raw chemical compound solution that is mixed with water and air to produce finished foam; may be protein, synthetic, aqueous film forming, high expansion, or alcohol types. (2) Raw foam liquid as it rests in its storage container before the introduction of water and air. *Also see* Class A Foam Concentrate, Class B Foam Concentrate, Aqueous Film Forming Foam (AFFF), Foam Solution, Foam System, and Finished Foam.

Foam Eductor — Type of foam proportioner used for mixing foam concentrate in proper proportions with a stream of water to produce foam solution. *Also see* Foam Solution and Foam Proportioner.

Foam Monitor — Master stream appliance used to apply foam.

Foam Proportioner — Device that injects the correct amount of foam concentrate into the water stream to make the foam solution. *Also see* Foam Solution and Foam Eductor.

Foam Solution — Result of mixing the appropriate amount of foam concentrate with water; exists between the proportioner and the nozzle or aerating device that adds air to create finished foam. *Also see* Foam Concentrate, Foam Proportioner, Foam Eductor, and Finished Foam.

Foam Stability — Relative ability of foam to withstand spontaneous collapse or breakdown from external causes. *Also see* Finished Foam and Foam Blanket.

Foam System — Extinguishing system that uses a foam concentrate such as aqueous film forming foam (AFFF) as the primary extinguishing agent; usually installed in areas where there is a risk for flammable liquid fires. *Also see* Aqueous Film Forming Foam (AFFF) and Foam Concentrate.

Fork Pockets — Transverse openings in the base of a container that permit entry of forklift devices.

Formal Decontamination — *See* Technical Decontamination.

Frangible — Breakable, fragile, or brittle.

Freezing Point — Temperature at which a liquid becomes a solid at normal atmospheric pressure. *Also see* Melting Point.

Freight Container — *See* Container (1).

Frostbite — Local freezing and tissue damage caused by prolonged exposure to extreme cold. *Also see* Hypothermia.

Full Structural Protective Clothing—*See* Personal Protective Equipment (PPE).

Full Trailer — Truck trailer constructed so that all of its own weight and that of its load rests upon its own wheels; it does not depend upon a truck tractor to support it. A semitrailer equipped with a truck tractor is considered a full trailer. *Also see* Semitrailer and Truck Tractor.

Fume — Suspension of particles that form when material from a volatilized (vapor state) solid condenses in cool air.

G

Gamma Radiation — Very high-energy ionizing radiation composed of gamma rays. *Also see* Alpha Radiation, Beta Radiation, Ionizing Radiation, and Radiation (2).

Gamma Ray — High-energy photon (packet of electromagnetic energy) emitted from the nucleus of an unstable (radioactive) atom; one of three types of radiation emitted by radioactive materials; most penetrating and potentially lethal of the three types. *Also see* Alpha Particle, Beta Particle, Gamma Radiation, and Radioactive Material (RAM).

Gas — Compressible substance, with no specific volume, that tends to assume the shape of a container. Molecules move about most rapidly in this state. *Also see* Compressed Gas.

Gas Chromatogram — Chart from a gas chromatograph tracing the results of analysis of volatile compounds by display in recorded peaks. *Also see* Gas Chromatograph.

Gas Chromatograph — Device to detect and separate small quantities of volatile liquids or gases through instrument analysis.

Gas Chromatography — Characterizing volatilities and chemical properties of compounds that evaporate enough at low temperatures (about 120°F or 49°C) to provide detectable quantities in the air through the use of instrument analysis in a gas chromatograph. *Also see* Gas Chromatograph.

GEBMO — Acronym for General Emergency Behavior Model.

General Emergency Behavior Model (GEBMO) — Model used to describe how hazardous materials are accidentally released from their containers and how they behave after the release. *Also see* Engulf (1).

Genetic Effect — Mutations or other changes that are produced by irradiation of the germ plasma; changes produced in future generations.

GHS — Abbreviation for Globally Harmonized System of Classification and Labeling of Chemicals (GHS).

Globally Harmonized System of Classification and Labeling of Chemicals (GHS) — International classification and labeling system for chemicals and other hazard communication information such as material safety data sheets.

Global Positioning System (GPS) — System for determining a position on the earth's surface by calculating the difference in time for the signal from a number of satellites to reach a receiver on the ground.

GPS — Abbreviation for Global Positioning System.

Gross Decontamination — Quickly removing the worst surface contamination, usually by rinsing with water from handheld hoselines, emergency showers, or other water sources. *Also see* Decontamination.

Gross Weight — Weight of a vehicle or trailer together with the weight of its entire contents.

H

Half-life — Time required for half the amount of a substance in or introduced into a living system or ecosystem to be eliminated or disintegrated by natural processes; period of time required for any radioactive substance to lose half of its strength or reduce by one-half its total present energy.

Halogenated Agents—Chemical compounds (halogenated hydrocarbons) that contain carbon plus one or more elements from the halogen series. Also called *halogenated hydrocarbons.*

Halogenated Hydrocarbons — *See* Halogenated Agents.

Hazard — Condition, substance, or device that can directly cause injury or loss; the source of a risk. *Also see* Target Hazard, Hazard or Risk Analysis, Hazard Class, and Hazard Assessment.

Hazard Area — Established area from which bystanders and unneeded rescue workers are prohibited. *Also see* Hazard-Control Zones.

Hazard Assessment — Formal review of the hazards that may be encountered while performing the functions of a fire and emergency services responder; used to determine the appropriate level and type of personal and respiratory protection that must be worn. *Also see* Hazard, Risk Management Plan, Target Hazard, and Hazard or Risk Analysis.

Hazard Class — Group of materials designated by the U.S. Department of Transportation (DOT) that shares a major hazardous property such as radioactivity or flammability. *Also see* Hazard, Hazardous Material, Hazardous Chemical, and Hazardous Substance.

Hazard-Control Zones — System of barriers surrounding designated areas at emergency scenes intended to limit the number of persons exposed to a hazard and to facilitate its mitigation; major incident has three zones: restricted (hot), limited access (warm), and support (cold). U.S. EPA/OSHA term: *site work zones.* Also called *scene-control zones* and *control zones.* *Also see* Hazard Area and Initial Isolation Zone.

Hazard or Risk Analysis — Identification of hazards or risks and the determination of the appropriate response to that hazard or risk; combines hazard assessment with risk management concepts. *Also see* Hazard, Hazard Assessment, and Risk Management Plan.

Hazardous Atmosphere — Any atmosphere that may or not be immediately dangerous to life or health but that is oxygen deficient, contains a toxic or disease-producing contaminant, or contains a flammable or explosive vapor or gas. *Also see* Immediately Dangerous to Life or Health (IDLH).

Hazardous Chemical — Any chemical that is a physical hazard or health hazard to people; defined by the U.S. Occupational Safety and Health Administration (OSHA). *Also see* Hazardous Material.

Hazardous Material — (1) Any substance or material that possesses an unreasonable risk to health and safety of persons and/or the environment if it is not properly controlled during handling, storage, manufacture, processing, packaging, use, disposal, or transportation. (2) Substance or material in quantities or forms that may pose an unreasonable risk to health, safety, or property when stored, transported, or used in commerce (U.S. Department of Transportation definition). *Also see* Dangerous Good (1), Corrosive Material, Hazardous Substance, Hazardous Waste, Hazardous Chemical, Material, and Product.

Hazardous Materials Incident — Emergency, with or without fire, that involves the release or potential release of a hazardous material. *Also see* Hazardous Material.

Hazardous Materials Regulations (HMR) — Regulations developed and enforced by the U.S. Department of Transportation.

Hazardous Substance — Any substance designated under the U.S. Clean Water Act and the Comprehensive Environmental Response, Compensation, and Liability Act (CERCLA) as posing a threat to waterways and the environment when released. *Also see* Hazardous Material and Extremely Hazardous Substance.

Hazardous Waste — Discarded materials with no monetary value that can have the same hazardous properties it had before being used; regulated by the U.S. Environmental Protection Agency (EPA) because of public health and safety concerns. *Also see* Hazardous Material.

Hazardous Waste Operations and Emergency Response (HAZWOPER) — U.S. regulations in Title 29 (Labor) *CFR* 1910.120 for cleanup operations involving hazardous substances and emergency response operations for releases of hazardous substances. *Also see Code of Federal Regulations (CFR).*

HAZWOPER — Acronym for Hazardous Waste Operations and Emergency Response.

Head — (1) Front and rear closure of a tank shell. (2) Alternate term for pressure, especially pressure due to elevation.

Health Canada — Agency responsible for developing health policy, enforcing health regulations, promoting disease prevention, and enhancing healthy living in Canada.

Health Hazard — Material that may directly affect an individual's health once it enters or comes in contact with the body. *Also see* Physical Hazard.

Heat Cramps — Heat illness resulting from prolonged exposure to high temperatures; characterized by excessive sweating, muscle cramps in the abdomen and legs, faintness, dizziness, and exhaustion. *Also see* Heat Exhaustion, Heat Stroke, Heat Rash, and Heat Stress.

Heat Exhaustion — Heat illness caused by exposure to excessive heat; symptoms include weakness, cold and clammy skin, heavy perspiration, rapid and shallow breathing, weak pulse, dizziness, and sometimes unconsciousness. *Also see* Heat Cramps, Heat Stroke, Heat Rash, and Heat Stress.

Heating Tube — Tube installed inside a tank to heat the contents. Also called *fire tube.*

Heat Rash — Condition that develops from continuous exposure to heat and humid air; aggravated by clothing that rubs the skin; reduces an individual's tolerance to heat. *Also see* Heat Exhaustion, Heat Cramps, Heat Stroke, and Heat Stress.

Heat Stress — Combination of environmental and physical work factors that compose the heat load imposed on the body; environmental factors include air, temperature, radiant heat exchange, air movement, and water vapor pressure. Physical work contributes because of the metabolic heat in the body; clothing also has an effect. *Also see* Heat Exhaustion, Heat Stroke, Heat Rash, and Heat Cramps.

Heat Stroke — Heat illness caused by heat exposure, resulting in failure of the body's heat regulating mechanism; symptoms include (a) high fever of 105 to 106°F (40.5°C to 41.1°C), (b) dry, red, and hot skin, (c) rapid, strong pulse, and (d) deep breaths or convulsions; may result in coma or possibly death. Also called *sunstroke. Also see* Heat Exhaustion, Heat Cramps, Heat Rash, and Heat Stress.

Heavy Metal — Generic term referring to lead, cadmium, mercury, and other elements that are toxic in nature; term may also be applied to compounds containing these elements. Also called *toxic element.*

Hematotoxic Agent (Hemotoxin) — Chemical that damages blood cells.

Hemispherical — Half a sphere in shape.

Hemispherical Head — End of a tank that is in the shape of half of a sphere. Usually found on pressure tanks.

Hemispheric Release — Semicircular or dome-shaped pattern of airborne hazardous material that is still partially in contact with the ground or water. *Also see* Cloud, Cone, and Plume.

HEPA — Acronym for High Efficiency Particulate Air.

Hepatotoxic Agent (Hepatotoxin) — Chemical that damages the liver.

High Efficiency Particulate Air (HEPA) Filter — Respiratory protection filter designed and certified to protect the user from particulates in the air.

High Explosive — One that decomposes extremely rapidly (almost instantaneously) and has a detonation velocity faster than the speed of sound. *Also see* Explosive (1), Low Explosive, Ammonium Nitrate and Fuel Oil (ANFO), and Detonation.

High-Pressure Tank — Cargo tank truck that carries liquefied gases. *Also see* Cargo Tank Truck.

Hitch — Connecting device at the rear of a vehicle used to pull a full trailer with provision for easy coupling.

HMR — Abbreviation for Hazardous Materials Regulations.

Homogeneous — Substance having uniform structure or composition throughout.

Hopper — (1) Any of various receptacles used for temporary storage of a material. (2) Tank holding a liquid and having a device for releasing its contents through a pipe. (3) Freight car with a floor sloping to one or more hinged doors for discharging bulk contents. (4) Funnel-shaped bin used for the storage of dry solid materials such as corn, which discharges from the bottom.

Horizontal Pressure Vessel — Pressurized storage tank characterized by rounded ends; capacity may range from 500 to 40,000 gallons (1 893 L to 151 416

L). Examples of materials stored: propane, butane, ethane, and hydrogen chloride. *Also see* Pressure Vessel and Spherical Pressure Vessel.

Horizontal Storage Tank — Atmospheric storage tank that is laid horizontally and constructed of steel. *Also see* Atmospheric Storage Tank.

Hydrocarbon Fuel — Petroleum-based organic compound that contains only hydrogen and carbon. *Also see* Polar Solvent Fuel and Liquefied Compressed Gas.

Hygroscopic — Ability of a substance to absorb moisture from the air.

Hypergolic — Chemical reaction between a fuel and an oxidizer that causes immediate ignition on contact without the presence of air; example: contact of fuming nitric acid and unsymmetrical dimethylhydrazine. *Also see* Hypergolic Materials.

Hypergolic Materials — Materials that ignite when they come into contact with each other. The chemical reactions of hypergolic substances vary from slow reactions that may barely be visible to reactions that occur with explosive force. *Also see* Hypergolic.

Hypothermia — Abnormally low body temperature. Also called *systemic hypothermia*. *Also see* Frostbite.

Hypoxia — Condition caused by a deficiency in the amount of oxygen reaching body tissues.

I
_____

IAP — Abbreviation for Incident Action Plan.

IBC — Abbreviation for Intermediate Bulk Container.

IC — Abbreviation for Incident Commander.

ICS — Abbreviation for Incident Command System.

IDLH — Abbreviation for Immediately Dangerous to Life or Health.

IED — Abbreviation for Improvised Explosive Device.

Ignition — Beginning of flame propagation or burning; the start of a fire. *Also see* Autoignition and Ignition Temperature.

Ignition Temperature — Minimum temperature to which a fuel (other than a liquid) in air must be heated in order to start self-sustained combustion independent of the heating source. *Also see* Autoignition Temperature, Autoignition, and Ignition.

Illegal Clandestine Lab — Laboratory established to produce or manufacture illegal or controlled substances such as drugs, chemical warfare agents, explosives, or biological agents. *Also see* Meth Lab, Explosive (2), and Chemical Warfare Agent.

Illegal Dump — Site where chemicals are disposed of illegally.

Immediately Dangerous to Life or Health (IDLH) — Any atmosphere that poses an immediate hazard to life or produces immediate irreversible, debilitating effects on health; represents concentrations above which respiratory protection should be required; expressed in parts per million (ppm) or milligrams per cubic meter (mg/m^3). Companion measurement to the permissible exposure limit (PEL). *Also see* Hazardous Atmosphere, Permissible Exposure Limit (PEL), Recommended Exposure Limit (REL), Threshold Limit Value (TLV®), and Short-term Exposure Limit (STEL).

Immiscible — Incapable of being mixed or blended with another substance. *Also see* Miscibility, Soluble, and Insoluble.

IMO — Abbreviation for International Maritime Organization.

IMO Type 5 — *See* Pressure Intermodal Tank.

Impingement — Come into sharp contact with.

IM Portable Tank — *See* Nonpressure Intermodal Tank.

Improvised Explosive Device (IED) — Device that is categorized by its container and the way it is initiated; usually homemade, constructed for a specific target, and contained in almost anything. *Also see* Explosive (1 and 2).

Improvised Nuclear Device (IND) — Device that results in the formation of a nuclear-yield reaction (nuclear blast); low-yield device is called a *mini-nuke*. *Also see* Suitcase Bomb and Radiation (2).

IMS — Abbreviation for Incident Management System.

Incapacitant — Chemical agent that produces a temporary disabling condition that persists for hours to days after exposure has occurred. *Also see* Riot Control Agent.

Incendiary Device — Any mechanical, electrical, or chemical device used intentionally to initiate combustion and start a fire. Also called *explosive device*. *Also see* Incendiary Thermal Effect.

Incendiary Thermal Effect — Thermal heat energy resulting from the fireball created by the burning of combustible gases or flammable vapors and ambient air at very high temperatures during an explosion.

Incident Action Plan (IAP) — Written or unwritten plan for the disposition of an incident; contains the overall strategic goals, tactical objectives, and support requirements for a given operational period during an incident; required for all incidents but may not be in writing on relatively small ones.

Incident Commander (IC) — Person in charge of the incident management system and responsible for the management of all incident operations during an emergency.

Incident Command System (ICS) — Management system of procedures for establishing and maintaining command and control of an incident; developed in California in the early 1970s to address the resource management needs associated with large-scale wildland fires. Also known as the *California FIRESCOPE Incident Command System*.

Incident Management System (IMS) — Management system developed by the National Fire Service Incident Management System Consortium, combining pre-existing command systems into one.

IND — Abbreviation for Improvised Nuclear Device.

Individual Container — Product container used to transport materials in small quantities; includes bags, boxes, and drums. *Also see* Packaging (1).

Industrial Packaging — Container used to ship radioactive materials that present limited hazard to the public and the environment (such as smoke detectors). *Also see* Packaging (1); Type A Packaging; Type B Packaging; Strong, Tight Container; and Excepted Packaging.

Inert Gas — Gas that does not normally react chemically with a base or filler metal. *Also see* Simple Asphyxiant.

Ingestion — Taking in food or other substances through the mouth. *Also see* Routes of Entry.

Inhalation — Taking in materials by breathing through the nose or mouth. *Also see* Routes of Entry.

Inhibitor — Material that is added to products that easily polymerize in order to control or prevent an undesired reaction. Also called *stabilizer*. *Also see* Polymerization.

Initial Isolation Distance — Distance within which all persons are considered for evacuation in all directions from a hazardous materials incident. *Also see* Protective Action Distance, Protective Action Zone, Isolation Perimeter, and Initial Isolation Zone.

Initial Isolation Zone — Circular zone (with a radius equivalent to the initial isolation distance) within which persons may be exposed to dangerous concentrations upwind of the source and may be exposed to life-threatening concentrations downwind of the source. *Also see* Initial Isolation Distance, Isolation Perimeter, and Hazard-Control Zones.

Injection — Process of taking in materials through a puncture or break in the skin. *Also see* Routes of Entry.

Insoluble — Incapable of being dissolved in a liquid (usually water). *Also see* Immiscible, Soluble, Emulsion, and Miscibility.

Intermediate Bulk Container (IBC) — Rigid (RIBC) or flexible (FIBC) portable packaging (other than a cylinder or portable tank) designed for mechanical handling with a maximum capacity of not more than three 3 cubic meters (3,000 L, 793 gal, or 106 ft³) and a minimum capacity of not less than 0.45 cubic meters (450 L, 119 gal, or 15.9 ft³) or a maximum net mass of not less than 400 kilograms (882 lbs). *Also see* Packaging (1).

Intermodal Container — Freight container designed and constructed to be used interchangeably in two or more modes of transport. Also called *intermodal tank container*. *Also see* Container (2), Refrigerated Intermodal Container, Intermodal Reporting Marks, and Container Vessel.

Intermodal Reporting Marks — Series of letters and numbers stenciled on the sides of intermodal tanks that may be used to identify and verify the contents of the tank or container. *Also see* Intermodal Container and Railcar Initials and Numbers.

Intermodal Tank Container — *See* Intermodal Container.

Internal Floating Roof Tank — Fixed-site vertical storage tank that combines both the floating roof and closed roof design. Also called *covered floating roof tank*. *Also see* Atmospheric Storage Tank, Floating Roof Storage Tank, and External Floating Roof Tank.

International Maritime Organization (IMO) — Specialized agency of the United Nations devoted to maritime affairs; has developed and promoted the adoption of more than 30 conventions and protocols and 700 codes and recommendations dealing with maritime safety; main purposes are safer shipping and cleaner oceans.

Inversion — (1) Increase of temperature with height in the atmosphere. Vertical motion in the atmosphere is inhibited allowing for smoke buildup. A *normal* atmosphere has temperature decreasing with height. *Also see* Atmospheric Stability. (2) Atmospheric phenomenon that allows smoke to rise until its temperature equals the air temperature and then spread laterally in a horizontal layer. Also called *night inversion*.

Ionization — Process in which a charged portion of a molecule (usually an electron) is given enough energy to break away from the atom; results in the formation of two charged particles or ions: (a) molecule with a net positive charge and (b) free electron with a negative charge.

Ionizing Radiation — Radiation that has sufficient energy to remove electrons from atoms resulting in a chemical change in the atom. *Also See* Radiation (2) and Nonionizing Radiation.

Irritant/Irritating Material — Liquid or solid that upon contact with fire or exposure to air emits dangerous or intensely irritating fumes.

Irritating Agent — *See* Riot Control Agent.

Isolation Perimeter — Outer boundary of an incident that is controlled to prevent entrance by the public or unauthorized persons. *Also see* Initial Isolation Distance and Initial Isolation Zone.

Isotope — Atoms of a chemical element with the usual number of protons in the nucleus, but an unusual number of neutrons; has the same atomic number but a different atomic mass from normal chemical elements. *Also see* Radionuclide.

J

Jacket — Metal cover that protects tank insulation.

Jurisdiction — (1) Legal authority to operate or function. (2) Boundaries of a legally constituted entity.

L

Label — Four-inch-square (102 mm) diamond marker required on individual shipping containers containing hazardous materials that are smaller than 640 cubic feet (18 m³). *Also see* Package Marking, Placard, and Marking.

Lading — Freight or cargo that composes a shipment. *Also see* Bill of Lading and Shipping Papers.

LC$_{50}$ — Abbreviation for Lethal Concentration.

LD$_{50}$ — Abbreviation for Lethal Dose.

Leach — To pass out or through by percolation (gradual seepage).

LEL — Abbreviation for Lower Explosive Limit.

LEPC — Abbreviation for Local Emergency Planning Committee.

LERP — Abbreviation for Local Emergency Response Plan.

Lethal — Deadly; resulting in death.

Lethal Concentration (LC$_{50}$) — Concentration of an inhaled substance that results in the death of 50 percent of the test population; the lower the value the more toxic the substance; an inhalation exposure expressed in parts per million (ppm), milligrams per liter (mg/liter), or milligrams per cubic meter (mg/m³). *Also see* Concentration (1).

Lethal Dose (LD$_{50}$) — Concentration of an ingested or injected substance that results in the death of 50 percent of the test population; the lower the value the more toxic the substance; an oral or dermal exposure expressed in milligrams per kilogram (mg/kg). *Also see* Dose.

Level A Protection — Highest level of skin, respiratory, and eye protection that can be given by personal protective equipment (PPE) as specified by the U.S. Environmental Protection Agency (EPA); consists of positive-pressure self-contained breathing apparatus (SCBA), totally encapsulating chemical-protective suit, inner and outer gloves, and chemical-resistant boots. *Also see* Chemical Protective Clothing (CPC), Special Protective Clothing, and Personal Protective Equipment (PPE).

LFL — Abbreviation for Lower Flammable Limit.

Lifter Roof Storage Tank — Atmospheric storage tank designed so that the roof floats on a slight cushion of vapor pressure; liquid-sealed roof floats up and down with vapor pressure. When the vapor pressure exceeds a designated limit, the roof lifts to relieve the excess pressure. *Also see* Atmospheric Storage Tank and Floating Roof Storage Tank.

LIP Service — Emergency incident management priorities of *L*ife safety, *I*ncident stabilization and control, and *P*rotection of property and the environment.

Liquefied Compressed Gas — Gas that under the charging pressure is partially liquid at 70°F (21°C). Also called *liquefied gas*. *Also see* Compressed Gas, Liquefied Natural Gas (LNG), Liquefied Petroleum Gas (LPG), and Nonliquefied Gas.

Liquefied Flammable Gas Carrier — Tanker used to transport liquefied natural gas (LNG) and liquefied petroleum gas (LPG) (propane and butane for example); generally uses large insulated spherical tanks for product storage. *Also see* Tanker.

Liquefied Gas — *See* Liquefied Compressed Gas.

Liquefied Natural Gas (LNG) — Natural gas stored under pressure as a liquid. *Also see* Liquefied Compressed Gas, Gas, and Hydrocarbon Fuel.

Liquefied Petroleum Gas (LPG) — Any of several petroleum products, such as propane or butane, stored under pressure as a liquid. *Also see* Liquefied Compressed Gas, Gas, and Hydrocarbon Fuel.

Liquid Oxygen (LOX) — Oxygen that is stored under pressure as a liquid.

LNG — Abbreviation for Liquefied Natural Gas.

Local Emergency Planning Committee (LEPC) — Community organization responsible for local emergency response planning. *Also see* Local Emergency Response Plan (LERP).

Local Emergency Response Plan (LERP) — Plan required by U.S. Environmental Protection Agency (EPA) that is prepared by the Local Emergency Planning Committee (LEPC) detailing how local emergency response agencies will respond to community emergencies.

Lower Explosive Limit (LEL) — *See* Lower Flammable Limit (LFL).

Lower Flammable Limit (LFL) — Lower limit at which a flammable gas or vapor will ignite; below this limit the gas or vapor is too *lean* or *thin* to burn (too much oxygen and not enough gas). Also called *lower explosive limit (LEL)*. *Also see* Flammable Limit and Upper Flammable Limit (UFL).

Low Explosive — One that decomposes rapidly but does not produce an explosive effect unless it is confined; rather it burns rapidly. *Also see* High Explosive, Explosive (2), and Detonation.

Low-Pressure Chemical Tank — Cargo tank truck designed to carry various chemicals such as flammables, corrosives, or poisons with pressures not to exceed 40 psi (276 kPa) {2.76 bar} at 70°F (21°C). *Also see* Cargo Tank Truck.

Low-Pressure Storage Tank — Class of fixed-facility storage tanks that are designed to have an operating pressure ranging from 0.5 to 15 psi (3.45 kPa to 103 kPa) {0.03 bar to 1.03 bar}. *Also see* Pressure Vessel, Pressure Storage Tank, Noded Spheroid Tank, Spheroid Tank, and Atmospheric Storage Tank.

LOX — Acronym for Liquid Oxygen.

LPG — Abbreviation for Liquefied Petroleum Gas.

M

Manhole — *See* Manway.

Manifold — (1) Top portion of a pump casing. (2) Device used to join a number of discharge pipelines to a common outlet.

Manway — (1) Hole through which a person may go to gain access to an underground or enclosed structure. (2) Openings usually equipped with removable, lockable covers large enough to admit a person into a tank trailer or dry bulk trailer. Also called *manhole*.

Marking — Descriptive name, identification number, weight, or specification along with instructions, cautions, or UN marks required on outer packagings of hazardous materials. *Also see* Package Marking, Label, and Placard.

Mass Decontamination — Conducting gross decontamination of multiple people at one time with or without a formal decon corridor or line. *Also see* Decontamination, Decontamination Corridor, and Gross Decontamination.

Material — Generic term used by first responders for a substance involved in an incident. *Also see* Product and Hazardous Material.

Material Safety Data Sheet (MSDS) — Form provided by the manufacturer and blender of chemicals that contains information about chemical composition, physical and chemical properties, health and safety hazards, emergency response procedures, and waste disposal procedures of a specified material.

Mechanical Trauma — Injury, such as an abrasion, puncture, or laceration, resulting from direct contact with a fragment or a whole container.

Melting Point — Temperature at which a solid substance changes to a liquid state at normal atmospheric pressure. *Also see* Freezing Point.

Metabolism — Conversion of food into energy and waste products.

Meth Lab — Illegal clandestine laboratory established to produce illegal methamphetamine (meth). *Also see* Illegal Clandestine Lab.

Mininuke — *See* Improvised Nuclear Device (IND).

Miscibility — Two or more liquids' capability to mix together. *Also see* Immiscible, Soluble, and Insoluble.

Mist — Finely divided liquid suspended in the atmosphere; is generated by liquids condensing from a vapor back to a liquid or by breaking up a liquid into a dispersed state by splashing, foaming, or atomizing. *Also see* Aerosol.

Mixture — Substance containing two or more materials not chemically united.

Monitor — (1) Measure radioactive emissions from a substance with monitoring device. (2) Closely follow radio communications. (3) Observe and record the activities of an individual performing a function.

MSDS — Abbreviation for Material Safety Data Sheet.

Mutagen — Material that causes changes in the genetic system of a cell in ways that can be transmitted during cell division; effects may be hereditary.

N

National Fire Protection Association (NFPA) — U.S. nonprofit educational and technical association located in Quincy, MA, devoted to protecting life and property from fire by developing fire protection standards and educating the public. *Also see* NFPA Labeling System and NFPA 704 Placard.

National Incident Management System (NIMS) — U.S. national incident management plan that creates a unified structure for federal, state, and local lines of government for incident response.

National Institute for Occupational Safety and Health (NIOSH) — U.S. government agency under the Centers for Disease Control and Prevention (CDC), U.S. Department of Health and Human Services, that helps ensure that the workplace and associated equipment are safe; investigates workplaces, recommends safety measures, and reports about on-the-job fire injuries.

Nephrotoxic Agent (Nephrotoxin) — Chemical that damages the kidneys.

Nerve Agent — Toxic agent that attacks the nervous system by affecting the transmission of impulses. *Also see* Chemical Warfare Agent.

Neurotoxic Agent (Neurotoxin) — Chemical that damages the central nervous system.

Neutron — Part of the nucleus of an atom that has a neutral electrical charge yet produces highly penetrating radiation; ultrahigh energy particle that has a physical mass like alpha or beta radiation but has no electrical charge. *Also see* Radiation (2).

NFPA — Abbreviation for National Fire Protection Association.

NFPA 704 Labeling System — System for identifying hazardous materials in fixed facilities. *Also see* NFPA 704 Placard.

NFPA 704 Placard — Color-coded, symbol-specific placard affixed to a structure to inform of fire hazards, life hazards, special hazards, and reactivity potential. The placard is divided into sections that identify the degree of hazard according to health, flammability, and reactivity as well as special hazards. *Also see* NFPA 704 Labeling System.

Night Inversion — *See* Inversion (2).

NIMS — Acronym for National Incident Management System.

NIOSH — Acronym for National Institute for Occupational Safety and Health.

Noded Spheroid Tank — Low-pressure fixed facility storage tank held together by a series of internal ties and supports that reduce stress on the external shell. *Also see* Pressure Storage Tank, Spheroid Tank, and Low-Pressure Storage Tank.

Nonbulk Packaging — Package that has the following characteristics: (a) maximum capacity of 119 gallons (450 L) or less as a receptacle for a liquid, (b) maximum net mass of 882 pounds (400 kg) or less and a maximum capacity of 119 gallons (450 L) or less as a receptacle for a solid, and (c) water capacity of 1,000 pounds (454 kg) or less as a receptacle for a gas. *Also see* Packaging (1) and Bulk Packaging.

Noncombustible — Incapable of supporting combustion under normal circumstances. *Also see* Combustion and Nonflammable.

Nonflammable — Incapable of combustion under normal circumstances; normally used when referring to liquids or gases. *Also see* Noncombustible and Flammable.

Nonflammable Gas — Compressed gas not classified as flammable. *Also see* Flammable Gas, Compressed Gas, and Gas.

Nonintervention Mode — *See* Nonintervention Strategy.

Nonintervention Operations — Operations in which responders take no direct actions on the actual problem. *Also see* Defensive Operations and Offensive Operations.

Nonintervention Strategy — Strategy for handling fires involving hazardous materials where the fire is allowed to burn until all of the fuel is consumed. Also called *nonintervention mode*. *Also see* Defensive Strategy, Strategy, and Offensive Strategy.

Nonionizing Radiation — Series of energy waves composed of oscillating electric and magnetic fields traveling at the speed of light. Examples: ultraviolet radiation, visible light, infrared radiation, microwaves, radio waves, and extremely low frequency radiation. *Also See* Radiation (2) and Ionizing Radiation.

Nonliquefied Gas — Gas, other than a gas in a solution, that under the charging pressure is entirely gaseous at 70°F (21°C). *Also see* Liquefied Compressed Gas and Gas.

Nonpersistent Agent — Chemical agent that generally vaporizes and disperses quickly (less than 10 minutes). *Also see* Persistent Agent and Vapor Pressure.

Nonpressure Intermodal Tank — Portable tank that transports liquids or solids at a maximum pressure of 100 psi (689 kPa) {6.9 bar}. Also called *IM portable tank. Also see* Pressure Intermodal Tank and Intermodal Container.

Nonpressure Liquid Tank — Cargo tank truck used to carry flammable liquids (such as gasoline and alcohol), combustible liquids (such as fuel oil), Division 6.1 poisons, and liquid food products. *Also see* Cargo Tank Truck.

Nonpressure Storage Tank — *See* Atmospheric Storage Tank.

Noxious — Physically harmful or destructive to living beings; unwanted or troublesome.

NRC — Abbreviation for Nuclear Regulatory Commission.

Nuclear Radiation — *See* Radiation (2).

Nuclear Regulatory Commission (NRC) — U.S. agency that regulates commercial nuclear power plants and the civilian use of nuclear materials as well as the possession, use, storage, and transfer of radioactive materials.

O

Objective — (1) Purpose to be achieved by tactical units at an emergency. (2) Specific, measurable, achievable statement of intended accomplishment.

Occupancy — (1) General fire service term for a building, structure, or residency. (2) Building code classification based on the use to which owners or tenants put buildings or portions of buildings.

Occupational Safety and Health Administration (OSHA) — U.S. federal agency that develops and enforces standards and regulations for occupational safety in the workplace.

ODP — Abbreviation for Office for Domestic Preparedness.

Offensive Mode — *See* Offensive Strategy.

Offensive Operations — Operations in which responders take aggressive, direct action on the material, container, or process equipment involved in an incident. *Also see* Defensive Operations and Nonintervention Operations.

Offensive Strategy — Overall plan for incident control established by the Incident Commander (IC) in which responders take aggressive, direct action on the material, container, or process equipment involved in an incident. *Also see* Defensive Strategy, Strategy, and Nonintervention Strategy.

Office for Domestic Preparedness (ODP) — U.S. agency under the Department of Homeland Security that issues federal emergency responder guidelines for events involving weapons of mass destruction.

OI — Abbreviation for Operating Instruction.

Open-Top Floating Roof Tank — *See* External Floating Roof Tank.

Operating Instruction (OI) — *See* Predetermined Procedures.

Operational Level — Level of training established by the National Fire Protection Association allowing first responders to take defensive actions at hazardous materials incidents. *Also see* Awareness Level and Operations Plus.

Operations Plus — Level of training allowing first responders to take defensive actions at all hazardous materials incidents, plus offensive actions when dealing with gasoline, diesel fuel, natural gas, and liquefied petroleum gas (LPG).

Organic Peroxide — Any of several organic derivatives of the inorganic compound hydrogen peroxide.

ORM-D — Abbreviation for Other Regulated Materials.

OSHA — Acronym for Occupational Safety and Health Administration.

Other Regulated Material (ORM-D) — Material that does not meet the definition of hazardous material and is not included in any other hazard class but possess enough hazardous characteristics that it requires some regulation; presents limited hazard during transportation because of its form, quantity, and packaging. *Also see* Material and Hazardous Material.

Outlet Valve — Valve farthest downstream to which a discharge hose is attached in a tank piping system.

Overturn Protection — Protection for fittings on top of a tank in case of rollover; may be combined with flashing rail or flashing box.

Oxidation — Chemical process that occurs when a substance combines with oxygen; common example is the formation of rust on metal.

Oxidizer — Any substance or material that yields oxygen readily and may stimulate the combustion of organic and inorganic matter. *Also see* Strong Oxidizer.

P

Package Marking — Descriptive name, instructions, cautions, weights, and specification marks required on the outside of hazardous materials containers. *Also see* Marking, Label, and Placard.

Packaging — (1) Broad term the U.S. Department of Transportation (DOT) uses to describe shipping containers and their markings, labels, and/or placards. *Also see* Bulk Packaging, Combination Packaging, Composite Packaging, Excepted Packaging, Individual Container, Industrial Packaging, Intermediate Bulk Container (IBC), Bulk Packaging, Type A Packaging, Type B Packaging, Nonbulk Packaging, and Strong, Tight Container. (2) Readying a victim for transport.

Parts Per Million (ppm) — Method of expressing the concentration of very dilute solutions of one substance in another, normally a liquid or gas, based on volume expressed as a ratio of the volume of contaminants (parts) compared to the volume of air (million parts).

PASS — Acronym for Personal Alert Safety System.

Patient Decontamination — Removing contamination from injured patients or victims. *Also see* Decontamination.

PCB — Abbreviation for Polychlorinated Biphenyl.

PEL — Acronym for Permissible Exposure Limit.

PEL-C — Acronym for Permissible Exposure Limit/ Ceiling Limit

Penetration — Process in which a hazardous material enters an opening or a puncture in a protective material. *Also see* Routes of Entry.

Permeation — Process in which a chemical passes through a protective material on a molecular level.

Permissible Exposure Limit (PEL) — Maximum time-weighted concentration at which 95 percent of exposed, healthy adults suffer no adverse effects over a 40-hour workweek; an 8-hour time-weighted average unless otherwise noted; expressed in either parts per million (ppm) or milligrams per cubic meter (mg/m³). *Also see* Immediately Dangerous to Life or Health (IDLH), Recommended Exposure Limit (REL), Short-Term Exposure Limit (STEL), Threshold Limit Value (TLV®), and Permissible Exposure Limit/Ceiling Limit (PEL-C).

Permissible Exposure Limit/Ceiling Limit (PEL-C) — Maximum concentration to which an employee may be exposed at any time, even instantaneously, as established by Occupational Safety and Health Administration (NIOSH). *Also see* Permissible Exposure Limit (PEL).

Peroxidizable Compound — Material apt to undergo spontaneous reaction with oxygen at room temperature and form peroxides and other products.

Persistence — Length of time a chemical agent remains effective without dispersing. *Also see* Persistent Agent, Nonpersistent Agent, and Dispersion.

Persistent Agent — Chemical agent that remains effective in the open (at the point of dispersion) for a considerable period of time. *Also see* Persistence, Nonpersistent Agent, and Dispersion.

Personal Alert Safety System (PASS) — Electronic lack-of-motion sensor that sounds a loud tone when an emergency responder becomes motionless; can also be triggered manually. *Also see* Personal Protective Equipment (PPE).

Personal Protective Equipment (PPE) — General term for the equipment worn by fire and emergency services responders; includes helmets, coats, pants, boots, eye protection, gloves, protective hoods, self-contained breathing apparatus (SCBA), and personal alert safety system (PASS) devices. When working with hazardous materials, bands or tape are added around the legs, arms, and waist. Also called *full structural protective clothing*. *Also see* Chemical Protective Clothing (CPC) and Special Protective Clothing (1).

Petroleum Carrier — Tank vessel that transports crude or finished petroleum products. *Also see* Tanker.

pH — Measure of acidity of an acid or the level of alkaline in a base. *Also see* Acid, Alalki, and Base.

Photon — Packet of electromagnetic energy.

Physical Hazard — Material that presents a threat to health because of its physical properties. *Also see* Health Hazard and Physical Properties.

Physical Properties — Those properties that do not involve a change in the chemical identity of a substance; however, they affect the physical behavior of the material inside and outside the container, which involves the change of the state of the material; examples: boiling point, specific gravity, vapor density, and water solubility. *Also see* Boiling Point, Specific Gravity, Vapor Density, Chemical Properties, and Water Solubility.

Pictogram — Drawing or symbol that indicates information.

PIN — Acronym for Product Identification Number.

Placard — Diamond-shaped sign that is affixed to each side of a structure or vehicle transporting hazardous materials to inform people of fire hazards, life hazards, special hazards, and reactivity potential; indicates the primary class of the material and, in some cases, the exact material being transported; required on containers that are 640 cubic feet (18 m³) or larger. *Also see* Label, Marking, and Package Marking.

Plume — Irregularly shaped pattern of an airborne hazardous material where wind and/or topography influence the downrange course from the point of release. *Also see* Cloud, Cone, and Hemispheric Release.

Poison — Any material that when taken into the body is injurious to health. *Also see* Convulsant and Toxin.

Polar Solvent Fuel — Flammable liquids that have an attraction for water, much like a positive magnetic pole attracts a negative pole. Examples: alcohol, ketone, and lacquer. *Also see* Flammable Liquid and Hydrocarbon Fuel.

Polychlorinated Biphenyl (PCB) — Toxic compound found in some old oil-filled electric transformers.

Polymerization — Reactions in which two or more molecules chemically combine to form larger molecules; reaction can often be violent. *Also see* Inhibitor.

Posttraumatic Stress Disorder (PTSD) — Manifestation of critical incident stress symptoms occurring 30 days to years after the initial critical incident. *Also see* Critical Incident Stress (CIS) and Stress (3).

Pounds Per Square Inch (psi) — Unit for measuring pressure in the English or Customary System. Its International System equivalents are kilopascals (kPa) and bar.

PPE — Abbreviation for Personal Protective Equipment.

ppm — Abbreviation for Parts Per Million.

Predetermined Procedures — Standard methods or rules in which an organization performs routine functions in addition to operating actions to perform at every possible type of emergency incident. Also known as *standard operating procedure (SOP)*, *standard operating guideline (SOG)*, and *operating instruction (OI)*.

Pre-Incident Survey — Survey of a facility or location made before an emergency occurs in order to prepare for an appropriate emergency response. Sometimes called *preplan*.

Preplan — *See* Pre-Incident Survey.

Pressure Intermodal Tank — Liquefied gas container designed for working pressures of 100 to 500 psi (689 kPa to 3 447 kPa) {6.9 bar to 34.5 bar}. Also known as *Spec 51* or *IMO Type 5*. *Also see* Nonpressure Intermodal Tank and Intermodal Container.

Pressure Storage Tank — Class of fixed facility storage tanks divided into two categories: low-pressure storage tanks and pressure vessels. *Also see* Low-Pressure Storage Tank, Pressure Vessel, and Atmospheric Storage Tank.

Pressure Tank Railcar — Tank railcars that carry flammable and nonflammable liquefied gases, poisons, and other hazardous materials. They are recognizable by the valve enclosure at the top of the car and the lack of bottom unloading piping.

Pressure Vessel — Fixed-facility storage tank with operating pressures above 15 psi (103 kPa) {1.03 bar}. *Also see* Low-Pressure Storage Tank, Pressure Storage Tank, and Spherical Pressure Vessel.

Prilled — Converted into spherical pellets.

Primary Label — Label placed on the container of a hazardous material to indicate the primary hazard. *Also see* Subsidiary Label.

Product — Generic term used in industry to describe a substance that is used or produced in an industrial process. *Also see* Material and Hazardous Material.

Product Identification Number (PIN) — Number assigned by the United Nations and used in the *Emergency Response Guidebook (ERG)* to identify specific product names.

Proportioner — *See* Foam Proportioner.

Proportioning Valve — Valve used to balance or divide the air supply between the aeration system and the discharge manifold of a foam system.

Protective Action Distance — Downwind distance from a hazardous materials incident within which protective actions should be implemented. *Also see* Initial Isolation Distance, Protective Action Zone, and Protective Actions.

Protective Action Zone — Area immediately adjacent to and downwind from the initial isolation zone, which is in imminent danger of being contaminated by airborne vapors within 30 minutes of material release. *Also see* Initial Isolation Zone, Protective Action Distance and Protective Actions.

Protective Actions — Steps taken to preserve health and safety of emergency responders and the public. *Also see* Protective Action Distance and Protective Action Zone.

psi — Abbreviation for Pounds Per Square Inch.

PTSD — Abbreviation for Posttraumatic Stress Disorder.

Pyrophoric — *See* Air-Reactive Materials.

R

R — Abbreviation for Roentgen.

rad — Acronym for Radiation Absorbed Dose.

Radiated Heat — *See* Radiation (1).

Radiation — (1) Transmission or transfer of heat energy from one body to another at a lower temperature through intervening space by electromagnetic waves such as infrared thermal waves, radio waves, or X rays. Also called *radiated heat.* (2) Energy from a radioactive source emitted in the form of waves or particles; emission of radiation as a result of the decay of an atomic nucleus; process know as *radioactivity.* Also called *nuclear radiation.* *Also see* Ionizing Radiation, Nonionizing Radiation, Radiation Absorbed Dose (rad), Radioactive Material (RAM), Radioactive Particles, Alpha Radiation, Beta Radiation, and Gamma Radiation.

Radiation Absorbed Dose (rad) — English System unit used to measure the amount of radiation energy absorbed by a material. Its International System equivalent is gray. *Also see* Radiation (2) and Radioactive Material (RAM).

Radioactivity — *See* Radiation (2).

Radioactive Material (RAM) — Material whose atomic nucleus spontaneously decays or disintegrates, emitting radiation. *Also see* Radiation (2), Curie (Ci), and Becquerel (Bq).

Radioactive Particles — Particles emitted during the process of radioactive decay; three types: alpha, beta, and gamma. *Also see* Alpha Particle, Beta Particle, Gamma Ray, and Radiation (2)

Radiography — Process of making a picture on a sensitive surface by a form of radiation other than light.

Radioisotope — *See* Radionuclide.

Radiological Dispersal Device (RDD) — Device that spreads radioactive contamination over the widest possible area by detonating conventional high explosives wrapped with radioactive material. Also called *dirty bomb.*

Radionuclide — Unstable atom with an unusual number of neutrons. Also called *radioisotope. Also see* Isotope.

Radiopharmaceutical — Radioactive drug used for diagnostic or therapeutic purposes.

Railcar Initials and Numbers — Combination of letters and numbers stenciled on rail tank cars that may be used to get information about the car's contents from the railroad's computer or the shipper. Also called *reporting marks. Also see* Intermodal Reporting Marks.

RAM — Acronym for Radioactive Material.

Rapid Relief — Fast release of a pressurized hazardous material through properly operating safety devices caused by damaged valves, piping, or attachments or holes in the container.

RDD — Abbreviation for Radiological Dispersal Device.

Reaction (Chemical) — *See* Chemical Reaction.

Reactive Material — Substance capable of or tending to react chemically with other substances; examples: materials that react violently when combined with air or water. *Also see* Air-Reactive Material, Water-Reactive Material, and Reactivity.

Reactivity — Ability of two or more chemicals to react and release energy and the ease with which this reaction takes place. *Also see* Chemical Reaction and Reactive Material.

Recommended Exposure Limit (REL) — Recommended value expressing the maximum time-weighted dose or concentration to which workers should be exposed over a 10-hour period as established by National Institute for Occupational Safety and Health (NIOSH). *Also see* Permissible Exposure Limit (PEL), Short-Term Exposure Limit (STEL), and Threshold Limit Value (TLV®).

Reefer — *See* Refrigerated Intermodal Container.

Refrigerated Intermodal Container — Cargo container having its own refrigeration unit; also called *reefer. Also see* Intermodal Container, and Container Vessel.

Refrigerated Liquid — *See* Cryogen.

Refrigeration Unit — Cooling equipment used to maintain a constant temperature within a given space.

Regulations — Rules or directives of administrative agencies that have authorization to issue and enforce them.

Rehab — Abbreviation for Rehabilitation.

Rehabilitation (Rehab) — (1) Allowing emergency responders to rest, rehydrate, and recover during an incident; also refers to a station at an incident where personnel can rest, rehydrate, and recover. (2) Activities necessary to repair environmental damage.

REL — Abbreviation for Recommended Exposure Limit.

Relay Emergency Valve — Combination valve in an air brake system that controls brake application and also provides for automatic emergency brake application should a trailer become disconnected from the towing vehicle.

rem — Acronym for Roentgen Equivalent in Man.

Reporting Marks — *See* Railcar Initials and Numbers.

Research and Special Programs Administration (RSPA) — U.S. Department of Transportation (DOT) agency that carries out and enforces the hazardous materials regulations (HMR) through a program of regulation, enforcement, emergency response education and training, and data collection and analysis.

Resources — All of the immediate or supportive assistance available, or potentially available, for assignment to help control an incident, including personnel, equipment, control agents, agencies, and printed emergency guides.

RIBC — Abbreviation for Rigid Intermediate Bulk Container.

Rickettsia — Specialized bacteria that live and multiply in the gastrointestinal tract of arthropod carriers (such as ticks and fleas). *Also see* Bacteria and Virus.

Rigid Intermediate Bulk Container (RIBC) — *See* Intermediate Bulk Container (IBC)

Ring Stiffener — Circumferential tank shell stiffener that helps to maintain the tank's cross section.

Riot Control Agent — Chemical compound that temporarily makes people unable to function by causing immediate irritation to the eyes, mouth, throat, lungs, and skin. Also called *tear gas or irritating agent. Also see* Incapacitant.

Risk Analysis — *See* Hazard or Risk Analysis.

Risk Management Plan — Written plan that identifies and analyzes the exposure to hazards, selection of appropriate risk management techniques to handle exposures, implementation of chosen techniques, and monitoring of the result of using those techniques. *Also see* Hazard or Risk Analysis and Hazard Assessment.

Roentgen (R) — English System unit used to measure radiation exposure, applied only to gamma and X-ray radiation; the unit used on most U.S. dosimeters. *Also see* Radiation (2), Radioactive Material (RAM), Roentgen Equivalent in Man (rem), Gamma Radiation, and Radiation Absorbed Dose (rad).

Roentgen Equivalent in Man (rem) — English System unit used to express the radiation absorbed dose (rad) equivalence as pertaining to a human body; applied to all types of radiation; used to set radiation dose limits for emergency responders. *Also see* Roentgen (R), Radiation (2), Radioactive Material (RAM), and Radiation Absorbed Dose (rad).

Roll-On/Roll-Off Vessel — Ship with large stern and side ramp structures that are lowered to allow vehicles to be driven on and off the vessel. *Also see* Cargo Vessel.

Rotary Gauge — Gauge for determining the liquid level in a pressurized tank.

Routes of Entry — Pathways by which hazardous materials get into (or affect) the human body; commonly listed routes are inhalation, ingestion, skin contact, injection, absorption, and penetration (for radiation). *Also see* Radiation (2) and Permeation.

RSPA — Acronym for Research and Special Programs Administration.

Rupture Disk — Safety device that fails at a predetermined pressure and thus protects a pressure vessel from being overpressurized.

S

Safety Can — Flammable liquid container, usually 5 gallons (19 L) or less, that has a self-closing spout and has been approved by a suitable testing agency.

Safety Chain — Chain connecting two vehicles to prevent separation in the event the primary towing connection breaks.

Safety Relief Valve — Device on cargo tanks with an operating part held in place by a spring. The valve opens at preset pressures to relieve excess pressure and prevent failure of the vessel.

SAR — Abbreviation for Supplied-Air Respirator.

SARA — Acronym for Superfund Amendments and Reauthorization Act.

SCBA — Abbreviation for Self-Contained Breathing Apparatus.

Scene-Control Zones — *See* Hazard-Control Zones.

Secondary Contamination — Contamination of people, equipment, or the environment outside the hot zone without contacting the primary source of contamination; sometimes called *cross contamination*. *Also see* Contamination, Decontamination, and Hazard-Control Zones.

Secondary Decontamination — Taking a shower after having completed a technical decontamination process. *Also see* Decontamination and Technical Decontamination.

Seismic Effect — Earth vibration created by an explosion that is similar to an earthquake.

Self-Contained Breathing Apparatus (SCBA) — Respirator worn by the user that supplies a breathable atmosphere that is carried in or generated by the apparatus and is independent of the ambient atmosphere. *Also see* Supplied-Air Respirator (SAR).

Semitrailer — Freight trailer that when attached is supported at its forward end by the fifth wheel device of the truck tractor; often refers to a trucking rig composed of a tractor and a semitrailer. *Also see* Fifth Wheel.

Sensitizer — *See* Allergen.

SETIQ — Abbreviation for the Emergency Transportation System for the Chemical Industry (Mexico).

Shelter in Place — Having occupants remain in a structure or vehicle in order to provide protection from a rapidly approaching hazard. *Also see* Evacuation.

Shipping Papers — Shipping order, bill of lading, manifest, waybill, or other shipping document issued by the carrier. *Also see* Bill of Lading, Lading, Consist, Waybill, and Air Bill.

Short-Term Exposure Limit (STEL) — Fifteen-minute time-weighted average that should not be exceeded at any time during a workday; exposures should not last longer than 15 minutes nor be repeated more than four times per day with at least 60 minutes between exposures. *Also see* Immediately Dangerous to Life or Health (IDLH), Permissible Exposure Limit (PEL), Recommended Exposure Limit (REL), and Threshold Limit Value (TLV®).

Shrapnel Fragmentation — Small pieces of debris thrown from a container or structure that ruptures from containment or restricted blast pressure.

Side Rails — Upper side rails: main longitudinal frame members of a tank used to connect the upper corner fittings. Lower side rails: main longitudinal frame members of a tank used to connect the lower corner fittings.

Simple Asphyxiant — Any inert gas that displaces or dilutes oxygen below the level needed by the human body. *Also see* Asphyxiant and Inert Gas.

Site Work Zones — *See* Hazard-Control Zones.

Skin Contact — Occurrence when a chemical or hazardous material (in any state — solid, liquid, or gas) contacts the skin or exposed surface of the body (such as the mucous membranes of the eyes, nose, or mouth). *Also see* Routes of Entry.

Slurry — (1) Watery mixture of insoluble matter such as mud, lime, or Plaster of Paris. (2) Thick mixture formed when a fire-retardant chemical is mixed with water and a viscosity agent.

SOG — Abbreviation for Standard Operating Guideline.

Soluble — Capable of being dissolved in a liquid (usually water). *Also see* Insoluble, Immiscible, Water Solubility, and Miscibility.

Somatic — Pertaining to all tissues other than reproductive cells.

SOP — Abbreviation for Standard Operating Procedure.

Sorbent — Granular, porous filtering material used in vapor- or gas-removing respirators.

Sorption — Method of removing contaminants; used in vapor- and gas-removing respirators.

Spec 51 — *See* Pressure Intermodal Tank.

Special Protective Clothing — (1) Chemical protective clothing specially designed to protect against a specific hazard or corrosive substance. *Also see* Chemical Protective Clothing (CPC) and Personal Protective Equipment (PPE). (2) High-temperature protective clothing including approach, proximity, and fire entry suits.

Specification Marking — Stencil on the exterior of tank cars indicating the standards to which the tank car was built.

Specific Gravity — Weight of a substance compared to the weight of an equal volume of water at a given temperature. Specific gravity less than 1 indicates a substance lighter than water; specific gravity greater than 1 indicates a substance heavier than water. *Also see* Physical Properties.

Specific Heat — Amount of heat required to raise the temperature of a specified quantity of a material and the amount of heat necessary to raise the temperature of an identical amount of water by the same number of degrees.

Spherical Pressure Vessel — Round-shaped fixed facility pressure vessel. *Also see* Pressure Vessel.

Spheroid Tank — Round- or oval-shaped fixed facility low-pressure storage tank. *Also see* Low-Pressure Storage Tank, Noded Spheroid Tank, and Pressure Storage Tanks.

Splitter Valve — Valve installed to divide a pipeline manifold.

Spontaneous Combustion — *See* Spontaneous Ignition.

Spontaneous Heating — Heating resulting from chemical or bacterial action in combustible materials that may lead to spontaneous ignition. *Also see* Spontaneous Ignition.

Spontaneous Ignition — Combustion of a material initiated by an internal chemical or biological reaction producing enough heat to cause the material to ignite. Also called *spontaneous combustion.*

Stabilization — (1) Stage of an incident when the immediate problem or emergency has been controlled, contained, or extinguished. (2) Process of providing additional support to key places between an object of entrapment and the ground or other solid anchor point to prevent unwanted movement.

Stabilizer — *See* Inhibitor.

Standard Operating Guideline (SOG) — *See* Predetermined Procedures.

Standard Operating Procedure (SOP) — *See* Predetermined Procedures.

Standard Transportation Commodity Code (STCC Number) — Numerical code used by the rail industry on the waybill to identify the commodity.

STCC Number — *See* Standard Transportation Commodity Code.

STEL — Acronym for Short-Term Exposure Limit.

Strategic Goals — Broad statements of desired achievement to control an incident; achieved by the completion of tactical objectives. *Also see* Strategy, Tactical Objectives, and Tactics.

Strategy — Overall plan for incident attack and control established by the Incident Commander (IC). *Also see* Tactics, Nonintervention Strategy, Defensive Strategy, and Offensive Strategy.

Stress — (1) State of tension put on a shipping container by internal or external chemical, mechanical, or thermal changes. (2) Factors that work against the strength of any piece of apparatus or equipment. (3) Any condition causing bodily or mental tension. *Also see* Critical Incident Stress (CIS) and Posttraumatic Stress Disorder (PTSD).

Strong Oxidizer — Material that encourages a strong reaction (by readily accepting electrons) from a reducing agent (fuel). *Also see* Oxidizer.

Strong, Tight Container — Packaging used to ship materials of low radioactivity. *Also see* Excepted Packaging, Industrial Packaging, Type A Packaging, Type B Packaging, and Packaging (1).

Subsidiary Label — Label indicating a secondary hazard associated with a material. *Also see* Primary Label.

Suffocate — To die from being unable to breathe; to be deprived of air or to stop respiration by strangulation or asphyxiation.

Suitcase Bomb — Small, suitcase- or backpack-sized nuclear weapon. *Also see* Improvised Nuclear Device (IND).

Sunstroke — *See* Heat Stroke.

Superfund Amendments and Reauthorization Act (SARA) — U.S. law that in 1986 reauthorized the Comprehensive Environmental Response, Compensation, and Liability Act (CERCLA) to continue cleanup activities around the country and included several site-specific amendments, definitions, clarifications, and technical requirements.

Supplied-Air Respirator (SAR) — Atmosphere-supplying respirator for which the source of breathing air is not designed to be carried by the user; not certified for fire-fighting operations. Also known as an *Airline Respirator. Also see* Self-Contained Breathing Apparatus (SCBA).

Surface Contamination — Contamination that is limited to the surface of a material. *Also see* Contamination, Decontamination, and Contaminant.

Systemic Effect — Something that affects an entire system rather than a single location or entity.

Systemic Hypothermia — *See* Hypothermia.

T

Tactical Objectives — Specific operations that must be accomplished to achieve strategic goals. *Also see* Strategic Goals and Tactics.

Tactics — Methods of employing equipment and personnel on an incident to accomplish specific tactical objectives in order to achieve established strategic goals. *Also see* Tactical Objectives, Strategy, and Strategic Goals.

Tanker — Vessel (ship) that exclusively carries liquid products in bulk; also called *tank vessel. Also see* Chemical Carrier, Liquefied Flammable Gas Carrier, and Petroleum Carrier.

Tank Motor Vehicle — *See* Cargo Tank Truck.

Tank Truck — *See* Cargo Tank Truck.

Tank Vessel — *See* Tanker

Target Hazard — Facility in which there is a great potential likelihood of life or property loss in the event of an attack or natural disaster. *Also see* Hazard and Hazard Assessment.

TC — Abbreviation for Transport Canada.

Tear Gas — *See* Riot Control Agent.

Technical Assistance — Personnel, agencies, or printed materials that provide technical information on handling hazardous materials or other special problems.

Technical Decontamination — Using chemical or physical methods to thoroughly remove contaminants from responders (primarily entry team personnel) and their equipment; usually conducted within a formal decontamination line or corridor following gross decontamination; also called *formal decontamination. Also see* Decontamination, Gross Decontamination, and Decontamination Corridor.

Teratogen — Chemical that interferes with the normal growth of an embryo, causing malformations in the developing fetus.

Terrorism — Unlawful use of force or violence against persons or property for the purpose of intimidating or coercing a government, the civilian population, or any segment thereof, in furtherance of political or social objectives; defined by the U.S. Federal Bureau of Investigation (FBI). *Also see* Chemical Attack and Biological Attack.

Threshold Limit Value (TLV®) — Concentration of a given material in parts per million (ppm) that may be tolerated for an 8-hour exposure during a regular workweek without ill effects. *Also see* Threshold Limit Value/Ceiling (TLV®/C), Short-Term Exposure Limit (STEL), Threshold Limit Value/Short-Term Exposure Limit (TLV®/STEL), Permissible Exposure Limit (PEL), Recommended Exposure Limit (REL), and Threshold Limit Value/Time Weighted Average (TLV®/TWA).

Threshold Limit Value/Ceiling (TLV®/C) — Maximum concentration of a given material in parts per million (ppm) that should not be exceeded, even instantaneously. *Also see* Threshold Limit Value (TLV®), Threshold Limit Value/Short-Term Exposure Limit (TLV®/STEL), Short-Term Exposure Limit (STEL), Permissible Exposure Limit (PEL), Recommended Exposure Limit (REL), and Threshold Limit Value/Time Weighted Average (TLV®/TWA).

Threshold Limit Value/Short-Term Exposure Limit (TLV®/STEL) — Fifteen-minute time-weighted average exposure that should not be exceeded at any time nor repeated more than four times daily with a 60-minute rest period required between each STEL exposure. These short-term exposures can be tolerated without suffering from irritation, chronic or irreversible tissue damage, or narcosis of a sufficient degree to increase the likelihood of accidental injury, impair self-rescue, or materially reduce worker efficiency. TLV/STELs are expressed in parts per million (ppm) and milligrams per cubic meter (mg/m³). *Also see* Short-Term Exposure Limit (STEL), Permissible Exposure Limit (PEL), Recommended Exposure Limit (REL), Threshold Limit Value (TLV®), Threshold Limit Value/Ceiling (TLV®/C), and Threshold Limit Value/Time Weighted Average (TLV®/TWA).

Threshold Limit Value/Time-Weighted Average (TLV®/TWA) — Maximum airborne concentration of a material to which an average, healthy person may be exposed repeatedly for 8 hours each day, 40 hours per week without suffering adverse effects; based upon current available data; are adjusted on an annual basis. *Also see* Threshold Limit Value (TLV®), Threshold Limit Value/Ceiling (TLV®/C), Permissible Exposure Limit (PEL), Recommended Exposure Limit (REL), Short-Term Exposure Limit (STEL), and Threshold Limit Value/Short-Term Exposure Limit (TLV®/STEL).

TIC — Abbreviation for Toxic Industrial Chemical.

TIH — Abbreviation for Toxic Inhalation Hazard.

TIM — Abbreviation for Toxic Industrial Material.

TLV® — Abbreviation for Threshold Limit Value.

TLV®/C — Abbreviation for Threshold Limit Value/Ceiling.

TLV®/STEL — Abbreviation for Threshold Limit Value/Short-Term Exposure Limit.

TLV®/TWA — Abbreviation for Threshold Limit Value/Time-Weighted Average.

Ton Container — Pressurized tank with a capacity of 1 short ton or approximately 2,000 pounds (907 kg or 0.9 tonne).

Toxic Atmosphere — Any area, inside or outside a structure, where the air is contaminated by a poisonous substance that may be harmful to human life or health if it is inhaled, swallowed, or absorbed through the skin. *Also see* Toxic Gas.

Toxic Element — *See* Heavy Metal.

Toxic Gas — Poisonous gas that contains poisons or toxins that are hazardous to life; many gaseous products of combustion are poisonous; toxic materials generally emit poisonous vapors when exposed to an intensely heated environment. *Also see* Gas, Toxic Material, and Toxin.

Toxic Industrial Chemical (TIC) — *See* Toxic Industrial Material (TIM).

Toxic Industrial Material (TIM) — Industrial chemical that is toxic at certain concentration and is produced in quantities exceeding 30 tons per year at any one production facility; readily available and could be used by terrorists to deliberately kill, injure, or incapacitate people. Also called *toxic industrial chemical (TIC)*. *Also see* Chemical Attack and Terrorism.

Toxic Inhalation Hazard (TIH) — Liquid or gas known to be a severe hazard to human health during transportation.

Toxicity — Ability of a substance to do harm within the body. *Also see* Toxin.

Toxic Material — Substance classified as a poison, asphyxiant, irritant, or anesthetic that can be poisonous if inhaled, swallowed, absorbed, or introduced into the body through cuts or breaks in the skin. *Also see* Toxic Gas, Asphyxiant, and Toxin.

Toxic Substances Control Act (TSCA) — U.S. law enacted in 1976 to give the Environmental Protection Agency (EPA) the ability to track the 75,000 industrial chemicals currently produced or imported into the United States.

Toxin — Substance that has the property of being poisonous. *Also see* Toxic Material, Biological Toxin, Toxic Gas, Toxicity, Poison, and Toxic Material.

Train Consist — *See* Consist.

Transport Canada (TC) — Agency responsible for developing and administering policies, regulations, and programs for a safe, efficient, and environmentally friendly transportation system in Canada; contributing to Canada's economic growth and social development; and protecting the physical environment.

Truck Tractor — Powered motor vehicle designed to pull a truck trailer. *Also see* Truck Trailer.

Truck Trailer — Vehicle without motor power; primarily designed for transportation of property rather than passengers; drawn by a truck or truck tractor. *Also see* Full Trailer.

TSCA — Abbreviation for Toxic Substances Control Act.

Tube Trailer — *See* Compressed-Gas Tube Trailer.

Type A Packaging — Container used to ship radioactive materials with relatively high radiation levels. *Also see* Packaging (1), Excepted Packaging, Industrial Packaging, Type B Packaging, and Strong, Tight Container.

Type B Packaging — Container used to ship radioactive materials that exceeds the limits allowed by Type A packaging such as materials that would present a radiation hazard to the public or the environment if there were a major release. *Also see* Packaging (1), Excepted Packaging, Industrial Packaging, Type A Packaging, and Strong, Tight Container.

U

UC — Abbreviation for Unified Command.

UEL — Abbreviation for Upper Explosive Limit.

UFL — Abbreviation for Upper Flammable Limit.

Unified Command (UC) — Shared command role that allows all agencies with responsibilities for an incident to manage the incident by establishing a common set of incident objectives and strategies.

Unit Loading Device — Container used to ship materials on an airplane.

Unstable Material — Material that readily undergoes chemical changes or decomposition.

Upper Explosive Limit (UEL) — *See* Upper Flammable Limit (UFL).

Upper Flammable Limit (UFL) — Upper limit at which a flammable gas or vapor will ignite. Above this limit, the gas or vapor is too rich to burn (lacks the proper quantity of oxygen). *Also see* Flammable Limit, Flammable Range, and Lower Flammable Limit (LFL).

USCG — Abbreviation for U.S. Coast Guard.

U.S. Coast Guard (USCG) — U.S. military, multi-mission, and maritime service, whose mission is to protect the public, the environment, and U.S. economic interests in U.S. ports and waterways, along the coasts, on international waters, or in any maritime region as required to support national security.

Utilidor — Insulated, heated conduit built belowground or supported aboveground to protect contained water, steam, and sewage lines from freezing.

V

Vapor — Gaseous form of a substance that is normally in a solid or liquid state at room temperature and pressure; formed by evaporation from a liquid or sublimation from a solid. *Also see* Vapor Density, Vapor Pressure, Vapor Dispersion, Vapor Suppression, and Vaporization.

Vapor Density — Weight of a given volume of pure vapor or gas compared to the weight of an equal volume of dry air at the same temperature and pressure. Vapor density less than 1 indicates a vapor lighter than air; vapor density greater than 1 indicates a vapor heavier than air. *Also see* Vapor and Physical Properties.

Vapor Dispersion — Action taken to direct or influence the course of airborne hazardous materials. *Also see* Vapor and Dispersion.

Vaporization — Process of evolution that changes a liquid into a gaseous state; rate of vaporization depends on the substance involved, heat, and pressure. *Also see* Vapor and Vapor Density.

Vapor Pressure — Measure of the tendency of a substance to evaporate; pressure at which a vapor is in equilibrium with its liquid phase for a given temperature. *Also see* Vapor and Boiling Point.

Vapor Suppression — Action taken to reduce the emission of vapors at a hazardous materials spill. *Also see* Vapor and Hazardous Material.

Venturi Principle — Physical law stating that when a fluid is forced under pressure through a restricted orifice, there is an increase in the velocity of the fluid passing through the orifice and a corresponding decrease in the pressure exerted against the side of the constriction. Because the surrounding air is under greater atmospheric pressure, it is forced into the area of lower pressure.

Vesicant — *See* Blister Agent.

Violent Rupture — Immediate release of chemical or mechanical energy caused by rapid cracking of the container.

Virus — Simplest type of microorganism that can only replicate itself in the living cells of its host; unaffected by antibiotics. *Also see* Bacteria and Rickettsia.

Volatile — Changing into vapor quite readily at a fairly low temperature. *Also see* Vapor and Vaporization.

Volatility — Ability of a substance to vaporize easily at a relatively low temperature. *Also see* Vapor, Volatile, and Vaporization.

Vomiting agent — Chemical warfare agent that causes violent, uncontrollable sneezing, cough, nausea, vomiting, and a general feeling of bodily discomfort. *Also see* Chemical Warfare Agent.

W

Water Gel — Chemical solution that is gelled or partially solidified to make it easier to use or handle; example: gelatin dynamite (gelignite).

Water-Reactive Material — Substance, generally a flammable solid, that reacts in varying degrees when mixed with water or exposed to humid air. *Also see* Air-Reactive Material, Reactivity, and Reactive Material.

Water Solubility — Ability of a liquid or solid to mix with or dissolve in water. *Also see* Physical Properties, Insoluble, Dilution, and Soluble.

Waybill — Shipping paper used by a railroad to indicate origin, destination, route, and product. Each car has a waybill that the conductor carries. *Also see* Shipping Papers and Consist.

WHMIS — Acronym for Workplace Hazardous Materials Information System.

Workplace Hazardous Materials Information System (WHMIS) — Canadian law requiring that hazardous products be appropriately labeled and marked.

X

X Ray — High-energy photon produced by the interaction of charged particles with matter.

Index

I

IAEA (International Atomic Energy Agency), 432

IAPs. *see* incident action plans (IAPs)

IBCs (intermediate bulk containers), 144–145

ICs. *see* Incident Commanders (ICs)

ID numbers. *see* identification (ID) numbers (U.N.), 156–158

IDs (incapacitating doses), 77

ICS (Incident Command System), 230

identification (ID) numbers (U.N.), 156–158

identification of hazardous materials in problem-solving process, 249. *see also* clues to presence of hazardous materials

IEDs (improvised explosive devices), 476–478, 482–486

IFSTA. *see* International Fire Service Training Association (IFSTA)

ignition, preventing
- at flammable/combustible liquid spills, 414–415
- at flammable gas leaks, 406
- at flammable solid spills, 416
- at oxidizing substances and organic peroxides incidents, 423, 424
- vapor suppression and, 296

ignition sources, 49

ignition temperature, 47, 48

illegal clandestine labs, 486–495, 507–508

illegal dumps, 495–496

ILO (International Labour Organization) (Canada) MSDS requirements, 208

immiscibility and miscibility, 52–53

IMO (International Maritime Organization (IMO), 432

improvised explosive devices (IEDs), 476–478, 482–486

improvised nuclear devices (INDs), 456

IMS. *see* Incident Management System (IMS)

incapacitants, 475

incapacitating doses (IDs), 77

incendiary incidents
- special operational considerations, 503
- terrorist attacks, 457–458

incendiary thermal effects, 87

incident action plans (IAPs)
- accountability systems, 247
- developing, 270–271
- evaluating, 273
- implementing, 272–273
- overview, 237, 266–268, 271

Incident Command System (ICS), 230

Incident Commanders (ICs)
- checklists for hazardous materials incidents, 533
- establishing and transferring command, 237–238
- in IMS structure, 232, 234

incident management. *see also* incident action plans (IAPs)
- evaluating, 273
- management structure, 228–247

priorities at incidents, 228

problem-solving process, 228, 248–273

Incident Management System (IMS)
- compared to ICS, FGC, and NIMS, 230
- elements of, 231–237, 274. *see also specific elements*
- organizational levels, 231, 232, 273. *see also specific levels*
- positions specific to hazardous materials incidents, 239–240

incident management systems
- establishing and transferring command, 237–238
- overview, 228–231
- predetermined procedures and emergency response plans, 240–247
- problem-solving process, 248–273
- unified command, 238–239

incident scenario sample, 95–109

incidents. *see* hazardous materials incidents

India, methyl isocyanate in Bhopal, 10

indicator papers and pH meters, 220

INDs (improvised nuclear devices), 456

industrial packaging, 151

infectious substances. *see* biological weapons; poisonous materials and infectious substances (Class 6 hazards)

inflammable, 48

information gathering as part of problem-solving process, 249–251

ingestion, 67–68, 71

inhalation, 67, 71. *see also* air contaminants; respiratory irritants

inhibitors, 58

initial isolation distance and initial isolation zone
- defined, 284
- described, 280–281
- in *ERG*, 214–215
- strategic goals and tactical objectives, 290–291

initial response phase, 210

initial survey as part of problem-solving process, 249–252

initials (reporting marks) and numbers on rail tank cars, 179, 181

injection, 72

integrated contingency plans, 271

intermediate bulk containers (IBCs), 144–145

intermodal containers
- placards, labels and markings, 180–183, 184
- types of, 134–138

International Atomic Energy Agency (IAEA), 432

International Fire Service Training Association (IFSTA)
- principles of risk management, 254
- problem-solving system model, 248

International Labour Organization (ILO) (Canada) MSDS requirements, 208

International Maritime Organization (IMO), 432

tankers, 138–140, 141
tanks (containers)
>corrosives in, 434
>at fixed facilities, 114–118
>flammable and combustible liquids in, 413–414
>intermodal, 134–138
>marine vessels, 138–143
>overview, 134–135
>on railcars, 118–124
>on trucks, 124–134
>unit loading devices, 143–144
Task level of Command in IMS, 232
tastes as clue to presence of hazardous materials, 216
TC. *see* Transport Canada (TC)
tear gas (chlorobenzylidene malononitrile or CS), 473, 474
tearing containers, 257
technical advisors and command personnel, 243–244
technical (formal) decontamination, 374–375, 380–383
Technical Specialist (Hazardous Materials Reference/ Science Technical Specialist), 240
Technician-Level responders
>decontamination and contamination reduction, 377
>exposure limits and, 81
>leak control and confinement, 299
>oxidizing substances and organic peroxides, 424
>roles of, 270
>ton containers and, 146
TECP (totally encapsulating chemical-protective) suits, 332, 348, 350
telecommunications centers and telecommunicators, predetermined procedures for, 242, 243–244
temperature
>cold temperature hazards, 61–62
>firefighter safety and, 362–366
>maximum safe storage temperature (MSST), 424
>thermal hazards, 58, 61–63, 256
>vapor pressure and, 50
teratogens, 84
termination phase of incidents, 314, 319
terrorism and terrorist attacks. *see also* criminal activities
>defined, 443–445
>potential targets, 445–447
>safety briefings, 235
>types of attacks, 447–486. *see also specific types of attacks*
tetryl, 481
thermal hazards. *see also* temperature
>container failure and, 256
>as defined in TRACEM model, 58
>overview, 61–63
threshold limit value-ceiling (TLV®-C), 77, 78
threshold limit value-short-term exposure limit (TLV®-STEL), 79

threshold limit value-time-weighted average (TLV®-TWA), 79
threshold limit value (TLV®), 77, 78
TIH (toxic inhalation hazard), 216
TIMs. *see* toxic industrial materials (TIMs)
TLV® (threshold limit value), 77, 78
TNT (trinitrotoluene), 481
ton containers, 145–146
tools and equipment. *see specific tasks; specific tools*
totally encapsulating chemical-protective (TECP) suits, 332, 348, 350
totes (flexible intermediate bulk containers), 144, 146
toxic and infectious substances. *see* poisonous materials and infectious substances (Class 6 hazards)
toxic industrial materials (TIMs)
>blood agents (cyanide agents) as, 464
>defined, 458
>terrorist attacks using, 475–476
toxic inhalation hazard (TIH), 216
Toxic Substances Control Act (TSCA), 23
TRACEM (TRACEMP) model, 58–61
training
>Canadian requirements for, 11–12
>Mexican requirements for, 12
>online training program (U.S.), 9–10
>with other emergency services organizations in the area, 230, 447
>U.S. requirements for, 11
trains. *see* railways
transborder shipments, shipping paper requirements, 205, 206
transfer of command, 234, 237–238
Transport Canada (TC). *see also* Canadian Transport Emergency Center (CANUTEC)
>cargo tank truck specifications, 124–125, 128, 129, 131
>emergency response center operated by, 32
>regulations and definitions, 25
>shipping paper requirements, 203
>transportation placards, labels, and markings, 172, 174–177
Transportation of Dangerous Goods Directorate, 32
transportation of hazardous materials. *see also* containers
>hazard classes
>>gases, 403–404, 404–412
>>oxidizing substances and organic peroxides, 422
>>poisonous materials and infectious substances, 425–426
>>radioactive materials, 431–433, 433–434, 557–561
>locations where incidents are likely, 112–113
>regulations and definitions for hazardous materials, 17–22. *see also specific agencies and regulations*
>shipping paper requirements, 205
>statistics about, 36, 37

630 Index

U.S. Office of Pipeline Safety, 36
U.S. online training program, 9–10
U.S. Sandia National Laboratories, 382
USAR (urban search and rescue) operations, 343–344.
    see also search and rescue operations

V

V-agent (VX), 461, 463
vacuuming as chemical decontamination method, 382
vapor- and gas-removing filters in APRs, 339
vapor densities, 52
vapor pressures, 50–51
vapor-protective clothing, 332–333, 344
vapor-tight totally encapsulating chemical-protective (TECP) suits, 332, 348, 350
vaporization of cryogenic and liquefied gases, 61
vapors. *see also* fumes; gases
    control and confinement
        dispersion, 298
        suppression, 295–297
        ventilation, 297
    decontamination operations at chemical warfare incidents, 503
    defined, 46
    extinguishment affecting, 305
    foam concentrates affecting, 314
    PPE and, 327, 349–350, 350–351
    primary (direct) contamination and, 372
ventilation, 297
vesicants (blister agents), 463–464, 465–467
vessel cargo carriers, 138–143
victims
    decontamination operations and, 375, 383–386, 386–390, 436
    evidence collection and, 393
violent ruptures. *see* boiling liquid expanding vapor explosions (BLEVEs)
viral agents, 448
visual clues to presence of hazardous materials, 216, 217–218
vomiting agents, 475

W

warm zones (decontamination corridors)
    defined, 284
    described, 283, 376, 391–393
    sample layout of, 384
washing as chemical decontamination method, 382–383
waste. *see* hazardous waste
Waste Isolation Pilot Plant (WIPP), 433
water gels/slurries, 481
water-reactive materials, 57, 297. *see also* flammable solids, spontaneously combustible materials, and dangerous-when-wet materials (Class 4 hazards)

water solubility, 52–53, 53–54
water used for extinguishment
    at flammable gas leaks, 407, 408, 409
    overview, 305–306
water used in decontamination operations
    at chemical warfare incidents, 504–506
    at corrosives emergencies, 436
    dilution as control tactic, 299
    dissolution as control tactic, 299
    exposure protection, 304
    overview, 377
    vapor dispersion, 298
waterways
    decontamination site selection and, 391
    likelihood of hazardous materials incidents, 113
    shipping papers on ships and barges, 205
    transporting radioactive materials, 432
weapons of mass destruction (WMD), 31, 448
wet methods of decontamination, 378–379
WHMIS (Canadian Workplace Hazardous Materials Information System), 190–191, 192, 208
WIPP (Waste Isolation Pilot Plant), 433
withdrawal. *see also* nonintervention strategies at hazardous materials incidents
    BLEVEs, 302
    distances recommended for, 195, 198
    at explosives on fire (or threatened by fire) emergencies, 400
    at oxidizing substances and organic peroxides incidents, 423, 425
    as tactical objective, 305
WMD (weapons of mass destruction), 31, 448
Workplace Hazardous Materials Information System (WHMIS) (Canada), 190–191, 192, 208
workplace labels, WHMIS requirements, 191
written resources. *see also* record-keeping; reports, verbal; standard operating procedures (SOPs) and predetermined procedures; *specific resources*
    Clue 5 to presence of hazardous materials, 202–216
    predetermined procedures complying with, 240
    requirements for shipping papers, 531
    UN identification numbers (ID) in, 157

X

X rays, 64–65

Y

Yvorra, James G., 248

Indexed by Kerri Kells.